Margaret Atwood

A Reference Guide
1988–2005

Shannon Hengen
Ashley Thomson

The Scarecrow Press, Inc.
Lanham, Maryland • Toronto • Plymouth, UK
2007

SCARECROW PRESS, INC.

Published in the United States of America
by Scarecrow Press, Inc.
A wholly owned subsidiary of
The Rowman & Littlefield Publishing Group, Inc.
4501 Forbes Boulevard, Suite 200, Lanham, Maryland 20706
www.scarecrowpress.com

Estover Road
Plymouth PL6 7PY
United Kingdom

British Library Cataloguing in Publication Information Available

Library of Congress Cataloging-in-Publication Data
Hengen, Shannon Eileen.
  Margaret Atwood : a reference guide, 1988–2005 / Shannon Hengen, Ashley Thomson.
      p. cm.
  Includes bibliographical references and indexes.
  ISBN-13: 978-0-8108-5904-3 (hardcover : alk. paper)
  ISBN-10: 0-8108-5904-1 (hardcover : alk. paper)
  1. Atwood, Margaret Eleanor, 1939– Bibliography. 2. Atwood, Margaret Eleanor,
1939– Interviews. 3. Women and literature–Canada–Bibliography. I. Thomson, Ashley.
II. Title.
Z8046.947.H46 2007
[PR9199.3.A8]
016.818'5409–dc22   2006038788

♾™ The paper used in this publication meets the minimum requirements of American
National Standard for Information Sciences—Permanence of Paper for Printed Library
Materials, ANSI/NISO Z39.48-1992. Manufactured in the United States of America.

Contents

Preface vii

Introduction.. ix

An Atwood Chronology.. xiii

1988

    Atwood's Works... 1

    Adaptations of Atwood's Works 4

    Quotations.. 4

    Interviews 4

    Scholarly Resources 5

    Reviews of Atwood's Works.. 15

1989

    Atwood's Works... 17

    Quotations.. 21

    Interviews 21

    Scholarly Resources 22

    Reviews of Atwood's Works.. 29

1990

    Atwood's Works... 33

    Adaptations of Atwood's Works 36

    Quotations.. 37

    Interviews 37

    Scholarly Resources 39

    Reviews of Atwood's Works.. 51

    Reviews of Adaptations of Atwood's Works 52

1991

    Atwood's Works... 55

    Adaptations of Atwood's Works 59

    Quotations.. 59

    Interviews 59

    Scholarly Resources 60

    Reviews of Atwood's Works.. 69

    Reviews of Adaptations of Atwood's Works 71

Contents

1992

Atwood's Works...72
Quotations...76
Interviews 76
Scholarly Resources 77
Reviews of Atwood's Works..88
Reviews of Adaptations of Atwood's Works 90

1993

Atwood's Works...91
Adaptations of Atwood's Works 96
Quotations...97
Interviews 97
Scholarly Resources 99
Reviews of Atwood's Works..109

1994

Atwood's Works...114
Quotations...118
Interviews 118
Scholarly Resources 120
Reviews of Atwood's Works..133
Reviews of Adaptations of Atwood's Works 135

1995

Atwood's Works...136
Adaptations of Atwood's Works 141
Quotations...141
Interviews 142
Scholarly Resources 143
Reviews of Atwood's Works..154
Reviews of Adaptations of Atwood's Works 156

1996

Atwood's Works...157
Adaptations of Atwood's Works 161
Quotations...161
Interviews 162
Scholarly Resources 163
Reviews of Atwood's Works..173
Reviews of Adaptations of Atwood's Works 177

1997

Atwood's Works...178
Adaptations of Atwood's Works 183
Quotations...183
Interviews 185
Scholarly Resources 186
Reviews of Atwood's Works..196

1998

Atwood's Works...199
Adaptations of Atwood's Works 204
Quotations...204
Interviews 205

Scholarly Resources 207
Reviews of Atwood's Works 220

1999

Atwood's Works 221
Adaptations of Atwood's Works 226
Quotations 226
Interviews 227
Scholarly Resources 228
Reviews of Atwood's Works 237
Reviews of Adaptations of Atwood's Works 237

2000

Atwood's Works 238
Adaptations of Atwood's Works 242
Quotations 243
Interviews 244
Scholarly Resources 249
Reviews of Atwood's Works 259

2001

Atwood's Works 263
Adaptations of Atwood's Works 268
Quotations 268
Interviews 270
Scholarly Resources 273
Reviews of Atwood's Works 281
Reviews of Adaptations of Atwood's Works 282

2002

Atwood's Works 283
Adaptations of Atwood's Works 287
Quotations 288
Interviews 289
Scholarly Resources 291
Reviews of Atwood's Works 299
Reviews of Adaptations of Atwood's Works 301

2003

Atwood's Works 302
Adaptations of Atwood's Works 309
Quotations 309
Interviews 310
Scholarly Resources 316
Reviews of Atwood's Works 323
Reviews of Adaptations of Atwood's Works 328

2004

Atwood's Works 330
Adaptations of Atwood's Works 336
Quotations 336
Interviews 337
Scholarly Resources 343
Reviews of Atwood's Works 350
Reviews of Adaptations of Atwood's Works 352

Contents

2005

Atwood's Works 354

Quotations 363

Interviews 364

Scholarly Resources 369

Reviews of Atwood's Works 375

Reviews of Adaptations of Atwood's Works 377

Margaret Atwood on the Web 378

Author Index 387

Subject Index 402

About the Authors 439

Preface
Shannon Hengen

The work of a bibliographer such as Ashley Thomson, who compiled this work, is as meticulous and invaluable as it is thankless. An exhaustive compilation, this book represents something like a monument in Canadian literary criticism, belied by its modest title: a reference guide. For to peruse these pages carefully is to make a passage through significant moments in the life not just of the writer, Margaret Atwood, but of her generation. The critical reception of her forty-four published books having been recorded, we chart cultural history.

Why, for example, have so many scholars been drawn to the 1985 dystopian novel, *The Handmaid's Tale*? What important ethos in North American or indeed Western life was so articulated by Offred and those who oppressed her? While many scholarly treatments of the novel address the literary issue of genre—Is it dystopian? feminist? anti-feminist? anti-utopian?—concerns beyond the literary never fail to emerge, most importantly among them: Is North America's future to be guided by the religious right? If not, then by whom or what?

That Atwood's work stimulates opposing views seems an indication of its ability to observe a segment of North American life—middle class, mainstream—with striking clarity. Critics do not agree if the oeuvre is, for example, baldly nationalistic, or if its wide international appeal implies much broader concerns than those involving Canada's identity. Is it modern or postmodern—that is, does the work seem deliberately well wrought, a thing complete unto itself, or do experimental techniques such as indeterminacy and lack of closure express profound contemporary uncertainties? Does the oeuvre qualify as postcolonial in the extent and kind of views of imperial power expressed in it? Why is her work, so engaging on the page, so challenging to adapt to film, among Western culture's most easily consumed media? While critics agree that myth and folklore underlie many of her stories, we disagree in her attitude to them: Are they destructive and unavoidable in their appeal, or are they malleable and useful? And, is she a comic writer; if so, how?

The growing scholarly field of cultural studies has opened literary analysis to issues that connect Atwood's work intimately with its material contexts: attitudes to madness and illness, for example, and to violence, the body, social mores, youth and aging—all issues that recur in Atwood's writing. While literary critics often address one another and strictly technical questions, we also increasingly move into dialogue with the greater world and so analyze Atwood's work in relation to forces beyond fiction. Atwood and nature, a theme to which critics have returned again and again over the years, for example, becomes a question of Atwood and the environmental movement.

Influenced by the cultural imagination, Atwood is also a shaper of it. How influential her work has been is made obvious by the sheer heft of this volume, one that all readers of her work will need.

Introduction
Ashley Thomson

Margaret Atwood: A Reference Guide, 1988-2005 is the successor to Judith McCombs and Carole L. Palmer's *Margaret Atwood: A Reference Guide* (Boston: Hall, 1991). Both books celebrate the impact of Canada's best-known living author—so well known in fact that she is sometimes mistaken for an American.

While the new book picks up where McCombs and Palmer left off, retaining the chronological arrangement of entries from the original as well as author and subject indexes, it is different from its predecessor title in three significant ways. First, instead of concentrating solely on Atwood's books as did McCombs and Palmer's, this book attempts to include all of Atwood's works, from books, to articles, to short stories, to letters to the editor, to individual poetry. Adaptations of Atwood's works are also included as are some of her comments that have been quoted publicly. Second, references about Atwood are more finely arranged. Rather than listing them alphabetically by author, the new guide sorts them first by type: Interviews, Scholarly Resources, and Reviews. Third, while the new book attempts to provide annotations for many Interviews and Scholarly Resources, unlike McCombs and Palmer, physical limitations of the new manuscript precluded extensive excerpts from reviews.

As far as possible, the individual citations in this guide reflect the Modern Language Association (MLA) format, although sharp-eyed readers will note some variations that deserve to be explained. The pure MLA format is possible in a research paper with an alphabetical list of citations at its end. The citations in this reference guide are not, of course, initially organized alphabetically but by date. This explains why the book does not follow MLA, which places the date of original publication ahead of the date that an item was republished (MLA 5.6.17). Instead this book lists the dates of republication first, with date of original publication second, as, for example, 1988 ©1972. Similarly, reprints of scholarly articles are not listed by date of original publication (MLA 5.6.7) but by date of republication with a note that the article is "Reprinted from." In addition to being primarily organized by date, this reference guide is indexed. That explains why it does not follow the MLA style for translations (MLA 5.6.13) which make no reference to the language of the original work.

There are other instances where the MLA style has not been followed primarily for reasons of clarity. For example, in numbering pages, MLA prescribes page ranges like this: 57-59 when they are under 100; over 100, 157-59, dropping the 1. We have included the complete run. We have also provided fuller information for newspaper articles than MLA typically suggests (5.7.5). On the other hand, our format for book reviews is far more compact than MLA prescribes (5.7.7). This time, space was the dictator.

Like its predecessor, this book grew out of the annual checklists prepared for the Margaret Atwood Society, an affiliate of the Modern Language Association. Since 1988 these checklists have been published in the fall issue of the *Newsletter of the Margaret Atwood Society*. As joint authors of annual checklists, the authors of this book are painfully aware that citations come to light sometimes several years after their date of publication. Thus in preparing this book, extensive research took place to verify existing references and to uncover new ones. Almost all references are available through interlibrary loan (and those that could not be obtained in this way were dropped from the guide). The major exception to this rule of thumb were theses, some of which are only available from the university of origin. The authors thought, however, that knowledge of the existence of such theses would be of interest to students beginning to undertake their own.

In 2006-2007, the Margaret Atwood Society newsletter will begin to publish peer-reviewed articles on Atwood, as well as the ongoing checklists, designed to be annual updates to this book, and the newsletter's title will change to *Margaret Atwood Studies*. Next year's issue, covering references by and about Atwood for 2006, will include Atwood's new books *The Tent* (Toronto: McClelland and Stewart, 2006), "a highly imaginative collection of mini-fictions," and *Moral Disorder* (New York: Nan A. Talese, 2006), which the publisher describes as "her moving new book of fiction, [which] could be seen either as a collection of ten stories that is almost a novel or as a novel broken up into ten stories. It resembles a photograph album—a series of clearly observed moments that trace the course of a life, and also the lives intertwined with it—those of parents, of siblings, of children, of friends, of enemies, of teachers, and even of animals. And as in an album, times change: the 30s, the 40s, the 50s, the 60s, the 70s and 80s, the present time—all are here. The settings are equally varied: large cities, suburbs, farms, northern forests..."

In the area of scholarly resources, the 2006 checklist will include at least three other new books. The first is *The Cambridge Companion to Margaret Atwood*, edited by Coral Ann Howells (Cambridge, UK; New York: Cambridge University Press, 2006). All chapters in this book will be indexed, including one by the coauthor of this book, Shannon Hengen. The second title is *Waltzing Again: New and Selected Conversations with Margaret Atwood*, edited by Earl J. Ingersoll (Princeton, NJ: Ontario Review Press; New York: Distributed by W.W. Norton & Co., 2006); the book is a collection of recent interviews. The third title is *Atwood on Her Work: "Poems Open the Doors. Novels Are the Corridors,"* edited by Christine Evain and Reena Khandpur (Nantes: Université de Nantes, 2006). This work, which reprints some of Atwood's poems, also includes four critical essays, including one by Hengen. Its highlight, however, is an extended interview with Atwood herself by the two coeditors. In many ways the book symbolizes Atwood's international appeal.

Readers of this guide will find at least one significant value-added in the annual checklists which appear in the Atwood newsletter and forthcoming journal—a complete section devoted to Atwood "In the News." To get a flavor of her many activities, consult the Atwood Chronology on pages xiii-xiv, although this short synopsis really does not do justice to her (almost daily) activity. Of course, those not wanting to wait for the checklists could do worse than set up an alert for Margaret Atwood on Google Alerts, (http://www.google.com/alerts), one of the more useful tools of its kind.

There is now so much information about Atwood in print that readers may be shocked to discover that a simple Google search on "Margaret Atwood" will generate nearly 2,330,000 other references. Because not all users of this guide will have ready access to the citations in it, the authors asked Alain Lamothe, the electronic reference librarian at Laurentian University, to provide a succinct guide to the best of what is currently available. Lamothe's chapter appears on pages 378-386.

The authors want to thank not only Alain Lamothe but several categories of other contributors. From the Margaret Atwood Society these include predecessor bibliographers who have graciously permitted us to use their work as a basis of our own: Carol L. Palmer (1988-1991), Loretta P. Koch (1991-1994), Barbara G. Preece (1994), Danette Dimarco (1995-1999), and Cynthia Kuhn (2000-2001). Ashley Thomson has been working on the checklists since 1995, and in 2002, Shannon Hengen joined as coauthor. Also to be thanked are Jerome Rosenberg, who edited the newsletter until 2005, and Ted Sheckels, who replaced him and who will be the founding editor of *Margaret Atwood Studies.*

From the University of Toronto, which houses the Margaret Atwood Archives, we owe thanks to Jennifer Toews, who is in charge of the Atwood collection and who has been most generous in sharing her knowledge, including some extensive verification of entries.

At Laurentian University, thanks are due to Dr. Liette Vasseur, Associate Vice-President (Research), Dr. Susan Silverton (Vice-President Academic), Dr. John Isbister (Dean of Humanities), and Lionel Bonin (Director of the Library), all of whom supported this project both financially and otherwise. In the library we owe thanks to Diane Tessier and Dan Leduc (interlibrary loans), and we received assistance from researcher Rachel Desjardins. Dr. Lisa Laframboise, a freelance editor, contributed significantly to the preparation of the indexes. Mel Chomiak, a professor of computer science, also assisted in this area.

At Scarecrow Press, we owe thanks to Martin Dillon, who enthusiastically embraced the project; Stephen Ryan, our patient editor; and Sally Craley, one of the most personable production editors we have ever known.

An Atwood Chronology
1988–2005[i]

1988   *Cat's Eye*; promoted to Companion of the Order of Canada; receives Aggie, a bronze statue named after the YWCA's founder, Agnes Blizard, upon being named a Woman of Distinction by Metro Toronto's YWCA

1989   Writes screenplay for *Cat's Eye*, 1989-1991; wins Canadian Booksellers' Association Award and City of Toronto Book Award; writer-in-residence at Trinity University, San Antonio, Texas

1990   *Selected Poems: 1966-1984* (Oxford) and *For the Birds*; receives Order of Ontario and Centennial Medal from Harvard University; attends Berlin Film Festival for premier of Volker Schlondorff's film *The Handmaid's Tale*

1991   *Wilderness Tips*; Clarendon Lectures at the University of Oxford; family spends winter in France (1991-1992)

1992   *Good Bones*; receives Trillium Award from Ontario Government for *Wilderness Tips*

1993   *The Robber Bride*

1994   *Good Bones and Simple Murders* (Doubleday); wins Trillium Award for *The Robber Bride*; named Chevalier dans l'Ordre des Arts et des Lettres by the government of France; receives *Sunday Times'* Award for Literary Excellence

1995   *Strange Things: The Malevolent North in Canadian Literature*; *Morning in the Burned House*; and *Princess Prunella and the Purple Peanut*; *The New Oxford Book of Canadian Short Stories in English* (coedited with Robert Weaver); series of radio interviews in French with Quebec writer Victor-Lévy Beaulieu; receives Trillium Award *Morning in the Burned House* and International Humourous Writers Award from the Swedish Humour Association[ii]

1996   *Alias Grace*, which wins Giller Prize; *The Labrador Fiasco*; receives Norwegian Order of Literary Merit and is named Canadian Booksellers Association Author of the Year

1997   *The Journals of Susanna Moodie* (with illustrations by Charles Pachter); *A Quiet Game and Other Early Works*; *In Search of Alias Grace*

1998   *Eating Fire: Selected Poetry 1965-1995* (Virago); receives honorary doctorate from the University of Oxford

1999   Receives London Literature Award

2000   *The Blind Assassin*, which wins Booker prize; Empson Lectures at the University of Cambridge; attends premier in Copenhagen of Poul Ruders's opera *The Handmaid's Tale*

2001   Wins Hammett Prize for *The Blind Assassin* from the North American Branch of the International Association of Crime Writers; receives honorary doctorate from the University of Cambridge and from Algoma University College; wins place on Canada's Walk of Fame, the first fiction writer so honored

2002   *Negotiating with the Dead: A Writer on Writing*

2003   *Oryx and Crake* and *Rude Ramsey and the Roaring Radishes*; attends London premier of *The Handmaid's Tale* opera

2004   *Bottle* (Hay Festival Press); *Bashful Bob and Doleful Dorinda*; and *Moving Targets: Writing with Intent, 1982-2004*; Toronto premier of The *Handmaid's Tale* opera; receives honorary doctorate from Harvard University

2005   *Curious Pursuits: Occasional Writing, 1970-2005*; receives honorary doctorate from the Université de la Sorbonne Nouvelle, Paris[iii]; *The Penelopiad*

---

[i] Based on chronology provided by Atwood finding aid available in the Fisher Library at the University of Toronto. 5-7. See http://www.library.utoronto.ca/fisher/collections/findaids/atwood.pdf.

[ii] Once asked about the best award she ever won, she replied: "Well, I'd never pick and choose, but who would have ever guessed I'd win the Swedish humor award? My publishers went to accept it and the prize was a crystal ball or bowl—I never did find out because they took it back to their office and someone stole it." See Finbar O'Reilly, "Atwood on Awards and Almost Dying." *National Post* 13 June 2001: A13.

[iii] According to Atwood, "My most intoxicating honour was having a 236-ton sewer tunnelling machine in Hull [Quebec] named after me." See *The Express* 18 October 2003: Section: Columns: 51.

~ 1988 ~

Atwood's Works

1. "Adrienne Rich: Of Woman Born." *Prose Pieces: Essays and Stories [by] Sixteen Modern Writers*. Ed. Pat C. Hoy and Robert Diyanni. New York: Random House, 1988. 491-493. Book review with some questions. Reprinted from *Second Words: Selected Critical Prose*, ©1982.
2. "Afterword." *A Jest of God.* By Margaret Laurence. Toronto: McClelland and Stewart, 1988. 211-215.
3. "An Angel." *Translation* 20 (Spring 1988): 43-44. Prose poem.
4. "The Animals in That Country." *15 Canadian Poets X2*. Ed. Gary Geddes. Toronto: Oxford UP, 1988. 396-397. Reprinted from *The Animals in That Country*, ©1968.
5. *Bluebeard's Egg and Other Stories*. London: Virago, 1988 ©1987.
6. *Bodily Harm. Selections.* [Sound recording]. Read by Margaret Atwood. Columbia, MO: American Audio Prose Library, 1988.
7. *Cat's Eye*. Toronto: McClelland and Stewart; New York: Doubleday; London: Bloomsbury, 1988. Elaine Risley, a successful artist approaching 50, returns to Toronto where she confronts her past and especially her relationship with her childhood friend and tormentor, Cordelia.
8. *Cat's Eye*. [Sound recording]. Read by Sandra Scott. Toronto: CNIB, 1988. 10 cassettes (13:55 hrs.).
9. "Cherished Moments." *Life* 11.10 (Fall 1988): 155. Comments on a snapshot of herself on a fishing trip when she was 4 years old.
10. *Crónica de uma serva.* Mem Martins, Portugal: Publicações Europa-América, 1988. Portuguese translation of *The Handmaid's Tale* by A. Martins Lopes.
11. *Dancing Girls and Other Stories.* Toronto: Seal Books, 1988 ©1977.
12. *Dancing Girls and Other Stories.* [Sound recording]. Read by Aileen Seaton. Toronto: CNIB, [1988?]. 6 sound cassettes (360 min.).
13. "Death of a Young Son by Drowning." *15 Canadian Poets X2*. Ed. Gary Geddes. Toronto: Oxford UP, 1988. 402-403. Reprint.
14. *Die Unmöglichkeit der Nähe*. Frankfurt: Ullstein, 1988. German translation of *Life Before Man*.
15. *Dikter*. Stockholm: Prisma, 1988. Selected poems in Swedish.
16. "Dreams of the Animals." *The Canadian Children's Treasury*. Contributing editors Frances Hanna and Sandra Martin. Toronto: Key Porter Books, 1988. [166-167]. Poem. Reprinted from *Procedures for Underground*, ©1970.

17. *The Edible Woman.* [Sound recording]. Read by Barbara Byers. Toronto: CNIB, 1988. 8 sound cassettes (660 min.).

18. "Five Poems for Dolls." *15 Canadian Poets X2.* Ed. Gary Geddes. Toronto: Oxford UP, 1988. 406-408. Reprinted from *Two-Headed Poems,* ©1978.

19. "Foreword." *Cambridge Guide to Literature in English.* Ed. Ian Ousby. Cambridge: Cambridge UP; Rushden: Hamlyn Publishing Group, 1988. [i].

20. "Game after Supper." *15 Canadian Poets X2.* Ed. Gary Geddes. Toronto: Oxford UP, 1988. 403-404. Reprinted from *Procedures for Underground,* ©1971.

21. "Giving Birth." *Prose Pieces: Essays and Stories [by] Sixteen Modern Writers.* Ed. Pat C. Hoy and Robert Diyanni. New York: Random House, 1988. 504-513. Reprinted from *Dancing Girls and Other Stories,* ©1977.

22. "Great Unexpectations: An Autobiographical Foreword." *Margaret Atwood: Vision and Forms.* Ed. Kathryn VanSpanckeren and Jan Garden Castro. Carbondale, IL: Southern Illinois UP, 1988. xiii-xvi. Reprinted from *Ms.* (July-August 1987).

23. *The Handmaid's Tale.* [Sound recording]. Read by Betty Harris. Charlotte Hall, MD: Recorded Books, 1988. 8 sound cassettes.

24. *Il racconto dell'ancella.* Milan: A. Mondadori, 1988. Italian translation of *The Handmaid's Tale* by Camillo Pennati.

25. "In the Right Place at the Right Time: The Thing from the Briny Deep." *New York Times Magazine* 137 (13 March 1988): 44, 88.

26. *Interlunar.* London: J. Cape, 1988 ©1984.

27. "Introducing *The CanLit Foodbook.*" *Literary Gastronomy.* Ed. David Bevan. Amsterdam: Rodopi, 1988. 51-56.

28. "It Is Dangerous to Read Newspapers." *The Heath Introduction to Poetry.* 3rd ed. Lexington, MA, and Toronto: D.C. Heath, 1988. 533. Reprinted from *The Animals in That Country,* ©1968-1969.

29. "Late August." *Deep Down: The New Sensual Writing by Women.* Ed. Laura Chester. Boston and London: Faber and Faber, 1988. 311. Poem. Reprinted from "Circe/Mud Poems" in *Selected Poems 1965-1975,* ©1976-1978.

30. *La servante écarlate.* [Sound recording]. Read by René Chouteau. Longueil: Institut Nazareth et Louis-Braille, 1988. 8 cassettes. French version of *The Handmaid's Tale.*

31. *La vie avant l'homme.* [Sound recording]. Read by René Chouteau. Longueuil: Institut Nazareth et Louis-Braille, 1988. 8 cassettes. French version of *Life Before Man.*

32. *Lichamelijk Letsel.* Amsterdam: Bert Bakker, 1988 ©1983. Dutch translation of *Bodily Harm* by Tineke Funhoff.

33. *Marquée au corps.* [Sound recording]. Read by René Chouteau. Longueuil: Institut Nazareth et Louis-Braille, 1988. 7 cassettes. French version of *Bodily Harm.*

34. "Newsreel: Man and Firing Squad." *15 Canadian Poets X2.* Ed. Gary Geddes. Toronto: Oxford UP, 1988. 405-406. Reprint.

35. "A Night in the Royal Ontario Museum." *15 Canadian Poets X2.* Ed. Gary Geddes. Toronto: Oxford UP, 1988. 397-398. Reprinted from *The Animals in That Country,* ©1968.

36. "Notes Towards a Poem That Can Never Be Written." *15 Canadian Poets X2.* Ed. Gary Geddes. Toronto: Oxford UP, 1988. 409-411. Reprinted from *True Stories,* ©1981.

37. *Oeil-de-chat.* Paris: Robert Laffont [1988]. French translation of *Cat's Eye* by Hélène Filion.

38. "Of Food and Fiction." *Canadian Living* 13.1 (23 January 1988): 30-34, 37-38. "A cook's tour of Canadian literature includes recipes."

39. *Olho de gato*. [Lisbon]: Publicaçes Europa-América, 1988. Portuguese translation of *Cat's Eye*.

40. "On Being a 'Woman Writer': Paradoxes and Dilemmas." *Prose Pieces: Essays and Stories [by] Sixteen Modern Writers*. Ed. Pat C. Hoy and Robert Diyanni. New York: Random House, 1988. 494-503. Article followed by some questions. Reprinted from *Second Words: Selected Critical Prose*, ©1982.

41. "Pollution: A Call to Arms." *Toronto Star* 29 October 1988: Section: Life: H1. (1343 w).

42. "Progressive Insanities of a Pioneer." *15 Canadian Poets X2*. Ed. Gary Geddes. Toronto: Oxford UP, 1988. 399-402. Reprinted from *The Animals in That Country*, ©1968.

43. "Rape Fantasies." *Story and Structure*. 7th ed. Ed. Laurence Perrine. New York: Harcourt Brace Jovanovich, 1988. 519-526. Reprinted from *Dancing Girls and Other Stories*, ©1977.

44. "[Review of *Second Words*]." *Critical Essays on Margaret Atwood*. Ed. Judith McCombs. Boston: Hall, 1988. 251-253. Tongue-in-cheek review of her own book (by Margarets Atwood). Reprinted from *Globe and Mail* 20 November 1982: L2.

45. *Siniparran Muna*. Helsinki: Kirjayhtymä, 1988. Finnish translation of *Bluebeard's Egg and Other Stories* by Matti Kannosto.

46. *Slušskinjina priška*. Zagreb [Croatia]: Globus, 1988. Croatian translation of *The Handmaid's Tale*.

47. "Summers on Canada's Rideau Canal." *Architectural Digest* June 1988: 84, 88, 90-91.

48. *Surfacing*. London: Virago Press, 1988 ©1972. With a new introduction by Francine du Plessix Gray.

49. "Theology." *Translation* 20 (Spring 1988): 44-45. Reprinted in *Harper's* 277 (September 1988): 36-37. Short story.

50. "They Eat Out." *15 Canadian Poets X2*. Ed. Gary Geddes. Toronto: Oxford UP, 1988. 404-405. Reprinted from *Power Politics*.

51. "This Is Nothing." *New York Times* 8 May 1988: Section: 7: 47. Poem. Reprinted from *Atwood's Selected Poems II: Poems Selected & New 1976-1986*, ©1987.

52. "Tillie Olsen: *Silences*." *Prose Pieces: Essays and Stories [by] Sixteen Modern Writers*. Ed. Pat C. Hoy and Robert Diyanni. New York: Random House, 1988. 488-490. Book review with some questions. Reprinted from *Second Words: Selected Critical Prose*, ©1982-1984.

53. "Tips for the Sophisticated Traveler: In the Right Place at the Right Time; the Thing from the Briny Deep." *New York Times* 13 March 1988: Section 6: 44.

54. *Tjenerindens fortaelling*. Copenhagen: Lindhardt og Ringhof, 1988. Danish translation of *The Handmaid's Tale*.

55. *Tornare a galla*. Milan: Serra e Riva, 1988. Italian translation of *Surfacing* by Fausta Libardi.

56. "Variation on the Word *Sleep*." *Homes* September 1988: 141. Also in *Toronto Life* 22.12 (August 1988): H41 and in *Deep Down: The New Sensual Writing by Women*. Ed. Laura Chester. Boston; London: Faber and Faber, 1988. 86. Poem. Excerpt from "Notes Towards a Poem That Can Never Be Written" Selected *Poems II. Poems Selected and New 1978-1986*, ©1987.

57. "The Whirlpool Rapids." *Editor's Choice*. v. 4. Compiled by George E. Murphy Jr. New York: Bantam, 1988. 13-20. Short story. Reprinted from *Redbook*, November 1986.
58. "A Woman's Issue." *15 Canadian Poets X2*. Ed. Gary Geddes. Toronto: Oxford UP, 1988. 412-413. Reprinted from *True Stories*, ©1981.

Adaptations of Atwood's Works

59. CHATMAN, Stephen. "You Are Happy for Contralto and Piano." [Toronto: Canadian Music Centre?], 1988. 1 score (10 p.). Atwood poem set to music. "Commissioned for Maureen Forrester by Music in the Morning."
60. PINTER, Harold. *The Handmaid's Tale*. Draft dated 1988. A screenplay adapted from the novel. Source: WorldCat.

Quotations

61. "[Quote]." *Toronto Star* 25 June 1988: Section: Insight: D6. Article titled "Free Trade: Pro and Con" quotes Atwood: "If Canada is going to hitch its wagon to a star, why not a rising star, rather than one hovering so close to burn-out."
62. COMMIRE, Anne, ed. *Something about the Author*. Vol. 50. Detroit, MI: Gale, 1988. 38-43. Biocritical entry on Atwood as an author of children's books; includes a lengthy section of Atwood quotes.

Interviews

63. "The *Booktalk* Interview with Margaret Atwood." *Booktalk* 3.1 (Autumn 1988): 1, 3.
64. BRANS, Jo. "Using What You're Given." *Listen to the Voices: Conversations with Contemporary Writers*. Dallas: Southern Methodist UP, 1988. 125-147. Slightly revised and reprinted from *Southwest Review* 68.4 (Autumn 1983).
65. CASTRO, Jan Garden. "An Interview with Margaret Atwood, 20 April 1983." *Margaret Atwood: Vision and Forms*. Ed. Kathryn VanSpanckeren and Jan Garden Castro. Carbondale, IL: Southern Illinois UP, 1988. 215-232. Transcribed from American Audio Prose Library, cassette 1983.
66. GILLEN, Francis X. "A Conversation: Margaret Atwood and Students." *Margaret Atwood: Vision and Forms*. Ed. Kathryn VanSpanckeren and Jan Garden Castro. Carbondale, IL: Southern Illinois UP, 1988. 233-243.
67. GOULD, Allan M. "How 3 Famous Women Cope with Success." *Chatelaine* 61.4 (April 1988): 141, 143.
68. HAAG, Ed. "International Atwood / Margaret Atwood: Magicienne des mots." *Canadian* (Vernon, BC) 2.5 (September 1988): 50, 52-58.
69. LANGER, Beryl Donaldson. "Interview with Margaret Atwood." *Australian-Canadian Studies* 6:1 (1988): 125-136.
70. ROSS, Jean W. "C A Interview." *Contemporary Authors* 24. New rev. ser. Detroit, MI: Gale, 1988. 22-25.

71. RUBBO, Michael. *Margaret Atwood: Once in August*. New York: Brighton Video, 1988 ©1984. "An intimate view of one of Canada's most elusive literary figures, Margaret Atwood, in an interview with filmmaker Michael Rubbo."
72. TWIGG, Alan. "Margaret Atwood." *Strong Voices: Conversations with Fifty Canadian Authors*. Madeira Park, BC: Harbour Publishing Co., 1988. 6-11. Revised version of interview from *Vancouver Free Press* 9-15 November 1979.
73. VEVAINA, Coomi S. "Forging a Canadian Identity." *World Press Review* 35.6 (June 1988): 60. From an interview in the *Times of India* (New Delhi) in which Atwood discusses her writing, her criteria for good fiction, the effect of colonialism on Canadian culture, and her affinities with writers from other cultures with colonial pasts.

Scholarly Resources

74. ABITEBOUL, Maurice. "Le romanesque et le grotesque dans 'The Man from Mars' de Margaret Atwood ou le mythe démythifié." *Études canadiennes / Canadian Studies* 24 (1988): 87-98. "In 'The Man from Mars,' one of the best-known stories written by M. Atwood, a close textual analysis reveals all the structural elements of a conventional fairy tale. The story narrates the adventures of a pathetically inadequate 'knight,' desperately trying to conquer the lady with whom he has fallen in love at first sight. But the story is treated as a parody of the genre and is actually a demythification [sic] of the tale. Yet this does not affect the emotional impact of the story which is a realistic version of the old tale." (Author).
75. BAER, Elizabeth R. "Pilgrimage Inward: Quest and Fairy Tale Motifs in *Surfacing*." *Margaret Atwood: Vision and Forms*. Ed. Kathryn VanSpanckeren and Jan Garden Castro. Carbondale, IL: Southern Illinois UP, 1988. 24-34. Sees *Surfacing* as a "loup-garou" story centering around a metamorphosis theme and a female character with intelligence and magic powers.
76. BARBOUR, Douglas. [Review of *Two-Headed Poems*]. *Critical Essays on Margaret Atwood*. Ed. Judith McCombs. Boston: Hall, 1988. 208-212. Reprinted from *Fiddlehead* 121 (Spring 1979): 138-142.
77. BARR, Marleen. "Blurred Generic Conventions: Pregnancy and Power in Feminist Science Fiction." *Reproductive and Genetic Engineering* 1.2 (1988): 167-174. A discussion of science fiction and reproductive technology from Alien to Femininity (1987) to include the merger of sex, reproduction, and silence in *The Handmaid's Tale*.
78. BENTON, Carol L. "Raised Eyebrows: The Comic Impulse in the Poetry of Margaret Atwood." PhD thesis. Southern Illinois University at Carbondale, 1988. 171 pp. Drawing from Iser's phenomenology of reading, employs "reading as rehearsal" to study comedy in Atwood's poetry. For more see: *DAI-A* 50.10 (April 1990): 3105.
79. BLODGETT, E. D. "On *Surfacing*: A Response to Margaret Atwood." *Peace, Development and Culture: Comparative Studies of India and Canada*. Ed. Harold Coward. [Calgary]: Shastri Indo-Canadian Institute, ©1988, printed 1990. 83-94. Not only in Atwood, surfacing is a theme in other Canadian, border fiction. This paper was presented at a conference in 1988 for the 20th anniversary of the Institute; at the conference, Atwood presented a slide and sound program in which she "discussed her own self-discovery as a Canadian."

80. BLOTT, Anne. "Journey to Light [*Interlunar*]." *Critical Essays on Margaret Atwood*. Ed. Judith McCombs. Boston: Hall, 1988. 275-279. Reprinted from *Fiddlehead* 146 (Winter 1985): 90-95.

81. BOSSERT, Rex Thomas. "Oneiric Architecture: A Study in the Ideology of Modern Utopian Fiction." PhD thesis. Stanford University 1988. 327 pp. The last chapter looks at the "feminization" or personalization of the utopia in works by Atwood, Le Guin, and Lessing. For more see *DAI-A* 49.09 (March 1989): 2664.

82. BOUTELLE, Ann Edwards. "Margaret Atwood, Margaret Laurence, and Their Nineteenth-Century Forerunners." *Faith of a (Woman) Writer*. Ed. Alice Kessler-Harris and William McBrien. *Contributions in Women's Studies*, no. 86. New York, Westport, CT: Greenwood Press, 1988. 41-47. Atwood has inherited the literary tradition of Susanna Moodie, and she and Laurence have drawn from Catherine Parr-Traill.

83. BOWERING, George. "Desire and the Unnamed Narrator." *Descant* 19.3 (Fall 1988): 18-24. *Surfacing*'s narrative goes beyond the nationalist, feminist, or ecological; it falls between the views of Barthes and Kristeva to create a new metaphor, a figuration of the relationship between nature and woman.

84. BREWSTER, Elizabeth. "Powerful Poetry [*Power Politics*]." *Critical Essays on Margaret Atwood*. Ed. Judith McCombs. Boston: Hall, 1988. 35-36. Reprinted from *Edmonton Journal* 16 April 1971: 60.

85. BROMBERG, Pamela S. "The Two Faces of the Mirror in *The Edible Woman* and *Lady Oracle*." *Margaret Atwood: Vision and Forms*. Ed. Kathryn VanSpanckeren and Jan Garden Castro. Carbondale, IL: Southern Illinois UP, 1988. 12-23. Explores image and reality in *The Edible Woman* and *Lady Oracle*, "exposing the rhetoric and politics of women's entrapment in the mirror of gender."

86. BROWN, Russell. "Atwood's Sacred Wells [*Dancing Girls*, Poetry, and *Surfacing*]." *Critical Essays on Margaret Atwood*. Ed. Judith McCombs. Boston: Hall, 1988. 213-229. Reprinted from *Essays on Canadian Writing* 17 (Spring 1980): 5-43.

87. BUCHBINDER, David. "Weaving Her Version: The Homeric Model and Gender Politics in Selected Poems." *Margaret Atwood: Vision and Forms*. Ed. Kathryn VanSpanckeren and Jan Garden Castro. Carbondale, IL: Southern Illinois UP, 1988. 122-141. Classical allusions and repertoire of structures, patterns, and linguistic features are used to resolve problems of gender politics. Atwood's new version is "part of an old yet always new discourse."

88. BUTT, William. "Canada's Mental Travellers Abroad." *World Literature Written in English* 28:2 (Autumn 1988): 287-307. *Lady Oracle* and *Bodily Harm* are included in an overview of writing "by and about Canadians who have traveled to other lands."

89. CAENEPEEL, Mimo. "Margaret Atwood's *Surfacing*: The Politics of Victimization." *Journal of the Department of English* (University of Calcutta) 23.1-2 (1988-89): 25-39. The self-discovery theme is furthered by the narrative use of pronominal reference.

90. CAMERON, Elspeth. "In Darkest Atwood [*Murder in the Dark*]." *Critical Essays on Margaret Atwood*. Ed. Judith McCombs. Boston: Hall, 1988. 254-256. Reprinted from *Saturday Night* 98.3 (March 1983): 70-72.

91. CAMPBELL, Josie P. "The Woman as Hero in Margaret Atwood's *Surfacing*." *Critical Essays on Margaret Atwood*. Ed. Judith McCombs. Boston: Hall, 1988. 168-179. Reprinted from *Mosaic* 11.3 (Spring 1978): 17-28.

92. CARRINGTON, Ildikó de Papp. "Demons, Doubles, and Dinosaurs: *Life Before Man*, *The Origin of Consciousness*, and 'The Icicle.'" *Critical Essays on Margaret Atwood*. Ed. Judith McCombs. Boston: Hall, 1988. 229-245. Reprinted from *Essays on Canadian Writing* 33 (Fall 1986): 68-88.

93. DAVEY, Frank. "Alternate Stories: The Short Fiction of Audrey Thomas and Margaret Atwood." *Reading Canadian Reading*. Winnipeg: Turnstone Press, 1988. 151-166. "Reprinted from *Canadian Literature* 109."

94. ———. "Atwood's Gorgon Touch [Seven Books of Poetry, from *Double Persephone* to *You Are Happy*]." *Critical Essays on Margaret Atwood*. Ed. Judith McCombs. Boston: Hall, 1988. 134-153. Reprinted from *Studies in Canadian Literature* 2.2 (Summer 1977): 146-163.

95. ———. "*Margaret Atwood: A Feminist Poetics*." *Reading Canadian Reading*. Winnipeg: Turnstone Press, 1988. 63-85. Davey discusses reception of his book of this title.

96. ———."'Translating Translating Apollinaire': The Problematizing of Discourse in Some Recent Canadian Texts." *Cross-Cultural Studies: American, Canadian, and European Literatures: 1945-1985*. Ed. Mirko Jurak. Ljubljana, Yugoslavia: English Department, Filozofka Fakulteta, Edvard Kardelj University of Ljubljana, 1988. 41-46. Discusses *The Handmaid's Tale* as an example of "transgressive translation" in a study of translation as the transformation of "one or more discourses into another."

97. DAVIDSON, Arnold E. "Future Tense: Making History in *The Handmaid's Tale*." *Margaret Atwood: Vision and Forms*. Ed. Kathryn VanSpanckeren and Jan Garden Castro. Carbondale, IL: Southern Illinois UP, 1988. 113-121. Historical notes bring up questions of boundaries between fiction and history and the construction and conditioning of history by academics.

98. ———. "The Poetics of Pain in Margaret Atwood's *Bodily Harm*." *American Review of Canadian Studies* 18.1 (Spring 1988): 1-10. Atwood's new commitment to telling the painful truth is illustrated by the "calculus of suffering" that transforms the protagonist and through the complex, non-escapist ending.

99. De VOOGD, Peter J. "A Handmaid's Harm: Or, Margaret Atwood's Dystopia." *External and Detached: Dutch Essays on Contemporary Canadian Literature*. Ed. Charles Forceville, August J. Fry, and Peter J. de Voogd. *Canada Cahiers*, no. 4. Amsterdam: Free UP, 1988. 29-35. Although similar in structure, style, and content, the dystopian *The Handmaid's Tale* is less successful than *Bodily Harm*.

100. FOSTER, John Wilson. "The Poetry of Margaret Atwood [Six Books of Poetry, from *The Circle Game* to *You Are Happy*]." *Critical Essays on Margaret Atwood*. Ed. Judith McCombs. Boston: Hall, 1988. 153-167. Reprinted from *Canadian Literature* 74 (Autumn 1977): 5-20.

101. FREIBERT, Lucy M. "Control and Creativity: The Politics of Risk in Margaret Atwood's *The Handmaid's Tale*." *Critical Essays on Margaret Atwood*. Ed. Judith McCombs. Boston: Hall, 1988. 280-291.

102. FULFORD, Robert. *Best Seat in the House: Memoirs of a Lucky Man*. Toronto: Collins, 1988. See especially Chapter 10, "Mythology, Politics, and Atwood." 185-205. In this chapter Fulford discusses cultural nationalism and politics in Atwood's life and works as she participated in their creation.

103. GADPAILLE, Michelle. *The Canadian Short Story: Perspectives on Canadian Culture*. Toronto: Oxford UP, 1988. See especially "Margaret Atwood." 82-98. Discusses *Dancing Girls*, *Bluebeard's Egg*, and *Murder in the Dark*, addressing

Atwood's ability to transcend the boundaries of the short story form and her continual challenging of the language.

104. GARRETT-PETTS, W. F. "Reading, Writing, and the Postmodern Condition: Interpreting Margaret Atwood's *The Handmaid's Tale.*" *Open Letter* 7.1 (Spring 1988): 74-92. *The Handmaid's Tale'*s history as narrative links the postmodern reading experience with didactic intentions and issues of power, identity, and self-expression.

105. GEDDES, Gary. "Notes on the Poets: Margaret Atwood." *15 Canadian Poets X2.* Toronto: Oxford UP, 1988. 521-522. Outlines themes and techniques in Atwood's works; includes a brief biographical statement.

106. GERSTENBERGER, Donna. "Revisioning Cultural Norms: The Fiction of Margaret Atwood and Alice Walker." *Cross-Cultural Studies: American, Canadian, and European Literatures: 1945-1985.* Ed. Mirko Jurak. Ljubljana, Yugoslavia: English Department, Filozofka Fakulteta, Edvard Kardelj University of Ljubljana, 1988. 47-51. *Surfacing* and *The Color Purple* provide hopeful alternatives to the norms of gender and race created through language and other cultural systems.

107. GLOVER, Douglas. "Her Life Entire." *Books in Canada* 17.7 (October 1988): 11-14. Introduces *Cat's Eye*, which is "as thematically diverse and complex as anything she has written."

108. GRACE, Sherrill E. "In Search of Demeter: The Lost, Silent Mother in *Surfacing.*" *Margaret Atwood: Vision and Forms.* Ed. Kathryn VanSpanckeren and Jan Garden Castro. Carbondale, IL: Southern Illinois UP, 1988. 35-47. *Surfacing* keynotes are loss and silence in a "double-voiced discourse of Demeter & Persephone within a wilderness quest."

109. GRAY, Francine du Plessix. "Nature as Nunnery [*Surfacing*]." *Critical Essays on Margaret Atwood.* Ed. Judith McCombs. Boston: Hall, 1988. 131-134. Reprinted from *New York Times Book Review* 17 July 1977: 3, 29.

110. GREENE, Gayle. "*Life Before Man*: 'Can Anything Be Saved?'" *Margaret Atwood: Vision and Forms.* Ed. Kathryn VanSpanckeren and Jan Garden Castro. Carbondale, IL: Southern Illinois UP, 1988. 65-84. Achieves modernist goal by freeing "narrative from plot so that she can focus on inner events that are the real adventures." Studies time and experience of time, seeing hope through change in individuals.

111. GREENE, Sharon Elaine. "The Body Politic: Women, Language, and Revolution in Three Contemporary Novels." PhD thesis. Emory University, 1988. 253 pp. Explores the female body, language, and revolution against patriarchy in *Bodily Harm* and works by Naipaul and Didion. For more see *DAI-A* 49.06 (December 1988): 1599.

112. GROSSKURTH, Phyllis. "Survival Kit." *Critical Essays on Margaret Atwood.* Ed. Judith McCombs. Boston: Hall, 1988. 66-70. Reprinted from *New Statesman* 24 August 1973: 254-255.

113. HELLER, Arno. "Die Literarische Dystopie in Amerika mit einer Exemplarischen Erorterung von Margaret Atwoods *The Handmaid's Tale.*" *Utopian Thought in American Literature: Untersuchungen zur literarischen Utopie und Dystopie in den U.S.A.* Ed. Arno Heller, Walter Holbling, and Waldemar Zacharasiewicz. Buchreiche zu den Arbeiten aus Anglistik und Amerikanistik, Band 1. Tubingen: Gunter Narr, 1988. 185-204. Within the scope of the American dystopian tradition, *The Handmaid's Tale* goes beyond the conventional dystopic narrative and achieves individualistic, conservative goals.

114. HELWIG, David. "[Review of *The Animals in That County*]." *Critical Essays on Margaret Atwood*. Ed. Judith McCombs. Boston: Hall, 1988. 32-33. Reprinted from *Queen's Quarterly* 76 (Spring 1969): 161-162.

115. HENGEN, Shannon Eileen. "Margaret Atwood's Power." PhD thesis. University of Iowa, 1988. 200 pp. The gaining of power by Atwood's female characters, combined with a leftist political view, forms a complex definition of Canadianness. For more see *DAI-A* 49.08 (February 1989): 2224.

116. HINZ, Evelyn J. "The Religious Roots of the Feminine Identity Issue: Margaret Laurence's *The Stone Angel* and Margaret Atwood's *Surfacing*." *Margaret Laurence: An Appreciation*. Ed. Christl Verduyn. Peterborough, ON: Broadview Press, 1988. 82-100. "Reprinted from *Journal of Canadian Studies/Revue d'études canadiennes* 22.1 (Spring 1987)."

117. HITE, Molly. "Writing—and Reading—the Body: Female Sexuality and Feminist Fiction." *Feminist Studies* 14.1 (Spring 1988): 121-142. The patriarchally created image of the female body is taken apart and demystified in *Lady Oracle* and works by Walker, Lessing, and Wittig.

118. HJARTARSON, Paul. "The Literary Canon and Its Discontent: Reflections on the Cultural Reproduction of Value." *Canadian Issues/Thèmes canadiens* 10.5 (1988): 67-80. Highlights *The Handmaid's Tale* and Kroetsch's *Badlands* to illustrate the contingency of aesthetic value and the impact of gender and cultural forces on the formation of a Canadian literary canon.

119. HUTCHEON, Linda. *The Canadian Postmodern: A Study of Contemporary English-Canadian Fiction*. Toronto; New York; Oxford: Oxford UP, 1988. See especially "Process, Product, and Politics: The Postmodernism of Margaret Atwood." 138-159. Atwood's work represents the epitome of the postmodern paradox. It expresses the tension between the process and the result of art and develops political and moral responsibility in the reader.

120. IRVINE, Lorna. "The Here and Now of *Bodily Harm*." *Margaret Atwood: Vision and Forms*. Ed. Kathryn VanSpanckeren and Jan Garden Castro. Carbondale, IL: Southern Illinois UP, 1988. 85-100. Abridged version of "Atwood's Parable of Flesh." Reprinted from *Sub/Version*, Toronto: ECW Press, 1986. A superficial, heavily coded plot articulates and liberates the female body.

121. ———. "Murder and Mayhem: Margaret Atwood Deconstructs." *Contemporary Literature* 29.2 (Summer 1988): 265-276. *Murder in the Dark*'s textual games give insight to other works; deconstructed language has redemptive possibilities and allows new structures.

122. KANE, Patricia. "A Woman's Dystopia: Margaret Atwood's *Handmaid's Tale*." *Notes on Contemporary Literature* 18.5 (November 1988): 9-10. The success of *The Handmaid's Tale* as a dystopia lies in the central character who "does not identify with victims and cares only about a man's love."

123. KINGDEN, Elizabeth. "A Faulty Diagnosis of Society's Ills as Seen in Margaret Atwood's *Handmaid's Tale*." *Cross-Canada Writer's Quarterly* 10.2 (1988): 7, 32. The premise of population decline is one of several problems that make *The Handmaid's Tale* "a seriously flawed work."

124. KURIBAYASHI, Tomoko. "The Desire for Transformation: A Study of the Significance of Clothes in Atwood's Fiction." MA thesis. University of Alberta, 1988. Also available on microfiche from Canadian Theses Service (1989).

125. LANGER, Beryl Donaldson. "Class and Gender in Margaret Atwood's Fiction." *Australian-Canadian Studies* 6.1 (1988): 73-101. Confrontation of the social and

moral dilemmas of the late 20th century's "new class" is one of the greatest strengths of Atwood's fiction.

126. LARKIN, Joan. "Soul Survivor [*Surfacing* and *Power Politics*]." *Critical Essays on Margaret Atwood.* Ed. Judith McCombs. Boston: Hall, 1988. 48-52. Reprinted from *Ms.* May 1973: 33-35.

127. LAURENCE, Margaret. "[Review of *Surfacing*]." *Critical Essays on Margaret Atwood.* Ed. Judith McCombs. Boston: Hall, 1988. 45-47. Reprinted from *Quarry* 4 (Spring 1973): 62-64.

128. LILIENFELD, Jane. "Circe's Emergence: Transforming Traditional Love in Margaret Atwood's *You Are Happy*." *Critical Essays on Margaret Atwood.* Ed. Judith McCombs. Boston: Hall, 1988. 123-130. Reprinted from Worcester *Review* 5 (Spring 1977): 29-31, 33-37.

129. LOZAR, Tom. "America in the Canadian Mind." *Cross-Cultural Studies: American, Canadian, and European Literatures: 1945-1985.* Ed. Mirko Jurak. Ljubljana, Yugoslavia: English Department, Filozofka Fakulteta, Edvard Kardelj University of Ljubljana, 1988. 379-85. Examines varieties of nationalism and internationalism in Canadian literature and culture. "Anti-Americanism of the *Surfacing/Survival* type is part of the Canadian intellectual's uniform."

130. LYNCH, Denise E. "Personalist Plot in Atwood's *Bodily Harm*." *Studies in the Humanities* 15.1 (June 1988): 45-57. The parallel structure and complexity of *Bodily Harm*'s plot builds a personalist consciousness of "creative non-victim" for the reader and the protagonist.

131. MacLULICH, T. D. "Atwood's Adult Fairy Tale: Lévi-Strauss, Bettelheim, and *The Edible Woman*." *Critical Essays on Margaret Atwood.* Ed. Judith McCombs. Boston: Hall, 1988. 179-197. Reprinted from *Essays on Canadian Writing* 11 (Summer 1978): 111-129.

132. MALLINSON, Jean. *Margaret Atwood.* Toronto, ON: ECW Press, 1988.

133. MANDEL, Ann. "[Review of *True Stories*]." *Critical Essays on Margaret Atwood.* Ed. Judith McCombs. Boston: Hall, 1988. 245-251. Reprinted from *Fiddlehead* 131 (January 1982): 63-70.

134. MANDEL, Eli. "Atwood Gothic [*You Are Happy, Surfacing, Survival, The Animals in That Country, The Circle Game* and *Power Politics*]." *Critical Essays on Margaret Atwood.* Ed. Judith McCombs. Boston: Hall, 1988. 114-123. Reprinted from *Malahat Review: Margaret Atwood: A Symposium.* Ed. Linda Sandler. 41 (January 1977): 165-174.

135. McCOMBS, Judith. "Country, Politics, and Gender in Canadian Studies: A Report from Twenty Years of Atwood Criticism." *Canadian Issues/Thèmes canadiens* 10.5 (1988): 27-47. Lack of warmth is a key issue in 20 years of Atwood criticism by men and women in Canada and the United States.

136. ———. "Politics, Structure, and Poetic Development in Atwood's Canadian-American Sequences: From an Apprentice Pair to 'The Circle Game' to 'Two-Headed Poems.'" *Margaret Atwood: Vision and Forms.* Ed. Kathryn VanSpanckeren and Jan Garden Castro. Carbondale, IL: Southern Illinois UP, 1988. 142-162. Sees works in two stages of development and documents changes in treatment of Canadian-American themes beginning in early unpublished papers.

137. McCOMBS, Judith, ed. *Critical Essays on Margaret Atwood.* Boston: G. K. Hall, 1988. 306. Reprints a "range of the best obtainable and still-key Atwood criticism." Individual entries indexed in this section. Detailed introduction complements and gives perspective to the selections.

138. McMILLAN, Ann. "The Transforming Eye: *Lady Oracle* and Gothic Tradition." *Margaret Atwood: Vision and Forms*. Ed. Kathryn VanSpanckeren and Jan Garden Castro. Carbondale, IL: Southern Illinois UP, 1988. 48-64. Perception and transformation equal the "transforming eye" that allows the heroine maturity and insight into a Gothic tradition that is no longer an "instrument of patriarchy." Some comparison with *Northanger Abbey*.

139. MONTIGNY, Denise de. "Giving Birth = [Donner naissance]." MS thesis. University of Ottawa, 1988. 219 pp. French translation with commentary. Also available on microfiche from Canadian Theses Service (1989).

140. NABAR, Vrinda. "Self-Discovery Through Integration with One's Past: Reflections on Margaret Atwood's *Surfacing*." *Peace, Development and Culture: Comparative Studies of India and Canada*. Ed. Harold Coward. Calgary: Shastri Indo-Canadian Institute, ©1988, printed 1990. 73-82. Relates Atwood's remarks to Indo-English literature and says that tradition is a different experience from the Canadian one; this paper was presented at a conference in 1988 for the 20th anniversary of the institute.

141. NAULTY, Patricia Mary. "'I Never Talk of Hunger': Self-Starvation as Women's Language of Protest in Novels by Barbara Pym, Margaret Atwood, and Anne Tyler." PhD thesis. Ohio State University, 1988. Anorexic behavior in *Quartet in Autumn*, *The Edible Woman*, and *Dinner at the Homesick Restaurant* is a language of protest against women's prescribed roles in a dysfunctional society. For more see *DAI-A* 50.01 (July 1989): 140.

142. NEWMAN, Christina. "In Search of a Native Tongue [*Surfacing*]." *Critical Essays on Margaret Atwood*. Ed. Judith McCombs. Boston: Hall, 1988. 43-45. Reprinted from *Maclean's* September 1972: 88.

143. ONDAATJE, Michael. "[Review of *The Circle Game*]." *Critical Essays on Margaret Atwood*. Ed. Judith McCombs. Boston: Hall, 1988. 29-32. Reprinted from *Canadian Forum* April 1967: 22-23.

144. ONLEY, Gloria. "Power Politics in Bluebeard's Castle [*Power Politics, The Edible Woman, Surfacing, Survival, Procedures for Underground* and 'Polarities']." *Critical Essays on Margaret Atwood*. Ed. Judith McCombs. Boston: Hall, 1988. 70-89. Reprinted from *Canadian Literature* 60 (Spring 1974): 21-42.

145. OSADNIK, Waclaw M. "Margaret Atwood's *Life Before Man* as a Comment on Contemporary Human Relationships." *Studies in Semiotics and Poetics of Canadian and English Literature*. Ed. Waclaw M. Osadnik. Vienna: S. & B. Publishers, 1988. 17-24.

146. ———. "The Semiotic Interpretation of Ritualistic Behaviour in the Literary Work: Margaret Atwood: *Surfacing*." *Studies in Semiotics and Poetics of Canadian and English Literature*. Ed. Waclaw M. Osadnik. Vienna: S. & B. Publishers, 1988. 1-16.

147. PIERCY, Marge. "Margaret Atwood: Beyond Victimhood [*Survival, The Edible Woman, Surfacing* and Five Books of Poetry]." *Critical Essays on Margaret Atwood*. Ed. Judith McCombs. Boston: Hall, 1988. 53-66. Reprinted from American *Poetry Review* 2 (November-December 1973): 41-44.

148. PURDY, A. W. "Atwood's Moodie [*The Journals of Susanna Moodie*]." *Critical Essays on Margaret Atwood*. Ed. Judith McCombs. Boston: Hall, 1988. 38-42. Reprinted from *Canadian Literature* 47 (Winter 1971): 80-84.

149. REDEKOP, Magdalene. "Charms and Riddles [*Bluebeard's Egg*]." *Critical Essays on Margaret Atwood*. Ed. Judith McCombs. Boston: Hall, 1988. 256-258. Reprinted from *Canadian Forum* January 1984: 30-31.

150. RILEY, Ruby J. "Childbirth in Literature." MA thesis. University of Houston, 1988. 70 pp. Unlike writers of an earlier age, Atwood, Doris Lessing, and Toni Morrison use birth scenes for a variety of purposes. For more see *MAI* 27.03 (Fall 1989): 352.

151. ROBINSON, Sally. "The 'Anti-Logos Weapon': Multiplicity in Women's Texts." *Contemporary Literature* 29.1 (Spring 1988): 105-124. Uses French feminist theories of Hélène Cixous, Luce Irigaray, and Julia Kristeva in analysis of *Surfacing*, Joanna Russ's *The Female Man*, and Bertha Harris's *Lover*.

152. ROGERS, Jaqueline Eleanor McLeod. "Aspects of the Female Novel: Experience, Pattern, Selfhood." PhD thesis. University of Manitoba, 1988. Studies the difference in principles and content between female novels and the traditional novel, covering the chronological period from Aphra Behn's *Oroonoko* to *The Handmaid's Tale*. For more see *DAI-A* 49.04 (October 1988): 808.

153. ROSOWSKI, Susan J. "Margaret Atwood's *Lady Oracle*: Fantasy and the Modern Gothic Novel." *Critical Essays on Margaret Atwood*. Ed. Judith McCombs. Boston: Hall, 1988. 197-208. An earlier version was published in *Research Studies* 49.2 (June 1981): 87-98.

154. RUBENSTEIN, Roberta. "Nature and Nurture in Dystopia: *The Handmaid's Tale*." *Margaret Atwood: Vision and Forms*. Ed. Kathryn VanSpanckeren and Jan Garden Castro. Carbondale, IL: Southern Illinois UP, 1988. 101-112. Inversions of nature and nurture themes "connect the personal and political dimensions of victimization and survival in explicitly female and feminist terms."

155. ———. "Pandora's Box and Female Survival: Margaret Atwood's *Bodily Harm*." *Critical Essays on Margaret Atwood*. Ed. Judith McCombs. Boston: Hall, 1988. 259-275. Reprinted from *Journal of Canadian Studies* 20.1 (Spring 1985): 120-135.

156. SAN, Shusmita. "*Bluebeard's Egg and Other Stories*: Margaret Atwood's Portraits of the Resilient Woman." MA thesis. Eastern Washington University, 1988. Source: WorldCat.

157. SCHLUETER, June. "Canlit/Victimlit: *Survival* and *Second Words*." *Margaret Atwood: Vision and Forms*. Ed. Kathryn VanSpanckeren and Jan Garden Castro. Carbondale, IL: Southern Illinois UP, 1988. 1-11. Support of Atwood's victim premise in *Survival* and how it is broadened in *Second Words*.

158. SKELTON, Robin. *The Memoirs of a Literary Blockhead*. Toronto: Macmillan of Canada, 1988. This humorous autobiography by the poet and writer tells of Skelton's life in England and Canada, but focuses on his experiences with other literary figures, such as Atwood, as well as Ezra Pound, Milton Acorn, and Dorothy Livesay.

159. ———. "[Review of *The Journals of Susanna Moodie* and *Procedures for Underground*]." *Critical Essays on Margaret Atwood*. Ed. Judith McCombs. Boston: Hall, 1988. 34-35. Reprinted from *Malahat Review* 17 (January 1971): 133-134.

160. STAELS, Hilde. "Margaret Atwood." *Post-war Literatures in English: A Lexicon of Contemporary Authors*. Ed. Johannes Willem Bertens. Alphen aan den Rijn: Samson Uitgeverij; Groningen: Wolters-Noordhoff, 1988: 1-10. Biography and critical essay followed by Bibliography of Primary Sources, A1, and Bibliography of Secondary Sources, B1-B3.

161. STEVEN, Laurence. "Margaret Atwood's 'Polarities' and George Grant's Polemics." *American Review of Canadian Studies* 18.4 (Winter 1988): 443-454. Outlines a relationship between Grant's *Technology and Empire* and Atwood's "Polarities." Finds a foreshadowing of this connection in the Grant epigraphs in *Survival*.

162. STEVENS, Peter. "Dark Mouth [*Procedures for Underground*]." *Critical Essays on Margaret Atwood*. Ed. Judith McCombs. Boston: Hall, 1988. 37-38. Reprinted from *Canadian Literature* 50 (Autumn 1971): 91-92.

163. STILLMAN, Peter. "Public and Private in Margaret Atwood's *The Handmaid's Tale* and *Bodily Harm*." *Q/W/E/R/T/Y* 8 (1988): 207-215.

164. STOUCK, David. "Margaret Atwood." *Major Canadian Authors: A Critical Introduction to Canadian Literature in English*. 2nd rev. and exp. ed. Lincoln; London: University of Nebraska Press, 1988. 273-294. New edition adds a critical essay on Atwood's novels and poetry through *The Handmaid's Tale*.

165. STOW, Glenys. "Nonsense as Social Commentary in *The Edible Woman*." *Journal of Canadian Studies/Revue d'études canadiennes* 23.3 (Fall 1988): 90-101. Parallel nonsense devices, events, and characters in *The Edible Woman* and Lewis Carroll's *Alice* stories express a common view of society and its conventions.

166. SULLIVAN, Rosemary. "Breaking the Circle [*The Circle Game, Survival, The Journals of Susanna Moodie, The Animals in That Country* and *Surfacing*]." *Critical Essays on Margaret Atwood*. Ed. Judith McCombs. Boston: Hall, 1988. 104-114. Reprinted from *Malahat Review: Margaret Atwood: A Symposium*. Ed. Linda Sandler. 41 (January 1977): 30-41.

167. THOMAS, Sue. "Mythic Reconception and the Mother/Daughter Relationship in Margaret Atwood's *Surfacing*." *ARIEL* 19.2 (April 1988): 73-85. Mother and daughter relationships are reflected by grail motifs, quest structure, Freudian symbolism, and biblical myth.

168. TSCHACHLER, Heinz. "The Reconstruction of Myth in James Dickey's *Deliverance* and Margaret Atwood's *Surfacing*, or, the Ideology of Form." *Cross-Cultural Studies: American, Canadian, and European Literatures: 1945-1985*. Ed. Mirko Jurak. Ljubljana, Yugoslavia: English Department, Filozofka Fakulteta, Edvard Kardelj University of Ljubljana, 1988. 65-77. *Deliverance*, a "mythic novel," and *Surfacing*, a "novel on mythic themes," imaginatively articulate a modern reconstruction of the mythic quest.

169. TURNER, Alden R. "Atwood's Playing Puritans in *The Handmaid's Tale*." *Cross-Cultural Studies: American, Canadian, and European Literatures: 1945-1985*. Ed. Mirko Jurak. Ljubljana, Yugoslavia: English Department, Filozofka Fakulteta, Edvard Kardelj University of Ljubljana, 1988. 85-91. *The Handmaid's Tale* is written in the American literary tradition of "fiction founded on fact." Offred survives by creating an oral narrative that "develops a literary pattern of playing puritans."

170. VanSPANCKEREN, Kathryn. "Introduction." *Margaret Atwood: Vision and Forms*. Ed. Kathryn VanSpanckeren and Jan Garden Castro. Carbondale, IL: Southern Illinois UP, 1988. xix-xxvii. Overview of essays in the "new, comprehensive critical collection encompassing Atwood's recent work." The study is "particularly interested in Atwood's feminism."

171. ———. "Shamanism in the Works of Margaret Atwood." *Margaret Atwood: Vision and Forms*. Ed. Kathryn VanSpanckeren and Jan Garden Castro. Carbondale, IL: Southern Illinois UP, 1988. 183-204. Shamanic images in poetry and fiction show spiritual tradition of Amerindian. Focus on descents and nature-oriented vision supports a feminist interpretation.

172.   VanSPANCKEREN, Kathryn and Jan Garden CASTRO, eds. *Margaret Atwood: Vision and Forms.* With an autobiographical foreword by Margaret Atwood. Carbondale, IL: Southern Illinois UP, 1988. Individual essays listed separately in this section.

173.   VOGT, Kathleen. "Real and Imaginary Animals in the Poetry of Margaret Atwood." *Margaret Atwood: Vision and Forms.* Ed. Kathryn VanSpanckeren and Jan Garden Castro. Carbondale, IL: Southern Illinois UP, 1988. 163-182. Examines the dominance of animals in poetry, alive, dead, real, and metamorphic. Animals reflect the relationship between human and other.

174.   WALKER, Nancy. "Ironic Autobiography: From *The Waterfall* to *The Handmaid's Tale.*" *Women's Studies* 15.1-3 (1988): 203-220. Narrators with two selves in *The Handmaid's Tale*, Fay Weldon's *Female Friends*, Margaret Drabble's *The Waterfall*, and Nora Ephron's *Heartburn* communicate verbal and situational irony to reveal the absurd forces that have continued to subordinate women over the past 20 years.

175.   WALL, Kathleen. "*Surfacing*: The Matriarchal Myth Re-surfaces." *The Callisto Myth from Ovid to Atwood: Initiation and Rape in Literature.* Kingston, Montreal: McGill-Queen's UP, 1988. 155-170. Archetype for *Surfacing* is the Callisto myth in a two-encounter form. The violation and renewal experiences "give the narrator psychological virginity."

176.   WIDMER, Kingsley. *Counterings: Utopian Dialectics in Contemporary Contexts.* Ann Arbor, MI; London: UMI Research Press, 1988. See especially "Antifemtopian Feminism and Atwood." 75-80. Ambiguous feminism and dystopian ironies in *The Handmaid's Tale* form an "antifemtopianism" that is part of a larger utopian dialect.

177.   WIEDE-BEHRENDT, Ingrid. "Dangling Woman: Die hintergründigen Romane der Anglokanadierin Margaret Atwood." *Literatur in Wissenschaft und Unterricht* 21.2 (1988): 108-128. Atwood is a storyteller of the highest order dealing with the problems of the contemporary woman and the sweet Canadians. Her enigmatic novels are similar to the double vision of René Magritte's paintings.

178.   WILD-BICANIC, Sonia. "Dependence and Resolution in the Novels of Margaret Atwood." *Cross-Cultural Studies: American, Canadian, and European Literatures: 1945-1985.* Ed. Mirko Jurak. Ljubljana, Yugoslavia: English Department, Filozofka Fakulteta, Edvard Kardelj University of Ljubljana, 1988. 79-83. Reminiscent of Wordsworth's "Resolution and Independence," Atwood's novels focus on psychological and spiritual regeneration and "independence through resolution."

179.   WILOCH, Thomas. Atwood entry. *Contemporary Authors.* Ed. Deborah A. Straub 24. New rev. ser. Detroit, MI: Gale Research Co., 1988. 17-22, 25-26. Biographical entry with a primary bibliography and an essay on critical reception of novels, mainly *The Handmaid's Tale.*

180.   WILSON, Sharon R. "Sexual Politics in Margaret Atwood's Visual Art." *Margaret Atwood: Vision and Forms.* Ed. Kathryn VanSpanckeren and Jan Garden Castro. Carbondale, IL: Southern Illinois UP, 1988. 205-214. Like poetry and fiction, Atwood's "watercolors represent recurrent, archetypal images of power politics." Taped interview and color reproductions enrich discussion of 8 paintings.

181.   WOODCOCK, George. "Margaret Atwood: Poet as Novelist [*Power Politics, The Circle Game, The Edible Woman, The Journals of Susanna Moodie, The Animals in That Country, Survival* and *Surfacing*]." *Critical Essays on Margaret Atwood.*

Ed. Judith McCombs. Boston: Hall, 1988. 90-104. Reprinted from The *Canadian Novel in the Twentieth Century*. Ed. George Woodcock. Toronto: McClelland and Stewart, 1975. 312-327.

182. WURST, Gayle. "Cultural Stereotypes and the Language of Identity: Margaret Atwood's *Lady Oracle*, Maxine Hong Kingston's *The Woman Warrior*, and Alice Walker's *The Color Purple*." *Cross-Cultural Studies: American, Canadian, and European Literatures: 1945-1985*. Ed. Mirko Jurak. Ljubljana, Yugoslavia: English Department, Filozofka Fakulteta, Edvard Kardelj University of Ljubljana, 1988. 53-64. Three diverse novels use the common process of awakening consciousness to break through restrictive stereotypes.

183. YORK, Lorraine M. "'Violent Stillness': Photography and Postmodernism in Canadian Fiction." *Mosaic* 21.2-3 (Spring 1988): 193-201. Includes a short discussion on the use of photography in Atwood's work.

184. ZAMOST, Julie. "Recovery of the Mother." MA thesis. Sonoma State University, 1988. Discusses Atwood's *Surfacing*.

Reviews of Atwood's Works

185. *Bluebeard's Egg and Other Stories*. Boston: Houghton Mifflin, 1986; London: J. Cape, 1987; New York: Ballantine, 1987; London: Virago, 1988.
    English Studies 69.5 (October 1988): 419. By J. M. BLOM and L. R. LEAVIS.
    Fiction (London) July 1988: 32. By Helen HAYWARD.
    Illinois Writers Review 7.1 (Spring 1988): 8-13. By Brad HOOPER.
    Kliatt Young Adult Paperback Book Guide 22.1 (January 1988): 24-25. By B.E.L.

186. *Canlit Foodbook*. Toronto: Totem Books, 1987.
    CM 16.4 (July 1988):134-35. By Sharon A. McLENNAN McCUE.

187. *Cat's Eye*. Toronto: McClelland and Stewart, 1988; New York: Doubleday, 1988; London: Bloomsbury, 1988.
    Atlantic Provinces Book Review 15.4 (November-December 1988): 12. By Allan DONALDSON.
    Book of the Month Club News December 1988: 2-3. By David Willis McCULLOUGH.
    Booklist 85.8 (15 December 1988): 665. By D[enise] P. D[ONAVIN].
    Canadian Churchman 114.10 (December 1988): 16. By Sheila MARTINDALE.
    Kirkus Reviews 56.24 (15 December 1988): 1754-1755. By Jim KOBAK.
    Malahat Review 85 (December 1988): 131-132. By Constance ROOKE.
    Now (Toronto) 8.9 (3-9 November 1988): 49. By John OUGHTON.
    Quill and Quire 54.10 (October 1988): 18. By Robert FULFORD.
    Saturday Night 103.11 (November 1988): 66-67, 69. By Alberto MANGUEL.
    Toronto Star 1 October 1988: Section: Magazine: M3. By Ken ADACHI. (1669 w.)

188. *Der Report der Magd*. Translated by Helga Pfetsch. Dusseldorf: Claassen, 1987. [*The Handmaid's Tale*.]
    Argument (Hamburg) 169 (1988): 426-427. By Ingrid WIEDE-BEHRENDT.

189. *Essai sur la littérature canadienne*. Translated by Hélène Filion. Montreal: Boreal, 1987. [*Survival*.]
    Actualité 13.3 (March 1988): 150.

Nuit Blanche 30 (December 1987-January 1988): 68. By Marie-Christine PIOFFET.

190. *The Handmaid's Tale.* [Sound recording]. Read by Betty Harris. Charlotte Hall, MD: Recorded Books, 1988. 8 sound cassettes.

　　　Library Journal 113.17 (15 October 1988): 66. By Janet MORGAN.

191. *The Handmaid's Tale.* Toronto: McClelland and Stewart, 1985; Boston: Houghton Mifflin, London: J. Cape, 1986; New York: Fawcett Crest, London: Virago, 1986

　　　Emergency Librarian 16.1 (September-October 1988): 54. By Nicholas WHITLE. High school student review.

　　　Library Journal 113.17 (15 October 1988): 66. By Janet MORGAN.

　　　Stand 30 (Winter 1988): 77. By Peter LEWIS.

192. *Interlunar.* Toronto: Oxford UP, 1984.

　　　Sunday Times (London) 20 November 1988: G12. By David PROFUMO.

193. *Meurtre dans la nuit.* Translated by Hélène Filion. Montreal: Éditions du Remue-ménage, 1987. [*Murder in the Dark.*]

　　　Resources for Feminist Research/Documentation sur la recherche féministe 17.128. By Christine KLEIN-LATAUD.

194. *New Oxford Book of Canadian Verse in English.* Toronto; New York: Oxford UP, 1982.

　　　In Defence of Art: Critical Essays and Reviews. Ed. with an introduction by Aileen Collins. Kingston, ON: Quarry Press, 1988: 244-47. Reprint of *Globe and Mail* 11 December 1982. By Louis DUDEK.

195. *Oxford Book of Canadian Short Stories in English.* Toronto; New York: Oxford UP, 1986.

　　　Washington Post 19 May 1988: Section: Style: C 15. By Dennis DRABELLE. (797 w.)

196. *Selected Poems II.* Toronto: Oxford UP, 1986; Boston: Houghton Mifflin, 1987. US edition does not include the 13 selections from *Murder in the Dark* and 34 additional poems that appear in the Canadian publication.

　　　America 158.18 (7 May 1988): 490. *Includes Selected Poems: 1965-1975.* Boston: Houghton Mifflin, 1987. By Robert HOSMER.

　　　American Book Review 10.3 (July-August 1988): 21. By Miriam LEVINE.

　　　Canadian Literature 116 (Spring 1988): 185-187. By Lorraine YORK.

　　　Choice 25.9 (May 1988): 1398. By Jerome H. ROSENBERG.

　　　Kenyon Review 10.3 (Summer 1988): 136-139. Includes *Selected Poems: 1965-1975.* Boston: Houghton Mifflin, 1987. By Dave SMITH.

　　　New York Times Book Review 3 April 1988: 12. By Harold BEAVER.

197. *La Servante écarlate.* Translated by Sylviane Rue. Paris: Laffont, 1987. [*The Handmaid's Tale.*]

　　　Bulletin critique du livre français 506 (February 1988): 196.

　　　Châtelaine 29.2 (February 1988): 17. By Mireille SIMARD.

~ 1989 ~

Atwood's Works

198. "[Advice on Writing.]" *Form*. [Videorecording]. s.l.: Institute of Contemporary Arts, 1989. 25 min. Authors give advice about writing professionally. This program focuses on form and genre. In addition to Atwood, Brian Aldiss, Maya Angelou, Elaine Feinstein, P. D. James, Robert Leeson, Deborah Moggach, Christopher Priest, Ruth Rendell, and Fay Weldon appear.

199. "Afterword." *Sudden Fiction International: Sixty Short-Short Stories*. Ed. Robert Shapard and James Thomas. New York and London: Norton, 1989. 62-64.

200. "Age of Lead." *Toronto Life* 23.12 (August 1989): 36-39, 50-51, 54. Short fiction.

201. *The Best American Short Stories, 1989*. Selected from US and Canadian magazines by Margaret Atwood with Shannon Ravenel. Boston: Houghton Mifflin, 1989.

202. "Biographobia: Some Personal Reflections on the Act of Biography." *Nineteenth-Century Lives: Essays Presented to Jerome Hamilton Buckley*. Ed. Laurence S. Lockridge, John Maynard, and Donald D. Stone. Cambridge; New York: Cambridge UP, 1989. 1-8.

203. *Bluebeard's Egg and Other Stories*. New York: Fawcett Crest, 1989 ©1986. Paperback. ed.

204. *Bodily Harm*. Toronto; New York: Bantam, 1989 ©1981.

205. "Bowering Pie…Some Recollections." *Essays on Canadian Writing* 38 (Summer 1989): 3-6. Traces the events that led to a personal encounter with Canadian poet George Bowering in 1967.

206. "Cat's Eye." *Seventeen* 48 (August 1989): 310-313, 329-331.

207. *Cat's Eye*. Toronto: McClelland-Bantam; New York: Bantam Books; London: Bloomsbury, 1989 ©1988.

208. *Cat's Eye*. [Braille]. Toronto: CNIB, 1989. 9v.

209. *Cat's Eye*. [Sound recording]. Read by Kate Nelligan. New York: Bantam Audio Pub, 1989. 2 sound cassettes. 180 min.

210. *Dancing Girls and Other Stories*. New York: Bantam, 1989 ©1982.

211. *Danshingu garusu, Magaretto Atouddo tanpenshu*. Tokyo: Hakusuisha, 1989. Japanese translation of *Dancing Girls and Other Stories* by Kishimoto Sachiko. Title romanized.

212. "Death by Landscape." *Saturday Night* 104.7 (July 1989): 46-53. Short fiction. Also published in *New Woman*. November 1989: 148-156.

213. "Death of a Young Son by Drowning." *Poetry by Canadian Women*. Ed. Rosemary Sullivan. Toronto: Oxford UP, 1989. 153-154. Originally published 1970.

214. *Der Report der Magd: Roman*. Frankfurt: Fischer Taschenbuch Verlag, 1989. German translation of *The Handmaid's Tale*.

215. "Earth." *Poetry by Canadian Women*. Ed. Rosemary Sullivan. Toronto: Oxford UP, 1989. 160-161. Originally published 1981.

216. *The Edible Woman*. Toronto: McClelland and Stewart; New York: Warner Books; London: Virago Press, 1989 ©1969.

217. *The Edible Woman*. [Sound recording]. Read by Barbara Byers. [Toronto]: CNIB, 1989. 8 sound cassettes in 1 cont. (11:00 hrs.).

218. *En la superficie*. La Habana: Editorial Arte y Literatura, 1989. Spanish translation of *Surfacing* by Ana Busquet.

219. "Game after Supper." *The Faber Book of 20th Century Women's Poetry*. Ed. Fleur Adcock. London; Boston: Faber and Faber, 1989. 269. Reprinted from *Procedures for Underground*, ©1970.

220. "The Grave of the Famous Poet." *The Houghton Mifflin Anthology of Short Fiction*. Boston: Houghton Mifflin, 1989. 23-30. Reprinted from *Dancing Girls and Other Stories*, ©1982.

221. "Great Aunts." *Family Portraits: Remembrances by Twenty Distinguished Writers*. Ed. Carolyn Anthony. New York: Doubleday, 1989. 3-16.

222. "Habitation." *The Faber Book of 20th Century Women's Poetry*. Ed. Fleur Adcock. London; Boston: Faber and Faber, 1989. 270. Reprinted from *Procedures for Underground*, ©1970.

223. *The Handmaid's Tale*. Toronto: McClelland-Bantam; New York: Ballantine Books; Fawcett Crest, 1989 ©1985.

224. *The Handmaid's Tale*. [Sound recording]. Brantford, ON: W. Ross MacDonald School, 1989.

225. "Happy Endings." *Sudden Fiction International: Sixty Short-Short Stories*. Ed. Robert Shapard and James Thomas. New York; London: Norton, 1989. 55-59. Reprinted from *Murder in the Dark*, ©1983.

226. *Hē historia tes porphyres doules*. Athens: Hestia, 1989. Greek translation of *The Handmaid's Tale* by Paulos Matesis.

227. *Heaven on Earth*. [Video recording]. Screenplay by Margaret Atwood and Peter Pearson. [New York] : SVS, 1989. 1 videocassette (ca. 100 min.). "Between 1867 and 1914 many orphaned British children were sent to Canada to find new homes. They were called home children. An emotional story of the lives of some of these children, based on historical events." (Publisher).

228. "Helpful Hints." *Conde Nast Traveler* (February 1989): 40. Travel advice.

229. "Introduction." *The Dry Wells of India: An Anthology Against Thirst: Selected Poems Entered in the Canadian Poetry Contest 1987-88*. Ed. George Woodcock. Madeira Park, BC: Harbour Publishing, 1989. i-ii. Atwood was one of the judges of this contest, along with Al Purdy and Woodcock. [Ed. note: The title page references a Foreword by Atwood, not an Introduction.]

230. "Introduction." *Women Writers at Work: The Paris Review Interviews*. Ed. George Plimpton. New York: Viking Press, 1989. xi-xviii.

231. "Introduction: Reading Blind." *The Best American Short Stories 1989*. Selected from US and Canadian magazines by Margaret Atwood with Shannon Ravenel. Boston: Houghton Mifflin, 1989. xi-xxiii.

232. *Katteøje*. Viborg [Denmark]: Lindhardt og Ringhof, 1989. Danish translation of *Cat's Eye* by Lisbeth Møller-Madsen.

233. *Katteøyet*. [Oslo]: Aschehoug, 1989. Norwegian translation of *Cat's Eye* by Inger Gjelsvik.

234. *Kattöga*. Stockholm: Prisma, 1989. Swedish translation of *Cat's Eye* by Maria Ekman.

235. *Kissansilmä*. Helsinki: Kirjayhtymä, 1989. Finnish translation of *Cat's Eye* by Matti Kannosto.

236. *Lady Oracle*. London: Virago Press, 1989 ©1976.

237. "Late August." *Touching Fire: Erotic Writings by Women*. Ed. Louise Thornton, Jan Sturtevant, and Amber Coverdale Sumrall. New York: Carroll and Graf, 1989. 104. Reprinted from *Selected Poems 1965-1975*; biographical sketch of Atwood on 211 includes quote on her "sense of the erotic."

238. *Life Before Man*. Toronto: McClelland-Bantam; London: Virago Press, 1989 ©1979.

239. "The Man from Mars." *Between Worlds*. Ed. Maggie Goh and Craig Stephenson. Oakville, ON: Rubicon Publishing, 1989. 64-84. Also in: *New Worlds of Literature*. Ed. Jerome Beaty and J. Paul Hunter. New York: Norton, 1989. 651-667. Includes study questions: 667-668. Reprinted from *Dancing Girls and Other Stories*, ©1977-1982.

240. *Meng Duan Chang Ye*. Taipei: Huang guan chu ban she, 1989. Chinese translation of *Bodily Harm* by Zhang Huiqian Yi.

241. *Murder in the Dark*. [Sound recording]. Read by Clare Coulter. Toronto: Coach House/Music Gallery, 1989. 1 sound cassette. (ca. 90 min.). [Side A]: "Autobiography," "Making Poison," "The Boys' Own Annual," "Before the War," "Horror Comics," "Boyfriends," "The Victory Burlesque," "Fainting," "Raw Materials," "Murder in the Dark," "Simmering," "Women's Novels 1 & 2," "[Side B]: Women's Novels 3-7," "Happy Endings," "Bread," "The Page," "Mute," "She," "Worship," "Iconography," "Liking Men—Strawberries," "Him," "Hopeless," "A Parable," "Hand," "Everlasting," "Instructions for the Third Eye."

242. "My Brother." *Harper's Magazine* 278 (March 1989): 36, 38.

243. "Note from an Italian Postcard Factory." *Canadian Travellers in Italy*. Ed. Barry Callaghan. Toronto: Exile Editions, 1989. 146-47. Reprinted from *Two-Headed Poems*, ©1978-1980.

244. "Noted with Pleasure." *New York Times Book Review* 19 February 1989: 35. Short excerpt from *Cat's Eye*.

245. "Notes Towards a Poem That Can Never Be Written." *Poetry by Canadian Women*. Ed. Rosemary Sullivan. Toronto: Oxford UP, 1989. 158-160. Originally published 1981.

246. "Nothing." *Poetry by Canadian Women*. Ed. Rosemary Sullivan. Toronto: Oxford UP, 1989. 161-162.

247. *O femeie obisnuit*. Bucharest: Editura Univers, 1989. Romanian translation of *The Edible Woman*.

248. *O Lago Sagrado*. São Paulo: Editora Globo, 1989. Portuguese translation of *Surfacing* by Cacilda Ferrante.

249. *Pani Wyrocznia*. Warsaw: Panstwowy Instytut Wydawn, 1989. Polish translation of *Lady Oracle* by Zofia Uhrynowska-Hanasz.

250. *The Poetry of Margaret Atwood*. [Sound recording]. Read by Pamela Rabe. Sydney: ABC Radio, 1989. 1 sound cassette.

251. "Preface." *The Canadian Green Consumer Guide*. Prepared by The Pollution Probe Foundation. Toronto: McClelland & Stewart, 1989. 2-3.

252. Promotional blurb, front wrapper for Valerie Martin's *A Recent Martyr*. New York: Vintage Contemporaries, 1989 ©1987.

253. "The Public Woman as Honorary Man." *Los Angeles Times Book Review* 2 April 1989: 3. Review of *The Warrior Queens* by Antonia Fraser.

254. "Significant Moments in the Life of My Mother." *Close Company: Stories of Mothers and Daughters*. Ed. Christine Park and Caroline Heaton. New York: Ticknor and Fields, 1989. 5-20. Reprinted from *Bluebeard's Egg and Other Stories*, ©1986.

255. "Siren Song." *The Faber Book of 20ᵗʰ Century Women's Poetry*. Ed. Fleur Adcock. London; Boston: Faber and Faber, 1989. 272. Reprinted from *You Are Happy*, ©1974.

256. "Snake Woman." *Till All the Stars Have Fallen: Canadian Poems for Children*. Selected by David Booth. Toronto: Kids Can Press, 1989. 64. Reprinted from *Interlunar*, ©1984.

257. *Survival: A Thematic Guide to Canadian Literature*. [Sound recording]. Brantford, ON: W. Ross MacDonald School, 1989.

258. "There Is Only One of Everything." *Poetry by Canadian Women*. Ed. Rosemary Sullivan. Toronto: Oxford UP, 1989. 154-155. Originally published 1974.

259. "Time to Sink the Sub," by Atwood and John Polanyi. *Globe and Mail* 8 February 1989: A7. Letter supporting review of military defense programs and cancellation of nuclear submarine proposal.

260. "True North." *Travels in the Americas*. Ed. Jack Newcombe. New York: Weidenfeld & Nicolson, 1989. 233-244. "Reproduced from *Saturday Night* magazine, January 1987."

261. "Two Poems." *Canadian Woman Studies* 10.4 (Winter 1989): 9-10. Reprints "Last Day" from *True Stories* and Anna Akhmatova's "Boris Pasternak," with a preliminary essay.

262. *Ublízení na Tele*. Prague [Czechoslovakia]: Odeon, 1989. Czech translation of *Bodily Harm* by Hana Zantovská.

263. *Upp till ytan*. Stockholm: Litteraturframjandet, 1989. Swedish translation of *Surfacing*.

264. "'Waking at 3 A.M.'" *Field* 41 (1989): 29-33. About William Edgar Stafford's poem "Waking at 3 A.M."

265. "Weight." *Chatelaine* 62.11 (November 1989): 155-158, 160, 162.

266. "When It Happens." *Finding Courage: Writings by Women*. Ed. Irene Zahava. Freedom, CA: Crossing Press, 1989. 9-17. Reprinted from *Dancing Girls and Other Stories*, 1982 ©1977.

267. "Wilderness Tips." *Saturday Night* 104.7 (July 1989): 46-53.

268. "Woman Skating." *The Faber Book of 20ᵗʰ Century Women's Poetry*. Ed. Fleur Adcock. London; Boston: Faber and Faber, 1989. 270-271. Reprinted from *Procedures for Underground*, ©1970.

269. "The Woman Who Could Not Live with Her Faulty Heart." *Poetry by Canadian Women*. Ed. Rosemary Sullivan. Toronto: Oxford UP, 1989. 156-157. Originally published 1978.

270. "Writing Utopia." Unpublished speech, 1989. An answer to the question: How did *The Handmaid's Tale* get written? [Ed. note: Reprinted in *Curious Pursuits: Occasional Writing 1970-2005*. London: Virago, 2005. 85-94.]

271. "You Begin." *Poetry by Canadian Women*. Ed. Rosemary Sullivan. Toronto: Oxford UP, 1989. 155-156. Originally published 1978.

Quotations

272. "[Quote]." *Los Angeles Times* 9 April 1989: Section: Book Review: 12. One of the lines from Atwood's review of *The Warrior Queens* by Antonia Fraser which appeared in the 2 April edition of the paper quoted under the heading "Critic's Choice": "A lore-packed historical essay. Fraser has assembled a remarkable group of women who displayed superior courage and outmanoeuvred the cream of the male crop. Fascinating to read."

273. "[Quote]." *New York Times* 12 March 1989: Section: 7: 1. Atwood joins 27 other writers born in 21 countries in encouraging Salman Rushdie, author of *Satanic Verses*, then hiding in England with a price on his head having been accused by the Iranian revolutionary leader Ayatollah Ruhollah Khomeini of slandering Islam in his novel. The Ayatollah called for his death. "You're the one in trouble; tell us what we can do to best support you. It's all too easy to pop off the handle and say what is on my mind without reflecting on your position. We feel deeply the horror of your position. And remember: You are worth a great deal more to the Ayatollah alive than dead, because dead you are no longer something to be waved around."

Interviews

274. "The Handmaid's Vision." *Journal* (Providence) 12 March 1989. NewsBank 1989: 34: C9-11.

275. *The MacNeil/Lehrer NewsHour* 7 July 1989, Friday, Transcript #3510. Available from Lexis-Nexis. On origins and meaning of *Cat's Eye.* Excerpt: "My notes on this book date back to 1964. And I took a couple of tries at it over the years and it never really happened or got finished. So for me it's partly here's something I've been thinking about for all these years, and I finally managed to do it. What a relief."

What did she do? "I've written a novel that covers 50 years of time, which I never attempted before, and I've written a novel that deals with a somewhat neglected subject. And when I say neglected, I don't mean only in literature but in life, because even psychoanalysts tended to tell us that the years up to 6 were very important and then the years of adolescence were very important, but that space in-between, particularly for little girls, between 8 and about 12, tended to be not dealt or not looked at and somewhat dismissed. But as anyone who's ever been a little girl or had little girls will tell you, that is a very emotionally intense and important time. So I dealt with that. It's usually only dealt with in juvenile fiction such as *Anne of Green Gables* or those novels about English boarding schools. And I attempted that in a novel for adults, risky business."

And, on the difference between writing poetry and novels: "If you wired up the brain of a poet at the moment of composition, you would find that certain parts of the brain lit up. I was very intrigued by some wiring up of musicians that they did and they found that musicians' brains lit up in quite different ways from the brains of ordinary people listening to music. So it would be fun to wire up a poet right at the instant of composing a poem and then wire up a novelist and monitor his brain while he was composing a novel. And I think you would find that different areas lit up. I think you would find that poetry is much more connected with the left-handed, right-sided part of the brain, and that the novel has more to do with the right hand and the left side."

276. "A Vampire by the Mausoleum: It Was Not Margaret Atwood." *Houston Chronicle* 5 March 1989. NewsBank 1989: 34: C12-13.
277. ANDERSON, Jon. "Margaret Atwood Reigns." *Chicago Tribune* 19 March 1989: Section 6: 1, 6.
278. BENATAR, Giselle. "Under the Spell of the 'Cat's Eye.'" *Los Angeles Herald Examiner* 7 March 1989. NewsBank 1989: 34:C4-5.
279. BRAMPTON, Sally. "The Credible Woman." *The Guardian* (Manchester) 26 October 1989:17.
280. CHRISTY, Marian. "Conversations: The Mean Games Girls Play." *Boston Globe* 15 March 1989: Section: Living: 45. Atwood interviewed when in town to promote *Cat's Eye*.
281. COLTRERA, Francesca. "Atwood Has 'Eye' for a Best-Seller." *Boston Herald* 12 March 1989. NewsBank 1989: 34:C8.
282. FORSBERG, M[yra]. "Journey to the Screen." *New York Times* 2 April 1989: Section 2: 13. Brief comments on Natasha Richardson as Offred and Harold Pinter's screenplay of *The Handmaid's Tale*.
283. GERACIMOS, Ann. "Margaret Atwood's Tale: Literary Feminism." *Washington* (DC) *Times* 27 February 1989. NewsBank 1989: 34:C14.
284. HUBBARD, Kim. "Reflected in Margaret Atwood's *Cat's Eye*, Girlhood Looms as a Time of Cruelty and Terror." *People Weekly* 31.9 (8 March 1989): 205-206.
285. LEE, Hermione. *Margaret Atwood: Writers Talk Ideas of Our Time*. [Video-recording] Northbrook, IL; Peasmarsh, Near Rye, East Sussex, UK: The Roland Collection, 1989. 1 videocassette (52 min.). Atwood talks about themes of women "breaking out," literature informed by fairy tales, visual imagery as inspiration, mythology in contemporary literature, comparing the short story with the novel, autobiography as source material, writing as a woman from the male point of view, and using humor.
286. MANSNERUS, Laura. "Different Brands of Meanness." *New York Times Book Review* 5 February 1989: 35.
287. PERI, Camille. "Witchcraft." *Mother Jones* 14.3 (April 1989): 28, 30-31, 44-45.
288. PULLINGER, Kate. "An Archaeology of Sisterhood." *Independent* (London) 2 January 1989: 15.
289. SANDS, Melissa. "Hindsight." *Châtelaine* 62 (February 1989): 61, 63.
290. STREITFELD, David. "Neighbors to the North." *Washington Post Book Review* 12 March 1989: 15. Atwood reflects on being a "Canadian writer." Interview includes the first Canadian joke she ever heard: The road to Heaven forks. The right branch has a sign that says: To Heaven. The sign on the left branch: Panel discussion on Heaven. All the Canadians go to the left.

Scholarly Resources

291. "Margaret (Eleanor) Atwood." *Short Story Criticism: Excerpts from Criticism of the Work of Short Fiction Writers*. Ed. Sheila Fitzgerald. Vol. 2. Detroit, MI: Gale, 1989. 1-23. An anonymous biocritical essay, accompanied by excerpts from Onley, Hofsess, Hill, Cameron, Woodcock, Grace, Thompson, Tyler, Flower, Mezei, Abley, Carrington, Davey, with a bibliography of additional works.
292. ADAMS, Carol J. "Feminism, the Great War, and Modern Vegetarianism." *Arms and the Woman: War, Gender, and Literary Representation*. Ed. Helen M. Cooper, Adrienne Auslander Munich, and Susan Merrill Squier. Chapel Hill; London: Uni-

versity of North Carolina Press, 1989. 244-267. Women share oppression with animals; giving up meat is also giving up male dominance. *The Edible Woman* illustrates these themes in Marian's choice of food.

293. AUGIER, Valérie. "An Analysis of *Surfacing* by Margaret Atwood." *Commonwealth Essays and Studies* 11.2 (Spring 1989): 11-17.

294. BACHINGER, Katrina. "Gender Positions: The Intertextuality of Gender Difference in Margaret Atwood, Katherine Mansfield, Joyce Carol Oates, Edgar Allan Poe, Sir Philip Sidney and others." Habilitationsschrift [i.e., PhD thesis]. University of Salzburg, 1989.

295. BARTKOWSKI, Frances. *Feminist Utopias*. Lincoln; London: University of Nebraska Press, 1989. See especially "No Shadows without Light: Louky Bersianik's *The Euguelionne* and Margaret Atwood's *The Handmaid's Tale*." 133-158. This final chapter pairs Atwood's anglophone and Bersianik's francophone texts to demonstrate a synthesis of feminist fiction and theory; discusses geopolitical questions, the power of language, marginality, identity, and difference.

296. BERGMANN, Harriet F. "'Teaching Them to Read': A Fishing Expedition in *The Handmaid's Tale*." *College English* 51.8 (December 1989): 847-854. *The Handmaid's Tale*'s statements on authorship, reading, and patriarchal language are revealed through Offred, who learns to "read the world," and by the "Historical Notes," where women's history is misread.

297. BILLI, Mirella. "Margaret Atwood." *Belfagor* (Florence) 44.4 (July 1989): 417-435. Discusses Atwood's career, poetry, and novels through *The Handmaid's Tale*.

298. BOUSON, J. Brooks. *The Empathic Reader: A Study of the Narcissistic Character and the Drama of the Self*. Amherst: University of Massachusetts Press, 1989. See especially chapter entitled "Comic Storytelling as Escape and Narcissistic Self-Expression in Atwood's *Lady Oracle*." 154-168. Follows Joan's comic experiences of self-creation and self-annihilation in a psychoanalytic approach to the mother-daughter relationship in *Lady Oracle*.

299. BURACK, Cynthia. "Bringing Women's Studies to Political Science: The Handmaid in the Classroom." *NWSA Journal* 1.2 (Winter 1988-89): 274-283. Uses *The Handmaid's Tale* to teach political concepts and to overcome the "pedagogical orthodoxy" of the classroom.

300. BUSS, Helen. "Maternality and Narrative Strategies in the Novels of Margaret Atwood." *Atlantis* 15.1 (Fall 1989): 76-83. Explores the ethics of mothering in Atwood's novels, finding *The Handmaid's Tale* the most politically and aesthetically developed and *Cat's Eye* the most optimistic.

301. CAMPBELL, Elizabeth A. "The Woman Artist as Sibyl: Sappho, George Eliot, and Margaret Atwood." *Nassau Review* 5.5 (1989): 6-14.

302. CARRERA SUAREZ, Isabel. "Metalinguistic Features in Short Fiction by Lessing and Atwood: From Sign and Subversion to Symbol and Deconstruction." *Short Fiction in the New Literatures in English: Proceedings of the Nice Conference of the European Association for Commonwealth Literature and Language Studies*. Ed. Jacqueline Bardolph. Nice: Fac. des Lettres & Sciences Humaines de Nice, 1989. 159-164.

303. COWART, David. *History and the Contemporary Novel*. Crosscurrents/Modern Critiques/Third Series. Carbondale and Edwardsville, IL: Southern Illinois UP, 1989. See especially "The Way It Will Be: Puritanism and Patriarchy: *The Handmaid's Tale*." 105-119. Sees *The Handmaid's Tale* as a "complex historical meditation" that mirrors the Old Testament and the Puritan age. Identifies illusions to the Bible, Little Red Riding Hood, Chaucer's Wife of Bath, and *The Waste Land*.

304. CULPEPER, Richard. "Recognition and Rejection of Victimization in the Novels of Margaret Atwood." MA thesis. University of Waterloo, 1989. Also available on microfiche from Canadian Theses Service (1992).

305. DELBAERE-GARANT, Jeanne. "*Surfacing*: Retracing the Boundaries." *Commonwealth Essays and Studies* 11.2 (Spring 1989): 1-10.

306. DETWEILER, Robert. *Breaking the Fall: Religious Readings of Contemporary Fiction*. London: Macmillan, 1989. See especially Chapter 6: "Scheherazade's Fellowship: Telling against the End." 159-191. This chapter contains an extensive discussion of *The Handmaid's Tale.*

307. DIVASSON, Lourdes. "The Short Stories of Margaret Atwood: A Visible Link between Her Poetry and Longer Fiction." Short Fiction in the New Literatures in English: Proceedings of the Nice Conference of the European Association for Commonwealth Literature and Language Studies. Ed. Jacqueline Bardolph. Nice: Fac. des Lettres & Sciences Humaines de Nice, 1989. 153-157.

308. DIVASSON CILVETI, Lourdes. "*The Handmaid's Tale*: Una Forma de supervivencia." *Revista Canaria de Estudios Ingleses* 19-20 (1989): 211-220.

309. DOBRIS, Catherine Aileen. "Weaving the Utopian Vision: A Rhetorical Analysis of Feminist Utopian Fiction." PhD thesis. Indiana University, 1989. 256 pp. An analysis of 9 novels, includes *The Handmaid's Tale* and Piercy's *Woman on the Edge of Time* as the "female" perspective. For more see *DAI-A* 50.07 (January 1990): 1846.

310. EDWARDS, Jannie. "Margaret Atwood and the Politics of Consumption." MA thesis. University of Alberta, 1989. 100 pp. Also available on microfiche from Canadian Theses Service (1990). Focus on *The Edible Woman, Lady Oracle*, and *Surfacing.*

311. ENS, Kelly Linda. "Writing the Female Body in Three Canadian Women's Novels." MA thesis. McMaster University, 1989. 68 pp. Atwood's *Bodily Harm*, Marian Engel's *The Honeyman Festival*, and Margaret Laurence's *The Stone Angel.*

312. FERNS, Chris. "The Value/s of Dystopia: *The Handmaid's Tale* and the Anti-Utopian Tradition." *Dalhousie Review* 69.3 (Fall 1989): 373-382. *The Handmaid's Tale* possesses significant differences from Zamyatin's, Huxley's, and Orwell's dystopias; for example, *The Handmaid's Tale* relies on more subversive tactics.

313. FITTING, Peter. "Recent Feminist Utopias: World Building and Strategies for Social Change." *Mindscapes: The Geographies of Imagined Worlds*. Ed. George E. Slusser and Eric S. Rabkin. Carbondale and Edwardsville, IL: Southern Illinois UP, 1989. passim. *The Handmaid's Tale* is one of the novels that "mark an end to the feminist utopianism of the 1970s."

314. FOLEY, Michael. "Satiric Intent in the 'Historical Notes' Epilogue of Margaret Atwood's *The Handmaid's Tale*." *Commonwealth Essays and Studies* 11.2 (Spring 1989): 44-52.

315. GEORGE, Jacqueline A. "The Mirror's Frame: A Study of the Unifying Framework of Experience, Symbol and Metaphor in the Development of Identity and Self-Knowledge in the Novels of Margaret Atwood." MA thesis. St. Bonaventure University (NY), 1989.

316. GIVNER, Jessie. "Mirror Images in Margaret Atwood's *Lady Oracle*." *Studies in Canadian Literature* 41.1 (1989): 139-146. Recognizes a relationship between *Lady Oracle* and Irigaray's feminist theory. Examines the unconventional use of mirrors and the recurring use of loose ends, disrupted frames, and ellipses.

317. GODARD, Barbara. "Palimpsest: Margaret Atwood's *Bluebeard's Egg*." *Recherches Anglaises et Nord-Américaines* 20 (1987): 51-60. A shift in Atwood's narrative techniques of embedding and *mise en abyme* creates an illusion of deepened "human understanding."

318. GRIESINGER, Emily Ann. "Before and After *Jane Eyre*: The Female Gothic and Some Modern Variations." PhD thesis. Vanderbilt University, 1989. 417 pp. *Surfacing* is one of the novels examined to illustrate that the modern female gothic often entails rejection or revision of the earlier tradition. For more see *DAI-A* 51.02 (August 1990): 511.

319. HARKNESS, David L. "Alice in Toronto: The Carrollian Intertext in *The Edible Woman*." *Essays on Canadian Writing* 37 (Spring 1989): 103-111. Identifies and explicates a series of intertextual links between Lewis Carroll's work and *The Edible Woman*.

320. HEIDENREICH, Rosmarin. *The Postwar Novel in Canada: Narrative Patterns and Reader Response*. Waterloo, ON: Wilfrid Laurier UP, 1989. See especially "Social Norms and Perspectival Patterns. Graduated Perspectives: Margaret Atwood's *The Edible Woman*." 22-28. The novel's characters represent a group of perspectives, or norms, to be explored, not a hierarchical ordering of perspectives.

321. HIRSCH, Marianne. *The Mother/Daughter Plot: Narrative, Psychoanalysis, Feminism*. Bloomington, IL; Indianapolis: Indiana UP, 1989. See especially "Feminist Family Romances. Life before Oedipus: Atwood's *Surfacing*." 140-145. This section examines how *Surfacing* "exemplifies and puts into question" the feminist family romance of revisionary psychoanalytic theories.

322. HITE, Molly. *The Other Side of the Story: Structures and Strategies of Contemporary Feminist Narrative*. Ithaca, NY; London: Cornell UP, 1989. See especially "Other Side, Other Woman: *Lady Oracle*." 127-167. *Lady Oracle*'s two-sided story of self and other, reality and unreality, with its Gothic elements, and Irigarayan otherness, succeeds in creating "representation with a difference."

323. HOEPPNER, Kenneth. "Frye's Theory of Romance, Popular Romance and Atwood's *Lady Oracle*." *ACLALS Bulletin* 8.1 (1989): 74-87.

324. HOWELLS, Coral Ann. "Free-Dom, Telling, Dignidad: Margaret Laurence, 'A Gourdful of Glory,' Margaret Atwood, *The Handmaid's Tale*, Sarah Murphy, *The Pleasure of Miranda*." *Commonwealth Essays and Studies* 12.1 (Autumn 1989): 39-46.

325. HUGGAN, Graham. "Maps and Mapping Strategies in Contemporary Canadian and Australian Fiction." PhD thesis. University of British Columbia, 1989. Atwood is discussed as one of "three significant precursors of the contemporary period of literary cartography." For more see *DAI-A* 50.12 (June 1990): 3941.

326. ———. "Resisting the Map as Metaphor: A Comparison of Margaret Atwood's *Surfacing* and Janet Frame's *Scented Gardens for the Blind*." *Kunapipi* 11.3 (1989): 5-15. Atwood and Frame challenge the status of map as metaphor, reacting against authoritarian representation and strategies of restriction in the notion of mapping.

327. HUTCHEON, Linda. Afterword to *The Edible Woman*. New Canadian Library, Ed. David Staines. Toronto: McClelland and Stewart, 1989. 313-319. Sees *The Edible Woman* as a "kind of model" for Atwood's following work. The delicate balance of the ironic and serious is the "mark of Atwood's already mature writing."

328. JONES, Dorothy. "Not Much Balm in Gilead." *Commonwealth Essays and Studies* 11.2 (Spring 1989): 31-43.

329. KALB, John Douglas. "Articulated Selves: The Attainment of Identity and Per-
      sonal Voice through Language and Storytelling in Works by Twentieth-Century
      American Authors." PhD thesis. Michigan State University, 1989. 254 pp. Atwood
      is one of several authors who illustrate this process. For more see *DAI-A* 50.07
      (January 1990): 2053.

330. KALER, Anne K. "'A Sister, Dipped in Blood': Satiric Inversion of the Formation
      Techniques of Women Religious in Margaret Atwood's Novel *The Handmaid's
      Tale.*" *Christianity and Literature* 38.2 (Winter 1989): 43-62. *Handmaid's Tale*
      incorporates Frye's groups of fiction (satire, fantasy, etc.) through a framework of
      inversions of pre-Vatican II religious tradition. The historical notes section is an
      inversion of scholarship.

331. KAUFFMAN, Linda. "Special Delivery: Twenty-first Century Epistolarity in *The
      Handmaid's Tale.*" *Writing the Female Voice: Essays on Epistolary Literature.*
      Ed. Elizabeth C. Goldsmith. Boston: Northeastern UP, 1989. 221-244. "Forms of
      masculine writing vs. feminine speech" in *Handmaid's Tale* belong to the tradition
      of epistolary literature. The novel combines epistolary poetics with apocalyptic
      politics.

332. KEITH, W. J. "Margaret Atwood." A Sense of Style: Studies in the Art of Fiction
      in English-Speaking Canada. Toronto: ECW Press, 1989. 175-194.

333. ———. *Margaret Atwood's* The Edible Woman*: A Reader's Guide* (Canadian
      Fiction Studies 3) Toronto: ECW Press, 1989. 79.

334. KETTERER, David. "Margaret Atwood's *The Handmaid's Tale*: A Contextual
      Dystopia." *Science Fiction Studies* 16.2 (July 1989): 209-217. The preceding and
      succeeding historical circumstances in *Handmaid's Tale* make it a unique work of
      contextual dystopia. This quality is overlooked in Mary McCarthy's negative re-
      view.

335. KIZUK, A. R. "The Father's No and the Mother's Yes: Psychological Intertexts in
      Davies's *What's Bred in the Bone* and Atwood's *The Handmaid's Tale.*" *Atlantis*
      14.2 (Spring 1989): 1-9. Unstable structures and self-interpreting devices in these
      fictional biographies by Atwood and Davies subvert modern psychological
      "truths" and myths.

336. LANE, Patrick. "The Unyielding Phrase." *Canadian Literature* 122-123 (Autumn-
      Winter 1989): 57-64. Atwood and Newlove shock the reader into understanding
      and use history to create their imagined truths. Atwood's reimagined *The Journals
      of Susanna Moodie* relates Moodie's "failure of the imagination" and inability to
      be "transformed."

337. LARSON, Janet L. "Margaret Atwood and the Future of Prophecy." *Religion and
      Literature* 21.1 (Spring 1989): 27-61. *The Handmaid's Tale* adds to feminist bibli-
      cal hermeneutics by expanding the prophetic tradition and exposing its patriarchal
      roots.

338. LECKER, Robert, Jack DAVID, and Ellen QUIGLEY, eds. *Canadian Writers and
      Their Works.* Toronto: ECW Press, Fiction Series 2 (1989) passim. Discusses At-
      wood's comments on wild animals as a theme in Canadian literature.

339. LECLAIRE, Jacques. "Enclosure and Disclosure in *Surfacing* by Margaret At-
      wood." *Commonwealth Essays and Studies* 11.2 (Spring 1989): 18-23.

340. LEWOCHKO, Mary. "Circular Patterns of Change in the Feminine Quest for Self-
      Identity in the Novels of Margaret Atwood and Alice Munro." MA thesis. Concor-
      dia University, 1989. Also available on microfiche from Canadian Theses Service
      (1990).

341. LUCAS, Linda E. "The Reconstructive Vision of the Third Eye in Margaret Atwood's *The Handmaid's Tale*." MA thesis. University of Western Ontario, 1989. 113 pp.

342. MANDERSON, Jill. "The Nameless Voice: A Comparison of Narrative Voice in Margaret Atwood's Early Poems and *Surfacing*." MA thesis. Dalhousie University, 1989. Also available on microfiche from Canadian Theses Service (1990).

343. McCOMBS, Judith. "Country, Politics, and Gender in Canadian Studies: A Report from Twenty Years of Atwood Criticism." *Literatures in Canada/Littératures au Canada*. Ed. Deborah C. Poff. Montreal: Association for Canadian Studies, 1989. 27-47.

344. ———. "'Up in the Air So Blue': Vampires and Victims, Great Mother Myth and Gothic Allegory in Margaret Atwood's First, Unpublished Novel." *Centennial Review* 33.3 (Summer 1989): 251-257. The Great Mother myth and Gothic elements are predominant in Atwood's first unpublished novel. These themes are reformulated in the *The Edible Woman*.

345. MEINDL, Dieter. "Gender and Narrative Perspective in Margaret Atwood's Stories." *Recherches Anglaises et Nord-Américaines* 22 (1989): 5-15.

346. NAGY, Erzsébet. "Possible Approaches to Translation Analysis: Margaret Atwood, *Surfacing*. " MA thesis. Eötvös Lorand University, 1989.

347. NEW, W. H. *A History of Canadian Literature*. London: Macmillan, 1989. passim. Many scattered references; survey-essay on Atwood. 292-295.

348. PALMER, Paulina. *Contemporary Women's Fiction: Narrative Practice and Feminist Theory*. New York; London; Toronto; Sydney; Tokyo: Harvester Wheatsheaf, 1989. passim. Most of Atwood's novels are discussed with particular attention to *Bodily Harm* and *The Handmaid's Tale*.

349. PATTERSON, Helen Jayne. "A World of Women's Words: Elements of Form in the Poetry of Margaret Atwood." PhD thesis. York University, 1989. Also available on microfiche from Canadian Theses Service (1989). A "stylistic, psychological, and semiotic" analysis of Atwood's feminist writing. For more see *DAI-A* 50.09 (March 1990): 2902.

350. PATTON, Marilyn. "Cannibal Craft: The Eaten Body in the Writings of Herman Melville and Margaret Atwood." PhD thesis. University of California at Santa Cruz, 1989. 446 pp. In a study of cannibalism as narrative trope, uncovers the major cultural concerns in Atwood's novels through *Bodily Harm*. For more see *DAI-A* 50.09 (March 1990): 2899.

351. PEEL, Ellen. "Subject, Object, and the Alternation of First- and Third-Person Narration in Novels by Alther, Atwood, and Drabble: Toward a Theory of Feminist Aesthetics." *Critique* 30.2 (Winter 1989): 107-122. Alternating narration is part of a "feminist aesthetic" that examines the self/other problem in *Kinflicks*, *The Edible Woman*, and *The Waterfall*.

352. POEHLS, Alice O'Toole. "Repetition and Reading: Word Rhythms in Henry James and Margaret Atwood." PhD thesis. University of North Dakota, 1989. 170 pp. "This study develops a method of reading the novel which emphasizes single-word repetitions as they rhythmically occur in the artistic text. By analyzing these word rhythms, a reader can disrupt the habitual production of the novel based on the fictional events of the story and, instead, focus on the textual events of the artistic form. Chapter Four presents a reading of Margaret Atwood's *Surfacing*. Atwood's text evokes Sigmund Freud's essay, 'The Uncanny,' by performing the uncanny, both as a theme and as an experience for the reader and/or the narrator. Examination of word rhythms in the text, however, demonstrates that Freudian as-

sociations, like all linguistic forms, are relational and subjective. The psychic and geographic journeys of the narrator in *Surfacing* are much like the reader's journey through the novel: recollection and repetition continually subsidize the text." (Author). For more see *DAI-A* 51.01 (July 1990): 164.

353. QUINN, Antoinette. "Atwood and Autobiography: The Opening Sequence of *Murder in the Dark.*" *Recherches Anglaises et Nord-Américaines* 22 (1989): 17-25.

354. RAO, Eleonora. "Margaret Atwood's *Lady Oracle*: Writing Against Notions of Unity." *British Journal of Canadian Studies* 4.1 (1989): 136-156. Atwood's "revised version of Gothic Romance" challenges genre hierarchies and conventional iconography of woman, breaks down generic representations of character, and emphasizes plural subjectivity.

355. ROBERTS, Claudette M. "Presence, Absence, and the Interface in Twentieth-Century Literature and Painting." PhD thesis. Ohio State University, 1989. 186 pp. Presence and absence are no longer viewed as binary opposites; several juxtapositions, including Atwood and Picasso, are used as demonstrations. For more see *DAI-A* 51.03 (September 1990): 843.

356. ROOKE, Constance. "Atwood's Hands." *Fear of the Open Heart: Essays on Contemporary Canadian Writing.* Toronto: Coach House Press, 1989. 163-174. Describes many of the hand images found in Atwood which Rooke sees as part of the language Atwood uses.

357. ———. "Interpreting *The Handmaid's Tale*: Offred's Name and 'The Arnolfini Marriage.'" *Fear of the Open Heart: Essays on Contemporary Canadian Writing.* Toronto: Coach House Press, 1989. 175-196. Makes case for June being Offred's real name; discusses novel's similarities to this van Eyck painting.

358. RUBENSTEIN, Roberta. "Bodily Harm: Paranoid Vision in Contemporary Fiction by Women." *LIT: Literature, Interpretation, Theory* 1.1-2 (1989): 137-149. Discusses multidimensional interpretations of women's hostile worlds in *Bodily Harm*, *The Handmaid's Tale*, and works by Lessing, Drabble, and others.

359. SCHENK, Susan Jean. "'Burning Dinner Is Not Incompetence but War': Marriage and Madness in Contemporary Domestic Fiction." PhD thesis. University of Western Ontario, 1989. Sixteen novels by various writers, including Atwood, are examined. For more see *DAI-A* 50.05 (November 1989): 1315.

360. SCOBIE, Stephen. *Signature Event Cantext.* Edmonton: NeWest Press, 1989. passim. Mentions Atwood a few times, with main focus on *The Journals of Susanna Moodie* as a "documentary poem," which is viewed as distinctly Canadian.

361. SPRIET, Pierre. "Margaret Atwood's Post-Modernism in *Murder in the Dark.*" *Commonwealth Essays and Studies* 11.2 (Spring 1989): 24-30.

362. STURGESS, Charlotte. "Subtexts of Displacement in Margaret Atwood's *Dancing Girls and Other Stories.*" *Recherches Anglaises et Nord-Américaines* 22 (1989): 27-32.

363. TOMPKINS, Cynthia Margarita. "The Spiral Quest in Selected Inter-American Female Fictions: Gabrielle Roy's *La Route d'Altamont*, Marta Lynch's *La Señora Ordonez*, Erica Jong's *Fear of Flying*, Margaret Atwood's *Surfacing*, and Clarice Lispector's *Agua Viva* (Argentina, Brazil, Canada, United States)." PhD thesis. Pennsylvania State University, 1989. 289 pp. Reveals "the absence of the public sphere," and a cross-cultural, gender-oriented "intermediate stage of the female Bildungsroman," in women's spiral quest novels. For more see *DAI-A* 50.07 (January 1990): 2045.

364. WAUGH, Patricia. *Feminine Fictions: Revisiting the Postmodern*. London and New York: Routledge, 1989. See especially "Contemporary Women Writers: Challenging Postmodernist Aesthetics. Margaret Atwood." 179-189. Body image and food images form the discussion of *The Edible Woman* and *Lady Oracle*; Atwood mentioned in passing elsewhere in book also.

365. WEINER, Deborah. "'Difference That Kills'/Difference That Heals: Representing Latin America in the Poetry of Elizabeth Bishop and Margaret Atwood." *Comparative Literature East and West: Traditions and Trends*. Selected Conference Papers. Literary Studies: East and West, Vol. 1. Ed. Cornelia Moore and Raymond A. Moody. Honolulu: College of Languages, Linguistics, and Literature, University of Hawaii and the East-West Center, 1989. 208-219. Contrasts difference, epistemology, aesthetics, and ethics; Atwood's *True Stories* breaks down dichotomies, producing a "stronger and more resilient affirmation."

366. WILSON, Sharon R. "Fairy-Tale Cannibalism in *The Edible Woman*." *Cooking by the Book: Food in Literature and Culture*. Ed. Mary Anne Schofield. Bowling Green, OH: Bowling Green State University Popular Press, 1989. 78-88. Identifies Atwood's use of a fairy-tale intertext focused on food, tracing patterns from "The Robber Bridegroom" and "Fitcher's Bird" in *The Edible Woman*.

367. WORKMAN, Nancy V. "Sufi Mysticism in Margaret Atwood's *The Handmaid's Tale*." *Studies in Canadian Literature* 14.2 (1989): 10-26.

368. YARNALL, Judith H. "The Transformations of Circe: The History of an Archetypal Character." PhD thesis. McGill University, 1989. In the 20th century, Atwood and Joyce brought about a more positive view of Circe. For more see *DAI-A* 50.04 (October 1989): 943.

Reviews of Atwood's Works

369. *Best American Short Stories.* Selected by Margaret Atwood with Shannon Ravenel. Boston: Houghton Mifflin, 1989.
   Hartford Courant (CT) 29 October 1989. NewsBank 1989: 104: F12. By Robert DAHLIN.
   Library Journal 114.17 (15 October 1989): 101. By Frank PISNO.
   New York Times 15 November 1989: C25. By Nona BALAKIAN.
   Oregonian (Portland) 10 December 1989. NewsBank 1990: 1: D10-11. By Paul PINTARICH.
   Philadelphia Inquirer 24 December 1989. NewsBank 1990: 1: D12-13. By Andrew LEVY.
   Publishers Weekly 236.10 (8 September 1989): 63. By Penny KAGANOFF.
   Sun (Baltimore) 19 November 1989. NewsBank 1989: 121: C1. By Joan MOONEY.
   Times-Dispatch (Richmond, VA) 24 December 1989. NewsBank 1990: 1: D14. By Sharon Lloyd STRATTON.

370. *Cat's Eye.* Toronto: McClelland and Stewart, 1988; New York: Doubleday, 1988; London: Bloomsbury, 1988.
   America 160 (6 May 1989): 435-437. By Richard BAUTCH.
   Arkansas Democrat-Gazette 19 March 1989: s.p. (930 w). ANON. Available from Lexis-Nexis.
   Atlanta Journal 19 March 1989: M10. By Chris VERNER.

30

~ **1989** ~

Book of the Month Club News Spring 1989: 2-3.

Books (London) 22 January 1989: 17. By Kate PULLINGER.

Boston Globe 29 January 1989: Section: Books: A14. By Gail CALDWELL. (1123 w).

Boston Herald 22 January 1989. NewsBank 1989: 13: C10. By Judith WYNN.

Chicago Tribune 29 January 1989: Section 14: 6. By Jody DAYNARD.

Christian Science Monitor 20 April 1989: 11. By Marilyn GARDNER.

CM 17.1 (January 1989): 15. By Joanne K. A. PETERS.

Cosmopolitan 206.2 (February 1989): 52. By Louise BERNIKOW.

Daily News (New York) 5 March 1989. NewsBank 1989: 34: D7-8. By Sherryl CONNELLY.

Economist 311 (6 May 1989): 88.

The Guardian (London) 27 January 1989: s.p. By Stephen FENDER. (674 w). Available from Lexis-Nexis.

The Guardian (London) 12 April 1989: 17. By Elayne RAPPING.

Hartford Courant (CT) 12 February 1989. NewsBank 1989: 25: B11. By Jocelyn McCLURG.

Houston Chronicle 5 March 1989. NewsBank 1989: 34: D9.

The Independent 28 January 1989: Section: Weekend Books: 29. By Jill NEVILLE. (537 w).

Inside Books February 1989: 19, 21. By Barbara MITCHELL.

Jerusalem Post 7 April 1989: Section: Book: s.p. By Frances GERTLER. (896 w). Available from Lexis-Nexis.

Jerusalem Post 29 December 1989: Section: Book: s.p. By S. T. MERAVI.

Journal (Providence) 29 January 1989. NewsBank 1989: 13: C11. By Beverly Lyon CLARK.

Journal of Commonwealth Literature 24.2 (1989): 40. By W. H. NEW.

Library Journal 114.2 (1 February 1989): 81. By Barbara HOFFERT.

Listener 121 (26 January 1989): 26. By Judy COOKE.

Literary Review (London) 127 (January 1989): 22-23. By Susannah HERBERT.

London Review of Books 11.2 (19 January 1989): 3, 5. Includes discussion of *Interlunar.* By Dinah BIRCH.

Los Angeles Times Book Review 19 February 1989: 3, 13. By Richard EDER.

Mademoiselle 95 (February 1989): 94, 96. By Joyce MAYNARD.

Minneapolis Star and Tribune 26 February 1989. NewsBank 1989: 34: D5-6.

Modern Maturity 32.2 (April-May 1989): 32. By Digby DIEHL.

Ms. 17.9 (March 1989): 38, 41. By Alison LURIE.

Nation 248.22 (5 June 1989): 776-779. By Lillian S. ROBINSON.

New Leader 72.5 (6 March 1989): 19. By Carole CLEAVER.

New Republic 200.15 (10 April 1989): 38-40. By Hermione LEE.

New Statesman and Society 2.34 (27 January 1989): 37. By Carole ANGIER.

New York 22.7 (13 February 1989): 80, 82. By Rhoda KOENIG.

New York Review of Books 36.7 (27 April 1989): 50-51. By Robert TOWERS.

New York Times 28 January 1989: 16. By Caryn JAMES. (995 w).

New York Times Book Review 5 February 1989: 1, 35. By Alice McDERMOTT. (1457 w).

New York Times Book Review 17 December 1989: 32. By George JOHNSON.

New Yorker 65.15 (29 May 1989): 108-110. By Judith THURMAN.

Newsweek 20 March 1989: Section: The Arts: 80C. By Peter S. PRESCOTT. (405 w).

Observer (London) 29 January 1989: 49. By Claire TOMALIN.

Oregonian (Portland) 12 February 1989. NewsBank 1989: 25: B14. By Paul PINTARICH.

Orlando Sentinel 12 February 1989. NewsBank 1989: 25: B13. By Nancy PATE.

People Weekly 31 (27 February 1989): 22-23. By Susan TOEPFER.

Philadelphia Inquirer 12 February 1989. NewsBank 1989: 25: C1-3. By Janet BURROWAY.

Publishers Weekly 235.2 (13 January 1989): 74. By Sybil STEINBERG.

Publishers Weekly 236.18 (3 November 1989): 88. ANON.

Punch 296 (27 January 1989): 49-50. By David BENEDICTUS.

Queen's Quarterly 96.2 (Summer 1989): 478-480. By Christine OVERALL.

Radcliffe Quarterly December 1989: 34. By Hope Hale DAVIS.

San Francisco Chronicle 22 January 1989: Section: Review: 1, 7. By Paul SKENAZY.

School Library Journal 35.11 (July 1989): 98-99. By Alice CONLON.

Seventeen 48 (August 1989): 126. ANON.

Spectator 262 (28 January 1989): 32-33. By Anita BROOKNER.

St. Louis Post Dispatch 5 March 1989: C5. By Lynn THEODORE. (1094 w).

St. Petersburg Times 12 March 1989: Section: Books: 6D. By Kit REED. (937 w).

Sunday News Journal (Wilmington, DE) 12 February 1989. NewsBank 1989: 25:B12. By Gary SOULSMAN.

Sunday Times (London) 29 January 1989: G7. By Peter KEMP. (747 w).

Time 133.6 (6 February 1989): 70 [66 in the Canadian edition]. By Stefan KANFER.

The Times (London) 26 January 1989: 19. By Philip HOWARD. (506 w).

The Times (London) 22 July 1989: 40. By Philip HOWARD.

Times-Picayune (New Orleans) 12 February 1989: E7-8. By Susan LARSON.

TLS 3-9 February 1989: 113. By Shena MacKAY.

Tribune (Oakland, CA) 26 February 1989. NewsBank 1989: 34: D1-2. By Diana KETCHAM.

University of Toronto Quarterly 59:1 (Fall 1989): 13. By Dennis DUFFY.

USA Today 24 February 1989: D4. By Michele SLUNG.

Village Voice 21 March 1989: 49-50. By Sharon THOMPSON.

Vogue 179.2 (February 1989): 238. By Katha POLLITT.

Washington Post Book World 19 February 1989: 1, 4. By Isabel COLEGATE (796 w).

Washington Times (DC) 20 February 1989. NewsBank 1989: 25: C4-5. By Bruce BAWER.

Women's Review of Books 6.10-11 (July 1989): 3-4. By Helen YGLESIAS.

371.   *The Handmaid's Tale.* London: J. Cape, 1986; London: Virago, 1987.

Books 3.1 (April 1989): 19. By Michael BARBER.

Sunday Times (London) 22 January 1989: G8. By Austin MacCURTAIN.

372.   *Interlunar*. Toronto: Oxford UP, 1984.

    London Review of Books 11.2 (19 January 1989): 3, 5. Includes discussion of *Cat's Eye*. By Dinah BIRCH.

    Poetry Review 79.3 (Autumn 1989): 61-62. By Sheenagh PUGH.

    TLS 18-24 (August 1989): 903. By Lawrence NORFOLK.

373.   *Murder in the Dark: Short Fictions and Prose Poems*. Toronto: Coach House Press, 1983; London: Jonathan Cape, 1984.

    Short Story Criticism. Ed. Sheila Fitzgerald. Vol. 2. Detroit, MI: Gale Research, 1989. 18-20. By Ildiko [De Papp] CARRINGTON. Reprints the April 1984 review of *Murder in the Dark* from *Women's Review of Books*.

374.   *La Servante écarlate*. Translated by Sylviane Rue. Paris: Laffont, 1987. [*The Handmaid's Tale*.]

    Études (Paris) 370.4 (April 1989): 557. By Joelle TURIN.

375.   *Selected Poems II*. Toronto: Oxford UP, 1986; Boston: Houghton Mifflin, 1987.

    Chronicles March 1989: 28-29. By Paul RAMSEY.

    World Literature Today 63.1 (Winter 1989): 103-104. By Joan Trodden KEEFE.

~ 1990 ~

Atwood's Works

376. "The Age of Lead." *New Statesman and Society* 3 (20 July 1990): 24-29. Also in *Colours of a New Day: Writing for South Africa*. Ed. Sarah Lefanu and Stephen Hayward. Calcutta: Seagull Books, 1990, 204-219, and in *Lear's* September 1990: 114-119, 144-146.

377. *Anadyse.* Athens: Ekdoseis Hestia, 1990 ©1972. Greek translation of *Surfacing*.

378. "The Boys' Own Annual, 1911." *The Faber Book of Contemporary Canadian Short Stories*. Selected by Michael Ondaatje. London; Boston: Faber and Faber, 1990. 62-63. Except for title and copyright pages, the same as 1990 Viking (US) edition titled *From Ink Lake: Canadian Stories*. Selected by Michael Ondaatje. Reprinted from *Murder in the Dark*, ©1983.

379. "Case of the Crazed Cashier." *Toronto Life* 24.4 (March 1990): 46-47.

380. *Cat's Eye.* Boston: G. K. Hall, 1990 ©1988. Large print edition.

381. "Christmas Carols." *In the Gold of Flesh: Poems of Birth and Motherhood*. Ed. Rosemary Palmeira. London: The Women's Press, 1990. 155. Reprinted from *True Stories*, ©1981.

382. "Death by Landscape." *Harper's* August 1990: 49-57 and in *The Oxford Book of Canadian Ghost Stories*. Ed. Alberto Manguel. Toronto; Oxford; New York: Oxford UP, 1990. 221-237. Reprinted from *Saturday Night* 104.7 (July 1989): 46-53.

383. "Death of a Young Son by Drowning." *In the Gold of Flesh: Poems of Birth and Motherhood*. Ed. Rosemary Palmeira. London: The Women's Press, 1990. 133. Reprinted from *The Journals of Susanna Moodie*, ©1970.

384. *Deklina Zgodba.* Ljubljana: Mladinska knjiga, 1990. Slovenian translation of *The Handmaid's Tale* by Miriam Drev.

385. *Den Berömde Poetens Grav, Och Andra Noveller*. Stockholm: Bokförlaget Prisma, 1990. Swedish translation of various Atwood short stories by Maria Ekman. Includes: "Betty," "Polariteter," "Den berömde poetens grav," "Hårsmycken," "När det hander," "Poeternas liv," "Viktiga ögonblick i mors liv," "Orkanen Hazel," "Loulou, ellar Språkets hemliv," "Blåskäggs ägg," "Saltträdgården," "Solupp-gång," "Några avslöjanden."

386. *Der lange Traum: Roman*. Frankfurt am Main: Fischer Taschenbuch, 1990. German translation of *Surfacing* by Reinhild Böhnke.

387. "Deserved Mention." *Globe and Mail* 17 July 1990: A14. Letter to editor acknowledging David (Fire) Young, whose efforts were overlooked in an article on the Baffin Island Writers.

388. *Die Unmöglichkeit der Nähe: Roman*. Frankfurt am Main: Fischer Taschenbuch Verlag, 1990. German translation of *Life Before Man* by Werner Waldhoff.

389. "A Double-Bladed Knife: Subversive Laughter in Two Stories by Thomas King." *Canadian Literature* 124-125 (Spring-Summer 1990): 243-250. Reprinted in *Na-*

tive Writers and Canadian Writing. Ed. W. H. New. Vancouver, BC: UBC Press, 1990. 243-250.

390. *El huevo de Barba Azul*. Barcelona: Alcor, 1990. Spanish translation of *Bluebeard's Egg* by Eduardo G. Murillo.

391. "[Excerpt]." *Erotica: An Anthology of Women's Writing*. Ed. Margaret Reynolds. London: Pandora, 1990. 18-21. Published in the United States as *Erotica: Women's Writings from Sappho to Margaret Atwood*. Ed. Margaret Reynolds. New York: Fawcett Columbine, 1990. 18-21. Reprinted from *The Handmaid's Tale*.

392. "Eventual Proteus." *The Virago Book of Love Poetry*. Ed. Wendy Mulford. London: Virago Press, 1990. 168-169.

393. "An Exchange: Defense of PEN." *Books in Canada* 19.1 (January-February 1990): 10-13.

394. "The Female Body." *Michigan Quarterly Review* 29.4 (Fall 1990): 490-493. Also in *Solo Square III*. Ed. Alberto Manguel. London: Bloomsbury, 1990. 68-71. Prose poem.

395. "A Flying Start." *That Reminds Me ... Canada's Authors Relive Their Most Embarrassing Moments*. Ed. Marta Kurc. Toronto: Stoddart, 1990. 11-13. What a flying squirrel did to Atwood on live TV.

396. *For the Birds*. Toronto: Douglas & McIntyre, 1990. 54. Illustrated by John Bianchi. Juvenile.

397. "Foreword." *Ambivalence: Studies in Canadian Literature*. Ed. Om P. Juneja and Chandra Mohan. New Delhi: Allied Publishers, 1990. v-vi.

398. "Foreword." *Barbed Lyres: Canadian Venomous Verse*. Toronto: Key Porter Books, 1990. xiii-xvi. Poems from contest conducted by *This Magazine*; idea for contest came from Atwood, who was one of the judges.

399. "Frogless." *Paris Review* 33.117 (Winter 1990): 67. Poem.

400. "Giving Birth." *Black Water 2: More Tales of the Fantastic*. Ed. Alberto Manguel. New York: Clarkson Potter, 1990. 528-542. Also in *We Are the Stories We Tell: The Best Short Stories by North American Women Since 1945*. Ed. Wendy Martin. New York: Pantheon, 1990. 134-149. Reprinted from *Dancing Girls and Other Stories*, ©1977-1982.

401. "Hack Wednesday." *New Yorker* 66.31 (17 September 1990): 38-47. Short story.

402. *The Handmaid's Tale*. [Sound recording]. Read by Joanna David. Bath, UK: Chivers Audio Books, 1990. 8 sound cassettes.

403. "Haunted by Their Nightmares." *Toni Morrison: Modern Critical Views*. Ed. Harold Bloom. New York; Philadelphia: Chelsea House, 1990. 143-147. Review of *Beloved* originally published in the *New York Times Book Review* 15 September 1987: 1, 79-50.

404. "Homelanding." *Tesseracts3*. Ed. Candas Jane Dorsey and Gary Truscott. Victoria: Porcépic Books, 1990. 83-86. Speculative fiction. "First appeared in *Elle* (UK ed.) 1989; also appeared in *Ms. Magazine*, 1990."

405. "If You Can't Say Something Nice, Don't Say Anything at All." *Language in Her Eye: Views on Writing and Gender by Canadian Women Writing in English*. Ed. Libby Scheier, Sarah Sheard, and Eleanor Wachtel. Toronto: Coach House Press, 1990. 15-25.

406. "In Search of the Rattlesnake Plantain." *Vital Lines: Contemporary Fiction about Medicine*. Ed. Jon Mukand. New York: St. Martin's Press, 1990. 14-23. Reprinted from *Bluebeard's Egg and Other Stories*, ©1986-1987.

407. "Isis in Darkness." *Granta* 31 (Spring 1990): 186-206. *Granta* issue title: *The General*. Ed. Isabel Hilto. New York: Granta U.S.A., 1990. Short story.

408. *Jijo no Monogatari*. Tokyo: Shinchosha, 1990. Japanese translation of *The Handmaid's Tale*. Title romanized.

409. "Kat." *New Yorker* 66.3 (5 March 1990): 38-44. Short story. Republished later as "Hairball."

410. *Katteoog*. Amsterdam: Uitgeverij Bert Bakker, 1990. Dutch translation of *Cat's Eye*.

411. *Katzenauge*. Frankfurt am Main: S. Fischer, 1990. German translation of *Cat's Eye* by Charlotte Franke.

412. *Life Before Man*. London: Virago Press, 1990 ©1982.

413. "The Loneliness of the Military Historian." *TLS* 14-20 September 1990: 976. Reprinted in *Harper's* 281 (December 1990): 17-18. Poem.

414. "The Man from Mars." *The Faber Book of Contemporary Canadian Short Stories*. Selected by Michael Ondaatje. London and Boston: Faber and Faber, 1990. 273-293. Except for title and copyright pages, the same as 1990 Viking (US) edition titled *From Ink Lake: Canadian Stories*, selected by Michael Ondaatje. Also in *The World of the Short Story: A Twentieth-Century Collection*. Ed. Clifton Fadiman. New York; Avenel, NJ: Wing Books, 1990 ©1986. [769]-785. Reprinted from *Dancing Girls and Other Stories*, ©1977.

415. "Marsh, Hawk." *The Nation 1865-1990: Selections from the Independent Magazine of Politics and Culture*. Ed. Katrina vanden Heuvel. New York: Thunder's Mouth Press, 1990. 501-502. Poem; reprinted from *The Nation* 7 July 1973.

416. "My Life as a Bat." *Antaeus* 64-65 (Spring-Autumn 1990): 172-175. Prose poem.

417. "Nine Beginnings." *The Writer on Her Work*. Vol. 1. Ed. Janet Sternburg. New York: Norton, 1990. 150-156.

418. "Obstacle Course." *The Critical Response to Tillie Olsen*. Ed. Kay Hoy Nelson and Nancy Huse. Westport, CT: Greenwood, 1994. 250-251. Review of Olsen's *Silences*. Reprinted from *New York Times Book Review* 30 July 1978: 1, 27.

419. *Occhio di Gatto*. Milan: A. Mondadori, 1990. Italian translation of *Cat's Eye* by Marco Papi.

420. *Oeil-de-chat: roman*. Paris: Éditions R. Laffont, 1990. French translation of *Cat's Eye* by Hélène Filion.

421. *Ojo de gato*. Barcelona: Ediciones B, 1990. Spanish translation of *Cat's Eye* by Jordi Mustieles.

422. *Olho de gato*. São Paulo, Brasil: Marco Zero, 1990. Portuguese translation of *Cat's Eye* by Maria José Silveira.

423. *Orjattaresi*. Helsinki: Kirjayhtymä, 1990. Finnish translation of *The Handmaid's Tale* by Matti Kannosto.

424. "The Page." *Ellipse* 44 (1990): 84-87. Prose poem. Reprinted from *Murder in the Dark*; French translation on facing pages.

425. "[Poems]." *Margaret Atwood*. [Sound recording]. Read by Margaret Atwood. New York: Academy of American Poets, [1990s] ©1978. 1 sound cassette. Recorded 11 April 1978 at the Solomon R. Guggenheim Museum.

426. "Progressive Insanities of a Pioneer." *Acquario* 3 December 1990: 55-57.

427. Promotional blurb, back dust jacket for Valerie Martin's *Mary Reilly*. New York: Doubleday, 1990.

428. "The Santa Claus Trap." *Canadian Christmas Stories in Prose and Verse*. Ed. Don Bailey and Daile Unruh. Kingston, ON; Clayton, NY: Quarry Press, 1990. 11-23. Verse narrative; reprinted from *The Weekend Magazine*.

429. "Scrooge McDuck vs. the Trickster." *TLS* 16-22 (March 1990): 282. Essay on Native Indian writing in Canada.

430. *Selected Poems: 1966-1984.* Toronto: Oxford UP, 1990. 320. "This selection of Margaret Atwood's poetry is a substantial introduction to her work, drawing from *The Circle Game, The Animals in That Country, Procedures for Underground, The Journals of Susanna Moodie* (complete), *Power Politics, You Are Happy, Two-Headed Poems, True Stories,* and *Interlunar.*"

431. *La servante écarlate.* Paris: J'ai Lu, 1990. French translation of *The Handmaid's Tale* by Sylviane Rué.

432. "The Sin Eater." *The Daemonic Imagination: Biblical Text and Secular Story.* Ed. Robert Detweiler and William G. Doty. Atlanta, GA: Scholars Press, 1990. 209-220. Reprinted from *Dancing Girls and Other Stories*, ©1977-1982.

433. "A Slave to His Own Liberation." *New York Times Book Review* 16 September 1990: 1, 30. Review of *The General and His Labyrinth* by Gabriel García Márquez.

434. "Small Requiem." *Canadian Forum* 69 (November 1990): 31. Poem; first published in *Canadian Forum* in 1959.

435. *Surfacing.* New York: Fawcett; London: Virago, 1990 ©1972.

436. *Surfacing, Life Before Man, The Handmaid's Tale.* New York: Quality Paperback Book Club, 1990. "This edition was specially created in 1990 for Quality Paperback Book Club." Appears to be photographic offsets of earlier editions.

437. "This Is a Photograph of Me." *Acquario* 3 December 1990: 54.

438. "Three Chronicles." *This Magazine* 24.3 (September 1990): 38-41; also in *Ms.* 1.2 (September-October 1990): 80-83. Short story.

439. *Tjenerinnens beretning.* [Oslo]: Aschehoug, 1990. Norwegian translation of *The Handmaid's Tale* by Mereta Alfsen.

440. *Ull de gat.* Barcelona: Edicions de l'Eixample, 1990. Catalan translation of *Cat's Eye* by Roser Berdagué i Costa.

441. "Uncles." *Saturday Night* 105.6 (July-August 1990): 52-59.

442. *Verletzungen: Roman.* Frankfurt am Main: Fischer Taschenbuch, 1990 ©1982. German translation of *Bodily Harm* by Werner Waldhoff.

443. *Vynáranie.* Bratislava: Smena, 1990. Slovak translation of *Surfacing* by Katarína Karovicová.

444. "Weight." Vogue 180 (August 1990): 328-331, 384.

445. *You Are Happy.* New York: Harper & Row, 1990 ©1974. Based on a photocopied reproduction [Berkeley: University of California, Library Photographic Service, 1990?].

Adaptations of Atwood's Works

446. *The Handmaid's Tale.* [Motion Picture]. Screenplay by Harold Pinter; directed by Volker Schlondorff. United States: Cinecom Entertainment Group, 1990. 12 reels of 12 on 6 (ca. 9324 ft.).

447. *The Handmaid's Tale.* [Videorecording]. Screenplay by Harold Pinter; directed by Volker Schlondorff. New York: HBO Video, 1990. VHS tape 1 videocassette (109 min.).

Quotations

448. "[Quote]." *Canadian Dreams and American Control: The Political Economy of the Canadian Film Industry*. By Pendakur, Manjunath. Detroi, MI: Wayne State UP, 1990. 251. Forequote for Chapter 8; reprinted from *Globe and Mail* 5 November 1987: A7; originally, remarks made at Parliamentary hearing on free trade.
449. "[Quote]." *Public Perspective* 1.6 (September-October 1990): 26. Article reviewing Seymour Martin Lipset's *Continental Divide: The Values and Institutions of the United States and Canada* quotes Atwood: "If the national mental illness of the United States is megalomania, that of Canada is paranoid schizophrenia."
450. "[Quote]." *Singular Texts/Plural Authors: Perspectives on Collaborative Writing*. By Lisa Ede and Andrea Lunsford. Carbondale, IL: Southern Illinois UP, 1990. 69. Fifty-word quotation disagreeing with the notion of "the writer as an enclosed self."

Interviews

451. "[Interview]." *Writers on Writing: Creative Writing Course*. [Videorecording]. Northbrook, IL: Roland Collection, 1990 ©1988. 6 videocasettes plus study guide. The authors on these tapes talk about how and why they began to write, where they found their inspiration, and how they see their role as a writer, in personal and public terms. These 6 videos are based on the series, "Writers talk ideas of our times," and are copied from "Writers in conversation" programs. With a study guide containing 48 tasksheets designed to develop literary appreciation and to bridge the gap between the professional author and the student writer. Atwood appears on the 5th videocassette which covers the topics of form and genre.
452. *Lifetime I, Canadian Personalities Package*. [Videorecording]. [Toronto]: CTV Television Network, 1990. 1 videocassette (41 min.). Among those interviewed, Atwood talks about herself, women, and her latest project, *The Handmaid's Tale* (10 min.).
453. *Not a Love Story: A Film about Pornography*. [Videorecording]. Ho-Ho-Kus, NJ: National Film Board of Canada Library, 1990. VHS tape, 1 videocassette (ca. 69 min.). Atwood is one of several interviewed.
455. BAER, Susan. "*Handmaid* Author Supports Film." *Chicago Sun-Times* 31 March 1990: 15.
456. GODDARD, Peter. "Margaret Atwood on Words, Films and Puritans." *Toronto Star* 4 March 1990: Section: Entertainment: C1. (1091 w). Atwood reflects on earlier attempts to adapt her novels as movies, and refutes the criticism that *The Handmaid's Tale* was made by men: "There are not very many female producers around, there are not very many female directors, and there are not very many female script writers. It's an underpopulated area, although there are more people moving into it…. If it had been an entirely female team, they never would have got the money to make the movie. People would have taken one look at the subject and said, 'Oh, no, it's total propaganda. We don't want to touch it.'"

In response to the question: **Who exactly should be entrusted with this essentially feminist story? Wouldn't the only choice to direct have been a woman?** Atwood replied: "I don't think gender is any guarantee of anything. They might have gone over backwards in the other direction—i.e., 'We don't want people to think we're strident, so let's make everything a bit softer.' Remember, the jury that picked Kingsley Amis for the Booker Prize (which won over *The Handmaid's Tale*) was all female, except for one person."

458. INGERSOLL, Earl G., ed. *Margaret Atwood: Conversations*. Ontario Review Press Critical Series. Willowdale, ON: Firefly Books; Princeton, NJ: Ontario Review Press, 1990. 251 pp. Contents: Graeme Gibson. "Dissecting the Way a Writer Works." 3-19. Conducted in 1972 and published in his *Eleven Canadian Novelists*. Toronto: Anansi, 1973.—Levenson, Christopher. "Magical Forms of Poetry." 20-32. Conducted on 4 April 1972 and published in *Manna* 2 (1972).—Gibson, Mary Ellis. "Thinking about the Technique of Skiing When You're Halfway Down the Hill." 33-39. Conducted in February 1976 and published in *Chicago Review* 27 (1976): 105-113.—Sandler, Linda. "A Question of Metamorphosis." 40-57. Conducted during March and April 1976 and published in *The Malahat Review* 41 (1977): 7-27.—Struthers, J. R. (Tim). "Playing Around." 58-68. Conducted in October 1976 and published in *Essays on Canadian Writing* 6 (1977): 18-27.—Oates, Joyce Carol. "My Mother Would Rather Skate Than Scrub Floors." 69-85. Conducted in February 1978 and published in *New York Times Book Review* 21 May 1978.—Davidson, Jim. "Where Were You When I Really Needed You." 86-98. Conducted 6 March 1978 and published in *Meanjin* 37 (1978): 189-205.—Hammond, Karla. "Defying Distinctions." 99-108. Conducted 8 July 1978 and published in *Concerning Poetry* 12.2 (1979): 73-81.—Hammond, Karla. "Articulating the Mute." 109-120. Conducted 8 July 1978 and published in *American Poetry Review* 8.5 (1979): 27-29.—Twigg, Alan. "Just Looking at Things That Are There." 121-130. Conducted in 1979 and published in his *Strong Voices: Conversations with Fifty Canadian Authors*. Madeira Park, BC: Harbour Publishing, 1988.—Gerald, Gregory Fitz and Kathryn Crabbe. "Evading the Pigeonholers." 131-139. Conducted on 13 September 1979 and published in *Midwest Quarterly* 28.4 (1987): 525-539. [Ed. note: Journal also lists Earl G. Ingersoll as a third interviewer.] Brans, Jo. "Using What You're Given." 140-151. Conducted in 1982 and published in *Southwest Review* 68.4 (Autumn1983): 301-315.—Ross, Catherine Sheldrik and Copry Bieman Davies. "More Room for Play." 152-161. Conducted 20 January 1983 and published in *Canadian Children's Literature* 42 (1986).—Mendez-Egle, Beatrice. "Witness Is What You Must Bear." 162-170. Conducted in 1983 and published in *Margaret Atwood: Reflection and Reality*, Edinburg, TX: Pan American University, 1987.—Walker, Sue. "Managing Time for Writing." 171-176. Conducted February 1985 and published in *Negative Capability* 5 (1985).—Meese, Elizabeth. "The Empress Has No Clothes." 177-190. Conducted in April 1985 and published in *Black Warrior Review* 12.1 (1985): 88-108.—Hancock, Geoff. "Tightrope-Walking Over Niagara Falls." 191-220. Conducted 12-13 December 1986 and published in his *Canadian Writers at Work*. Toronto: Oxford, UP, 1987.—Lyons, Bonnie. "Using Other People's Dreadful Childhoods." 221-234. Conducted 14 February 1987 and published in *Shenandoah* 3.2 (1987: 69-89.—Ingersoll, Earl. "Waltzing Again." 234-238. Conducted in November 1989 and published in *Ontario Review* 32 (1990): 7-11.

459. ———. "Waltzing Again': A Conversation with Margaret Atwood." *Ontario Review* 32 (1990): 7-11.

460. JOHNSTON, Sheila. "The Ultimate Sexploitation Movie: Sheila Johnston Talked to Margaret Atwood about Double Standards at Play in the Screen Adaptation of Her Novel *The Handmaid's Tale*." *The Independent* (London) 26 October 1990:

Section: Listings: 6. Although she was currently adapting her latest novel, *Cat's Eye*, for the screen, Atwood did not write the script for *The Handmaid's Tale*; Harold Pinter was responsible for that. "I think I was too close to it. There is a lot of layering of time, a lot of meditational prose and inner monologue. All that had to go and I didn't feel up to doing that. The other practical reason was the subject matter, the 'horrible feminist propaganda' factor. As it was, it was very difficult to get it financed; a lot of people were scared silly by it. So with that and a female screenwriter, the chances of it ever being made were very low." That said, Atwood was not dazzled with the results, she stated.

461. MALCOLM, Andrew H. "Margaret Atwood Reflects on a Hit." *New York Times* 14 April 1990: Section: Arts: 13. Atwood pronounced herself happy with the movie version. "This story," she said, "could have been the most gross sexploitative film ever, sort of 'maidens on a sexual rampage.'"

462. MOORE, Micki. "Margaret Atwood: What Didn't Happen to Me That Happens to a Lot of Women Is That Their Self-Confidence Gets Damaged at a Fairly Early Stage of Childhood." *Toronto Star* 22 March 1990: Section: Life: F1. (2059 w). Questions about her career and marriage.

463. MORRIS, Mary. "The Art of Fiction CXXI." *Paris Review* 117 (Winter 1990): 69-88. Representation of the theme of survival in her works; consideration of survival as an intellectual and political struggle; challenges of being a poet.

464. PERRY, Gerald. "*Handmaid's Tale* Depicts Futuristic Puritans in Harvard Square." *Boston Globe* 4 March 1990: B39. Reprint: *Los Angeles Times* 4 March 1989 Section: CAL: 38-39, 90.

465. WOODWARD, Calvin. "Margaret Atwood, a Very Lively 'Bug on a Pin.'" *Toronto Star* 15 August 1990: B3. Atwood reflects on what it is like to be under constant examination.

Scholarly Resources

466. "Atwood, Margaret." *The Feminist Companion to Literature in English: Women Writers from the Middle Ages to the Present*. By Virginia Blain, Patricia Clements, and Isobel Grundy. New Haven, CT; London: Yale UP, 1990. 38-39. Biographical sketch and discussion of Atwood's themes and impact of her work.

467. *Literary History of Canada: Canadian Literature in English*. Vol. 4. 2nd ed. Toronto: University of Toronto Press, 1990, passim. Covering 1972-1984, includes Atwood as one of Canada's best poets and novelists.

468. ALLISON, Alida Louise. "Eurydice: The Lost Voice (Virgil)." PhD thesis. University of California, Riverside, 1990. 274 pp. Atwood is discussed as one of the 20th-century women writers who have portrayed the character of Eurydice. For more see *DAI-A* 51.07 (January 1991): 2371.

469. ANDERSON, Michele E. "Two Cultures, One Consciousness: A Comparative Study of Canadian Women's Literature in French and in English." PhD thesis. Indiana University, 1990. 498 pp. Similarities are greater than differences for Atwood, Blais, Hébert, and Laurence. For more see *DAI-A* 51.10 (April 1991): 3415.

470. ARMBRUSTER, Jane. "Memory and Politics: A Reflection on *The Handmaid's Tale*." *Social Justice* 17.3 (Fall 1990): 146-152. *The Handmaid's Tale* is a springboard to urge looking back to the feminist movement and reviving consciousness raising of 20-plus years ago.

471. ARNOLD, David Scott. "Hidden Since the Foundation of the World: Girard, Turner, and Two Mythic Readings." *The Daemonic Imagination: Biblical Text and Secular Story.* Ed. Robert Detweiler and William G. Doty. American Academy of Religion. Studies in Religion. Ed. Lawrence S. Cunningham, no. 60. Atlanta: Scholars Press, 1990. 137-148. Girard's concept of mimeticism to interpret Mark's Gospel story of the Gerasene demoniac and Turner's concept of liminality to understand "The Sin Eater" are the mythic perspectives for these stories.

472. ATHERTON, Stanley S. "Atwood, Horwood, Kreiner, and Wright: The Caribbean Connection." *Tensions between North and South: Studies in Modern Commonwealth Literature and Culture.* Proceedings of the Eighth Commonwealth Literature Conference. Ed. Edith Mettke. Würzburg: Königshausen and Neumann, 1990. 28-36. Includes *Bodily Harm*, an ironic exploration of outsider involvement in local politics, in an analysis of Canadian fiction set in the Caribbean where the focus is on tensions that result from lack of understanding and an inability to suffer personal consequence.

473. BACHINGER, Katrina. "The Rhetorics of Desperation and Re-Definition in the Evolution of the Ape Feminine: Margaret Atwood's 'Under Glass.'" *Crisis and Creativity in the New Literatures in English Canada,* ed. Geoffrey Davis. *Cross/Cultures: Readings in the Post/Colonial Literatures in English,* ed. Gordon Collier, Hena Maes-Jelinek, and Geoffrey Davis, 2. Amsterdam; Atlanta, GA: Rodopi, 1990. 185-198. The banality of "Under Glass" gives it "paradigmatic status." Atwood's use of desperation speech followed by the rhetoric of re-definition brings on "epistemological evolution" and a re-visioning of the ape feminine.

474. BANERJEE, Chinmoy. "Alice in Disneyland: Criticism as Commodity in *The Handmaid's Tale.*" *Essays on Canadian Writing* 41 (Summer 1990): 74-92. Atwood's parody, duplicity, and concern with aesthetics make *The Handmaid's Tale* a "pseudo-dystopia." The novel's structure "generates two levels of response": naive consumption and sophisticated enjoyment.

475. ———. "Atwood's Time: Hiding Art in *Cat's Eye.*" *Modern Fiction Studies* 36.4 (Winter 1990): 513-522. The psychological narration forms an understanding of the novel in artistic and literary terms.

476. BAUGHMAN, Cynthia. "The Handmaid's Tale." *The Pinter Review: Annual Essays* (1990): 92-96.

477. BERAN, Carol L. "The Canadian Mosaic: Functional Ethnicity in Margaret Atwood's *Life Before Man.*" *Essays on Canadian Writing* 41 (Summer 1990): 59-73. The *Life Before Man* manuscripts show Atwood's concern with Lesje's ethnicity and altering of key scenes, affirming the characters' "movement from existential isolation toward social integration."

478. ———. "Images of Women's Power in Contemporary Canadian Fiction by Women." *Studies in Canadian Literature* 15.2 (1990): 55-76. Works by Aritha Van Herk and Alice Munro are discussed along with *The Handmaid's Tale* and *Cat's Eye*; *Survival* heralded an interest in power as a theme.

479. BLAISE, Clark. *The Border as Fiction.* [Orono, ME]: Borderlands Project, 1990. 1-12. *Bodily Harm* and *The Handmaid's Tale* are mentioned in essay on the symbolism of borders, primarily the Canadian and United States border; printed and bound with BROWN (see 483).

480. BOUCHARD, Guy. "Science-fiction et utopie: Margaret Atwood." *Imagine: Regards sur la science-fiction et les littératures de l' imaginaire* 11.4 (September 1990): 109-136.

481. BOUSON, J. Brooks. "The Anxiety of Being Influenced: Reading and Responding to Character in Margaret Atwood's *The Edible Woman*." *Style* 24.2 (Summer 1990): 228-241. Bouson compares the reading experience to psychoanalytic countertransference and examines how the self-deficient Marian invites reader participation and interpretation.

482. BOWEN, Deborah. "Mimesis, Magic, Manipulation: A Study of the Photograph in Contemporary British and Canadian Novels." PhD thesis. University of Ottawa, 1990. 443 pp. Atwood, and other Canadian writers, ascribe to Roland Barthes's thesis of "the intransigent value of appearances." For more see *DAI-A* 52.12 (June 1992): 4337.

483. BROWN, Russell. *Borderlines and Borderlands in English Canada: The Written Line*. [Orono, ME]: Borderlands Project, 1990. 13-70. Atwood's novels and her critical writings are referred to frequently in this essay discussing Canadian literature in terms of opposites and two sides of existence; printed and bound with BLAISE (above).

484. BRUNTON, Rosanne D. "Feminine Discourses in the Fantastic: A Reading of Selected Inter-American Writers." PhD thesis. Pennsylvania State University, 1990. 213 pp. "This dissertation analyses four contemporary novels from the perspectives of the Inter-American, the fantastic, and the feminine. The texts discussed are Isabel Allende's *La casa de los espíritus*, Margaret Atwood's *Surfacing*, Toni Morrison's *Beloved*, and Simone Schwarz-Bart's *TiJean L'horizon*. The development of Inter-American literary conventions—as having distinct qualities that relate to the Inter-American environment and experience—is discussed. The fantastic is defined as a literary mode that articulates the awareness of magic in certain Inter-American cultures. The feminine aspect of the study relates to themes and techniques in the texts that emanate from female experiences." (Author). For more see *DAI-A* 51.09 (March 1991): 3063.

485. BUCK, M. Laurel. "The Spiritual Dimension of the Struggle of Marian Engel's Heroines to Shape Their Lives toward Wholeness." MA thesis. University of Calgary, 1990. 186 pp. "While Engel shares with such writers as Margaret Laurence, Alice Munro and Margaret Atwood the creation of women engaged in a struggle toward wholeness of life, the exploration of the spiritual dimension is distinctive in her work." (Author). For more see *MAI* 30.03 (Fall 1992): 483.

486. BURDETTE, Martha. "Sin Eating and Sin Making: The Power and Limits of Language." *The Daemonic Imagination: Biblical Text and Secular Story*. Ed. Robert Detweiler and William G. Doty. American Academy of Religion. Studies in Religion. Ed. Lawrence S. Cunningham, no. 60. Atlanta: Scholars Press, 1990. 159-168. Psychoanalytic literary criticism to interpret the Gospel of Mark tale and "The Sin Eater."

487. CARRIKER, Kitti. "Literary Automata: Lacanian and Figurative Approaches to the Self-Created Miniature." PhD thesis. University of Notre Dame, 1990. 330 pp. Many writers are discussed; for Atwood, "the body of the doll appears as an object and imperfect imitation of the human subject it represents." For more see *DAI-A* 51.07 (January 1991): 2383.

488. DAÑOBEITIA, María Luisa. "*The Journals of Susanna Moodie* and *Roughing It in the Bush*: An Interpretation Based on Social Adjustment." *Revista Española de Estudios Canadienses* 1.1 (September 1990): 45-70. Uses these two works to illustrate that more educated and wealthier immigrants have a more difficult time adjusting to a new culture.

489. DECONCINI, Barbara. "Narrative Hunger." *The Daemonic Imagination: Biblical Text and Secular Story.* Ed. Robert Detweiler and William G. Doty. American Academy of Religion. Studies in Religion. Ed. Lawrence S. Cunningham, no. 60. Atlanta, GA: Scholars Press, 1990. 111-122. Loss, remembrance, a desire to make sense of things are themes in this narrative and involve the reader in the story.

490. DESJARDINS, Louise. "Comparaison entre *Power Politics* de Margaret Atwood et *Bloody Mary* de France Théoret ou Comment on disait je t'aime dans les années soixante-dix." *Metonymies: Essais de literature canadienne comparée / Essays in Comparative Canadian Literature.* Ed. Larry Shouldice. Sherbrooke: Département de letters et communications, Université de Sherbrooke, 1990. [57]-74. [Ed. note: The Table of Contents incorrectly lists the page numbers as 49-66.]

491. DETWEILER, Robert, and William G. DOTY, ed. *The Daemonic Imagination: Biblical Text and Secular Story.* American Academy of Religion. Studies in Religion. Ed. Lawrence S. Cunningham, no. 60. Atlanta: Scholars Press, 1990. 232. Papers presented at 1987 colloquy, sponsored by American Academy of Religion; Atwood's "The Sin Eater" and the narrative of the Gerasene demoniac from the Gospel of Mark are the subjects of the papers; the papers on Atwood appear here as individual entries.

492. DEV, Jai. "A Study of Margaret Atwood's *Surfacing*: Lessons for M. Phil. (English) Course, Option VII (Semester II), Commonwealth Fiction, Perspectives of Historico-Cultural Identity." Patiala: Dept. of Correspondence Courses, Punjabi University, 1990. Available from the National Library of Canada.

493. DIVASSON CILVETI, Lourdes. "*The Handmaid's Tale*: Una Forma de Supervivencia." *Revista Canaria de Estudios Ingleses* 19-20 (November 1989-April 1990): 211-219. Irony is examined as a seldom-mentioned feature of this novel.

494. DOTY, William G. "Afterword: Sacred Pigs and Secular Cookies: Mark and Atwood Go Postmodern." *The Daemonic Imagination: Biblical Text and Secular Story.* Ed. Robert Detweiler and William G. Doty. American Academy of Religion. Studies in Religion. Ed. Lawrence S. Cunningham, no. 60. Atlanta, GA: Scholars Press, 1990. 191-206. Discusses the essays presented and the themes set forth in postmodern interpretation.

495. DOWNEY, Mike. "German Stories." *Cinema Papers* 80 (August 1990): 24-26. *The Handmaid's Tale* is one of 3 films from German directors discussed here.

496. EPSTEIN, Grace Ann. "Fluid Bodies: Narrative Disruption and Layering in the Novels of Doris Lessing, Toni Morrison and Margaret Atwood." PhD thesis. Ohio State University, 1990. 181 pp. These writers are aware of oppressive appropriation of women in traditional novels, and their narratives try to escape that fate. For more see *DAI-A* 51.12 (June 1991): 4117.

497. FIGUEIRA, Dorothy. "The Redemptive Text." *The Daemonic Imagination: Biblical Text and Secular Story.* Ed. Robert Detweiler and William G. Doty. American Academy of Religion. Studies in Religion. Ed. Lawrence S. Cunningham, no. 60. Atlanta, GA: Scholars Press, 1990. 149-158. The hermeneutics theories of Hans-Georg Gadamer are employed to understand these texts through a mixture of familiarity and strangeness with the text.

498. FITTING, Peter. "The Turn from Utopia in Recent Feminist Fiction." *Feminism, Utopia, and Narrative.* Ed. Libby Falk Jones and Sarah Webster Goodwin. Tennessee Studies in Literature, Vol. 32. Knoxville: University of Tennessee Press, 1990. 141-158. *The Handmaid's Tale* is one of 4 novels that illustrate recent feminist preoccupation with a dystopian patriarchical society; the value of these novels lies in the reminder that vigilance is needed in our world.

499. FOLEY, Michael. "'Basic Victim Positions' and the Women in Margaret Atwood's *The Handmaid's Tale*." *Atlantis* 15.2 (Spring 1990): 50-58. Applies the four types of victims as presented in *Survival* to the female characters of *The Handmaid's Tale*, finding the narrator the most interesting.

500. FULLBROOK, Kate. *Free Women: Ethics and Aesthetics in Twentieth-Century Women's Fiction*. Philadelphia: Temple UP, 1990. See especially "Margaret Atwood: Colonisation and Responsibility." 171-193. In a book examining statements and texts by women writers of significant ethical and aesthetic achievement, this chapter is devoted to the themes of change, responsibility, and refusal of innocence in Atwood's novels.

501. GILBERT-MACEDA, Ma Teresa. "Metafora en lo alto de los cielos, metaforas al fondo de la calle: El uso de la metafora en *Life Before Man*, de Margaret Atwood." *Epos: Revista de Filologia* 6 (1990): 511-520.

502. GILLESPIE, Tracey. "Elements of the Gothic in the Novels of Margaret Atwood." MA thesis. University of Alberta, 1990. 109 pp. Also available on microfiche from Canadian Theses Service (1991). "Atwood's three most strongly Gothic novels—*Lady Oracle, Bodily Harm,* and *The Handmaid's Tale*—chronicle the lives of 'Gothic' heroines who manage to break out of male-defined roles and forge their own identities, independent of patriarchal society's narrow parameters of female identity. In Atwood's hands, the Gothic becomes a political tool that disrupts the status quo and subverts dominant ideology. Her novels offer alternative endings to the standard Gothic's happily-ever-after marriages. By refusing to re-encapsulate the female fears and anxieties she raises, Atwood challenges our society's destructive stereotypes of gender and genre." (Author). For more see *MAI* 30.02 (Summer 1992): 218.

503. GOODWIN, Ken. "Revolution as Bodily Fiction: Thea Astley and Margaret Atwood." *Antipodes* 4.2 (Winter 1990): 109-114. Explores the politics of decolonization and the issues of fear and identity related to revolution in the inwardly personal *Bodily Harm* and the outwardly political *Beachmasters*.

504. GOTSCH-THOMSON, Susan. "The Integration of Gender into the Teaching of Classical Social Theory: Help from *The Handmaid's Tale*." *Teaching Sociology* 18 (January 1990): 69-73. Uses *The Handmaid's Tale* as a reference point for introducing gender issues and feminist perspectives in the classroom.

505. GRANOFSKY, Ronald. "Fairy-Tale Morphology in Margaret Atwood's *Surfacing*." *Mosaic* 23.4 (Fall 1990): 51-65. Vladimir Propp's *Morphology of the Folktale* is employed to interpret the female narrator's subversion of the fairy-tale element.

506. GREENE, Gayle. "Margaret Laurence's *Diviners* and Shakespeare's *Tempest*: The Uses of the Past." *Women's Re-Visions of Shakespeare*. Ed. Marianne Novy. Urbana; Chicago: University of Illinois Press, 1990. 166-167. Brief mention of *Surfacing* and *Lady Oracle* in comparison to Laurence's *Diviners* and as "feminist quest novels."

507. HALES, Lesley Ann. "Sorcery to Spirituality in Margaret Atwood's *Cat's Eye*." *Month* 23.9-10 (September-October 1990): 382-387. View of Elaine's spiritual search, pointing out the elements of the Catholic Church present in the journey.

508. HAMMER, Stephanie Barbé. "The World as It Will Be? Female Satire and the Technology of Power in *The Handmaid's Tale*." *Modern Language Studies* 20.2 (Spring 1990): 39-49. Satire in this novel appears in both its traditional form and as a reaction to the male satiric canon.

509. HAWKINS, Harriett. *Classics and Trash: Traditions and Taboos in High Litera-
      ture and Popular Modern Genres*. Toronto; Buffalo: University of Toronto Press,
      1990, passim. *Cat's Eye* and *Lady Oracle* illustrate the theme of a woman's con-
      flict between artistic talent and romantic love.

510. HENNEBERGER, Sandra. "Strange and Playful Paradigms in Margaret Atwood's
      Poetry." *Women's Studies* 17 (1990): 277-288. "The concept of dual-track, sepa-
      rate modes of consciousness within a single person, as explored in *Two-Headed
      Poems* by Margaret Atwood reflects her complex view of language." (Author).

511. HERRICK, Jim. "A Humanist Warning: *The Handmaid's Tale*." *New Humanist*
      106.4 [i.e., 105] (December 1990): 13. Compares film and novel.

512. HORNER, Avril, and Sue ZLOSNIK. *Landscapes of Desire: Metaphors in Mod-
      ern Women's Fiction*. New York; London; Toronto; Sydney; Tokyo; Singapore:
      Harvester Wheatsheaf, 1990. See especially "Beyond Boundaries and Back Again:
      Margaret Atwood's *Surfacing*." 181-202. Examines water and nature as means for
      the narrator to find herself and come to terms with her past.

513. JAIDEV. "'How Did We Get Bad?' The Lessons of *Surfacing*." *Ambivalence:
      Studies in Canadian Literature*. Foreword by Margaret Atwood. Ed. Om P. Juneja
      and Chandra Mohan. New Delhi: Allied Publishers, 1990: 276-283. These lessons
      are cultural, and thus political, and the power expressed is an important and rele-
      vant lesson, more so for Third World countries than for Canada.

514. JARRETT, Mary. "The Presentation of Montreal in Mavis Gallant's 'Between
      Zero and One' and of Toronto in Margaret Atwood's *Cat's Eye*." *Études canadi-
      ennes / Canadian Studies* 29 (1990): 173-181. "Mavis Gallant's portrayal of Mont-
      real in her story story...and Margaret Atwood's portrayal of Toronto in her
      novel...at first appear very similar. Each city is perceived through the eyes of the
      female protagonist, and each appears more of less disconcerting, not to say repel-
      lant. But the painter Elaine Risley is eventually reconciled to her Toronto whereas
      the writer Linnet Muir cannot be reconciled to her Montreal." (Author).

515. JENA, Seema. *Carving a Pattern out of Chaos: Withdrawal, a Narrative Device in
      Women's Writing*. New Delhi: Ashish Pub. House, 1990. Focus on the works of
      Atwood as well as of Anita Desai.

516. JUNEJA, Om P., and Chandra MOHAN, ed. *Ambivalence: Studies in Canadian
      Literature*. Foreword by Margaret Atwood. New Delhi: Allied Publishers, 1990.
      304. Many scattered references in addition to chapters specifically on Atwood; see
      Jaidev, Singh, and Vevaina in this section.

517. KAUFFMAN, Linda. "Special Delivery: Twenty-First-Century Epistolarity in *The
      Handmaid's Tale*." *Courage and Tool: The Florence Howe Award for Feminist
      Scholarship 1974-1989*. Ed. Joanne Glasgow and Angela Ingram. New York:
      Modern Language Association of America, 1990. 218-237. Reprinted from *Writ-
      ing the Female Voice: Essays in Epistolary Literature*. Ed. Elizabeth Goldsmith.
      Boston: Northeastern UP, 1989.

518. KITCH, Sally L. "A Worm in the Apple: French Critical Theory and the Metaphor
      of the Child in the Work of Atwood and Broner." *Rocky Mountain Review of Lan-
      guage and Literature* 44.1-2 (1990): 35-49. Applies French theories of discourse
      by Kristeva and others, to "the child as maternal metaphor," and linguistic/cultural
      structures in *Life Before Man* and *A Weave of Women*.

519. KLAPPERT, Peter. "I Want, I Don't Want: The Poetry of Margaret Atwood." *Get-
      tysburg Review* 3.1 (Winter 1990): 217-230. Atwood's 2 volumes of selected po-
      ems show a move from precision and pessimism to greater accessibility and com-

passion. "Modulation" begins in *You Are Happy*, with a "reflective tone" evolving in *Interlunar*.

520.   KLARER, Mario. "Frau und Utopie: Funktion von Geschlecht in der literarischen Utopie mit exemplarischen Analysen anglo-amerikanischer Frauenromane." PhD thesis. Leopold-Franzens Universitaet Innsbruck (Austria), 1990. 307 pp. Translation of German title: "Woman and Utopia: The Function of Gender in Literary Utopias with Illustrative Analyses of Anglo-American Women's Novels." "This study deals with the role of gender in the utopian tradition, considering works by both male and female authors. A general introduction to the most recent trends in feminist literary theory provides the theoretical framework for the subsequent three major chapters: The first examines gender-specific issues in male utopias ranging from Greco-Roman, medieval and early modern to contemporary Anglo-American literary utopias. The second surveys the female tradition of the genre starting in the Middle Ages and culminating in the feminist works of the last two decades. The third and last part of this study is devoted to independent analyses of four utopian novels by female authors. Common to all four texts is a metafictional or metatheoretical approach, i.e. reflections on gender in relation to writing. Mary Shelley's *Frankenstein* implies a gendered critique of science; Margaret Atwood's *The Handmaid's Tale* reflects on gender and media of expression; Sally Miller Gearhart's *The Wanderground* problematizes gender as a criterion for the production of texts and Ursula Le Guin's *The Dispossessed* links gender with narrative techniques. The overall aim of this investigation is to trace the question of gender in both utopian traditions, putting special emphasis on metafictional aspects in the works of Anglo-American female writers." (Author). For more see *DAI-C* 54.04 (Winter 1993): 983.

521.   ———. "The Gender of Orality and Literacy in Margaret Atwood's *The Handmaid's Tale*." *AAA: Arbeiten aus Anglistik und Amerikanistik* 15.2 (1990): 151-170. Relates recent anthropological and ethnological scholarship, and recent feminist literary theory, to the political and gender implications of the oral tradition and literacy concepts in *The Handmaid's Tale*. In German.

522.   KOLODNY, Annette. "Margaret Atwood and the Politics of Narrative." *Studies on Canadian Literature*. Ed. Arnold E. Davidson. New York: The Modern Language Association of America, 1990. 90-109.

523.   KORTE, Barbara. "Margaret Atwoods Roman *The Handmaid's Tale*: Interpretationshinweise für eine Verwendung im Englischunterricht der Sekundarstufe II." *Die Neueren Sprachen* 89.3 (June 1990): 224-242. Atwood's dystopia relates to conditions of contemporary world; this contrasts with the dystopian works that are often taught in Germany.

524.   ———. "Textuelle Interdependenzen in Margaret Atwoods Roman *The Handmaid's Tale*." *Zeitschrift der Gesellschaft für Kanada-Studien* 10.1 (1990): 15-25. More than her other novels, *The Handmaid's Tale* opens up another dimension of interpretation by way of other texts. With this intertextual dimension, *The Handmaid's Tale* demonstrates subtly the value and the persistence of these traditions.

525.   KRÓTKI, Karol Jósef, and Guy C. GERMAIN. "Demographic concerns in Belles-lettres: Insights from the Writings of Günter Grass and Margaret Atwood." Edmonton: Population Research Laboratory, University of Alberta, 1990. 12. (Research discussion paper, University of Alberta. Population Research Laboratory, no. 61).

526.   KUESTER, Martin Herbert. "History as Parody: Parodic Structures in Contemporary English-Canadian Historical Novels." PhD thesis. University of Manitoba,

1990. Both *Bodily Harm* and *The Handmaid's Tale* use parodies; Atwood's feminism marks her as distinct from male postmodernism. For more see *DAI-A* 53.01 (July 1992): 155.

527.   LANGER-DEVINE, Maureen C. "Literary Reconceptualizations of Woman and Nature." DPhil thesis. Universitaet für Bildungswissenschaften Klagenfurt (Austria), 1990. 170 pp. "This study analyses the concepts of woman and nature from the frame of reference of the discourses of ecofeminism and gynocriticism in seven North American feminist novels: *Surfacing* (Margaret Atwood), *The Diviners* (Margaret Laurence), *The Color Purple* (Alice Walker), *The Women of Brewster Place* (Gloria Naylor), *Woman on the Edge of Time* (Marge Piercy), *The Wanderground* (Sally Gearhart), *Housekeeping* (Marilynne Robinson)." (Author). For more see *DAI-C* 53.03 (Fall 1992): 399.

528.   LECKER, Robert, Jack DAVID, and Ellen QUIGLEY, eds. *Canadian Writers and Their Works*. Fiction Series. Vol. 5. Toronto: ECW Press, 1990. passim. Atwood briefly mentioned in chapter on Ernest Buckler.

529.   ———. *Canadian Writers and Their Works*. Poetry Series. Vol. 4. Toronto: ECW Press, 1990. passim. A few comments on Atwood in chapters on F. R. Scott and A. J. M. Smith.

530.   ———. *Canadian Writers and Their Works*. Poetry Series. Vol. 7. Toronto: ECW Press, 1990, passim. Scattered references to Atwood in several chapters.

531.   LECLAIRE, Jacques. "Margaret Atwood's *Cat's Eye* as a Portrait of the Artist." *Commonwealth Essays and Studies* 13.1 (1990): 73-80. Art's creation harks back to the artist's personal experiences; however, being an artist is part of a larger world, "among several possible ways of being."

532.   LEE, Jerrine Emma. "Myth and Belief in Margaret Atwood's Domestic Fiction." MA thesis. University of Victoria, 1990. 128 pp. Also available on microfiche from Canadian Theses Service (1991). "This study examines Atwood's use of classical mythology, fairy tale, and realism to challenge traditional ideas about home as a place and about woman's place in society. Close readings of *The Edible Woman*, *Lady Oracle*, and *Life Before Man* as well as selected stories from two collections, *Dancing Girls* and *Bluebeard's Egg*, show how Atwood uses revisionary mythopoesis and realistic details to create both settings and characters which undercut the concepts of these two domestic, and largely patriarchal, assumptions." (Author). For more see *MAI* 30.03 (Fall 1992): 484.

533.   LUCKING, David. "In Pursuit of the Faceless Stranger: Depths and Surfaces in Margaret Atwood's *Bodily Harm*." *Studies in Canadian Literature* 15.1 (1990): 76-93. Through turning Rennie's experience inside out, the illusions that keep the world apart from her are subverted.

534.   McGUIRE, Ann. "Margaret Atwood and English Studies: An Intellectual Context for Her Early Prose." PhD thesis. University of Western Australia, 1990. 292 pp.

535.   McVANN, Mark. "Destroying Death: Jesus in Mark and Joseph in 'The Sin Eater.'" *The Daemonic Imagination: Biblical Text and Secular Story*. Ed. Robert Detweiler and William G. Doty. American Academy of Religion. Studies in Religion. Ed. Lawrence S. Cunningham, no. 60. Atlanta, GA: Scholars Press, 1990. 123-136. Both stories are that of divine mediators and life transformations in which uncrossable boundaries are crossed.

536.   MICHAEL, Magali Cornier. "Feminism and the Postmodernist Impulse: Doris Lessing, Marge Piercy, Margaret Atwood, and Angela Carter." PhD thesis. Emory University, 1990. 132 pp. The thesis offers "specific readings of Doris Lessing's *The Golden Notebook*, Marge Piercy's *Woman on the Edge of Time*, Margaret At-

wood's *The Handmaid's Tale*, and Angela Carter's *Nights at the Circus*. Each of these novels has roots in the dominant themes of Anglo-American literature, yet each also testifies to various disruptive postmodern strategies that have been appropriated to feminist ends. My analyses of these four novels focus among other things on Lessing's use of narrative disruptions and of madness, Piercy's placing of worlds in confrontation, Atwood's unveiling of the gap that exists between official 'History' and women's histories, and Carter's appropriation of fantasy and carnivalization. Furthermore, I attempt to join these specific readings to a general consideration of the potential contribution of these authors' disruptive strategies to feminist criticism as well as to contemporary literature." (Author). For more see *DAI-A* 51.05 (November 1990): 1609.

537. MOREY, Ann-Janine. "The Old In/Out." *The Daemonic Imagination: Biblical Text and Secular Story*. Ed. Robert Detweiler and William G. Doty. American Academy of Religion. Studies in Religion. Ed. Lawrence S. Cunningham, no. 60. Atlanta: Scholars Press, 1990. 169-180. Feminist interpretation of Mark and Atwood's narratives, focusing on attack by demons and the irony that for females, rescue may be worse than the attack.

538. MURPHY, Patrick D. "Reducing the Dystopian Distance: Pseudo-Documentary Framing in Near-Future Fiction." *Science-Fiction Studies* 17.1 (March 1990): 25-40. Atwood's "post-future history" pseudo-documentary in *The Handmaid's Tale*, and the "contemporaneous journalistic" technique in Murphy and Strieber's *Warday and the Journey Onward*, bring the tenor and vehicle closer together to produce an enhanced cognitive experience.

539. MURRAY, Heather. "The Woman in the Preface: Atwood's Introduction to the 'Virago' Edition of Moodie's *Roughing It in the Bush*." *Prefaces and Literary Manifestoes/Prefaces et manifestes litteraires*. Ed. E. D. Blodgett and Anthony Purdy. Edmonton: University of Alberta, 1990. 90-97. (Conference organized by the Research Institute for Comparative Literature at the University of Alberta, 12-14 November 1987).

540. MURRAY, Shauna. "Narrative Strategies in Margaret Atwood's 'Bluebeard's Egg.'" *British Journal of Canadian Studies* 5.1 (1990): 127-140.

541. NESTOR, Theo Pauline. "The Cottage Novel: A Study of Three Novels by Canadian Women." MA thesis. San Francisco State University, 1990. On Atwood's *Surfacing*, Margaret Laurence's *Diviners*, and Audrey Thomas's *Intertidal Life*.

542. NORRIS, Ken. "'The University of Denay, Nunavit': The 'Historical Notes' in Margaret Atwood's *The Handmaid's Tale*." *American Review of Canadian Studies* 20.3 (Autumn 1990): 357-364. Discusses several ways this device furthers Atwood's plot and its interpretation.

543. PAGET, Elsie. "*The Handmaid's Tale*: Margaret Atwood's Use of Carnival and the Postmodern." MA thesis. McMaster University, 1990. 123 pp.

544. PALETTA, Anna. "From Subordinate to Subversive: Feminist Fiction as an Instrument in Expanding and Changing the Social Meaning of Gender." MA thesis. University of Victoria, 1990. 204 pp. Also available on microfiche from Canadian Theses Service (1991). This thesis "looks at contemporary feminist fiction as counter-hegemonic cultural production, i.e., as an instrument in expanding and changing the social meaning of gender. A theory is developed which posits that counter-hegemonic feminist fiction accomplishes three political objectives: unmasking women's subordination, creating models of resistance to it, and prefiguring systems towards which change can move." (Author). Novels studied include

The Handmaid's Tale, Alice Walker's *The Color Purple*, and Alice Munro's *Lives of Girls and Women*. For more see *MAI* 30.03 (Fall 1992): 567.

545. PARRY, Sally E. "Becoming a Jezebel: Taking on Roles in Margaret Atwood's *The Handmaid's Tale*." *Exercise Exchange* 36.1 (Fall 1990): 26-27. Outlines a college-level classroom exercise for exploring societal roles in *The Handmaid's Tale*.

546. PECK, Elizabeth G. "More Than Ideal: Size and Weight Obsession in Literary Works by Marge Piercy, Margaret Atwood, and Andre Dubus." *Platte Valley Review* 18.1 (Winter 1990): 69-75. The narrator of *Lady Oracle* uses eating and being fat as a means of exercising control over her mother.

547. PELLAUER, David. "Narrative Identity and Religious Identity." *The Daemonic Imagination: Biblical Text and Secular Story*. Ed. Robert Detweiler and William G. Doty. American Academy of Religion. Studies in Religion. Ed. Lawrence S. Cunningham, no. 60. Atlanta: Scholars Press, 1990. 99-110. Discussion centering on Paul Ricoeur's *Time and Narrative* as a means of understanding "The Sin Eater."

548. PIUSINSKA-WOZNIAK, Maria. "An American Aspect of the Search for the Canadian Identity: Hugh MacLennan's *The Precipice* and Margaret Atwood's *Surfacing*." *Kwartalnik Neofilologiczny* 37.4 (1990): 343-354. In both novels, "the Canadian state of mind is identified with innocence as its dominating feature."

549. QUIGLEY, Theresia Maria (FIAND). "The Evolution of the Child Protagonist in the Quebec and English-Canadian Adult Novel." PhD thesis. Université de Sherbrooke, 1990. 274 pp. Atwood one of several writers examined. For more see *DAI-A* 52.11 (May 1992): 3934.

550. RIBEIRO, Ofelia. "A Different Thread: An Analysis of the Diary Form in the Representation of the Female Self." MA thesis. Concordia University (Canada), 1990. 168 pp. "The contemporary woman author has experimented with different techniques in an attempt to find a form appropriate for her complex concerns as both woman and author. The extensive use of the diary in fictional form is a case in point as it utilizes and transforms what is primarily a nonfictional structure into a literary one. How this is done is examined using both a theoretical and a practical approach. The use of theoretical criticism, notably feminist literary criticism, permits a critique of the differences inherent in literature written by men versus that written by women as well as how these differences translate into praxis. A historical perspective of the development of the diary, both in its fictional and its nonfictional form, will reveal how extensively it has been used in the past as well as how it is currently being employed. Several novels, Doris Lessing's *The Golden Notebook*, Alice Walker's *The Color Purple*, and Margaret Atwood's *The Handmaid's Tale*, will form the thrust of the literary interpretation of the contemporary diary novel in an effort to examine the nature of the representation of the female self." (Author). For more see *MAI* 30.04 (Winter 1992): 1027.

551. RICHARDS, Mary Elizabeth. "The Politics of Language in Margaret Atwood's Later Fiction." PhD thesis. University of Nebraska–Lincoln, 1990. 253 pp. "Margaret Atwood is a Canadian author who believes that language is inherently political. In her fiction, linguistic acts of influence and control are made visible in the characters' interactions, revealing the political nature of interpersonal communication. Although critics have examined language in Atwood's earlier works, the present study addresses the relationship between language and power in Atwood's later prose published from 1979 through 1988, including analysis of four novels and one short story from the collection *Bluebeard's Egg*. The Introduction assesses the role of language in the practice of Atwood's art and in her theory of writing. In

addition, it contrasts Atwood's views on language with current thought in Feminist Criticism and Linguistic Theory in order to provide a context for understanding her assumptions. After this background, Chapter One explores the communication problems and strategies of three characters in *Life Before Man* (1979) as they deal with conflicts in their relationships. The second chapter contrasts the characters' use of language in the short story 'Loulou; or, The Domestic Life of the Language' and discusses Loulou's attempt to determine how the words of others affect her identity. Chapter Three analyzes the main character's development in *Bodily Harm* (1981); Rennie Wilford changes her attitude toward language and vows to use her professional writing to reflect and affect the realities of her society. *The Handmaid's Tale* (1985) is the subject of Chapter Four, which examines how Offred, the narrator, overcomes restrictions on communication in her future world and uses her voice to undermine the totalitarian Republic of Gilead...." (Author). For more see *DAI-A* 51.11 (May 1991): 3739.

552. ROWLANDS, Helen Caroline Anne. "The Relationship of Textuality to Concepts of the Self in the Novels of Margaret Atwood." MSc. Econ. thesis. University of Cardiff, 1990.

553. SANDIN, Maria. "Moten med skuggan: Om kvinnors sjalvblivelse." *Kulturtidskriften HORISONT* 37.5 (1990): 2-7. Treatment of women in Atwood compared to Inger Edelfeldt. Swedish.

554. SINGH, Sunaina. "Escape as Evolution in *Lady Oracle* and *Where Shall We Go This Summer?*" *Ambivalence: Studies in Canadian Literature.* Foreword by Margaret Atwood. Ed. Om P. Juneja and Chandra Mohan. New Delhi: Allied Publishers, 1990. 160-170. Joan's flight allows her to evaluate her life and return to a more positive reality.

555. SPARROW, Fiona. "'This Place Is Some Kind of a Garden': Clearings in the Bush in the Works of Susanna Moodie, Catherine Parr-Traill, Margaret Atwood and Margaret Laurence." *Journal of Commonwealth Literature* 25.1 (1990): 24-41. Moodie's texts are called on by Atwood to illustrate the value of good art and good order in the wilderness.

556. THOMPSON, Lars, and Becci HAYES. *Companions to Literature: A Teacher's Guide for* The Handmaid's Tale*, Margaret Atwood.* Mississauga, ON: S.B.F. Media, ©1990.

557. TIGER, Virginia. "Cultures of Occupation and the Canadian [Con]Script[ion]: 'Lessing Changed My Life.'" *In Pursuit of Doris Lessing: Nine Nations Reading.* Ed. Claire Sprague. New York: St. Martin's Press, 1990. 89-101. *Survival* and *Second Words* referred to in passing.

558. TSCHACHLER, Heinz. "Margaret Atwoods *Surfacing* (1972), George Grants Kanada und Die 'Tragische Weltanschauung.'" *Ökologie und Arkadien: Natur und nordamerikanische Kultur der siebziger Jahre.* Frankfurt am Main; Bern; New York; Paris: Peter Lang, 1990. 247-296.

559. VAN BERKEL, Elizabeth Christine. "The Female Artist's Room as a Metaphor for Language in Canadian Postmodern Fiction." MA thesis. Dalhousie University, 1990. 129 pp. "This thesis involves the application of feminist ideas expressed in Virginia Woolf's essay 'A Room of One's Own' to five Canadian novels. Four of these five, *The Handmaid's Tale*, *Beautiful Losers*, *Intertidal Life*, and *Ana Historic*, are here regarded as postmodern fiction while *The Fire-Dwellers*, as it is most commonly, is described as modern, though a modernist text comparable in theme to *The Handmaid's Tale*. All five novelists, including Laurence, use the female artist's room as a metaphor for language, as a structure, both physical and

psychological, which parallels her/his protagonist's experience of language. They imply that the female artist's creativity is inhibited in a society with patriarchal origins. In making conscious what has been true at least since Woolf's day, these five Canadian novels accurately reflect the concerns of many Canadian novelists. As postmodern writers, they advocate a suspicion for all norms and institutions which are socially approved. And as writers with strong feminist concerns, they both appeal to and expand upon the opinions of Woolf." (Author). For more see *MAI* 30.04 (Winter 1992): 1037.

560.   VEVAINA, Coomi S. "Wastelanders in This New Gilead: An Analysis of Margaret Atwood's *The Handmaid's Tale*." *Ambivalence: Studies in Canadian Literature*. Foreword by Margaret Atwood. Ed. Om P. Juneja and Chandra Mohan. New Delhi: Allied Publishers, 1990. 221-240. Detailed examination of setting and plot.

561.   WAGENER, Christel. "Margaret Atwood: Katzenauge." *Weimarer Beiträge: Zeitschrift für Literaturwissenschaft, Ästhetik und Kulturtheorie* 36.11 (1990): 1815-1820. Primarily about *Cat's Eye*. In German.

562.   WALKER, Nancy A. *Feminist Alternatives: Irony and Fantasy in the Contemporary Novel by Women*. Jackson; London: UP of Mississippi, 1990, passim. Includes *The Handmaid's Tale*, *Lady Oracle*, *Surfacing*, and *Cat's Eye*, with works by Piercy, Godwin, Drabble, Weldon, Lessing, Walker, and others, in a study of "unacceptable fantasies" and irony in realistic women's novels.

563.   WALL, Kathleen. "Healing the Divisions: Goddess Figures in Two Works of Twentieth-Century Literature." *Goddesses in Religions and Modern Debate*. Ed. Larry W. Hurtado. University of Manitoba. Studies in Religion, Vol. 1. Atlanta: Scholars Press, 1990. 205-226. Atwood's female deity in *Surfacing* is more grounded in the real world than is Lessing's in *Marriages*; however, similarities exist between the 2 figures.

564.   WILSON, Sharon R. "Fairy-Tale Cannibalism in *The Edible Woman*." *Cooking by the Book: Food in Literature and Culture*. Ed. Mary Anne Schofield. Bowling Green, OH: Popular, 1990. 78-88.

565.   ———. "A Note on Margaret Atwood's Visual Art and *Bodily Harm*." *Antipodes* 4.2 (Winter 1990): 115-116. Explicates 2 of Atwood's art works, relating the imagery to *Bodily Harm*.

566.   WILT, Judith. "'We Are Not Dying': Abortion and Recovery in Four Novels by Women." *Abortion, Choice, and Contemporary Fiction: The Armageddon of the Maternal Instinct*. Chicago and London: University of Chicago Press, 1990. 67-100. *Surfacing*, and 3 other novels by Didion, Felicitas, and Piercy, convey beginnings, birth, and survival through an abortion theme.

567.   WITHIM, Philip. "Arrival as Departure in Margaret Atwood's *Surfacing* and *Bodily Harm*." *Aspects of Commonwealth Literature*. Vol. 1. London: University of London, Institute of Commonwealth Studies, 1990. 76-84. Atwood's concerns broaden from the more private issues of *Surfacing* to the more social ones of *Bodily Harm*; still, both have a sub-theme of male oppression. The paper concludes with a short discussion of these themes in Atwood's other novels.

568.   WOODCOCK, George. *Introducing Margaret Atwood's* Surfacing. Canadian Fiction Studies, No. 4. Toronto: ECW Press 1990. 74. Contains a brief Atwood chronology, chapters on "the importance of the work," and "critical reception," and a section on "reading the text," which details Atwood's individual expression, structure and plot, use of metaphor, character development, ambiguous themes, and the narrator's rite of passage.

569. WRIGHT, Terence R. "Margaret Atwood and St. Mark: The Shape of the Gaps." *The Daemonic Imagination: Biblical Text and Secular Story.* Ed. Robert Detweiler and William G. Doty. American Academy of Religion. Studies in Religion. Ed. Lawrence S. Cunningham, no. 60. Atlanta, GA: Scholars Press, 1990. 181-190. Wolfgang Iser's theory of "implied reader" offers the chance to fill in the gaps in these stories and form answers to spiritual questions.

570. WYATT, Jean. *Reconstructing Desire: The Role of the Unconscious in Women's Reading and Writing.* Chapel Hill; London: University of North Carolina Press, 1990. See especially "Toward a More Creative Autonomy: *To the Lighthouse, Violet Clay, Bodily Harm,* 'How I Came to Write Fiction,' and *On Not Being Able to Paint.*" 103-125. This chapter discusses the female artist characters in these works in terms of their having to choose between work and love and their belief that they must keep total autonomy from emotional ties.

571. YORK, Lorraine M. "The Habits of Language: Uniform(ity), Transgression and Margaret Atwood." *Canadian Literature* 126 (Autumn 1990): 6-19. For Atwood heroines, the uniform often marks the limits and the transgression, and the struggle between the two.

572. ZUO, Qiang-hua. *On Cat's Eye.* s.l.: Sichuan International Studies University, 1990.

Reviews of Atwood's Works

573. *Barbed Lyres: Canadian Venomous Verse.* Toronto: Key Porter Books, 1990.
   Quill and Quire 56.11 (November 1990): 20. By Mark GERSON.

574. *Best American Short Stories.* Selected by Margaret Atwood with Shannon Ravenel. Boston: Houghton Mifflin, 1989.
   Arizona Daily Star (Tucson) 14 January 1990. NewsBank 1990: 11: C14-D1. By Christine WALD-HOPKINS.
   San Francisco Chronicle 21 January 1990: Section: Sunday Review: 4. By Cathy HO. (745 w).

575. *Cat's Eye.* Toronto: McClelland and Stewart; New York: Doubleday; London: Bloomsbury, 1988.
   Belles Lettres 5.3 (Spring 1990): 9. By B. A. St. ANDREWS.
   Booklist 86.10 (15 January 1990): 994. ANON.
   Canadian Literature 127 (Winter 1990): 135-138. By Sherrill GRACE.
   Cross-Canada Writers' Magazine 12.1 (1990): 27-28. By Veronica ROSS.
   Hudson Review 42.4 (Winter 1990): 664-665. By Gary KRIST.
   Landfall 44.1 (March 1990): 78-79. By Katherine MAYNARD.
   Library Journal 115.1 (January 1990): 50.
   Magill's Literary Annual 1(1990) Pasadena, CA; Englewood Cliffs, NJ: Salem Press, 1990: 91-93. By Steven G. KELLMAN.
   Presbyterian Record 114.3 (March 1990): 30. By Bertram Deh ATWOOD.
   Sojourners (Washington, DC) 19.4 (May 1990) 40-42. By Karen PETERSON.

576. *The Edible Woman.* Toronto: McClelland and Stewart; London: Virago, 1989 ©1969.
   CM 18.1 (January 1990): 24. By Ellen ROBSON.
   Times (London) 4 March: 38. By Sabine DURRANT. Also reviews Virago's reissued *Lady Oracle, Bodily Harm,* and *The Handmaid's Tale.*

577. *For the Birds*. Toronto: Douglas & McIntyre, 1990. 54 pp.
   Toronto Star 13 December 1990: Section: Neighbors: W12. By Kim
   PITTAWAY. (698 w).
578. *The Handmaid's Tale*. New York: Fawcett, 1985; Fawcett Crest, [1987].
   English Journal 79.6 (October 1990): 82-83. By Judith S. CHELTE.
   Progressive 54.9 (September 1990): 40-42. By Gene BLUESTEIN.
   Reading Women 1.1 (January-February 1990): 1, 8.
579. *The Handmaid's Tale*. Recorded Books.
   Book World 20.51 (23 December 1990): 8. Audio versions of *Cat's Eye* (Bantam) and *Bluebeard's Egg* (Brilliance) are also reviewed. By Vic SUSSMAN.
580. *Margaret Atwood: Conversations*. Ed. Earl G. Ingersoll. Princeton, NJ: Ontario
   Review Press; Willowdale, ON: Firefly Books, 1990.
   Booklist 86.18 (15 May 1990): 1772. By Ray OLSON.
   Books in Canada 19.8 (November 1990): 40-41. By Brian FAWCETT.
   CM 18.6 (November 1990): 289. ANON.
   Vancouver Sun 18 August 1990: D18. By Karenn KRANGLE.
   Winnipeg Free Press 15 September 1990: 22. By Maggie DWYER.
581. *Murder in the Dark*. Toronto: Coach House Press, 1983.
   Malahat Review 92 (Fall 1990): 121. By Jay RUZESKY.
582. *Œil-de-chat*. Translated by Hélène Fillion. Paris: Robert Laffont, 1990. [*Cat's Eye*.]
   L'Actualité 15.13 (1 September 1990): 77. By Gilles MARCOTTE.
   Châtelaine 31.9 (September 1990): 32. By Monique ROY.
   Nuit blanche 42 (December 1990-February 1991): 10-13. By Cécilia
   WIKTOROWICZ.
583. *Selected Poems: 1966-1984*. Toronto: Oxford UP, 1990.
   Books in Canada 19.9 (December 1990): 49. By Barbara CAREY.
   Toronto Star 22 December 1990: Section: Weekend: H17. By Don
   RUTLEDGE. (751 w).

Reviews of Adaptations of Atwood's Works

584. *The Handmaid's Tale*. [Motion Picture]. Screenplay by Harold Pinter; directed by
   Volker Schlondorff. United States: Cinecom Entertainment Group, 1990. 12 reels
   of 12 on 6 (ca. 9324 ft.).
   Anglican Journal 116. 5 (May 1990): 15. By Philip JEFFERSON.
   Boston Globe 9 March 1990: Section: Arts & Film: 25. By Jay CARR. (874 w).
   Boston Globe 18 March 1990: Section: Arts & Film: B31. By John KOCH. (879 w).
   Boston Herald 9 March 1990. FTV NewsBank 1990: 42: E10-11. By James
   VERNIERE.
   Catholic New Times 14.9 (29 April 1990): 6. By Paul CONSTABILE.
   Chicago Sun-Times 16 March 1990. FTV NewsBank 1990: 42: E8-9.
   By Roger EBERT.
   Christian Science Monitor 10 April 1990: Section: The Arts: 15. By David
   STERRITT. (553 w).
   Daily (Los Angeles) 7 March 1990. FTV NewsBank 1990: 42: D14. By Tom
   JACOBS.

Dallas Times Herald 16 March 1990. FTV NewsBank 1990: 42: F3. By David
  KRONKE.

Denver Post 16 March 1990. FTV NewsBank 1990: 42: E3-4. By Roger
  EBERT.

Detroit News 16 March 1990. FTV NewsBank 1990 42: E12. By Susan
  STARCK.

English Review 1 (April 1991): 36-37. By Bernard RICHARDS.

Feminisms 3.2 (1 March 1990): 16-17. By Mary SULLIVAN.

Film Journal 93.3 (March 1990): 13-14. By David NOH.

Films in Review 41.6-7 (June-July 1990): 368. By Nathaniel BIRD.

Gay Community News 17.34 (11 March 1990): 9. By Natalie DIFFLOTH.

The Guardian (London) 1 November 1990: s.p. By Derek MACOLM. (265 w).
  Available from Lexis-Nexis.

Hartford (CT) *Courant* 16 March 1990. FTV NewsBank 1990: 42: E5.
  By Malcolm L. JOHNSON.

The Humanist 50.3 (May-June 1990): 25. By Edd DOERR.

The Humanist 50.3 (May-June 1990): 26-28, 44. Companion review to Doerr
  (above). By Michael CALLERI.

*The Independent (*London) 4 November 1990: Section: Sunday Review: 17.
  By Anthony LAKE. (1354 w).

Journal (Atlanta, GA) 16 March 1990. FTV NewsBank 1990: 42: E6-7.
  By Eleanor RINGEL.

Legal Times 2 April 1990: Section: After Hours: 54. By Louise P.
  ZANAR. (1089 w).

Los Angeles 35 (April 1990): 178. By Merrill SHINDLER.

Los Angeles Times 16 March 1990: Section: Calendar: 36. By Peter RAINER.
  (1108 w).

New Directions for Women 19.3 (May-June 1990): 7. By Laura FLANDERS.

New Internationalist 213 (November 1990): 30.

New Republic 202.12 (19 March 1990): 26-27. By Stanley KAUFFMANN.

New York Post 7 March 1990. FTV NewsBank 1990: 42: E14-F1. By David
  EDELSTEIN.

New York Times 9 March 1990: Section: C: 17. By Janet MASLIN. (968 w).

Newsweek 26 March 1990: Section: The Arts: 54. By Jack KROLL.
  (390 w).

Off Our Backs 20.6 (June 1990): 12-13. By D. A. CLARKE.

Oregonian (Portland) 16 March 1990. FTV NewsBank 1990: 42: F2. By Ted
  MAHAR.

Pinter Review: Annual Essays 1990. Ed. Francis Gillen and Steven H. Gale.
  Tampa, FL: University of Tampa, ©1990 [appeared 1992]. 92-96. By Cynthia
  BAUGHMAN.

Positif 355 (September 1990): 77. By Philippe ROUYER.

La revue du cinéma 463 (September 1990): 46. By François CHEVASSU.

Roanoke Times & World News (Roanoke, VA) 12 May 1990: Section: Extra:
  E8. By Donnell STONEMAN. (757 w).

Rolling Stone 22 March 1990: 36. By Peter TRAVERS.

St. Louis Post-Dispatch 6 September 1990: Section: Everyday Magazine: 4E.
  By Rita KEMPLEY. (1347 w).

St. Petersburg Times 17 March 1990: Section: Floridian: 1D. By Clark PERRY. (701 w).

San Diego Magazine 42 (April 1990): 56, 58. By Richard PIETSCHMANN.

San Francisco Chronicle 9 March 1990: Section: Daily Datebook: E1. By Judy STONE. (1174 w).

San Francisco Examiner 9 March 1990. FTV NewsBank 1990: 42: E1-2. By Barbara SHULGASSER.

Savvy Woman January 1990: 20. By Lee LORDEAUX.

Screen World 1991 Vol. 42. New York: Crown, 1991. 24. By John WILLIS.

Seattle Post-Intelligencer 9 March 1990: Section: What's Happening: s.p. By William ARNOLD. (608 w). Available from Lexis-Nexis.

Seattle Times 9 March 1990: Section: Tempo: 20. By Michael UPCHURCH. (912 w).

Séquences 147-148 (September 1990): 107-108. By Martin GIRARD.

Spare Rib 218 (November 1990): 19. By Rukhsana AHMAD.

Spin 6 (May 1990): 65. By Katherine DIECKMANN.

Star-Ledger (Newark, NJ) 7 March 1990. FTV NewsBank 1990: 42: E13. By Richard FREEDMAN.

Texas Observer 82 (23 March 1990): 18-19. By Steven G. KELLMAN.

TLS 2-8 (November 1990): 1181. By John CLUTE.

Toronto Life 24.8 (May 1990): 99. By Martin KNELMAN.

Toronto Star 9 March 1990: Section: Entertainment: D14. By Peter GODDARD. (982 w).

United Church Observer 53.11 (May 1990): 40. By David WILSON.

Us 19 March 1990: 60. By Joy Gould BOYUM.

USA Today 7 March 1990: Section: Life: 4D. By Mike CLARK. (346 w).

Variety 14 February 1990: 32. From Berlin Film Festival showing.

Village Voice 35.11 (13 March 1990): 76. By Georgia BROWN.

Washington Post 13 September 1990: Section: Style: D1. By Rita KEMPLEY. (799 w).

Washington Times 9 March 1990: Section: Life; Arts & Entertainment: Movies: E3. By Gary ARNOLD. (797 w).

~ 1991 ~

Atwood's Works

585. "L'âge du plomb." *Le Serpent à plumes* 13 (Autumn 1991): 3-8. French translation of "The Age of Lead."

586. "The Age of Lead." *Best English Short Stories III.* Ed. Giles Gordon and David Hughes. New York; London: W. W. Norton, 1991. 1-15. Originally published in England under the title *Best Short Stories, 1991.* "Story first published in *New Statesman & Society*, 20 July 1990." Also in Canadian *Short Stories, Fifth Series.* Selected by Robert Weaver. Toronto: Oxford University Press, 1991. 1-16 and in *Colors of a New Day: Writings for South Africa.* Ed. Sarah Lefanu and Stephen Hayward. New York: Pantheon Books, 1991. 204-219. Republished in *Wilderness Tips.*

587. "The Bog Man." *Playboy* 38.1 (January 1991): 106-108, 203-206. Republished in *Wilderness Tips.*

588. "Books: What Writers Are Reading." *Ms.* 2.1 (July-August 1991): 82. Mentions books she has recently read.

589. *Cat's Eye.* Bath: Chivers, 1991. Large print edition.

590. *Chia hsiang.* Beijing: Chong-kuo wen lien ch'u pien she, 1991. Chinese translation of *Surfacing.* Title romanized.

591. "Concerning Franklin and His Gallant Crew." *Books in Canada* 20.4 (May 1991): 20-26. "This is a condensed version of one of Margaret Atwood's 1991 Clarendon Lectures at Oxford University, delivered in April of this year."

592. "Dance of the Lepers." *Quarry* 40.1-2 (Winter-Spring 1991): 10-11. Originally published in French in *Le Sabord.*

593. *Die essbare Frau.* Frankfurt: Fischer, 1991. German translation of *The Edible Woman.*

594. "A Double-Bladed Knife: Subversive Laughter in Two Stories by Thomas King." *Canadian Literature* 124-125 (Spring-Summer 1991): 243-251.

595. "Down." *Mississippi Valley Review* 20.2 (Spring 1991): 75-77. Poem and biographical sketch.

596. "Dream 2: Brian the Still-Hunter." *Cries of the Spirit: A Celebration of Women's Spirituality.* Ed. Marilyn Sewell. Boston: Beacon Press, 1991. 230-231. Reprinted from *The Journals of Susanna Moodie*, ©1970.

597. *The Edible Woman.* New York; Toronto; London; Sydney; Auckland: Bantam Books, 1991 ©1969.

598. "Eggnog and Tears." *New York Times Book Review* 24 November 1991: 7. Excerpt from short story "Hack Wednesday"; accompanies review of collection *Wilderness Tips* (see 761).

599. "Elegy for the Giant Tortoises." *The Forgotten Language: Contemporary Poets and Nature*. Ed. Christopher Merrill. Salt Lake City: Peregrine Smith Books, 1991. 12. Reprinted from *Selected Poems*, ©1976.

600. "Eli, from Time to Time." *Essays on Canadian Writing* 45-46 (1991): 67-68.

601. [Excerpt.] *Sinclair Ross's* As for Me and My House: *Five Decades of Criticism*. Ed. David Stouck. Toronto; Buffalo; London: University of Toronto Press, 1991. 29-30. Excerpt from *Survival*; portion excerpted is from chapter "The Paralyzed Artist," in which Atwood discusses the character of Philip Bentley.

602. *Fantasie di Stupor*. Milan: La Tartaruga, 1991. Italian translation of *Dancing Girls and Other Stories*.

603. *Family Cooking Celebration: Kitchen Discoveries for All Ages! From the Food for Thought Culinary Art School in Seattle*. Seattle, WA: Pepper Mill Press, 1991. By Atwood and Victory Crealock.

604. "The Female Body." *The Best American Essays 1991*. Ed. Joyce Carol Oates. Series Ed. Robert Atwan. New York: Ticknor and Fields, 1991. 9-12. Also in *Critical Fictions: The Politics of Imaginative Writing*. Ed. Philomena Mariani. Seattle, WA: Bay Press, 1991. 157-160. Reprinted from *Michigan Quarterly Review*; republished in *Good Bones*, ©1992.

605. "Fishing for Eel Totems." *Uncommon Waters: Women Write about Fishing*. Ed. Holly Morris. Seattle, WA: Seal Press, 1991. 179. Poem.

606. "Five Poems for Grandmothers (excerpt)." *Cries of the Spirit: A Celebration of Women's Spirituality*. Ed. Marilyn Sewell. Boston: Beacon Press, 1991. 89-90. Reprinted from *Two-Headed Poems*, ©1978-1980.

607. "Foreword." *Homeward Bound*. By Elliot Hayes. Toronto: Playwrights Canada Press, 1991. [7]-9.

608. *Fru Orakel*. [Copenhagen]: Lindhardt og Ringhof, 1991. Danish translation of *Lady Oracle* by Lisbeth Møller-Madsen.

609. "The Great Communicator." *Globe and Mail* 24 January 1991. Tribute to Northrop Frye. Reprinted in *Canadian Literature* 129 (Summer 1991): 242-243 (as "Northrop Frye: 1912-1991"); *Journal of Canadian Poetry* 6 (1991): 1-3 (as "Northrop Frye Remembered by His Students"); *Michigan Quarterly Review* 30.4 (Fall 1991): 647-649 (as "Northrop Frye Remembered"); *Chronicle of Higher Education* 38.12 (13 November 1991): B5 (in part, as "Northrop Frye as Critic and Teacher").

610. *Haendu Meidu*. Seoul: T`ukpyolsi: Toso Ch`ulp`an Ch`ongdamsa, 1991. Korean translation of *The Handmaid's Tale*. Title romanized.

611. *The Handmaid's Tale*. Abridged edition. [Sound recording]. Read by Julie Christie. London: Random Century Audiobooks, ©1991. 2 sound cassettes (ca. 180 min). Abridgement by Betty Stephenson.

612. "Heaven on Earth." By Atwood and Peter Pearson. Script for 90-minute drama, encore production on PBS, 22 December 1991; previously presented in the United Kingdom on BBC and in Canada on CBC; recipient of Edgar Dale Award for writing. Information obtained from Mobil Masterpiece Theatre press release.

613. "Hurricane Hazel." *Worlds Unrealized: Short Stories of Adolescence by Canadian Writers*. Vol. 1. Ed. Andrew Garrod and Janet Webster. St. John's, NF: Breakwater, 1991. [30]-49. Reprinted from *Bluebeard's Egg and Other Stories*, ©1984.

614. "If You Can't Say Something Nice, Don't Say Anything at All." *The Thinking Heart: Best Canadian Essays*. Ed. George Galt. Kingston, ON; Clayton, NY: Quarry Press, 1991. 13-23.

615. "It Is Dangerous to Read Newspapers." *Cries of the Spirit: A Celebration of Women's Spirituality*. Ed. Marilyn Sewell. Boston: Beacon Press, 1991. 174. Poem. Reprinted from *The Animals in That Country*, ©1968, 1969.

616. *Izranjanje*. Zagreb [Croatia]: Mladost, 1991. Croat translation of *Surfacing* by Nedeljka Paravić.

617. *Kavyavishva Shreni: Margaret Atwood*. Gandhinagar: Gujarati Sahitya Akademi (Britain), 1991. Gujarati translation of some Atwood poetry by Nita Ramaiya. [Ed. note: Gujarati, the language of Ghandi, is the official language of Gujarat state, on the west coast of India, with an area of 196,024 square kilometers. Within the Republic of India, Gujarat borders with Rajasthan, Madhyapradesh, and Maharashtra; it also borders with Pakistan to the northwest. The languages spoken in the areas contiguous to the Gujarat within India are Marwari, Hindi, and Marathi. The 1991 census of India reports 40,673,814 speakers, accounting for approximately 5 percent (4.85%) of the population.]

618. *Lekhak, Margaret Atwood*. Ahamadabad [India]: Gujarat Sahitya Akademi, 1991. Selected poems translated into Gujarati. Title romanized.

619. "The Loneliness of the Military Historian." *Canadian Literature* 128 (Spring 1991): 3-4. Poem excerpt used within editorial, "Discontent's Winter," by W. H. New.

620. *Los Diarios de Susanna Moodie*. Valencia [Spain]: Pre-Textos, 1991. Spanish translation of *The Journals of Susanna Moodie* by Lidia Taillefer and Álvaro García. Text in Spanish with original text in English on opposite pages.

621. *Margaret Atwood*. [Sound recording]. New York: The Academy of American Poets, 1991. 1 sound cassette (60 min.). Atwood reads selections from her poetry. Originally recorded at the Solomon R. Guggenheim Museum, in 1978.

622. "Marriage and Cooking." *Stitches: A Patchwork of Feminist Humor and Satire*. Ed. Gloria Kaufman. Bloomington; Indianapolis: Indiana University Press, 1991. 25-27. Reprinted from *Lady Oracle*.

623. "Murder in the Dark." *Great Canadian Murder and Mystery Stories*. Ed. Don Bailey and Daile Unruh. Kingston, ON; Clayton, NY: Quarry Press, 1991. 14-15. Title piece from *Murder in the Dark*.

624. "A Night in the Royal Ontario Museum." *The Actor's Book of Monologues for Women from Non-Dramatic Sources*. Collected and introduced by Stefan Rudnicki. New York; London; Victoria; Toronto; Auckland: Penguin Books, 1991. 246-247. Reprinted from *Selected Poems*, ©1976, 1978.

625. "Nine Beginnings." *The Writer on Her Work, Volume II: New Essays in New Territory*. Ed. Janet Sternburg. New York; London: Norton, 1991. 150-156.

626. *Oeil-de-chat*. Paris: Éditions J'ai lu, 1991. French translation of *Cat's Eye* by Hélène Filion.

627. *Oraklet*. Stockholm: Bokförlaget Prisma, 1991. Swedish translation of *Lady Oracle* by Ingela Bergdahl.

628. "Poèmes de serpent." *Lèvres urbaines* 20 (1991): 9-17.

629. *Poems 1965-1975*. London: Virago, 1991. "Offset from the Houghton Mifflin USA edition 1976"; new introduction by Margaret Atwood.

630. "Preface." *The Canadian Green Consumer Guide*. Revised and expanded. Prepared by Pollution Probe. Toronto: McClelland and Stewart, 1991 ©1989. 2-3.

631. "Remarks Made at Northrop Frye's Memorial Service, University of Toronto, February 1991." *Brick* 40 (Winter 1991): 3. Republished as "Tribute to H. Northrop Frye 1912-1991." *University of Toronto Quarterly* 61.1 (Fall 1991): 4-5. One of 16 tributes delivered at Frye's memorial service.

632. "Resurrection." *Cries of the Spirit: A Celebration of Women's Spirituality*. Ed. Marilyn Sewell. Boston: Beacon Press, 1991. 253-254. Reprinted from *The Journals of Susanna Moodie*, ©1970.

633. "Scarlet Ibis." *Modern Stories in English*. 3rd ed. [Ed.] W. H. New and H. J. Rosengarten. Mississaugua, ON: Copp Clark Pitman, 1991. 14-27. Reprinted from *Bluebeard's Egg*, ©1983.

634. *Shen zun: Jianada wen hsueh zhu di ji nan*. Beijing: Chong-kuo wen lien ch'u pien she, 1991. Chinese translation of *Survival: A Thematic Guide to Canadian Literature*.

635. "Solstice Poem (excerpt)." *Cries of the Spirit: A Celebration of Women's Spirituality*. Ed. Marilyn Sewell. Boston: Beacon Press, 1991. 138. Reprinted from *Two-Headed Poems*, ©1978.

636. "Spelling." *Images of Women in Literature*. 5th ed. Ed. Mary Ann Ferguson. Boston: Houghton Mifflin, 1991. 533-534. Poem. Reprinted from *True Stories*, ©1981-1982.

637. *Stories from Wilderness Tips*. [Sound recording]. Read by Helen Shaver. New York: Bantam Audio, 1991. Two cassettes containing the following stories: "True Trash"; "Hairball"; "Wilderness Tips"; "Hack Wednesday."

638. "Three Eyes." *West Coast Line* 25.3 (1991): 142-143. Poem.

639. "Three Praises." *The Forgotten Language: Contemporary Poets and Nature*. Ed. Christopher Merrill. Salt Lake City: Peregrine Smith Books, 1991. 13. Reprinted from *Selected Poems*, ©1976.

640. *Tips für die Wildnis: Short Stories*. Frankfurt am Main: S. Fischer, 1991. German translation of *Wilderness Tips* by Charlotte Franke.

641. "True North." *The Canadian Essay*. Selected and introduced by Gerald Lynch and David Rampton. Toronto: Copp Clark Pitman, 1991. 303-313. Reprinted from *Saturday Night* 102.1 (January 1987): 141-148; photograph and literary biography, 289-290.

642. "True Trash." *Saturday Night* 106.6 (July-August 1991): 18-28. Short story; reprinted in *Wilderness Tips* (see 650); excerpt reprinted in *Globe and Mail* 24 August 1991: Section C: 5.

643. [Untitled.] Porritt, Jonathon. *Save the Earth*. Atlanta, GA: Turner, 1991. 194. Short statement of concern.

644. *Variation on the Word* Sleep. [San Francisco]: Pacific Editions, 1991. "This is an accordian [sic] book designed and executed by Charles Hobson in an edition of 20. The monotype has been printed on BFK Gray Rives and accented with pastel. The box, a replica of one found on the Borgo S. Jacopa in Florence, provided the spark for the solution to the long-nagging question of how to respond visually to Margaret Atwood's extraordinary poem." (Colophon).

645. *Verletzungen*. Frankfurt: Fischer, 1991. German translation of *Bodily Harm*.

646. "The Way They Were." *Books in Canada* 20.4 (May 1991): 12. Atwood describes her life at age 20; includes poem "Woman on the Subway."

647. "Weight." *The Best of Cosmopolitan Fiction*. Ed. Kate Figes. London: Serpent's Tail, 1991. 187-199. Reprinted from *Wilderness Tips*, ©1990.

648. "Where Is How." *Publishers Weekly* 238.35 (8 August 1991): 8-11. Essay describing the connection between location and a writer's creativity.

649. "Wilderness Tips." *New Yorker* 66.53 (18 February 1991): 26-36. Reprinted in *Wilderness Tips* (below).

650. *Wilderness Tips.* Toronto: McClelland and Stewart; New York: Nan A. Talese/Doubleday; London: Bloomsbury, 1991. Short story collection. Includes: "True Trash," "Hairball" (appeared as "Kat" in *The New Yorker*), "Isis in Darkness," "The Bog Man," "Death by Landscape," "Uncles," "The Age of Lead," "Weight," "Wilderness Tips," "Hack Wednesday."

651. *Wilderness Tips.* [Bath, UK]: Paragon / Chivers Press, 1991. Large print edition.

652. "Writing the Male Character." *The Canadian Essay.* Selected and introduced by Gerald Lynch and David Rampton. Toronto: Copp Clark Pitman, 1991. 291-302. Reprinted from *Second Words: Selected Critical Prose*; photograph and literary biography, 289-290.

Adaptations of Atwood's Works

653. *Computer Music.* [Sound recording]. Texts by Atwood set to music. Washington, DC: Smithsonian Folkways Records, 1991. 1 sound cassette. Includes the following pieces: "Prisms," "Any Resemblance Is Purely Coincidental," "Music in Circular Motions," "Speeches for Dr. Frankenstein," "Canadian Coastlines."

Quotations

654. "[Quotes]." *Falser Than a Weeping Crocodile and Other Similes.* By Elyse Sommer and Mike Sommer. Detroit, MI; Chicago; Washington, DC; London: Visible Ink Press, 1991. Atwood quotes appear under several headings.

Interviews

655. FRASER, Matthew. "Atwood in Paris: Canada's Most Famous Author Leads a Quest for Peanut Butter and Her French Ancestors." *Gazette* (Montreal) 8 December 1991: Section F: 1.

656. JOHNSON, Jeri. "Face to Face: A Conversation Between Margaret Atwood and Jeri Johnson." *English Review* (Deddington, UK) 2 (November 1991): 27-32.

657. MacLAREN, Sherrill. *Invisible Power: The Women Who Run Canada.* Toronto: Seal Books, 1991. See especially 368-373.

658. MARCHAND, Philip. "Atwood Lends Her Celebrity to Ontario." *Toronto Star* 7 September 1991: Section: Weekend: G1. (1491 w). Before heading to France to work on next novel, Atwood interviewed about *Wilderness Tips.*

659. RICHARDS, Bernard. "Future Imperfect." *Oxford Today: The University Magazine* 4.1 (29 September 1991): 31.

660. ROSS, Val. "I've Always Been Funny." *Globe and Mail* 24 August 1991 Section C: 1, 5.

661. RUBBO, Michael. *Atwood and Family.* [Videorecording]. [Montreal]: National Film Board of Canada, 1991. HS tape 1 videocassette (30 min.). "Filmmaker Michael Rubbo visits writer Margaret Atwood and family at their northern island cottage. Atwood presents her views on her work and its influences, on being a Canadian, a female and a writer. Her parents and husband (Graeme Gibson) relate pertinent anecdotes." (Publisher). Filmed in 1985.

662. SACKVILLE-WEST, Sophia. "Novel Perceptions." *The Observer Magazine* 1 September 1991: 35, 42.
663. STACEY, Wendy. "Her Good Books." *Sunday Times Magazine* 3 March 1991: 11.

Scholarly Resources

664. "Atwood, Margaret." *20th-Century Culture: A Dictionary of the Arts and Literature of Our Time*. By David Brownstone and Irene Franck. New York: Prentice Hall, 1991. 21. Brief entry.
665. "Atwood, Margaret." *Contemporary Authors*. Ed. James G. Lesniak. New Revision Series. Vol. 33. Detroit, MI; London: Gale Research, 1991. 9-14. Updated biographical and critical essay.
666. "Atwood, Margaret." *The Writer's Directory 1992-94*. 10th ed. Chicago; London: St. James Press, 1991. 37-38. List of publications, awards, and academic positions held.
667. ASH, Susan. "Urgent Journeys: Two Women Travellers." *Australian-Canadian Studies: A Journal for the Humanities & Social Sciences* 9.1-2 (1991): 53-65. Treatment of the traveler in *Bodily Harm* and Janet Frame's *The Carpathians*.
668. BAZIN, Nancy Topping. "Women and Revolution in Dystopian Fiction: Nadine Gordimer's *July's People* and Margaret Atwood's *The Handmaid's Tale*." *Selected Essays: International Conference on Representing Revolution 1989*. Ed. John Michael Crafton. Carrollton: West Georgia College International Conference, 1991. 115-127.
669. BEHUNIAK-LONG, Susan. "Feminism and Reproductive Technology." *Choice* 29.2 (October 1991): 243-251. In this "Bibliography Essay," *The Handmaid's Tale* is mentioned (244) in a discussion of feminist fiction concerned with this issue.
670. BERAN, Carol L. "'At Least Its Voice Isn't Mine': The Concept of Voice in Margaret Atwood's *Lady Oracle*." *Weber Studies* 8.1 (Spring 1991): 54-71. Atwood uses 3 voices for the narrator, and the 3 are combined as a voice for herself, the author.
671. BORSTAD, Louise Marie. "An Analysis of the Disease of Anorexia Nervosa in the Novel *The Edible Woman* by Margaret Atwood." MA thesis. St. Cloud State University, 1991.
672. BROWN, Julie. "Our Ladies of Perpetual Hell: Witches and Fantastic Virgins in Margaret Atwood's *Cat's Eye*." *Journal of the Fantastic in the Arts* 4.3 [15] (1991): 40-52.
673. CALVERT, Michelle. "The Body as Topos: The Discursive Mapping of the Feminine Subject in Selected Works of Canadian Art and Literature." MA thesis. Carleton University, 1991. 187 pp. Also available on microfiche from Canadian Theses Service (1992). "This thesis utilizes selected feminist and poststructural theories of gendered subjectivity to explore the work of four Canadian women artists and writers. It suggests that the body as topos represents a central organizing metaphor which highlights the position of women's bodies as always-already marked and positioned within dominant discursive and social practices. This analysis addresses Margaret Atwood's *The Handmaid's Tale*, Audrey Thomas's *Mrs. Blood* and *Intertidal Life*, Janice Gurney's appropriational art, and Genevieve Cadieux's multimedia installations." (Author). For more see *MAI* 31.01 (Spring 1993): 13.

674. CARRINGTON, Ildikó de Papp. "Definitions of a Fool: Alice Munro's 'Walking on Water' and Margaret Atwood's Two Stories about Emma: 'The Whirlpool Rapids' and 'Walking on Water.'" *Studies in Short Fiction* 28.2 (Spring 1991): 135-149. Although similar in origin of themes, the two writers differ in their narrative approach. [Ed. note: Munro's "Walking on Water" was published in 1974 in *Something I've Been Meaning to Tell You*; in 1986 Margaret Atwood also published a short story entitled 'Walking on Water.' Appearing originally in *Chatelaine*, it was republished in a longer version in the second, American edition of *Bluebeard's Egg.*]

675. CUDER-DOMÍNGUEZ, Pilar. "El Romance y la Literatura Canadiense: Margaret Atwood." *Revista Española de Estudios Canadienses* 1.2 (May 1991): 278-303.

676. DAVIDSON, Arnold E. "Canada in Fiction." *The Columbia History of the American Novel*. Ed. Emory Elliott et al. New York: Columbia University Press, 1991. 558-585. Short references; also, biographical sketch of Atwood on 756.

677. DeMARCO, Donald. *Biotechnology and the Assault on Parenthood*. San Francisco: Ignatius Press, 1991. See especially "The Politicization of Motherhood." 70-71. This section contains a brief mention of *The Handmaid's Tale*.

678. DHAR, T. N. "First Person Singular: The Raised Feminine Consciousness in Atwood's *The Edible Woman*." *Feminism and Recent Fiction in English*. Ed. Sushil Singh. New Delhi: Prestige Books, 1991. 268-276.

679. DUPRIEZ, Bernard. *A Dictionary of Literary Devices*. Translated and adapted by Albert W. Halsall. Toronto; Buffalo, NY: University of Toronto Press, 1991. Contains several references to Atwood; translation of *Gradus: Les précédes littéraires*.

680. ELLIOTT, Marilyn O. Mercer. "Words on Paper: An Exploration of the Creative Process in Six Stories. (Original writing)." MA thesis. Texas Woman's University, 1991. 165 pp. "Many writers, writing out of a love of language, a need for expression, a desire to be heard, choose fiction as their vehicle for universal truth. In drawing upon personal experience as a source of that truth, writers discover and/or experience the creative process, the art of writing, insight into a subjective past, and enrichment through the creative act. As a demonstration of that process, this thesis employees autobiographical elements as a source for original fiction purporting to evoke recognition of truth in the reader. Preparation included reading essays by Margaret Atwood, Eudora Welty, Joyce Carol Oates, and Alice Munro on fiction as a literary art form." For more see *MAI* 30.01 (Spring 1992): 29.

681. EMBERLEY, Julia. "We Will Not Play Body to Your Territory: A Response." *Room of One's Own* 14.4 (December 1991): 82-96. Response to Henderson article (see 695).

682. EPSTEIN, Hugh. "'Where He Is Not Wanted': Impression and Articulation in 'The Idiots' and 'Amy Foster.'" *Conradiana* 23.3 (1991): 217-232. Discussion of *Surfacing* (224) to illustrate the artist's relationship to the world.

683. FAWCETT, Brian. *Unusual Circumstances, Interesting Times*. Vancouver: New Star Books, 1991. See especially Chapter 8, "Margaret Atwood's Achievement." 75-79. Reprinted from *Books in Canada*; Fawcett, in the "Introduction," implies revision from journal publication; Atwood mentioned in two other essays also.

684. FITZ, Earl E. *Rediscovering the New World: Inter-American Literature in a Comparative Context*. Iowa City: University of Iowa Press, 1991. Section on *Surfacing* (214-221) in Chapter 10 "The Conflict between Civilization and Barbarism." 211-232; scattered references to Atwood elsewhere.

685. FRASER, Wayne. *The Dominion of Women: The Personal and the Political in Canadian Women's Literature*. Contributions in Women's Studies, No. 116. New

York; Westport, CT; London: Greenwood Press, 1991. 190. Chapters 5, 6, and 7 deal extensively with Atwood: covering anti-Americanism in her early novels, comparing *Lady Oracle* and Laurence's *The Diviners*, and commenting on her political role in the 1980s.

686. GASPAROTTI, Alessandra. *Surfacing*: Margaret Atwood e la messinscena del passato. *Il Lettore di Provincia* 23 (April 1991): 53-62.

687. GERNES, Sonia. "Transcendent Women: Uses of the Mystical in Margaret Atwood's *Cat's Eye* and Marilynne Robinson's *Housekeeping*." *Religion and Literature* 23.3 (Autumn 1991): 143-165. Atwood's representation is more intellectual than the mythology presented by Robinson, but both seek answers in a spiritual quest.

688. GILBERT, Sandra M., and Susan GUBAR. "'Infection in the Sentence: The Woman Writer and the Anxiety of Authorship' from *The Madwoman in the Attic* (1979)." *Feminisms: An Anthology of Literary Theory and Criticism*. Ed. Robyn R. Warhol and Diane Price Herndl. New Brunswick, NJ: Rutgers University Press, 1991. *Lady Oracle* mentioned (297) to illustrate the crippling effects of culture upon a woman author.

689. GLICKMAN, Susan. "The Waxing and Waning of Susanna Moodie's 'Enthusiasm.'" *Canadian Literature* 130 (Autumn 1991): 7-26. Says Moodie's poetry differs from Atwood's portrayal.

690. GREENE, Gayle. *Changing the Story: Feminist Fiction and the Tradition*. Bloomington; Indianapolis: Indiana University Press, 1991. See especially chapter entitled "Margaret Atwood's *Lady Oracle*." 166-190. The Gothic theme in *Lady Oracle* is analyzed as it goes past the conventional ending to create a happier present. Also, *The Edible Woman* is discussed in the chapter, "Mad Housewives and Closed Circles" (58-85), and there are numerous other comments on Atwood throughout the book.

691. ———. "Feminist Fiction and the Uses of Memory." *Signs* 16.2 (Winter 1991): 290-321. *Bodily Harm, Lady Oracle*, and *Cat's Eye* are discussed in this examination of the structure of the narrative; other women authors discussed extensively as well.

692. GULICK, Angela Michelle. "*The Handmaid's Tale* by Margaret Atwood: Examining Its Utopian, Dystopian, Feminist and Post Modernist Traditions." MA thesis. Iowa State University, 1991.

693. HANSEN, Elaine Tuttle. "Mothers Tomorrow and Mothers Yesterday, but Never Mothers Today: *Woman on the Edge of Time* and *The Handmaid's Tale*." *Narrating Mothers: Theorizing Maternal Subjectivities*. Ed. Brenda O. Daly and Maureen T. Reddy. Knoxville: University of Tennessee Press, 1991. 21-43. The "missing mother" with the "lost daughter" is a theme in both novels to present views of mothering.

694. HAUGHTON, Rosemary. "Women and the Church." *Thought* 66.263 (December 1991): 398-412. *The Handmaid's Tale* is briefly mentioned as illustration of women's treatment in a theocracy.

695. HENDERSON, Jennifer. "Birdwatching the Postcolonial Way." *Room of One's Own* 14.4 (December 1991): 51-56. Discusses critical approach to Canadian literature in which female characters represent Canada and says this approach is in keeping with Atwood's *Survival*.

696. HENGEN, Shannon. "'Metaphysical Romance': Atwood's PhD Thesis and *The Handmaid's Tale*." *Science-Fiction Studies* 18.1 (March 1991): 154-156. Themes

of good and evil, nature, and power are traced back to Atwood's uncompleted thesis.

697. HOWELLS, Coral Ann. "A Question of Inheritance: Canadian Women's Short Stories." *Determined Women: Studies in the Construction of the Female Subject, 1900-90.* Ed. Jennifer Birkett and Elizabeth Harvey. Savage, MD: Barnes & Noble, 1991. 108-120. Resistance and revision in tradition are examined in stories by Atwood ("Bluebeard's Egg"), Munro ("Heirs of the Living Body"), and Thomas ("Crossing the Rubicon").

698. HUMM, Maggie. *Border Traffic: Strategies of Contemporary Women Writers.* Manchester; New York: Manchester University Press, 1991. See especially Chapter 4 "Going Through the Green Channel: Margaret Atwood and Body Boundaries." 123-159. Several novels, including *The Edible Woman*, *The Handmaid's Tale*, and *Surfacing*, are discussed.

699. HUTCHEON, Linda. *Splitting Images: Contemporary Canadian Ironies.* Toronto; Oxford; New York: Oxford UP, 1991. passim. Atwood's works frequently cited as portraying this cultural theme.

700. HUTCHISON, Beth. "Essential Fictions: Masquerade, Mimicry, and Self-Enactments in Contemporary North American Fiction." PhD thesis. University of Washington, 1991. 200 pp. Several novels examined including *Cat's Eye*. For more see *DAI-A* 52.08 (February 1992): 2924.

701. INGERSOLL, Earl G. "Margaret Atwood's *Cat's Eye*: Re-Viewing Women in a Postmodern World." *Ariel: A Review of International English Literature* 22.4 (October 1991): 17-27. Argues that similarities between Elaine Risley and Atwood's life are not coincidental.

702. JUMP, Harriet Devine. "Margaret Atwood: Taking the Capital W off Woman." *Diverse Voices: Essays on Twentieth-Century Women Writers in English.* Ed. Harriet Devine Jump. New York: St. Martin's Press; London: Harvester Wheatsheaf, 1991. 98-121. Draws from *The Handmaid's Tale*, *Cat's Eye*, and other novels, poems, and essays to define Atwood's complex and evolving approach to gender.

703. KAMBOURELI, Smaro. *On the Edge of Genre: The Contemporary Canadian Long Poem.* Toronto; Buffalo, NY; London: University of Toronto Press, 1991. 56-57, 87. Briefly mentions *The Journals of Susanna Moodie*.

704. KAMMLER, Heike. "Observers and Prophets of Our Time and Our Future: Women in Dystopian Fiction by Margaret Atwood and Doris Lessing." MA thesis. University of Florida, 1991. Study of *The Handmaid's Tale* and Lessing's *Four-gated City*.

705. KEITH, W. J. *An Independent Stance: Essays on English-Canadian Criticism and Fiction.* Erin, ON: The Porcupine's Quill, 1991. See especially "Atwood as (Infuriating) Critic." 54-61. This review essay on *Second Words* first appeared in *Canadian Forum* (February 1983); Keith is critical of Atwood's efforts as a critic; this version restores some sentences left off the end in the earlier printing, and see also "Interpreting and Misinterpreting 'Bluebeard's Egg': A Cautionary Tale." 278-288. Warns against fitting a particular theory, in this case a feminist one, to a work of literature and ignoring other evidence.

706. KERTZER, J. M. "Genius Loci: The Ghost in Canadian Literature." *Canadian Literature* 130 (Autumn 1991): 70-89. Brief mentions, especially of *Survival*, scattered throughout the article.

707. KOLODNY, Annette. "Margaret Atwood and the Politics of Narrative." *Studies on Canadian Literature: Introductory and Critical Essays.* New York: Modern Language Association of America, 1991. 90-109.

708. LeBIHAN, Jill. *"The Handmaid's Tale, Cat's Eye*, and *Interlunar*: Margaret Atwood's Feminist(?) Futures(?)."* Narrative Strategies in Canadian Literature: Feminism and Postcolonialism.* Ed. Coral Ann Howells and Lynette Hunter. Buckingham, UK; Bristol, PA: Open UP, 1991. 93-107. Postfeminism, postmodernism, and postmodernist feminism mark a crossroad in these works, in both a literary and a critical sense.

709. LECKER, Robert, ed. *Canadian Canons: Essays in Literary Value.* Toronto; Buffalo, NY; London: University of Toronto Press, 1991. passim. Essays by various contributors in which Atwood is frequently mentioned.

710. LECLAIRE, Jacques. "La metropole: Image du pouvoir dans les romans de Margaret Atwood." *Études canadiennes / Canadian Studies* 30 (1991): 89-93. "The maze of the metropolis is the background of the cruel power game: who wields power over whom and how. It also embodies socio-economic and moral pressures. In order to survive everybody must foil the other's attempts and also establish his own power at least over some space. Finally in the novels [from *The Edible Woman* to *Cat's Eye*] the metropolis becomes the image of human power, as opposed to nature where man is confronted with other forms of power." (Author abstract).

711. LETCHER, Bettina Havens. "In the Belly of This Story: The Role of Fantasy in Four American Women's Novels of the 1980s." PhD thesis. University of Rhode Island, 1991. 199 pp. *The Handmaid's Tale* is examined along with Gould's *Subject to Change*, Morrison's *Beloved*, and Silko's *Ceremony*; fantasy provides the change for a radical new self which is taken in by the social community. For more see *DAI-A* 52.10 (April 1992): 3602.

712. LITTLE, Philippa Susan. "Images of Self-Feminine and Feminist Subjectivity in the Poetry of Sylvia Plath, Anne Sexton, Margaret Atwood, and Adrienne Rich (1950-1980)." PhD thesis. University of London, Queen Mary and Westfield College, 1991.

713. LOCKETT, Jacqueline Rose. "Margaret Atwood: The Treatment of Women's Biology in *The Edible Woman, Surfacing*, and *The Handmaid's Tale*." MA thesis. (Women's Studies). University of Natal, 1991. 106 pp.

714. LOWE, Julia. "Re-inscribing the Mother: Feminist Theory and Fiction." MA thesis. Carleton University, 1991. 97 pp. Also available on microfiche from Canadian Theses Service (1992). "This thesis [examines] the different ways feminist theory and literature has [sic] defined the multiple meanings of the maternal which have been suppressed by the patriarchal paradigm....[In contrast to other works studied] a Lacanian reading of Margaret Atwood's *Lady Oracle* [shows] the mother is incapable of liberating her daughter from patriarchal law." (Author). For more see *MAI* 31.02 (Summer 1993): 563.

715. MAYS, Lynda Graham. "Women as Daughters, Wives, and Mothers in the Novels of Margaret Atwood." MLS (Master of Liberal Studies) thesis. Rollins College, 1991.

716. McCOMBS, Judith. "Contrary Rememberings: The Creating Self and Feminism in *Cat's Eye*." *Canadian Literature* 129 (Summer 1991): 9-23. Multi-layered and fluid, the feminist and literary self is also affected by "pre-literary and non-literary concepts of the self."

717. McCOMBS, Judith, and Carole L. PALMER. *Margaret Atwood: A Reference Guide.* Boston: G. K. Hall and Company, 1991. 735. An annotated bibliography covering writing about Margaret Atwood from 1962 to 1988, with a literary intro-

duction by McCombs that supplements her 1988 introduction to *Critical Essays on Margaret Atwood*.

718. McDONALD, Christie. "Changing the Facts of Life: The Case of Baby M." *Sub-Stance* 64 (1991): 31-48. On 42, The *Handmaid's Tale* is cited as relevant to the Baby M case. [Ed. note: Baby M (born 27 March 1986) was the name given to the child in an American custody case between the surrogate mother hired to carry her, and the child's biological father. Mary Beth Whitehead, the surrogate mother, was artificially inseminated with William Stern's sperm. Contrary to popular belief (as well as what was stated in the surrogacy contract), Mr. Stern's wife, Elizabeth, was not infertile, but rather there was a possibility she had multiple sclerosis. When Whitehead gave birth to a daughter whom she named "Sara Elizabeth Whitehead," she refused to give her up to the Sterns. A New Jersey court awarded custody of Melissa (as the Sterns had named her) to the Sterns in 1987, but this ruling was overturned by the Supreme Court of New Jersey on 2 February 1988. The Supreme Court remanded the case to family court. On remand, the lower court awarded William Stern custody and Mary Beth Whitehead visitation rights.]

719. MEYERS, Helene. "Femicidal Fears in Contemporary Fiction: Feminist Thought and the Female Gothic." PhD thesis. Indiana University, 1991. 267 pp. *Bodily Harm* one of several texts examined in a study which "charts the intersections between the female gothic tradition, feminist theory, and contemporary women's fiction." For more see *DAI-A* 52.09 (March 1992): 3277.

720. MILLER, Jane. *Seductions: Studies in Reading and Culture*. Cambridge, MA: Harvard University Press, 1991. See especially "Feasters and Spoilsports." 136-164. Section VI of this chapter (159-162) contains the discussion of *Cat's Eye*, focusing on differences in male and female childhoods.

721. MINER, Madonne. "'Trust Me': Reading the Romance Plot in Margaret Atwood's *The Handmaid's Tale*." *Twentieth-Century Literature* 37.2 (Summer 1991): 148-168. Episodes in the novel, such as the Scrabble game, show how to put together plot elements to obtain additional readings of the text.

722. MOLNÁR, Judith. "The Coalescence of Natural and Mental Landscapes in Margaret Atwood's *The Journals of Susanna Moodie*." *Hungarian Studies in English* 22 (1991): 127-132. *The Journals of Susanna Moodie* reflect the mental and physical landscape of Canada through the changes in Moodie's psychological and spiritual development.

723. MOOS, Patricia Danelle. "Reflections of Motherhood in Three Novels by Margaret Atwood." MA thesis. McMaster University, 1991. 83 pp. *The Edible Woman*, *The Handmaid's Tale*, and *Surfacing*.

724. NEW, W. H. "Canadian Literature. Atwood/Power." *Encyclopedia of Literature and Criticism*. Ed. Martin Coyle, Peter Garside, Malcolm Kelsall, and John Peck. Detroit, MI; New York: Gale Research, 1991. 1172-1175. Discusses Atwood as both part of and different from the Ontario literary tradition; touches on her feminism and her cultural nationalism with the message that no writer can be neutral regarding the issues of society.

725. NISCHIK, Reingard M. *Mentalstilistik: Ein Beitrag zu Stiltheorie und Narrativik dargestellt am Erzählwerk Margaret Atwoods*. Tübingen: Narr, 1991. Atwood's works are considered in terms of choice of words, transitive systems, syntax, types of narrative transmission and mental stylistics, speech acts and mental stylistics, and sexist versus non-sexist language.

726. ———. "'Où maintenant? Quand maintenant? Qui maintenant?' Die namenlose Ich-Erzahlfigur im Roman." *Poetica: Zeitschrift für Sprach- und Literaturwissens-chaft* 23.1-2 (1991): 257-275.

727. PATTON, Marilyn. "*Lady Oracle*: The Politics of the Body." *Ariel: A Review of International English Literature* 22.4 (October 1991): 29-48. Speaks to the influence of myth and Robert Graves's *The White Goddess* upon Atwood; in this novel, Atwood confronts the White Goddess myth and both destroys and celebrates her.

728. PETERSON, Nancy Jean. "The Politics of Language: Feminist Theory and Contemporary Works by Women of Color." PhD thesis. University of Wisconsin-Madison, 1991. 340 pp. "This dissertation discusses works by women of color that thematize and enact the politics of language of profound concern to feminist critics and theorists. Using texts authored mainly by white, bourgeois women, most feminists have argued that women are disempowered in/by 'mal(e)functioning' language (Mary Daly). Women of color share with poststructuralist feminists such as Luce Irigaray and Hélène Cixous skepticism about representation and the adequacies of any language to inscribe their multiple differences. However, rather than articulating an anxiety of language that marks texts by many white women writers and theorists (e.g. Daly, Margaret Atwood, Margaret Homans), women of color emphasize their creative agency, their ability to re-form language and genre; this quality they share with pragmatist feminists such as Alicia Ostriker, Mae Henderson, and Adrienne Rich." (Author). For more see *DAI-A* 53.03 (September 1992): 812.

729. POWERS, Meredith A. *The Heroine in Western Literature: The Archetype and Her Reemergence in Modern Prose*. Jefferson, NC; London: McFarland, 1991. 167, 168, 193. Very brief mention of Atwood.

730. QUIGLEY, Theresia M. *The Child Hero in the Canadian Novel*. Toronto: NC Press, 1991. 183. The emphasis in *Lady Oracle* is on escaping from the pain of childhood and that in *Cat's Eye* is on coming to terms with childhood traumas; both novels parallel similar themes in other Canadian novels written at the same time.

731. RAO, Eleonora. "Strategies for Identity: The Fiction of Margaret Atwood." PhD thesis. University of Warwick (United Kingdom), 1991. 407 pp. This thesis "focuses on problems pertaining to the questions of genre, identity and female subjectivity. The thesis is thematically structured. Chapter One, 'The Question of Genre: Creative Reappropriations,' explores the plurality of genres and narrative styles present in the novels. The second Chapter 'A Proliferation of Identities: Doubling and Intertextuality,' examines constructions of the self in the light of psychoanalytic theories of language and subjectivity which conceive of the subject as heterogeneous and in constant process. Chapter Three, 'Cognitive Questions,' discusses the text's emphasis on sense receptivity and the epistemological question they [i.e., The Cognitive Questions] pose in relation to language, reality and interpretation. Chapter Four, 'Writing the Female Character,' analyses Atwood's configurations of femininity, sexual politics and sexual difference." (Author). For more see *DAI-A* 53.03 (September 1992): 813.

732. REESMAN, Jeanne Campbell. "Dark Knowledge in *The Handmaid's Tale*." *CEA Critic* 53.3 (Spring-Summer 1991): 6-22. The female voice is characterized by hermeneutic fiction, particularly dualism, dialogue, and ambiguity in place of a single truth.

733. RIBEIRO, Ofelia. "A Different Thread: An Analysis of the Diary Form in the Representation of the Female Self." MA thesis. Concordia University, 1991. Also

available on microfiche from Canadian Theses Service (1991). "A historical perspective of the development of the diary, both in its fictional and its nonfictional form, will reveal how extensively it has been used in the past as well as how it is currently being employed. Several novels, Doris Lessing's *The Golden Notebook*, Alice Walker's *The Color Purple*, and Margaret Atwood's *The Handmaid's Tale*, form the thrust of the literary interpretation of the contemporary diary novel in an effort to examine the nature of the representation of the female self." (Author).

734. ROCARD, Marcienne. "Margaret Atwood's *Surfacing* and Alma Luz Villanueva's *The Ultraviolet Sky*: The Spiritual Journeys of Two Women Artists: One Anglo-Canadian and One Mexican American." *Recherches anglaises et nord-américaines* 24 (1991): 155-161.

735. RODRÍGUEZ, Ileana. "De lecturas y escrituras. De la nota al texto. Centrando 'Nolite te Bastardes Carborundorum.'" *Revista de Critica Literaria Latinoamericana* 17.33 (1991): 59-68. *The Handmaid's Tale* is part of this discussion on reading and writing, women and literacy, and limitations on women.

736. ROSENFELT, Deborah Silverton. "Feminism, 'Postfeminism,' and Contemporary Women's Fiction." *Tradition and the Talents of Women*. Ed. Florence Howe. Urbana; Chicago: University of Illinois Press, 1991. 268-291. Traces the development from feminist texts to a different set of characteristics common in novels starting in the mid-eighties; *The Handmaid's Tale* is described in terms of these features.

737. RYAN, Bryan, ed. *Major 20th-Century Writers: A Selection of Sketches from Contemporary Authors*. Detroit, MI: Gale Research, 1991. 146-151. Integrates a wide range of critical work on Atwood into an outline of her literary career; includes brief biographical notes, primary bibliography, and a list of sources.

738. SCHISSEL, Wendy L. "The Keepers of Memory: Canadian Mythopoeic Poets and Magic Realist Painters." PhD thesis. University of Calgary, 1991. 256 pp. "By 'raiding' many feminist theoretical approaches, we can also find analogies between the works of Margaret Atwood and Mary Pratt. Whether or not Atwood and Pratt's intentions are as critical as we read them, when we approach their arts through feminist subjectivities, we recognize a common challenge in the poetry and painting to phallocentric assumptions about the representations of women." (Author). For more see *DAI-A* 53.10 (April 1993): 3520.

739. SÖDERLIND, Sylvia. *Margin/Alias: Language and Colonization in Canadian and Québécois Fiction*. Toronto; Buffalo, NY; London: University of Toronto Press, 1991. 264 pp. A few references to Atwood.

740. STAELS, Hilde. "Fiction and the Seduction of Its Designs: A Study of Narrative Discourse in the Novels of Margaret Atwood." PhD thesis. Katholieke Universiteit Leuven, 1991. 381 pp.

741. STAHLMAN, Susan Jane. "Escapees from the Attic: A Study of George Eliot, Virginia Woolf, and Margaret Atwood." MA thesis. University of Mississippi, 1991. 110 pp. Chapter on Margaret Atwood (68-97) concentrates on *Surfacing*.

742. STEWART, Margaret. "The Seeing Eye, the Speaking Voice: Investigations of Voice in Margaret Atwood's *The Handmaid's Tale* and *Cat's Eye*." MA thesis. University of Guelph, 1991. 155 pp. Also available on microfiche from Canadian Theses Service (1992). This thesis "is premised upon the conviction that throughout all of Atwood's utterances the reader hears a consistent voice speaking, and that the firm presence of the author is detectable in her work. The thesis explores various means of affirming this authorial voice. These include metafictive elements, connections between fictive and extra-fictive works, recurrences in the fic-

68   ~ 1991 ~

tion, linked image patterns, and the tone of authority that is so characteristic of Atwood. In addition, the paper investigates the stylistic and grammatical idiosyncrasies that support and contribute to the authoritative tone of the texts." (Author). For more see *MAI* 31.02 (Summer 1993): 572.

743. STOCKS, Anthony G. "Atwood, Margaret (Eleanor)." *Contemporary Poets.* 5th ed. Ed. Tracy Chevalier. Chicago; London: St. James Press, 1991. 26-29. Biography, bibliography, short critical essay on her poetry.

744. STURGESS, Charlotte. "Text and Territory in Margaret Atwood's 'Unearthing Suite.'" *Études canadiennes / Canadian Studies* 31 (1991): 81-87. "The short story 'Unearthing Suite' defines narration as the ongoing conflict of form and process. Governing these polarities in search of resolution is Atwood's metaphor of nature as a signifying force akin to language, ending this duality." (Author).

745. SWEARINGEN, C. Jan. *Rhetoric and Irony: Western Literacy and Western Lies.* New York; Oxford: Oxford University Press, 1991. 216-217, 247. Mentions character Cordelia from *Cat's Eye*.

746. TEMPLIN, Charlotte. "Atwood's *The Handmaid's Tale*." *Explicator* 49.4 (Summer 1991): 255-256. Offers evidence that the novel is set in the 21st century, not in the 20th.

747. TENNANT, Colette Giles. "Margaret Atwood's Transformed and Transforming Gothic." PhD thesis. Ohio State University, 1991. 268 pp. "Whereas Gothic literature typically portrays women as victims, Atwood's use of the genre seeks to alert and inform women readers so that they can avoid victimization. Atwood also transforms traditional elements of the Gothic genre so that her novels seem more modern and 'psychological.' The four elements of the traditional Gothic that Atwood employs and yet transforms are: the use of settings, the role of men, the prevalence of violence, and the transformation of characters." (Author). For more see *DAI-A* 52.09 (March 1992): 3289.

748. TRACY, Laura. *The Secret Between Us: Competition Among Women.* Boston; Toronto; London: Little, Brown, 1991. 61 pp. Refers to Atwood and *Cat's Eye* to illustrate harm of revenge.

749. VEVAINA, Coomi S. "The Theme of Alienation and Survival in the Novels of Margaret Atwood and the Manawaka Novels of Margaret Laurence." PhD thesis. S.N.D.T. Women's University, Bombay, 1991.

750. WILLIAMS, David. *Confessional Fictions: A Portrait of the Artist in the Canadian Novel.* Toronto; Buffalo; London: University of Toronto Press, 1991. passim. *Lady Oracle* and *Survival* mentioned.

751. WILSON, Rob. *American Sublime: The Genealogy of a Poetic Genre.* Madison; London: University of Wisconsin Press, 1991. 70-71. Brief mention of Atwood's work in compiling the *New Oxford Book of Canadian Verse in English*.

752. WILSON, Sharon R. "Atwood, Margaret." *Bénet's Reader's Encyclopedia of American Literature.* Ed. George Perkins, Barbara Perkins, and Phillip Leininger. New York: HarperCollins, 1991. 52-53. Brief bio-critical sketch.

753. ———. "Eyes and I's." *International Literature in English: Essays on the Major Writers.* Ed. Robert L. Ross. New York; London: Garland, 1991. 225-239. Critical essay concentrates upon *Cat's Eye* as the Atwood novel most concerned with vision, stating that Elaine's identity ("I") is dependent on her artistic vision ("eye"). Essay accompanied by biographical and bibliographical information.

754. WOODCOCK, George. "Atwood, Margaret (Eleanor)." *Contemporary Novelists.* 5th ed. Ed. Lesley Henderson and Noelle Watson. Chicago; London: St. James

Press, 1991. 57-60. Biography, bibliography, and critical essay on Atwood's fiction.

Reviews of Atwood's Works

755. *Cat's Eye*. Toronto: McClelland and Stewart; New York: Doubleday; London: Bloomsbury, 1988.
   Women's Studies 18.4 (1991): 445-455. By Gayle GREENE. Note length of this review.
756. *For the Birds*. Toronto; Vancouver: Douglas and McIntyre, 1990.
   Atlantic Provinces Book Review 18.1 (February-March 1991): 13. By Linda HODGINS.
   Canadian Book Review Annual 1990. Ed. Joyce M. Wilson. Toronto: Simon and Pierre, 1991. 456-457. By Alice KIDD.
   CM 19.2 (March 1991): 93-94. By Jennifer JOHNSON.
   Emergency Librarian 19.1 (September-October 1991): 57. By Joan McGRATH.
   Environment Views 14.2 (Fall 1991): 25.
   Probe Post 13.4 (Winter 1991): 36. By Bridget AMBROGIO.
   Quill and Quire 56.11 (November 1990): 11. By Pamela HICKMAN.
   Toronto Star 14 February 1991: Section: Neighbors: N12. By Kim PITTAWAY. (736 w).
757. *The Handmaid's Tale*. Boston: Houghton Mifflin, 1986; New York: Fawcett Crest, 1987.
   Odd Jobs: Essays and Criticism. New York: Knopf, 1991: 425-436. By John UPDIKE.
   Women's Studies International Forum 14.3 (1991): 231-233. By Theresa SAUTER-BAILLET.
758. *Poems 1965-75*. London: Virago, 1991.
   Poetry Wales 27.1 (June 1991): 69-70. By Gillian CLARKE.
759. *Selected Poems: 1966-1984*. Toronto: Oxford University Press, 1990.
   Canadian Book Review Annual 1990. Ed. Joyce M. Wilson. Toronto: Simon and Pierre, 1991. 206-207. By Shannon HENGEN.
   CM 19.1 (January 1991): 47. By Loÿs MAINGON.
   Sunday Times 10 March 1991 Section 6: 10. By Carol RUMENS.
   University of Toronto Quarterly 61.1 (Fall 1991): 57. By Ronald B. HATCH.
760. *La Servante écarlate*. Translated by Sylviane Rue. Paris: J'ai lu, 1989. [*The Handmaid's Tale*.]
   Femmes d'action 20.2 (November 1990-January 1991): 30. By Colette GODIN.
761. *Wilderness Tips*. Toronto: McClelland and Stewart; London: Bloomsbury; New York: Talese/Doubleday, 1991.
   Atlanta Journal and Constitution 15 December 1991: Section: N: 8. By Ann HUME. (647 w).
   Belles Lettres 7.1 (Fall 1991): 43. Plus brief annotation for *Margaret Atwood: Conversations* following review. By Suzanne BERNE.
   Booklist 87.21 (July 1991): 2011. By Ray OLSON.
   Books 5.6 [sic, 5] (November-December 1991): 21. ANON.
   Books in Canada 20.7 (October 1991): 29-32. By Brian FAWCETT.

Boston Globe 1 December 1991: Section: Books: A13. By Gail CALDWELL. (1096w).

Boston Herald 8 December 1991 LIT NewsBank 1992: 1: C10. By Mary KRAMER.

Canadian Forum 70 (November 1991): 30-33. By Sherrill GRACE.

Christian Science Monitor 27 December 1991: 14. By Merle RUBIN. (1069 w).

Financial Times (London) 14 September 1991: Section: Weekend: XVI. By Anthony CURTIS. (710 w).

Fortune 124.15 (30 December 1991): 137. By Gil SCHWARTZ.

The Guardian (London) 31 October 1991: s.p. By Claire MESSUD. (511 w). Available from Lexis-Nexis. "Atwood is not a natural short-story writer: most of the pieces in this collection strain for bigger things, squashing entire decades into flashy, occasionally sloppy, paragraphs. When she does pause to focus her prose, Atwood's revelations charm, or move, or evoke the wistfulness and reflection of maturity; but these moments alone are not sufficient to redeem the stories."

Hartford Courant (CT) 8 December 1991: Section: Arts: 3. By Jocelyn McCLURG. (1014 w).

Houston Chronicle 22 December 1991: Section: Zest: 13. By Sally POIVOIR. (759 w).

The Independent 13 October 1991: Section: Sunday Review: 38. By Hermione LEE. (588 w).

Kirkus Reviews 59.17 (1 September 1991): 1104. ANON.

Library Journal 116.13 (August 1991): 74. By Barbara HOFFERT.

Library Journal 116.18 (1 November 1991): 133. By Marnie WEBB.

London Review of Books 13.23 (5 December 1991): 20. By John BAYLEY.

Los Angeles Times Book Review 8 December 1991: 3. By Richard EDER. (1092 w).

Literary Review 159 (September 1991): 18. By Nicolette JONES.

Maclean's 104.37 (16 September 1991): 58. By John BEMROSE. (899 w).

Minneapolis Star and Tribune 24 November 1991 LIT NewsBank 1991: 95: C2-3. By Robert LACY.

New Statesman and Society 29 November 1991: 33. By Judy COOKE.

New York 24.47 (2 December 1991): 160. By Rhoda KOENIG.

New York Times (Late Edition) 26 November 1991: C18. By Michiko KAKUTANI. (917 w).

New York Times Book Review 24 November 1991: 7. By James WILCOX.

New York Times Book Review 1 December 1991: 65 (in Notable Books of the Year). Mentioned also, with short annotation, in "And Bear in Mind" section on p. 72, same issue.

The Observer (London) 15 September 1991: 62. By Nicci GERRARD. (353 w).

Paragraph 14.1 (1992): 21-22. By Lynn CROSBIE.

Publishers Weekly 238.44 (4 October 1991): 78. By Sybil STEINBERG.

Quill and Quire 57.8 (August 1991): 14. By Daniel JONES.

Quill and Quire 57.10 (October 1991): 27. By George WOODCOCK.

The Record (Kitchener-Waterloo, ON) 21 September 1991: Section: Books: D6. By John KELLY. (686 w).

San Francisco Review of Books 16.3 (1991): 52-53. By Suzanne SAMUEL.

The Spectator 267 (12 October 1991): 36-37. By Anita BROOKNER.

Sunday Times 22 September 1991: Section 7: 4. By Penny PERRICK. (546 w).

The Times 19 September 1991: Section: Features: s.p. By Victoria GLENDIN-NING. (797 w). Available from Lexis-Nexis.

TLS 13 September 1991: 20. By Aamer HUSSEIN.

Toronto Star 7 September 1991: Section: Weekend: G12. By Philip MAR-CHAND. (972 w). "A collection of stories in which feeling and the sympathetic imagination has by and large been successfully strangled."

Tribune Books (Chicago) 24 November 1991: Section 14: 3. By Clark BLAISE.

Tribune Books (Chicago) 8 December 1991: Section 14: 1.

Voice Literary Supplement December 1991: 9. By Carol ANSHAW.

Reviews of Adaptations of Atwood Works

762. *The Handmaid's Tale.* [Motion Picture]. Screenplay by Harold Pinter; directed by Volker Schlondorff. United States: Cinecom Entertainment Group, 1990. 12 reels of 12 on 6 (ca. 9324 ft.).

The Aurum Film Encyclopedia: Science Fiction. Ed. Phil Hardy. London: Aurum Press, 1991. 449.

Film Review 1991-2: Including Video Releases. London: Virgin Books, 1991. 54. By James CAMERON-WILSON.

Magill's Cinema Annual 1991: A Survey of the Films of 1990. Ed. Frank N. Magill. Pasadena, CA; Englewood Cliffs, NJ: Salem Press, 1991: 146-149. By Robert STRAUSS.

Nuclear Movies: A Critical Analysis and Filmography of International Feature Length Films Dealing with Experimentation, Aliens, Terrorism, Holocaust and Other Disaster Scenarios, 1914-1989. Jefferson, NC; London: McFarland, 1991: 188-189. By Mick BRODERICK.

The Time Out Film Guide. 2nd ed. Ed. Tom Milne. London: Penguin Books, 1991. 278. By Steve GRANT.

~ 1992 ~

Atwood's Works

763. *Ademden Önceki Yaşam*. Istanbul: Afa Yayinlari, 1992. Turkish translation of *Life Before Man*.
764. "Afterword." *Anne of Green Gables*. By L. M. Montgomery. Toronto: McClelland and Stewart (New Canadian Library), 1992. 331-336.
765. "Angela Carter: 1940-1992." Unpublished in 1992. Later published in *Curious Pursuits: Occasional Writing 1970-2005*. London: Virago, 2005. 155-157.
766. "The Art of Pachter: As Canadian as the Queen on a Moose." *Canadian Forum* 71.814 (November 1992): 17-20. Excerpted from "Foreword" to *Charles Pachter* (see 780).
767. "Bad News." *Mississippi Review* 21.1-2 (1992): 67-68.
768. "Betty." *Das grosse Frauen-Lesebuch*. Ed. Anne Rademacher and Georg Reuchlein. Munich: Wilhelm Goldmann, 1991. 109-131. In German.
769. "Bread." *Flash Fiction: Very Short Stories*. Ed. James Thomas, Denise Thomas, and Tom Hazuka. New York; London: W. W. Norton, 1992. 198-200. Reprinted from *Iowa Review* 12.2-3 (©1981).
770. "Bread from *Murder in the Dark*." *Loaves & Wishes: Writers Writing on Food*. Ed. Antonia Till. London: Virago, 1992. 69-70. A volume published to mark Oxfam's 50th anniversary.
771. "Comments." *University of Toronto Quarterly* 61.3 (Spring 1992): 82. Atwood's thoughts on the issue's topic of "allusion."
772. *Damizlik kiz'in öyküsü*. Istanbul: AFA Yayinlari, 1992. Turkish translation of *The Handmaid's Tale*.
773. *Den Ätbara Kvinnan*. Stockholm: Bökforlaget Prisma, 1992. Swedish translation of *The Edible Woman* by Vanja Lantz.
774. *Der Report der Magd*. Frankfurt: Fischer, 1992. German translation of *The Handmaid's Tale*.
775. *Die Essbare Frau: Roman*. Hildesheim [Germany]: Claassen, 1992. German translation of *The Edible Woman* by Werner Waldhoff.
776. "Eli, from Time to Time." *Essays on Canadian Writing* 45-46 (Winter-Spring 1991-92): 67-68. Reminiscence in "Eli Mandel Issue."
777. "[Excerpt]." *Erotica: Women's Writings from Sappho to Margaret Atwood*. Ed. Margaret Reynolds. New York: Fawcett Columbine, 1992. 18-21. From *The Handmaid's Tale*. Originally published in hard cover in Great Britain under the title: *Erotica: An Anthology of Women's Writing*.

778. "[Excerpts]." *View from the Typewriter*. [Videorecording]. Robert Duncan. Montreal: National Film Board of Canada, 1992. 1 videocasette. A celebration of Canada (people, places, culture) presented via readings from the works of leading literary figures matched up with illustrative documentary film footage. Featured authors are: Milton Acorn, Malcolm Lowry, Jack Hodgins, Earle Birney, Margaret Laurence, W. O. Mitchell, Farley Mowat, Hugh MacLennan, Leonard Cohen, and Margaret Atwood.

779. "Five Poems for Dolls." *Exile: A Literary Quarterly* 16.1 (1992): 425-426. David Annesley sketch of Atwood on p. [v].

780. "Foreword." *Charles Pachter*. By Bogomila Welsh-Ovcharov. Toronto: McClelland and Stewart, 1992. 1-5. Portrait of *Margaret Atwood with Mug I* reproduced opposite page 1.

781. "Gertrude Talks Back." *Sunday Times Books* (London) 23 August 1992: Section 6: 6-7. Short story; reprinted in *Good Bones* (see 782).

782. *Good Bones*. Toronto: Coach House Press; London: Bloomsbury, 1992. Contains the following: "Bad News," "The Little Red Hen Tells All," "Gertrude Talks Back," "There Was Once," "Unpopular Gals," "Let Us Now Praise Stupid Women," "The Female Body," "In Love with Raymond Chandler," "Stump Hunting," "Making a Man," "Epaulettes," "Cold-Blooded," "Men at Sea," "Alien Territory," "Adventure Story," "Hardball," "My Life as a Bat," "Theology," "An Angel," "Poppies: Three Variations," "Homelanding," "Third Handed," "Death Scenes," "Four Small Paragraphs," "We Want It All," "Dance of the Lepers," "Good Bones."

783. *Good Bones: A Poem*. Toronto: Harbourfront Reading Series, 1992. 8pp. "Printed in a limited ed. of 500 copies, of which 150 are signed and numbered by the author and 50 are *hors de commerce*."

784. "Gup." *In a Word: A Dictionary of Words That Don't Exist, But Ought To*. Ed. Jack Hitt and Deidre McFadyen. New York: Laurel, 1992. 80. Atwood contributed this coined word and its definition.

785. "Hairball." *Lovers: Stories by Women*. Ed. Amber Coverdale Sumrall. Freedom, CA: The Crossing Press, 1992. 140-149. Reprinted from *Wilderness Tips*, ©1991.

786. "I Learned to Read Before I Started School." *Toronto Star* 26 September 1992: Section: Weekend: K1. (1338 w). Books in childhood and youth read by Atwood.

787. "In Love with Raymond Chandler." *Sunday Times Books* (London) 23 August 1992: Section 6: 6. Short story; Reprinted in *Good Bones* (see 782).

788. "Isis in Darkness." *Caught in a Story: Contemporary Fairytales and Fables*. Ed. Christine Park and Caroline Heaton. London: Vintage, 1992. 58-81. Reprinted from *Wilderness Tips*, ©1991.

789. "Kat." *A Pocketful of Prose: Contemporary Short Fiction*. Ed. David Madden. Fort Worth; Philadelphia; San Diego; New York; Orlando; Austin; San Antonio; Toronto; Montreal; London; Sydney; Tokyo: Harcourt Brace Jovanovich College Publishers, 1992. 236-246. Reprinted from *New Yorker* 66.3 (5 March 1990): 38-44. Appears in *Wilderness Tips*, ©1991 as "Hairball."

790. *Katzenauge*. Frankfurt: Fischer, 1992. German translation of *Cat's Eye*.

791. *Kedi gözü*. Istanbul: AFA Yayinlari, 1992. Turkish translation of *Cat's Eye* by Suna Güler.

792. "La edad de plomo." *Revista de Occidente* 139 (December 1992): 7-24. "The Age of Lead" translated into Spanish by María Elena de Valdés.

793. *Lady Orakel: Roman*. Hildesheim [Germany]: Claassen, 1992. German translation of *Lady Oracle* by Werner Waldhoff.

794. "Let Us Now Praise Stupid Women." *This Magazine* 26.3 (September 1992): 20-21. Fictional poem; reprinted in *Good Bones* (see 782).

795. "Little Red Hen Tells All." *Zeitschrift für Kanada-Studien* 21.1 (1992): 7-12.

796. "Machine. Gun. Nest." *Exile: A Literary Quarterly* 16.4 (1992): 282-283. Poem.

797. "Making a Man." *Sunday Times Books* (London) 23 August 1992: Section 6: 6-7. Short story; reprinted in *Good Bones* (see 782).

798. *Murder in the Dark*. North Rocks, NSW: Royal N.S.W. Institute for Deaf & Blind Children, [1992]. Braille edition, 1 v.

799. "Murder in the Dark" (that is, "Worship," "Iconography," "Him," "Hopeless," "A Parable"). *Exile: A Literary Quarterly* 16.4 (1992): 78-80. All from Part IV of *Murder in the Dark*.

800. "Nationalism, Socialism and Feminism: Margaret Atwood in Scotland." *Twist and Shout: A Decade of Feminist Writing in* This Magazine. Toronto: Second Story Press, 1992. 1-16. Reprinted from *This Magazine* 13.5-6 (1979).

801. "Notes towards a Poem That Can Never Be Written." *Inside the Poem: Essays and Poems in Honor of Donald Stephens*. Ed. W. H. New. Toronto: Oxford UP, 1992. 2-4. Reprinted from *Selected Poems: 1966-1984*, ©1990.

802. *Opowiesc Podrecznej*. Warsaw: Panstwowy Instytut Wydawniczy, 1992. Polish translation of *The Handmaid's Tale* by Zofia Uhrynowska-Hanasz.

803. *Poems 1976-1986*. London: Virago, 1992. 147. "This edition offset from Houghton Mifflin first edition, 1987."

804. *The Poetry and Voice of Margaret Atwood*. [Sound recording]. New York: HarperCollins, 1992. 1 sound cassette (36 min.) Reissue of: Caedmon CDL 51537 (1977). Includes: "The Animals in That Country," "A Foundling," "The Landlady," "At the Tourist Center in Boston," "Roominghouse," "Winter," "Game After Supper," "Girl and Horse," "1928," "The Small Cabin," "Midwinter," "Presolstice," "6 A.M. Boston Summer Sublet," "Dreams of the Animals," "Cyclops," "Younger Sister, Going Swimming," "Power Politics," "They Eat Out," "My Beautiful Wooden Leader," "We Are Hard on Each Other," "At First I Was Given Centuries," "You Refuse to Own Yourself," "They Are Hostile Nations," "They Were All Inaccurate," "Tricks with Mirrors," "You Are Happy," "There Is Only One of Everything," "Late August," " Book of Ancestors."

805. "Poppies: Three Variations." *Saturday Night* 107.9 (November 1992): 68-69. Fiction. Appears in *Good Bones*.

806. "Preface." *The Canadian Green Consumer Guide*. [Sound recording]. Read by Chris Landry. Toronto: CNIB, 1992. 2 cassettes. Recorded from book with same title: Toronto: McClelland and Stewart, ©1989.

807. *Råd Fra Villmarken*. Oslo: Aschehoug, 1992. Norwegian translation of *Wilderness Tips* by Inger Gjelsvik.

808. *Råd I Vildmarken, Och Andra Berättelser*. Stockholm: Bokförlaget Prisma, 1992. Swedish translation of *Wilderness Tips* by Else Lundgren.

809. "Rape Fantasies." *The Heath Introduction to Fiction*. 4th ed. With a Preface on Fiction and Introductory Notes by John J. Clayton. Lexington, MA; Toronto: D. C. Heath, 1992. 864-871. Reprinted from *Dancing Girls and Other Stories*; brief description of Atwood's writings, 863-864.

810. "The Santa Claus Trap." *Canadian Christmas Stories in Prose and Verse*. Ed. Don Bailey and Daile Unruh. [Sound recording]. Read by Rick Book. Toronto: CNIB, 1992. 1 sound cassette. Recorded from book with same title: Kingston, ON: Quarry Press, ©1990.

811. "Shopping." *Ark of Ice: Canadian Futurefiction*. Ed. Lesley Choyce. Lawrence-town Beach, NS: Pottersfield Press, 1992. 243-249. Excerpt from *The Handmaid's Tale*, ©1985.

812. "Simmering." *The Great Big Book of Canadian Humour*. Ed. Allan Gould. Toronto: Macmillan, 1992. 70-72. Reprinted from *Murder in the* Dark, ©1983.

813. "The Sin Eater." *The Short Story: 30 Masterpieces*. 2nd ed. Ed. Beverly Lawn. New York: St. Martin's Press, 1992. 377-387. Reprinted from *Bluebeard's Egg and Other Stories*. Biographical sketch, 439.

814. *Stories from Wilderness Tips*. [Sound recording]. Read by Helen Shaver. Toronto: Bantam Audio Publishing, 1992. 2 sound cassettes (1 h 20 min). Canadian version of US edition, 1991.

815. *Surfacing*. London: Bloomsbury, 1992, ©1977.

816. *Suzana Mudi no nikki,* Tokyo: Kokubunsha, 1992. Japanese translation of *The Journals of Susanna Moodie* by Hirabayashi Mitoko, Kuno Sachiko, and Bevarii Karen. Title romanized.

817. "There Was Once." *Mississippi* Review 21.1-2 (1992): 69-71; also in *This Magazine* 26.3 (September 1992): 21-22. Prose poem; reprinted in *Good Bones* (see 782).

818. "Three-Eyes." *West Coast Line* 25.3 (Winter 1991-92): 142-143. Poem; in special issue, "'You Devise. We Devise.' A Festschrift for Phyllis Webb."

819. "To Salman Rushdie, a Letter from Margaret Atwood." *The Independent* 12 February 1992: Section: Editorial Page: 21.

820. "True Romances." *Exile: A Literary Quarterly* 16.1 (1992): 132-134. Prose piece; David Annesley sketch of Atwood on p. [v].

821. "Unearthing Suite." *Woman's Hour Book of Short Stories Volume II*. Selected and introduced by Pat McLoughlin. London: BBC Books, 1992. 265-281. "Shelley Thompson read this story on *Woman's Hour* in April 1992." Reprinted from *Bluebeard's Egg and Other Stories*, ©1986.

822. "Unpopular Gals." *Mississippi Review* 21.1-2 (1992): 72-74.

823. [Untitled.] *Exile: A Literary Quarterly* 16.2-3 (1992): 50-51. Unidentified, facsimile manuscript page and full-page photograph by John Reeves.

824. [Untitled.] *The Pleasure of Reading*. Ed. Antonia Fraser. London: Bloomsbury, 1992. 153-158. Essay and list of favorite books; essay illustrated by Karen Ludlow. "This book has been produced to commemorate the bicentenary of W. H. Smith."

825. [Untitled.] "Voices of the Nation." *Maclean's* 105.43 ("special issue—on sale from October 19, 1992"): 23. Response to question of how she was planning to vote in the October 26 referendum on the Charlottetown accord; photo accompanies her reply.

826. "Weight." *Legal Fictions: Short Stories about Lawyers and the Law*. Ed. Jay Wishingrad. Woodstock, NY: Overlook Press, 1992. 70-81. Reprinted from *Wilderness Tips*, ©1991.

827. *Wenken Voor De Wildernis (Verhalen)*. Amsterdam: Uitgeverij Bert Bakker, 1992. Dutch translation of *Wilderness Tips*.

828. *Wilderness Tips*. Toronto: Seal Books; London: Virago, 1992 ©1991. Paperback reprint.

829. "Women's Novels." *Likely Stories: A Postmodern Sampler*. Ed. George Bowering and Linda Hutcheon. Toronto: Coach House Press, 1992. 27-30. Also in *The Great Big Book of Canadian Humour*. Ed. Allan Gould. Toronto: Macmillan, 1992. 82-83. Reprinted from *Murder in the Dark*, ©1983.

Quotations

830. "[Quote]." *Contemporary Literary Criticism Yearbook 1991.* Ed. Roger Matuz et al. Detroit, MI: Gale Research, 1992: 275. Quote is from Atwood's *Globe and Mail* tribute to Frye which was quoted in the *New York Times* obituary; same quote appears on 276 in boldface.

831. "[Quote]." *The Last Word: A Treasury of Women's Quotes.* Carolyn Warner. Englewood Cliffs, NJ: Prentice Hall, 1992. 193. Unattributed quote is a comment on literature.

832. "[Quote]." *Making the News: Photo-mosaics by Bruce Johnson.* Halifax, NS: [The Art Gallery, Mount Saint Vincent University], 1992. [1]. Atwood quoted on Bruce Johnson by John Murchie: "He has changed profoundly the way we look at familiar iconography." A requote from John Allemang. "Queen, Moore & Charlie Go to France." *Globe and Mail* 12 October 1991: D1.

833. "[Quotes]." *The Beacon Book of Quotations by Women.* Compiled by Rosalie Maggio. Boston: Beacon Press, 1992. 4, 7, 68, 86, 120, 133, 307, 322. Eleven Atwood quotes.

834. "[Quotes]." *The New Quotable Woman.* Compiled and ed. by Elaine Partnow. New York and Oxford: Facts on File, 1992. 470. One quote from *Surfacing;* three from *The Handmaid's Tale.*

835. "[Quotes]." *Webster's II New Riverside Desk Quotations.* By James B. Simpson. Boston; New York; London: Houghton Mifflin, 1992. 27, 203. Reprinted from *The Journals of Susanna Moodie* and *Time.*

836. "[Quotes]." *Write to the Heart: Wit and Wisdom of Women Writers.* Ed. Amber Coverdale Sumrall. Freedom, CA: The Crossing Press, 1992. 17, 22, 50, 55, 78, 88, 93, 109, 121, 125, 147, 158, 162, 167. Fourteen Atwood quotes.

Interviews

837. *An Interview with Margaret Atwood.* [Sound recording]. Sydney: ABC Radio, 1992. 1 sound cassette (30 min.). Interview by Jill Kitson.

838. DREIFUS, Claudia. "Margaret Atwood: 'Respectability Can Kill You Very Quickly.'" *The Progressive* 56.3 (March 1992): 30-33. "In the interview, Atwood discusses the Canadian reputation for dullness, her fame, her new book, *Wilderness Tips,* the type of woman she writes about, her inspiration for *The Handmaid's Tale,* the mixing of art and politics, the Canadian feeling of being overwhelmed by the United States, her politics, her disdain for respectability, and her lack of political correctness." (Journal).

839. GUTTRIDGE, Peter. "The Handmaid and the Home Economist's Tale." *The Independent* 14 November 1992: 28. (1276 w). Atwood caught en route to Canada after 9 months in Provence. Some excerpts:

   Commenting **on the Margaret Atwood Society:** "I feel silly about the Society, as if I should be dead, I should be Robert Browning or somebody. I feel the same about being taught in university. But what can I do? If I dwelt on it I would probably get a terrible skin disease. I do, however, refuse to tell them the answers to these questions about the one true meaning of what I do. They have to figure that out for themselves."

On biographies: "I used to disapprove of biographies on principle, but with increasing age I've become as nosey as anyone else."

What about her own life? "Oh, I wouldn't recommend writing about me. There isn't any good Nancy Reagan stuff. But rather than anybody else doing it, maybe I'd better do it myself." She pauses. "In 20 years or so. I see no need for haste."

840. INGERSOLL, Earl G., and Philip HOWARD. *Margaret Atwood: Conversations.* London: Virago, 1992 ©1990.

841. KENYON, Olga. "Margaret Atwood Gives Voice." *Women's Voice in Literature and Society.* Ed. Maggie Allison and Anne White. Bradford, West Yorkshire: University of Bradford, Dept. of Modern Languages, [1992]. 15-27. (Bradford Occasional Papers No. 11). Explores, in part, how Atwood draws inspiration from other texts.

842. MARCHAND, Philip. "Atwood Experiments with 'Pieces.'" *Toronto Star* 25 September 1992: Section: Entertainment: C13. (505 w). On *Good Bones*—**why it was published by Coach House Press:** "It can do unclassifiable books. You can't say *Good Bones* is a novel, or a collection of short stories, or poetry. It's a book of... pieces." [Ed. note: See SLOPEN interview below.]

On its use in readings: "Because it's not poetry and it's not short stories, but it has some of the virtues of both. You can use quite condensed language, but there's an end to it after two or three pages."

843. MEYER, Bruce, and Brian O'RIORDAN. "Figure It Out: Margaret Atwood." *Lives and Works.* Windsor, ON: Black Moss Press, 1992. 1-8.

844. SLOPEN, Beverley. "Atwood's Erotica." *Toronto Star* 1 August 1992: Section: Weekend: G15. Atwood, then in France, queried about her entry in *Erotica: Women's Writing from Sappho to Margaret Atwood.* "You've got me there," Atwood answers. "I'm anthologized a great deal and they must have picked something from my published works, either poetry or fiction, and got permission from the publisher." Instead she preferred to talk about *Good Bones* as a small-format hardcover, priced at $18.95, of which the publisher is hoping to sell 20,000 copies. Atwood, who received no advance but was paid royalties, hoped the book would be successful enough to help put the small literary press in the black.

845. TIDMARSH, Andrew. "Dinosaurs, Comics, Conan—and Metaphysical Romance: Andrew Tidmarsh Talks to Margaret Atwood." *Interzone* 65 (1 November 1992): 23-25.

846. WHITE, Lesley. "A Heroine of the Struggle Casts a Cool Eye on Women." *Sunday Times* 16 August 1992: Section 2: 5. (1750 w).

Scholarly Resources

847. *100 Years of Critical Solitudes: Canadian and Québécois Criticism from the 1880s to the 1980s.* Ed. Caroline Bayard. Toronto: ECW Press, 1992. 356. Atwood mentioned in several essays.

848. "Atwood, Margaret." *Who's Who in Canadian Literature 1992-93.* By Gordon Ripley and Anne Mercer. Teeswater, ON: Reference Press, 1992. 9-11. Biographical facts and list of publications.

849. "Atwood, Margaret Eleanor." *Who's Who in Writers, Editors and Poets: United States and Canada 1992-1993.* 4th ed. Ed. Curt Johnson and Frank Nipp. Highland Park, IL: December Press, 1992. 19-20. Primarily a list of publications and awards.

850. "Atwood, Margaret Eleanor." *Who's Who of American Women.* 17th ed. 1991-1992. Wilmette, IL: Marquis Who's Who, Macmillan Information Company, 1991. 35. Biographical sketch.

851. "Atwood, Margaret Eleanor (born 1939)." *The Bloomsbury Guide to Women's Literature.* Ed. Claire Buck. New York; London; Toronto; Sydney; Tokyo; Singapore: Prentice Hall General Reference, 1992. 300-301. Biographical reference with short bibliography.

852. "Handmaid." *A Dictionary of Biblical Tradition in English Literature.* Ed. David Lyle Jeffrey. Grand Rapids, MI: William B. Eerdmans Publishing Company, 1992. 328. Reference to Atwood novel in definition of the word "handmaid."

853. ANDRE, Alestine. "Offred at the Roman Catholic Hostel." *Atlantis: A Women Studies Journal* 17.2 (Spring-Summer 1992): 104-105.

855. BACCOLINI, Raffaella. "Forme dell'Utopia 1: Breaking the Boundaries: Gender, Genre, and Dystopia; Atti del Convegno Internazionale di Bagni di Lucca 12-14 settembre 1990." *Per una definizione dell'utopia: Metodologie e discipline a confronto.* Ed. Nadia Minerva; introduction by Vita Fortunati. Ravenna: Longo, 1992. 137-146.

856. BALCOM, Ted. *Book Discussions for Adults: A Leader's Guide.* Chicago; London: American Library Association, 1992. 22. *The Handmaid's Tale* is mentioned as a selection for women's book discussion groups.

857. BARR, Marleen S. *Feminist Fabulation: Space/Postmodern Fiction.* Iowa City: University of Iowa Press, 1992. See especially "Hesitation, Self-Experiment, Transformation—Women Mastering Female Narrative." 183-224. Joan of *Lady Oracle* is able to rewrite her life, discarding patriarchal stories in favor of the woman's narrative.

858. BERAN, Carol L. "Intertexts of Margaret Atwood's *Life Before Man*." *American Review of Canadian Studies* 22.2 (Summer 1992): 199-214. Analysis of the influence of other cultural and literary texts upon this novel.

859. BESSNER, Neil. "Beyond Two Solitudes, After Survival: Postmodern Fiction in Canada." *Postmodern Fiction in Canada.* Ed. Theo D'haen and Hans Bertens. Amsterdam: Rodopi and Antwerpen: Restant: 1992. 9-25. Atwood's role in Canadian literature is examined, and *Surfacing* is seen as "a powerful novel with a compelling plot."

860. BLAKE, Marjorie Rose. "Speculative Fiction and Mothering: Marge Piercy's *Woman on the Edge of Time* and Margaret Atwood's *The Handmaid's Tale*." MA thesis. University of Victoria, 1992. 111 pp. Also available on microfiche from Canadian Theses Service (1992). Among other matters, this thesis focuses "on Piercy's and Atwood's employment of speculative fiction for their innovative explorations of mothering. [It delves] briefly into the development of new birth technologies and consider[s] how Piercy's and Atwood's conjectural visions shed light on the present sociological problems that influence women's quotidian decisions." (Adapted from Author). For more see *MAI* 31.04 (Winter 1993): 1493.

861. BÖK, Christian. "Sibyls: Echoes of French Feminism in *The Diviners* and *Lady Oracle*." Canadian Literature 135 (Winter 1992): 80-93. The female writer in both novels experiences the transformation of identity into being her own muse and is thus able to upset patriarchal creativity.

862. BOWER, Martha Gilman. "Seduction and Sedation: Doctors' Plunder of Female Space." *Misogyny in Literature: An Essay Collection.* Ed. Katherine Anne Ackley. New York; London: Garland Publishing, 1992. 225-245. References *The Hand-*

maid's Tale as a futuristic version of women as victims as men control their bodies through medicine.

863. BOWERING, George. "Atwood's Hook." *Open Letter*, Eighth Series 2 (Winter 1992): 81-90. The short poem "You fit into me / like a hook into an eye / a fish hook / an open eye" is analyzed as representative of many of the themes of Atwood's other works.

864. BRAIN, Tracy Eileen. "The Female Body in Women's Writing: From Sylvia Plath to Margaret Atwood." PhD thesis. University of Sussex, 1992.

865. BREWSTER, Elizabeth. "Autobiographical essay." *Contemporary Authors: Autobiography Series.* Vol. 15. Ed. Joyce Nakamura. Detroit, MI; London: Gale Research, 1992. 157-158. Mentions Atwood's influence and her inspiration for a poem, "Poem for a Young Sorceress."

866. BRITTON, Krista M. "Gilead Within: Margaret Atwood's Science Fiction." MA thesis. Kent State University, 1992.

867. BURNHAM, Julie E. "Voice and Origin in Margaret Atwood's Fiction." MA thesis. Rice University, 1992. 59 pp. "In contradiction to Lyotard, who posits an equal relationship between listener and speaker in *Just Gaming* and *The Postmodern Condition*, Atwood examines the ways in which women's voices are stifled by men's terroristic control of the speaking position. Her novels reveal a significant flaw in Lyotard's work: he ignores the effects which a political or hierarchical system has on his ideal language grid. Within contemporary patriarchal societies, Atwood's heroines must struggle against male dominance in order to fulfill what Lyotard calls 'the obligation to retell.' Irigaray argues that women's exclusion from discourse can be traced back to Plato's myth of the cave, in which both men and women are encouraged to forget their maternal origins. In Atwood's novels, women must return to and revalue their maternal origins in order to find a voice, and the stories they must retell are altered versions of those of the mother." (Author). For more see *MAI* 31.01 (Spring 1993): 85. [Ed. note: See Irigaray, "Plato's Hysteria." *Speculum of the Other Woman.* Tr. Gillian C. Gill. Ithaca, NY: Cornell UP, 1985. 243-364.]

868. CALDWELL, Larry W. "Wells, Orwell, and Atwood: (EPI)Logic and Eu/Utopia." *Extrapolation* 33.4 (Winter 1992): 333-345. Thomas More's *Utopia* is starting point for discussion of utopian fiction, defining that genre as indeterminate.

869. CAMPBELL-FURTICK, Cristy. "Psychological Escape in Four Novels of Margaret Atwood." MA thesis. Tarleton State University, 1992. 113 pp. "Finding their environments threatening and malevolent, the female protagonists in *The Edible Woman*, *Surfacing*, *Lady Oracle*, and *Life Before Man* withdraw psychologically. Their psychological escapes take many forms: fantasies, alternative worlds, delusions, hallucinations, and madness. While the behavior of these protagonists is irrational and illogical to the 'sane' world, it allows them to reintegrate their fragmented lives. The protagonists emerge from their psychological cocoons with clarity of vision, recognizing both their multiplicity and their complicity." (Author). For more see *MAI* 31.02 (Summer 1993): 569.

870. CARPENTER, Sherida Hughes. "Revisionist Mythmaking: The Female Poet's Break with Tradition." MA thesis. University of Alaska, Anchorage, 1992. 108 pp. "The revisionist mythmaking conducted by women poets of the past twenty years is marked by a discerning deconstruction of cultural myth. The process involves a comprehensive revising of the entire character and/or story from a female perspective. In their poetry, revisionists trace the roots of gender problems to various cultural myths and address the contemporary concerns which have resulted. Revision-

ist poets most often focus on literary structures such as the fairy tale, classical myth, and religious stories. While revisionist poetry has proliferated in recent years, Margaret Atwood, Anne Sexton and Sylvia Plath were among the early practitioners. Their work contains prime examples of this trend." (Author). For more see *MAI* 31.02 (Summer 1993): 562.

871. CHAKOVSKY, Sergei, and M. Thomas INGE, ed. *Russian Eyes on American Literature.* Jackson; London: UP of Mississippi and A. M. Gorky Institute of World Literature, 1992. passim. Atwood mentioned in several essays; includes discussion of her departmentalizing literature and her critique of Updike's *Witches.*

872. COLES EDITORIAL BOARD. Surfacing: *Notes.* Toronto: Coles, ©1992. Study guide.

873. COOKE, Nathalie. "Reading Reflections: The Autobiographical Illusion in *Cat's Eye.*" *Essays on Life Writing: From Genre to Critical Practice.* Ed. Marlene Kadar. Toronto; Buffalo; London: University of Toronto Press, 1992. 162-170. The autobiographical element in *Cat's Eye* is employed as a literary strategy by Atwood and is not simply a reflection of Atwood's life.

874. COWART, David. "Bridge and Mirror: Replicating Selves in *Cat's Eye.*" *Postmodern Fiction in Canada.* Ed. Theo D'haen and Hans Bertens. Amsterdam: Rodopi; Antwerp: Restant: 1992. 125-136. Art and memory provide the means to examine the dimension of time, the crucial element in this novel.

875. COX, Michele Lee. "Re-Vision as Revision: Women Narrating the Past in *The Woman Warrior, Housekeeping,* and *Cat's Eye.*" MA thesis. University of Montana, 1992.

876. DANIELS, Steven Robert. "In the Tracks of Gray Owl: Renaming and Transformation in Twentieth-Century Canadian Literature." MA thesis. University of North Carolina at Chapel Hill, 1992. Focus on Atwood, as well as Robert Kroetsch and Mordecai Richler.

877. DAVEY, Frank. "What's in a Genre: Margaret Atwood's 'Notes Towards a Poem.'" *Inside the Poem: Essays and Poems in Honor of Donald Stephens.* Ed. W. H. New. Toronto: Oxford UP, 1992. 48-54. Analyzes progression from notes to poem.

878. DEER, Glenn. "Rhetorical Strategies in *The Handmaid's Tale*: Dystopia and the Paradoxes of Power." *English Studies in Canada* 18.2 (June 1992): 215-233. The narrator is the powerful voice of Atwood who is responsible for the story's pain.

879. DESJARDINS, Louise. "Traduction de *Power Politics* de Margaret Atwood." MA thesis. Université de Sherbrooke, 1992. Also available on microfiche from Canadian Theses Service (1992).

880. DEVINE, Maureen. *Woman and Nature: Literary Reconceptualizations.* Metuchen, NJ; London: Scarecrow Press, 1992. Frequent mention of Atwood, especially *Surfacing*, throughout.

881. DiBENEDETTO, Tamra Elizabeth. "The Role of Language in Constructing Consciousness in Margaret Atwood's *The Handmaid's Tale.*" MA thesis. California State University, San Bernardino, 1992.

882. DONALDSON-TOSH, Kathy. "Siren's Song or Funeral Dirge: The White Goddess as Destroyer or Destroyed Woman in Selected Short Fiction of Margaret Atwood." MS thesis. Illinois State University, 1992.

883. DOPP, Jamie. "Reading through Subject-Positions: A Materialist Investigation of Subject-Positions with Readings of Three Exemplary Texts." PhD thesis. York University, 1992. 379 pp. Also available on microfiche from Canadian Theses Service (1993). A study of *The Handmaid's Tale* as well as Robertson Davies's

What's Bred in the Bone and Timothy Findley's *Famous Last Words*. For more see *DAI-A* 54.03 (September 1993): 922.

884. EVANS, F. E. M. (Francis Eric Mark). "Margaret Atwood: Words and the Wilderness." PhD thesis. University of Edinburgh, 1992. This study "is motivated by a desire to demonstrate the polysemous irreducibility of literary meaning and to suggest ways in which critical theory and textual practice may meaningfully interact and correspond." (Author). Examples used: *The Circle Game, The Edible Woman,* and *Survival.*

885. FENWICK, Julie. "The Silence of the Mermaid: *Lady Oracle* and *Anne of Green Gables*." *Essays on Canadian Writing* 47 (Fall 1992): 51-64. Points out parallels between the 2 novels regarding struggles with conventional expectations and choices for women.

886. FOX-GENOVESE, Elizabeth. "The New Female Literary Culture." *Antioch Review* 50.1-2 (Winter-Spring 1992): 260-282. "50th Anniversary Issue"; reprinted from 38.2 (Spring 1980). Survey article; compares Atwood with Gail Godwin.

887. GARLICK, Barbara. "*The Handmaid's Tale*: Narrative Voice and the Primacy of the Tale." *Twentieth-Century Fantasists: Essays on Culture, Society and Belief in Twentieth-Century Mythopoeic Literature*. Ed. Kath Filmer and David Jasper. New York: St. Martin's, 1992. 161-171.

888. GARRETT-PETTS, W. F. "A Rhetoric of Reading Contemporary Canadian Narratives: George Bowering, Margaret Atwood, and Robert Kroetsch." PhD thesis. University of Alberta, 1992. 264 pp. "This thesis argues for a rhetoric of reading to complement the rapid developments in text-oriented poetics that, despite a renewed interest in audience and process, continue to dominate contemporary critical discourse. A rhetoric of reading shifts the focus of critical attention from texts as aesthetic objects to texts as interactive elements in the 'contextualized production and reception of meaning.' This particular variation on a celebrated critical theme (that of discourse as enunciation) belongs to Linda Hutcheon, and this thesis constitutes both an elaboration and a critique of Hutcheon's critical stance." (Author). For more see *DAI-A* 53.12 (June 1993): 4327.

889. GIOIA, Dana. *Can Poetry Matter? Essays on Poetry and American Culture*. St. Paul, MN: Graywolf Press, 1992. See especially "Margaret Atwood." 186-187. Discussion of *Two-Headed Poems.*

890. GIVNER, Jessie. "Names, Faces and Signatures in Margaret Atwood's *Cat's Eye* and *The Handmaid's Tale*." *Canadian Literature* 133 (Summer 1992): 56-75. Autobiography and fiction set the relationship between the dichotomies expressed.

891. GODARD, Barbara. "Canadian? Literary? Theory?" *Open Letter*, Eighth Series 3 (Spring 1992): 5-27. Atwood not always studied solely in terms of her being a Canadian author; *Survival* is cited in discussion of Canadian literature.

892. HEILAND, Donna. "Postmodern Gothic: *Lady Oracle* and Its Eighteenth-Century Antecedents." *RSSI (Recherches sémiotiques / Semiotic Inquiry)* 12.1-2 (1992): 115-136. Both the male and female traditions of the Gothic portrayal of the sublime exist in this novel and together prove that the metahistory in the eighteenth century is pointless in the twentieth.

893. HEINIMANN, David. "An Ethical Critique of Men in Laurence and Atwood." PhD thesis. Université de Montréal, 1992. 331 pp. Also available on microfiche from Canadian Theses Service (1994). "The characterization in fiction of one sex by the other raises disputes among both. Accuracy and intent are argued to determine what the writer really meant. Agreement is difficult to achieve. Yet without it, we risk the devaluation of our literature....My examination of the novels of

82 ~ 1992 ~

Margaret Laurence and Margaret Atwood, plus Laurence's interconnected stories in *A Bird in the House*, concerns both the men who appear in them and what the narrators say about men. I raise questions about assumptions and intent, and I consider the consequences of the characterizations and comments." (Author). For more see *DAI-A* 55.05 (January 1995): 1967.

894. HELWIG, David. "L'autre littérature." *Possibles* 16.2 (1992): 107-111. Discussion of Canadian literature with Atwood and *Survival* mentioned.

895. HENDERSON, Jennifer. "Gender in the Discourse of English-Canadian Literary Criticism." *Open Letter*, Eighth Series 3 (Spring 1992): 47-57. Survey article with brief mention of Atwood's view of feminist writing.

896. HITE, Molly. *The Other Side of the Story: Structures and Strategies of Contemporary Feminist Narrative*. Ithaca, NY: Cornell UP, 1992. A study of Doris Lessing's *Golden Notebook*, Alice Walker's *Color Purple*, and Atwood's *Lady Oracle*.

897. HOOPER, Brad. *Short Story Writers and Their Work: A Guide to the Best*. 2nd ed. Chicago; London: American Library Association, 1992. 43. Guide to recommended short story collections; Atwood's work described with particular attention to *Bluebeard's Egg*.

898. HORIKAWA, Tetsushi. "Margaret Atwood and 'Self in Disguise'—Clothes: A Symbol of Disguise or of Reality?" *Kyoto Gaikokugo Daigaku Kenkyu Ronso* 39 (1992): 72-83. Clothing as a symbol of self in *The Edible Woman* and *Surfacing*.

899. HUTCHEON, Linda, ed. *Double Talking: Essays on Verbal and Visual Ironies in Canadian Contemporary Art and Literature*. Toronto: ECW Press, 1992. Atwood mentioned in several essays.

900. INGERSOLL, Earl. "Margaret Atwood's *The Handmaid's Tale*: Echoes of Orwell." *Journal of the Fantastic in the Arts* 5.4 (1992): 64-72.

901. JOHNSTON, Susan. "Reconstructing the Wilderness: Margaret Atwood's Reading of Susanna Moodie." *Canadian Poetry* 31 (Fall-Winter 1992): 28-54. Compares Moodie's world and the context of her writings with the interpretation of Atwood.

902. JONES, Michelle Lynne. "Laughing Hags: The Comic Vision as Feminist." PhD thesis. University of Alberta, 1992. 337 pp. "Feminist comedy allows writers to 'shatter the framework of institutions' (Cixous). Such revolutionary comedy mocks primary socialization, or the very roles or models affirmed by classic comedy....By examining [Atwood's, John Irving's, Barbara Pym's, and Muriel Spark's] mockery of three major ideological structures—the academy, the church, and the self—and by myself using a style reflective of such mockery, [this thesis attempts] to demonstrate the authors' comic concern with the price paid by the individual, and society, in adhering to conservative behavior and roles. Laughter is the best medicine for the ills of society, and is especially effective in breaking the chains of socialization." (Author). For more see *DAI-A* 53.12 (June 1993): 4310.

903. KAPLAN, E. Ann. *Motherhood and Representation: The Mother in Popular Culture and Melodrama*. London; New York: Routledge, 1992. passim. Various references to *The Handmaid's Tale*.

904. KAUFFMAN, Linda S. *Special Delivery: Epistolary Modes in Modern Fiction*. Chicago; London: The University of Chicago Press, 1992. See especially "Twenty-First Century Epistolarity in *The Handmaid's Tale*." 221-262. An earlier version appeared in *Writing the Female Voice: Essays on Epistolary Literature*, ©1989.

905. KEITH, W. J. *Literary Images of Ontario*. Toronto; Buffalo; London: University of Toronto Press, 1992. Atwood is one of many writers presented and is especially

predominant in the chapter "A Changing Toronto," where the use of the city in her fiction is discussed.

906. KETTERER, David. *Canadian Science Fiction and Fantasy*. Bloomington, IL; Indianapolis: Indiana UP, 1992. See especially "The International Arrival of Canadian Science Fiction. Margaret Atwood's *The Handmaid's Tale*: A Contextual Dystopia." 147-154. Terms *The Handmaid's Tale* a "contextual dystopia" because of its transitory nature with the "Historical Notes" indicating that Gilead did not last; in this sense, the novel differs from the traditional dystopian tale.

907. KIRTZ, Mary K. "'I Am Become a Name': The Representation of Ukrainians in Ross, Laurence, Ryga and Atwood." *Canadian Ethnic Studies / Études Ethniques au Canada* 24.2 (1992): 35-45. The power of naming is explored in four novels including *Life Before Man*.

908. KRÖLLER, Eva-Marie. *George Bowering: Bright Circles of Colour*. Vancouver: Talonbooks, 1992. passim. Four brief references to Atwood, including description of Charles Pachter's cover for *The Gangs of Kosmos* in which Atwood's image appears.

909. KRUK, Laurie Ann. "Voices of the 'Concerned Middle': The Short Stories of Six Canadian Women Writers." PhD thesis. University of Western Ontario, 1992. 317 pp. This "thesis, feminist in approach, examines voices of the 'concerned middle' through the 'female fictions' of six contemporary inheritors of the realist tradition in Canadian literature. With their short stories, Edna Alford, Sandra Birdsell, Joan Clark, Elisabeth Harvor, Carol Shields and Janette Turner Hospital continue the exploration of women's experience in patriarchal society initiated by Margaret Atwood, Margaret Laurence, Alice Munro and Mavis Gallant." (Author). For more see *DAI-A* 54.02 (August 1993): 526.

910. KRYWALSKI, Diether. *Knaurs Lexikon der Weltliteratur*. Munich: Droemer Knaur, 1992. See especially "Atwood, Margaret." 43. Brief biographical sketch.

911. KUESTER, Martin. *Framing Truths: Parodic Structures in Contemporary English-Canadian Historical Novels*. Toronto; London; Buffalo: University of Toronto Press, 1992. See especially Chapter 5: "Atwood: Parodies from a Feminist Point of View." 124-147. Analyzes *Bodily Harm* and *The Handmaid's Tale* as variations on traditional literary genres.

912. LANDIS, Kathleen M. "The Rhetoric of Madness." PhD thesis. University of Southern California, 1992. "This dissertation proposes a new category for contemporary fiction—'schizophrenic fiction'—in which madness plays a key rhetorical role. The rhetoric of madness inheres primarily in its function as a means of persuasion, used by a growing number of writers, consciously or unconsciously, to drive home their messages about life in the world today. Although the messages vary from one novel to the next, and a single text typically contains multiple messages, works of schizophrenic fiction all convey one central message: for many, life today is so painful, so oppressive, or so incomprehensible that their 'sanest' recourse is insanity. 'Insanity' in these cases takes the form of a schizophrenic psychic rift, which gives rise to two realities—one real, one imagined—in which an individual lives. Unlike clinical schizophrenia, however, which is triggered largely by brain abnormalities, fictionalized schizophrenia results directly and exclusively from external sources. To the schizophrenic characters, their access to alternate realities, whether temporary or permanent, is not viewed as a disease. Rather, it is a mechanism for coping with their lives, serving variously as a way to escape, to fill emotional voids, to feel empowered, and even to come to terms with losses. Five contemporary novels are examined: *Slaughterhouse-Five* by Kurt

Vonnegut, *The Tin Drum* by Gunter Grass, *Surfacing* by Margaret Atwood, *Mrs. Caliban* by Rachel Ingalls, and *Woman on the Edge of Time* by Marge Piercy." (Author). For more see *DAI-A* 53.09 (March 1993): 3209.

913. LAURET, Maria Laetitia Josephine. "Liberating Literature: American Women's Writing and Social Movements from the Thirties to the Present." DPhil thesis. University of Sussex (UK), 1992. 301 pp. Shows the new kind of writing emerging from the 1960s civil rights movements with critical discussions on the works of Marge Piercy, Alice Walker, Marilyn French, Agnes Smedley, Josephine Herbst, Ann Petry, Meridel LeSueur, Kate Millett, Audre Lorde, Maya Angelou, Margaret Atwood, and Sue Miller. For more see *DAI-C* 54.04 (Winter 1993): 986.

914. MANGUEL, Alberto. "À la découverte de la littérature canadienne." *Revue de l'Impériale* 76 (Summer 1992): 20-23. Atwood mentioned several times in this survey article.

915. MARSHALL, Tom. *Multiple Exposures, Promised Lands: Essays on Canadian Poetry and Fiction*. Kingston, ON: Quarry Press, 1992. See especially "Margaret Atwood's Cool." 73-78. In this collection of Marshall's essays, Atwood is mentioned in essays on other authors as well.

916. MASSÉ, Michelle A. *The Name of Love: Women, Masochism, and the Gothic*. Ithaca, NY; London: Cornell UP, 1992. See especially "Resisting the Gothic: Subversion and *Lady Oracle*." 250-264. Joan's splitting of her identity is her subversion until she finds she no longer needs to do so; then, she is able to act upon what she has learned.

917. MAYO, Kathleen A. The Struggle for Success in Achieving Self-Identity: A Thesis." MA thesis. State University of New York College at Oneonta, 1992. Atwood major author referenced.

918. McKAY, George. "'Time Back Way Back': 'Motivation' and Speculative Fiction." *Critical Quarterly* 34.1 (Spring 1992): 102-116. *The Handmaid's Tale* is one of several novels examined to study boundary between real and imaginary.

919. MILDON, Denis A. (Denis Albert). "Narrative Inquiry in Education in the Light of Contemporary Canadian Fiction." EdD thesis. University of Toronto, 1992. 358 pp. Also available on microfiche from Canadian Theses Service (1993). Atwood's fiction examined along with that of Timothy Findley, Michael Ondaatje, and Audrey Thomas.

920. MINER, Valerie. *Rumors from the Cauldron: Selected Essays, Reviews, and Reportage*. Ann Arbor: University of Michigan Press, 1992. See especially "Atwood in Metamorphosis: An Authentic Canadian Fairy Tale." 152-166. Essay on Miner's visit with Atwood; reprinted from *Her Own Woman*, ©1975.

921. MISHLER, Barbara Ensor. "Interpersonal Conflict in Women's Friendships: Patterns and Strategies from Women's Novels." PhD thesis. University of Oregon, 1992. "Novels offer a rich source of relevant situations in which to study conflict behavior among female friends. The value of this study lies in the fact that such conflict is studied within a realistic context which includes the consequences of decisions made during conflict episodes. [Alice Walker's] *The Color Purple*, [Atwood's] *Cat's Eye*, [Marilynne Robinson's] *Housekeeping*, and [Marge Piercy's] *Braided Lives*, all novels by women written during the 1980s, were analyzed for conflict scenes among women friends. Analysis was conducted for topic, personality type (independent/traditional), self-monitoring, self-esteem, strategies, and repair attempts. The most frequent topics were men and abandonment. No preference for strategy was found for independent or traditional personality types. Repair

attempts were infrequent and appeared only after extreme disagreement." (Author). For more see *DAI-A* 53.10 (April 1993): 3409.

922. MOREY, Ann-Janine. "Margaret Atwood and Toni Morrison: Reflections on Postmodernism and the Study of Religion and Literature." *Journal of the American Academy of Religion* 60.3 (Fall 1992): 493-513. Discusses *Surfacing* and *Beloved* as examples of women's fiction being outside and threatening to traditional religious reality.

923. ———. *Religion and Sexuality in American Literature.* Cambridge; New York; Melbourne: Cambridge UP, 1992. See especially "Fatal Abstractions: Metaphors of Embodiment in the Gynocentric Imagination." 200-235. Atwood, along with Mary Gordon, Marilynne Robinson, and Louise Erdrich, utilizes metaphors of flight and water to explore the establishment and crossing of boundaries.

924. MOYES, Lianne. "'Canadian Literature Criticism': Between the Poles of the Universal-Particular Antinomy." *Open Letter*, Eighth Series 3 (Spring 1992): 28-46. Discussion of Atwood's criticism speaks of her view of Canadian literature as involving psychology, sociology, and geography.

925. NELSON, Sandra. "Blood Taboo: A Response to Margaret Atwood's 'Lives of the Poets.'" *Mid-American Review* 12.2 (1992): 111-115. Personal reaction to the short story.

926. PACHE, Walter. "Margaret Atwood: *The Handmaid's Tale.*" Anglistentag 1991 Düsseldorf: Proceedings. Ed. Wilhelm G. Busse. Tübingen: Niemeyer, 1992. 386-400.

927. PATTON, Marilyn. "Tourists and Terrorists: The Creation of *Bodily Harm.*" *PLL: Papers on Language and Literature* 28.2 (Spring 1992): 150-173. The Margaret Atwood Papers, at the University of Toronto, Thomas Fisher Rare Book Library, were examined, and these manuscripts revealed a progression in Atwood's fiction of political themes, as an act in itself and not simply a setting for the fiction.

928. PERKIN-McFARLAND, Anne Louise. "Connection and Dislocation: Themes in Recent Short Stories by Canadian Women Writers." MA thesis. University of New Brunswick, 1992. 195 pp. Also available on microfiche from Canadian Theses Service (1992). In addition to Atwood, Janette Turner Hospital, Alice Munro, and Miriam Waddington are discussed. "Common themes emerge in the stories by these writers, most notably the theme of connection and dislocation. The term 'connection' is borrowed from Carol Gilligan who, using Nancy Chodorow's theories, explains that women's identities are dependent on ongoing relationships or connections. The term 'dislocation' is borrowed from the title of Janette Turner Hospital's collection of short stories. Dislocation is essentially the same as alienation, a theme which is found throughout Canadian literature." (Author). For more see *MAI* 31.03 (Fall 1993): 1024.

929. PICHECA, Donna M. "The Men We Love to Hate: A Study of Atwood's Male Characters." MA thesis. McMaster University, 1992. 89 pp.

930. POOLE, Ralph J. *Sind Frauen essbar? Zur Symptomatik des weiblichen Körpers im Werk Margaret Atwoods.* Egelsbach [Germany]: Verlag Hänsel-Hohenhausen, 1992. Study of anorexia nervosa in *Lady Oracle* and bulimia in *The Edible Woman*.

931. POST, Stephen G. "The Moral Meaning of Relinquishing an Infant: Reflections on Adoption." *Thought: A Review of Culture and Idea* 67.265 (June 1992): 207-220. *Surfacing* is discussed as a classic example in section titled "Abortion Trauma?"

932. RELKE, Diana M. A. "Myths of Nature and the Poetry of Canadian Women: An Alternative Reading of Literary History." *New Literatures Review* 23 (Summer

1992): 31-49. Atwood quoted and discussed regarding her literary criticism of Canadian poetry.

933. RINDISBACHER, Hans J. *The Smell of Books: A Cultural-Historical Study of Olfactory Perception in Literature.* Ann Arbor: The University of Michigan Press, 1992. Footnote on 229 discusses the olfactory in *The Handmaid's Tale* as a means of switching between the present and past of the novel's setting.

934. ROSS, Catherine. "Calling Back the Ghost of the Old-Time Heroine: Duncan, Montgomery, Atwood, Laurence, and Munro." *Such a Simple Little Tale: Critical Responses to L. M. Montgomery's* Anne of Green Gables. Ed. Mavis Reimer. Metuchen, NJ; London: The Children's Literature Association and Scarecrow Press, 1992. 39-55. Compares Anne and Joan of *Lady Oracle*, especially in their use of the mirror double.

935. SAGE, Lorna. *Women in the House of Fiction.* New York: Routledge, 1992. See especially Chapter 5, "Divided among Ourselves," 153-193, and most particularly 161-168 which discusses Atwood's place among postwar women novelists.

936. St. PETER, Christine. "Eye to I, Tail to Tale: Atwood, Offred and the Politicized Classroom." *Atlantis* 17.2 (Spring-Summer 1992): 93-103. Outline given of the discussion of *The Handmaid's Tale* in a women's studies course; novel is used to provide a common point of departure.

937. SALYER, Gregory. "Signs, Symbols, and the Sacred: Representation and Meaning in Contemporary Literature." PhD thesis. Emory University, 1992. 238 pp. "This dissertation in the field of Religion and Literature examines current conceptualizations of the sacred and representation. It attempts to provide an answer to the question of how the sacred can be understood and represented in light of poststructuralism's problematization of all representation....Chapter Two shows how the differences between signs and religious symbols and sacred symbols play out in the life of the female narrator of Margaret Atwood's *Surfacing*." (Author). For more see *DAI-A* 53.04 (October 1992): 1148.

938. SENKPIEL, Aron. "From the Wild West to the Far North: Literary Representations of North America's Last Frontier." *Desert, Garden, Margin, Range: Literature on the American Frontier.* Ed. Eric Heyne. New York: Twayne, 1992. passim. Atwood's writings mentioned in terms of northern quest literature.

939. SHOEMAKER, Adam. "Crossing at the Intersection: Native Australian and Canadian Writing." *Meridian* 11.1 (May 1992): 4-13. Atwood cited (9), saying humor is absent from writings about native peoples.

940. SMYTH, Jacqui. "'Divided Down the Middle': A Cure for *The Journals of Susanna Moodie*." *Essays on Canadian Writing* 47 (Fall 1992): 149-162. Argues that Atwood's "Afterword" is an integral part of the work and should be read with the poems, not discarded.

941. STAELS, Hilde. "Metaphor and Mind-Style in Margaret *Atwood's Cat's Eye*." *BELL: Belgian Essays on Language and Literature* (1992): 91-108.

942. STEIN, Karen F. "Margaret Atwood's *The Handmaid's Tale*: Scheherazade in Dystopia." *University of Toronto Quarterly* 61.2 (Winter 1991-92): 269-279. The narrator and the narrative itself are examined, including issues of language, creating a self, the desire to tell one's story and the fear of doing so, and the multiple interpretations of a narrative.

943. STREHLE, Susan. *Fiction in the Quantum Universe.* Chapel Hill; London: The University of North Carolina Press, 1992. See especially "Margaret Atwood: *Cat's Eye* and the Subjective Author." 159-189. Subject and object are structured ac-

cording to the new physics and are shown in the use Atwood makes of time and tense.

944. STROBEL, Christina. "On the Representation of Representation in Margaret Atwood's *Surfacing*." *Zeitschrift für Anglistik und Amerikanistik* 40.1 (1992): 35-43. Painting and film are represented in a power structure which is deconstructed in the same process.

945. STUMMER, Peter O. "Perception of Difference: The Conceptual Interaction of Cultures in Literary Discourse." *Us / Them: Translation, Transcription and Identity in Post-Colonial Literary Cultures*. Ed. Gordon Collier. Amsterdam; Atlanta: Rodopi, 1992. 307-337. Atwood's "The Man from Mars" is cited as an example of the clash of culture.

946. TAYLOR, Donna Joyce. "The Development of a Computer-Generated Promptbook for Performance Studies." MA thesis. Arizona State University, 1992. Uses selections from *The Handmaid's Tale*.

947. THIEME, John. "A Female Houdini: Popular Culture in Margaret Atwood's *Lady Oracle*." *Kunapipi* 14 (1992): 71-80. Discusses the treatment of popular culture in a variety of Margaret Atwood's works.

948. THOMPSON, Lee Briscoe. "Atwood and Drabble: Life after Radiance." *Re-Siting Queen's English: Text and Tradition in Post-Colonial Literatures*. Ed. Gillian Whitlock and Helen Tiffin. Amsterdam; Atlanta: Rodopi, 1992. 37-46. Compares and contrasts the works of Drabble and Atwood; concludes both portray ordinary life in a similar but different fashion.

949. TSCHACHLER, Heinz. "Janus, Hitler, the Devil, and Co.: On Myth, Ideology, and the Canadian Postmodern." *Postmodern Fiction in Canada*. Ed. Theo D'haen and Hans Bertens. Amsterdam: Rodopi; Antwerp: Restant: 1992. 27-66. Atwood's use of myth and nationalism is examined, especially regarding victims and survival.

950. WALKER FIELDS, Ingrid. "Paranoia, Politics, and the Popular Imagination: Conspiracy in Contemporary American Literature." PhD thesis. University of California, Santa Cruz, 1992. 216 pp. "The postmodern American novel is acutely concerned with conspiracy theory as a form of narrative and political authority. In the works of Pynchon, Doctorow, Atwood and DeLillo, conspiracy emerges as the focal point of public memory and social resistance. This study traces conspiracy as a literary metaphor for a transformation in the American national identity, from a public besieged with internal enemies to one which identifies its own government as the internal enemy. Against these dynamics, narrative memory in the postmodern novel becomes a means of reconstructing and authorizing the political, personal and historical self. I identify three periods in this century's construction of conspiracy narratives: we have moved from a government-authorized narrative to a popular response to this narrative, back to the social text of this conspiracy dialectic, in search of a comprehensive construct." (Author). For more see *DAI-A* 53.12 (June 1993): 4325.

951. WEBB, Janeen. "Feminism and Science Fiction." *Meanjin* 51.1 (1992): 185-198. Examines *The Handmaid's Tale* in terms of female complicity leading to the situation described in the novel.

952. WEBER, Jean Jacques. *Critical Analysis of Fiction: Essays in Discourse Stylistics*. Amsterdam; Atlanta: Rodopi, 1992. See especially "The Process of Schema Liberation: Margaret Atwood's *Surfacing*." 65-81. A semiotic approach is used to analyze this novel by examining all meanings of the title.

953. WESSELING, Lies, and José van DIJCK. "The Issue of Responsibility in Margaret Atwood's *The Handmaid's Tale*." Against Patriarchal Thinking: Proceedings of
the 6th Symposium of the International Association of Women Philosophers
(IAPh) 1992. Ed. Maja Pellikaan-Engel. Amsterdam: VU UP, 1992. 243-251.

954. WHALEN, Terence. "The Future of a Commodity: Notes Toward a Critique of
Cyberpunk and the Information Age." *Science-Fiction Studies* 19.1 (March 1992):
75-88. Brief contrast of *The Handmaid's Tale* with cyberpunk fiction.

955. WHALEN-BRIDGE, John. "Outside the Whale: Reading the American Political
Novel in the Age of Reagan." PhD thesis. University of Southern California, 1992.
"There is a specific kind of book we call 'the political novel.' Only when we take
the American resistance to politicized literature into account can we appreciate the
artistry with which American novelists have presented political visions. [This the-
sis] critically reviews academic studies to demonstrate that definitions not
grounded in a particular historical moment are insufficient. Critics and theorists
reviewed include Speare, Milne, Blotner, Howe, Jameson, and Pease. A definition
of the political novel is then tested....[The chapter entitled] '*The Handmaid's Tale*
and the (Impure) Art of the Political Novel' examines the freedom with which a
non-American author artistically deploys the thematic of 'impurity' to organize an
anti-Fundamentalist political novel." (Author). For more see *DAI-A* 54.04 (October 1993): 1371.

956. WOOD, Diane S. "Bradbury and Atwood: Exile as Rational Decision." *The Literature of Emigration and Exile*. Ed. James Whitlark and Wendell Aycock. Lub-
bock: Texas Tech UP, 1992. 131-142. Choosing the hard life of the exile is prefer-
able to staying in a repressive society where books and reading are the objects of
government suppression.

957. YORK, Lorraine. "Prayers for Canadian Daughters: Gender Specificity and The
Parental Advice Poem." *Atlantis* 18.1-2 (Summer-Fall 1992): 60-69. "There are a
number of recent Canadian poems which offer advice to daughters, and all of them
revise the best-known twentieth-century example of this sub-genre: William Butler
Yeats's 'Prayer for My Daughter' (1921). Most of these are by women poets such
as Margaret Atwood, Mary di Michele, and Jan Conn, who re-write Yeats by turning his patriarchal advice upside-down; their strategy is one of contradiction and
correction. The case of Michael Ondaatje's 'To a Sad Daughter' complicates this
dynamic of corrective challenge, however, since, as a male poet whose subject position is inevitably gendered 'male,' Ondaatje must struggle with the Yeatsian authority within himself before he can proceed to revise his poetic Father. The process of revising the advice poem is subtly informed by the gender of the poetic re-
visor." (Journal abstract).

Reviews of Atwood's Works

958. *Cat's Eye.* Toronto: McClelland and Stewart; New York: Doubleday; London:
Bloomsbury, 1988.
    Indian Journal of Canadian Studies 1 (1992): 118-119. By Charu MAINI.

959. *For the Birds.* Toronto; Vancouver: Douglas and McIntyre, 1990.
    CCL: Canadian Children's Literature 65 (1992): 83-85. By J. GELLERT.

960. *Good Bones.* Toronto: Coach House Press; London: Bloomsbury, 1992.
    Books in Canada 21.7 (October 1992): 40-41. By Gary DRAPER.
    Financial Post (Toronto) 86.38 (21 September 1992): Section 1: S6.

By Araminta WORDSWORTH.

Globe and Mail (Toronto) 19 September 1992: C8. By Eve DROBOT.

Hamilton Spectator (ON) 17 October 1992: Section: Weekend: W4. By
   John LEVESQUE. (432 w).

Maclean's 105.40 (5 October 1992): s10-s11. By John BEMROSE. (1025 w).

Quill and Quire 58.10 (October 1992): 21. By Nancy WIGSTON.

Sunday Times (London) 8 November 1992: Section 6: 10. By Penny PERRICK.
   (653 w).

TLS 6 November 1992: 20. By Peter KEMP.

Toronto Star 26 September 1992: Section: Weekend: K9. By Philip
   MARCHAND. (841 w).

961. *The Handmaid's Tale.* [Sound recording]. Read by Joanna David. Bath, UK:
      Chivers Audio Books, 1990. 8 sound cassettes.
      Kliatt: Young Adult Paperback Book Guide 26 (January 1992):53. By Hugh M.
         FLICK.

962. *Margaret Atwood: Conversations.* Ed. Earl G. Ingersoll. Princeton, NJ: Ontario
      Review Press; Willowdale, ON: Firefly Books, 1990.
      Canadian Literature 132 (Spring 1992): 170-172. By Janice FIAMENGO.

963. *Poems 1976-1986.* London: Virago, 1992.
      The Herald (Glasgow) 30 January 1992: 14. By Julie Maurice. (779 w). Excerpt:
         "For poetry, it is remarkably unpoetic. It is difficult to imagine anyone finding
         a line or couplet from this book recurring rhythmically in their thoughts. Nor
         is striking sense imagery, which seals a corner of the world in a verbal crystal,
         a notable feature of her work. In fact there is none of that peculiarly poetic
         pleasure of slow savouring and careful unpeeling of sounds and sense, no lilt
         or tumble or exuberant wordy expressionism. Instead there are concentrated,
         hotly cerebral representations of life in the northern, civilised world at the end
         of the twentieth century; a life easy in itself, but uneasy at the messages it re-
         ceives from the edges of the global village."
      New Statesman and Society 14 February 1992: 41. By Michèle ROBERTS.
      Times Saturday Review (London) 8 February 1992: 33. By Adrian DANNATT.

964. *Selected Poems: 1966-1984.* Toronto: Oxford UP, 1990.
      Journal of Canadian Poetry 7 (1992): 7-13. By David JARRAWAY.

965. *Stories from Wilderness Tips.* [Sound recording]. Read by Helen Shaver. New
      York: Bantam Audio, 1991.
      Booklist 88.16 (15 April 1992): 1547. By Nancy McCRAY.
      Library Journal 117.3 (15 February 1992): 218, 220. By Rochelle RATNER.
      Publishers Weekly 239.2 (6 January 1992): 30. By John ZINSSER.

966. *Wilderness Tips.* Toronto: McClelland and Stewart; New York: Talese/Doubleday;
      London: Bloomsbury, 1991.
      Berkshire Eagle (Pittsfield, MA) 12 January 1992 LIT NewsBank 1992: 8:
         A14-B1. By Isabel K. ROCHE.
      The Bookwatch 13.2 (February 1992): 8. ANON.
      British Book News (August 1992): 569. Review/announcement of Virago edi-
         tion. ANON.
      Canadian Book Review Annual 1991. Ed. Joyce M. Wilson. Toronto: Simon
         and Pierre, 1992. 173. By Sarah ROBERTSON.
      Chicago Sun Times 8 December 1991 LIT NewsBank 1992: 1: C8-9. By Martin
         BRADY.

Detroit News 26 February 1992 LIT NewsBank 1992: 25: A14. By
   Domenica MARCHETTI.
Glamour January 1992: 72. By Laura MATHEWS.
*Grolier's Masterplots 1992 Annual: Essay-Reviews of 100 Outstanding Books
   Published in the United States during 1991*. Danbury, CT: Grolier Enterprises,
   1992. 386-389. By Elizabeth J. JEWELL.
Houston Chronicle 22 December 1991 LIT NewsBank 1992 1: C11. By Sally
   POIVOIR.
Kansas City Star 16 February 1992 LIT NewsBank 1992: 15: B1. By Charles G.
   MASINTON.
Magill's Literary Annual 1992 Vol. 2. Ed. Frank N. Magill. Pasadena, CA;
   Englewood Cliffs, NJ: Salem Press, 1992. 900-904. By Thomas L. ERSKINE.
Miami Herald 15 December 1991 LIT NewsBank 1992: 1: C6. ANON.
Milwaukee Journal 5 January 1992 LIT NewsBank 1992: 8: B4. By Steven
   BLACKWOOD.
Orlando Sentinel 22 December 1991 LIT NewsBank 1992: 1: C7. ANON.
Pittsburgh Post Gazette 27 January 1992 LIT NewsBank 1992: 9: E9. By Bob
   HOOVER.
Pittsburgh Press 23 February 1992 LIT NewsBank 1992: 15: B2. By Susan Har-
   ris SMITH.
San Francisco Examiner 9 December 1991 LIT NewsBank 1992 1: C4-5.
   By Cyra McFADDEN.
Seattle Times 12 January 1992: Section: Books: K7. By Melinda BARGREEN.
   (736 w).
University of Toronto Quarterly 62.1 (Fall 1992): 43. By T. L. CRAIG.
Washington Post 6 January 1992 Section: Style: C3. By Evelyn TOYNTON.
Women's Review of Books 9.4 (January 1992): 6-7. By Gayle GREENE.
World Literature Today 66.4 (Autumn 1992): 720. By B. A. St. ANDREWS.

Reviews of Adaptations of Atwood's Works

967.   *The Handmaid's Tale*. [Motion Picture]. Screenplay by Harold Pinter; directed by
   Volker Schlondorff. United States: Cinecom Entertainment Group, 112 reels of 12
   on 6 (ca. 9324 ft.).
      *Fantastic Cinema Subject Guide: A Topical Index to 2500 Horror, Science Fic-
      tion, and Fantasy Films*. Jefferson, NC; and London: McFarland, 1992. 245.
      By Bryan SENN and John JOHNSON.
      The Screenplay's the Thing: Movie Criticism 1986-1990. Hamden, CT: Archon
      Books, 1992. 250-253. By Bruce BAWER.
      Variety Movie Guide. New York; London; Toronto; Sydney; Tokyo; Singapore:
      Prentice Hall, 1992. 253.

~ 1993 ~

Atwood's Works

968. *A noiva ladra*. São Paulo: Marco Zero, ©1993. Portuguese translation of *The Robber Bride* by Maria J. Silveira.

969. "Afterword." *The Diviners*. By Margaret Laurence. Chicago: University of Chicago Press, 1993. 383-389. Reprinted from "Face to Face," *Maclean's*, May 1974.

970. "Afterword." *A Jest of God*. By Margaret Laurence. Chicago: University of Chicago Press, 1993. 211-215. Reprinted from 1988 edition, published by New Canadian Library / McClelland and Stewart.

971. "Alien Territory." *Michigan Quarterly Review* 32.4 (Fall 1993): 510-516. Special issue, "The Male Body (Part One)." Reprinted from *Good Bones*, ©1992.

972. *Aohige no tamago*. Tokyo: Chikuma Shobo, 1993. Japanese translation of *Bluebeard's Egg*. Title romanized.

973. "At the Tourist Centre in Boston." *The Broadview Anthology of Poetry*. Ed. Herbert Rosengarten and Amanda Goldrick-Jones. Peterborough, ON: Broadview Press, 1993. 828-829. Reprinted from *Selected Poems 1966-1984*.

974. "Bad News." *Mississippi Review* 21.1-2 (Spring 1993): 67-68. Short story. "Excerpted from *Good Bones*."

975. "Bearfeet." *Voix parallèles / Parallel Voices*. Ed. Andre Carpentier and Matt Cohen. Montreal: XYZ Editeur; Kingston, ON: Quarry Press, 1993. 145-151.

976. "Bearfeet." *Quarry* 42.1 (April 1993): 9-21. "Excerpted from *Parallel Voices / Voix parallèles*, co-published by Quarry Press and XYZ Editeur, in May 1993."

977. "Beloved." *Toni Morrison: Critical Perspectives Past and Present*. Ed. Henry Louis Gates Jr. and K. A. Appiah. New York: Amistad, 1993. 32-35. A review of Toni Morrison's *Beloved* reprinted from the *New York Times* 13 September 1987.

978. "Betty." *I Know Some Things: Stories about Childhood by Contemporary Writers*. Ed. Lorrie Moore. New York: Faber and Faber, 1993. 6-20. Reprinted from *Dancing Girls*, ©1977.

979. "Blind Faith and Free Trade." *The Case against Free Trade: GATT, NAFTA and the Globalization of Corporate Power*. San Francisco: Earth Island Press; Berkeley, CA: North Atlantic Books, 1993. 92-96. Reprinted from the *Ottawa Citizen*, 19 December 1987: B3.

980. "Cold-Blooded." *The Penguin Book of Lesbian Short Stories*. Ed. Margaret Reynolds. London; New York: Penguin, 1993. 384-[386]. Reprinted from *Good Bones*, ©1992.

981. *Dancing Girls and Other Stories*. New York; Toronto; London; Sydney; Auckland: Bantam Books, 1993 ©1977 ©1982. Same stories as 1977 Canadian edition.

982. *Dansende Meisjes*. Amsterdam: B. Bakker, 1993. Translation into Dutch of short stories selected from *Bluebeard's Egg and Other Stories* and *Dancing Girls and Other Stories* by Barbara de Lange.

983. "Death of a Young Son by Drowning." *The Broadview Anthology of Poetry*. Ed. Herbert Rosengarten and Amanda Goldrick-Jones. Peterborough, ON: Broadview Press, 1993. 833-834. Reprinted from *Selected Poems 1966-1984*.

984. *Die Giftmischer: Horror-Tips und Happy-Ends*. Frankfurt am Main: Fischer Tachenbuch, 1993 ©1985. German translation of *Murder in the Dark* by Anna Kamp.

985. "Dream 1: The Bush Garden." *The Broadview Anthology of Poetry*. Ed. Herbert Rosengarten and Amanda Goldrick-Jones. Peterborough, ON: Broadview Press, 1993. 834. Reprinted from *Selected Poems 1966-1984*.

986. "Dump Bins and Shelf Strips." *A Virago Keepsake to Celebrate Twenty Years of Publishing*. London: Virago, 1993. 6-8. Atwood's relationship with her British publishers.

987. "[Early writing, selections]." *First Words: Earliest Writing from Favorite Contemporary Authors*. Collected and ed. Paul Mandelbaum. Chapel Hill: Algonquin Books, 1993. 8-23. Selections of Atwood's prose and poetry written between ages of 15 through 19. Titles are "A Representative," "Three Cheers for Corona!," "1956—and For Ever," "First Snow," "The English Lesson," "Pause Before Transition," "A Cliché for January." Also includes 2-page facsimile of handwritten manuscript of "A Cliché for January," 3 photographs of Atwood (age 14, 20, and adult), and margin notes relating these pieces to her later works.

988. *The Edible Woman*. [Sound recording]. [Brantford]: WRMS, 1993. (Peterborough: Ontario Audio Library Service). 2 tape reels.

989. "[Excerpt]." *Great Beginnings: Opening Lines of Great Novels*. By Georgianne Ensign. New York: HarperCollins, 1993. 164. *Cat's Eye* is one of the selections.

990. "[Excerpt]." *Washington Post* 5 September 1993: Section: Book Page: X8. (166 w). From *The Robber Bride*

991. "[Excerpt]." *Women Without Men: Female Bonding and the American Novel of the 1980s*. By Donald J. Greiner. Columbia: University of South Carolina Press, 1993. 103. Excerpt from Atwood's review of *During the Reign of the Queen of Persia* (reprinted from *New York Times Book Review*, 12 June 1983).

992. *For the Birds*. Scarborough, ON: Nelson Canada, 1993 ©1990.

993. "Further Arrivals." *The Broadview Anthology of Poetry*. Ed. Herbert Rosengarten and Amanda Goldrick-Jones. Peterborough, ON: Broadview Press, 1993. 832-833. Reprinted from *Selected Poems 1966-1984*.

994. *Good Bones*. Toronto: Coach House Press; London: Virago, 1993 ©1992. 153. "First paperback edition." Same pieces as in hardcover Coach House Press edition, ©1992.

995. *Good Bones*. [Sound recording]. Read by Barbara Karmazyn. Vancouver, BC: Library Services Branch, 1993. 2 sound cassettes in 1 cont. (2:25 hrs.). "This audiobook is for the exclusive use of persons unable to read print because of a physical or visual disability." (Container).

996. "Grimms Remembered." *The Reception of Grimm's Fairy Tales: Responses, Reactions, Revisions*. Ed. Donald Haase. Detroit, MI: Wayne State UP, 1993. 290-292.

997. *The Handmaid's Tale*. Oxford: Heinemann New Windmills, 1993 ©1986.

998. *The Handmaid's Tale*. Charlesbourg, QU: Braille Jymico, 1993. Braille ed., abridged in 4 v.

999. "Happy Endings." *How Stories Mean*. Ed. John Metcalf and J. R. (Tim) Struthers. Erin, ON: Porcupine's Quill, 1993. 170-173. Reprinted from *Murder in the Dark: Short Fictions and Prose Poems*, ©1983.

1000. "He/She/It." *Queen's Quarterly* 100.1 (Spring 1993): 140-141. Poem. Reprinted from *Queen's Quarterly* 71.1 (Spring 1964): 40-41.

1001. "Homelanding." *The Norton Book of Science Fiction: North American Science Fiction, 1960-1990*. Ed. Ursula K. Le Guin and Brian Attebery. New York; London: W. W. Norton, 1993. 794-796. First published in *Tesseracts3*, 1990.

1002. *Hur Man Gör En Man: Och Andra Tidsenliga Betraktelser*. Stockholm: Prisma, 1993. Swedish translation of *Good Bones*.

1003. "In My Ravines." *Queen's Quarterly* 100.1 (Spring 1993): 142-143. Poem. Reprinted from *Queen's Quarterly* 71.1 (Spring 1964): 42-43.

1004. "Is/Not." *Love's Witness: Five Centuries of Love Poetry by Women*. Ed. Jill Hollis. New York: Carroll & Graf, 1993. 191. Reprinted from *Poems 1965-1975*, Virago. Also in *The Broadview Anthology of Poetry*. Ed. Herbert Rosengarten and Amanda Goldrick-Jones. Peterborough, ON: Broadview Press, 1993. 838-839.

1005. "Journey to the Interior." *The Broadview Anthology of Poetry*. Ed. Herbert Rosengarten and Amanda Goldrick-Jones. Peterborough, ON: Broadview Press, 1993. 827-828. Reprinted from *Selected Poems 1966-1984*.

1006. *Lady Oracle*. [Sound recording]. Edmonton: Alberta Education, 1993. 4 cassettes.

1007. *Lakomyi Kusochek*. St. Petersburg: Severo-Zapad, 1993. Russian translation of *The Edible Woman* by N. Tolstoi. Title romanized.

1008. "Letters to Salman Rushdie." *The Rushdie Letters: Freedom to Speak, Freedom to Write*. Ed. Steve MacDonogh in association with Article 19. Lincoln: University of Nebraska Press, 1993. "First published in 1993 in Great Britain and Ireland by Brandon Book Publishers Ltd., Dingle, Co. Kerry, Ireland. Published simultaneously in the United States by the University of Nebraska Press." Atwood is one of 25 writers contributing to this compilation.

1009. *Life Before Man; Cat's Eye*. London: Bloomsbury, 1993.

1010. "Life Is Short." *Voix parallèles / Parallel Voices*. Ed. Andre Carpentier and Matt Cohen. Montreal: XYZ Editeur; Kingston, ON: Quarry Press, 1993. 33-37. Atwood translation of "La vie est courte" by Monique Proulx.

1011. "Life Is Short." *Quarry* 42.1 (April 1993): 27-30. Atwood translation of "La vie est courte" by Monique Proulx. "Excerpted from *Parallel Voices / Voix parallèles*, co-published by Quarry Press and XYZ Editeur, in May 1993."

1012. "The Lively Dead." *Book World* (*Washington Post*) 23.36 (5 September 1993): 8. Excerpt from *The Robber Bride*.

1013. "The Loneliness of the Military Historian." *Book Group Companion to Margaret Atwood's* The Robber Bride. New York: Nan A. Talese / Doubleday, 1993. 22-24. Reprinted from *The Times Literary Supplement*, 14-20 September 1990. Poem.

1014. "Making Poison." *Myths and Voices: Contemporary Canadian Fiction*. Ed. David Lampe. Fredonia, NY: White Pine Press, 1993. 61-62.

1015. *Margaret Atwood Reads*. [Sound recording]. New York: Caedmon, 1993 ©1977. 1 sound cassette. Includes "The Animals in That Country," "A Foundling," "The Landlady," "At the Tourist Center in Boston," "Roominghouse, Winter," "Game After Supper," "Girl and Horse, 1928," "The Small Cabin," "Midwinter, Presolstice," "6 A.M., Boston Summer Sublet," "Dreams of the Animals," "Cyclops," "Younger Sister, Going Swimming," "Power Politics," "They Eat Out," "My

Beautiful Wooden Leader," "We Are Hard on Each Other," "At First I Was Given Centuries," "You Refuse to Own Yourself," "They Are Hostile Nations," "They Were All Inaccurate," "Tricks with Mirrors," "You Are Happy," "There Is Only One of Everything," "Late August," "Book of Ancestors." [Ed. note: Also published in 1992 under different title, *The Poetry and Voice of Margaret Atwood*, and by a different publisher—New York: HarperCollins.]

1016. "Margaret Atwood's Address to the American Booksellers Association Convention: Miami, Florida; June 1, 1993." *Book Group Companion to Margaret Atwood's* The Robber Bride. New York: Nan A. Talese / Doubleday, 1993. 7-13.

1017. "Monet's Olympia." *Ploughshares* 19.4 (1993): 83-84. Poem.

1018. "More and More." *Love's Witness: Five Centuries of Love Poetry by Women*. Ed. Jill Hollis. New York: Carroll & Graf, 1993. 267. Reprinted from *"Poems 1965-1975*, Virago."

1019. "Murder in the Dark." *Myths and Voices: Contemporary Canadian Fiction*. Ed. David Lampe. Fredonia, NY: White Pine Press, 1993. 63-65. Reprinted from *Murder in the Dark*.

1020. "Murder in Turkey." *New York Review of Books* 40.9 (13 May 1993): 57. Letter to the editors on murder of 13 journalists since January 1992; Atwood one of 20 writers signing letter.

1021. "Peau d'ours." *Voix parallèles / Parallel Voices*. Ed. Andre Carpentier and Matt Cohen. Montreal: XYZ Editeur; Kingston, ON: Quarry Press, 1993. 152-159. French translation of "Bearfeet" by Monique Proulx.

1022. "Peau d'ours." *Quarry* 42.1 (April 1993): 15-21. French translation of "Bearfeet" by Monique Proulx. "Excerpted from *Parallel Voices / Voix parallèles*, co-published by Quarry Press and XYZ Editeur, in May 1993."

1023. *The Poetry of Gwendolyn MacEwen. Volume One: The Early Years*. Ed. Margaret Atwood and Barry Callaghan. Introduction and introductory notes (vii-xii) by Margaret Atwood. Toronto: Exile Editions, 1993.

1024. "Progressive Insanities of a Pioneer." *The Broadview Anthology of Poetry*. Ed. Herbert Rosengarten and Amanda Goldrick-Jones. Peterborough, ON: Broadview Press, 1993. 830-832. Reprinted from *Selected Poems 1966-1984*.

1025. Promotional blurb, back dust-jacket flap for Thomas King's *Green Grass, Running Water*. Boston; New York: Houghton Mifflin, 1993. Reprinted from *Canadian Literature*.

1026. "Provence: Romans vs. Celts." *New York Times* 12 September 1993: Section 6: 17. (3751 w). Reflections on Provence (France) where she had spend some time the previous year.

1027. "Rape Fantasies." *Fiction: A HarperCollins Pocket Anthology*. [Ed.] R. S. Gwynn. New York: HarperCollins College Publishers, 1993. 294-301. Reprinted from *Dancing Girls and Other Stories*, ©1977.

1028. "The Robber Bride." *Saturday Night* October 1993: 56-61. "Excerpted from *The Robber Bride*"; photograph of Atwood by Suzanne Langevin; illustrations by Balvis Rubess.

1029. "The Robber Bride." *Sunday Times Books* 10 October 1993: Section 6: I-IV. "Chapter five is extracted from *The Robber Bride*"; photograph of Atwood by Lawrence Barns.

1030. *The Robber Bride*. Toronto: McClelland and Stewart, 1993. 546 pp. US edition: New York: Nan A. Talese / Doubleday, 1993. 466 pp. "A signed first edition of this book has been privately printed by The Franklin Library." UK edition: London: Bloomsbury, 1993. Limited edition of "150 copies, numbered and signed by the author" available from London Limited Editions (information from promotional letter from London Limited Editions). Three middle-aged women have little in common except Zenia, who slithered into their lives and stole their men, their money, and their self-respect. They believe that Zenia died years ago in Beirut, but her reappearance creates turmoil.

1031. *The Robber Bride.* Toronto: McClelland and Stewart; New York: Nan A. Talese / Doubleday, 1993. Large print edition.

1032. *The Robber Bride.* [Sound recording]. Read by Blythe Danner. New York: Bantam Doubleday Dell Audio Pub., 1993.

1033. "The Robber Bridegroom." *Book Group Companion to Margaret Atwood's* The Robber Bride. New York: Nan A. Talese / Doubleday, 1993. 20. Reprinted from *Selected Poems II: Poems Selected and New 1976-1986,* ©1986.

1034. *Rouva Oraakkeli.* Helsinki: Kirjayhtymä, 1993. Finnish translation of *Lady Oracle* by Marja Haapio.

1035. "The Santa Claus Trap." *Canadian Christmas Stories in Prose and Verse.* Ed. Don Bailey and Daile Unruh. Toronto: CNIB, 1993. Braille ed., 4 v. Based on 1990 edition.

1036. *Senhora do Oráculo.* [Lisbon]: Circulo de Leitores, 1993. Portuguese translation of *Lady Oracle* by Maria Antónia Vasconcelos.

1037. "She." *Book Group Companion to Margaret Atwood's* The Robber Bride. New York: Nan A. Talese / Doubleday, 1993. 21-22. Poem. Reprinted from *Selected Poems II: Poems Selected and New 1976-1986.*

1038. "Siren Song." *Book Group Companion to Margaret Atwood's* The Robber Bride. New York: Nan A. Talese / Doubleday, 1993. 20-21. Poem. Also published in *The Green Book of Poetry.* Compiled and ed. Ivo Mosley. Kirstead, UK: Frontier, 1993, 252-253, and in Poetry*: A HarperCollins Pocket Anthology.* Ed. R. S. Gwynn. New York: HarperCollins College Publishers, 1993. 290-291. Reprinted from *You Are Happy,* ©1974.

1039. "Spotty-Handed Villainesses: Problems of Female Bad Behaviour in the Creation of Literature." Originally delivered as an address in the Cheltenham Lecture Series, University of Gloucester, 8 October 1993. Later published in *Moving Targets: Writing with Intent 1982-2004.* By Margaret Atwood. Toronto: Anansi, 2004. 157-172, and in *Curious Pursuits: Occasional Writing 1970-2005.* London: Virago, 2005, 171-186, as well as in *Writing with Intent: Essays, Reviews, Personal Prose, 1983-2005.* New York: Carroll & Graf Publishers, 2005. 125-138.

1040. "There Was Once." *Mississippi Review* 21.1-2 (Spring 1993): 69-71. "Excerpted from *Good Bones.*"

1041. "This Is a Photograph of Me." *Book Group Companion to Margaret Atwood's* The Robber Bride. New York: Nan A. Talese / Doubleday, 1993. Back cover. Reprinted from *The Circle Game,* ©1966.

1042. "This Is a Photograph of Me." *The Broadview Anthology of Poetry.* Ed. Herbert Rosengarten and Amanda Goldrick-Jones. Peterborough, ON: Broadview Press, 1993. 827. Reprinted from *Selected Poems 1966-1984,* ©1990.

1043. "Thoughts from Underground." *The Broadview Anthology of Poetry.* Ed. Herbert Rosengarten and Amanda Goldrick-Jones. Peterborough, ON: Broadview Press, 1993. 834-835. Reprinted from *Selected Poems 1966-1984,* ©1990.

1044. *Tip Om Overlevelse: Noveller.* [Copenhagen]: Lindhardt og Ringhof, 1993 ©1991. Danish translation of *Wilderness Tips* by Lisbeth Møller-Madsen.

1045. "Tricks with Mirrors." *The Broadview Anthology of Poetry*. Ed. Herbert Rosengarten and Amanda Goldrick-Jones. Peterborough, ON: Broadview Press, 1993. 836-838. Reprinted from *Selected Poems 1965-1975*.

1046. *Ukabiagaru = Surfacing*. Tokyo: Shinsuisha, 1993. Japanese translation of *Surfacing*. Title romanized.

1047. "Unpopular Gals." *Mississippi Review* 21.1-2 (Spring 1993): 72-74. "Excerpted from *Good Bones*."

1048. "Variation on the Word *Sleep*." *Into the Garden: A Wedding Anthology*. Ed. Robert Haas and Stephen Mitchell. New York: HarperCollins, 1993. 30-31. Reprinted from *Selected Poems II: Poems Selected and New 1976-1986*, ©1987.

1049. "Variations on the Word *Love*." *Love's Witness: Five Centuries of Love Poetry by Women*. Ed. Jill Hollis. New York: Carroll & Graf, 1993. 20-21. Reprinted from *True Stories*, Cape.

1050. *Verletzungen: Roman*. Hildesheim: Claassen, 1993. German translation of *Bodily Harm* by Werner Waldhoff.

1051. "The Victory Burlesk." *Myths and Voices: Contemporary Canadian Fiction*. Ed. David Lampe. Fredonia, NY: White Pine Press, 1993. 59-60. Reprinted from *Murder in the Dark*.

1052. "Waking at 3 A.M." *On William Stafford: The Worth of Local Things*. Ed. Tom Andrews. Ann Arbor: University of Michigan Press, 1993. 249-252. Reprinted from *Field* 41 (Fall 1989).

1053. "Werewolf Movies." *The Faber Book of Movie Verse*. Ed. Philip French and Ken Wlaschin. London; Boston: Faber and Faber: 1993. 339-340. Reprinted from *Poems 1976-1986* (1992) and from *Selected Poems II: Poems Selected & New 1976-1986* (1986).

1054. "Why I Write: To Give as Well as Receive." *Quill and Quire* 59.8 (August 1993): 1, 21. "Text of a talk given at the American Booksellers Association convention in June." See also: *Toronto Star* 5 June 1993: Section: Weekend: G11. (1053 w).

1055. *Wilderness Tips*. New York; Toronto; London; Sydney; Auckland: Bantam Books, 1993. 297. Same stories as US and Canadian hardcover editions, 1991. At end, 16 unnumbered pages of excerpts from other Atwood titles published by Bantam: *The Edible Woman, Bodily Harm, Dancing Girls and Other Stories, Cat's Eye*.

1056. *Wilderness Tips*. Bath [England]: Chivers Press; Hampton, NH: Eagle Large Print, 1993, 1991. Large print edition.

1057. *Wilderness Tips*. [Sound recording]. Read by Denica Fairman. Bath, UK: Sterling Audio: Chivers Audio, 1993. 6 sound cassettes (8 hr., 18 min.).

1058. "A Woman's Issue." *Ain't I a Woman! A Book of Women's Poetry from Around the World*. Ed. Illona Linthwaite. New York; Avenel, NJ: Wings Books, 1993. 135-136. Reprinted from *True Stories*, Oxford UP, ©1981.

1059. "Women's Novels." *Harper's* 286.1716 (May 1993): 32-33. Reprinted from *Murder in the Dark*, ©1983.

Adaptations of Atwood's Works

1060. *Bestiary: For Soprano, Clarinet, Horn and Piano*. Musical Score: Printed music , 1993. 1 score (31 p.) + score in C (36 p.) + parts. Includes Atwood poem, "Landcrab" set to music by David Garner for San Francisco's Beaumont Ensemble. Copy of score available in the San Francisco Academy of Music. (Worldcat); see also Garner's website http://www.davidgarner.com /pages/Chamber_ Music7.php? project_id=7.

Quotations

1061. "[Quote]." *21st Century Dictionary of Quotations*. Ed. The Princeton Language Institute. Produced by The Philip Lief Group, Inc. New York: Dell (Laurel), 1993. 469.
1062. "[Quote]." In advertisement in *The Green Bird* playbill, Yale Repertory Theatre, 27 November-18 December 1993: 19.
1063. "[Quote]." *Toronto Star* 7 March 1993: Section: People: D4. In article headed "What Canadians Say," Atwood is quoted: "A divorce is like an amputation; you survive but there is less of you." [1972].
1064. "[Quote]." *Toronto Star* 1 May 1993: Section: Weekend: J16. Atwood quoted in connection with upcoming joke book, *All Men Are Bastards*: "What do you call field full of men? A vacant lot."
1065. "[Quotes]." *The Columbia Dictionary of Quotations*. Compiled by Robert Andrews. New York: Columbia UP, 1993. 96, 116, 352, 575, 711, 994, 1019.
1066. "[Quotes]." *The Harper Book of Quotations*. 3rd ed. Ed. Robert I. Fitzhenry. New York: HarperCollins (HarperPerennial), 1993. 78, 159, 269, 484. Four Atwood quotes. "This book is published in Canada by Fitzhenry and Whiteside Limited under the title *The Fitzhenry and Whiteside Book of Quotations*, Revised and Enlarged."
1067. "[Quotes]." *Northrop Frye: A Visionary Life*. By Joseph Adamson. Toronto: ECW Press, 1993. passim. Various comments on Frye from Atwood's written and spoken tributes. Includes 1983 photo (66) of Frye, George Ignatieff, and Atwood when she received an honorary degree at the University of Toronto.
1068. "[Quotes]." *The Penguin Dictionary of Twentieth-Century Quotations*. Compiled by J. M. Cohen and M. J. Cohen. London; New York; Victoria; Toronto; Auckland: Viking, 1993. 16-17. Six quotes.

Interviews

1069. BANCROFT, Colette M. "Author Atwood Is Fascinated with Dynamics of Her Villain." *Arizona Daily Star* (Tucson), 7 November 1993: LIT NewsBank 1993: 94: B3-4.
1070. CLOSE, Ajay. "Thief of Hearts." *Scotland on Sunday* 10 October 1993: s.p. (1349 w). Available from Lexis-Nexis.
1071. CRAIG, Paul. "Atwood Shares Tales, Truths in Davis." *Sacramento Bee* 16 February 1993: LIT NewsBank 1993: 26: B3-4.
1072. DENISON, D. C. "The Interview: Margaret Atwood." *Boston Globe* 19 December 1993: LIT NewsBank 1993: 6: B11-12.
1073. GOOCH, Brad. "A Handmade Tale." *The Advocate* (Los Angeles) 2 November 1993: 52-53.
1074. GRAEBER, Laurel. "Zenia Is Sort of Like Madonna." *New York Times Book Review* 31 October 1993: 22. Sidebar to Moore's review of *The Robber Bride* (see 1201).

1075. ITALIE, Hillel. "Atwood Enjoys Surprising Readers." *Chicago Sun-Times* 26 December 1993: Section: Show: 16C. (761 w). On occasion of the publication of *The Robber Bride*.

1076. KELLAWAY, Kate. "Oracle and Private Joker." *The Observer* (London) 10 October 1993: 16. (1109 w). Excerpt: "As a young writer, she was patronised or described as 'cute.' When she was the same age as her interviewers, they were 'jealous' of her achievements and now that she is older than most of the journalists she meets, she enjoys being the sage, likes to give advice. 'If I were an uncle I would be avuncular. I say things like 'Time will heal all—I even have the shawl.' Does she also like to ask for advice? 'I have no need to ask for advice, except on technical matters.'"

1077. LEVESQUE, John. "In This Corner: Margaret Atwood." *Hamilton Spectator* (ON) 1 November 1993: Section: Now: D1. (931 w). In anticipation of a reading in Hamilton. A testy interview.

1078. LYALL, Sarah. "An Author Who Lets Women Be Bad Guys." *New York Times* 23 November 1993: Section: C: 13. (1221 w). Atwood on the women in *The Robber Bride*. Zenia has "been around since Delilah, so why wouldn't she come back? She'll be back in another form, in another book."

1079. MARCHAND, Philip. "Atwood's Warrior Woman Confronts Feminist Notion." *Toronto Star* 9 October 1993: Section: Weekend: J5. (846 w). About Atwood's interest in military history and how military historians are much like novelists.

1080. McELROY, James. "The Ancient Mariner Experience: An Interview with Margaret Atwood." *Writing on the Edge* 5.1 (Fall 1993): 45-52.

1082. RICHARDS, Beth. "Interview with Margaret Atwood." *Prairie Schooner* 67.4 (Winter 1993): 8-12. Focus on *Cat's Eye*.

1083. RITCHIE, Harry. "Come into the Garden." *Sunday Times Books* 10 October 1993: Section 6: 8-9. Photograph of Atwood by Sally Soames. An interview conducted in the back yard of her home. **On the Margaret Atwood Society:** "I don't think you should give it the same weight as the Rolling Stones Fan Club. It seems to be an assemblage of academics. I thought of sending them a T-shirt for their opening meeting with 'Atwood Lives' on it. The best thing that an academic ever said to me was, 'You've written enough for us by now.' In other words, drop dead and we can deal with your texts. Some critics prefer a writer to be dead, because then the writer can never write anything that will contradict what has been said by the critic."

1084. ROSS, Val. "Playing the Atwood Guessing Game." *Globe and Mail* 7 October 1993: Section: C: 1-2.

1085. SMITH, Stephen. "Atwood Tells Story Behind Latest Novel." *Financial Post* 87.40 (2 October 1993): S6.

1086. STEPHENSON, Anne. "Atwood at Her Best: 'Feminist' Novelist Achieves Acclaim as Author, Respect as Person." *Arizona Republic* (Phoenix) 15 November 1993: LIT NewsBank 1993: 94: B1-2.

1087. WACHTEL, Eleanor. *Writers and Company*. Toronto; New York; London; Sydney; Auckland: Alfred A. Knopf Canada, 1993. 190-203. "Interview prepared in collaboration with Sandra Rabinovitch."

1088. WINEGAR, Karin. "Atwood Gives Us a Wicked Woman." *Star Tribune* (Minneapolis, MN): Section: Variety: 1E. (1232 w). Interview by telephone about *The Robber Bride* in advance of Atwood's visit to Minneapolis. This tricky, shapeshifting Zenia, says Atwood, is most like the author herself. "She tells huge whoppers that she tries to get other people to believe, and what is a novel but huge whoppers that you try to get other people to believe?" said Atwood. "The difference is I put labeling on mine that says at the front 'this is fiction.' And Zenia doesn't. But if she weren't such a manipulative operator, maybe she'd be a novelist." She added: "The original story, 'The Robber Bridegroom' is a tale of a wicked maiden-devouring monster—so why did I change it? Well, I was sitting around one day thinking to myself, where have all the Lady Macbeths gone? Gone to Ophelias, every one, leaving the devilish tour de force parts to be played by bass-baritones. Or to put it another way: if all women are well behaved by nature—or if we aren't allowed to say otherwise for fear of being accused of anti-femaleism—then they are deprived of moral choice, and there isn't much left for them to do in books except run away a lot. Or, to put it another way: equality means equally bad as well as equally good."

Scholarly Resources

1089. "Atwood, Margaret (1939–)." *Modern Mystery, Fantasy and Science Fiction Writers*. Compiled and ed. Bruce Cassiday. New York: Continuum, 1993. 30-37. Collection of excerpts from reviews and essays on *The Handmaid's Tale*.

1090. *Book Group Companion to Margaret Atwood's* The Robber Bride. New York: Nan A. Talese / Doubleday, 1993. 28 pp. Intended to promote reading and discussion of Atwood's new novel; contents are "Introduction to the Book Group Companion," "Margaret Atwood: Biography," "From Sandra Martin's Review of *The Robber Bride* from *Quill and Quire*," "Margaret Atwood's Address to the American Booksellers Association Convention 1993," "'The Robber Bridegroom' by the Brothers Grimm, Translation by Jack Zipes," "Selected Poems of Margaret Atwood," "Topics for Group Discussion," "Miscellany"; primary items and review excerpt cited separately in this section. Also available online: http://www.randomhouse.com /resources/bookgroup/robberbride_bgc.html.

1091. AGUIAR, Sarah Appleton. "Nolite Te Bastardes Carborundorum: Body Politics and *The Handmaid's Tale*." *Postscript: A Journal of Graduate School Criticism and Theory* 1.1 (1993): 49-63.

1092. AHEARN, Catherine. "An Archetype of Pain: From Plath to Atwood and Musgrave." *Still the Frame Holds: Essays on Women Poets and Writers*. Ed. Sheila Roberts and Yvonne Pacheco Tevis. San Bernardino: Borgo, 1993. 137-156.

1093. AHERN, Stephen. "'Meat like You like It': The Production of Identity in Atwood's *Cat's Eye*." *Canadian Literature* 137 (Summer 1993): 8-17. Elaine is unable to resolve her problem because she is treated both as a subject, able to work toward her own goals, and as an object, judged by a society rooted in patriarchal ideology.

1094. ANDRIANO, Joseph. "*The Handmaid's Tale* as Scrabble Game." *Essays on Canadian Writing* 48 (Winter 1992-93): 89-96. Analysis of the game and its use of words in the nonword Gilead.

1095. BACCOLINI, Raffaella. "'What's in a Name?': Language and Self-Creation in Women's Writing." *The Representation of the Self in Women's Autobiography*. Ed. Vita Fortunati and Gabriella Morisco. Bologna: Univ. of Bologna, 1993. 44-64. Focus on Atwood.

1096. BARR, Marleen S. *Lost in Space: Feminist Science Fiction and Beyond*. Chapel Hill; London: University of North Carolina Press, 1993. See especially "Ms. Sammler's Planet: Margaret Atwood, Saul Bellow, and Joanna Russ Rescue the

Female Child's Story." 196-222. Barr sees *Cat's Eye* as logical follow-up to the dystopian *The Handmaid's Tale*; speculative science fiction allows the female childhood story to be recaptured.

1097. BEDDOES, Julie. "Changing Moodie: Author Constructions in a Canadian 'Classic.'" *English Studies in Canada* 19.3 (September 1993): 363-377. Comments upon Atwood's influence in recognizing Moodie and quotes from Atwood's "Afterword" in her *The Journals of Susanna Moodie*.

1098. BERAN, Carol. *Living over the Abyss: Margaret Atwood's* Life Before Man. Toronto: ECW Press, 1993. 99 pp. Presents background to novel and summary of its critical reception as well as exploring the novel's themes and issues.

1099. BIEBER, David C. "The Machinery of Patriarchy: Masculinity in the Fiction of Margaret Atwood." MA thesis. Carleton University, 1993. Also available on microfiche from Canadian Theses Service (1993). "Critical discussion of Margaret Atwood's fiction has centred upon her representation of femininity as a subject position within patriarchy; her female characters reveal a limited range of acceptable roles for women, ones which fit into and perpetuate the power relations of a society that Atwood has described as a machine which either incorporates or destroys the individual. Recent work in gender theory strengthens the argument that masculinity is also a subject position created by the culture accompanying a patriarchal order. Atwood's male characters accordingly reveal the constructed nature of conventional masculinity, and its function in positioning individual men into roles which work to maintain the machine of the given social order. Atwood subverts the (re)production of patriarchy at the level of the individual subject by positioning some of her male characters outside the hierarchical roles of dominance or submission forming the parameters of conventional gender difference. The result is a body of work which explores the conservative nature of masculinity as the function of an historically specific hierarchical social organization." (Author). For more see *MAI* 32.03 (June 1994): 804.

1100. BIGNELL, Jonathan. "Lost Messages: *The Handmaid's Tale*, Novel and Film." *British Journal of Canadian Studies* 8.1 (1993): 71-84.

1101. BLODGETT, E. D. "Is a History of the Literatures of Canada Possible?" *Essays on Canadian Writing* 50 (Fall 1993): 1-18. Uses Atwood's *Lady Oracle* and *The Handmaid's Tale* as examples of literary history. Also quotes Atwood's *Survival* to support the concept of literary history.

1102. BOILY, Lise. "On the Semiosis of Corporate Culture." *Semiotica* 93.1-2 (1993): 5-31. Atwood's *Survival* is used to support the concept that Canadian literature reflects the sociocultural context.

1103. BOUSON, J. Brooks. *Brutal Choreographies: Oppositional Strategies and Narrative Design in the Novels of Margaret Atwood*. Amherst: University of Massachusetts Press, 1993. 204. Atwood's first 7 novels reveal a common use of narrative forms to enact her psychological and political themes.

1104. BRADFORD, Kelly Jean. "Margaret Atwood: The Significance of Storytelling." MA thesis. Western Illinois University, 1993.

1105. CARRINGTON, Ildikó de Papp. "Margaret Atwood (1939–)." *ECW's Biographical Guide to Canadian Novelists*. Ed. Robert Lecker, Jack David, and Ellen Quigley. Toronto: ECW Press, 1993. 239-243. Biographical sketch.

1106. CHANDLER, Joel C. "Gender and the Search for Meaning in Margaret Atwood's *Surfacing* and Thomas McGuane's *Ninety-Two in the Shade*." MA thesis. Georgia State University, 1993.

1107. CHANDRA, Suresh. "Women's Liberation in the Fiction of Margaret Atwood and Shashi Deshpande." *Meerut Journal of Comparative Literature and Language* 6.2 (1993): 77-85.

1108. CLARK, Miriam Marty. "After Epiphany: American Stories in the Postmodern Age." *Style* 27.3 (Fall 1993): 387-94. Selfhood and meaning in Atwood and American writers are examined.

1109. CLAYTON, Jay. The Pleasures of Babel: Contemporary American Literature and Theory. New York; Oxford: Oxford UP, 1993. passim. References to *Bodily Harm* and *Surfacing*.

1110. COLES EDITORIAL BOARD. The Edible Woman. *Notes*. Toronto: Coles, ©1993. 121 pp. Study notes.

1111. CONBOY, Sheila C. "Scripted, Conscripted, and Circumscribed: Body Language in Margaret Atwood's *The Handmaid's Tale.*" *Anxious Power: Reading, Writing, and Ambivalence in Narrative by Women.* Ed. Carol J. Singley and Susan Elizabeth Sweeney. Albany: State University of New York Press, 1993. 349-362. Reading and language, grounded in the body, are oppressive for women rather than expressive.

1112. CONDÉ, Mary. "The Male Immigrant in Two Canadian Stories." *Kunapipi* 15.1 (1993): 103-109. Alice Munro's "Oranges and Apples" and Margaret Atwood's "Wilderness Tips."

1113. ———. "Visible Immigrants in Three Canadian Women's Fictions of the Nineties." *Études canadiennes / Canadian Studies: Revue Interdisciplinaire des études canadiennes en France* 19.34 (1993): 91-100. Atwood's "Wilderness Tips" set off against Sky Lee's *Disappearing Moon Café* and Alice Munro's "Oranges and Apples."

1114. CROSBIE, Lynn. "Like a Hook into a Cat's Eye: Locating Margaret Atwood's Susie." *Tessera* 15 (1993): 30-41.

1115. CROWDER, Diane Griffin. "Separatism and Feminist Utopian Fiction." *Sexual Practice / Textual Theory: Lesbian Cultural Criticism.* Ed. Susan J. Wolfe and Julia Penelope. Cambridge, MA; Oxford: Blackwell, 1993. 244-245. Dystopian visions are examined in *The Handmaid's Tale.*

1116. CUDER-DOMINGUEZ, Pilar. "La Narrativa de Margaret Atwood como romance." PhD thesis. Sevilla: Universidad de Sevilla, 1993. 362 pp.

1117. DAVEY, Frank. *Post-National Arguments: The Politics of the Anglophone-Canadian Novel since 1967.* Toronto; Buffalo; London: University of Toronto Press, 1993. See especially "Individualist Nationalism: *Cat's Eye*." 223-239. Develops chapter's thesis based on localisms found in the novel.

1118. DeBOER, Ron B. "Margaret Atwood and the Cultural Landscape." MA thesis. University of Waterloo, 1993. 97 pp. Also available on microfiche from Canadian Theses Service (1993). "In the context of this paper's problematization of modern advertising, gender roles within advertising, and culture at large, Atwood's feminist agenda in works from *The Circle Game* to *Good Bones* continues to discover truths about the role of women in society. Atwood problematizes women's positions in society, drawing in her works images of entrapment, dismemberment, immobility, and binary oppositions in meaning between head and the body. While many of Atwood's characters 'emerge' from her novels with greater understanding and realization, all are constructs of a male-empowered consumer marketplace which emits violent sexual imagery, whether through glamorized rape scenes in advertising or commonplace notions about pornography portrayed as acceptable. Finally, the premise of this paper is to show that modern society's insistence that women have the freedom to do as they please is a thin veneer, strategically coated by a consumer-based power structure that, in fact, ensnares women attempting to live out an ideal of freedom. Atwood's Gileadian society in *Handmaid's Tale* serves as true freedom to women, a freedom from the constraints and entrapments of cosmetic surgery, make-up, fashion consciousness, weight-loss obsession and sexual violence." (Author). For more see *MAI* 32.01 (February 1994): 56.

1119. DUNCKER, Patricia. "Heterosexuality: Fictional Agendas." *Heterosexuality: A Feminism and Psychology Reader*. Ed. Sue Wilkinson and Celia Kitzinger. London; Newbury Park; New Delhi: Sage Publications, 1993. 137-149. *Life Before Man*, *The Edible Woman*, and Jenny Diski's *Nothing Natural* are examined with regard to heterosexuality as a social and sexual institution.

1120. DURIX, Carole, and Jean-Pierre DURIX. *An Introduction to the New Literatures in English*. Paris: Longman France, 1993. 206 pp. Section on Atwood (151-154) provides an introduction to her work as an important Canadian writer.

1121. EPSTEIN, Grace A. "*Bodily Harm*: Female Containment and Abuse in the Romance Narrative." *Genders* 16 (Spring 1993): 80-93. A meaningful narrative is constructed over the romance narrative as Rennie struggles for control of her body and her story.

1122. ———. "Nothing to Fight For: Repression of the Romance Plot in Harold Pinter's Screenplay of *The Handmaid's Tale*." *Pinter Review: Annual Essays 1992-93*. Ed. Francis Gillen and Steven H. Gale. Tampa, FL: University of Tampa Press, 1993. 54-60.

1123. FARWELL, Marilyn R. "Toward a Definition of the Lesbian Literary Imagination." *Sexual Practice / Textual Theory: Lesbian Cultural Criticism*. Ed. Susan J. Wolfe and Julia Penelope. Cambridge, MA; Oxford: Blackwell, 1993. 66. A mention of Atwood's review of Adrienne Rich's *Diving into the Wreck*.

1124. FEE, Margery. *The Fat Lady Dances: Margaret Atwood's* Lady Oracle. Toronto: ECW Press, 1993. 95. Presents background to novel and summary of its critical reception as well as exploring the novel's themes and issues.

1125. FILIPCZAK, Dorota. "Is There No Balm in Gilead? Biblical Intertext in *The Handmaid's Tale*." *Literature and Theology* 7.2 (June 1993): 171-185. Traces the use of Gilead in the Bible and its associations that appear in *The Handmaid's Tale* to see whether it is used to enforce the structure of that society or whether the society is a consequence of the Biblical reality.

1126. FINNELL, Susanna. "Unwriting the Quest: Margaret Atwood's Fiction and *The Handmaid's Tale*." *Women and the Journey: The Female Travel Experience*. Ed. Bonnie Frederick and Susan H. McLeod. Pullman: Washington State UP, 1993. 199-215. The traditional quest/journey motif takes on a new subject, the female, in Atwood's novels, especially *The Handmaid's Tale*.

1127. FRYE, Northrop. *The Eternal Act of Creation: Essays, 1979-1990*. Ed. Robert D. Denham. Bloomington; Indianapolis: Indiana UP, 1993. Atwood's poem "Journey to the Interior" is briefly discussed in essay titled "Levels of Cultural Identity" (177); Atwood quoted in "Introduction" (xvii-xviii) as to the great influence Frye had upon Canadian literature.

1128. GADPAILLE, Michelle. "Odalisques in Margaret Atwood's *Cat's Eye*." *Metaphor and Symbolic Activity* 8.3 (1993): 221-226. Odalisques are examined as a metaphor for sexual and imperial domination in *Cat's Eye*. [Ed. note: An odalisque was a female slave or concubine in the Ottoman seraglio, tending to the harem of the Turkish sultan. The word appears in a French form, and originates from the Turkish odalık, meaning "chambermaid," from oda, "chamber" or "room." Various writers spell the word as odahlic, odalisk, and odaliq. An odalisque was not a concubine of the harem, but she could possibly become one. Odalisques were the virgin slaves of the harem, where they were at the bottom of the social ladder, serving not the sultan himself but rather his concubines and wives as personal chambermaids.]

1129. GERNES, Sonia. *North American Women Writers: Spirit and Society.* [Video-recording]. Florence, KY: Brenzel Pub.; Chicago: Public Media Education, 1993. VHS tape, 2 videocassettes (170 min.). On the tape, Professor Sonia Gernes discusses 6 women authors—Edith Wharton, Flannery O'Connor, Toni Morrison, Marilynne Robinson, Leslie Marmon Silko, and Margaret Atwood—reviewing their work and highlighting important themes.

1130. GERRY, Thomas M. F. *Contemporary Canadian and U.S. Women of Letters: An Annotated Bibliography.* New York: Garland, 1993. Includes Atwood.

1131. GREENE, Gayle, Ann Rosalind JONES, and Linda S. KAUFFMAN, eds. *Changing Subjects: The Making of Feminist Literary Criticism.* London; New York: Routledge, 1993. Passing mention of Atwood in chapters by Gayle Greene

1132. GRIFFIN, Gabriele. *The Influence of the Writings of Simone Weil on the Fiction of Iris Murdoch.* San Francisco: Mellen Research UP, 1993. 49-50. *The Handmaid's Tale* and *Surfacing* are cited, the former as an example of differences between men and women and the latter as an example of rebirth.

1133. GROENING, Laura Smith. *E. K. Brown: A Study in Conflict.* Toronto; Buffalo, NY; London: University of Toronto Press, 1993. 90, 118. Brief mention of Margaret Atwood.

1134. HENGEN, Shannon. Margaret Atwood's Power: Mirrors, Reflections and Images in Select Fiction and Poetry. Toronto: Second Story Press, 1993.

1135. HERMES, Liesel. "Modern Women Writers: Versuch Einer Einführung." *Neusprachliche Mitteilungen aus Wissenschaft und Praxis* 46.4 (1993): 217-227. Includes discussion of Atwood's "Happy Endings."

1136. HERNDL, Diane Price. *Invalid Women: Figuring Feminine Illness in American Fiction and Culture, 1840-1940.* Chapel Hill; London: University of North Carolina Press, 1993. Uses quote from *The Handmaid's Tale* ("An invalid, one who has been invalidated") as forequote to "Introduction" and as discussion in summary on page 218 to define nuance of title.

1137. HOLTZE, Elizabeth A. "Sirens and Their Song." *Woman's Power, Man's Game: Essays on Classical Antiquity in Honor of Joy K. King.* Ed. Mary DeForest. Wauconda, IL: Bolchazy-Carducci Publishers, 1993. 392-414. Cites "Siren Song" and "Circe/Mud Poems" to illustrate that the Siren tells the story from her perspective rather than from the male adventurer; this changes one's view of the singers and suggests that women poets will offer a different interpretation.

1138. HORNE, Helen Marion. "Revisionist Mythmaking: The Use of the Fairy Tale Motif in the Works of Angela Carter, Margaret Atwood and Anne Sexton." MLitt thesis. University of Newcastle upon Tyne, 1993. 123 pp.

1139. HOWELLS, Coral Ann. *Margaret Atwood,* The Handmaid's Tale: *Notes.* Beirut: York Press; Harlow: Longman, 1993. 88. Cover title: *York Notes on* The Handmaid's Tale.

1140. HUTCHEON, Linda. "Eruptions of Postmodernity: The Postcolonial and the Ecological." *Essays on Canadian Writing* 51-52 (Winter 1993-Spring 1994): 146-163. Discussion of Canada's identity; *Survival* briefly mentioned.

1141. INGERSOLL, Earl. "Margaret Atwood's *The Handmaid's Tale*: Echoes of Orwell." *Journal of the Fantastic in the Arts* 5.3 (1993): 64-72. Compares Offred and Winston as narrators.

1142. IRVINE, Lorna. *Collecting Clues: Margaret Atwood's* Bodily Harm. Toronto: ECW Press, 1993. 113 pp. Presents background to novel and summary of its critical reception as well as exploring the novel's themes and issues.

1143. JACKSON, Kevin. "The Trappings of Disaster." *Sight and Sound* 3.5 (May 1993): 38-39. Critical essay on science-fiction films with references to *The Handmaid's Tale*.

1144. JEFFRIES, Lesley. *The Language of Twentieth-Century Poetry*. New York: St. Martin's Press, 1993. 102. Atwood poem, "Woman Skating," very briefly analyzed in chapter, "Grammatical Structure."

1145. JORGENSEN, Mary Crew. "The Voices of Mothers and Daughters in Three Novels by Margaret Atwood." MA thesis. University of South Dakota. 1993. 65 pp.

1146. KANAAR, Kay. "A Comparison of Margaret Atwood's Dystopian Text, *The Handmaid's Tale*, and Catherine Helen Spence's Utopian Text, *Handfasted*." MA thesis. University of Wollongong, 1993.

1147. KING, Bruce. "Introduction: A Changing Face." *The Later Fiction of Nadine Gordimer*. Ed. Bruce King. New York: St. Martin's Press, 1993. 10. Mention of Atwood with comment that Atwood and Gordimer relationship worthy of further study.

1148. LANCASHIRE, Ian. "Computer-Assisted Critical Analysis: A Case Study of Margaret Atwood's *Handmaid's Tale*." *The Digital Word: Text-Based Computing in the Humanities*. Ed. George P. Landow and Paul Delany. Cambridge, MA; London: MIT Press, 1993. 293-318. An analysis of *The Handmaid's Tale*, novel and screenplay, by TACT, a computerized text retrieval and analysis tool, suggests that computer programs like this help critics give a more objective review of a work.

1149. LANE, R. D. "Cordelia's 'Nothing': The Character of Cordelia and Margaret Atwood's *Cat's Eye*." *Essays on Canadian Writing* 48 (Winter 1992-93): 73-88. The concept of nothing is present in both *King Lear* and *Cat's Eye* and represents both unlimited possibilities and desperate isolation.

1150. LANE, Richard. "Anti-Panoptical Narrative Structures in Two Novels by Margaret Atwood." *Commonwealth Essays and Studies* 16.1 (Autumn 1993): 63-69. Discusses memory-narratives in *Cat's Eye* and *Surfacing*.

1151. LeBIHAN, Jill. "The Conditions of a Documentary Genre: Nineteenth-Century Documents in the Writing of Contemporary Canadian Women (with Particular Reference to Margaret Atwood's *The Journals of Susanna Moodie*, Margaret Laurence's *The Diviners*, Susan Swan's *The Biggest Modern Woman of the World* and Daphne Marlatt's *Ana Historic*)." PhD thesis. University of Leeds, 1993. 311 pp.

1152. LECKER, Robert. "Privacy, Publicity, and the Discourse of Canadian Criticism." *Essays on Canadian Writing* 51-52 (Winter 1993-Spring 1994): 32-82. *Survival* is described as a book of criticism that is addressed to the public; for this reason it is attacked by the critics, theorizes Lecker.

1153. LONGO, Maria Luisa. "La città di Margaret Atwood." Doctoral thesis. Università degli studi della Basilicata, Potenza, 1993. 199 pp.

1154. LOPEZ, Barbara Leaman. "Typers. (Original composition)." MA thesis. San Jose State University, 1993. 53 pp. "This thesis develops the poem 'A Place: Fragments' by Margaret Atwood." (Author). For more see *MAI* 31.04 (Winter 1993): 1422.

1155. MACKLIN, Lisa A. "Feminism in the Selected Science Fiction Novels of Margaret Atwood and Marge Piercy." MA thesis. Texas Woman's University, 1993. 99 pp. "The rise of the women's movement is paralleled by an increased recognition of writing by women. Science fiction, although previously dominated by male themes, allows feminist writers to create new societies without the restraints of tradition." (Author). For more see *MAI* 32.03 (June 1994): 805.

1156. MacLENNAN, Jennifer Margaret. "The Gift of Voice: The Role of Self-Projection in the Rhetorical Appeal of Margaret Atwood's Nonfiction." PhD thesis. University of Washington, 1993. 293 pp. "The projection of self through discourse is, as Aristotle argued, a significant aspect of effective rhetorical appeal. Nevertheless, the study of this dimension of written discourse has been complicated by modern critical assumptions and the parallel notion of literary persona. This dissertation attempts to set ethos and persona into the broader framework of voice and to establish a coherent critical method for approaching voice in literary nonfiction, before moving on to demonstrate its contribution to the rhetorical force of Margaret Atwood's nonfiction prose." (Author). For more see *DAI-A* 54.01 (January 1994): 2584.

1157. MALLINSON, Jean. "Margaret Atwood (1939-)." *ECW's Biographical Guide to Canadian Poets*. Ed. Robert Lecker, Jack David, and Ellen Quigley. Toronto: ECW Press, 1993. 247-249. Biographical sketch.

1158. MASEL, C. "Late Landings: Reflections on Belatedness in Australian and Canadian Literature." *Recasting the World: Writing after Colonialism*. Ed. Jonathan White. Baltimore, MD: Johns Hopkins UP, 1993. 161-189. About Margaret Atwood as well as David Malouf.

1159. MEINDL, Dieter. "Between Eliot and Atwood: Faulkner as Ecologist." *Faulkner, His Contemporaries, and His Posterity.* Ed. Waldemar Zacharasiewicz. Tübingen: Francke, 1993. 301-308.

1160. MILINDER, Le'Ann. "Margaret Atwood's Evaluation of Friendship between Women: From *Lady Oracle* to *Cat's Eye*." ALM thesis. Harvard University, 1993. 81 pp.

1161. MONTELARO, Janet J. "Discourses of Maternity and the Postmodern Narrative: A Study of Lessing, Walker, and Atwood." PhD thesis. Louisiana State University, Baton Rouge, 1993. 402 pp. "Doris Lessing's *The Golden Notebook*, Alice Walker's *The Color Purple,* and Margaret Atwood's *The Handmaid's Tale* are narrated by women whose social identities are partially constructed through activities traditionally associated with mothering....In *The Handmaid's Tale*, the patriarchal society of Gilead equates women's sexuality with the reproductive-maternal function. Read according to Luce Irigaray's critique of phallogocentrism, Atwood's novel exposes the role of scopophilia in Gilead's subordination of women and its regulation of their sexuality. Visual metaphors such as the convex mirror and its reflection of masculinity in the pregnant Handmaid signify the repression of the feminine. Atwood's textual echoes of John Ashbery's 'Self-Portrait in a Convex Mirror,' like Irigaray's subversive mimicry, serve to deconstruct the specular logic of Gilead's patriarchy." (Author). For more see *DAI-A* 54.08 (February 1994): 3043.

1162. MONTRESOR, Jaye Berman, ed. *The Critical Response to Ann Beattie*. Westport, CT; London: Greenwood Press, 1993. passim. Brief mentions of Atwood in several essays.

1163. MOODY, Gayle Lawson. "The Quest for Selfhood: Women in the Novels of Margaret Atwood." PhD thesis. Baylor University, 1993. 182 pp. "Anthropological studies show that the role the patriarchy has created for women arose from man's knowledge of his paternity and from his need for offspring to inherit property he had accumulated....Focusing on the novels of Atwood, this dissertation examines the female characters in Atwood's novels and the roles they choose to occupy or the roles they attempt to create for themselves. The first role examined is that of the oppressive mother or substitute mother. The second role examined is the one occupied by women who attempt to usurp the male subject position. And the final role examined is the one created by women who define an individual sense of self-hood. These women who create their own identities are more productive than those who accept defined roles." (Author). For more see DAI-A 54.11 (May 1994): 4097.

1164. MYCAK, Sonia. "Divided and Dismembered: The Decentred Subject in Margaret Atwood's *Bodily Harm.*" *Canadian Review of Comparative Literature / Revue canadienne de littérature comparée* 20.3-4 (September-December 1993): 469-478. The theme of identity-formation is explored in *Bodily Harm.*

1165. NISCHIK, Reingard M. "Speech Act Theory, Speech Acts, and the Analysis of Fiction." *Modern Language Review* 88.2 (April 1993): 297-306. Speech act theory is used to analyze two short stories, "Uglypuss" and "Polarities."

1166. NOVY, Marianne. "Introduction." *Cross-Cultural Performances: Differences in Women's Re-Visions of Shakespeare.* Ed. Marianne Novy. Urbana; Chicago: University of Illinois Press, 1993. 10-11. Footnote reference to "Gertrude Talks Back." Reprinted from *Good Bones.*

1167. O'BRIEN, Peter. "An Interview with Al Purdy." *Essays on Canadian Writing* 49 (Summer 1993): 147-162. Poet Al Purdy on Atwood as a poet: "She's not as good at poems as she is at fiction. To me what a poet ought to be is to be able to write in many different modes, to have many different voices. I hope I have more than one myself, but I think Atwood generally sounds just like Atwood. I don't want to always sound like me. I want to have every poem as different as I can make it." And what is that voice?: "What there is in Atwood's poems is an unmistakably female voice that is generally rather cold, as it was in the Moodie poems, saying things quite nasty about men (as, for instance, Erin Mouré does). However, she is so clever, she is so brilliant, that what she has to say gets listened to, and should be."

1168. O'KEEFE, Bernard. "An Approach to *The Handmaid's Tale.*" *English Review* 3.3 (February 1993): 10-13. Describes teaching the book at a boys' boarding school.

1169. OUSBY, Ian. "Atwood, Margaret (Eleanor)." *The Cambridge Guide to Literature in English.* Cambridge: Cambridge UP, 1993. 42. Biographical sketch.

1170. PAYANT, Katherine B. *Becoming and Bonding: Contemporary Feminism and Popular Fiction by American Women Writers.* Westport, CT; London: Greenwood Press, 1993. passim. Series of references to Atwood and her place in contemporary feminist popular fiction.

1171. PURDY, Al. *Reaching for the Beaufort Sea: An Autobiography.* Madeira Park, BC: Harbour Publishing, 1993. passim. Contains several references to Atwood (230-231, 235, 237, 253-255, 276, 278, 283 and 288-289).

1172. RAMAIYA, Nita P. "The Exploration of the Self in the Poetry of Margaret Atwood." PhD thesis. S.N.D.T. Women's University, 1993.

1173. RAO, Eleonora. "Le Immagini della Differenza nell'Ultima Margaret Atwood: Ripensare un'Etica." *I Linguaggi della Passione.* Ed. Romana Rutelli and Anthony Johnson. Udine [Italy]: Campanotto, 1993. 427-433. *Bodily Harm*, *Cat's Eye*, and *You Are Happy.*

1174. ———. *Strategies for Identity: The Fiction of Margaret Atwood.* New York: Peter Lang Publishing, 1993.

1175. REICHENBÄCHER, Helmut. "Von *The Robber Bridegroom* zu *Bodily Harm*: Eine Analyse unveröffentlichter Entwürfe Margaret Atwoods." *ZAA: Zeitschrift für Anglistik und Amerikanistik.* Berlin; Munich; Vienna; Zürich; New York: Langenscheidt, 1993. 54-65. Study of the manuscripts and typescripts for *Bodily Harm* show the evolution of the title, the beginning versions of the novel, and the changes in setting.

1176. ROBERTS, Nancy. "Reader as Woman: Gender and Identification in Novels." PhD thesis. University of British Columbia, 1993. 232 pp. Also available on microfiche from Canadian Theses Service (1993). "The main body of the thesis is a consideration of four novels (*Clarissa*, *The Scarlet Letter*, *Portrait of a Lady*, and *Tess of the d'Urbervilles*), all of which are centered around a heroine defined by her suffering. In my sixth and final chapter, I turn to the work of two twentieth-century female authors, Margaret Atwood and Angela Carter, to see in what ways they 'talk back' to the tradition which has defined woman as other, to see in what ways, if any, they re-define the possibility of female heroism, and, finally, to consider the implications for the reader." (Author). For more see DAI-A 54.08 (February 1994): 3020.

1177. ROSE, Ellen Cronan. "The Good Mother: From Gaia to Gilead." *Ecofeminism and the Sacred.* Ed. Carol J. Adams. New York: Continuum, 1993. 149-167. Brief mention of *The Handmaid's Tale* in discussion of environmental pollution causing a crisis in fertility.

1178. SCHOLTMEIJER, Marian. *Animal Victims in Modern Fiction: From Sanctity to Sacrifice.* Toronto; Buffalo; London: University of Toronto Press, 1993. 330. Brief mention of Atwood's statement in *Survival* identifying Canada with animal victims.

1179. SEXTON, Melanie. "The Woman's Voice: The Post-Realist Fiction of Margaret Atwood, Mavis Gallant and Alice Munro." PhD thesis. University of Ottawa, 1993. 484 pp. Also available on microfiche from Canadian Theses Service (1993). "Since Margaret Atwood, Mavis Gallant, and Alice Munro do not frequently employ experimental or overtly metafictional forms, they are often read as realist writers in contradistinction to postmodernists. In fact, the assumptions upon which their work rests have little in common with the assumptions underlying realism, and they are as resoundingly post-realist as their postmodern counterparts.... [These writers] do not construct fictions that attempt to mirror life—they recognize the power of voice to construct the world. They are therefore not the naive or conservative 'realists' they are sometimes read as. In fact, their work, like that of the postmodernists, challenges and deconstructs the assumptions of realism. However, whereas language for the postmodernists has become little more than a play of empty signifiers, for these women writers it is still vitally allied to power." (Author). For more see *DAI-A* 54.11 (May 1994): 4098.

1180. SHARPE, Martha. "Autonomy, Self-Creation, and the Woman Artist Figure in Woolf, Lessing, and Atwood." MA thesis. McGill University, 1993. 159 pp. Also available on microfiche from Canadian Theses Service (1994). "This thesis traces the self-creation and autonomy of the woman artist figure in Virginia Woolf's *To the Lighthouse*, Doris Lessing's *The Golden Notebook*, and Margaret Atwood's *Cat's Eye*....Drawing on the work of women moral theorists, this thesis suggests that women's self-creation and autonomy result in an undervalued but nevertheless workable solution to the public/private rift." (Author). For more see *MAI* 32.06 (December 1994): 1527.

1181. ———. "Margaret Atwood and Julia Kristeva: Space-Time, the Dissident Woman Artist, and the Pursuit of Female Solidarity in *Cat's Eye*." *Essays on Canadian Writing* 50 (Fall 1993): 174-189. A discussion of Julia Kristeva's space-time theory in regard to the protagonist Elaine Risley in *Cat's Eye*. Risley's art signifies space and ultimately communicates meaning beyond language.

1182. SHELTON, Robert. "The Social Text as Body: Images of Health and Disease in Three Recent Feminist Utopias." *Literature and Medicine* 12.2 (1993): 161-177. *The Handmaid's Tale* plus Marge Piercy's *Woman on the Edge of Time* (1976) and Johanna Russ's *The Female Man* (1975).

1183. SIMMONS, Jes. "Atwood's [You Fit into Me]." *The Explicator* 51.4 (Summer 1993): 259-260. Compares men's and women's interpretations of this poem; why male readers miss the poem's full meaning and find the last lines redundant.

1184. SMITH, Erin. "Gender and National Identity in *The Journals of Susanna Moodie* and *Tamsen Donner: A Woman's Journey*." *Frontiers* 13.2 (1993): 75-88. Moodie represents to Atwood much of the Canadian character which Atwood reinterprets as a poet.

1185. SPECTOR, Judith Ann. "Marriage, Endings, and Art in Updike and Atwood." *Midwest Quarterly* 34.4 (Summer 1993): 426-445. Comparison of Updike's *Marry Me* and Atwood's *Lady Oracle*. Explores the concept of identity within a marriage.

1186. SPIVAK, Gayatri Chakravorty. *Outside in the Teaching Machine*. New York; London: Routledge, 1993. Reference to "Giving Birth."

1187. STURGESS, Charlotte Jane. "A Politics of Location: Subjectivity and Origins in the Work of Mavis Gallant, Alice Munro and Margaret Atwood." PhD thesis. University of London, 1993.

1188. SUGARS, Cynthia. "On the Rungs of the Double Helix: Theorizing the Canadian Literatures." *Essays on Canadian Writing* 50 (Fall 1993): 19-44. Atwood is cited as one of many literary critics who believe Canadian literature encompasses both French Canadian and English Canadian literature. Quebec is perceived as a microcosm of Canada.

1189. SUTHERLAND, Katherine. "Bloodletters: Configurations of Female Sexuality in Canadian Women's Writing." PhD thesis. York University, 1993. Also available on microfiche from Canadian Theses Service (1993). "This study examines female sexuality in the writing of Canadian women from the eighteenth to the twentieth century in both French and English. The primary texts include works by Frances Brooke, Anna Brownell Jameson, Sara Jeanette Duncan, Laure Conan, Frances Beynon, Emily Carr, Elizabeth Smart, Anne Hebert, Margaret Atwood, and Alice Munro." (Author).

1190. TAYLOR, Linda Anne. "Depictions of Oppression and Subversion in *Handmaid's Tale* and *Cat's Eye*." MA thesis. Central Washington University, 1993. 98 pp.

1191. TEMPLIN, Charlotte. "Names and Naming Tell an Archetypal Story in Margaret Atwood's *The Handmaid's Tale*." *Names: A Journal of Onomastics* 41.3 (1993): 143-157.

1192. TOMC, Sandra. "'The Missionary Position': Feminism and Nationalism in Margaret Atwood's *The Handmaid's Tale*." *Canadian Literature* 138-139 (Fall-Winter 1993): 73-87. *The Handmaid's Tale* is influenced by Atwood's concept of Canada's relationship with the United States and provides an unexpected conservative representation of women.

1193. WHITE, Roberta. "Margaret Atwood: Reflections in a Convex Mirror." *Canadian Women Writing Fiction*. Ed. Mickey Pearlman. Jackson: UP of Mississippi, 1993. 53-69. Essay on Atwood's novels concentrating on the development of the 3-dimensional aspect of the main characters.

1194. WILSON, Sharon Rose. *Margaret Atwood's Fairy-Tale Sexual Politics*. Toronto: ECW Press; Jackson: UP of Mississippi, 1993. Examines Atwood's works in terms of folklore motifs; includes study of her visual art in that context as well.

1195. ———. "Margaret Atwood's Visual Art." *Essays on Canadian Writing* 50 (Fall 1993): 129-173. An essay on Margaret Atwood, the visual artist, which compares the visual and literary images of her works.

1196. WOODCOCK, George. *George Woodcock's Introduction to Canadian Fiction*. Toronto: ECW Press, 1993. See especially "Realism and Neo-Realism: Margaret Laurence, Margaret Atwood, Matt Cohen, Marian Engel, Rudy Wiebe." 135-153. Atwood is characterized as an "ironically didactic realist." She and Laurence, Cohen, Engel, and Wiebe are discussed as Canadian realists. See also "The Translucent Glass: D. G. Jones, Gwendolyn MacEwen, Margaret Atwood, Dennis Lee, Patrick Lane, Robin Skelton." 141-156. Atwood and the careers of five of her contemporaries are examined. Atwood's poetry is described as more visual in recent years. The theme of survival is evident in her poetry and literature.

1197. ZIRKER, Herbert. "Margaret Atwood, *The Handmaid's Tale*: A Variety of Literary Utopias." *Studying and Writing the Difference: Essays in Canadian Culture(s) and Society*. Ed. Hans Braun and Wolfgang Kloos. Trier: Universität Trier, Forschungsstelle Zentrum fur Kanada-Studien, 1993. 125-139.

1198. ZONDERVAN, Jean Marie. "Margaret Atwood's *Cat's Eye*: Character Development in Visual Images." MA thesis. Stephen F. Austin State University, 1993. 54 pp. "The fiction of Margaret Atwood is laden with powerful images, and her most recent novel *Cat's Eye* is perhaps exceptional in its use of visual images....The goal of this interpretation is not to come to a comprehensive conclusion about their meaning, but to illustrate that an understanding of the power of Atwood's images comes in discerning their woven strata of experience that must be taken together." (Author). For more see *MAI* 32.02 (April 1994): 433.

Reviews of Atwood's Works

1199. *Good Bones*. Toronto: Coach House Press; London: Bloomsbury, 1992.
Australian Book Review 148 (February-March 1993): 54-55. By Carolyn UEDA.
British Book News August 1993: 534. Review/announcement of Virago edition.
Canadian Book Review Annual 1992. Ed. Joyce M. Wilson. Toronto: Canadian Book Review Annual, 1993. 182. By Noreen MITCHELL.
Canadian Literature 138-139 (Fall-Winter 1993): 105-106. By Neil BESNER.
Paragraph 15.1 (Summer 1993): 36. By Lisa SCHMIDT.
University of Toronto Quarterly 63.1 (Fall 1993): 47-48. By Aritha VAN HERK.
West Coast Line 27.2 (1993): 143. By Billy LITTLE.

1200. *The Oxford Book of Canadian Short Stories in English*. Selected by Margaret Atwood and Robert Weaver. Toronto: Oxford UP, 1986.
New Renaissance 8.3 (1993): 138-142. By Ruth MOOSE.

1201. *The Robber Bride.* Toronto: McClelland and Stewart; London: Bloomsbury; New
York: Talese/Doubleday, 1993.

  The Advocate (Los Angeles) 2 November 1993: 72. By Brad GOOCH.

  Arizona Daily Star (Tucson) 7 November 1993: LIT NewsBank 1993: 94: B5-6.
  By Colette M. BANCROFT.

  Arkansas Democrat (Little Rock) 24 October 1993: LIT NewsBank 1993: 85:
  C14. By Celia STOREY.

  Atlantic Monthly 272.6 (December 1993): 142. By Phoebe-Lou ADAMS.

  Booklist 90.2 (15 September 1993): 101. By Donna SEAMAN.

  Books in Canada 22.7 (October 1993): 30-31. By Joan THOMAS.

  British Book News December 1993: 748-751. Part of survey, "Fiction '93." By
  Valentine CUNNINGHAM.

  Buffalo News 24 October 1993: Section: Book Reviews: 7. By Charles A.
  BRADY. (1187 w).

  Chicago Sun-Times 31 October 1993: Section: Show: 12. By Wendy SMITH.
  (961 w).

  Christian Science Monitor 19 November 1993: Section: Books: 19. By Merle
  RUBIN. (1069 w). Excerpt: "Readers may well enjoy Atwood's crisp writing,
  neatly interwoven plotting, sharp-eyed descriptions, and wry sense of humor.
  But those who imagine *The Robber Bride* to be a work of large significance
  with anything profound or new to say about gender, power, love, hate, or the
  nature of good and evil, are simply kidding themselves."

  Cosmopolitan November 1993: 30. By Chris CHASE.

  Denver Post 25 November 1993: LIT NewsBank 1993: 94: B10. By Maureen
  HARRINGTON.

  Elle 9.3 (November 1993): 84. By Leslie BRODY.

  Entertainment Weekly 12 November 1993: 55. By Tom DE HAVEN.

  Financial Post 87.40 (2 October 1993): S10. By Araminta WORDSWORTH.

  Financial Times 16 October 1993: Section: Books: 20. By Anthony THORN-
  CROFT. (313 w).

  Glamour December 1993: 170. By Sara NELSON.

  The Guardian 5 October 1993: Section 2: 12-13. By Noah RICHLER. (934 w).
  Excerpt: "Even if you've not read the early Atwood, there is the feeling of
  having been this way before. And too, there is something of the Empress here,
  poverty at the core which no pretension to greater ideas will disguise. There is
  no battle going on, and Zenia, on whom this novel so much depends, is not a
  mystery, but an irritant who should just be shooed away. Perhaps, in sharper
  hands, she might have made a wonderful novel of laughter, mischief, and
  pain, but this novel is as much a charade as Zenia is, and no end of wordy references—to the Gulf, the IRA, Lebanon, AIDS or Gerald Bull—will help a
  story which finally depends on Charis's tarot cards for its weight and ring of
  truth."

  Hamilton Spectator (ON) 30 October 1993: Section: Weekend: 4. By Sandra
  HUNTER. (784 w).

  Harper's October 1993: 26. By Patrick GALE.

  Hartford Courant 14 November 1993: LIT NewsBank 1993: 94: B11. By Kitty
  BENEDICT.

  The Herald (Glasgow) 9 October 1993: 8. By Carl MacDOUGALL. (751 w).

  Houston Chronicle 21 November 1993: Section: Zest: 22. By Rich QUACK-
  ENBUSH. (907 w).

The Independent 17 October 1993: Section: Sunday review Page: 47. By Salman RUSHDIE. (866 w). Excerpt: "*The Robber Bride* is a tale of small, private catastrophes. Its villain unleashes nothing grander than domestic and emotional violence. But it is vividly written, acutely observed and is very possibly the most intelligently tongue-in-cheek novel of the year. It is as good as ever to hear Margaret Atwood's dry, droll, spiky voice. Why the novel is being published too late to make the Booker shortlist, however, remains a mystery."

The Independent 23 October 1993: Section: Weekend Books: 32. By Helen BIRCH. (930 w).

Kirkus Reviews 61.19 (1 October 1993): 1215. ANON.

Library Journal 118.12 (July 1993): 58. "Prepub Alert" also announces large print edition and abridged audio. By Barbara HOFFERT and Mark ANNICHIARICO.

Library Journal 118.16 (1 October 1993): 125. By Barbara HOFFERT.

Literary Review October 1993: 53. By Elizabeth IMLAY.

Los Angeles Times 14 November 1993: Section: Book Review: 3. By Richard EDER. (1122 w). Excerpt: "It is rather poor Atwood country, flat and sometimes marshy. The road that leads through it winds at excessive length to take in a great deal of uninteresting scenery. It could have cut across and reached the same destination much faster."

Maclean's 106.40 (4 October 1993): 55. By Judith TIMSON. (918 w).

Minneapolis Star and Tribune 31 October 1993: LIT NewsBank 1993: 85: D1. By Dave GOLDSMITH.

Ms. "International Bookshelf." 4.3 (November-December 1993): 65.

The Nation 257.20 (13 December 1993): 734-737. By Linda HUTCHEON.

New York 26.45 (15 November 1993): 93. By Rhoda KOENIG.

New York Review of Books 40.21 (16 December 1993): 14, 16. By Gabriele ANNAN.

New York Times 26 October 1993: Section: C: 20. By Michiko KAKUTANI. (841 w). Excerpt: "In a shorter, more focused book, [Atwood's] cartoonlike approach to writing might have resulted in a kind of darkly colored fairy tale, but for all her narrative skills, Ms. Atwood is unable to ever really lift her story into that magical realm of fable. Her characters remain exiles from both the earthbound realm of realism and the airier altitudes of allegory, and as a result, their story does not illuminate or entertain; it grates."

New York Times Book Review 31 October 1993: 1, 22. By Lorrie MOORE.

New York Times Book Review 7 November 1993: 30. In "And Bear in Mind" section.

New York Times Book Review "Notable Books of the Year 1993." 5 December 1993: 64.

News and Observer (Raleigh, NC) 28 November 1993: LIT NewsBank 1993: 94: B14-C1. By Karen C. BLANSFIELD.

Newsweek 122.19 (8 November 1993): Section: The Arts: 81. By Laura SHAPIRO. (349 w).

The Observer (London) 10 October 1993: 16. By Eavan BOLAND. (524 w).

The Oregonian (Portland) 7 November 1993: LIT NewsBank 1993: 94: C2-3. By Paul PINTARICH.

People Weekly 40.21 (22 November 1993): 34-35. By Susan TOEPFER.

Philadelphia Inquirer 14 November 1993: LIT NewsBank 1993: 94: C4-5. By Edward HOWER.

Publishers Weekly 240.32 (9 August 1993): 100. "Fall Announcements Issue."

Publishers Weekly 240.37 (13 September 1993): 84. By Sybil S. STEINBERG.

Publishers Weekly 240.44 (1 November 1993): 46. "PW's Best Books 1993" survey. By Sybil STEINBERG.

Quill and Quire September 1993: 59. Excerpt of this review in *Book Group Companion to Margaret Atwood's* The Robber Bride. New York: Nan A. Talese / Doubleday, 1993. 4-6. By Sandra MARTIN.

The Record (Kitchener-Waterloo) 16 October 1993: Section: Books: D6. By John KIELY. (692 w). Excerpt: "Some advice to Atwood: 'Plan a holiday, take a trip, get out of Toronto, get out of Ontario, leave these people be. It is done and it is over. The life has gone out of this writing and the soul has long ago fled. Leave us and come back with something fresh, come back with something more than a reputation.'"

St. Louis Post-Dispatch 14 November 1993: Section: Everyday Magazine: 5C. By Lynn Z. BLOOM. (1294 w).

San Diego Union 7 November 1993: LIT NewsBank 1993: 94: B7. By Glenda WINDERS.

San Jose Mercury News 14 November 1993: LIT NewsBank 1993: 94: B8-9. By Madeleine BLAIS.

Seattle Times 12 December 1993: Section: Books: 12. By Melinda BARGREEN. (909 w).

The Spectator 271.8623 (16 October 1993): 32. ANON.

The Spectator 271.8628 (20 November 1993): 37. In "Books of the Year" section. By Anita BROOKNER.

The Star-Ledger (Newark, NJ) 7 November 1993: LIT NewsBank 1993: 94: B13. By Roger HARRIS.

Sunday Times 17 October 1993: Section 6: 13. By Peter KEMP. (856 w).

The Times 30 September 1993: Section: Features: s.p. By Christine KONING. (696 w). Available from Lexis-Nexis.

Times-Picayune (New Orleans, LA) 7 November 1993: Section: Travel: E7. By Susan LARSON. (862 w).

TLS 8 October 1993: 27. By Claire MESSUD.

Toronto Star 2 October 1993: Section: Weekend: G14. By Philip MARCHAND. (829 w).

Tribune Books (Chicago) 21 November 1993: Section 14: 1, 4. By Philip GRAHAM.

Vogue (British) 159.10 (October 1993): 92. By Glyn MAXWELL.

Vogue 183.11 (November 1993): 200. By Victoria GLENDINNING.

Washington Post 7 November 1993: Section: Book World: 11. By Francine PROSE. (836 w).

Washington Times 28 November 1993: Section: Books: B7. By Jennifer PINKERTON. (867 w).

1202. *The Robber Bride.* (4 cassettes, abridged). New York: Bantam Audio, 1993. Audio.

Book Alert (Baker and Taylor) 15.11 (November 1993): 32. ANON.

1203. *Wilderness Tips.* Toronto: McClelland and Stewart; London: Bloomsbury; New York: Talese/Doubleday, 1991.

Canadian Literature 137 (Summer 1993): 75-76. By Sherrill GRACE.

Jerusalem Post 19 November 1993: Section: Books: 28. By Frances GERTLER. (311 w).

New York Times Book Review 7 March 1993: 24. Review/announcement of Bantam edition.

New York Times Book Review 6 June 1993: 56. List of paperbacks "from the New and Noteworthy column since the 1992 Christmas issue." By Laurel GRAEBER.

Tribune Books (Chicago) 21 February 1993: Section 14: 8. Bantam edition noted in "Also Worth Reading" column.

~ 1994 ~

Atwood's Works

1205. "Alien Territory." *The Male Body: Features, Destinies, Exposures*. Ed. Laurence Goldstein. Ann Arbor: University of Michigan Press, 1994. 1-7.

1206. "Asparagus." *This Magazine* 28.4 (November 1994). Insert between pages 24 and 25.

1207. "Betty." *Coming of Age: Short Stories about Youth and Adolescence*. [Ed.] Bruce Emra. Lincolnwood, IL: National Textbook Co., 1994. 250-265. Short story in high school text followed by study questions, 265-266.

1208. "Book Tour Comics." *Publishers Weekly* 241.4 (24 January 1994): 14. Also published in *Brick: A Literary Journal* 48 (Spring 1994): 63. A comic strip used by Atwood on her Christmas card in 1993.

1209. "Book Tour Comix #911." *Brick: A Literary Journal* 50 (Fall 1994): 37.

1210. "Bored." *Atlantic Monthly* 274.6 (December 1994): 102. Poem.

1211. *Cat's Eye*. London: Bloomsbury, 1994.

1212. "Cell." *This Magazine* 28.4 (November 1994). Insert between pages 24 and 25.

1213. "Cold-Blooded." *The Penguin Book of Lesbian Short Stories*. Ed. Margaret Reynolds. New York: Viking, 1994. 384-386. Reprinted from *Good Bones*, Bloomsbury, ©1992.

1214. "Cressida to Troilus: A Gift." *This Magazine* 28.4 (November 1994). Insert between pages 24 and 25.

1215. "Dancing." *Saturday Night* 109.10 (December 1994): 150. Poem.

1216. "Daphne and Laura and So Forth." *Field: Contemporary Poetry and Poetics* 51 (Fall 1994): 48.

1217. *De roofbruid*. Amsterdam: Bert Bakker, 1994. Dutch translation of *The Robber Bride*.

1218. "Death by Landscape." [Sound recording]. Read by Sondra Bolton. *The Oxford Book of Canadian Ghost Stories*. Ed. Alberto Manguel. Toronto: CNIB, 1994. Originally published 1990.

1219. *Der Salzgarten: Short stories*. Frankfurt am Main: S. Fischer, 1994. German translation of *Bluebeard's Egg* (©1983) by Charlotte Franke.

1220. *Die Räuberbraut: Roman*. Frankfurt am Main [Germany]: S. Fischer, 1994. German translation of *The Robber Bride* by Brigitte Walitzek.

1221. *The Edible Woman*. Toronto: McClelland and Stewart, 1994 ©1969. With an afterword by Linda Hutcheon.

1222. *Faire surface: Roman*. Paris: Serpent à plumes, 1994. French translation of *Surfacing* by Marie-France Girod.

1223. "February." *This Magazine* 28.4 (November 1994). Insert between pages 24 and 25.

1224. "The Female Body." *Minding the Body: Women Writers on Body and Soul*. Ed. Patricia Foster. New York; London; Toronto; Sydney; Auckland: Doubleday, 1994. 89-93. Contains her famous quote about Barbie: "If a real woman was built like that, she'd fall flat on her face."

1225. "Gathering." *Toronto Sun* 31 July 1994: Section: Sunday Magazine: M21. Also published in *Because You Loved Being a Stranger: 55 Poets Celebrate Patrick Lane*. Ed. Susan Musgrave. Madeira Park, BC: Harbour, 1994. 14. In the book, Atwood also comments on Lane on p. 113.

1226. "Germaine Greer (Part One)." *One on One: The Imprint Interviews*. Ed. Leanna Crouch. Toronto: Somerville House, 1994. 37-50. Originally taped for broadcast on TV Ontario on 7 October 1992.

1227. "Germaine Greer (Part Two)." *One on One: The Imprint Interviews*. Ed. Leanna Crouch. Toronto: Somerville House, 1994. 183-195. Originally taped for broadcast on TV Ontario on 7 October 1992.

1228. *Good Bones*. [Sound recording]. Read by Deborah Kipp. Toronto: CNIB, 1994. 1 cassette. Recorded from 1992 title.

1229. *Good Bones and Simple Murders*. New York: Nan A. Talese / Doubleday, 1994. 164. Contains the following: "Murder in the Dark," "Bad News," "Unpopular Gals," "The Little Red Hen Tells All," "Gertrude Talks Back," "There Was Once," "Women's Novels," "The Boys' Own Annual, 1911," "Stump Hunting," "Making a Man," "Men at Sea," "Simmering," "Happy Endings," "Let Us Now Praise Stupid Women," "The Victory Burlesk," "She," "The Female Body," "Cold-Blooded," "Liking Men," "In Love with Raymond Chandler," "Simple Murders," "Iconography," "Alien Territory," "My Life as a Bat," "Hardball," "Bread," "Poppies: Three Variations," "Homelanding," "The Page," "An Angel," "Third Handed," "Death Scenes," "We Want It All," "Dance of the Lepers," "Good Bones."

1230. *Good Bones and Simple Murders*. Rockland, MA: Wheeler Pub., 1994. Large print edition.

1231. "The Grunge Look." *Writing Away: The PEN Canada Travel Anthology*. Ed. Constance Rooke. Toronto: McClelland and Stewart, 1994. 1-11.

1232. "Hair Jewellery." *The Oxford Book of Modern Women's Stories*. Ed. Patricia Craig. Oxford; New York: Oxford UP, 1994. 379-392. Reprinted from *Dancing Girls and Other Stories*.

1233. "Helen of Troy Does Counterdancing." *This Magazine* 28.4 (November 1994). Insert between pages 24 and 25.

1234. *Hoch oben im Baum*. Frankfurt am Main: Fischer Taschenbuch Verlag, 1994. German translation of *Up in the Tree* (1978) by Peter Maiwald. Juvenile.

1235. "I Wish I'd Written." *The Guardian* (London) 18 November 1994: Section: Guardian Features Page: T18. (322 w). Answer: *The Tale of Mr. Tod*, by Beatrix Potter.

1236. "Islands of the Mind." *Without a Guide: Contemporary Women's Travel Adventures*. Ed. Katherine Govier. Toronto: Macfarlane Walter & Ross, 1994. 19-31. "Originally published in *Quest*."

1237. "King Lear in Respite Care." *Field: Contemporary Poetry and Poetics* 51 (Fall 1994): 52-53.

1238. *La voleuse d'hommes: Roman*. [Paris]: R. Laffont, 1994. French translation of *The Robber Bride* by Anne Rabinovitch.

1239. "Let Us Now Praise Stupid Women." *This Magazine* 263 (September 1994): 20.

1240. "Liking Men." *Wild Women: Contemporary Short Stories by Women Celebrating Women*. Ed. Sue Thomas. Introduction by Clarissa Pinkola Estés. Woodstock, NY: The Overlook Press, 1994. 57-58. Reprinted from *Murder in the Dark*, ©1983.

1241. "MacEwen, Gwendolyn (1941-87)." *Encyclopedia of Post-Colonial Literatures in English*. Ed. Eugene Benson and L. W. Conolly. Vol. 2. London: Routledge, 1994. 933-935.

1242. "Man in a Glacier." *Field: Contemporary Poetry and Poetics* 51 (Fall 1994): 54-55.

1243. "Man Looks." *Vice Versa* 46-47 (October-December 1994): 15. Poem.

1244. "Manet's Olymmpia." *Vice Versa* 46-47 (October-December 1994): 14. Poem.

1245. *Margaret Atwood*. [Sound recording]. [San Francisco]: City Arts of San Francisco, 1994. 1 sound cassette (58:45 min.). Margaret Atwood reads her poems and prose on the subject of "bad female behavior." Recorded live at the Herbst Theatre in 1994.

1246. "Me, She, and It." *Antæus* 73-74 (Spring 1994): 7. Also Atwood sketch of herself, as paper doll, on p. 6. This issue, edited by Daniel Halpern, has theme of "Who's Writing This: Notations on the Authorial."

1247. "Miss July Grows Older." *This Magazine* 28.4 (November 1994). Insert between pages 24 and 25.

1248. "Monet's Olympia." *Ploughshares* 19.4 (Winter 1993-94): 83-84. Theme issue, "Borderlands," guest edited by Russell Banks and Chase Twichell.

1249. *Murder in the Dark: Short Fictions and Prose Poems*. London: Virago Press, 1994 ©1983.

1250. "My Canada Includes." *Maclean's* 3 January 1994: 18. Her exact words: "A few years ago, a taxi driver was murdered in Toronto. All the other taxi drivers drove around City Hall with their lights on. It was big news. In our great neighbour to the south, his death might not have made the newspaper. That kind of crime is pretty rare in Canada. I have noticed something else in the past year. I had been going to the hospital a lot because my father was sick. Everywhere I went, people held the door for me. Canadians are door-holders. There is a consideration for others here that I like. It's a part of our character."

1251. "N Atmosferische Scheiding." *Viva* 5 (31 January-7 February 1994): 52-26.

1252. *The New Oxford Book of Canadian Verse in English*. [Sound recording]. Read by Joan Dahl. Vancouver: CILS, 1994. 12 cassettes (17 hr.). Recorded from 1982 title.

1253. "Norrie Banquet Ode." *The Legacy of Northrop Frye*. Ed. Alvin A. Lee and Robert D. Denham. Toronto; Buffalo; London: University of Toronto Press, 1994. 171-173. Text of remarks made and original poem read at "The Legacy of Northrop Frye" conference in October 1992. Poem and portion of remarks also in the *Northrop Frye Newsletter* 6.1 (Fall 1994): 38-39.

1254. "Not Just a Pretty Face." *Women's Review of Books* 11.4 (January 1994): 6-7. A keynote presentation at *The Women's Review of Books* 10th anniversary conference, November 1993.

1255. "Obstacle Course." *The Critical Response to Tillie Olsen*. Ed. Kay Hoyle Nelson and Nancy Huse. Westport, CT: Greenwood Press, 1994. 250-251. Review of *Silences*. Reprinted from *the New York Times Book Review* 30 July 1978: 1, 27.

1256. *The Poetry of Gwendolyn MacEwen. Volume Two: The Later Years*. Ed. Margaret Atwood and Barry Callaghan. Introduction and introductory notes by Rosemary Sullivan. Toronto: Exile Editions, 1994.

1257. *Polaridades y otros cuentos de Margaret Atwood*. [Caracas]: Asociación venezo-lana de estudios canadienses, 1994. Spanish translation of several Atwood short stories by various translators. Includes Introducción: "Identidad, espacio y otras afinidades culturales en la narrativa de Margaret Atwood" [11]-24; Los Cuentos: "Polaridades" [27]-54, "Betty" [57]-77, "El Hombre de Marte" [81]-105; "Marga-ret Atwood: Invención y Militancia: Conversación con la Profesora Elaine New-ton" [107]-111.

1258. *Polarities: Selected Stories*. Stuttgart: Philipp Reclam jun., 1994. Intended as a textbook for second language learners, the text in English and German. German translated by Reingard M. Nischik.

1259. "[Poster]." Celebrated Writers Series—Kurt Vonnegut Jr., Michael Ondaatje, Richard Wilbur, Timothy Findley, Margaret Atwood, 1994—poster. [Stratford: The Festival], 1994. 1 item; 48 x 63 cm.

1260. "Questioning the Dead." *Field: Contemporary Poetry and Poetics* 51 (Fall 1994): 49.

1261. "Red Fox." Field: Contemporary Poetry and Poetics 51 (Fall 1994): 50-51.

1262. *Resurgir*. Barcelona: Muchnik Editores, 1994. Spanish translation of *Surfacing* by Ana Poljak.

1263. *The Robber Bride*. Toronto: McClelland-Bantam; London: Virago, 1994 ©1993. Paperback.

1264. *The Robber Bride*. [Sound recording]. Read by Barbara Caruso. Prince Frederick, MD: Recorded Books, 1994. 15 sound cassettes (21.5 hrs.).

1265. *Rövarbruden*. [Sweden]: Rabén Prisma, 1994. Swedish translation of *The Robber Bride* by Ulla Danielsson.

1266. *Røverbruden*. [Copenhagen]: Lindhardt og Ringhof, 1994. Danish translation of *The Robber Bride* by Lisbeth Møller-Madsen.

1267. "Running with the Tigers." *Flesh and the Mirror: Essays on the Art of Angela Carter*. Ed. Lorna Sage. London: Virago, 1994. 117-135. One of 13 essays honor-ing novelist Carter, who died in 1992.

1268. *Ryövärimorsian*. Helsingissä: Otava, 1994. Finnish translation of *The Robber Bride* by Kristiina Drews.

1269. "Sekhmet, the Lion-Headed Goddess of War, Violent Storms, Pestilence, and Re-covery from Illness, Contemplates the Desert in the Metropolitan Museum of Art." *New Letters* 60.4 (1994): 28-29.

1270. "Silencing the Scream." *Profession 94*. New York: Modern Language Association of America, 1994. 44-47. "A version of this paper was presented at the 1993 MLA convention in Toronto."

1271. "Simmering." *Wild Women: Contemporary Short Stories by Women Celebrating Women*. Ed. Sue Thomas. Introduction by Clarissa Pinkola Estés. Woodstock, NY: Overlook Press, 1994. 59-61. Reprinted from *Murder in the Dark*, ©1983.

1272. "Simple Murders." *Antæus* 75-76 (Autumn 1994): 11-12. Short story.

1273. "Siren Song." *An Introduction to Poetry*. 8th ed. By X. J. Kennedy and Dana Gioia. New York: HarperCollins, 1994. 309-310.

1274. "Statuary." *New Letters* 60.4 (1994): 30-31.

1275. *Surfacing*. Toronto: McClelland and Stewart; London: Virago, 1994 ©1972. Pa-perback.

1276. *Tips für die Wildnis: Short Stories*. Frankfurt am Main: Fischer Taschenbuch, 1994. German translation of *Wilderness Tips* (1991) by Charlotte Franke.

1277. "Tre poesie." *Rivista di studi canadesi* 7 (1994): 9-18.

1278. "Up." *New Letters* 60.4 (1994): 31-32.

1279. "The War in the Bathroom." *First Fiction: An Anthology of the First Published Stories by Famous Writers*. Ed. Kathy Kiernan and Michael M. Moore. Introduction by Jane Smiley. Boston; New York; Toronto; London: Little, Brown, 1994. 16-25. "Originally published in *Alphabet* Magazine (London, Ontario)."
1280. "What I'd Be If I Were Not a Writer." *Brick: A Literary Journal* 50 (Fall 1994): 15.
1281. *Where to Start Is the Problem, Because Nothing Begins*. [Menlo Park, CA]: Kepler's Books, 1994. 1 broadside. Printed in dark brown on tan paper; text superimposed on engraving in medium brown of 3 draped figures; colophon on verso. Title from first line. "This is a gift for the New Year, 1994, from Kepler's Books and Magazines. From *The Robber Bride* by Margaret Atwood ... Engraving by Pierre Milan © 1550. Okeanos Press Design." (Colophon).
1282. *Wilderness Tips*. Stockport, UK: National Library for the Blind, 1994. Braille ed., 5 v.
1283. "You Fit into Me." *An Introduction to Poetry*. 8th ed. By X. J. Kennedy and Dana Gioia. New York: HarperCollins, 1994. 112.

Quotations

1284. "[Quote]." *Narcissism and the Literary Libido: Rhetoric, Text, and Subjectivity*. By Marshall W. Alcorn Jr. New York; London: New York UP, 1994. 63. From poem, "Tricks with Mirrors:" "There is more to a mirror / than you looking at / your full-length body / flawless but reversed." Forequote to chapter, "Projection and the Resistance of the Signifier: A Reader-Response Theory of Textual Presence."
1285. "[Quote]." *Toronto Star* 21 July 1994: Section: Life: F5. Article by Marlene Habib entitled "Perspectives on Women's Bodies: Female Authors Offer Views on Perils They Faced Growing Up" quotes Atwood on Barbie: "If a real woman was built like that, she'd fall flat on her face."

Interviews

1286. *The True Story of Frankenstein.* [Videorecording]. New York: ICFT, Ltd.: A&E Home Video, ©1994. 1 videocassette (VHS) (100 min.). Atwood among those interviewed.
1287. BARGREEN, Melinda. "Villainesses Come to Memorable Life in Margaret Atwood's Polished Pages." *Seattle Times* 4 February 1994: Section: Arts, Entertainment: F1. On her "oeuvre": "It's not that I'm prolific," she claims. "I'm old." Also, "I never talk about things that aren't published," she says, bending the brim of her black-velvet hat to a better angle. "Perhaps it's superstition, the fear of naming that which has not yet appeared. But I don't, because whatever it is might end up being one of those manuscripts that I put away in a drawer. I don't publish everything I've written."
1288. CALLWOOD, June. "Margaret Atwood." *June Callwood's National Treasures*. Toronto: Stoddart and Vision TV, 1994. 11-39.
1289. CONTINELLI, Louise. "On the Streets of Toronto with Margaret Atwood." *Buffalo News* (NY) 25 December 1994: Section: Lifestyles: 1. (2160 w).
   Atwood comments **on setting *The Robber Bride* in Toronto**: "It was a somewhat daring thing to do. People in Canada didn't think it was real unless it was

New York, Paris or London. But when you live in a smaller city, you know that lots of other people have written about New York, Paris or London. So you have more of a wide open field with Toronto. It would be similar with Buffalo."

On why she writes: It's not the money or the prizes that keep Atwood at her art: "I suppose I write for some of the same reasons I read: to live a double life; to go places I haven't been; to examine life on earth; to come to know people in ways, and at depths, that are otherwise impossible; to be surprised. Whatever their other reasons, I think all writers write as part of this sort of continuum: to give back something of what they themselves have received."

1290. DAVIES, Linda. "Interview." *Glimmer Train Stories* 11 (Summer 1994): 25-34.

1291. ENGELER, Beth. *Margaret Atwood [et al]*. [Sound recording]. [Troy, NY: Sage Colleges; Albany, NY: WAMC Public Radio, 1994. 1 sound cassette (8 min.). "She chilled us with *The Handmaid's Tale* and charmed us with *Wilderness Trips* [sic]. Now, Canadian writer Margaret Atwood is out with a new collection of short stories called *Good Bones and Simple Murders*. Beth Engeler has a profile." Cassette also includes a story on the emerging female market for videogames as well as a profile of Beverly Carter Sexton. Recorded 9 December 1994.

1292. FOX, Sue. "Margaret Atwood." *The Times* 7 May 1994: Section: Features: s.p. (866 w). Available from Lexis-Nexis. Focuses on her youth. In high school, looking at pay-scales, Atwood noticed that home economists commanded the highest salaries. "I opted for extra lessons in domestic subjects but I should have chosen typing instead." It is a constant regret that she made the wrong decision. "I can knit, crochet, set in a zipper and make excellent blancmange, but I barely type with four fingers. My handwriting is so bad, no one else can read it."

1293. GARRON, Rebecca. "Air of Turbulence." *Prairie Fire* 15.3 (Autumn 1994): 24-34.

1294. GREENWOOD, Gillian. *Margaret Atwood*. [Videorecording]. Sydney: SBS, 1994. 1 videocassette (VHS) (51 min.). Atwood discusses her life and work, especially *The Robber Bride*, while dramatizations from the book accompanied by commentary support the points made. Broadcast on 14 February 1994.

1295. HELLMAN, Mary. "In the Company of Women: No Halos Allowed in Atwood's Literary World." *San Diego Union* 25 January 1994: LIT NewsBank 1994: 6: B8-10.

1296. HOOVER, Bob. "Author Adds Her Share to List of Literature's Wicked Women." *Pittsburgh Post-Gazette* (PA) 7 December 1994: Section: Arts & Entertainment: B1. Atwood interviewed by phone from New York mostly focussing on her hometown of Toronto.

1297. KELLY, M. T. "Margaret Atwood." *One on One: The Imprint Interviews*. Ed. Leanna Crouch. Toronto: Somerville House, 1994. 151-162. Reprint of interview which took place 29 August 1991 on the topic of *Wilderness Tips*. Originally broadcast on TV Ontario.

1298. LYDEN, Jack. "Interview with Margaret Atwood." NPR: All Things Considered 5 February 1994: Transcript # 1384-5. (1081w). Available from Lexis-Nexis. On Zenia and bad women.

1299. LYKE, M. L. "Three Cheers for the Femme Fatale; The World Gets a Fascinating Villainess in Margaret Atwood's Wicked New Novel." *Seattle Post-Intelligencer* 4 February 1994: Section: Living: D1. (1078 w). Atwood interviewed in Seattle before reading. **On her writing style:** "Tidy answers aren't her style. That goes for books as well as interviews; Atwood, daughter of an Ottawa entomologist, likes language that 'jumps the tracks.' Fiction that 'pushes against expectation.' She calls it exploratory fiction; 'I don't write novels that tie things up.' 'People ask, 'Why don't the men resist Zenia? Why aren't they stronger?' says Atwood, who is in the process of negotiating movie rights for the highly filmable tale. 'I tell them, 'If they did, there wouldn't be a story.'"

1300. MILLER, Lauri. "On the Villainess." *San Francisco Review of Books* 19.1 (February-March 1994): 30-32, 34.

1301. NEIDORF, Robin M. "What Margaret Atwood Said to Me." *Iowa Woman* 14.2 (1994): 39-40.

1302. PINTARICH, Paul. "Margaret Atwood Relishes Life's Enigmas." *The Oregonian* (Portland) 28 January 1994: LIT NewsBank 1994: 12: D1-2.

1303. SEAMAN, Donna. "The Booklist Interview: Margaret Atwood." *Booklist* 90.10 (15 January 1994): 898-899.

1304. SUJAN, Deehra, *Margaret Atwood [et al.]* [Sound recording]. Troy, NY: Sage Colleges; Albany, NY: WAMC Public Radio, 1994. "*The Handmaid's Tale* is perhaps Canadian author Margaret Atwood's most well-known novel. Deehra Sujan caught up with Atwood in Amsterdam." (3:58). This interview is one of 4 on program (2 September 1994).

1305. YOST, Barbara. "Skipping Tea with Margaret Atwood." *Bloomsbury Review* 14.5 (September-October 1994): 3, 16-17.

Scholarly Resources

1306. "Atwood, Margaret." *The Writer's Directory 1994-96.* 11th ed. Ed. Miranda H. Ferrara and George W. Schmidt. Detroit, MI; London; Washington, DC: St. James Press, ©1994. 45. List of publications, awards, and academic positions held.

1307. "Atwood, Margaret (Eleanor)." *The Concise Columbia Encyclopedia.* 3rd ed. New York: Columbia UP, 1994. 55. Biographical reference.

1308. "Atwood, Margaret Eleanor." *Larousse Dictionary of Writers.* Ed. Rosemary Goring. Edinburgh; New York: Larousse, 1994. 44. Biographical reference.

1309. "Margaret Atwood." *Great Women Writers: The Lives and Works of 135 of the World's Most Important Women Writers, from Antiquity to the Present.* Ed. Frank N. Magill. New York: Henry Holt, 1994. 20-24. Biographical and literary sketch of Atwood.

1310. "Margaret Atwood." *Poetry Criticism: Excerpts from Criticism of the Works of the Most Significant and Widely Studied Poets of World Literature.* Vol. 8. Ed. Drew Kalasky. Detroit, MI, Washington DC, London: Gale Research, 1994. 1-44. Primarily excerpts of critical pieces on Atwood's poetry; also contains a brief biography and bibliography.

1311. ADAMS, Alice E. "*The Handmaid's Tale*: A Banished Mother." *Reproducing the Womb: Images of Childbirth in Science, Feminist Theory, and Literature.* Ithaca, NY; London: Cornell UP, 1994. 104-114. Analysis of the novel, with some comparison to Huxley's *Brave New World.*

1312. AISENBERG, Nadya. *Ordinary Heroines: Transforming the Male Myth.* New York: Continuum, 1994. passim. Brief discussion of Atwood's message in the transformation of the new heroine in a postmodern setting.

1313. ALAIMO, Stacy. "Cartographies of Undomesticated Ground: Nature and Feminism in American Women's Fiction and Theory." PhD thesis. University of Illinois at Urbana–Champaign, 1994. 304 pp. This thesis "examines how American women writers from the early nineteenth century to the present have rearticulated the gendered ideologies of nature. Insights from feminist theory, cultural studies, and interdisciplinary postmodern theories of nature enable me to reveal how women's texts transform the representations promoted by literary, popular, and political discourses." (Author). Chapter 4 includes references to Atwood. For more see *DAI-A* 55.09 (March 1995): 2825.

1314. ALLEN, Lisa F. "Vision Quest: The Search for Creative Harmony in Two Novels by Margaret Atwood." MA thesis. Kent State University, 1994. 86 pp.

1315. AMENDE, Coral. *Legends in Their Own Time*. New York; London; Toronto; Sydney; Tokyo; Singapore: Prentice Hall General Reference, 1994. See especially "Atwood, Margaret," 13.

1316. BACH, Susanne. "Bildliche Bildung-Natur- und Zivilisationsparadigmen in Margaret Atwoods *Cat's Eye*." Das Natur / Kultur-Paradigma in Der Englischsprachigen Erzählliteratur Des 19 und 20. Jahrhunderts: Festschrift Zum 60. Geburtstag Von Paul Goetsch. Ed. Konrad Groß, Kurt Müller, and Meinhard Winkgens. Tübingen: Narr, 1994. 380-397.

1317. BALDWIN, Dean, and Gregory L. MORRIS. *The Short Story in English: Britain and North America: An Annotated Bibliography*. Metuchen, NJ; London: Scarecrow Press and Pasadena; Englewood Cliffs, NJ: Salem Press, 1994. 35. Two sources cited for study of Atwood.

1318. BALESTRA, Gianfranca. "Topografie della mente: Analisi di 'Polarities' di Margaret Atwood." *Moderni e post moderni: Studi sul racconto canadese del Novecento*. Abano Terme: Piovan Editore, 1994. 25-41. Analysis in Italian of "Polarities" from *Dancing Girls*.

1319. BATSTONE, Kathleen Loren. "Unlocking Pandora's Box: Female Desire in Three Works by Canadian Female Writers." MA thesis. Acadia University, 1994. 88 pp. Also available on microfiche from Canadian Theses Service (1994). A study of *Lady Oracle* as well as Alice Munro's *Lives of Girls and Women* and Audrey Thomas's *Songs My Mother Taught Me*. For more see *MAI* 33.04 (August 1995): 1082.

1320. BEARD, William. "The Canadianness of David Cronenberg." *Mosaic* 27.2 (June 1994): 113-133. *Survival* and *Second Words* cited; Frye/Atwood model discussed.

1321. BENNETT, Donna. "English Canada's Postcolonial Complexities." *Essays on Canadian Writing* 51-52 (Winter 1993-Spring 1994): 164-210. Describes *Surfacing* as an example of postcolonial literature. Also cites Atwood as a writer who is able to "articulate the nature of the Canadian experience."

1322. BENTLEY, D. M. R. *Mimic Fires: Accounts of Early Long Poems on Canada*. Kingston; Montreal; London; Buffalo: McGill-Queen's UP, 1994. passim. Two references to *The Journals of Susanna Moodie*.

1323. BERG, Temma F. "Sisterhood Is Fearful: Female Friendship in L. M. Montgomery." *Harvesting Thistles: The Textual Garden of L. M. Montgomery: Essays on Her Novels and Journals*. Ed. Mary Henley Rubio. Guelph: Canadian Children's Press, 1994. 36-49. Influence of Montgomery seen in *Lady Oracle* and, especially, *Cat's Eye*.

1325. BISHOP, M. G. H. "The Genius of Disease. Culture Dependent Illness: Keats, Mozart and Margaret Atwood." *Journal of the Royal Society of Medicine* 87.2 (February 1994): 67-69. *The Handmaid's Tale* is used as an example of culture dependent sickness.

1326. BOOKER, M. Keith. *Dystopian Literature: A Theory and Research Guide*. Westport, CT; London: Greenwood Press, 1994. See especially "Margaret Atwood: *The Handmaid's Tale* (1985)," 78-83, which is a summary of plot and theme as well as

"Skepticism Squared: Western Postmodernist Dystopias," 141-172, which cites *The Handmaid's Tale* as an example of Western postmodernist dystopian fiction. Suggests that it represents a change for feminist writers who traditionally wrote from a utopian viewpoint.

1327. CAMINERO-SANTANGELO, Marta. "Moving Beyond 'The Blank White Spaces': Atwood's Gilead, Postmodernism, and Strategic Resistance." *Studies in Canadian Literature / Études en littérature canadienne* 19.1 (1994): 20-42. Suggests that *The Handmaid's Tale* represents postmodern feminism by its depiction of resistance to society's order and the restraints put upon this resistance. Also references *Surfacing*.

1328. CARRERA SUAREZ, Isabel. "'Yet I Speak, Yet I Exist': Affirmation of the Subject in Atwood's Short Stories." *Margaret Atwood: Writing and Subjectivity: New Critical Essays*. Ed. Colin Nicholson. New York: St. Martin's Press, 1994. 230-247. Traces the evolution of the subject and language from *Dancing Girls* to *Bluebeard's Egg* to *Wilderness Tips*.

1330. CHEN, Zhongming. "Theorising about New Modes of Representation and Ideology in the Postmodern Age: The Practice of Margaret Atwood and Li Ang." *Canadian Review of Comparative Literature / Revue canadienne de littérature comparée* 21.3 (September 1994): 341-354. Both writers "achieve postmodern irony with a feminist cutting edge," "break down traditional symbolic or semiotic systems," and "subvert patriarchal ideologies."

1331. CHOE, Okyoung. "Margaret Atwood's *The Handmaid's Tale*: A Survival Story." *Canadian Literature: Introductory and Critical Essays*. Ed. Sang Ran Lee, Kwangsook Chung, and Myungsoon Shin. Yonsei University: Center for Canadian Studies, Institute of East and West Studies, published by Seoul Press, 1994. 147-158. Discusses *The Handmaid's Tale* as a representative Canadian novel.

1332. COLES EDITORIAL BOARD. *Atwood*—The Edible Woman: *Notes*. Toronto: Coles, 1994. 121. Study guide.

1333. COOLEY, Dennis. "Nearer by Far: The Upset 'I' in Margaret Atwood's Poetry." *Margaret Atwood: Writing and Subjectivity: New Critical Essays*. Ed. Colin Nicholson. New York: St. Martin's Press, 1994. 68-93. Discusses difference between the early and the later poetry in terms of the speaker's role.

1334. DAVEY, Frank. "Agony Envy: Margaret Atwood's 'Notes Towards a Poem.'" *Canadian Literature: Recent Essays*. Ed. Manorama Trikha. New Delhi: Pencraft International, 1994. 249-259. "Notes Towards a Poem That Can Never Be Written" was first published in *True Stories*, ©1981.

1335. ———. *Canadian Literary Power*. Edmonton: NeWest, 1994. See especially Chapter 6: "Agony Envy: Atwood's 'Notes Towards a Poem.'" 151-165. "Notes Towards a Poem That Can Never be Written" was originally published in *True Stories*, ©1981.

1336. ———. *Karla's Web: A Cultural Investigation of the Mahaffy-French Murders*. Toronto: Penguin, 1994. Murder in its cultural context includes references to Atwood's *Bodily Harm* (194-198), *The Edible Woman* (152), *The Handmaid's Tale* (198-201,) and *Surfacing* (213-214).

1337. DAVIDSON, Arnold E. *Coyote Country: Fictions of the Canadian West*. Durham, NC; London: Duke UP, 1994. passim. Four references to Atwood's works.

1338. DE ANGELIS, Valerio Massimo. "'It Isn't a Story I'm Telling': *The Handmaid's Tale* come romanzo storico." *Rivista di studi canadesi* 7 (1994): 87-96.

1339. DEER, Glenn. *Postmodern Canadian Fiction and the Rhetoric of Authority*. Montreal; Kingston; London; Buffalo, NY: McGill-Queen's UP, 1994. See especially

"*The Handmaid's Tale*: Dystopia and the Paradoxes of Power," 110-129, which analyzes *The Handmaid's Tale* as a narrative and the power given to the narrator.

1340. DEVANEY, Sheila Ann. "The Reconfiguration of Civilization and Nature in Margaret Atwood's *Surfacing* and *The Handmaid's Tale*." MA thesis. University of North Carolina at Wilmington, 1994. 58 pp.

1341. DODSON, Danita Joan. "Women's Utopia: The 'Imagined Community' in Other Worlds." PhD thesis. University of Southern Mississippi, 1994. 335 pp. *The Handmaid's Tale* discussed along with Charlotte Perkins Gilman's *Herland*, Marge Piercy's *Woman on the Edge of Time*, Buchi Emecheta's *Rape of Shavi*, Bessie Head's *Question of Power*, and Alice Walker's *Color Purple*. For more see *DAI-A* 56.03 (September 1995): 922.

1342. DONAWERTH, Jane L., and Carol A. KOLMERTEN. "Introduction." *Utopian and Science Fiction by Women: Worlds of Difference*. Ed. Jane L. Donawerth and Carol A. Kolmerten. Syracuse, NY: Syracuse UP, 1994. 12. Reference to *The Handmaid's Tale* as failed female heroism.

1343. DOPP, Jamie. "Subject-Position as Victim-Position in *The Handmaid's Tale*." *Studies in Canadian Literature / Études en littérature canadienne* 19.1 (1994): 43-57. A critique of *The Handmaid's Tale*. The author suggests that, unlike most critical commentary, *The Handmaid's Tale* depicts patriarchy rather than opposing it.

1344. EVANS, Mark. "Versions of History: *The Handmaid's Tale* and Its Dedicatees." *Margaret Atwood: Writing and Subjectivity: New Critical Essays*. Ed. Colin Nicholson. New York: St. Martin's Press, 1994. 177-188. Relates influence of the dedicatees, Mary Webster and Perry Miller, on this novel.

1345. FINDLEY, Timothy. "Atwood, Margaret." *Encyclopedia of Post-Colonial Literatures in English*. Vol. 1. Ed. Eugene Benson and L. W. Conolly. London; New York: Routledge, 1994. 75-77. Biographical reference.

1346. FORTH, Sarah S. "Women's Responses to Evil: A Literary and Theological Study." PhD thesis. Northwestern University, 1994. 226 pp. "This study investigates women's responses to evil through close readings of imaginative works of literature by three contemporary North American women: Annie Dillard, Margaret Atwood, and Paule Marshall. The intent is to discover resources that enable women to generate creative alternatives to evil....Readings of the three literary 'friends' under consideration—*Holy the Firm* by Annie Dillard, *Bodily Harm* by Margaret Atwood, and *Praisesong for the Widow* by Paule Marshall—demonstrate that each provides distinct responses to evil. Dillard offers to a suffering world her gift of artistic sacrifice; Atwood prescribes subversion of the existing, unjust social order; and Marshall limns for us a sanctified prophet struggling for her people through a return to the spiritual blessings of her African and Black church heritage. Commonalities also exist among the three works...." (Author). For more see *DAI-A* 56.03 (September 1995): 985.

1347. GARDNER, Laurel J. "Pornography as a Matter of Power in *The Handmaid's Tale*." *Notes on Contemporary Literature* 24.5 (November 1994): 5-7. Contends that the power described in *The Handmaid's Tale* is more reprehensible than pornography.

1348. GEBBIA, Alessandro. "'Surviving *Survival*': *Survival* ovvero istruzioni per l'uso." *Rivista di studi canadesi* 7 (1994): 117-124.

1349. GILBERT, Emily. "Home / City / Nation: Identity, Ideology and Place in Toronto Women's Literature." MA thesis. York University, 1994. 218 pp. Also available on microfiche from Canadian Theses Service (1995). "This thesis explores some of the issues relating to identity, ideology and place in some Canadian women's novels set in the city of Toronto in the middle 1970s. At this time, not only was the city undergoing radical changes, but women's place and role in the city were also changing. The urban fiction depicts many of these transformations. Three novels will be examined in detail: Margaret Atwood's *Lady Oracle* (1976), Helen Weitlzweig's *Basic Black with Pearls* (1980) and Marian Engel's *Lunatic Villas* (1981)." (Author). For more see *MAI* 34.01 (February 1996): 70.

1350. GILBERT, Sandra M., and Susan GUBAR. *No Man's Land: The Place of the Woman Writer in the Twentieth Century. Vol. 3: Letters from the Front.* New Haven, CT; London: Yale UP, 1994. passim. Atwood discussed in several sections, especially *The Edible Woman* and *Lady Oracle.*

1351. GILBERT-MACEDA, Ma Teresa. "Madres e hijas en la narrativa de Margaret Atwood." *Estudios de la mujer en el ámbito de los países de habla inglesa.* Ed. Margarita Ardanaz et al. Madrid: Universidad Complutense de Madrid, 1994. 333-340.

1352. GLASBERG, Ronald P. "The Dynamics of Domination: Levi's *Survival in Auschwitz*, Solzhenitsyn's *The Gulag Archipelago*, and Atwood's *The Handmaid's Tale.*" *Canadian Review of Comparative Literature / Revue canadienne de littérature comparée* 21.4 (December 1994): 679-693. Sees the 3 accounts as variations on a theme with elements in common; although Atwood's is fiction, the other two works are literary nonfiction.

1353. GODARD, Barbara. "My (m)Other, My Self: Strategies for Subversion in Atwood and Hébert." *Canadian Literature: Recent Essays.* Ed. Manorama Trikha. New Delhi: Pencraft International, 1994. 149-164. Based on a lecture delivered in 1981. Focus on *Lady Oracle.*

1354. GOLDENSOHN, Barry. "Euridice Looks Back." *American Poetry Review* 23 (November-December 1994): 43-52. Goldensohn "examines poetic representations of the myth of Eurydice and Orpheus and argues that in a century when the understanding of women's lives is changing so dramatically, Eurydice's voice can be very attractive to the poet once she is transformed from the passive, sentimental victim to something else—usually a defiant, angry woman, or one more passionate about death than love. Analyzing several poems that employ the myth, including those of Atwood, he finds that in all of them Eurydice and Orpheus mirror a complex debate that reflects the enormous change in the status of women and women artists." (Journal).

1355. GOMEZ, Christine. "From Being an Unaware Victim to Becoming a Creative Non-victim: A Study of Two Novels of Margaret Atwood." *Perspectives on Canadian Fiction.* Ed. Sudhakar Pandey. New Delhi: Prestige Books, 1994. 73-93. *The Edible Woman* and *The Handmaid's Tale.*

1356. GORING, Rosemary, ed. *Larousse Dictionary of Literary Characters.* Edinburgh; New York: Larousse, 1994. Contains entries for characters from Atwood's first 7 novels.

1357. GRACE, Sherrill E. "Atwood, Margaret (Eleanor)." *The Oxford Companion to Twentieth-Century Poetry in English.* Ed. Ian Hamilton. Oxford; New York: Oxford UP, 1994. 20-21. Biographical reference.

1358. ———. "Gender as Genre: Atwood's Autobiographical 'I.'" *Margaret Atwood: Writing and Subjectivity: New Critical Essays.* Ed. Colin Nicholson. New York: St. Martin's Press, 1994. 189-203. This theme is especially present in *Lady Oracle, The Handmaid's Tale*, and *Cat's Eye.*

1359. ———. "Quest for the Peaceable Kingdom: Urban/Rural Codes in Roy, Laurence and Atwood." *Canadian Literature Recent Essays.* Ed. Manorama Trikha. New Delhi: Pencraft International, 1994. 149-164.

1360. GRANT, Cynthia, Susan SEAGROVE, and Peggy SAMPLE. "'Penelope' Based on the "Circe / Mud Cycle" by Margaret Atwood." *Canadian Theatre Review* 78 (Spring 1994): 42-58. "A documentation of the process and three productions of this work inspired by the poetry of Margaret Atwood, Greek tragedy and epics."

1361. GREGORY, Eileen. "Dark Persephone and Margaret Atwood's *Procedures for Underground.*" *Images of Persephone: Feminist Readings in Western Literature.* Ed. Elizabeth T. Hayes. Gainesville; Tallahassee; Tampa; Boca Raton; Pensacola; Orlando; Miami; Jacksonville: UP of Florida, 1994. 136-152. Examines the representation of underground in Atwood's poetry.

1362. HANSOT, Elisabeth. "Selves, Survival, and Resistance in *The Handmaid's Tale.*" *Utopian Studies* 5.2 (1994): 56-69. Includes a discussion of the public persona of the handmaid in the book, the distinction between memory and dream and how the element of resistance was portrayed.

1363. HARKER, John W. "'Plain Sense' and 'Poetic Significance': Tenth-Grade Readers Reading Two Poems." *Poetics: Journal for Empirical Research on Literature, the Media and the Arts* 22.3 (1994): 199-218.

1364. HOLLINGER, Veronica. "Putting on the Feminine: Gender and Negativity in *Frankenstein* and *The Handmaid's Tale.*" *Negation, Critical Theory, and Postmodern Textuality.* Ed. Daniel Fischlin. Dordrecht: Kluwer Acad, 1994. 203-224.

1365. HORNE, H. "Revisionist Mythmaking: The Use of the Fairy Tale Motif in the Works of Angela Carter, Margaret Atwood and Anne Sexton." MLitt thesis. University of Newcastle upon Tyne, 1994.

1366. HOWELLS, Coral. "*Cat's Eye:* Elaine Risley's Retrospective Art." *Margaret Atwood: Writing and Subjectivity: New Critical Essays.* Ed. Colin Nicholson. New York: St. Martin's Press, 1994. 204-218. The paintings and the retrospective exhibition provide a means to examine the female as a subject in various forms of autobiography.

1367. ———. "Margaret Atwood's Canadian Signature: From *Surfacing* and *Survival* to *Wilderness Tips.*" *British Journal of Canadian Studies* 9.2 (1994): 205-215.

1368. HUGGAN, Graham. *Territorial Disputes: Maps and Mapping Strategies in Contemporary Canadian and Australian Fiction.* Toronto; Buffalo, NY; London: University of Toronto Press, 1994. passim. Several passages in which *Surfacing* and *The Handmaid's Tale* are discussed in terms of their charting a course in a search for identity.

1369. HUNG, Mei-hwa. "In Search of Female Self in Margaret Atwood's *Surfacing.*" MA thesis. Tamkang University, 1994. 91 pp.

1370. JACOBSOHN, Rachel W. *The Reading Group Handbook: Everything You Need to Know, from Choosing Members to Leading Discussions.* New York: Hyperion, 1994. Atwood works appear on several suggested lists.

1371. JOHNSON, Constance Hochstein. "The Journey: Walking with Mary Oliver, Margaret Atwood, and Adrienne Rich." MA thesis. Hamline University, 1994. 69 pp.

1372. KAUR, Iqbal. *Margaret Atwood's* Surfacing: *A Critical Study.* Chandigarh [India]: Arun, ©1994.

1373. KEEFER, Janice Kulyk. "Hope against Hopelessness: Margaret Atwood's *Life Before Man.*" *Margaret Atwood: Writing and Subjectivity: New Critical Essays.* Ed. Colin Nicholson. New York: St. Martin's Press, 1994. 153-176. Analyzes the bleakness of this novel, especially its place in the progression of Atwood's fiction.

1374. KEITH, W. J. "Interpreting and Misinterpreting 'Bluebeard's Egg': A Cautionary Tale." *Margaret Atwood: Writing and Subjectivity: New Critical Essays.* Ed. Colin Nicholson. New York: St. Martin's Press, 1994. 248-257. Relates experience in reading an essay on "Bluebeard's Egg"; in doing so, makes point of necessity of reading what the story really says and not fitting the story to a theory.

1375. LAHAIE, Christiane. "Alice s'en va au cinéma, ou comment museler le roman féministe [Alice Goes to the Movies, Or How to Muzzle the Feminist Novel]." *Recherches Feministes* 7.2 (1994): 81-94. "Turning a novel into a film is never easy, especially when the novel is a feminist one. In that case, narrative structures may express subversion through female protagonists' discourse or non-discourse. But does the difficulty result from the medium's limitations, or from dominant cinematic habits which usually depict women solely as objects of male discourse? An analysis of *Laura Laur* by Suzanne Jacob and its cinematographic version by Brigitte Sauriol, as well as of *The Handmaid's Tale* by Margaret Atwood and Volker Schlöndorff's movie, should allow us to verify the following hypothesis: Laura Laur and Offred, two exceptional fictional protagonists, become victims of underexposure when becoming stars of the big screen." (Journal summary).

1376. LAL, Malashri. "'What Home Shall a Woman Find?' A Feminist Critique of Margaret Atwood and Anita Desai." *The India-Canada Relationship: Exploring the Political Economic and Cultural Dimensions.* Ed. J. S. Grewal and Hugh Johnston. New Delhi; Thousand Oaks, CA: Sage Publications, 1994. 380-391. "The novels selected for discussion are Margaret Atwood's *Surfacing* (1973) and Anita Desai's *Where Shall We Go This Summer* (1975)."

1377. LAMB, Martha Moss. "Margaret Atwood's 'Trick Hip': Transcending Duality with Imagination." MA thesis. Florida Atlantic University, 1994. 73 pp.

1378. LAURENT, Delphine. "La créativité féminine dans l'oeuvre de Margaret Atwood: *Surfacing, Lady Oracle, Cat's Eye.*" MLM [Maîtrise de letters modernes] thesis, Université de Bourgogne, 1994. 123 pp.

1379. LAURET, Maria. *Liberating Literature: Feminist Fiction in America.* London; New York: Routledge, 1994. See especially section in chapter, "Backlash Fictions of the 1980s," 176-183, on *The Handmaid's Tale* which suggests a "hostility to feminism" in this novel.

1380. LEDYARD, M. D. "Metaphoric Landscape in the Novels of Virginia Woolf and Margaret Atwood." MPhil thesis. St. Andrews, 1994.

1381. LITTLE, Judy. "Humoring the Sentence: Women's Dialogic Comedy." *American Women Humorists: Critical Essays.* Ed. Linda A. Morris. New York; London: Garland Publishing, 1994. 155-170. Brief mention of Atwood's poem, "The Landlady," as an example of women's comic style.

1382. LOMBARDI, Giancarlo. "Leggere 'a rebours': Strategie d'interpretazione storico-testuale in *The Robber Bride.*" *Rivista di studi canadesi* 7 (1994): 105-116.

1383. LONG, Michael. "Theory into Practice: Establishing the Postmodernity of Atwood's 'Loulou; or, The Domestic Life of the Language.'" *Postscript: A Journal of Graduate School Criticism and Theory* 1.2 (1994): 61-70.

1384. LUTWACK, Leonard. *Birds in Literature.* Gainesville; Tallahassee; Tampa; Boca Raton; Pensacola; Orlando; Miami; Jacksonville: UP of Florida, 1994. See Chapter 5, "Literature and the Future of Birds," 231-254, and especially 234-236 which discusses Atwood's descriptions of people's attitude to the wild in *Surfacing* and *Bluebeard's Egg.*

1385. MARINOVICH, Sarolta. "The Discourse of the Other: Female Gothic in Contemporary Women's Writing." *Neohelicon* 21.1 (1994): 189-205. Atwood's "Giving Birth" is examined along with works by Flannery O'Connor and Doris Lessing.

1386. MARRA, Giulio. "*Surfacing*: A Journey to Innocence." *Rivista di studi canadesi* 7 (1994): 45-52.

1387. MARTINEZ-ZALCE, Graciela. "Margaret Atwood and Octavio Paz: Convergence and Divergence." *Voices of Mexico* 28 (July-September 1994): 42-44. *Survival* and Paz's *The Labyrinth of Solitude* are used as examples of essays that are central to understanding the cultural identity of Canada and Mexico.

1388. MASCARO, Patricia Ellen. "Word and Flesh: Gender Utopias and Dystopias in Three Canadian Science Fiction Novels." MA thesis. University of Windsor, 1994. 163 pp. Also available on microfiche from Canadian Theses Service (1995). "Many Canadian authors are turning to speculative fiction genres, instead of more realistic genres, to tell their tales. In the cases of William Gibson, Margaret Atwood, and Elisabeth Vonarburg, each author has used the speculative fiction genre of utopian science fiction to satirically depict restrictive gender roles that exist in contemporary Euro-American society." (Author). For more see *MAI* 34.02 (April 1996): 532.

1389. MATTHEWS, Patricia Shaw. "Pre-Revolt in 2100: A Handmaid's Tale." *Niekas* 44 (1994): 12-13.

1390. McCOMBS, Judith. "From 'Places, Migrations' to *The Circle Game*: Atwood's Canadian and Female Metamorphoses." *Margaret Atwood: Writing and Subjectivity: New Critical Essays*. Ed. Colin Nicholson. New York: St. Martin's Press, 1994. 51-67. Traces these changes through examination of manuscript material.

1391. MEINDL, Dieter. "Gender and Narrative Perspective in Margaret Atwood's Stories." *Margaret Atwood: Writing and Subjectivity: New Critical Essays.* Ed. Colin Nicholson. New York: St. Martin's Press, 1994. 219-229. Discusses the stories from *Dancing Girls and Other Stories* and *Bluebeard's Egg* and concludes that the "short stories display a gender-based rather than a language-based conception of reality."

1392. MITCHELL, E. "Narration, Ideology and the Construction of the Female Subject in the Fiction of Margaret Atwood and Angela Carter." MA thesis. Kent (England), 1994.

1393. MOGFORD, Sheilagh A. "Taking Up Space: Power and Self-Discovery in Women's Literature." MA thesis. University of Northern Colorado, 1994. 97 pp. "In literary works dealing with marginalized groups or individuals, struggles to 'fit' within the larger society and culture are often set up against a backdrop of struggles with personal, physical, and emotional space. The question of space, or lack of it, is evident in many literary periods and genres, most significantly in works which illustrate struggle within a power structure." (Author). Uses examples from *The Edible Woman, Lady Oracle,* and *The Robber Bride.* For more see *MAI* 33.02 (April 1995): 340.

1394. MUZYCHKA, Martha Deborah. "Telling Tales about Ourselves: The Integration of Identity as a Narrative Strategy in Selected Examples of Women's Writing." MA thesis. Memorial University, 1994. 176 pp. Also available on microfiche from Canadian Theses Service (1995). Includes study of "*Cat's Eye,* in which Atwood invests her writing with an awareness of such contemporary issues as personal growth, self-awareness and the philosophy that the personal is political." (Author). For more see *MAI* 33.06 (December 1995): 1670.

1395. NICHOLSON, Colin. "Living on the Edges: Constructions of Post-Colonial Sub-jectivity in Atwood's Early Poetry." *Margaret Atwood: Writing and Subjectivity: New Critical Essays*. Ed. Colin Nicholson. New York: St. Martin's Press, 1994. 11-50. In the Canadian paradigm of Atwood's poetry, the female is placed as the subject, and the meaning comes from this positioning.

1396. NICHOLSON, Colin, ed. *Margaret Atwood: Writing and Subjectivity: New Critical Essays*. New York: St. Martin's Press, 1994. 261 pp. Also published in Great Britain by Macmillan. Essays appear here as individual entries.

1397. NILSEN, Helge Normann. "Four Feminist Novels by Margaret Atwood." *American Studies in Scandinavia* 26.2 (1994): 126-139. Cites *The Edible Woman*, *Surfacing*, *Lady Oracle*, and *Bodily Harm* as novels that present the theme that women are oppressed in Western society and have limited options to overcome this.

1398. ———. "Sukzessive und simultane Aufspaltung der Erzählinstanz im Erzählwerk Margaret Atwoods." *Orbis Litterarum* 49.4 (1994): 233-251. Narrative techniques, especially in the early and middle phases, are examined.

1399. NISCHIK, Reingard M. "Sukzessive und simultane Aufspaltung der Erzählinstanz im Erzählwerk Margaret Atwoods." *Orbis Litterarum: International Review of Literary Studies* 49.4 (1994): 233-251.

1400. NOVY, Marianne. *Engaging with Shakespeare: Responses of George Eliot and Other Women Novelists*. Athens; London: University of Georgia Press, 1994. passim. Images of Shakespeare appear in *Life Before Man* and *Cat's Eye*; a note refers to "Gertrude Talks Back" as Gertrude is rewritten as a Shakespearean woman; *Survival* is also mentioned in terms of rewriting Shakespeare's tragedies.

1401. OSBORNE, Carol. "Constructing the Self through Memory: *Cat's Eye* as a Novel of Female Development." *Frontiers* 14.3 (1994): 95-112. The use of memory as a tool for contemporary novelists is explored in *Cat's Eye*.

1402. PALUMBO, Alice. "The Maple Curtain: New Writing on Margaret Atwood." *Paragraph: Canadian Fiction Review* 16.3 (Winter-Spring 1994-95): 25-28. Review-essay on 4 new secondary works on Margaret Atwood.

1403. ———. "Writing Moral Stories: Genre and Gothic in Lynn Crosbie." *Open Letter* 8.9 (Summer 1994): 86-96. Cites *Lady Oracle*; also describes Atwood as a Gothic poet.

1404. PARKER, Peter, ed. *The Reader's Companion to the Twentieth-Century Novel*. London: Fourth Estate and Helicon, 1994. Profiles two novels, *The Edible Woman* (442-443) and *The Handmaid's Tale* (592-593).

1405. PEARCE, Lynne. *Reading Dialogics*. London; New York; Melbourne; Auckland: Edward Arnold, 1994. passim. Two references to *The Handmaid's Tale*.

1406. PEARLMAN, Mickey. *What to Read: The Essential Guide for Reading Group Members and Other Book Lovers*. New York: HarperPerennial, 1994. 34, 164. Brief synopsis of *The Robber Bride* and *The Handmaid's Tale*.

1407. PIRÉ, Luciana. "Parole e meraviglia: La poesia di Margaret Atwood." *Rivista di studi canadesi* 7 (1994): 53-64.

1408. POLLVOGT, Lieselotte. "Another Mode of Meaning: Navigating Discourse in Novels by Margaret Atwood, Marge Piercy, and Thomas Pynchon." MA thesis. University of North Carolina at Chapel Hill, 1994. 58 pp.

1409. PONTUALE, Francesco. "*Survival*, ovvero: Ma la letteratura canadese è davvero cosí catastrofica?" *Rivista di studi canadesi* 7 (1994): 35-44.

1410. PORTELLI, Alessandro. *The Text and the Voice: Writing, Speaking, and Democracy in American Literature*. New York: Columbia UP, 1994. passim. Brief mentions of *Cat's Eye* and *The Handmaid's Tale*.

1411. PORTER-LADOUSSE, Gillian. "The Retreating Sign: The Obsolescent Bridge in Margaret Atwood's *Cat's Eye*." *Commonwealth: Essays and Studies* 17.1 (Autumn 1994): 51-57. Analysis of the symbolism of the bridge in this novel.

1412. POTTER, Nick. "Tropics of Identity in Margaret Atwood's *Surfacing*." *Swansea Review* (1994): 462-469.

1413. PRABHAKAR, M. "Margaret Atwood's *The Edible Woman*: Guide to Feminism." *New Quest* 105 (1994): 149-154.

1414. PRINGLE, Mary M. "'The Desire of the Woman Which Is for the Desire of the Man': Feminist Readings in Austen and Atwood." PhD thesis. University of North Dakota, 1994. 134 pp. "Three novels by Jane Austen are compared to three novels by Margaret Atwood in the context of reading and writing as feminist activity. Anna G. Jonasdottir's theoretical discussion of male authority supported by women's alienated love elaborates the apparent truth of W. B. Yeats's observation that 'the desire of the woman...is for the desire of the man,' the thematic link between the three essays which focus on women's concerns regarding work, maternity, and professionalism. Austen and Atwood are presented as early and late forms of a bright, coherent, middle-class female subjectivity that has remained remarkably coherent over two centuries and two continents. Austen's *Northanger Abbey* and Atwood's *Lady Oracle* are compared as two metagothics....In the comparison between *Mansfield Park* and *The Edible Woman*, the significance of women's potential, symbolic, and actual maternal functions is discussed in the context of woman as commodity. *Persuasion* and *Life Before Man* are compared as sites for the presentation of professionalism as an ascendant ideology allowing for both the advancement and control of the middle class." (Author). For more see *DAI-A* 55.12 (June 1995): 3854.

1415. QUARTERMAINE, Peter. "Margaret Atwood's *Surfacing*: Strange Familiarity." *Margaret Atwood: Writing and Subjectivity: New Critical Essays*. Ed. Colin Nicholson. New York: St. Martin's Press, 1994. 119-132. *Surfacing* follows the pattern set out in *Survival*—of literature providing both a mirror of the world and a map of the mind.

1416. RAMAKRISHNAN, E. V. "'To Trust Is to Let Go': Vision and Reality in Atwood's *Surfacing*." *Perspectives on Canadian Fiction*. Ed. Sudhakar Pandey. New Delhi: Prestige Books, 1994. 106-112.

1417. RAO, Eleonora. "Margaret Atwood's *Lady Oracle:* Writing against Notions of Unity." *Margaret Atwood: Writing and Subjectivity*. Ed. Colin Nicholson. New York: St. Martin's, 1994. 133-152. The variety of genres parodied provides a study of the fiction from within the story, much as Jane Austen did in *Northanger Abbey*.

1418. RAO, T. Nageshwara. "Male Mapping and Female Trapping: Parodic Deconstruction in Atwood's *Lady Oracle*." *Perspectives on Canadian Fiction*. Ed. Sudhakar Pandey. New Delhi: Prestige Books, 1994. 113-120.

1419. RATHBURN, Frances Margaret. "The Ties That Bind: Breaking the Bonds of Victimization in the Novels of Barbara Pym, Fay Weldon and Margaret Atwood." PhD thesis. University of North Texas, 1994. 294 pp. "In this study of several novels each by Barbara Pym, Fay Weldon, and Margaret Atwood, I focus on two areas: the ways in which female protagonists break out of their victimization by individuals, by institutions, and by cultural tradition, and the ways in which each author uses a structural pattern in her novels to propel her characters to solve their dilemmas to the best of their abilities and according to each woman's personality and strengths....The chapter on Atwood includes detailed analysis of *Surfacing* and *Cat's Eye*, with brief discussions of *The Edible Woman, The Handmaid's Tale*, and *The Robber Bride*." (Author). For more see *DAI-A* 56.01 (July 1995): 189.

1420. RICCIARDI, Caterina. "'Second Words' per Margaret Atwood." *Rivista di studi canadesi* 7 (1994): 7-8.

1421. ROSS, Robert L. "Canadian Literature." *The Reader's Adviser. Vol. 2: The Best in World Literature.* 14th ed. Ed. Robert DiYanni (vol. ed.) and Marion Sader (series ed.). New Providence, NJ: R. R. Bowker, 1994. 902-907. Quotes *Survival* as an introduction to Canadian literature; *Oxford Book of Canadian Short Stories in English* is mentioned; includes a brief biographical sketch and bibliography.

1422. RUSSOTTO, Márgara. "Identidad, espacio y otras afinidades culturales en la narrativa de Margaret Atwood." *Revista Venezolana de estudios canadiense* 1.1 (March 1994): 59-69. Survey article on Atwood's works.

1423. SALAT, M. F. "A Delicious Fare: Margaret Atwood's *The Edible Woman*." *Perspectives on Canadian Fiction*. Ed. Sudhakar Pandey. New Delhi: Prestige Books, 1994. 94-105.

1424. SANFILIPPO, Matteo. "Margaret Atwood, il Canada e gli Stati Uniti." *Rivista di studi canadesi* 7 (1994): 19-34.

1425. SCACCHI, Anna. "Lo specchio barocco e la chiesa quacchera: La morte dell'autore in *Lady Oracle*." *Rivista di studi canadesi* 7 (1994): 65-76.

1426. SCANNAVINI, Anna. "'Where Then Do Babies Come From?' La difficile generazione del testo in *The Handmaid's Tale*." *Rivista di studi canadesi* 7 (1994): 97-104.

1427. SCHALL, Birgitta. "Von der Version zur Vision: Von der Melancholie zur Trauer. Postmoderne Text- und Blickökonomien bei Margaret Atwood." PhD thesis. University of Munich, 1994.

1428. SHANDS, Kerstin W. *The Repair of the World: The Novels of Marge Piercy*. Westport, CT; London: Greenwood Press, 1994. passim. Atwood's writings on Piercy, especially her critique of *Woman on the Edge of Time*, are discussed.

1429. SHAW, Monica Leigh. "The Balanced One Survives: Gender Roles and Women in Margaret Atwood's *Surfacing, Bodily Harm* and *Cat's Eye*." MA thesis. University of Alabama (Huntsville), 1994. 111 pp. "In her novels *Surfacing, Bodily Harm*, and *Cat's Eye*, Margaret Atwood describes a woman's successful journey towards self-knowledge and ending the victimization she has suffered as a result of the patriarchal feminine gender role....Atwood's vision implies that women and men inherently possess traits patriarchally attributed to both the masculine and the feminine, and that accepting these traits is a first step toward overcoming the patterns of dominance and submission in patriarchal society's relationships, both personal and political." (Author). For more see *MAI* 33.04 (August 1995): 1085.

1430. SINGH, Sunaina. *The Novels of Margaret Atwood and Anita Desai: A Comparative Study in Feminist Perspectives*. New Delhi: Creative Books, 1994.

1431. SISK, David Warner. "Claiming Mastery over the Word: Transformations of Language in Six Twentieth-Century Dystopias." PhD thesis. University of North Carolina at Chapel Hill, 1994. 405 pp. "The present study examines the central roles language plays in six representative dystopian novels in English: Aldous Huxley's *Brave New World*, George Orwell's *Nineteen Eighty-Four*, Anthony Burgess's *A Clockwork Orange*, Margaret Atwood's *The Handmaid's Tale*, Russell Hoban's *Riddley Walker*, and Suzette Haden *Elgin's Native Tongue I and II*....Dystopia has emerged as the dominant branch of speculative fiction better suited to examine the repressive bases upon which such upheavals are founded. Speculative fiction offers alternative views of human development by constantly posing variations on the theme of 'What if....?' Dystopian authors seize upon language as a topic guaranteed to excite reader interest and empower didactic concerns. Throughout these novels, language is the principal weapon through which oppressors seize and maintain power. At the same time, language also serves as the primary tool by which the oppressed resist and rebel." (Author). For more see *DAI-A* 55.07 (January 1995): 1972.

1432. SMITH, Bonnie Lynne. "The Sleeping Beauty Subtext in Rosario Ferré's 'La Bella Durmiente' and Margaret Atwood's 'Bluebeard's Egg.'" MA thesis. Florida Atlantic University, 1994. 92 pp. "The well-known Grimms' fairy tale 'Sleeping Beauty' forms the subtext of two recent literary works, Rosario Ferre's novella 'La bella durmiente' (1976) and Margaret Atwood's short story 'Bluebeard's Egg' (1983). Both contemporary authors suggest that certain negative aspects inherent in the Sleeping Beauty paradigm should not persist in women's literature, unless the texts lead to transformation and self-realization of the heroines. This study demonstrates how the authors expose the fallacy in the paradigm, depart from it, and refigure it by transforming their heroines into characters quite distinct from the Grimm prototype....As the characters distance themselves from hegemonic patriarchal traditions, each author's work is also removed from the referent of masculine literary traditions and returned to its origins, the oral tale." (Author). For more see *MAI* 33.03 (June 1995): 728.

1433. SNODGRASS, Mary Ellen. The Handmaid's Tale: *Notes.* Lincoln, NE: Cliffs Notes; New York: Hungry Minds, 1994. 85 pp.

1434. STAELS, Hilde. "Canada en de Conditie Van De Vrouw: Margaret Atwood over Kolonisatie." *The Empire Writes Back (again): Vergelijkende literatuurwetenschap en post-koloniale literatuurstudie.* Ed. Luc Herman. Antwerp: Vlaamse Vereniging voor Algemene en Vergelijkende Literatuurwetenschap, 1994. 37-48.

1435. STILLMAN, Peter, and Anne S. JOHNSON. "Identity, Complicity, and Resistance in *The Handmaid's Tale.*" *Utopian Studies* 5.2 (1994): 70-86.

1436. STRONG, Amy L. "That Glaring, Hideously Difficult White Space: Feminist Visions in *To the Lighthouse* and *Lady Oracle.*" MA thesis. University of North Carolina at Chapel Hill, 1994. 40 pp.

1437. TANTAKIS, Penny. "'I Am the Market': A Critique of the Commodity in Selected Fiction by Margaret Atwood." MA thesis. Carleton University, 1994. 133 pp. Also available on microfiche from Canadian Theses Service (1994). "This thesis explores the nature and development of Margaret Atwood's materialist vision of culture. Drawing upon Marxist, poststructuralist and psychoanalytic theories, my theoretical framework allows me to move beyond traditional historical materialism and extend the notion of the commodity to map out the materiality of sign systems operating in Atwood's work and culture. I suggest that my theoretical paradigm, when applied to *The Edible Woman, Lady Oracle, The Handmaid's Tale,* and *The Robber Bride,* engages issues of subjectivity and hegemony on a spectacular stage of late capitalism." (Author). For more see *MAI* 33.03 (June 1995): 733.

1438. THOMPSON, Dawn. "A Politics of Memory: Cognitive Strategies of Five Women Writing in Canada." PhD thesis. University of British Columbia, 1994. 194 pp. Also available on microfiche from Canadian Theses Service (1994). A study of *Surfacing,* plus Nicole Brossard's *Picture Theory,* Beatrice Culleton's *In Search of April Raintree,* Marlene Nourbese Philip's *Looking for Livingstone,* and Régine Robin's *Québécoite.* For more see *DAI-A* 55.08 (February 1995): 2381.

1439. TRABATTONI, Grazia. "The Edible Atwood: Il cibo negli scritti di Margaret Atwood." *Rivista di studi canadesi* 7 (1994): 77-86.

1440. TRAPANI, Hilary Jane. "Violence, Postcoloniality and (Re)Placing the Subject: A Study of the Novels of Margaret Atwood." MA thesis. University of Hong Kong, 1994. 72 pp.

1441. TROUARD, Dawn. "Diverting Swine: The Magical Relevancies of Eudora Welty's Ruby Fisher and Circe." *The Critical Response to Eudora Welty's Fiction.* Ed. Laurie Champion. Westport, CT; London: Greenwood Press, 1994. 337, 354. Brief mention of Atwood's *Second Words*.

1442. TRUMAN, James C. W. "We Lived in the Blank White Spaces at the Edges of Print: Patriarchy and Resistance in *The Handmaid's Tale* and *Cat's Eye*." MA thesis. University of North Carolina at Chapel Hill, 1994. 78 pp.

1443. TUCKER, Lindsey. *Textual Escap(e)ades: Mobility, Maternity, and Textuality in Contemporary Fiction by Women*. Westport, CT; London: Greenwood Press, 1994. See especially Chapter 2, "Writing to the Other Side: Metafictional Mobility in Atwood's *Lady Oracle*," 35-53.

1444. VAN HERK, Aritha. "Smoke and Mirrors." *Journal of Canadian Studies / Revue d'études canadiennes* 29.3 (Fall 1994): 158-162. Brief mention of Atwood in discussion of *The Canadian Essay* (ed. Lynch and Rampton, 1991).

1445. VOKEY, Krista R. "Tingles of Terror: The Neo-Gothic Fiction of Margaret Atwood and Jane Urquart." MA thesis. Memorial University, 1994. 207 pp. For more see *MAI* 33.06 (December 1995): 1678.

1446. VOROS, Joseph J. (Joseph John). "The Fantastic, the Uncanny, and the Marvelous: Aspects of the Unreal in Three Canadian Novels." MA thesis. University of Manitoba, 1994. Also available on microfiche from Canadian Theses Service (1997). "The thesis examines Margaret Atwood's *The Handmaid's Tale*, Timothy Findley's *Not Wanted on the Voyage*, and Robert Kroetsch's *What the Crow Said* in relation to structural paradigms established by Tzvetan Todorov and Sigmund Freud." (Author). For more see *MAI* 35.05 (October 1997): 1154.

1447. WAGNER-MARTIN, Linda. *Telling Women's Lives: The New Biography*. New Brunswick, NJ: Rutgers UP, 1994. 26, 28. The criticism that Atwood and other female writers receive differs from that of male authors.

1448. WARD, David. "*Surfacing*: Separation, Transition, Incorporation." *Margaret Atwood: Writing and Subjectivity: New Critical Essays*. Ed. Colin Nicholson. New York: St. Martin's Press, 1994. 94-118. Draws upon Arnold van Gennep's *Les rites de passage* to analyze *Surfacing*.

1449. WEAR, Delese, and Lois Lacivita NIXON. *Literary Anatomies: Women's Bodies and Health in Literature*. Albany: State University of New York Press, 1994. passim. *The Handmaid's Tale* and "Giving Birth" are cited.

1450. WECZERKA, Margrit. "Die struktur von Margaret Atwood's *The Handmaid's Tale*." MA thesis. Christian-Albrechts-Universitat zu Kiel, 1994. 86 pp.

1451. WEISS, Allan. "The Salt Garden." *Reference Guide to Short Fiction*. Ed. Noelle Watson. Detroit, MI; London; Washington, DC: St. James Press, 1994. 883-884. Summary and critique.

1452. WHEELER, Kathleen. *"Modernist" Women Writers and Narrative Art*. New York: New York UP, 1994. 2, 13, 146. Slight references to Atwood.

1453. WILLS, Deborah. "Representing Resistance: Feminist Dystopia and the Revolting Body." PhD thesis. University of Alberta, 1994. Also available on microfiche from Canadian Theses Service (1995). "This dissertation explores the possibilities and impossibilities of resistance elaborated within twentieth-century feminist dystopian narrative. It argues that these texts consistently, although to differing degrees, deflate and undermine the viability of strategies of insurgence, even while representing cultures which demand such strategies." (Author). See especially Chapter 2, which studies *The Handmaid's Tale.* For more see *DAI-A* 56.04 (October 1995): 1351.

1454. WILSON, Rob. "Techno-Euphoria and the Discourse of the American Sublime." *National Identities and Post-Americanist Narratives.* Ed. Donald E. Pease. Durham, NC; London: Duke UP, 1994. 226-227. Footnote reference to *Survival* in which Atwood describes the Canadian sublime.

1455. WOLMARK, Jenny. *Aliens and Others: Science Fiction, Feminism and Postmodernism.* Iowa City: University of Iowa Press, 1994. 100-107. Section of a chapter is devoted to Atwood; it is suggested that *The Handmaid's Tale* is used as a metaphor in the reexamination of gender relations.

1456. WOODCOCK, George. "Atwood, Margaret (Eleanor)." *Reference Guide to Short Fiction.* Ed. Noelle Watson. Detroit, MI; London; Washington, DC: St. James Press, 1994. 36-38. Biography of Atwood; includes list of publications and bibliographical references.

1457. YORK, Lorraine M. "Home Thoughts or Abroad? A Rhetoric of Place in Modern and Postmodern Canadian Political Poetry." *Essays on Canadian Writing* 51-52 (Winter 1993-Spring 1994): 321-339. Cites work from *The Animals in That Country, True Stories*, and *Two-Headed Poems* within a discussion of literary place in Canadian poetry.

1458. ———. "Wilderness Tips." *Reference Guide to Short Fiction.* Ed. Noelle Watson. Detroit, MI; London; Washington, DC: St. James Press, 1994. 974-975. Summary and critique of the short story.

Reviews of Atwood's Works

1459. *Cat's Eye.* Toronto: McClelland and Stewart; New York: Doubleday; London: Bloomsbury, 1988.
    Indian Review of Books 4.1 (October-December 1994): 8-9. By Shashi DESHPANDE.

1460. *Good Bones and Simple Murders.* New York: Talese / Doubleday, 1994.
    Times Union (Albany, NY) 6 December 1994: Section: Life & Leisure: C2. By Susan CAMPBELL. (501 w).

1461. *The Handmaid's Tale.* Toronto: McClelland and Stewart, 1985; Boston: Houghton Mifflin; London: J. Cape, 1986; New York: Fawcett Crest, London: Virago, 1986.
    Utopian Studies 5.2 (1994): 70 By Peter G. STILLMAN and S. Anne JOHNSON.

1462. *An Interview with Margaret Atwood.* American Audio Prose Library; Margaret Atwood reading "Unearthing Suite." American Audio Prose Library; Margaret Atwood reads from *The Handmaid's Tale* and talks about this futuristic fable of misogyny as compared to Orwell's *1984.* A Moveable Feast #17. Audio.
    Canadian Literature 141 (Summer 1994): 121-123. By Nancy ROBERTS.

1463. *The Robber Bride*. Toronto: McClelland and Stewart; London: Bloomsbury; New York: Talese / Doubleday, 1993.

> *Belles Lettres: A Review of Books by Women* 9.3 (Spring 1994): 2-4. By B. A. ST. ANDREWS.
>
> *BorderCrossings: A Magazine of the Arts* 13.2 (April 1994): 56-58. By Wayne TEFS.
>
> *Canadian Book Review Annual 1993*. Ed. Joyce M. Wilson. Toronto: CBRA, 1994, entry number 3002. By Sarah ROBERTSON.
>
> *Canadian Forum* 72.827 (March 1994): 44-45. By Sherrill GRACE.
>
> *Courier Mail* (AU) 8 January 1994: Section: Weekend: F6. By David MYERS. (854 w).
>
> *The Cresset* 57.4 (February 1994): 29-30. By Meridith BRAND.
>
> *Dictionary of Literary Biography Yearbook: 1993*. Ed. James W. Hipp. Detroit, MI; London: Gale Research, 1994: 15. Atwood with others in "The Year in the Novel" survey. By George GARRETT and Kristin van OGTROP.
>
> *Herizons* 8.1 (Spring 1994): 30. By Kathy PRENDERGAST.
>
> *Iowa Woman* 14.2 (1994): 40. By Marie Kester KROHN,
>
> *Jerusalem Post* 18 February 1994: Section: Books: 27. By Richard EDER. (614 w).
>
> *Missouri Review* 17.1 (1994): 185.
>
> *National Review* 46.2 (7 February 1994): 66-68. By Maggie GALLAGHER.
>
> *New Republic* 210.1 (3 January 1994): 36-39. By Ann HULBERT. (3207 w).
>
> *New Yorker* "Books Briefly Noted." 69.47 (24 January 1994): 95. ANON.
>
> *Paragraph: The Canadian Fiction Review* 15.3-4 (Winter 1993-Spring 1994): 40-41. By Alice PALUMBO.
>
> *Partisan Review* 61.1 (Winter 1994): 80-95. By Pearl K. BELL. Review includes 9 other novels.
>
> *Pittsburg Post-Gazette* 2 January 1994: Section: Entertainment: E5. By Betsy KLINE. (568 w).
>
> *Rapport: West Coast Review of Books, Art and Entertainment* 17.6 (January-February 1994): 24. By Paulette KOZICK.
>
> *Roanoke Times & World News* 20 March 1994: Section: Horizon: B4. By Mary Ann JOHNSON. (444 w).
>
> *St. Petersburg Times* (FL) 2 January 1994: Section: Perspective: 7d. By David WALTON. (603 w).
>
> *Seattle Times* 4 February 1994: LIT NewsBank 1994: 12: D3. By Melinda BARGREEN.
>
> *University of Toronto Quarterly* 64.1 (Winter 1994): 28-29. By T. L. CRAIG.
>
> *Women's Review of Books* 11.4 (January 1994): 15. By Carol ANSHAW. See also: *Women's Review of Books* "Letters." 11.6 (March 1994): 4. Letters respond to Carol Anshaw's review of *The Robber Bride*.
>
> *World and I: A Chronicle of Our Changing Era* 9.2 (February 1994): 310-315. By Roberta RUBENSTEIN.

1464. *The Robber Bride* (4 cassettes, abridged). New York: Bantam Audio, 1993. Audio.
    Forbes FYI: A Supplement to Forbes Magazine 153.6 (14 March 1994): S52.
       By Katherine A. POWERS.
    Houston Chronicle 15 January 1994: Section: Houston: 2. By Louis B. PARKS.
       (232 w).
    Library Journal 119.3 (15 February 1994): 206. By Rochelle RATNER.
    Times Union (Albany, NY) 11 January 1994: Section: Life Leisure: C2. (191 w).
       By Jon W. SPARKS.
1465. *Surfacing*. London: Virago, 1994; *Good Bones*. London: Virago, 1994.
    TLS 1 July 1994: 22. ANON.

Reviews of Adaptations of Atwood's Works

1466. *The Handmaid's Tale*. [Motion picture]. Screenplay by Harold Pinter; directed by
    Volker Schlondorff. United States: Cinecom Entertainment Group, 1990. 12 reels
    of 12 on 6 (ca. 9324 ft.).
    Halliwell's Film Guide 1994. Ed. John Walker. New York: HarperPerennial,
       1994. 517.

~ 1995 ~

Atwood's Works

1467. *A impostora*. Lisboa: Édição Livros do Brasil, 1995. Portuguese translation of *The Robber Bride* by Eduardo Saló.

1468. "The Age of Lead." *The Best of Best Short Stories of 1986-1995*. Ed. Gordon and David Hughes. London: Minerva, 1995. 21-34. Reprinted from *New Statesman and Society* 3 (20 July 1990): 24-29. Also appears in *Wilderness Tips*.

1469. "Autobiography." *Models of the Universe: An Anthology of the Prose Poem*. Selected and ed. Stuart Friebert and David Young. Oberlin, OH: Oberlin College Press, 1995. 238. Prose poem. Reprinted from *Murder in the Dark*, ©1983.

1470. "Ava Gardner Reincarnated as a Magnolia." *Michigan Quarterly Review* 34.4 (Fall 1995): 582-585. Poem. Reprinted from *Morning in the Burned House*.

1471. "Bad News." *Mississippi Review* (October 1995): s.p. Reprinted from *Good Bones*. Source: http://www.mississippireview.com/1995/07atwood.html (1 May 2006).

1472. "Before." *Antigonish Review* 102-103 (Summer 1995): 219-220. Poem.

1473. "Before the War." *Models of the Universe: An Anthology of the Prose Poem*. Selected and ed. Stuart Friebert and David Young. Oberlin, OH: Oberlin College Press, 1995. 241. Reprinted from *Murder in the Dark*, ©1983.

1474. "Bodily Harm." *For She Is the Tree of Life: Grandmothers through the Eyes of Women Writers*. Ed. Valerie Kack-Smith. Berkeley, CA: Conari Press, 1995. 159-164. Reprinted from 1983 Atwood novel.

1475. "The Bog Man." *The Cosmopolitan Book of Short Stories*. Ed. Kate Figes. London: Penguin, 1995. 147-163. Reprinted from *Wilderness Tips*. Bloomsbury, ©1991.

1476. *Bones and Murder*. London: Virago, 1995. Stories, poems, drawing, musings elected from two earlier collections, *Good Bones* and *Murder in the Dark*.

1477. "Bored." *The Best American Poetry of 1995*. Ed. Richard Howard and David Lehman. New York: Simon & Schuster, 1995. 21-22. Poem. Originally published *Atlantic Monthly* 274.6 (December 1994): 102.

1479. "The Boys' Own Annual, 1911." *From Ink Lake: Canadian Stories*. Selected by Michael Ondaatje. Toronto: Vintage, 1995. 62-63. Reprinted from *Murder in the Dark*, © 1983.

1480. "Canada Council Wants Writers' Money." *Globe and Mail* 10 May 1995: A13. Letter re: Canada Council wanting to take over the administration of the Public Lending Right Commission.

1481. "Cannibal Lecture: How Could a Culture So Apparently Boring as Ours Have Embraced the Flesh-Devouring Wendigo?" *Saturday Night* 110.9 (November

1995): 81-82, 84, 87+. Reprinted from *Strange Things: The Malevolent North in Canadian Literature*, ©1995.

1482. *Cat's Eye*. New York: Bantam Books, 1995.

1483. *Cat's Eye*. [Sound recording]. Read by Barbara Caruso. Prince Frederick, MD: Recorded Books; Oxford: Isis Audio Books, 1995. Compact disc, 14 sound discs (15 hr., 15 min.)

1484. "Christmas Carols." *Mother Songs: Poems for, by and about Mothers*. Ed. Sandra M. Gilbert, Susan Gubar, and Diana O'Hehir. New York: Norton, 1995. 330-331. Reprinted from *Selected Poems II: Poems Selected and New 1976-1986*, ©1987.

1485. "A Christmas Lorac." *Globe and Mail* 23 December 1995: C1, C15. Short story.

1486. "Come Back Madame Benoit." *Globe and Mail* 4 November 1995: C1, C8. A cookery expert has much in common with politicians.

1487. "Death by Landscape." *The Oxford Book of Adventure Stories*. Ed. Joseph Bristow. Oxford: Oxford UP, 1995. 385-400. Short story reprinted from *Wilderness Tips*, ©1991.

1488. *Die Unmöglichkeit der Nähe: Roman*. Frankfurt am Main: Fischer Taschenbuch Verlag, 1995. German translation of *Life Before Man* by Werner Waldhoff.

1489. "*Dream 2*: Brian the Still-Hunter." *Women on Hunting*. Ed. Pam Houston. Hopewell, NJ: Ecco Press, 1995. 19-20. Poem. Reprinted from *The Journals of Susanna Moodie*, ©1970.

1490. "[Excerpt]." *Bite to Eat Place: An Anthology of Contemporary Food Poetry and Poetic Prose*. Ed. Andrea Adolph, Donald L. Vallis, and Anne F. Walker. Oakland, CA: Redwood Coast Press, 1995. 171-173. Reprinted from *Murder in the Dark*, ©1983.

1491. "[Excerpt]." *Motherhood from 1920 to the Present Day: Women's Voices*. Ed. Vivien Devlin. Edinburgh: Polygon, 1995. 166. Reprinted from *Surfacing*, ©1972.

1492. "Fainting." *Models of the Universe: An Anthology of the Prose Poem*. Selected and ed. Stuart Friebert and David Young. Oberlin, OH: Oberlin College Press, 1995. 240. Prose poem. Reprinted from *Murder in the Dark*, ©1983.

1493. "Favorite Words." *Sun* (Baltimore) 3 December 1995: Section: Perspective: 4j. "30 years ago, my favorite words were 'Chthonic' and 'igneous' (I was in my Pre-Cambrian Shield phase). They then became 'Jungoid,' 'musilagenous,' and 'larval.' (Biology took over). Right now they are 'diaphanous' and 'lunar.' The latter especially, as it combines rock and light, solidity and inaccessibility, with a suggestion of tidal and howling wolves." Reprinted from *The Logophile's Orgy: Favorite Words of Famous People*. By Lewis Burke Frumkes. New York: Delacorte, 1995. 3-4.

1494. "February: A Poem." *Financial Post* 21 January 1995: 32.

1495. "Foreword." *The Book Group Book: A Thoughtful Guide to Forming and Enjoying a Stimulating Book Discussion Group*. 2nd ed. Ed. Ellen Slezak. Chicago: Chicago Review Press, 1995. ix-xi. In the section on "What to Read," several Atwood titles are recommended.

1496. "Foreword/Preface." *People Who Make a Difference / Des gens peu ordinaires*. Ed. Irene Carroll. Toronto: Penguin, 1995. 1-2. Book of celebrity photographs, proceeds of which go to AIDS research. According to Carroll, Atwood's "participation was key" in making this book happen. See *Montréal Gazette* 8 October 1995: F3.

1497. "Frogless." *Los Angeles Times* 24 September 1995: Section: Book Review: 6. Poem reprinted from *Morning in the Burned House*.

1498. "From Cave Series." *River Styx* 42-43 (1995): 58.

1499. "Gertrude Talks Back." *Wicked: Women's Wit and Humour from Elizabeth I to Ruby Wax*. Ed. Fidelis Morgan. London: Virago Press, 1995. 282-283. Reprinted from *Good Bones*, Virago, ©1992.

1500. "Girl without Hands." *Carnage Hall* 6 (1995): 16. Poem.

1501. *Good Bones*. [Sound recording]. Read by Deborah Kipp. [Toronto]: CNIB, [between 1992 and 1995]. 3 cassettes (1 container). 2:42 hours.

1502. *Good Bones & Simple Murders*. New York: Doubleday, 1995. Large Print Book Series also published in Rockland, MA, by Wheeler. Short-story pieces and prose poems. "The US collection contains work reprinted from both *Murder in the Dark* (published in Canada by Coach House Press in 1983, and in England by Virago in 1994) and *Good Bones* (published in Canada by Coach House Press in 1992, in England in hardcover by Bloomsbury in 1992, and in paperback by Virago in 1993)." (Atwood homepage).

1503. *Gute Knochen*. Berlin: Berlin Verlag, 1995. German translation of *Good Bones* by Brigette Walitzek.

1504. *The Handmaid's Tale*. Brantford, ON: W. Ross MacDonald, 1995. 2 v. Large print edition.

1505. *Het leven vóór de mens*. Amsterdam: B. Bakker, 1995. Dutch translation of *Life Before Man* by Heleen ten Holt.

1506. "How Many Canadas?" *New York Times* 5 November 1995: Section 4: 15: C2. On results of Quebec vote on separation. Reprinted as "Canada's Gnawed Cuticles Point Towards the Future" in *International Herald Tribune* 7 November 1995: Section: Opinion.

1507. "If You Can't Say Something Nice, Don't Say Anything at All." *Meanjin* 54.2 (1995): 197-[210]. Reprint of the essay on gender issues titled "If You Can't Say Something Nice, Don't Say Anything at All," which appeared in *Language in Her Eye: Views on Writing and Gender by Canadian Women Writing in English*. Ed. Libby Scheier, Sarah Sheard, and Eleanor Wachtel. Toronto: Coach House Press, 1990. 15-25.

1508. "In the Secular Night." Poem. Appears http://www.library.utoronto.ca/canpoetry /atwood/poem1.htm (1 May 2006) and is a reprint from *Morning in the Burned House*, ©1995.

1509. "Instructions for the Third Eye." *River Styx* 42-43 (1995): 56-57.

1510. "International Book of the Year: *Mr. Sandman* by Barbara Gowdy." *Times Literary Supplement* 1 December 1995: 12.

1511. "The Islands." *Images of Nature: Canadian Poets and the Group of Seven*. Compiled by David Booth. Toronto: Kids Can Press, 1995. 20. Poem.

1512. "It Is Dangerous to Read Newspapers." *Whole Earth Review* 86 (22 September 1995): 77. Reprinted from *Oxford Book of War Poetry*. Ed. Jon Stallworthy. Oxford; New York: Oxford UP, ©1984.

1513. *Katzenauge: Roman*. Frankfurt: Fisher Taschenbuch Verlag, 1995. German translation of *Cat's Eye* by Charlotte Franke.

1514. *Kocie oko*. Warsaw: Panstwowy Instytut Wydawniczy, 1995. Polish translation of *Cat's Eye* by Magdalena Konikowska.

1515. *La troisième main*. Lachine, QU: La pleine lune, 1995. French translation of *Good Bones* by Hélène Filion.

1516. "Late August." *Bite to Eat Place: An Anthology of Contemporary Food Poetry and Poetic Prose*. Ed. Andrea Adolph, Donald L. Vallis, and Anne F. Walker. Oakland, CA: Redwood Coast Press, 1995. 52. Excerpt from *You Are Happy* (Oxford UP) and *Selected Poems 1965-1975* (Oxford UP).

1517. "Livre de voûte: Un livre clé." *Sabord* 41 (Autumn 1995): 33-34. James Reaney's *The Bully* was an influential book on Atwood.

1518. Loupení jehňátek: Román o lstivosti, kráse a svedených muzích. Prague: Sulc a spol., 1995. Czech translation of *The Robber Bride* by Drahomíra Hlínková.

1519. "Making Poison." *Models of the Universe: An Anthology of the Prose Poem.* Selected and ed. Stuart Friebert and David Young. Oberlin, OH: Oberlin College Press, 1995. 237. Prose poem. Reprinted from *Murder in the Dark*, ©1983.

1520. "Marrying the Hangman." *This Ain't No Healing Town: Toronto Stories.* Ed. Barry Callaghan. Toronto: Exile Editions, 1995. [15]-18. Reprinted from *Selected Poems 1966-1984*, ©1990.

1521. "Me, She, and It." *Who's Writing This? Notations on the Authorial I with Self-Portraits.* Ed. Daniel Halpern. Hopewell, NJ: Ecco Press, 1995. 16-18. Features sketch of Atwood by herself, with autograph.

1522. *Morning in the Burned House.* Toronto: McClelland and Stewart; Boston: Houghton Mifflin; London: Virago, 1995. Poetry. Contains the following: "Asparagus" (13), "Ava Gardner Reincarnated as a Magnolia" (30), "Bored" (91), "Cell" (47), "Cressida to Troilus: A Gift" (28), "Dancing" (90), "Daphne and Laura and So Forth" (26), "Down" (72), "February" (11), "A Fire Place" (116), "Flowers" (93), "Frogless" (56), "Girl Without Hands" (112), "Half-Hanged Mary" (58), "Helen of Troy Does Counter Dancing" (33), "In the Secular Night" (6), "King Lear in Respite Care" (85), "The Loneliness of the Military Historian" (49), "Man in a Glacier" (81), "A Man Looks" (37), "Manet's Olympia" (24), "Marsh Languages" (54), "Miss July Grows Older" (21), "The Moment" (109), "Morning in the Burned House" (126), "Oh" (101), "The Ottawa River by Night" (103), "Owl Burning" (70), "A Pink Hotel in California" (76), "Red Fox" (16), "Romantic" (45), "A Sad Child" (4), "Sekhmet, the Lion-Headed Goddess of War, Violent Storms, Pestilence, and Recovery from Illness, Contemplates the Desert in the Metropolitan Museum of Art" (39), "Shapechangers in Winter" (120), "The Signer" (114), "Statuary" (118), "The Time" (98), "Two Dreams" (96), "Two Dreams, 2" (99), "Up" (110), "Vermilion Flycatcher, San Pedro River, Arizona" (107), "A Visit" (88), "Waiting" (8), "Wave" (83), "You Come Back" (3).

1523. *Morning in the Burned House.* [Sound recording]. Vancouver, BC: Crane Library, 1995. Recorded from book, 1995.

1524. "Morning in the Burned House." *The Independent* 21 May 1995: Section: Review: 30. The poem. Also published in *North American Review* 280.4 (July 1995): 11.

1525. "Murder in the Dark." *This Ain't No Healing Town: Toronto Stories.* Ed. Barry Callaghan. Toronto: Exile Editions, 1995. 189-190. Reprinted from *Murder in the Dark*, 1983.

1526. "The Nature of Gothic." *Carnage Hall* 6 (1995): 16. Poem.

1527. *New Oxford Book of Canadian Short Stories.* Toronto; New York; Oxford: Oxford UP, 1995. Co-edited with Robert Weaver. Contains "Introduction" by Atwood (xii-xv) and "True Trash" (247-266), reprinted from *Wilderness Tips*.

1528. "Not So Grimm: The Staying Power of Fairy Tales." *Los Angeles Times* 29 October 1995: Section: Book Review: 1. Review of Marina Warner's *From the Best to the Blond: On Fairy Tales and Their Tellers.* (1468 w). Reprinted in *Philadelphia Inquirer* 12 November 1995: Section K:2 C:1 and *Toronto Star* 30 December 1995: G14.

1529. "Owl and Pussycat, Some Years Later." *Paper Guitar: 27 Writers Celebrate 25 Years of Descant Magazine.* Ed. Karen Mulhallen. Toronto: HarperCollins, 1995. 15-20. Poem.

1530. "A Parable." [Title romanized]. *Najkrace price na svetu*. Belgrade: Cicero, 1995. 155. Serbo-Croation (Cyrillic) translation of "A Parable" from *Wilderness Tips*.

1531. *The Poetry of Gwendolyn MacEwen*. Vol. 1: *The Early Years*; Vol. 2: *The Later Years* [Braille ed.]. Toronto: CNIB, 1995. Co-edited with Barry Callaghan.

1532. *Politique de pouvoir*. Montréal: L'Hexagone, 1995. Poetry. Bilingual edition. French translation of *Power Politics* by Louise Desjardins.

1533. *Princess Prunella and the Purple Peanut*. Toronto: Key Porter; New York: Workman Pub.; Bath, UK: Barefoot Books, 1995. Children's book. Author donating proceeds to Woodcock Fund, which helps writers in mid-career who need money to finish their works.

1534. "Rage Deferred." *Women's Review of Books* 12.10-11 (July 1995): 28. With Jill Piggott.

1535. "Rape Fantasies." *Fiddlehead* 185 (1995): 91-99. Short story.

1536. *Robber Bride*. Toronto: Seal Books; New York: Bantam, 1995. Paper edition. Reprint of 1993 hard-cover version.

1537. *The Robber Bride*. [Sound recording]. Read by Barbara Caruso. Oxford: Isis Audio Books, ©1995. 14 sound cassettes (1260 min.).

1538. *Sabaibaru: Gendai Kanada bungaku nyumon*. Tokyo: Ochanomizu Shobo, 1995. Japanese translation of *Survival: A Thematic Guide to Canadian Literature* by Kato Yukako. Title romanized.

1539. "The Santa Claus Trap." *Favourite Christmas Stories from Fireside Al*. Selected and introduced by Alan Maitland. Toronto; New York; London: Viking, 1995. [18]-28. Poem.

1540. "The Signer." *Toronto Star* 11 February 1995: L3. Poem. Reprinted from *Morning in the Burned House*.

1541. "The Sin Eater." *This Ain't No Healing Town: Toronto Stories*. Ed. Barry Callaghan. Toronto: Exile Editions, 1995. 214-225. Reprinted from *Bluebeard's Egg*, 1982 ©1977.

1542. "Spelling." *Mother Songs: Poems for, by and about Mothers*. Ed. Sandra M. Gilbert, Susan Gubar, and Diana O'Hehir. New York: Norton, 1995. 89-90. Reprinted from *True Stories* (1981).

1543. "Statuary." *Toronto Star* 11 February 1995: L3. Poem. Reprinted from *Morning in the Burned House*.

1544. *Strange Things: The Malevolent North in Canadian Literature*. Oxford: Clarendon Press; Toronto; New York: Oxford UP, 1995. Atwood writes of the imaginative mystique of the Canadian North. In discussing the work of writers like Robert Service, Robertson Davies, Alice Munro, and Margaret Laurence, she talks of northern folklore, myth, and imagery. Originally presented as the Clarendon Lectures at Oxford University, 1991.

1545. "There Was Once." *Mississippi Review* (October 1995): s.p. Reprinted from *Good Bones*. Source http://www.mississippireview.com/1995/07atwood.html (1 May 2006).

1546. "There Was Once." *Wicked: Women's Wit and Humour from Elizabeth I to Ruby Wax*. Ed. Fidelis Morgan. London: Virago Press, 1995. 153-155. Reprinted from *Good Bones*, Virago, ©1992.

1547. "The Trappers." *Women on Hunting*. Ed. Pam Houston. Hopewell, NJ: Ecco Press, 1995. [21]-22. Poem. Reprinted from *The Animals in That Country*, ©1968.

1548. "True Trash." *Favourite Summer Stories from Front Porch Al*. Selected and introduced by Alan Maitland. Toronto: Viking, 1995. 261-288.

1549. "Uglypuss." *Points of View: An Anthology of Short Stories*. Rev. ed. [Ed.] James Moffett and Kenneth R. McElheny. New York: Penguin, 1995. 484-507. Reprinted from *Bluebeard's Egg*, 1983 ©1986.

1550. "Unpopular Gals." *Mississippi Review* (October 1995): s.p. Reprinted from *Good Bones*. Source: http://www.mississippireview.com/1995/07atwood.html (1 May 2006).

1551. "The Victory Burlesk." *This Ain't No Healing Town: Toronto Stories*. Ed. Barry Callaghan. Toronto: Exile Editions, 1995. 157-158. Prose poem. Reprinted from *Murder in the Dark*, ©1983. Index title: "At the Victory Burlesk." Also in *Models of the Universe: An Anthology of the Prose Poem*. Selected and ed. Stuart Friebert and David Young. Oberlin, OH: Oberlin College Press, 1995. 239.

1552. "A Visit." *Atlantic Monthly* (*US*) 275.5 (May 1995): 76. Poem.

1553. "When It Happens." *The Penguin Book of Modern Fantasy by Women*. Ed. A. Susan Williams and Richard Glyn Jones. London: Viking, 1995. 279-289. Short story first published in *Châtelaine* 1975, collected in *Dancing Girls and Other Stories*, Toronto: McClelland and Stewart, ©1977.

1554. *Wilderness Tips*. Toronto: McClelland and Stewart; London: Bloomsbury Classics, 1995, 1991.

1555. "The Woman Who Could Not Live with Her Faulty Heart." *On Doctoring: Stories, Poems, Essays*. New, revised, and expanded ed. Ed. Richard Reynolds and John Stone. New York: Simon & Schuster, 1995. 362-363. Reprinted from "Two-Headed Poems" in *Selected Poems II: Poems Selected and New 1976-1986*, ©1987.

1556. "You Come Back." *North America Review* 280.5 (September 1995): 52.

1557. "You Could Say." *Parnassus: Poetry in Review* 20.1-2 (1995): 334-337. A meandering answer to the question: What is the difference between a poem and a novel?

Adaptations of Atwood's Works

1558. *First Words: Earliest Writing from Favorite Contemporary Authors*. [Sound recording]. Collected and ed. Paul Mandelbaum. Read by various narrators. Beverly Hills, CA: Dove Audio, 1995. 4 sound cassettes (ca. 6 hr.). Includes some selections from Atwood.

Quotations

1559. "[Quote]." *Chicago Tribune* 17 July 1995: Section: Perspective: 11. "Canada must be the only country in the world where a policeman is used as a national symbol."

1560. "[Quote]." *The Guardian* 1 November 1995: Section: Foreign Page: 14. Article by Jonathan Freedland titled, "Quebec Gives Canada Splitting Headache," quotes Atwood: "Just because the faces of Anglos don't move around a lot when they talk doesn't mean they don't have feelings."

1561. "[Quote]." *Ottawa Citizen* 31 March 1995: A11. Includes Atwood commenting on poet known as the "Sweet Songstress of Saskatchewan" on the occasion of a new edition of *Sarah Binks: The Literary Biography of Paul Hiebert* (Toronto: McClelland and Stewart): "Sarah Binks—'The Sweet Songstress of Saskatchewan'—is without a doubt one of the most unjustly neglected of Canadian artists. Indeed, the entire Manure Spreader School of Poetry could scarcely have existed without her; and she has inspired several generations of Canadian literary critics with her pithy motto, 'Lay it on thick,' which students of literature will immediately recognize as a direct descendent of John Keats's famous admonition, 'Load every rift with ore.'"

1562. "[Quote]." *Toronto Star* 25 February 1995: G2. Article by Mitchell Smith entitled, "Dry-Land Sailors Scupper Plan to Bring Drake Home," quotes Atwood: "Some travelers think they want to go to foreign places but are dismayed when the places turn out actually to be foreign."

1563. "[Quotes]." *The Guardian* 18 November 1995: Section: Features: 34. On Atwood's birthday, *Guardian* quotes Atwood **about those who study her** ("This academic said to me, you've written enough for us by now. In other words, drop dead and we can deal with the texts"); **about journalists who visit and ask questions** ("If you're going to review the furniture which is what a lot of interviewers do these days—most of it belonged to my father-in-law"); **about activists who want her to be a propagandist for the moral superiority of women** ("Why should we all be sopranos? I don't think that feminism ought to mean that all men are bad"); and **about literary critics** ("They pressured me. Remember the 'Put your head in the oven or you're not a real poet' movement").

Interviews

1564. *Margaret Atwood.* [Sound recording]. [s.l.]: CBC Radio Works, ©1995. 1 cassette. (23 min.). Atwood interviewed by Peter Gzowski. Originally broadcast September 1993. The author discusses *The Robber Bride*.

1565. "What They're Reading." *Orlando Sentinel* 26 November 1995: Section: Arts & Entertainment: F9. Atwood has been reading *Athena* by John Banville (Knopf), a novel about a mysterious experience involving stolen paintings, a sexual liaison, and a serial killer: "Oh, I just loved it. I thought it was such a hoot. He's a master of metaphor."

1566. ABLEY, Mark. "Dire Things: An Interview with Margaret Atwood." *Poetry Canada Review* 15.2 (June 1995): 1, 3+.

1567. BADER, Rudolf. "Margaret Atwood, Toronto." *Anglistik: Mitteilungen des Verbandes deutscher Anglisten* 6.1 (March 1995): 7-18.

1568. BASBANES, Nicholas A. "Atwood Gets Lots of Attention without Trying." *Columbus Dispatch* 5 February 1995: Section: Features Accent & Entertainment: 6H.

1569. DORFMAN, Ariel. *Margaret Atwood.* [Videorecording]. [s.l.]: Distribution Access, 1995. VHS tape 2 videocassettes (ca. 53 min.). In Vol. 1 Dorfman talks to Atwood about her novel, *The Robber Bride*, and her children's book, *Princess Prunella and the Purple Peanut*; in Vol. 2 Dorfman interviews Atwood about her book of poems, *Morning in the Burned House*, and her novel, *Cat's Eye*.

1570. FEAY, Suzi. "Woman for All Seasons." *The Independent* 21 May 1995: Section: Review: 30. On poetry. (1187 w).

1571. GARRON, Rebecca. "An Interview with Margaret Atwood." *Clockwatch Review (A Journal of the Arts)* 10.1-2 (1995): 108-118.

1572. HABIB, Marlene. "Atwood Tempts Children with New Book on Ps." *Calgary Herald* 18 October 1995: C11. The author interviewed about *Princess Prunella*.

1573. MARCHAND, Philip. "Deep Down, Atwood's a Romantic." *Toronto Star* 1 February 1995: D1. Interview in connection with publication of *Morning in the Burned House*.

1574. O'BRIANT, Don. "The Writer Speaks: Atwood Puts Away Angst to Spin a Children's Tale." *Atlanta Journal and Constitution* 28 September 1995: Section: Features: 7G. Concerns *Princess Prunella and the Purple Peanut*. Includes some biographical material.

1575. PADDON, David. "The More Confounding It Is, the More Margaret Atwood She Is." *Vancouver Sun* 1 February 1995: C6. Interview in connection with publication of *Morning in the Burned House*. (705 w).

1576. ROCKBURN, Ken. *Medium Rare: Jamming with Culture*. Toronto: Stoddart, 1995. See especially "Peg o' My Heart." 61-72.

1577. STONE, John. "Not a Cash Crop: An Interview with Margaret Atwood." *Revista Española de Estudios Canadienses* 2.2-3 (1995): 243-253.

1578. WERTHEIMER, Linda. "Margaret Atwood Produces Proliferation of 'P's." *All Things Considered*. National Public Radio, 24 November 1995. Transcript #2041-6. Available from Lexis-Nexis.

Scholarly Resources

1579. "Margaret Atwood." *Who's Who in the League of Canadian Poets: Directory of Members 1995*. Compiled and ed. Jill Humphries. Toronto: League of Canadian Poets, 1995. 5. With photo. List of books in print, 139.

1580. ADHIKARI, Madhumalati. "Articulating Silence: Margaret Atwood's *The Handmaid's Tale*." *Canadian Literature Today*. Ed. R. K. Dhawan. New Delhi: Prestige, 1995. 154-165.

1581. ALLEN, Beverly. "From Multiplicity to Multitude: Universal Systems of Deformation." *Symposium* 49.2 (Summer 1995): 93ff. How Atwood (Milan Kundera and Gabriel Garcia Márquez) break down the traditional form and function of the novel.

1582. APTER, Terri. *Secret Paths: Women in the New Midlife*. New York: W. W. Norton, 1995. Refers to Elaine Risley, from *Cat's Eye*, making the journey through midlife. 151-152.

1583. BARAT, Urbashi. "*Cat's Eye*: Margaret Atwood's Portrait of the Artist as a Woman and a Survivor." *Canadian Literature Today*. Ed. R. K. Shawan. New Delhi: Prestige, 1995. 174-185.

1584. BEYER, Charlotte. "From Violent Duality to Multi-Culturalism: Margaret Atwood's Post-Colonial Cultural and Sexual Politics." *O Canada: Essays on Canadian Literature and Culture*. Ed. Jørn Carlesen and Tim Caudery. Aarhus, Denmark: Aarhus UP, 1995. 97-108.

1585. ———. "Margaret Atwood's Innovative Vision of Gender, Genre, Postmodernism and the City in *The Robber Bride*." *British Journal of Canadian Studies* 10.1 (1995): 146-155.

1586. ———. "The Writing of Margaret Atwood: Post-Colonialism, Feminism, Narrative." PhD thesis. University of Warwick, 1995. 365 pp.

1587. BHARATHI, V. "'Shifting Generic Boundaries': A Study of the Short Stories of Alice Munro, Margaret Laurence and Margaret Atwood." *Postmodernism and Feminism: Canadian Contexts*. Ed. Shirin Kudchedkar. New Delhi: Pencraft, 1995. 247-263.

1588. BLACK, Joseph, and J. L. BLACK. "Canada in the Soviet Mirror: English-Canadian Literature in Soviet Translation." *Journal of Canadian Studies / Revue d'études canadiennes* 30.2 (Summer 1995): 5-18. Focuses on period between 1918 and 1985 and includes some comments on Atwood translations.

1589. BLAZE, Margaret K. "Life Doesn't Have to End at Thirty: Some Advice from Kate Chopin, Margaret Drabble, Margaret Atwood, Jane Campion and Janet Frame." MA thesis. University of Wyoming, 1995. 84 pp. Insights from Atwood's *Surfacing* plus Chopin's *The Awakening*, Drabble's *The Waterfall*, Campion's *The Piano*, and Frame's *Autobiography*.

1590. BLOOM, Lynn Z., and Veronica MAKOWSKY. "Zenia's Paradoxes." *Literature, Interpretation, Theory* 6.3-4 (1995): 167-179. *The Robber Bride*. "Despite her devious, ambiguous, and often reprehensible tactics, Zenia is the secret ally of the trio of best friends whom she nominally betrays. Zenia, they maintain, understands and lives by the principle that to survive, to be happy, women must take control of their own lives and bond with other women to make this possible. They show that Zenia repeatedly takes the initiative to provide contexts and confrontations that ultimately force the women to understand their demeaning, self-destructive attachment to their partners—and so to understand themselves." (Author).

1591. BOUSON, J. Brooks. "Slipping Sideways into the Dreams of Women: The Female Dream Work of Power Feminism in Margaret Atwood's *The Robber Bride*." *Literature, Interpretation, Theory* 6.3-4 (1995): 149-266. "The article discusses the concept of the female dream work of power feminism in [this] novel....The novel explores women's collective fantasies of female power through the figure of the villainous Zenia. Openly questioning the radical feminist ideology that views women as free of the will to power, Atwood, in *The Robber Bride*, reflects on the resurgence of power feminism. The novel does the dream work of power feminism as it focuses attention, through the character of Zenia, on women's outlawed emotions and repressed fantasies of power and revenge." (Author).

1592. BOYNTON, Victoria Anne. "Sexciting Ethos: Women Speakers in Recent North American Writing." PhD thesis. State University of New York at Binghamton, 1995. 249 pp. "Start with an academic 'attitude.' Mix it with Judith Butler's body theory and Aristotle's notion of ethos, that messy conjunction of the believability of the speech and the 'character' of the speaker. Run it through baths of postmodern developers. Illuminate it with theories of social construction. Project it through a feminist lens. Here's what you get. You get a view of women speakers situated both within and beyond their conventional versions....You get the site of the sexed female body: exposed, spoken, figured, and invoked as power. This body-site isn't fixed but is instead dynamic, produced through citations of its governing conventions....Women speakers cite their sexed bodies in texts by Jane Tompkins, Nancy Miller, Margaret Atwood, Susan Minot, Sharon Olds, Anne Sexton, Rita Dove, Heather McHugh, Louise Erdrich, Leslie Silko, and Paula Gunn Allen." (Author). For more see *DAI-A* 56.02 (August 1995): 548.

1593. BRAIN, Tracy. "Figuring Anorexia: Margaret Atwood's *The Edible Woman*." *Literature, Interpretation, Theory* 6.3-4 (1995): 299-311. "In [this] novel written in 1965 and published in 1969, Atwood prefigures contemporary debate about the eating disorder anorexia nervosa. Though the word anorexia is never used in the text, Atwood examines the condition and its meanings with a sophistication rarely equalled in subsequent discussions of the illness. Atwood uses anorexia to address issues of gender, language, sexual politics and social dislocation." (Author).

1594. BROWN, Jane. "Constructing the Narrative of Women's Friendship: Margaret Atwood's Reflexive Fictions." *Literature, Interpretation, Theory* 6.3-4 (1995): 197-212. "Atwood's fiction has always moved women and their concerns from their peripheral places in traditional storytelling to a position of primacy. In her most recent fiction, she gives a central place to a subject that, until recently, has been distinctly peripheral in literature: the friendship of women. In novels such as *The Handmaid's Tale*, *Cat's Eye*, and *The Robber Bride*, Atwood explores the problem of how it can be possible, amidst the fragmentation and disjunction of the contemporary world, for women to establish community." (Author).

1595. BROWN, Lyn Mikel. "The Dangers of Time Travel: Revisioning the Landscape of Girls' Relationships in Margaret Atwood's *Cat's Eye*." *Literature, Interpretation, Theory* 6.3-4 (1995): 285-298. "The article traces the psychological roots of Elaine's—the central character of the novel—present-day feelings about herself and her life....It highlights, through Elaine, the trauma of a girl's life in patriarchal culture; not trauma as people usually think of it—acute emotional crisis or the psychological residues of physical or sexual assault—but the daily barrage of subtle and not-so subtle messages about being female in a male-defined culture that seep into girls' ears, into their speech, their feelings and thoughts; messages that first turn girls against each other, and then eventually, against themselves." (Author).

1596. BRYDON, Diana. "Atwood's Postcolonial Imagination: Rereading *Bodily Harm*." *Various Atwoods: Essays on the Later Poems, Short Fiction, and Novels*. Ed. Lorraine M. York. Concord, CA: Anansi, 1995. 89-116.

1597. CAMPBELL, Elizabeth. "Revisions, Reflections, Recreations: Epistolarity in Novels by Contemporary Women." *Twentieth Century Literature* 41.3 (Fall 1995): 332ff. Brief discussion of Atwood.

1598. CANTY, Joan F. "Does Eugenics = (E)utopia? Reproductive Control and Ethical Issues in Contemporary North American Feminist Fabulation." MA thesis. California State University, Stanislaus, 1995. 99 pp. Includes analysis of *The Handmaid's Tale*. For more see *MAI* 34.03 (June 1996): 970.

1599. CAPORALE BIZZINI, Silvia. "Power Politics: Literature and Foucauldian Analysis." *In-Between: Essays and Studies in Literary Criticism* 5.1 (1995): 23-39. Focus on *The Handmaid's Tale* and comparison to Marilyn French's *The Woman's Room*.

1600. CHEEVER, Leonard A. "Fantasies of Sexual Hell: Manuel Puig's *Pubis Angelical* and Margaret Atwood's *The Handmaid's Tale*." *Modes of the Fantastic: Selected Essays from the Twelfth International Conference on the Fantastic in the Arts*. Ed. Robert A. Latham and Robert A. Collins. Westport, CT: Greenwood Press, 1995. 110-121.

1601. CHRIST, Carol P. *Diving Deep and Surfacing: Women Writers on Spiritual Quest*. 3rd ed. Boston: Beacon Press, 1995. See especially Chapter 4: "Refusing to Be a Victim: Margaret Atwood." 41-53. Focus on *Surfacing*.

1602. CLARKE, Elizabeth. "How Feminist Can a Handmaid Be? Margaret Atwood's *The Handmaid's Tale*." *The Discerning Reader: Christian Perspectives on Literature and Theory*. Ed. David Barratt, Roger Pooley, and Leland Ryken. Leicester: Apollos; Grand Rapids, MI: Baker Books, 1995. 235-250.

1603. COMELLINI, Carla. "The Theme of Displacement in Three Canadian Women Writers: Margaret Laurence, Margaret Atwood and Edna Alford." *Rivisti di studi canadesi* 8 (1995): 145-164.

1604. COMISKEY, Barbara Anne. "Margaret Atwood: Fiction and Feminisms in Dialogue." PhD thesis. University of Lancaster, 1995. "Some commentators have been convinced that Atwood's texts are profoundly 'feminist' whilst others regard them as at best noncommittal and at worst misogynistic. This study asks why it might be that Atwood's works have been received so differently at various times and in different spheres, in terms of specific historical and discursive contexts (Part I) and of the textuality of her novels and short stories and their orientation to diverse 'reader-figures' (Part II). Selection of Atwood's texts in Part II is made from *The Edible Woman* (1969) to *The Robber Bride* (1993) and includes her two recent collections of short fiction." (Author).

1605. CONRAD, Peter. *To Be Continued: Four Stories and Their Survival.* Oxford: Clarendon Press, 1995. See especially 32ff. This book is derived from the Alexander Lectures in which, among other things, Conrad traces Chaucer's influence on *The Handmaid's Tale.*

1606. COOKE, Nathalie. "The Politics of Ventriloquism: Margaret Atwood's Fictive Confessions." *Various Atwoods: Essays on the Later Poems, Short Fiction, and Novels.* Ed. Lorraine M. York. Concord, CA: Anansi, 1995. 207-228.

1607. COOPER, Pamela. "Sexual Surveillance and Medical Authority in Two Versions of *The Handmaid's Tale.*" *Journal of Popular Culture* 28.4 (Spring 1995): 49-66. In literature and cinema.

1608. DEVI, N. Rama. "Edibility and Ambiguity in Margaret Atwood's *The Edible Woman.*" *Canadian Literature Today.* Ed. R. K. Dhawan. New Delhi: Prestige, 1995.

1609. DiMARCO, Danette. "Taking Their Word: Twentieth-Century Women Reinvent the Victorian." PhD thesis. Duquesne University, 1995. 323 pp. Includes discussion of how Atwood's *The Edible Woman* revises Lewis Carroll's Alice stories (1867 and 1971). For more see *DAI-A* 56.10 (April 1996): 3951.

1610. DJWA, Sandra. "Back to the Primal: The Apprenticeship of Margaret Atwood." *Various Atwoods: Essays on the Later Poems, Short Fiction, and Novels.* Ed. Lorraine M. York. Concord, CA: Anansi, 1995. 13-46.

1611. EDGECOMBE, Rodney Stenning. "Retrospectives in Patrick White and Margaret Atwood." *Quadrant* 39.7-8 (July-August 1995): 85-89.

1612. ENOS, Jennifer. "What's in a Name? Zenia and Margaret Atwood's *The Robber Bride.*" *Newsletter of the Margaret Atwood Society* 15 (1995): 14.

1613. FAND, Roxanne Joyce. "The Dialogic Self in Novels by Virginia Woolf, Doris Lessing and Margaret Atwood." PhD thesis. University of Hawaii, 1995. 315 pp. "A dialogic view of self as a continuous narrative tension between the integration and diversification of voices is exemplified in theme and form in Virginia Woolf's *The Waves*, Doris Lessing's *The Four-Gated City*, and Margaret Atwood's *Lady Oracle*....Atwood's Joan in *Lady Oracle,* lost in a maze of postmodern multiple personas, mocks herselves with internalized voices of society for avoiding the 'true' unitary identity she fears she lacks....Still preoccupied with herselves as objects of her own satire instead of validating them, she remains fixated on unity and disempowered in diversity, inverting and parodying the dialogic process that mobilizes integrity from diverse positions." (Author). For more see *DAI-A* 56.05 (November 1995): 1789.

1614. FILIPCZAK, Dorota. "'Is There No Balm in Gilead?' Biblical Intertext in Margaret Atwood's *The Handmaid's Tale.*" *Literature and Theology at Century's End.* Ed. Gregory Salyer and Robert Detweiler. Atlanta, GA: Scholars Press, 1995. 215-233.

1615. GINSBERG, Robert. "Literature and the Human Substance of Law." *Tamkang Review* 25.3-4 (Spring-Summer 1995): 87-110. Compares 4 short stories, including Atwood's "Weight," to explore how the literary art draws forth a poignant encounter with the humanity underlying law.

1616. GOMEZ, Christine. "Creating Female Space in Patriarchal/Colonial Power Structures: A Study of Margaret Atwood's *The Handmaid's Tale*." *Canadian Literature Today*. Ed. R. K. Dhawan. New Delhi: Prestige, 1995. 135-147.

1617. GRACE, Sherrill E. "'Franklin Lives': Atwood's Northern Ghosts." *Various Atwoods: Essays on the Later Poems, Short Fiction, and Novels*. Ed. Lorraine M. York. Concord, CA: Anansi, 1995. 146-166.

1618. GRANOFSKY, Ronald. *The Trauma Novel: Contemporary Symbolic Depictions of Collective Disaster*. New York: Peter Lang, 1995. Lengthy analysis of *Surfacing* (114-123) plus other relevant aspects of Atwood's works.

1619. HARIPRASANNA, A. "Margaret Atwood's *The Edible Woman*: An Expression of Feminine Sensibility." *Canadian Literature Today*. Ed. R. K. Dhawan. New Delhi: Prestige, 1995. 118-125.

1620. HENGEN, Shannon. "Zenia's Foreignness." *Various Atwoods: Essays on the Later Poems, Short Fiction, and Novels*. Ed. Lorraine M. York. Concord, CA: Anansi, 1995. 271-286.

1621. HERZIG-DANIELSON, Viola Angela. "The Aspect of Survival in Margaret Atwood's Novels *The Edible Woman* and *The Handmaid's Tale*." MA thesis. Oldenburg University, 1995.

1622. HITE, Molly. "An Eye for an I: The Disciplinary Society in *Cat's Eye*." *Various Atwoods: Essays on the Later Poems, Short Fiction, and Novels*. Ed. Lorraine M. York. Concord, CA: Anansi, 1995. 191-206.

1623. ———. "Optics and Autobiography in Margaret Atwood's *Cat's Eye*." *Twentieth Century Literature* 41.2 (Summer 1995): 135-159. "More than any other of Margaret Atwood's fictions, the 1988 novel *Cat's Eye* raises questions about the relation of the autobiographical 'real' to the meaning of a work of literature." (Author).

1624. HOLLIS, Hilda. "Between the Scylla of Essentialism and the Charybdis of Deconstruction: Margaret Atwood's *True Stories*." *Various Atwoods: Essays on the Later Poems, Short Fiction, and Novels*. Ed. Lorraine M. York. Concord, CA: Anansi, 1995. 117-145.

1625. HOLLISTER, Michael. "Spatial Cognition in Literature: Text-Centered Contextualization." *Mosaic* 28.2 (June 1995): 1-21. Reference to Atwood's *Surfacing* that illustrates "spatial dynamics of psychic growth."

1626. HOWELLS, Coral Ann. "The Figure of the Demonic Woman in Margaret Atwood's *The Handmaid's Tale*." *Postmodernism and Feminism: Canadian Contexts*. Ed. Shirin Kudchedkar. New Delhi: Pencraft, 1995. 133-141.

1627. ———. "'It All Depends on Where You Stand in Relation to the Forest': Atwood and the Wilderness from *Surfacing* to *Wilderness Tips*." *Various Atwoods: Essays on the Later Poems, Short Fiction, and Novels*. Ed. Lorraine M. York. Concord, CA: Anansi, 1995. 47-70.

1628. ———. *Margaret Atwood*. New York: St. Martin's Press; Basingstoke [UK]: Macmillan, 1995. Study focuses on Atwood's 8 novels, a book of short stories, and her analysis of Canadian literature.

1629. HOWLETT, Jeffrey Winslow. "Criminal Intuition: Late Twentieth-Century Novels of Confinement." PhD thesis. State University of New York at Binghamton, 1995. 242 pp. Includes discussion of Atwood's *Bodily Harm*. For more see *DAI-A* 56.04 (October 1995): 1355.

1630. KARRASCH, Anke. *Die Darstellung Kanadas im literarischen Werk von Margaret Atwood*. Trier, Germany: WVT Wissenschaftlicher Verlag, 1995. Originally presented as the author's thesis (doctoral), University of Wuppertal, 1995.

1631. KEITH, Cassandra M. "A Brief History of the Literature of English Canada." *RQ* 34.4 (22 June 1995): 447ff. Includes discussion of Atwood's place not only as author but as critic.

1632. KEITH, W. J. "Ethnicity, Canada and Canadian Literature." *Queen's Quarterly* 102.1 (Spring 1995): 100-111. Atwood cited for her ability to recreate half-Ukrainian, half-Jewish, character Lesje in *Life Before Man* (1979).

1633. KELLY, Darlene. "'Either Way, I Stand Condemned': A Women's Place in Margaret Atwood's *The Edible Woman* and Margaret Drabble's *The Waterfall.*" *English Studies in Canada* 21.3 (September 1995): 320-332.

1634. KENNEDY, Marjorie. "Fire of Roses: Two Short Stories and a Novel Excerpt." MFA thesis. Warren Wilson College, 1995. "Defamiliarizing the familiar in the stories of Margaret Atwood and John Cheever."

1635. KEULEN, Maggi. "'Where Is Here?' Or: The Importance of First Sentences in Novels." *Near Encounters: Festschrift for Richard Martin.* Ed. Hanjo Berressem and Bernd Herzogenrath. Frankfurt: Peter Lang, 1995. 151-159. Atwood compared to Aldous Huxley.

1636. KLARER, Mario. "Orality and Literacy as Gender-Supporting Structures in Margaret Atwood's *The Handmaid's Tale.*" *Mosaic* 28.4 (1 December 1995): 129-142.

1637. LAINE-WILLE, Ilona. "Literatur als Spiegel: Kulturkritik in Christa Wolfs *Kassandra* und Margaret Atwoods *Der Report der Magd.*" MA thesis. McGill University, 1995. Also available on microfiche from Canadian Theses Service (1996). German with abstracts in English and French.

1638. LAL, Malashri. "Canadian Gynocritics: Contexts of Meaning in Margaret Atwood's *Surfacing.*" *Perspectives on Women: Canada and India.* Ed. Aparna Basu. Bombay: Allied Pub. Ltd., 1995. 180-192.

1639. LANE, Patrick. "Lives of the Poets." *Geist* 7.17 (1995): 29-34. Memories of Canadian literary figures, including Atwood.

1640. LAPPAS, Catherine. "Rewriting Fairy Tales: Transformation as Feminist Practice in the Nineteenth and Twentieth Centuries." PhD thesis. St. Louis University, 1995. 169 pp. "Whether as subtext or intertext, the fairy tale appears consistently throughout the cultural productions of the nineteenth and twentieth centuries. Feminist criticism of the fairy tale contributes to understanding the control and victimization of female figures as a function of a patriarchal bias that proclaims its ahistoricity in order to justify the scripting of women's lives....In the twentieth century, feminist writers have reworked the old stories and have released aspects of feminine power previously curbed or suppressed. The tales inscribed in Anne Sexton's *Transformations* (1971), Angela Carter's *The Bloody Chamber* (1979), and Margaret Atwood's *Bluebeard's Egg (*1983) seize upon the polymorphism of the fairy tale both to reflect and to critique ideologies of late capitalism and to revise myths of patriarchy....The feminist rewrite invokes 'old' forms in order to reestablish a tradition of female storytelling particular to its historical and cultural context." (Author). For more see *DAI-A* 56.09 (March 1996): 3594.

1641. LAURENCE, Margaret. *A Very Large Soul: Selected Letters from Margaret Laurence to Canadian Writers.* Ed. with an introduction by J. A. Wainwright. Dunvegan, ON: Cormorant Books, 1995. Laurence's correspondence between 1962 and 1986 with such writers as Atwood, Timothy Findley, and Alice Munro.

1642. LAWN, Jennifer. "Our Bodies, Their Selves: Gender, Language, and Knowledge in Chapter Seventeen of *Cat's Eye.*" *Literature, Interpretation, Theory* 6.3-4 (1995): 269-283. "Those interested in Atwood's sexual politics in general, and the representation of female bodies in particular, will find a wealth of detail in [this chapter]. The chapter describes Elaine, the novel's protagonist, playing after school with the bully Cordelia and her cronies. It evokes the mystique and secrecy enveloping menstruation in 1950s Canada, including embarrassed silence, euphemism, pain, guilt, disgust, foreboding, mortification, melodrama, scorn, hyperbole, surreptitious behaviour, and intimations of contagion." (Author).

1643. MARTIN, Shannon. "A Palette of Unconventional Symbolism: Color Imagery in Three Margaret Atwood Novels." MA thesis. Western Kentucky University, 1995. 62 pp.

1644. MELLEY, Timothy Daniel. "Empire of Conspiracy: Paranoia and the Representation of Social Control in Post-World War II America." PhD thesis. Cornell University, 1995. 223 pp. "Since the Second World War, influential North American fictions have frequently represented individuals who are nervous—or paranoid—about the ways in which organizations, technologies, and social systems might govern individual action and identity. Since 'paranoid' claims always question consensus definitions of reality, the extraordinary postwar interest in paranoia is a register of postmodern challenges to 'the real.'...By examining Margaret Atwood's 'stalker' narratives, Chapter 3 argues that a woman's potentially paranoid fear of invisible male persecutors may powerfully illuminate social patterns of male violence, resisting the idea that such violence is individually motivated." (Author). Atwood discussed along with works of Joseph Heller, Thomas Pynchon, and Don DeLillo. For more see *DAI-A* 56.04 (October 1995): 1357.

1645. MERIVALE, Patricia. "From 'Bad News' to 'Good Bones': Margaret Atwood's Gendering of Art and Elegy." *Various Atwoods: Essays on the Later Poems, Short Fiction, and Novels.* Ed. Lorraine M. York. Concord, CA: Anansi, 1995. 252-270.

1646. MOHR, Dunja M. "Female Dystopia: Margaret Atwood's *The Handmaid's Tale.*" *Ahornblätter* 8 (1995): 62-80.

1647. ———. "Female Dystopia: Margaret Atwood's *The Handmaid's Tale* and Angela Carter's *Heros and Villains.*" MA thesis. Philipps-Universität Marburg, 1995.

1648. MONTELARO, Janet J. "Maternity and the Ideology of Sexual Difference in *The Handmaid's Tale.*" *Literature, Interpretation, Theory* 6.3-4 (1995): 233-256.

1649. MOURIER, P. F. "But How Can One Be Canadian." *Esprit* 11 (November 1995): 148-152. Margaret Atwood's view of national identity.

1650. MYCAK, Sonia. "The Split Subject in the Novels of Margaret Atwood: A Reading in Terms of Psychoanalytic and Phenomenological Theory." PhD thesis. University of New South Wales, 1995. 391 pp. "This dissertation is a close reading of five of Margaret Atwood's novels...with a view to exploring the divided self. As such it is a detailed theoretical investigation into the ways in which within *The Edible Woman, Lady Oracle, Life Before Man, Bodily Harm* and *Cat's Eye* subjective identity is dislocated, alienated, splintered and split." (Author). For more see *DAI-A* 57.01 (July 1996): 226.

1651. MYHAL, Bob. "Boundaries, Centres, and Circles: The Postmodern Geometry of *The Handmaid's Tale.*" *Literature, Interpretation, Theory* 6.3-4 (1995): 213-231. "Gilead, the near-future dystopian society of...*The Handmaid's Tale*, is founded on a carefully contrived but nevertheless distorted return to the extreme literal patriarchy of the Old Testament. In many ways Gilead marks a second coming of a highly restrictive, hierarchical, and rule-bound society. As an authoritarian society, Gilead is marked by rigid geographical, ideological, and personal boundaries. While the physical barriers are constant reminders of spatial limitations, the boundaries which shape Gilead society go beyond the purely geographical; indeed,

perhaps the more impermeable and intimidating barriers are those which exist between individuals in the form of strict gender and class segregation." (Author).

1653. NAVARRO, Emilia. "Women and War: Gendered Destruction." *ICLA '91 Tokyo:
The Force of Vision, II: Visions in History; Visions of the Other.* Ed. Earl Miner et
al. Tokyo: International Comparative Literature Association, 1995. 261-267. *Bodily Harm* compared to Marta Traba's *Conversación al sur.*

1654. NEWMAN, J. "Imaginary War Fiction at Colorado State University." *Popular
Culture in Libraries* 3.1 (1995): 95-97. Describes CSU's Imaginary Wars Collection that contains fiction by Margaret Atwood.

1655. ORAVITS, June Rapp. "Women as Generators of Knowledge: The Feminist Science Fiction of Margaret Atwood's, *The Handmaid's Tale,* and Marge Piercy's,
He, She and It." MA thesis. University of North Carolina at Wilmington, 1995. 43
pp.

1656. OSBORNE, Carol. "From Primals to Inner Children: Margaret Atwood's Reflections on Therapy." *Literature, Interpretation, Theory* 6.3-4 (1995): 181-195. "The
article discusses Margaret Atwood's reflections on therapy in her works. While direct commentary about psychologists or therapies appears infrequently in her novels, Atwood subtly incorporates aspects of contemporary psychotherapy in depict-
ing her characters' confrontations with the past. From the allusions in *Surfacing* to
primal therapy, to her indirect criticism of the recovery movement in *The Robber
Bride,* Atwood shows that not only has she been attuned to the impact that the psy-
chotherapeutic industry has had on society but also that she has become increasingly critical of its claims and influence." (Author).

1657. PALMER, Paulina. "Postmodern Trends in Contemporary Fiction: Margaret Atwood, Angela Carter, Jeanette Winterson." *Postmodern Subjects / Postmodern
Texts.* Ed. Jane Dowson and Steven Earnshaw. Amsterdam: Rodopi, 1995. 181-
199.

1658. PARKER, Emma. "You Are What You Eat: The Politics of Eating in the Novels
of Margaret Atwood." *Twentieth Century Literature* 41.3 (Fall 1995): 349-368.

1659. PERRAKIS, Phyllis Sternberg. "The Female Gothic and the (M)Other in Atwood
and Lessing." *Doris Lessing Newsletter* 17.1 (1995): 1. Reference to *Cat's Eye.*

1660. PRABHAKAR, M. "Language as 'Subversive Weapon' in Margaret Atwood's
The Handmaid's Tale." *Canadian Literature Today.* Ed. R. K. Dhawan. New
Delhi: Prestige, 1995. 166-173.

1661. ———. "Margaret Atwood's *Surfacing*: Blue-Print of Revolt." *Literary Half-
Yearly* 36.1 (1995): 70-79.

1662. ———. "Pen as a 'Weapon' in Margaret Atwood's *Bodily Harm.*" *Canadian Literature Today.* Ed. R. K. Dhawan. New Delhi: Prestige, 1995. 126-134.

1663. RAMAIYA, Nita. "Margaret Atwood's 'Machine. Gun. Nest': A Critical Note."
Indian Journal of Canadian Studies 4 (1995): 121-125. Comment on the poem, included with the article.

1664. RAO, Vimala Rama. "A Violin in the Void: The Voice of the Narrator in
Zamiatin's *We* and Atwood's *The Handmaid's Tale.*" *Canadian Literature Today.*
Ed. R. K. Dhawan. New Delhi: Prestige, 1995. 148-153.

1665. RASCHKE, Deborah. "Margaret Atwood's *The Handmaid's Tale*: False Borders
and Subtle Subversions." *Literature, Interpretation, Theory* 6.3-4 (1995): 257-268.
"Margaret Atwood's *The Handmaid's Tale* is, in part, a warning. Creating a nostalgia for pre-Gilead in which the narrator wistfully remembers the simple things
of earlier times, Atwood's tale, in romanticizing the past, masks the more pressing
problem of Gilead as the present, not the future. But there is more to this text than

de-evolution into some fundamentalist arcadia. Atwood's text is also about language and how language systems formulate how people think." (Author).

1666. REGIER, Ami M. "Collectibles, Fetishes, and Hybrid Objects: Object Discourses and Syncretic Female Identity in Recent Cross-Racial North American Women's Representation." PhD thesis. University of Southern California, 1995. 262 pp. This thesis documents "the emergence of a very contemporary aesthetics of collectibles, fetishes, and hybrid objects in recent North American cross-racial literary and visual production by women. Narratives of female collection practices configure female subjectivity through hybridity, excess, and accumulation, negating any singular notion of either personal or cultural identity. These texts revise the trope of the object, from its use to describe the position of women and minorities as objects of the investigations of sovereign, Western, implicitly male subjects, to an elaboration into a model of a more dialectical, material meeting point of self and other." (Author). The thesis includes an analysis of *Cat's Eye* and *The Edible Women*. For more see *DAI-A* 57.01 (July 1996): 209.

1667. ROSENBERG, Jerome H. *Margaret Atwood*. [Computer file]. 1 computer optical disc; 4 3/4 in. In Twayne's women authors on CD-ROM.

1668. SCHALL, Birgitta. *Von der Melancholie zur Trauer: Postmoderne Text- und Blickokonomien bei Margaret Atwood*. Trier, Germany: WVT Wissenschaftlicher Verlag, 1995.

1669. SHEPHERD, Valerie. "Narrative Survival: The Power of Personal Narration, Discussed Through the Personal Story-Telling of Fictional Characters, Particularly Those Created by Margaret Atwood." *Language and Communication* 15.4 (October 1995): 355-373.

1670. SHOJANIA, Moti Gharib. "Descartes' Doubting Daughters: The Care of the Self in the Fiction of Atwood, Laurence, and Munro." PhD thesis. University of Manitoba, 1995. 404 pp. This dissertation looks at the way the Cartesian mind/body problem is implicated in the practices surrounding the care of the self as foregrounded in the fiction of Margaret Atwood, Margaret Laurence, and Alice Munro. For more see *DAI-A* 58.04 (October 1997): 1288.

1671. SMITH, James Gregory. "The Dostoevskyan Dialectic in Selected North American Literary Works." PhD thesis. University of North Texas, 1995. 180 pp. "The Grand Inquisitor parable of *The Brothers Karamazov* is a blueprint for dystopian states delineated in anti-utopian fiction. Also, Dostoevsky's parable constitutes a powerful dialectical struggle between polar opposites which are presented in the following twentieth-century dystopias: Zamiatin's *We*, Bradbury's *Farenheit 451*, Vonnegut's *Player Piano*, and Atwood's *The Handmaid's Tale*. The dialectic in the dystopian genre presents a give and take between the opposites of faith and doubt, liberty and slavery, and it often presents the individual of the anti-utopian state with a choice. When presented with the dialectic, then, the individual is presented with the capacity to make a real choice; therefore, he is presented with a hope for salvation in the totalitarian dystopias of modern twentieth-century literature." (Author). For more see *DAI-A* 56.12 (June 1996): 4776.

1672. SMYTH, Donna. "Unlocking Pandora's Box: Female Desire in Three Works by Canadian Female Writers." MA thesis. Acadia University, 1995.

1673. SNYDER, Karyn. "Reality in Margaret Atwood's Poetry and the Dramatization of Reality in Her Novel *The Handmaid's Tale*." MA thesis. Drew University, 1995. 71 pp.

1674. SNYDER, Sharon Lynn. "The Work of Gender in Fictions of Science: A Study of Literary Amateurs in the Novels of Margaret Atwood, Richard Powers, Joan Didion, and Don DeLillo." PhD thesis. University of Michigan, 1995. 246 pp. "This study explores the reasons why current critical paradigms and reading lists of a contemporary literature of science emphasize masculinity as a standard trope of assessment. Because science and technology have been viewed as citadels of masculine endeavor, it comes as no surprise that literary criticism reflects these key suppositions as well. Rather than claim a mastery of complex scientific equations, theorems and disciplines, the novelists in this study more accurately use the novel as an interdisciplinary forum for analyzing the culture that surrounds scientific production. By exploring the figuration of gender and science within the fiction of four influential contemporary novelists—Joan Didion, Don DeLillo, Margaret Atwood and Richard Powers—a persistent story of women's disruptions of professional fields begins to unfold. Through an analysis of the ways in which these writers deploy characters in relation to traditionally masculine domains of power and authority, the significance and situation of gender in contemporary fictions of science can be given the centrality it deserves." (Author). For more see *DAI-A* 57.03 (September 1996): 1132.

1675. STAELS, Hilde. *Margaret Atwood's Novels: A Study of Narrative Discourse*. Tübingen, Germany: Francke Verlag, 1995.

1676. ———. "Margaret Atwood's *The Handmaid's Tale*: Resistance through Narrating." *English Studies* 76.5 (1 September 1995): 455-467.

1677. STAINES, David. *Beyond the Provinces: Literary Canada at Century's End*. Toronto: University of Toronto Press, 1995. Includes remarks on Atwood, most notably, on *The Handmaid's Tale*, 61-62.

1678. STOSKY, Sandra. "Changes in America's Secondary School Literature Programs." *Phi Delta Kappa* 76.8 (April 1995): 605ff. How world authors, including Atwood, are now studied as part of "American" literature.

1679. TAYLOR, Judith. "Persephone." *Poetry* 165.6 (March 1995): 321. Poem includes a reference to Margaret Atwood.

1680. UNES, Diana L. "A New Sense of Time in Female Development: Linearity and Cyclicity in Atwood's *Surfacing* and *Cat's Eye*." MA thesis. Eastern Illinois University, 1995. 55 pp.

1681. VERWAAYEN, Kimberly. "Re-Examining the Gaze in *The Handmaid's Tale*." *Open Letter* 9.4 (Fall 1995): 44-54.

1682. VESPERMANN, Susanne. *Margaret Atwood: Eine mythokritische Analyse ihrer Werke*. Augsburg, Germany: Bernd Wissner, 1995.

1683. VIPOND, Dianne. "The Body Politic in Margaret Atwood's 'True Trash.'" *Short Story* 3.1 (Spring 1995): 84-92.

1684. WAGNER, Monika. "The Other in Atwood: Maternity and Multiplicity in *The Robber Bride* and *Cat's Eye*." MS thesis. Monash University, 1995.

1685. WAGNER-MARTIN, Linda. "'Giving Way to Bedrock': Atwood's Later Poems." *Various Atwoods: Essays on the Later Poems, Short Fiction, and Novels*. Ed. Lorraine M. York. Concord, CA: Anansi, 1995. 71-88.

1686. WALKER, Nancy A. *The Disobedient Writer: Women and Narrative Tradition*. Austin: University of Texas Press, 1995. Study of writers, including Atwood, who revise classic texts in order to highlight classist, racist, or antifeminist messages.

1687. WEIN, Toni. "Margaret Atwood's Historical Notes." *Notes on Contemporary Literature* 25.2 (March 1995): 2-3. Re: *The Handmaid's Tale*.

1688. WEINSTEIN, Sheri M. "Heavy with the Unspoken: The Interplay of Absence and Presence in Margaret Atwood's *Cat's Eye*." MA thesis. McGill University, 1995. 148 pp. Also available on microfiche from Canadian Theses Service (1996). "This study explores the philosophical, linguistic and textual interplay of absence and presence in Margaret Atwood's novel *Cat's Eye*. The premise of the thesis is that the novel posits language as a problematic communicative medium; as such, language conveys that meanings of words are flexible, mutable and transient....This study concludes that absence/presence is a paradigm in *Cat's Eye* for the way in which words are (alternately as well as simultaneously) spoken and silent, understood and misunderstood, opposed and united." (Author). For more see *MAI* 34.05 (October 1996): 1765.

1689. WILLARD, Thomas. *"Life Before Man." Masterplots II: Women's Literature.* Ed. Frank McGill. Salem, CA: Salem Press, 1995. 1290-1294.

1690. ———. "Margaret Atwood." *Great Lives from History: American Women.* Ed. Frank McGill. Pasadena, CA: Salem Press, 1995. 108-112.

1691. WILLMOTT, Glenn. "O Say, Can You See: *The Handmaid's Tale* in Novel and Film." *Various Atwoods: Essays on the Later Poems, Short Fiction, and Novels.* Ed. Lorraine M. York. Concord, CA: Anansi, 1995. 167-190.

1692. YORK, Lorraine M. "'Over All I Place a Glass Bell': The Meta-Iconography of Margaret Atwood." *Various Atwoods: Essays on the Later Poems, Short Fiction, and Novels.* Ed. Lorraine M. York. Concord, CA: Anansi, 1995. 229-252.

1693. YORK, Lorraine M., ed. *Various Atwoods: Essays on the Later Poems, Short Fiction, and Novels.* Concord, CA: Anansi, 1995. Individual chapters indexed in this section.

1694. ZAMAN, Sobia. "The Feminist Appropriation of Dystopia: A Study of Atwood, Elgin, Fairbairns, and Tepper." MA thesis. University of Manitoba, 1995. 97 pp. Also available on microfiche from Canadian Theses Service (1997). "The feminist dystopia is a distinct generic category from the dystopia—a genre still defined by reference to a male lineage....I approach these texts [Atwood's *The Handmaid's Tale*, Suzette Elgin's *Native Tongue*, Zoe Fairbairns's *Benefits*, and Sheri Tepper's *The Gate to Women's Country*], from a feminist multidisciplinary stance. My thesis concludes with the assertion that the feminist dystopia is an ultimately empowering mode of discourse for the female writer in that it allows her to appropriate the three traditionally male roles of politician, prophet, and science fiction writer." (Author). For more see *MAI* 35.05 (October 1997): 1149.

1695. ZEUGE, Paula. "Beyond the Technologized Body: Body Imagery in the Poetry of Denise Levertov and Margaret Atwood since 1960." PhD thesis. Salve Regina University, 1995. 308 pp. "This study offers a new reading of the body imagery used by Denise Levertov and Margaret Atwood over the last thirty years. Their poetry offers a vivid and sensitive record of the powerful emotional issues that characterize these tumultuous decades. During this period, these two poets specifically rebel against what they perceive as a concept of women's bodies imposed upon them by an expanding and standardizing technology. Changes in their body imagery are examined along with relevant commentary from the writings of such thinkers as Julia Kristeva, Michel Foucault, Judith Butler, Peter Russell, and Fritjof Capra." (Author). For more see *DAI-A* 56.08 (February 1996): 3132.

1696. ZIMMERMAN, Barbara. "Shadow Play: Zenia, the Archetypal Feminine Shadow in Margaret Atwood's *The Robber Bride*." *Pleiades* 15.2 (1995): 70-82.

1697. ZORZI, Rosella Mamoli. "On Translating Margaret Atwood into Italian: A Few Practical Considerations." *Rivista di studi canadesi* 8 (1995): 97-100.

1698. ZUPANCIC, Metka. "Feministicna proza: Miti in utopija: Margaret Atwood, Chantal Chawaf, Helene Cixous, Madeleine Monette, Monique Larue, Berta Bojetu." *Primerjalna Knjizevnost* (Ljubljana, Slovenia) 18.2 (1995): 1-16. Feminist fiction (Canadian, French-Canadian, Slovenian).

Reviews of Atwood's Works

1699. *Bones and Murder*. London: Virago, 1995.
  Sunday Times 15 October 1995: Section: Features. By Pam BARRETT.
1700. *Cat's Eye*. [Sound recording]. Read by Barbara Caruso. s.l.: Recorded Books, 1995.
  Library Journal 120.10 (1 June 1995): 190(1). By Nan Blaine LYARD.
1701. *Good Bones and Small Murders*. New York: Doubleday, 1994. Also published as *Good Bones & Simple Murders* (Rockland, MA: Wheeler, 1995).
  Atlanta Constitution and Journal 29 January 1995: Section: Arts: N10. By Diane ROBERTS. (210 w).
  Atlantic Monthly 275.1 (January 1995): 109. By Phoebe-Lou ADAMS. (105 w).
  Chicago Sun-Times 15 January 1995: Section: Show: 20. Originally published in the *Washington Post* 8 January 1995: Section: Book World: X3. By Ursula K. Le GUIN. (627 w).
  Los Angeles Times 19 February 1995: Section: Book Review: 6. By Dick RORABACK. (270 w).
  Morning Call (Allentown, PA) 12 February 1995: Section: Arts & Travel: F3. By Nicholas BASBANES. (819 w).
  Palm Beach Post 26 March 1995: Section: Arts and Entertainment: 6j. By Ellen KANNER. (415 w).
  Roanoke Times & World News 12 February 1995: Section: Metro and Book: F6. By Mary Ann JOHNSON. (238 w).
  Seattle Times 2 January 1995: Section: Books: M2. ANON. (217 w).
  Virginia-Pilot (Norfolk) 4 January 1995: Section: Daily Break: E5. By Laura LAFAY. (471 w).
  Washington Post 8 January 1995: WBK3. By Ursula K. Le GUIN.
  Washington Times 12 February 1995: Section: Part B, Books and Short Fiction: B6. By Mark BAUTZ. (1081 w).
1702. *La voleuse d'hommes*. Paris: R. Laffont, 1994. [*The Robber Bride*]
  Actualité 20.391 (March 1995): 98. De Gilles MARCOTTE.
  Châtelaine (Fr.) 36.2 (February 1995): 20. ANON.
  Spirale 139 (February 1995): 16. ANON.
1703. *Morning in the Burned House*. London: Virago, 1995. Also published by Houghton Mifflin in the United States.
  Booklist 92.1 (1 September 1995): 32. By Ray OLSON.
  Books in Canada 24.2 (March 1995): 29-31. By Charlene DIEHL-JONES. (Includes brief interview).
  Border Crossings 14.2 (Spring 1995): 58-60.
  Calgary Herald 25 March 1995: C18. By Lorri NEILSEN. (497 w).
  Catholic New Times 19.20. (19 November 1995): Supplement 1,3. ANON.
  Economist 335.7918 (19 June 1995): 80. ANON. (387 w).
  Financial Post 89.4 (28 January 1995): 28. ANON.
  Globe and Mail 30 January 1995: C1. ANON.
  Halifax Chronicle Herald 2 June 1995: C2. ANON.

Irish Times 8 July 1995: Section: Weekend Supplement: Paperback Choice: 9. By Arminta WALLACE. (174 w).

Library Journal 120.14 (1 September 1995): 181. By C. STENSTROM.

Maclean's 108.6 (6 February 1995): 85(1). By John BEMROSE. (849 w).

Miami Herald 24 December 1995: Section I:3 C:3. By Peter SCHMITT.

Montréal Gazette 21 January 1995: 11. By Mark ABLEY. (991 w).

Ottawa Citizen 22 January 1995: Section: Books: B3. By Colin MORTON. (833 w).

Poetry Review 85.3 (Fall 1995): 14. By M. ROBERTS.

Publisher's Weekly 242.35 (28 August 1995): 107. By Dulcy BRAINARD. (182 w).

Quill & Quire 61.2 (February 1995): 25. ANON.

Sunday Telegraph 25 June 1995: Section: Books: 10. By Verson SCANNELL. (212 w).

The Times 6 July 1995: Section: Features: By Rachael CAMPBELL-JOHNSON. (472 w).

Winnipeg Free Press 19 February 1995: D5.

1704. *New Oxford Book of Canadian Short Stories in English*. Toronto: Oxford UP, 1995.

   Books in Canada 24.9 (December 1995): 26-27. By Bruce MEYER.

   Toronto Star 16 December 1995: L4. By Philip MARCHAND. (859 w).

1705. *The Poetry of Gwendolyn MacEwen*. Toronto: Exile Editions, 1993-1994. Ed. Margaret Atwood and Barry Callaghan.

   University of Toronto Quarterly 65.1 (Winter 1995): 75-76. By Rita TREGEBOV.

1706. *Politique de pouvoir*. Montréal: L'Hexagone, 1995. Translated by Louise Desjardins.

   University of Toronto Quarterly 65.1 (Winter 1995): 129. By Jane KOUSTAS.

1707. *Princess Prunella and the Purple Peanut*. Toronto: Key Porter Books, 1995.

   Atlanta Journal and Constitution 3 December 1995 Section: Arts: 11L. By Elizabeth WARD.

   Austin American-Statesman 10 November 1995: Section: Lifestyle: F2. ANON.

   Booklist 92.8 (15 December 1995): 702. By Hazel ROCHMAN.

   Books in Canada 24.9 (December 1995): 20.

   Calgary Herald 28 December 1995: N1. By Joan CRAVEN. (165 w).

   Des Moines Register 10 December 1995: Section: Opinion: 4. By Anita LARSEN.

   Globe and Mail 14 October 1995: E20. ANON.

   Los Angeles Times 3 December 1995: BR27. By Suzy SCHMIDT.

   Maclean's 11 December 1995: 52. By Patricia HLUCHY and Diane TURBIDE.

   Ottawa Citizen 11 November 1995: J5. ANON. (156 w).

   People 44.25 (18 December 1995): 29(1). ANON.

   Quill & Quire 61.9 (September 1995): 73. ANON.

   Times Educational Supplement 4145 (8 December 1995): SS12. ANON.

   Times Union (Albany, NY) 5 December 1995: Section: Life & Leisure: C1. By Nancy PATE. Also in *Orlando Sentinel* 26 November 1995: Section: Arts & Entertainment: F1.

   Toronto Star 7 October 1995: PJ20. By Arlene Perly RAE. (170 w).

   Vancouver Sun 2 December 1995: C9. By Patrick TRICKETT, a Grade 3 student. (141 w).

1708. *The Robber Bride.* Toronto: McClelland and Stewart, 1993.
    American Studies International 33.2 (October 1995): 1-16. By M. PAGE.
    Americas 47.5 (19 September 1995): 60. By Barbara MUJICA. (878 w).
    Canadian Literature 147 (Winter 1995): 157-159. By Aritha VAN HERK.
    Catholic New Times 19.20 (19 November 1995): 1, 3.
    Chicago Tribune 5 March 1995: Section: Tribune Books: 8. ANON. (197 w).
    Cosmopolitan 218.3 (March 1995): 28. By Chris CHASE
    Entertainment Weekly 267 (24 March 1995): 60(1). ANON. (51 w).
    Houston Chronicle 5 March 1995: Section: Zest: 21. ANON. (63 w).
    International Fiction Review 22.1-2 (1995): 114-116. By N. F. STOVEL.
    New York Times 26 February 1995: Section 7:28 C:1 By Laurel GRAEBER.
      (84 w).
    Orlando Sentinel 19 February 1995: Section: Arts & Entertainment: F12.
      By Nancy PATE. (139 w).
1709. *The Robber Bride.* Audiobook. Read by Blythe Danner.
    Booklist 91.10 (15 January 1995): 946. By Candace SMITH.
1710. *Strange Things: The Malevolent North in Canadian Literature.* Oxford: Clarendon Press, 1995.
    Booklist 92.3 (1 October 1995): 245. By Ray OLSON.
    Books in Canada 24.8 (November 1995): 48. By Scott ELLIS.
    Ottawa Citizen 31 December 1995: Section: Book: B3. By Joy GUGELER. (792 w).
    Quill & Quire 61.10 (October 1995): 31. ANON.
    Winnipeg Free Press 26 November 1995: D6. ANON.

Reviews of Adaptations of Atwood's Works

1711. *Good Bones.* Adapted for the stage and directed by Neta Gordon. At Helen Gardiner Phelan Playhouse, Toronto.
    Toronto Star 2 September 1995: D12. By Robert CREW.
1712. *The Robber Bride.* CBC Radio Adaptation.
    Toronto Star 3 September 1995: B5. By Sid ADILMAN.

~ 1996 ~

Atwood's Works

1713. *Alias Grace*. Toronto: McClelland and Stewart; New York: Doubleday; London: Bloomsbury, 1996. 470 pp. Novel. Set in 19th-century Canada, *Alias Grace* is partly presented by a first-person narrator who is a woman convicted of having murdered her employer. Grace Mark's narrative is evasive and unreliable concerning her involvement in the crime.

1714. *Alias Grace*. Amsterdam: B. Bakker, 1996. Dutch translation by Gerda Baardman and Tjadine Stheeman.

1715. *Alias Grace*. Berlin: Berlin Verlag, 1996. 622. German translation by Brigitte Walitzek.

1716. *Alias Grace.* [Sound recording]. Read by Elizabeth McGovern. Toronto; New York: Bantam Books-Audio, 1996. 4 cassettes. Abridged.

1717. *Alias Grace.* [Videorecording]. New York: Doubleday, 1996. A Doubleday Book Club video to be used in connection with a book study. 20 min. Order from Doubleday Marketing, 1540 Broadway, New York, NY 10035.

1718. "Ava Gardner Reincarnated as a Magnolia." *The Movies: Texts, Receptions, Exposures*. Ed. Laurence Goldstein and Ira Konigsberg. Ann Arbor: University of Michigan Press, 1996. 318-320.

1719. *Bluebeard's Egg*. Toronto: McClelland-Bantam; New York: Bantam Books, 1996. Paperback reissue of 1983 McClelland and Stewart cloth edition.

1720. *Bluebeard's Egg and Other Stories*. London: Vintage Books, 1996. Includes "Significant Moments in the Life of My Mother," "Hurricane Hazel," "Loulou; Or, The Domestic Life of the Language," "Uglypuss," "Two Stories about Emma: The Whirlpool Rapids, Walking on Water," "Bluebeard's Egg," "Spring Song of the Frogs," "Scarlet Ibis," "The Salt Garden," "In Search of the Rattlesnake Plantain," "The Sunrise," "Unearthing Suite."

1721. "Boat." *Unmuzzled Ox* 14.1-4 (1996): 20-21. Poem.

1722. *Bodily Harm*. New York: Bantam Books; London: Vintage, 1996. Originally published in London by Jonathan Cape, 1982.

1723. "The Case of Wei Jingsheng." *New York Review of Books* 43.3 (15 February 1996): 41-42. Atwood, with several other authors, demands release of Chinese human-rights activist by his government.

1724. *Cat's Eye*. New York: Bantam Doubleday Dell Publications, 1996.

1725. *Cat's Eye*. Madison, WI: Demco Media, 1996.

1726. *Dancing Girls and Other Stories.* New York: Bantam Books; London: Vintage, 1996 ©1982.

1727. "Daphne and Laura and So Forth." *The Year's Best Fantasy and Horror.* 9th annual collection. Ed. Ellen Datlow and Terri Windling. New York: St. Martin's Press, 1996. 367-368. Poem. Reprinted from *Morning in the Burned House,* ©1995.

1728. "Death by Landscape." *The Oxford Book of Adventure Stories.* Ed. Joseph Bristow. New York: Oxford UP, 1996. 385-400. Reprinted from *Wilderness Tips,* ©1991.

1729. *Death by Landscape.* Bredbury, UK: National Library for the Blind, 1996. Braille ed., 2 v. Short story.

1730. *Der Report der Magd.* Frankfurt am Main: Fischer Taschenbuch Verlag, 1996 ©1987. German translation of *The Handmaid's Tale* by Helga Pfetsch.

1731. *Die Räuberbraut: Roman.* Frankfurt am Main: S. Fischer, 1996 ©1994. German translation of *The Robber Bride* by Brigitte Walitzek.

1732. *Doña oráculo.* Barcelona: Muchnik Editores, 1996. Spanish translation of *Lady Oracle* by Sofía Carlota Noguera.

1733. *The Edible Woman.* New York: Bantam Books, 1996 ©1970.

1734. *Ein Morgen im verbrannten Haus: Gedichte.* Berlin: Berlin Verlag, 1996. German translation of *Morning in the Burned House* by Beatrice Howeg.

1735. *En he-hatul.* Tel-Aviv: Kineret, 1996. Hebrew translation of *Cat's Eye* by Shelomit Avi'asaf.

1736. [Excerpts]. *The Penguin Book of Women's Humor.* Introduction and ed. Regina Barreca. Toronto: Penguin Books, 1996. 34-37. Includes excerpts from "Their Attitudes Differ," "She Considers Evading Him," and "They Eat Out" (from *Power Politics*); "Aging Female Poet Sits on the Balcony" (from *Selected Poems II 1976-1986*); "Letters, Towards and Away" (from *The Circle Game* and from *Lady Oracle*).

1737. "Extract from *Cat's Eye.*" *When We Were Young: A Collection of Canadian Stories.* Selected and ed. Stuart McLean. Toronto; New York; London: Penguin, 1996. 97-116. Eight-year-old Elaine describes her first year at her new school.

1738. "[Favourite Books of 1996.]" *Maclean's* 30 December 1996: 15. "I really enjoyed Matt Cohen's novel *Last Seen.* It's a breakthrough book for him, and it's concerned with the bizarre and sometimes hilarious effects of grief....Dorothy Speak's *Object of Your Love* is a very accomplished book of short stories. They're straight-from-the-shoulder tales about passion gone wildly astray....Joan Didion's *The Last Thing He Wanted* is hard to describe because it's so offbeat. It reflects every paranoid nightmare that you've ever had about clandestine operations of government. Part spy thriller, part romance, it's a deft and gripping story from a very classy writer."

1739. "The Female Body." *Fireweed* 56 (December 1996): 22-24.

1740. "Hairball." *The Penguin Book of International Women's Stories.* Selected and with an introduction by Kate Figes. New York: Viking, 1996. 260-273. Reprinted from *Wilderness Tips,* ©1991.

1741. *The Handmaid's Tale.* London: Vintage, 1996.

1742. *The Handmaid's Tale.* New York: Fawcett Columbine/Ballantine, 1996. Large print edition.

1743. "Homelanding." *Virtually Now: Stories of Science, Technology, and the Future.* Ed. Jeanne Schinto. New York: Persea Books, 1996. 3-7. Reprinted from *Good Bones and Simple Murders,* ©1983, 1992, 1994.

1744. "Hurricane Hazel." *Woman's Hour 50th Anniversary Short Story Collection*. Ed. Di Speirs. London: Penguin, 1996. 85-109. Reprinted from *Bluebeard's Egg*, ©1987.

1745. "It All Comes Together for Cohen." *Globe and Mail* 28 September 1996: D17. Review of Matt Cohen's latest novel, *Last Seen*. Favorable review includes the following: "Cards on the table: I know Matt Cohen. More cards: I've known him for decades. Yet more cards: I once acted as his editor, back in the early '70s when I was giving blood for small Canadian literary publishing at the House of Anansi Press. The reader has a right to know such things."

1746. *La novia ladrona*. Barcelona: Ediciones B, 1996. Spanish translation of *The Robber Bride* by Jordi Mustieles.

1747. *La petite poule rouge vide son coeur: Nouvelles*. Paris: Le Serpent à plumes, 1996. French translation of *Good Bones* by Hélène Filion.

1748. *La voleuse d'hommes*. Paris: Librairie générale française, 1996. French translation of *The Robber Bride* by Anne Rabinovitch.

1749. "The Labrador Fiasco." *The Independent* 25 August 1996: Section: Books: 24-26. Also published in London as one of 10 "Birthday Quids" by Bloomsbury Press.

1750. *Lady Oracle*. New York: Bantam Books, 1996 ©1976.

1751. *Life Before Man*. New York: Bantam Books, 1996 ©1980.

1752. *Life Before Man*. London: Vintage, 1996 ©1979.

1753. *Ligava laupitaja*. Riga [Latvia]: Spriditis, 1996. Latvian translation of *The Robber Bride*.

1754. "Little Chappies with Breasts." *New York Times* 101.2 (June 1996): Section 7 (Book Review): 11:1. Review of Hilary Mantel's novel *An Experiment in Love*. (1432 w).

1755. *Mati gatas*. Athens: Vivliopoleion tes "Hestias" I. D. Kollarou, 1996. 508 pp. Greek translation of *Cat's Eye*.

1756. "Men at Sea." The Canadian Women Writers' Engagement Calendar 1996: 26-31.

1757. *Morgon i det brunna huset*. Stockholm: Rabaen, Prisma, 1996 ©1995. Swedish translation of *Morning in the Burned House* by Heidi von Born and Hans Nygren.

1758. *Morning in the Burned House*. New York: Houghton Mifflin Company, 1996.

1759. "Morning in the Burned House." *The Best American Poetry: 1996*. Ed. Adrienne Rich. New York: Scribner, 1996. 33-34. Reprinted from the *North American Review* 280.4 (July 1995): 11.

1760. *Mort en lisière: Nouvelles*. Paris: Laffont, 1996. 254 pp. French translation of *Wilderness Tips* by Francois Dupuigrenet-Desroussilles.

1761. "My Life as a Bat." *Sudden Fiction (Continued): 60 New Short-Short Stories*. Ed. Robert Shapard and James Thomas. New York: Norton, 1996. 17-21. Reprinted from *Antaeus 64/65* (Spring-Autumn 1990): 172-175. Reprinted from *Good Bones and Simple Murders*, ©1994.

1762. *New Oxford Book of Canadian Short Stories in English*. Ed. Margaret Atwood and Robert Weaver. Oxford: Oxford UP, 1996. Hardback.

1763. *The New Oxford Book of Canadian Short Stories in English*. Ed. Margaret Atwood and Robert Weaver. [Sound recording]. Read by Michael Haughn. Vancouver, BC: CILS [College and Institute Library Services], 1996. 19 cassettes (27 hr., 30 min.). Based on 1995 title.

1764. *The Oxford Book of Canadian Short Stories in English*. Ed. Margaret Atwood and Robert Weaver. [Sound recording]. [Brantford, ON]: W. Ross MacDonald School, 1996. 5 tape reels. Recorded from 1986 title.

160   ~ **1996** ~

1765. "P. K. Page as a Non-Snow Angel." *Malahat Review* 117 (Winter 1996): 100-101. Poem.

1766. "Paradoxes and Dilemmas, the Woman as Writer." *Feminist Literary Theory*: *A Reader*. 2nd ed. Ed. Mary Eagleton. Oxford: Blackwell, 1996. 103-105. Reprinted from *Women in the Canadian Mosaic*. Ed. Gwen Matheson. Toronto: Peter Martin Associates, 1976.

1767. "A Pioneer in Canadian Publishing." *Jack McClelland: The Publisher of Canadian Literature*. Guadalajara (Jalisco, México): Universidad de Guadalajara, 1996. 48. Text in English and Spanish. Spanish text in inverted pages. In Spanish: "Un pionero de la edición canadiense." *Jack McClelland: El editor de la literatura canadiense*. Guadalajara (Jalisco, México): Universidad de Guadalajara, 1996. 18. A book published as part of University of Guadalajara's international book fair that honored Canada in 1996.

1768. *Poetry of Gwendolyn MacEwen*. London: Virago, 1996. xvii 107. Selected and introduced by Margaret Atwood.

1769. *Power Politics*: *Poems*. Concord, CA: Anansi, 1996. 56. Reissue of the 1971 House of Anansi Press edition. No new material.

1770. *Princesse Prunelle et les pois pourpe*. Montreal: Phidal, 1966. 32. French translation of *Princess Prunella and the Purple Peanut* by Maryann Kovalski.

1771. "A Rich Dessert from a Saucy Carter." *Globe and Mail* 6 April 1996: C18. Review of *Burning Your Boats: The Collected Short Stories* by Angela Carter.

1772. *The Robber Bride*. [Sound recording]. Read by Barbara Caruso. Prince Frederick, MD: Recorded Books, 1996. 15 sound cassettes (21.5 hrs.).

1773. "Romantic." *New York Times* 28 January 1996: Section: 7 (Book Review): 35. Poem. Reprinted from *Morning in the Burned House*, ©1995.

1774. *Røverbruden*. Oslo: Aschehoug, 1996. Norwegian translation of *The Robber Bride*.

1775. "A Seasonal Insanity." *Boston Globe* 8 December 1996: Section: Books: N16. Excerpt from *Alias Grace*.

1776. *Stories from Wilderness Tips*. [Sound recording]. Read by Pat Barlow. Vancouver, BC: Province of British Columbia, 1996. 6 cassettes.

1777. *Strange Things: The Malevolent North in Canadian Literature*. Oxford: Oxford UP, 1996. (Clarendon Lectures in English Literature). Hardback.

1778. *Strange Things: The Malevolent North in Canadian Literature*. [Sound recording]. Vancouver, BC: Crane Library, 1996. 3 cassettes. Recorded from 1995 title.

1779. *Surfacing*. New York: Bantam Books, 1996 ©1972.

1780. *Survival*: *A Thematic Guide*. Toronto: McClelland and Stewart, 1996. Reprint of the 1992 House of Anansi Press edition.

1781. *Taberareru onna*. Tokyo: Shinchosha, 1996. Japanese translation of *The Edible Woman*. Title romanized.

1782. "There Was Once." *Only Connect: Readings on Children's Literature*. 3rd ed. Ed. Sheila Egoff, Gordon Stubbs, Ralph Ashley, and Wendy Sutton. Toronto; New York; Oxford: Oxford UP, 1996. [350]-352. Poem.

1783. "Through the One-Way Mirror." *Images through Literature*. [Ed.] John Borovilos. Scarborough, ON: Prentice Hall Canada, 1996. 168-171. Includes study questions, 172-173. Originally published in *The Nation* 22 March 1987.

1784. *True Trash*. Bredbury, UK: National Library for the Blind, 1996. Braille ed., 2 v. Short story.

1785. "Under the Thumb: How I Became a Poet." *Utne Reader* October 1996: 78-81, 107. Reprinted from *This Magazine* 29.6-7 (March-April 1996): 44.

1786. "A Voice from the Past." *Maclean's* 109.39 (23 September 1996): 44. Excerpt from *Alias Grace*.

1787. "Why I Write Poetry." *This Magazine* 29.6-7 (March-April 1996): 44.

1788. *Wilderness Tips*. New York: Bantam Books, 1996. 228 pp. Reprint.

1789. *Wilderness Tips*. [Sound recording]. Read by Pat Barlow. [Vancouver, BC]: Library Services Branch, Province of British Columbia, [1996]. 6 sound cassettes (7 hr., 55 min.). "This audiobook is for the exclusive use of persons unable to read print because of a physical or visual disability." (Container).

1790. "Wisdom from the Deep Freeze." *Globe and Mail* 16 July 1996: A13. Transcript of the convocation address delivered by Atwood after receiving an honorary doctor-of-letters degree from McMaster University on June 4.

1791. *Zbójecka narzeczona*. Poznan: Zysk i S-Ka Wydawn, 1996. Polish translation of *The Robber Bride* by Wieslaw Marcysiak.

Adaptations of Atwood's Works

1795. *The Handmaid's Tale = Tjenerindens fortælling*. [Musical Score]. Music by Poul Ruders; [English] libretto by Paul Bentley after Margaret Atwood's novel. [Copenhagen]: Edition Wilhelm Hansen, 1996. Printed music: Operas 1 vocal score (XXI, 563 pp.).

Quotations

1796. "[Quote]." *Evening Post* (Wellington, NZ) 6 April 1996: Section: Features and Opinion: 6. In article entitled "So Much Depravity: I'd Rather Have Hairy Maclary Any Day," Joanne Black quotes Atwood who wrote that she no longer wanted to read anything sad, violent, or disturbing: "Depression and squalor are for those under 25; they can take it, they can even like it, they still have enough time left."

1797. "[Quote]." *Globe and Mail* 27 April 1996: C1. Commenting at the Trillium Awards on the risk of publishing novels in the 1960s, Atwood noted that then "poetry was the preferred Canadian form....Publishers didn't think they could make a go of Canadian novels—too many pages."

1798. "[Quote]." *San Francisco Chronicle* 4 June 1996: Section: Daily Datebook: E10. In an article titled "Hate the Book; Love the Group, Though," Lara Adair quotes Atwood, who once wrote: "Book groups are to late 20th-century America what salons were to 18th-century Paris, and what improvement societies were to Victorians: in other words, an excuse for a party."

1799. "[Quote]." *Toronto Sun* 9 May 1996: Section: Entertainment: 7. In an article titled "Authors Festival Bigger Than Ever," Wilder Penfield III quotes Atwood on Al Purdy: "He writes like a cross between Shakespeare and a vaudeville comedian (so did Shakespeare)."

1800. "[Quote]." *Toronto Sun* 9 June 1996: Section: Comment: C3. In an article entitled "Busy as a Beaver Debunking Old Myths," John Dowling quotes Atwood's comment on the 1987 [sic] Free Trade Agreement between Canada and the United States: "Our national animal is the beaver, noted for its industrious habits and cooperative spirit. In medieval bestiaries it is also noted for its habit, when frightened, of biting off its own testicles and offering them to the pursuer. I hope we are not succumbing to some form of that impulse."

1801. "[Quote]." *Toronto Star* 29 December 1996: Section: Context: F4. In an article entitled "Notables and Non-entities," Lynda Hurst quotes Atwood's comment after losing the Booker Prize and $32,000 to fellow author Graham Swift: "It's not like a horse-race or the Olympics. Not having sex the night before won't help."

1802. "[Quote]." *Toronto Sun* 10 November 1996: Section: Comment: C10. In an article entitled "Heroine Addict: The Women I Worship," Heather Mallick quotes Atwood on sex: "Your body with head attached and my body with head attached coincide briefly."

1803. "[Quote]." *The Woman's Hour: 50 Years of Women in Britain*. By Jenni Murray. London: BBC Books, 1996. 249. Atwood on the word *feminist*: "Does feminist mean large unpleasant person who'll shout at you, or does feminist mean someone who believes women are human beings? If it's the latter, I'll sign up."

1804. "[Quotes]." *Canada Inside Out: How We See Ourselves; How Others See Us*. By David Olive. Toronto: Doubleday, 1996. Atwood quoted on 3, 25, 42, 53, and 56.

Interviews

1805. *Deux sollicitudes: Entretiens.* Trois-Pistoles [QU]: Editions Trois-Pistoles, 1996. This book is based on 20 interviews with Atwood broadcast between 26 January and 7 June 1996 on the stereo (FM) network of Radio-Canada as well as on interviews conducted with Victor-Levy BEAULIEU.

1806. ABLEY, Mark. "Don't Ask for the Truth." *The Guardian* 5 September 1996: Section: *Guardian* Features Page: 9. (2254 w).

1807. BATTERSBY, Eileen. "Out of Canada." *Irish Times* 16 April 1996: Section: Arts: 10. Interview with Atwood before her reading at the 10th Court Festival of Literature in Galway. Includes her remark that the Margaret Atwood Society, established in 1982 "embarrasses her" almost as much as the two aspiring biographers who are currently doing research on her. "I really think I should be dead or something, don't you?" (1827 w).

1808. BONE, James. "A Woman Possessed." *Times* (*London*) 14 September 1996: Section: Features: s.p. Available from Lexis-Nexis. Atwood, interviewed in her back yard with a splitting headache, faxes author the next day claiming she cannot remember a word she said to him. (2326 w).

1809. GUSSOW, Mel. "Author Atwood: Alternative Personalities in Life, Art." *Tulsa World* 31 December 1996: D3. (1050 w). Originally published in the *New York Times* 30 December 1996: Section: C: 9 as "The Alternate Personalities in an Author's Life and Art."

1810. KELLY, Karen. *Alias Grace [Holiday Reflection]*. [Sound recording]. Troy, NY: Sage Colleges; Albany, NY: WAMC Public Radio, 1996. 1 sound cassette (25 min., 9 sec.). Atwood interview about *Alias Grace* (18 min.) followed by short holiday message. Recorded 12 December 1996.

1811. LANGDON, Julia. "Not So Weird as Wonderful." *The Herald* (Glasgow) 4 October 1996: 21. (1587 w).

1812. MALLICK, Heather. "Alias Atwood: Our Finest Novelist's Books Speak for Themselves, but They Don't Say It All." *Toronto Sun* 29 September 1996: Section: Comments and Books: C10. (2595 w). Interview references a radio program, in which Atwood was asked some "desert island" questions. **What books might she take?** "Very long ones," Atwood said. **What writer would she choose to accompany her?** Another participant suggested James Joyce, rhapsodizing, "Ah, but he could talk!" Atwood quite rightly said Joyce would be useless—"couldn't boil an egg." She chose Boy Scout founder Lord Baden-Powell...because he could build a fire and do all the cooking. "And not only that, I wouldn't have to worry about—the SAYX."

1813. McLEAN, Sandy. "[Atwood Interviewed]." *U.P.I.* 29 October 1996: Section: Entertainment. Available from Lexis-Nexis. Atwood, interviewed at the rear of Toronto's Premier Dance Theatre, brought along a small slip of paper saved from that night's Chinese fortune cookie. It read: "Not every question deserves an answer."...Throughout the interview, which centered around her opinions concerning literary festivals, Atwood pointed to the fortune message sitting on the table whenever she didn't have an answer or chose to evade questions about what she's going to write about next or whether she is finished with the character from her latest book. (522 w).

1814. PATE, Nancy. "Princess Prunella: Playful Prose for Pint-Size Readers." *Sacramento Bee* 3 January 1996: Section: Scene: D9. On the origins of her new book. Includes Atwood's comment that she doubted she would pen another picture book any time soon. "I never predict the future in regard to my own writing, but I don't think it's really my métier. I mean really, what if that's what you're remembered for? Edward Lear painted wonderful pictures of parrots, but he's not remembered for parrot paintings but for his verse." (1027 w).

1815. PEPINSTER, Catherine. "The Writer's Tale: How a Story Chose an Author and Wowed the Critics." *The Independent* 20 September 1996: Section: News: 9. "In an exclusive interview, Atwood questioned the feminist label. She also talked about the precariousness of existence, temptresses and friends, why children should read Shakespeare and how she was 'chosen' to write *Alias Grace*." (808 w).

1816. SCHULTZ, Susy. "Atwood's *Alias:* She's Convincing as Always as Historical Writer." *Chicago Sun-Times* 22 December 1996: Section: SHO: 4. (1072 w).

1817. WONG, Jan. "An Audience with 'a Queen.'" *Globe and Mail* 7 September 1996: A6. Atwood admits she can't spell. "When I announced to my mother in high school I was going to be a writer, my mother said, 'You'd better learn to spell.' I said, 'Others will do that for me," and they have. In the interview, Atwood, at 5 feet 3.5 inches, comments: "I used to be 5-4 but I'm shrinking."

Scholarly Resources

1818. ARIAS-BEAUTELL, Eva. "Displacements, Self-Mockery, and Carnival in the Canadian Postmodern." *World Literature* (Spring 1996): 316-320.

1819. ATROPS, Lorene A. "The Evil Personality of Zenia in Margaret Atwood's *The Robber Bride*." MA thesis. University of Alaska, 1996. 93 pp. "In *People of the Lie*, M. Scott Peck defines evil personalities as individuals who are inherently different from other human beings, based upon the consistent destructiveness of their behaviors in human relationships. These intentional, destructive behaviors occur without any external cause or provocation. Peck's descriptions match the American Psychiatric Association's definitions of the antisocial and narcissistic personality disorders and apply to Zenia in Margaret Atwood's *The Robber Bride*....An analysis of Tony, Charis, and Roz identifies them as personalities who are not evil and who are primarily vulnerable to Zenia because of their misplaced trust in her." (Author). For more see *MAI* 34.06 (December 1996): 2167.

1820. BACCOLINI, Raffaella. "Journeying through the Dystopian Genre: Memory and Imagination in Burdekin, Orwell, Atwood, and Piercy." *Viaggi in Utopia.* Ed. Raffaella Baccolini, Vita Fortunati, and Nadia Minerva. Ravenna [Italy]: Longo, 1996. 347-357. Presented at a conference held 25-27 March 1993, Rimini, Italy.

1821. BARZILAI, Shuli. "Atwood's Female Quest-Romance: A Psychoanalytic Approach to *Surfacing.*" *Approaches to Teaching Atwood's* The Handmaid's Tale *and Other Works.* Ed. Sharon R. Wilson, Thomas B. Friedman, and Shannon Hengen. New York: Modern Language Association of America, 1996. 161-166.

1822. ———. "The Rhetoric of Ambivalence in Margaret Atwood's *Survival*: A Thematic Guide to Canadian Literature." *Precarious Present / Promising Future? Ethnicity and Identities in Canadian Literature.* Ed. Danielle Schaub, Janice Kulyk Keefer, and Richard E. Sherwin. Jerusalem, Israel: Magnes, 1996. 1-9.

1823. BELLIS, Miriam Hamilton. "Making and Unmaking the Self in the Novels of Fay Weldon, Margaret Atwood and Toni Morrison." PhD thesis. University of Miami, 1996. 275 pp. "Western thought has traditionally associated woman with body and man with mind. Weldon, Atwood, and Morrison offer in their novels a critique of this association of woman with physicality and address the complex relationship between the female body and subjectivity. They focus on violence directed toward that body, especially as represented in eating disorders, reproductive technologies, and 'cosmetic (re)construction' (e.g., hair dyeing and styling, makeup, elective plastic surgery). These forms of violence are used to contain and control the body, which is defined as a place of cultural unruliness and disorder. In addition to focusing on the violence others impose on female bodies that threatens the women's subjectivity, I also examine the violence that women practice, or cause to be practiced, on their own bodies and on those of other women when their subjectivity is threatened or denied." (Author). For more see *DAI-A* 57.12 (June 1997): 5143.

1824. BENNETT, Donna, and Nathalie COOKE. "A Feminist by Another Name: Atwood and the Canadian Canon." *Approaches to Teaching Atwood's* The Handmaid's Tale *and Other Works.* Ed. Sharon R. Wilson, Thomas B. Friedman, and Shannon Hengen. New York: Modern Language Association of America, 1996. 33-43.

1825. BENSON, Stephen. "Stories of Love and Death: Reading and Writing the Fairy Tale Romance." *Image and Power: Women in Fiction in the Twentieth Century.* Ed. Sarah Sceats and Gail Cunningham. London: Longman, 1996. 103-113. The quest and intertextuality are topics used in a comparative study of 4 novels: Margaret Atwood's *Lady Oracle*, Angela Carter's *The Bloody Chamber and Other Stories* and *The Magic Toyshop*, and Charlotte Brontë's *Jane Eyre.*

1826. BENTON, Carol L. "Reading as Rehearsal in a Communication Class: Comic Voicings in Atwood's Poetry." *Approaches to Teaching Atwood's* The Handmaid's Tale *and Other Works.* Ed. Sharon R. Wilson, Thomas B. Friedman, and Shannon Hengen. New York: Modern Language Association of America, 1996. 84-89.

1827. BERAN, Carol L. "The End of the World and Other Things: *Life Before Man* and *The Handmaid's Tale.*" *Approaches to Teaching Atwood's* The Handmaid's Tale *and Other Works.* Ed. Sharon R. Wilson, Thomas B. Friedman, and Shannon Hengen. New York: Modern Language Association of America, 1996. 128-134.

1828. BIESE, Eivor. "In Search of Voice in Margaret Atwood's *Surfacing.*" *New Courant* 6 (1996): 26-38.

1829. BJERRING, Nancy. "Feminism as Framework for Investigating Canadian Multi-culturalism." *Mosaic: A Journal for the Interdisciplinary Study of Literature* 29.3 (1996): 165-173.

1830. BOOKER, M. Keith. *A Practical Introduction to Literary Theory and Criticism.* White Plains, NY: Longman, 1996. See especially Chapter 14, "Approaches to *The Handmaid's Tale* by Margaret Atwood," 257-283. The work seen through the prism of various critical perspectives: The New Criticism, Deconstructive Criticism, Bakhtinian Criticism, and Foucauldian Criticism. Chapter 19 also contains two critical essays on Atwood, one by Stephanie Barbé Hammer and the other by Amin Malak, separately indexed.

1831. BOUSON, J. Brooks. "A Feminist and Psychoanalytic Approach in a Women's College." *Approaches to Teaching Atwood's* The Handmaid's Tale *and Other Works.* Ed. Sharon R. Wilson, Thomas B. Friedman, and Shannon Hengen. New York: Modern Language Association of America, 1996. 122-127.

1832. BRYDON, Diana. "Beyond Violent Dualities: Atwood in Postcolonial Contexts." *Approaches to Teaching Atwood's* The Handmaid's Tale *and Other Works.* Ed. Sharon R. Wilson, Thomas B. Friedman, and Shannon Hengen. New York: Modern Language Association of America, 1996. 49-54.

1834. CECIL, Lynn Anne. "Working from Nineteenth-Century Discourses: Margaret Atwood's Construction of Women in *The Edible Woman, Lady Oracle,* and *The Robber Bride.* MA thesis. University of Western Ontario, 1996. 89 pp. Also available on microfiche from Canadian Theses Service (1996). "Rather than ignoring mythology that centers on women, Atwood has instead attempted to 'transform it, rearrange it and shift the values' (in Van Varsveld 67) in order to create female characters who are multidimensional and difficult to categorize into one specific construction....Particularly in *The Edible Woman* (1969), *Lady Oracle* (1976), and *The Robber Bride* (1993), Atwood creates female characters around the discursive figures of the angel in the house, the maiden in the tower, the femme fatale, the mermaid, and the triple goddess, while transforming the values and meanings associated with such figures. Atwood subverts Victorian conceptions of womanhood and parodies twentieth-century men and women who continue to condone categorizing women according to such types." (Author). For more see *MAI* 34.06 (December 1996): 2168.

1835. CHAPMAN, Suzette. "Alternative Identities: Sexual Redefinition of Women in *The Last of the Mohicans, Jane Eyre, Democracy,* and *The Handmaid's Tale.*" MA thesis. University of Houston–Clear Lake, 1996. 160 pp. "In four important novels of nineteenth- and twentieth-century Anglo-American literature, subversive female protagonists address issues of social power and redefine literary heroism. The acquisition and concession of power can be traced through marginalized women in James Fenimore Cooper's *The Last of the Mohicans* (1826), Charlotte Brontë's *Jane Eyre* (1847), Joan Didion's *Democracy* (1984), and Margaret Atwood's *The Handmaid's Tale* (1985)....The[se women] counter gender discrimination, which is socialized biology, through sexuality, which is socialized sexual behavior. Sexual difference, the source of their victimization, becomes a solution....They apply a creative twist to Darwinian dominance and submission by overcoming culturally imposed limits based on biology and by proposing and enacting alternative sexualities." (Author). For more see *MAI* 35.03 (June 1997): 651.

1836. COOKE, John. *The Influence of Painting on Five Canadian Writers: Alice Munro, Hugh Hood, Timothy Findley, Margaret Atwood and Michael Ondaatje.* Lewiston, NY: Edwin Mellen Press, 1996.

1837. COWAN, Amy. "Transformations: Writing On / The Lesbian (Body)." *Canadian Woman Studies* 16.2 (Spring 1995): 53-57. "Within contemporary feminist texts, the body is a recurrent and often central text. This article examines two texts, one heterosexual, Margaret Atwood's 'Loulou, Or the Domestic Life of Language,'' and one lesbian, Rebecca Brown's 'Isle of Skye,' to analyze the way the relationship between the female body and language is configured." (Journal).

1838. D'ARCY, Chantal Cornut-Gentille, and José Ángel García LANDA, eds. *Gender I-deology: Essays on Theory, Fiction and Film*. Amsterdam; Atlanta, GA: Rodopi, 1996. Contains numerous references to *The Handmaid's Tale*. See especially FLORÉN, Celia, below.

1839. DAVIDSON, Arnold E. "Negotiating *Wilderness Tips*": *Approaches to Teaching Atwood's* The Handmaid's Tale *and Other Works*. Ed. Sharon R. Wilson, Thomas B. Friedman, and Shannon Hengen. New York: Modern Language Association of America, 1996. 180-186.

1840. DJWA, Sandra. "Canada." *The Oxford Guide to Contemporary Canadian Writing*. Ed. John Sturrock. Toronto: Oxford UP, 1996. 66-82. Atwood discussion: 72-74.

1841. EVANS, Gillian M. "Context Is All: Creativity, Criticism, and the Narrative Voice in the Novels of Margaret Atwood." MPhil thesis. University of Oxford, 1996.

1842. FARRELL, Kirby. "Thinking Through Others: Prosthetic Fantasy and the Cultural Moment." *Massachusetts Review* (Summer 1996): 213-235.

1843. FLORÉN, Celia. "A Reading of Margaret Atwood's Dystopia, *The Handmaid's Tale*." *Gender, I-deology: Essays on Theory, Fiction and Film*. Ed. Chantal Cornut-Gentille D'Arcy and José Ángel García Landa. Amsterdam; Atlanta, GA: Rodopi, 1996. 253-264.

1844. FRIEDMAN, Thomas B. "Using Atwood's *Survival* in an Interdisciplinary Canadian Studies Course." *Approaches to Teaching Atwood's* The Handmaid's Tale *and Other Works*. Ed. Sharon R. Wilson, Thomas B. Friedman, and Shannon Hengen. New York: Modern Language Association of America, 1996. 63-69.

1845. FRIEDMAN, Thomas B., and Shannon HENGEN. "Materials." *Approaches to Teaching Atwood's* The Handmaid's Tale *and Other Works*. Ed. Sharon R. Wilson, Thomas B. Friedman, and Shannon Hengen. New York: Modern Language Association of America, 1996. 7-20.

1846. FRANZKE, Anne Disney. "Through the Heart of the Shadow: A Study of the Literary Works of Margaret Atwood." MA thesis. Sonoma State University, 1996. 78 pp.

1847. GORJUP, Branko. "New Arrivals, Further Departures: The Euro-Immigrant Experience in Canada." *Ethnic Literature and Culture in the U.S.A., Canada and Australia*. Ed. Igor Maver. Frankfurt: Peter Lang, 1996. 263-271. Includes discussion of Atwood's *The Journals of Susanna Moodie*.

1848. HAMMER, Stephanie Barbé. "The World as It Will Be? Female Satire and the Technology of Power in *The Handmaid's Tale*." *A Practical Introduction to Literary Theory and Criticism*. M. Keith Booker. White Plains, NY: Longman, 1996. 409-419. Reprinted from *Modern Language Studies* 20.2 (Spring 1990): 39-49.

1849. HARTING, Heike. "The Profusion of Meanings and the Female Experience of Colonization: Inscriptions of the Body as Site of Difference in Tsitsi Dangarembga's *Nervous Conditions* and Margaret Atwood's *The Edible Woman*." *Fusion of Cultures*. Ed. Peter O. Stummer and Christopher Balme. Amsterdam: Rodopi, 1996. 237-246. (ASNEL Papers, 2. Cross/Cultures, 26).

1850. HELLER, Arno. "Margaret Atwood's Ecological Vision." *Nationalism vs. Internationalism: (Inter)National Dimensions of Literatures in English*. Ed. Wolfgang

Zach and Ken L. Goodwin. Tübingen: Stauffenburg, 1996. 313-318. Especially in *Surfacing*.

1851. HEWITT, Pamela. "Understanding Contemporary American Culture through *The Handmaid's Tale*: A Sociology Class." *Approaches to Teaching Atwood's* The Handmaid's Tale *and Other Works*. Ed. Sharon R. Wilson, Thomas B. Friedman, and Shannon Hengen. New York: Modern Language Association of America, 1996. 109-113.

1852. HOPE, Joan. "The Feminist Gaze: Feminism, Postmodernism, and Women's Bodies." PhD thesis. Indiana University, 1996. 241 pp. "This study examines the dialogue between feminism and postmodernism, primarily as it takes place in artistic and fictional representations of the female body....Particularly effective methods are to evoke and then foil the male gaze by shaping and reshaping the female body that it watches and to condition the reception of the image with language. Many performers, artists, and writers in England, Canada, and the United States have experimented with these techniques. I discuss works by Madonna, Mary Kelly, Cindy Sherman, Margaret Atwood, and by science fiction writers Ursula K. Le Guin, Suzy McKee Charnas, Joanna Russ, and Marge Piercy." (Author). For more see *DAI-A* 57.04 (October 1996): 1612.

1853. HOWELLS, Coral Ann. "Disruptive Geographies; Or, Mapping the Region of Woman in Contemporary Canadian Women's Writing in English." *Journal of Commonwealth Literature* 31.1 (1996): 115-126. Article includes analysis of *The Robber Bride*.

1854. HUFNAGEL, Jill. "Atwood's 'Variation on the Word *Sleep*.'" *The Explicator* 54.3 (Spring 1996): 188-191. On Atwood poem.

1855. ———. "The Uneasy Marriage of Feminism and Postmodernism in Six Twentieth-Century Novels by Women." PhD thesis. University of North Carolina, 1996. 224 pp. The study traces the feminist postmodern tradition through Djuna Barnes's *Nightwood* (1936), Margaret Atwood's *Surfacing* (1972), Joan Didion's *A Book of Common Prayer* (1977), Sandra Cisneros's *The House on Mango Street* (1984), Gloria Naylor's *Mama Day* (1988), and Jeanette Winterson's *Written on the Body* (1992). For more see *DAI-A* 57.07 (January 1997): 3291.

1856. INGERSOLL, Earl. "The Engendering of Narrative in Doris Lessing's *Shikasta* and Margaret Atwood's *The Handmaid's Tale*." *Visions of the Fantastic: Selected Essays from the Fifteenth International Conference on the Fantastic in the Arts*. Ed. Allienne Becker. Westport, CT: Greenwood Press, 1996. 39-47.

1857. JACOBSEN, Sally A. "Themes of Identity in Atwood's Poems and 'Rape Fantasies': Using *The Norton Anthology of Literature by Women*." *Approaches to Teaching Atwood's* The Handmaid's Tale *and Other Works*. Ed. Sharon R. Wilson, Thomas B. Friedman, and Shannon Hengen. New York: Modern Language Association of America, 1996. 70-76.

1858. JENNINGS, Rosalind Maria. "Disappearance in Deceptive Landscapes: Borderlines of Identity in the Canadian Wilderness with Particular Reference to Selected Works by Margaret Atwood, Robert Kroetsch, Michael Ondaatje and Aritha Van Herk." PhD thesis. University of York (UK), 1996. For more see *Index to Theses Accepted for Higher Degrees by the Universities of Great Britain and Ireland*. 47 (1998): 257.

1859. JOHNSON, Brian. "Language, Power, and Responsibility in *The Handmaid's Tale*: Towards a Discourse of Literary Gossip." *Canadian Literature* 148 (Spring 1996): 39-55. Focuses on the gossip in literature and ways in which the novel tests the power of gossip.

1860. ———. "Schools of Scandal: Gossip in Theory and Canadian Fiction." MA thesis. University of Manitoba, 1996. 205 pp. Also available on microfiche from Canadian Theses Service (1997). "Gossip in Margaret Atwood's *The Handmaid's Tale* develops the feminist articulation of gossip as a politically subversive discourse, but also suggests the dangers of gossip in its 'legitimized,' institutional form in ways that are illuminated, respectively, by M. M. Bahktin and Jacques Derrida's theories of language." (Author). For more see *MAI* 35.05 (October 1997): 1153.

1861. KADAR, Marlene. "*The Journals of Susanna Moodie* as Life Writing." *Approaches to Teaching Atwood's* The Handmaid's Tale *and Other Works.* Ed. Sharon R. Wilson, Thomas B. Friedman, and Shannon Hengen. New York: Modern Language Association of America, 1996. 146-152.

1862. KEMP, Mark Alexander Riach. "Backyards and Border Patrols: North American Nationalisms, Literature and the Impact of Postcolonialism." PhD thesis. University of Pittsburgh, 1996. 444 pp. "This dissertation argues that postcolonial cultural theory alters the way North America literary traditions are understood. For the last century, literary traditions have been constructed, studied, and taught predominantly to serve national agendas. A canon reflects 'the nation'—by which is most often meant the State—as an imagined community and a coherent system of values, symbols, and traits....To interrogate the relations between postcolonial and national reading attitudes, I examine the major works of four writers from the United States and Canada. Nathaniel Hawthorne and Herman Melville represent hypercanonized authors from the politically fraught and culturally rich antebellum period in the US. Although still in mid-career, Margaret Atwood and Michael Ondaatje have earned canonical status in Canada. All four authors both challenge and celebrate the concept and ideal of nation; they can thus provide a basis for interrogation of the State they are assumed to be serving and representing." (Author). For more see *DAI-A* 57.12 (June 1997): 5151.

1863. KIRTZ, Mary K. "Teaching Literature through Film: An Interdisciplinary Approach to *Surfacing* and *The Handmaid's Tale*." *Approaches to Teaching Atwood's* The Handmaid's Tale *and Other Works.* Ed. Sharon R. Wilson, Thomas B. Friedman, and Shannon Hengen. New York: Modern Language Association of America, 1996. 140-145.

1864. KORMALI, Sema. "Feminist Science Fiction: The Alternative Worlds of Piercy, Elgin, and Atwood." *Journal of American Studies of Turkey* 4 (1996): 69-77. Marge Piercy's *Woman on the Edge of Time* compared to Suzette Haden Elgin's *Native Tongue* and Atwood's *The Handmaid's Tale.*

1865. KURTZ, Roman. "All the Polarities: A Golden Age Revisited." *Fusion of Cultures?* Ed. Peter O. Stummer and Christopher Balme. Amsterdam: Rodopi, 1996. 119-128. *Surfacing* compared to Marie-Clare Blais's *Une Saison dans la vie d'Emmanuel* (*A Season in the Life of Emmanuel*) and Roch Carrier's *La Guerre, Yes Sir!*

1866. LAPPAS, Catherine. "'Gilded Cages' and 'Concave Mirrors': Female Prisons in Margaret Atwood and Angela Carter." *Feminism in Multi-Cultural Literature.* Ed. Antonio Sobejano-Moran. Lewiston, NY: Edwin Mellen Press, 1995. [85]-101. References *The Handmaid's Tale.*

1867. LAZ, C. "Science Fiction and Introductory Sociology: *The Handmaid* in the Classroom." *Teaching Sociology* 24.1 (January 1996): 54-63. Examines the pedagogical uses of science fiction in teaching sociology, with particular focus on *The Handmaid's Tale.*

1868. LECY, Maren. "Coloring in the Characters: A Study of the Symbolic and Metaphoric Uses of Color by Margaret Atwood, Charles Baxter, Zora Neale Hurston, and John Edgar Wideman." MALS thesis. Hamline University, 1996. 117 pp.

1869. LEE, So-Hee. "A Study on the Women's Work in *The Handmaid's Tale* Focused on the Handmaid's Work." *Feminist Studies in English Literature* 3 (1996): 187-212. In Korean; abstract in English.

1870. LEONARD, Garry. "A Practical Exercise: Popular Culture and Gender Construction in *Surfacing* and *Bodily Harm*." *Approaches to Teaching Atwood's* The Handmaid's Tale *and Other Works* Ed. Sharon R. Wilson, Thomas B. Friedman, and Shannon Hengen. New York: Modern Language Association of America, 1996. 90-98.

1871. LEVINE-KEATING, Helane. "Atwood's *You Are Happy:* Power Politics, Gender Roles, and the Transformation of Myth.*" Approaches to Teaching Atwood's* The Handmaid's Tale *and Other Works.* Ed. Sharon R. Wilson, Thomas B. Friedman, and Shannon Hengen. New York: Modern Language Association of America, 1996. 153-160.

1872. LOMBARDI, Giancarlo. "Mirrors of Their Own: Feminist Diary Fiction, 1952-1994." PhD thesis. Cornell University, 1996. 261 pp. "Constantly excluded from History, women have been forced to act as mere spectators to events which have nevertheless shaped their subjugated condition: the window thus remains their assigned place, and it is a window which often contains prison bars, if only at a symbolic level. The ideal coexistence of the internal and external world, that of the emotions and that of politics, lies at the core of most feminist fictional diaries, and my analysis of works by Alba de Cespedes, Dacia Maraini, Susanna Tamaro, Doris Lessing, Margaret Atwood, and Simone de Beauvoir is aimed at exploring its multifaceted, yet constant presence. Such a task will be carried out through the analysis of significant textual passages which most clearly reveal a struggle, occurring on one hand within the psyche of the diarist herself, and on the other, between the woman diarist and the phallogocentric society that resists her access to the written word." (Author). For more see *DAI-A* 57.04 (October 1996): 1607.

1873. LOTT, Lisa. "The Female Quest: Journeys Toward Re-Naming Identity and Re-Claiming Wholeness of Self in Novels by Carson McCullers, Harper Lee, Joan Didion and Margaret Atwood." MA thesis. University of Houston–Clear Lake, 1996. 60 pp. "Female protagonists in these novels represent different eras in history and share similar characteristics and problems. Each protagonist struggles to find her own identity, seeks to take control of her life, experiences feelings of isolation and 'otherness,' and becomes disillusioned with patriarchal female archetypes. Through quest, female characters push the established boundaries of 'otherness' and emerge re-defined, with a re-newed sense of self, and a re-claimed purpose." (Author). For more see *MAI* 35.03 (June 1997): 652.

1874. MacFARLANE, Susan Elizabeth Wilson. "Checking the Mainstream: The Architectonics of Canadian Literary Criticism." PhD thesis. University of Victoria, 1996. 323 pp. Also available on microfiche from Canadian Theses Service (1997). Includes analysis of Atwood's influence, especially of *Survival* on Canadian literary criticism. For more see *DAI-A* 58.05 (November 1997): 1716.

1875. MAHONEY, Elisabeth. "Writing So to Speak: The Feminist Dystopia.*" Image and Power: Women in Fiction in the Twentieth Century*. Ed. Sarah Sceats and Gail Cunningham. London: Longman, 1996. 29-40. *The Handmaid's Tale.*

1876. MALAK, Amin. "Margaret Atwood's *The Handmaid's Tale* and the Dystopian Tradition." *A Practical Introduction to Literary Theory and Criticism*. [Ed.] M.

Keith Booker. White Plains, NY: Longman, 1996. 419-425. Reprinted from *Canadian Literature* 112 (1987): 9-16.

1877. MANLEY, Kathleen E. B. "Atwood's Reconstruction of Folktales: *The Handmaid's Tale* and 'Bluebeard's Egg.'" *Approaches to Teaching Atwood's* The Handmaid's Tale *and Other Works*. Ed. Sharon R. Wilson, Thomas B. Friedman, and Shannon Hengen. New York: Modern Language Association of America, 1996. 135-139.

1878. MANUEL, Katrina. "On the Periphery: The Female Marginalized in Five Post-Colonial Novels." MA thesis. Memorial University, 1996. 114 pp. Also available on microfiche from Canadian Theses Service (1999) and as pdf file: http://www.nlc-bnc.ca/obj/s4/f2/dsk2/ftp04/MQ36150.pdf. "Margaret Atwood's *Cat's Eye*, Anita Desai's *Fire on the Mountain* and *In Custody*, Paule Marshall's *Brown Girl, Brownstones*, and Jean Rhys's *Wide Sargasso Sea* show the plight of marginalized women in addition to providing rich texts which address a number of pertinent and pressing issues." (Author). For more see *MAI* 37.04 (August 1999): 1082.

1879. MASON, Carol Ann. "Fundamental Opposition: Feminism, Narrative, and the Abortion Debate (Margaret Atwood, Charles Colson, Ellen Vaughn, Walter Kirn, Dorothy Allison, Arthur Miller, *Terminator 2*, *Jurassic Park*, *Species*, *2001: A Space Odyssey*, *ET*)." PhD thesis. University of Minnesota, 1996. 230 pp. Focuses on *The Handmaid's Tale*. For more see *DAI-A* 57.04 (October 1996): 1619.

1880. McCOMBS, Judith. "*Cat's Eye* as a Reenvisioned Portrait of the Artist: A Visual, Canadian Studies, and Feminist Approach." *Approaches to Teaching Atwood's* The Handmaid's Tale *and Other Works*. Ed. Sharon R. Wilson, Thomas B. Friedman, and Shannon Hengen. New York: Modern Language Association of America, 1996. 174-179.

1881. McMAHON, Daniel Jordan. "Maps of Myth-Reading: Utopias as Revolutionary Mythologies." PhD thesis. University of Maryland, 1996. 268 pp. "In the introductory chapter I define the vexed terms 'utopia,' 'myth,' and 'mythology' and establish the theoretical basis of my work. I examine theories of utopia and theories of mythology by such thinkers as Paul Ricoeur, Northrop Frye, Joseph Campbell, and Karl Mannheim. Succeeding chapters provide readings of utopias chosen for their explicit confrontation with a dominant mythology." (Author). Includes a chapter on *The Handmaid's Tale*. For more see *DAI-A* 57.10 (April 1997): 4381.

1882. MELLEY, Timothy. "'Stalked by Love': Female Paranoia and the Stalker Novel." *Differences: A Journal of Feminist Cultural Studies* 8.2 (1996): 68-100. References *The Edible Woman* and *Bodily Harm*.

1883. MERIVALE, Patricia. "'Hypocrite Lecteuse! Ma Semblable! Ma Soeur!' on Teaching *Murder in the Dark*." *Approaches to Teaching Atwood's* The Handmaid's Tale *and Other Works*. Ed. Sharon R. Wilson, Thomas B. Friedman, and Shannon Hengen. New York: Modern Language Association of America, 1996. 99-106.

1884. MICHAEL, Magali Cornier. *Feminism and the Postmodern Impulse: Post-World War II Fiction*. Albany, NY: State University of New York Press, 1996. Includes discussion of *The Handmaid's Tale*.

1885. MILLER, Kathy. "Cultural Geography: Nomadism, Friendship, and War in Margaret Atwood's *The Robber Bride*." *Dedalus: Revista Portuguesa de Literatura Comparada* 6 (1996): 71-80.

1886. MORRIS, Diana Marlene. "(Re)inscribing the Feminine: Gender and Sociopolitical Marginalization in the Fiction of Margaret Atwood and Toni Morrison."

PhD thesis. Ohio State University, 1996. 288 pp. "The conceptual framework for this project began to take shape as feminists began to debate feminism(s): theoretical versus activist perspectives; Anglo-American versus French perspectives; middle-class versus working-class perspectives; women of color versus Anglo-European perspectives; women of the 'third' world versus women of the 'first'; and so forth....Both Morrison and Atwood employ a similar strategy to a different end. Not the least of their concern is the complex way that they represent the effect of political feminization on their male characters, a matter which this study considers in detail. Each writer begins to redefine their ethnic/national group by confronting the effects of socio-political feminization by (1) de-inscribing the female body as the 'masculine' subject's object and (2) re-inscribing the feminine through an existentially-defined female presence. Through this process, both writers constitute a feminine subjective identity that is inseparable from their ethnic-national identity." (Author). For more see *DAI-A* 57.05 (November 1996): 2045.

1887. MYCAK, Sonia. *In Search of the Split Subject: Psychoanalysis, Phenomenology, and the Novels of Margaret Atwood.* Toronto: ECW Press, 1996.

1888. NELSON-BORN, Katherine A. "Trace of a Woman: Narrative Voice and Decentered Power in the Fiction of Toni Morrison. Margaret Atwood, and Louise Erdich." *Literature, Interpretation Theory* 7.1 (1996): 1-12. Most especially, *The Handmaid's Tale.*

1889. PADOLSKY, Enoch. "Italian-Canadian Writing and the Ethnic Minority/Majority Binary." *Social Pluralism and Literary History: The Literature of the Italian Emigration.* Ed. Francesco Loriggio. Toronto: Guernica, 1996. 248-268. Reference especially to *Lady Oracle.*

1890. PAILLOT, Patricia. "Miroirs à deux faces dans *The Robber Bride* de Margaret Atwood." *Annales du Centre de Recherches sur l'Amérique Anglophone* 21 (1996): 175. English summary.

1891. PALECANDA, Uma Devi Vaneeta K. "Re-Siting Memory: Reading Resistance Through Memorization in Three Margaret Atwood Novels." PhD thesis. West Virginia University, 1996. In the novels *Lady Oracle, The Handmaid's Tale,* and *Cat's Eye,* the author locates and names the sites of memory to show how Atwood's protagonists appropriate them as their loci of resistance. For more see *DAI-A* 57.12 (June 1997): 5158.

1892. PARKER, E. "The Politics of Eating: Food and Power in Contemporary Women's Fiction." PhD thesis. University of Birmingham, 1996. For more see *Index to Theses Accepted for Higher Degrees by the Universities of Great Britain and Ireland* 47 (1998): 257.

1893. PERRY, Susan. *A Study Guide to Margaret Atwood's* The Handmaid's Tale. Ballarat, Australia: Wizard Books, 1996. 48 pp.

1894. PYLVAINEN, Tina Tammy. "Dawn of Discovery: Margaret Atwood's *Morning in the Burned House.*" MA thesis. Lakehead University, 1996. 198 pp. Also available on microfiche from Canadian Theses Service (1999) and as .pdf file: http://www.nlc-bnc.ca/obj/s4/f2/dsk2/ftp04/MQ33435.pdf. Atwood's latest book of poetry "is a carefully structured exploration of the spiritual dimension of selfhood. The volume is divided into five sections which each serve as 'stages' of awareness, and the poetry is ordered in such a way that the sections themselves and the volume as a whole both convey a sense of progressive development." (Author). For more see *MAI* 37.03 (June 1999): 763.

1895. QUENTAL, Cheryl Mary. "Individual Awareness and Natural Consciousness: A Note on Two Novels of Margaret Atwood." *Canadian Literature and Society.* Ed.

K. S. Ramamurtti. New Delhi: Pencraft, 1996. 141-150. *Surfacing* and *Bodily Harm*.

1896. RAGLON, Rebecca. "Women and the Great Canadian Wilderness: Reconsidering the Wild." *Women's Studies* 25.5 (September 1996): 513-532. Analyzes contributions of Canadian women writers such as Atwood to wilderness theory.

1897. REGINALD, Robert. *Xenograffiti: Essays on Fantastic Literature.* San Bernardino, CA: Borgo Press, 1996. See especially "Margaret Atwood: The Young Woman in Agony" with Mary A. Burgess. 131-134.

1898. REITINGER, Douglas W. "The Culture of Consumption and Waste." PhD thesis. University of Nevada, 1996. 237 pp. Discussion of "transformational healing power of food" in works of several authors, including Atwood. For more see *DAI-A* 57.08 (February 1997): 3485.

1900. RESTUCCIA, Frances. "Tales of Beauty: Aestheticizing Female Melancholia." *American Imago* 53.4 (Winter 1996): 353-384. Women writers who fit the definition of melancholia proposed by Julia Kristeva include Atwood, Anita Brookner, and Margaret Drabble. Their works feature women who face suffering forced on them by social and cultural contexts which they can do nothing to stop.

1901. ROCARD, Marcienne. "Approche gothique du paysage canadien: 'Death by Landscape' de Margaret Atwood." *Caliban* 33 (1996): 147-156.

1902. ROSENBERG, Jerome. "'Who Is This Woman?'" *Approaches to Teaching Atwood's* The Handmaid's Tale *and Other Works.* Ed. Sharon R. Wilson, Thomas B. Friedman, and Shannon Hengen. New York: Modern Language Association of America, 1996. 28-32. Biography.

1903. SAINT-JACQUES, Bernard. "Identity and Nationalism in Canadian Literature." *Nationalism vs. Internationalism: (Inter)National Dimensions of Literatures in English.* Ed. Wolfgang Zach and Ken L. Goodwin. Tübingen, Germany: Stauffenburg, 1996. 299-306.

1904. SHECKELS, Theodore F., Jr. "A Writer for all Theories: Using Atwood's Works to Teach Critical Theory and Praxis." *Approaches to Teaching Atwood's* The Handmaid's Tale *and Other Works.* Ed. Sharon R. Wilson, Thomas B. Friedman, and Shannon Hengen. New York: Modern Language Association of America, 1996. 167-173.

1905. SHINN, Thelma J. *Women Shapeshifters: Transforming the Contemporary Novel.* Westport, CT; London: Greenwood Press, 1996. See especially Chapter 2: "The Word Made Man: Margaret Atwood." [41]-51. Focuses on *The Handmaid's Tale*.

1906. STAMBOVSKY, Phillip. *Myth and the Limits of Reason.* Amsterdam; Atlanta, GA: Editions Rodopi B.V., 1996. Contains commentary on works of Margaret Atwood and three other writers.

1907. STEIN, Karen. "Margaret Atwood's Modest Proposal: *The Handmaid's Tale*." *Canadian Literature* 148 (Spring 1996): 57-73. Swift's "Modest Proposal" and *The Handmaid's Tale*.

1908. STEWART, Bruce. Cat's Eye, *Margaret Atwood*. Harlow: Longman, 1996. 80 pp.

1909. TEEUWEN, Ruud. "Dystopia's Point of No Return: A Team-Taught Utopia Class." *Approaches to Teaching Atwood's* The Handmaid's Tale *and Other Works.* Ed. Sharon R. Wilson, Thomas B. Friedman, and Shannon Hengen. New York: Modern Language Association of America, 1996. 114-121.

1910. TEMPLIN, Charlotte. "Can One Read Literature Objectively?" *The Practice and Theory of Ethics.* Ed. Terry Kent, Marshall Bruce Gentry, and Dean Mary Moore. Indianapolis, IN: University of Indianapolis Press, 1996. 123-140. Treatment of Atwood by book reviewers compared to Erica Jong.

1911. VanSPANCKEREN, Kathryn. "The Trickster Text: Teaching Atwood's Works in Creative Writing Classes." *Approaches to Teaching Atwood's* The Handmaid's Tale *and Other Works*. Ed. Sharon R. Wilson, Thomas B. Friedman, and Shannon Hengen. New York: Modern Language Association of America, 1996. 77-83.

1912. VEVAINA, Coomi S. *Remembering Selves: Alienation and Survival in the Novels of Margaret Atwood and Margaret Lawrence*. New Delhi: Creative Books, 1996.

1913. VITALE, Ronald M. "Memory and the Quest for Self: A Jungian Reading of Alice Walker and Margaret Atwood." MA thesis. Villanova University, 1996. 79 pp.

1914. WEINHOUSE-RICHMOND, Linda. "The Politics of Motherhood." *Doris Lessing Newsletter* 18.1 (Summer 1996): 3, 10-14. Deals with Lessing's *The Marriages Between Zones Three, Four, and Five* and Atwood's *The Handmaid's Tale*.

1915. WELBY, Sharon Kay. "The Liminal Process of Healing in Three Women's Novels." MA thesis. San Diego State University, 1996. 106 pp. Atwood's *Surfacing*, Marilynne Robinson's *Housekeeping*, and Barbara Kingsolver's *Animal Dreams*.

1916. WILSON, Sharon. "Atwood's Intertextual and Sexual Politics." *Approaches to Teaching Atwood's* The Handmaid's Tale *and Other Works*. Ed. Sharon R. Wilson, Thomas B. Friedman, and Shannon Hengen. New York: Modern Language Association of America, 1996. 55-62.

1917. WILSON, Sharon R., Thomas B. FRIEDMAN, and Shannon HENGEN, eds. *Approaches to Teaching Atwood's* The Handmaid's Tale *and Other Works*. New York: Modern Language Association of America, 1996. 215 pp. Individual chapters indexed in this section.

1918. WORTHINGTON, Kim L. *Self as Narrative: Subjectivity and Community in Contemporary Fiction*. New York: Clarendon Press, 1996. Includes discussion of *Lady Oracle*.

1919. YORK, Lorraine M. "Satire: The No-Woman's Land of Literary Modes." *Approaches to Teaching Atwood's* The Handmaid's Tale *and Other Works*. Ed. Sharon R. Wilson, Thomas B. Friedman, and Shannon Hengen. New York: Modern Language Association of America, 1996. 43-48.

1920. ZIMMERMANN, Juta. *Metafiktion im anglokanadischen Roman der Gegenwart* Trier [Germany]: Wissenschaftlicher Verlag, 1996. Study of Atwood, Robert Kroetsch, Michael Ondaatje, and Kristjana Gunnars.

Reviews of Atwood's Works

1921. *Alias Grace*. Toronto: McClelland and Stewart, 1996. Also published by Bloomsbury in the UK and by Nan A. Talese/Doubleday in the US.
  Arizona Republican 1 December 1996: Section: Arts Plus: E12. By Anne STEPHENSON. (157 w).
  Atlanta Journal and Constitution 10 November 1996: Section: Arts: 10L. By Diane ROBERTS. (1038 w).
  Beaver 76.6 (December-January 1996): 42-48. By Chris RAIBLE.
  Book of the Month Club News Holiday 1996: 2-3. ANON.
  Booklist 93.2 (15 October 1996): 180. By Donna SEAMAN.
  Boston Globe 8 December 1996: Section: Books: N16. By Gail CALDWELL. (1379 w).
  Chatelaine 69.10 (October 1996): 18. By Gina MALLET.
  Chicago Sun-Times 24 November 1996: Section: Show: 15. By Wendy SMITH. (611 w).

Cincinnati Enquirer 31 December 1996: C04. By Kyrie O'CONNOR. (649 w).

Commercial Appeal (Memphis) 15 December 1996: Section: Fanfare: 3g.
   By Stephen DEUSNER. (778 w).

Daily Mail 14 September 1996: 36. By Val HENNESSY. (1267).

Daily News (New York) 13 November 1996: Section: New York Now: 37.
   By Sherryl CONNELLY. (507 w).

Daily Telegraph 21 September 1996: Section: Books: 8. By Maggie GEE.
   (509 w).

Dominion (Wellington, NZ) 9 November 1996: Section: Features (Books): 20.
   By Pauline SWAIN. (424 w).

Elle 136 (December 1996): 94. By Janice LEE.

Entertainment Weekly 355 (29 November 1996): 83. By Tom De HAVEN.
   (276 w).

Evening Post (Wellington, NZ) 25 October 1996: Section: Features/Books: 5.
   By Kim WORTHINGTON. (448 w).

Evening Standard 23 September 1996: 26. (747 w).

Glamour 94.11 (November 1996): 108. By Sara NELSON.

Globe and Mail 7 September 1996: C20. By Joan THOMAS.

Guardian 3 October 1996: Section: Features: T14. By Lindsay DUGUID.
   (1294 w).

Herald (Glasgow) 28 September 1996: 15. By Carl MACDOUGALL.   (960 w).

Houston Chronicle 8 December 1996: Section: Zest: 29. By Rich
   QUACKENBUSH. (989 w).

Independent 15 September 1996: Section: Books: 31. By Julie MYERSON. (854
   w). and 14 September 1996: Section: Books: 5. By Carole ANGIER. (719 w).

International Herald Tribune 24 December 1996: Section: Feature. By Christopher LEHMANN-HAUPT. (934 w).

Irish Times 14 September 1996: Section: Weekend: 9 (Supplement). By Eileen
   BATTERSBY. (1534 w).

Jerusalem Post 19 December 1996: Section: Books: 6. By Rachel MISKIN.
   (2454 w).

Kansas City Star 15 December 1996: Section: Arts: 19. By David WALTON.
   (782 w). Also published in *News & Record* (Greensboro, NC): Section: Ideas:
   F5.

Library Journal 121.18 (1 November 1996): 106. By Barbara HOFFERT.

Los Angeles Times 15 December 1996: Section: Book Review: 2. By Richard
   EDER. (1306 w). Also published in *Newsday* 15 December 1996: Section:
   Fanfare: C35.

Milwaukee Journal Sentinel 15 December 1996: Section: Cue: 15. By Whitney
   GOULD. (649 w).

Nation 263.19 (9 December 1996): 25-27. By Tom LECLAIR. (1791 w).

New York 29.47 (2 December 1996): 116-117. By Kim WALTER.

New York Review of Books 43.20 (19 December 1996): 4. By Hilary MANTEL.

New York Times 29 December 1996: Section: 7: 6. By Francine PROSE. (1403
   w). Also 12 December 1996: Section: C: 19. By Christopher LEHMANN-
   HAUPT.

New Statesman 9.423 (4 October 1996): 46-47. By Michele ROBERTS.

News and Observer (Raleigh, NC) 29 December 1996: G4. By Bruce ALLEN.
   (799 w).

Observer 22 September 1996: Section: *Observer* Review Page: 18. By Maureen
  FREELY. (1414 w).

Orlando Sentinel 1 December 1996: Section: Arts and Entertainment: F10.
  By Nancy PATE. (627 w).

Pittsburgh Post-Gazette 8 December 1996: Section: Arts and Entertainment: G9.
  By Geeta KOTHARI. (807 w).

Plain Dealer (Cleveland) 24 November 1996: Section: Books: 111. By Alicia
  METCALF-MILLER. (568 w).

Publishers Weekly 243.41 (7 October 1996): 58. By Sybil S. STEINBERG.

Record (Bergen) 8 December 1996: Section: Your Time: Y09. By Mary
  DeCICCO. (609 w).

Rocky Mountain News (Denver) 29 December 1996: 28D. By Marie ARANA-
  WARD. (734 w). Also published in the *Tampa Tribune* 29 December 1996:
  Section: Commentary: 5 and the *Washington Post* 22 December 1996: Sec-
  tion: Book World: X01.

St. Louis Post-Dispatch 22 December 1996: Section: Everyday Magazine: 5C.
  By Speer MORGAN. (492 w).

Sacramento Bee 15 December 1996: Section: Encore: 22. By Kyrie
  O'CONNOR. (867 w). Also published in the *Hartford Courant* 24 November
  1996: Section: Arts: G3.

Scotland on Sunday 15 September 1996: Section: Spectrum: 13. By Thomas
  MATTHEWS. (2200 w).

Scotsman 7 September 1996: 19. By Ali SMITH. (2067 w).

South China Morning Post 21 December 1996: Section: Books: 8. By Carolyn
  FORD. (560 w).

Spectator 277.8774 (14 September 1996): 36. By Anita BROOKNER.

Star Tribune (Pittsburgh) 8 December 1996: Section: Entertainment: 21F. By
  David WALTON. (745 w). Also published in *The Detroit News* 23 November
  1996: Section: HomeStyle: D35.

Sun-Sentinel (Fort Lauderdale, FL) 8 December 1996: Section: Arts and Leisure: 15D. By Ellen KANNER. (836 w).

Sunday Star-Times 24 November 1996: Section: Features (Books): 5. By Iain
  SHARP. (429 w).

Sunday Telegram (Worcester, MA) 29 December 1996: C5. By Nicholas A.
  BASBANES. (992 w). Also published in *The Patriot Ledger* 28 December
  1996: Section: Features: 33.

Sunday Telegraph 15 September 1996: Section: Books: 14. By Caroline
  MOORE. (616 w).

Sunday Times 8 September 1996: Section: features. By Peter KEMP. (862 w).

Tennessean 15 December 1996: Section: Showcase: 14S. By Ellen DAHNKE.
  (891 w).

Time 149.1 (16 December 1996): 76. By John SKOW. (472 w).

Times (London) 14 September 1996: Section: Features. By Elizabeth BUCHAN.
  (601 w).

Times Literary Supplement 4876 (13 September 1996): 23. By Lorna SAGE.

Times-Picayune 22 December 1996: Section: Travel: D5. By Mary A. McCAY.
  (767 w).

Wall Street Journal Eastern Edition 228.98 (15 November 1996): A12.
  By Ruben MERLE.

World Press Review 43.12 (December 1996): 43-44. By Joan SMITH.

1922. *La troisième main.* Lachine [QU]: La Pleine Lune, 1995. [*Good Bones*].
   Nuit blanche 63 (Spring 1996): 50-51. By Jean-Paul BEAUMIER.
1923. *La voleuse d'hommes.* Paris: Robert Laffont, 1994. [*The Robber Bride*].
   Nuit blanche 63 (Spring 1996): 50-51. By Jean-Paul BEAUMIER.
1924. *Morning in the Burned House.* London: Virago, 1995. Published in the US by
   Houghton Mifflin.
      Antioch Review 54.2 (Spring 1996): 248. By Molly BENDALL.
      Canadian Literature 149 (Summer 1996): 201. Recommended in review of
         1995 books by W. H. NEW.
      Chattanooga Free Press (25 February 1996): s.p. By Karin GLENDENNING.
         (747 w).
      Poetry 168.5 (August 1996): 281-302. By Sandra M. GILBERT. Comparative
         review.
      Santa Fe New Mexican 21 April 1996: Section: Outlook: D2. By Miriam
         SAGAN. (493 w).
      Star Tribune 21 January 1996: Section: Entertainment: 15F. By Fred ECKMAN.
         (368 w).
1925. *New Oxford Book of Canadian Short Stories in English.* Toronto: Oxford UP,
   1995.
      Canadian Living 21.3 (March 1996): 157. By Barbara PHILPS.
      Journal of Commonwealth Literature 32.1 (1996): 138-139. ANON.
      Observer 14 January 1996: Section: *Observer* Review Page: 16. By Kit STEAD.
         (187 w).
      Quill & Quire 62.1 (January 1996): 32. By Kim HUME.
      Times Literary Supplement 4847 (23 February 1996): 24. By Joyce Carol
         OATES.
1926. *Princess Prunella and the Purple Peanut.* Toronto: Key Porter Books, 1995.
      Children's Bookwatch (February 1996): 6.
      Publishers Weekly 243.1 (1 January 1996): 70. (203 w).
1927. *Strange Things: The Malevolent North in Canadian Literature.* Oxford: Clarendon
   Press, 1995.
      Canadian Forum 75.851 (July-August 1996): 42. By John MOSS.
      Canadian Geographic 116.1 (January-February 1996): 82. By Rudy WIEBE.
         (1137 w).
      Canadian Literature 149 (Summer 1996): 201. By W. H. NEW.
      New Republic 214.26 (24 June 1996): 33-40. By Andy LAMEY. (5920 w).
      New York Times 145.50411 (28 April 1996): 22. By Tom MacFARLANE.
         (226 w).
      New Zealand Listener 154.2935 (27 July 1996): 28. By Brian TURNER.

Reviews of Adaptations of Atwood's Works

1928. *The Edible Woman.* Radio play adapted by Dave Carley from the Margaret Atwood novel. Produced by Heather Brown and broadcast on CBC radio on 21 April
1996 at 10:05 p.m.
  Globe and Mail 20 April 1996: C4. By Christopher HARRIS.

~ 1997 ~

Atwood's Works

1929. *Alias Grace*. Toronto: Seal Books; New York: Doubleday; London: Virago, 1997 ©1996. Paperback edition.

1930. *Alias Grace*. Toronto: CNIB, 1997. Braille ed., 6 v.

1931. *Alias Grace*. Thorndike, ME: G. K. Hall; Bath [UK]: Windsor, 1997. Large print edition.

1932. *Alias Grace*. [Sound recording]. Read by Diana Quick. London: HarperCollins, 1997. 2 tapes (3 hr.).

1933. *Alias Grace*. [Sound recording]. Read by Shelley Thompson. Bath [UK]: Chivers Audio Books; Hampton, NH: Chivers North America, 1997. 12 sound cassettes (16 hr., 38 min.).

1934. *Alias Grace*. [Sound recording]. Read by Sandra Bolton. [Toronto]: Canadian National Institute for the Blind, 1997. 11 sound cassettes in one container (16:08 hr.). Restricted access: Available only to people with a print handicap.

1935. *Alias Grace*. [Copenhagen]: Lindhardt og Ronghof, 1997. Danish translation by Marit Lise Bøgh.

1936. *Alias Grace*. Stockholm: Rabén Prisma, 1997. Swedish translation by Ulla Danielsson.

1937. "The Animals in That Country." *Canadian Culture: An Introductory Reader*. Ed. Elspeth Cameron. Toronto: Canadian Scholar's Press, 1997. 299-300. Reprinted from *Selected Poems, 1966-1984*, ©1990.

1938. "Apple Jelly." *The Canadian Treasury of Cooking and Gardening*. By Mary Alice Downie and Barbara Robertson. Toronto: Key Porter Books, 1997. 45. Reprinted from *Two-Headed Poems*, ©1978.

1939. "Approximate Homes." *Writing Home: A PEN Canadian Anthology*. Ed. Constance Rooke. Toronto: McClelland and Stewart, 1997. 1-8. Includes photo of Atwood at a motel on her 8th birthday.

1940. "[Atwood Poems]." *Chung-Wai Literary Monthly* 300 (1997): 26-33. Includes: Tricks with Mirrors," 27-30; "Two-Headed Poems," 30-33; "This Is a Photograph of Me," 26-27.

1941. "Betty." *The Faber Book of Contemporary Stories about Childhood*. Ed. Lorrie Moore. London: Faber, 1997. 6-22. Reprinted from *Dancing Girls*, ©1977.

1942. "The Big, Bad Megacity Monster." *No Megacity*. [Sound recording]. Toronto: Protest Boy Records, 1997. 1 sound disc. Atwood's one of several performances.

1943. *Bluebeard's Egg*. Thorndike, ME: Thorndike Press; Bath, UK: Chivers Press, 1997 ©1986. Large print edition.

1944. "Bluebeard's Egg." *The Penguin Anthology of Stories by Canadian Women*. Selected by Denise Chong. Toronto: Viking, 1997. 211-243. Reprinted from *Bluebeard's Egg*, ©1986.

1945. Bluebeard's Egg *and Other Stories*. London: Vintage, 1997 ©1987.

1946. "The Bogman." *The Adventures of Chauncey Alcock [et al.]*. [Sound recording]. Grand Haven, MI: Brilliance Corp.: Playboy Audio, 1997. 2 sound cassettes (ca. 3 hr.).

1947. "Cat's Eye." *When We Were Young: A Collection of Canadian Stories*. Selected and intro. by Stuart McLean. Toronto: Penguin Books, 1997. 97-116. Excerpt from novel of same name in which 8-year-old Elaine describes her first year at her new school in Toronto.

1948. "Cheap, Gossipy Falsehoods Don't Belong in Obituary." *Toronto Star* 20 June 1997: Section: Letter: A24. Atwood commenting on obituary of Shirley Gibson, her partner's ex-wife, published in *Star* on 30 May. Section: News: A5. "An obituary should be the occasion for the celebration of a life, not an excuse for telling cheap, gossipy falsehoods. I'm referring to your 30 May account, 'Publisher and Poet Shirley Gibson.' First, it is a misrepresentation to state baldly that poet John Thompson 'killed himself.' He choked to death. That's kind of hard to arrange. Second, Graeme Gibson did not 'leave' Shirley for 'Margaret Atwood,' as you implied. Shirley was a strong character very much intent on making her own decisions; she would have been both insulted and amused by this suggestion. The marriage as such had been over for many years before I knew them, and both parties had been leading independent lives; this was hardly a secret. The decision for Graeme to move out was intensely mutual. He then lived on a farm near Beeton, by himself, for a year. Third, although I edited Shirley's book of poems, it was hardly 'Atwood influenced.' Shirley's poems came out of her own life, not out of my work. If anyone influenced her it was probably Anne Sexton. I hope you will see fit to publish this, both in justice to Shirley's life, which was a varied and accomplished one, and to alleviate the distress you have caused to survivors."

1949. "Crow Song." *Animal Farm and Related Readings*. By George Orwell. Evanston, IL: McDougal Littell, 1997. 128-129. Reprinted from *You Are Happy: Selected Poems 1965-1975*, ©1976.

1950. *Desde el Invierno: Veintitrés cuentos canadienses*. Compiled and intro. by Atwood and Graeme Gibson. La Habana: Ediciones Unión, 1997. Anthology of contemporary short fiction translated into Spanish and co-published by Union, the publishing arm of Cuba's writers and artists.

1951. *The Edible Woman*. London: Virago, 1997 ©1969.

1952. *The Enduring Enigma of Susanna Moodie*. [Videorecording]. Toronto: Upper Canada Moving Picture Co., 1997. VHS tape, 1 videocassette (59 min.). "Timothy Findley, Carol Shields, Margaret Atwood and Michael Peterman comment on the life and works of Susanna Moodie, and on her influence in contemporary Canadian literature. Findley reads from his novel *Headhunter*, Shields from her novel *Small Ceremonies*, and Atwood from her poetry, *The Journals of Susanna Moodie*. Each author tells what they see in her, and how they came to write about her." (Notes).

1953. "[Excerpt]." *In the House of Night: A Dream Reader*. Ed. Christopher Navratil. San Francisco: Chronicle Books, 1997. 154-156. From the dream sequence in *Lady Oracle* in which the central character reveals her relationship with her mother.

1954. "[Excerpt]." *The Muse Strikes Back: A Poetic Response by Women to Men*. Ed. Katherine McAlpine and Gail White. Brownsville, OR: Story Line Press, 1997.

31-32. Reprinted from "Circe/Mud Poems" originally published in *You Are Happy*, Oxford UP, ©1974.

1955. "[Excerpt]." *Parties: A Literary Companion.* Ed. Susanna Johnston. Woodstock, NY: Overlook Press, 1997. 102-103. First published in 1994 by Macmillan London Ltd. from *Cat's Eye*.

1956. "[Excerpt]." *Parties: A Literary Companion.* Ed. Susanna Johnston. Woodstock, NY: Overlook Press, 1994. 223-224. From *Life Before Man*, © 1979.

1957. "[Excerpt]." *Queen's Quarterly* 104.3 (Fall 1997): 436-449. Christine Hamelin's article, "Where Money Grew on Trees," the story of home children who came to Canada from Quarrier Homes in Scotland, contains an excerpt from Atwood poem "Death of a Son by Drowning."

1958. "[Excerpt]." *Washington Post* 1 June 1997 Section: Book World: X03. Story excerpts significant book reviews since 1972. Compare Atwood's "Niagara Falls" image in her 28 September 1980 review of E. L. Doctorow's *Loon Lake* with he use of that image in her 1997 Updike review (see "Momento Mori—but First, Carpe Diem" [#1978]): "What happens to a writer such as E. L. Doctorow when a novel such as *Ragtime* sells 220,000 copies in hardback, gets translated into 20 languages and wins the National Book Critics Circle Award for fiction? A writer of a certain kind would merely try to duplicate these lush results as quickly as possible. A writer who is more serious must either risk or perish. Everything in Doctorow's career to date indicates that he considers the novel a vehicle for social and moral commentary as well as an art form which should stretch the author's resources to their limits. But success on the *Ragtime* scale in America automatically makes it more difficult for a writer to take himself seriously, partly because other, less successful writers begin to discount him. Post-romantic inverse snobbery attached to sales figures is still with us. Does 220,000 hardback copies mean you're a schlock artist? Then there are all those critics gunning from the shrubberies. You've walked Niagara Falls on a tightrope once, but can you do it again?"

1959. "The Female Body." *The McGraw-Hill Reader: Issues Across the Disciplines.* 6th ed. Ed. Gilbert H. Muller. New York: McGraw-Hill, 1997. 243-246.

1960. "Five Poems for Grandmothers (excerpt) [i.e. Part III]." *Pearls of Wisdom from Grandma.* Ed. Jennifer Gates Hayes. New York: Regan Books, 1997. 50-51. Reprinted from *Selected Poems II: Poems Selected and New 1976-1986*, ©1987.

1961. "Gertrude Talks Back." *The Tragedy of Hamlet with Related Readings.* By William Shakespeare. Albany; London: International Thomson Pub., 1997. 167-168. Reprinted from *Good Bones*, ©1983.

1962. *Good Bones.* Toronto: McClelland and Stewart, 1997. Reprint of Coach House 1992 ed. with 5-page afterword by Rosemary Sullivan. (New Canadian Library Series).

1963. *Gute Knochen.* Munich: BTB, 1997. German translation of *Good Bones* by Brigitte Walitzek.

1964. *Ha-Kalah ha-shodedet.* [Tel Aviv]: Kineret, 1997. Hebrew translation of *The Robber Bride* by Yo'av Halevi.

1965. "Hairball." *High Infidelity: Twenty-Four Great Stories about Adultery by Some of Our Best Contemporary Authors.* Ed. John McNally. New York: Morrow, 1997. 224-237. Also in *The New Woman's Hour Book of Short Stories.* Ed. Di Speirs. London: Penguin, 1997. 8-21.

1966. "Half-Hanged Mary." *Wild Women.* Ed. Melissa Mia Hall. New York: Carroll & Graf, 1997. 5-17. Poem about Mary Webster, who was accused of witchcraft in the 1680s in a Puritan town in Massachusetts and hanged from a tree—where she stayed all night, by one account. When cut down, she was still alive and lived on another 14 years!

1967. "How I Became a Poet." *Prospect* 16 (February 1997): 29-46.

1968. *In Search of Alias Grace: On Writing Canadian Historical Fiction*. Ottawa: Ottawa UP, 1997. 37. (Charles R. Bronfman Lecture in Canadian Studies).

1969. *The Journals of Susanna Moodie*. Toronto: MacFarlane, Walter & Ross; New York: Houghton Mifflin; London, Bloomsbury, 1997. Trade edition of the 1980 limited edition (120 copies) collaboration between Atwood and Toronto artist Charles Pachter. Poems first published in 1970.

1970. *Kassisilm*. [Tallinn, Estonia]: Varrak, 1997. Estonian translation of *Cat's Eye* by Tiia Rinne.

1971. *Lady Oracle*. New York: Doubleday; London: Virago, 1997 ©1977. Paperback.

1972. *Lady Oracle*. Paris: Editions Autrement, 1997. French translation by Marlyse Piccand.

1973. *L'altra Grace*. Milan: Baldini and Castoldi, 1997. Italian translation of *Alias Grace* by Margherita Giacobino, although literally the title means "The Other Grace."

1974. "Late August." *The Canadian Treasury of Cooking and Gardening*. Ed. Mary Alice Downie and Barbara Robertson. Toronto: Key Porter Books, 1997. 167. Poem. Reprinted from *You Are Happy*, ©1974.

1975. *Life Before Man*. Bredbury, UK: National Library for the Blind, 1997. Braille ed., 6 v.

1976. "Loulou; Or, the Domestic Life of the Language." *Literature and Ourselves: A Thematic Introduction for Readers and Writers*. 2nd ed. [Ed.] Gloria Mason Henderson, Bill Day, and Sandra Stevenson Walker. New York: Longman, 1997. 970-982. Student study help, 982-983. Short story. Reprinted from *Bluebeard's Egg*, ©1983.

1977. *The Moment*. [Toronto]: Printed at the Massey College Press, 1997. Poem issued as a keepsake for a fundraising evening in support of the Thomas Fisher Rare Book Library on Wednesday, 5 November 1997; laid in a folder with the title, "An evening with Margaret Atwood," and a facsimile of Atwood's holograph manuscript poem on inside back cover. Issued in an edition of 100 copies.

1978. "Momento Mori—but First, Carpe Diem." *New York Times Book Review* 12 October 1997: 9:1. Enthusiastic review of John Updike's *Towards the End of Time* which begins: "*Towards the End of Time* is John Updike's 47th book, and it is deplorably good. If only he would write a flagrant bomb! That would be news. But another excellently written novel by an excellent novelist—what can be said? Surely no American writer has written so much, for so long, so consistently well. Such feats tend to be undervalued. They shouldn't be. Walking across Niagara Falls blindfolded on a tightrope for the 47th time is surely as remarkable as having made it across the first time, more remarkable perhaps; but the viewer's response is all too likely to be not a delighted 'How praiseworthy!' but a jaded 'What else did you expect?' And at 65, Updike isn't even old enough to be told he's performed well for his age...."

1979. "More and More." *Love Songs and Sonnets*. Selected and ed. Peter Washington. Toronto: Knopf, 1997. 173. Reprinted from *Poems 1965-75* published by Virago by permission of Little Brown.

1980. *Murder in the Dark: Short Fictions and Prose Poems*. Toronto: McClelland and Stewart, 1997. Reprint of 1983 Coach House Press edition with 7-page afterword by S. Heighton. (New Canadian Library Series).

1981. *Nam-i diger Grace*. Beyoglu, Istanbul: Oglak, 1997. Turkish translation of *Alias Grace* by Özden Arikan.

1982. "Nasturtiums." *The Canadian Treasury of Cooking and Gardening*. By Mary Alice Downie and Barbara Robertson. Toronto: Key Porter Books, 1997. 194. Reprinted from *Two-Headed Poems*, ©1978.

1983. *The New Oxford Book of Canadian Short Stories in English*. Selected and ed. Margaret Atwood and Robert Weaver. Toronto; New York; Oxford: Oxford UP, 1997. Paperback edition, printed with corrections.

1984. *Nimeltään Grace*. Helsinki: Kustannusosakeyhtiö Otava, 1997 ©1996. Finnish translation of *Alias* Grace by Kristiina Drews.

1985. "Our First Visit to Japan." *JF Toronto News* (Japan Foundation) Fall 1997: 1-2. With Graeme Gibson.

1986. "The Owl and the Pussycat, Some Years Later." *Verandah* 12 (1997): 5-8.

1987. *Pani Wyrocznia*. Poznan: Zysk i S-ka, 1997. Polish translation of *Lady Oracle* by Zofia Uhrynowska-Hanasz.

1988. "Poetic Process?" *A Field Guide to Contemporary Poetry and Poetics*. Ed. Stuart Friebert, David Walker, and David Young. Oberlin, OH: Oberlin College, 1997. 21. Reprinted from *Field* 4 (Spring 1971): 13-14.

1989. *Quiet Game and Other Early Works*. Ed. Kathy Chung and Sherrill Grace. Edmonton: Juvenilia Press, 1997. With an introduction by Sherrill Grace. Atwood writing at age 17.

1990. *Röövelpruut*. Tallinn [Estonia]: Eesti Raamat, 1997. Estonian translation of *The Robber Bride* by Maia Planhof.

1991. *Ryövärimorsian*. Helsinki: Otava, 1997. Finnish translation of *The Robber Bride* by Kristiina Drews.

1992. "Siren Song." *The Muse Strikes Back: A Poetic Response by Women to Men*. Ed. Katherine McAlpine and Gail White. Brownsville, OR: Story Line Press, 1997. 32-33. Reprinted from *You Are Happy*, Oxford UP, ©1974.

1993. "The Story of the Little Blue Harris and the Big Bad Megacity." *Toronto Star* 1 March 1997 Section Arts: L7. Speaking at an anti-megacity forum, Atwood spun her own tale of modern politics.

1994. *Toduk sinbu*. Seoul: Munhak Sasangsa, 1997. Korean translation of *The Robber Bride* in 2 v. by Kim Chin-jun omgim. Title romanized.

1995. "True Trash." *The New Oxford Book of Canadian Short Stories in English*. Selected and ed. Margaret Atwood and Robert Weaver. Toronto: Oxford UP, 1997. 247-266.

1996. *True Trash*. [Electronic resource]. Bredbury, UK: National Library for the Blind, 1997. Computer data (2 files: 25, 26 kb).

1997. "Underbrush Man." *Prairie Fire* 17.4 (Winter 1997): 6-14. Short story.

1998. *Vera spazzatura: E altri racconti*. Milan: La Tartaruga edizioni, 1997. Italian translation of *Wilderness Tips* by Francesca Avanzini.

1999. *Vulgo, Grace*. São Paulo, Brasil: Marco Zero, 1997. Portuguese translation of *Alias Grace* by Maria J. Silveira.

2000. "While He Writes, I Feel as If He Is Drawing Me." St. Paul [MN]: Hungry Mind Press, 1997 ©1996. 1 sheet. Broadside. From *Alias Grace*. Printed at Midnight Paper Sales for the occasion of Margaret Atwood's reading at the Hungry Mind on 8 January 1997. Limited edition of 90 numbered copies signed by the author.

2001. "The Writer: A New Canadian Life-Form." *New York Times Book Review* 18 May 1997: 9, 39:1. In an essay adapted from her acceptance speech for the 1997 National Arts Club Medal for Literature, Atwood discusses growing up in Canada and what it was like to be a writer in Canada, "a country in which you were relegated to a minor literary subcategory just by being a citizen of it." She also discusses the state of the novel in the 1990s and suggests that many are "shovels"—self-help books disguised as fiction.

2002. "A Writer's Life: This Master Storyteller Is Still Childhood Self, Poking Things to See What Happens." *F Digest* 151.908 (1997): 61-62.

Adaptations of Atwood's Works

2003. *Music for Art Galleries*. [Sound recording] Kitchener, ON: Clover Recordings, [1997?]. 1 sound disc. "All songs composed by Timothy Rempel....Includes song with words from the novel *Cat's Eye* by Margaret Atwood." Principally electronic music.

Quotations

2004. "[Quote]." *Books in Canada* 26.3 (April 1997): 12-13. In review of James Reaney's *The Box Social and Other* Stories, reviewer quotes Atwood's comment on one of these, "The Bully": "Strong in local atmosphere, which is not used however for the purposes of strict realism, combining the comic with the pathetic, proceeding by an associative dream language, resolving itself through image rather than through plot alone, it offered us a whole new way of looking at the possibilities of the world available to us....Without 'The Bully,' my fiction would have followed other paths. If there are such things as 'key' reading experiences, 'The Bully' was certainly one of mine." Reproduced from back cover of Reaney's *The Box Social and Other Stories*.

2005. "[Quote]." *Chattanooga Free Press* (TN) 16 March 1997: Section: Travel: L5. Article by Julie Johnson titled "Town Talk" begins with Atwood quote. "In the spring, at the end of the day you should smell like dirt."

2006. "[Quote]." *Globe and Mail* 25 June 1997: D1. After being named Author of the Year by the Canadian Booksellers Association, Atwood was quoted as saying: "I thought I was a bit over the hill to be given an award for my body...of work." The award was worth $2,000 and may have reflected the more than 100,000 Canadian sales of *Alias Grace*.

2007. "[Quote]." *The Guardian* (London) 3 December 1997: 17. In an article titled "Much Ado about Nothing," Atwood is quoted on Canada's "smaller neighbor syndrome": "If the national illness of the United States is megalomania, that of Canada is paranoid schizophrenia."

2008. "[Quote]." *Halifax Daily News* 12 January 1997: 49. Atwood is quoted on being Canadian: "In this country you can say what you like because no one will listen to you anyway."

2009. "[Quote]." *M2 Presswire* 13 October 1997. Available from Lexis-Nexis. In an article discussing the forthcoming *Oxford Dictionary of Literary Quotations* [see 2023], the writer quotes Atwood on deconstructionism: "Nobody was able to explain to me clearly (what deconstructionism was). The best answer I got was from a writer who said 'Honey, it's bad news for you and me.'"

2010. "[Quote]." *New York Times* 7 December 1997: Section: 6: 89. An article on Unitarianism quotes an earlier interview with Atwood "in which she said that if she ever decided to have a religious life, she would do it with the Unitarian church; the only problem was that the music was terrible."

2011. "[Quote]." *People* 24 March 1997: Section: Picks & Pans. A payout in the high 6 figures may have been the main reason Atwood sold the film rights for *Alias Grace* to Jodie Foster's Egg Pictures, but it wasn't the only reason. "I love the name of the production company....I've always been fond of eggs. I put eggs in my books a lot. It caught my attention immediately."

2012. "[Quote]." *The Province* [Vancouver] 28 October 1997: B9. On being surrounded by throngs pressing her for photos after she obtained 13th honorary degree from the University of Ottawa: "I begin to feel like Minnie Mouse at Disneyland, with a lot of happy students and Moms and Dads getting busy with the flash bulbs."

2013. "[Quote]." *Quill and Quire* 63.3 (March 1997): 15. Atwood weighing into debate about public lending rights: "Libraries want a free lunch, and they want our lunch."

2014. "[Quote]." *San Francisco Chronicle* 16 March 1997: Section: Sunday Review: 2. Atwood at a recent City Arts and Lectures appearance on the offhand way she began *Alias Grace*, noting that she was on European tour for another book when the first scene popped into mind. "It came to me vividly in the way that scenes often do. I wrote it down on a piece of hotel writing paper. It was much the same as the opening scene of the novel as it now exists. I recognized the locale...and the female figure in it....I thought it was a very bad idea for a novel, but this is what I usually think about my ideas for novels. The ones I actually write are the ones that overcome my own taste and judgement, and insist on being written anyway. So after a while I continued on with the writing."

2015. "[Quote]." *The Spectator* [Hamilton, ON] 13 February 1997: E9. Feminist Naomi Wolf reports that when Margaret Atwood asked women what they feared from men, they said, "We're afraid they'll kill us." When men were asked [what they feared about women], they said, "We're afraid they'll laugh at us." This quote is reproduced from *Men Are Lunatics, Women Are Nuts!!* Compiled with an introduction by Ronald B. Shwartz. Philadelphia: Running Press, 1996: 14.

2016. "[Quote]." *Star Tribune* [Minneapolis, MN] 3 November 1997: Section: Entertainment: 1F. Reference to comment made in late 1970s when Atwood compared the relationship between Canada and the United States to a one-way mirror: "They watch us, but we are too busy looking at ourselves to return the gaze."

2017. "[Quote]." *Sunday Telegraph* 2 March 1997: Section: Books: 15. On the problems of becoming a poet: "I did not know that 'poetess' was an insult...I did not know that wearing black was compulsory....[And] like all twenty-one year old poets, I thought I would be dead by 30. Sylvia Plath had not set a very helpful example. For a while there, you were made to feel that...you could not really be serious about it unless you had made at least one suicide attempt....I no longer feel I will be dead at 30, now it is 60."

2018. "[Quote]." *The Tennessean* 1 June 1997: Section: Home: 1G. Atwood on gardening: "Gardening is not a rational act."

2019. "[Quote]." *Time* 4 August 1997: Section: International Edition: 22. Atwood on Americans (as first spoken to a Parliamentary Committee): "About the only position they have adopted towards us, country to country, has been the missionary position, and we were not on top. I guess that is why the national wisdom vis-à-vis them has so often taken the form of lying still, keeping your mouth shut and pretending you like it."

2020. "[Quote]." *Toronto Star* 3 March 1997: Section: News: A1. In article entitled "Today's Megaday to Vote on Future Metro: Residents Speak Out about City of 2.3 Million." Nicolaas Van Rijn quotes Atwood who mused that the Toronto mega-city may have been inspired by "Larry, Curly and Al Leach" [Ontario's Minister of Municipal Affairs].

2021. "[Quote]." *Toronto Star* 31 October 1997: Section: Opinion: A29. Atwood commenting on the nature of Toronto: "We are all immigrants to this place, even those of us that were born here."

2022. "[Quote]." *Toronto Sun* 2 November 1997: Section: News: 2. Report of Atwood commenting on Toronto mayoralty candidates Mel Lastman, the eventual winner whom she opposed, and Barbara Hall, whom she supported: "We don't want (Toronto) tidied up into one homogenized shopping mall or parking lot....We don't want to be sold by our mayor; we want to be served by our mayor. Our mayor will be the mouth we are known by. To represent us, we want a mayor whose foot won't always be in their mouth."

2023. "[Quotes]." *The Oxford Dictionary of Literary Quotations*. Ed. Peter Kemp. New York: Oxford UP, 1997. Atwood is quoted 26 times.

Interviews

2024. CASCIATO, Paul. "Canadian Writer Margaret Atwood Wary of Praise." *Reuters World Service* 8 January 1997. Atwood comments on positive reviews of *Alias Grace*—and on losing the Booker.

2025. DODSON, Danita J. "An Interview with Margaret Atwood." *Critique: Studies in Contemporary Fiction* 38.2 (Winter 1997): 96-104. Atwood feels that *The Handmaid's Tale* was produced by studying the oppression of women.

2026. ENG, Monica. "Alias Atwood: Canadian Novelist Sees Future Writing of the Past." *Chicago Tribune* 8 January 1997: Section: Tempo: 2. Atwood answers audience questions at Glenbrook South High School in Glenview as part of the North Suburban Library Foundation's Literary Circle Series.

2027. EVENSON, Laura. "Wicked Wit of the North: Margaret Atwood Mines the Ambiguous in *Alias Grace*." *San Francisco Chronicle* 16 January 1997: Section: Daily Datebook: E1. (1151 w). Amusing interview in which Atwood reflects on her life. Includes several anecdotes including the time her high school home economics teacher told the class it could do a special project and could vote on what it could be. Instigated by Atwood, the group decided to put on a home economics opera. "It was about three fabrics—Orlon, Nylon and Dacron," she said. "I was Dacron. And they all lived with their father, old King Coal, spelled C-O-A-L, because they were all coal derivatives. Along came a natural-fiber character called Sir William Wooly, but he sang an aria about a terrible problem he had: He shrank from washing."

2028. GUSSOW, Mel. "The Alternate Personalities of Margaret Atwood." *International Herald Tribune* 7 January 1997: Section: Feature: 20. (1267 w). Also in *Dallas Morning News* 5 January 1997: Section: Arts: 4C. Atwood cherishes her wide international readership. "If we only write books for people writing academic papers, it would be a futile exercise."

2029. GZOWSKI, Peter. "Conversations with Writers IV: Margaret Atwood." *The Morningside Years*. Toronto: McCelland and Stewart, 1997: 168-176. Interview on occasion of publication of *Murder in the Dark*. Book also includes CD on which Atwood reads from *Princess Prunella and the Purple Peanut*.

2030. SALINE, Carol, and Sharon J. WOHLMUTH. "Margaret Atwood and Her Daughter, Margaret Atwood." *Mothers and Daughters*. New York: Doubleday, 1997. 62-65. Includes photo of both Margarets.

2031. SHARP, Iain. "A Writer Wary of Clumsy Dancers." *Sunday Star-Times* [Auckland] 23 February 1997: Section: Features. Notes that she can't write when she's traveling. "On planes I just behave like everyone else—I eat peanuts, read murder mysteries and look now and again at the in-flight movie."

2032. SNELL, Marilyn. "Margaret Atwood." *Mother Jones* 22.4 (July-August 1997): 24-27. In the interview Atwood states that she does not write her novels to express her political views (she claims she is a "Red Tory") and that her primary loyalty is to her art. She characterizes the women in her novels as people under pressure rather than victims. For comment on interview, see Heller, Daniel A. "Margaret Atwood." *English Journal* 86.8 (December 1997): 89-90.

Scholarly Resources

2033. "Atwood, Margaret." *Who's Who in Canadian Literature 1997-1998*. Comp. Gordon Ripley. Teeswater [ON]: Reference Press, 1997. 8-10. Biography.

2034. AGUIAR, Sarah Appleton. "Good Girls and Evil Twins: Constructing Zenia in Margaret Atwood's *The Robber Bride*." *Newsletter of the Margaret Atwood Society* 19 (Fall-Winter 1997): 5-6, 15-16.

2035. ANDRASZEK, Katharine. "The Feminist, Political, and Postmodern Aspects to Margaret Atwood." MA thesis. State University of New York College at Brockport, 1997. 82 pp.

2036. BELL, Virginia Ellen. "Narratives of Treason: Postnational Historiographic Tactics and Late Twentieth-Century Fiction in the Americas." PhD thesis. University of Maryland at College Park, 1997. 292 pp. In chapter four, *The Handmaid's Tale* and Carmen Boullosa's *Duerme* (Sleeping Beauty) are compared to discourse that produces a critical assessment of NAFTA. All 3 are discursive constructions of regionalism interested in the effects of global restructuring on women. For more see *DAI-A* 58.11 (May 1998): 4261.

2037. BENN JONES, Yvonne P. "Dystopian Feminism in Margaret Atwood's *The Handmaid's Tale*." MA thesis. Universidad de Puerto Rico, 1997. 76 pp.

2038. BOHNER, Jennifer Anne. "Sacrificing Solidarity for Self: Exploring Margaret Atwood's Solitary Feminists." MA thesis. California State University, Hayward, 1997. 67 pp.

2039. CAKEBREAD, C. (Caroline Marcus). "Voices from Beyond: Responses to Shakespeare in Six Novels by Contemporary Women Writers." PhD thesis. University of Birmingham, Shakespeare Institute, 1997. Study of *Cat's Eye* along with Gloria Naylor's *Mama Day*, Jane Smiley's *A Thousand Acres*, Barbara Trapido's *Juggling*, Anne Tyler's *Ladder of Years*, and Marina Warner's *Indigo*.

2040. CALL, Nancy J. "Marriage, Maternity and Beyond in Margaret Atwood's Novels." MA thesis. University of Vermont, 1997. 51 pp.

2041. CANNON, Elizabeth Monroe. "What 'Violent Violets' Want: Female Desire in Contemporary Women's Fiction." PhD thesis. University of Wisconsin–Madison, 1997. 314 pp. Includes analysis of *Lady Oracle*. For more see *DAI-A* 58.07 (January 1998): 2649.

2043. COMISKEY, B. "You Can Mean More Than One: Age, Gender and Atwood's Addresses." *Journal of Gender Studies* 6.2 (July 1997): 131-142. How Atwood appeals to academic and mainstream, feminist and non-feminist, readers.

2044. COOPER, Pamela. "'A Body Story with a Vengeance': Anatomy and Struggle in *The Bell Jar* and *The Handmaid's Tale*." *Women's Studies* 26.1 (January 1997): 89-124. Both books dwell on women's use of their own bodies and orifices as imperative to rebellion and subsequent freedom. Both also explore the common topography of gender and how women's struggle for survival and empowerment can be harnessed through the body. This is apparent in the perverse acts of consumption by the female protagonists in the novels which suggest interiority as a potent expression of will.

2045. COUPE, Laurence. *Myth*. London; New York: Routledge, 1997. From Dante to Shakespeare to Atwood, writers have felt the need to draw on archaic narrative patterns. See especially 190-194 for discussion of *The Handmaid's Tale*.

2046. DAVIDSON, Arnold E. *Seeing in the Dark: Margaret Atwood's* Cat's Eye. Toronto: ECW Press, 1997. (Canadian Fiction studies).

2047. DEERY, June. "Science for Feminists: Margaret Atwood's Body of Knowledge." *Twentieth-Century Literature: A Scholarly and Critical Journal* 43.4 (1997): 440-486. Focus on *Cat's Eye* and *The Robber Bride*.

2048. DELVILLE, Michel. "Murdering the Text: Genre and Gender Issues in Margaret Atwood's Short Short Fiction." *The Contact and the Culmination*. Ed. Marc Delrez, Bénédicte Ledent, and Juliette Dor. Liège, Belgium: L3-Liège Language and Literature, 1997. 57-67. Focus on *Murder in the Dark* (1983) and *Good Bones* (1992).

2049. DeROCCO, David. "Margaret Atwood." *Canadian Superlatives*. Virgil, ON; Lewiston, NY: FB Productions, 1997. 1. A literacy exercise focusing on Atwood.

2050. DODSON, Danita J. "'We Lived in the Blank White Spaces': Rewriting the Paradigm of Denial in Atwood's *The Handmaid's Tale*." *Utopian Studies* 8.2 (Spring 1997): 66-87. Atwood's novel portrays the United States as founded on a dream of equality and liberty which has been corrupted by marginalizing Native-Americans, African-Americans, and women. Puritan prejudice and conformity are intensified in the fictional Gilead, and those seeking to establish an ideal society have created a place for terror. Atwood suggests in this novel that global human rights will remain a fantasy until the repressive past has been acknowledged.

2051. DONELSON, Ken. "'Filth' and 'Pure Filth' in Our Schools: Censorship of Classroom Books in the Last Ten Years." *English Journal* 86.2 (February 1997): 21-25. *The Handmaid's Tale* is one of those attacked.

2052. DOSS, Michelle M. "Finding the Goddess Within: The Goddess Archetype in Margaret Atwood's *Surfacing*, *The Handmaid's Tale*, and *The Robber Bride*." MA thesis. Baylor University, 1997. 109 pp.

2053. DUNCAN, I. J. "Female Marginality in the Fiction of Margaret Atwood." PhD thesis. University of Strathclyde, 1997. Atwood portrays her female protagonists as outsiders, either exiles or invaders in their settings. In this study, "I consider Rennie Wilford's disempowering detachment in *Bodily Harm*, and the narrator's subversiveness in *The Handmaid's Tale*. It is the creative spirit, I shall argue, which constitutes the most effective resistance to the centralizing tendencies. When the protagonist acknowledges her distinctive creativity, and understands that it will enable her to make connections—with another, with an aspect of her self or her past—she is exploiting her marginality. In my concluding chapter, I summarise my main arguments, relating them to Atwood's most recent novel, *Alias Grace*."

(Author). For more see *Index to Theses Accepted for Higher Degrees by the Universities of Great Britain and Ireland* 48 (1999): 2697.

2054. EAGLETON, Mary. "Feminism and the Death of the Author: Margaret Atwood's *The Handmaid's Tale.*" *British Journal of Canadian Studies* 12.2 (1997): 281-297.

2055. EASUN, Sue. "'The Ice Is Its Own Argument': A Canadian Critic Takes a Second Look at *Bad Boy* and Her Own Modest Ambitions." *Canadian Children's Literature* 87 (1997): 5-14. Atwood's theories of national identity used to explicate Diana Wieler's novel.

2056. FEUER, Lois. "The Calculus of Love and Nightmare: *The Handmaid's Tale* and the Dystopian Tradition." *Critique: Studies in Contemporary Fiction* 38.2 (1997): 83-95. The novel affirms distrust for any unquestioned source of truth, which is a significant attitude in all dystopias. Dystopias offer worlds where the characters can choose freedom or happiness, but not both. *The Handmaid's Tale* has been most often compared to Orwell's *1984*, but Atwood's story offers a more vivid reality and a subtle feminist statement. Women in Atwood's novel have a central sense of the individual's importance. Individuality is crushed in *1984* but forms the source of politics and character in *The Handmaid's Tale*.

2057. FOERTSCH, Jacqueline. "The Bomb Next Door: Four Postwar Alterapocalyptics." *Genre: Forms of Discourse and Culture* 30.4 (1997): 333-358. References *The Handmaid's Tale* along with Paul Auster's *In the Country of Last Things*, Ray Bradbury's *Fahrenheit 451*, and George Orwell's *1984*.

2058. GARCÍA, Ana María. "Margaret Atwood y la trampa liberadora del cuerpo femenino." *Mujeres Que Escriben Sobre Mujeres (Que Esbriben)*. Vol. 1. Ed. Cristina Piña. Buenos Aires: Editorial Biblos, 1997. 51-80. Discussion of *El cuento de la criada*, a Spanish edition of *The Handmaid's Tale*. (Buenos Aires: Editorial Sudamericana, 1987).

2059. GARDINER, Heather. "The Portrayal of Old Age in English-Canadian Fiction." PhD thesis. University of Toronto, 1997. 226 pp. Also available on microfiche from Canadian Theses Service (1999) and as .pdf document: http://www.nlc-bnc.ca/obj/s4/f2/dsk2/ftp02/NQ27927.pdf. While not directly on Atwood, this thesis argues that "far from the notion of mere 'survival' suggested by Margaret Atwood in *Survival: A Thematic Guide to Canadian Literature* (1972), powerful elderly English-Canadian protagonists break away from the confinement of ageing bodies and explore new realities." (Author). For more see *DAI-A* 59.06 (December 1998): 2030.

2060. GATZ, Diana M. "Margaret Atwood's *Surfacing*: A Geography of the Mind." MA thesis. California State University, Dominguez Hills, 1997. 61 pp. "Addressing the problem of the narrator's split self in Margaret Atwood's *Surfacing*, the paper examines the themes of reciprocity between culture's artificiality, pollution of nature, sexual politics, and individual sterility. Close textual analysis focusing on Atwood's concern with how reality is constructed reveals the resonance of her images in archetypal symbols, psychological stages, a feminist revisioning of the quest pattern, and especially Atwood's invocation of goddess symbols and myth." (Author). For more see *MAI* 35.04 (August 1997): 943.

2061. GILBERT, E., and P. SIMPSON-HOUSLEY. "Places and Spaces of Dislocation: *Lady Oracle*'s Toronto." *Canadian Geographer / Geographe canadien* 41.3 (Fall 1997): 235-248.

2062. GORLIER, Claudio, and Anna VIACAVA. "Due romanzi di Margaret Atwood." *Indice dei Libri del Mese* 14.7 (1997): 8.

2063. GRACE, Dominick. "Margaret Atwood's Northern Utopia: Nunavut and *The Handmaid's Tale*." *Reflections on Northern Culture, Visions and Voices: Papers Presented at "Visions of the North, Voices of the North" Northern Culture Conference, Held at Nipissing University, North Bay, Ontario, May 24-26, 1996*. Ed. A. W. Plumstead, Laurie Kruk, and Anthony Blackburn. North Bay [ON]: Nipissing University, 1997. 75-82. "The novel concludes with a coda set in 2195 in Nunavit. The coda is key to our understanding of the novel." (Author).

2064. HAMMILL, Faye. "Sara Jeannette Duncan in the 'Camp of the Philistines.'" *Journal of Canadian Studies* 32.2 (Summer 1997): 154-170. The newspaper columns Duncan wrote in the 1880s explore English Canada's literary climate in relation to those of Great Britain and the United States, and this commentary is adapted and extended in her novel, *The Imperialist*. Duncan's own literary talents were not highly valued in Canada, and she was forced to seek recognition and publication abroad. Yet her veiled criticisms of Canada's "colonial" and philistine attitudes coexist in *The Imperialist* with an affirmation of her country's creative potential. Her analysis prefigures those offered almost a century later by Northrop Frye, D. G. Jones, and Margaret Atwood, and it is significant that these critics all omit Duncan from their reviews of Canadian literature.

2065. HANSEN, Elaine Tuttle. *Mother without Child*. Berkeley: U of California P, 1997. See especially "Mothers Yesterday and Mothers Tomorrow, but Never Mothers Today: *Woman on the Edge of Time* and *The Handmaid's Tale*." 158-183.

2066. HEINIMANN, David. "Ironized Man: *A Jest of God* and *Life Before Man*." *Canadian Literature* 154 (Autumn 1997): 52-67. The male characters in Laurence's *A Jest of God* and Atwood's *Life Before Man* were used to illustrate how misconceptions result in dysfunctional relationships between men and women. Laurence's Nick Kazlik and Atwood's Nate Schoenhof, together with the women they are involved with, should be viewed by readers as deserving of their sympathy.

2067. HOGSETTE, David S. "Margaret Atwood's Rhetorical Epilogue in *The Handmaid's Tale*: The Reader's Role in Empowering Offred's Speech Act." *Critique: Studies in Contemporary Fiction* 38.4 (Summer 1997): 262-278. Suggests Atwood thinks that effective and affective reading have a role in the communication through which women regain their voice and become "social agents."

2068. HOWELLS, Coral Ann. "*Morning in the Burned House*: At Home in the Wilderness." *The Contact and the Culmination: Essays in Honour of Hena Maes-Jelinek*. Ed. Marc Delrez and Bénédicte Ledent. Liège, Belgium: Liege Language and Literature, 1997. 69-78.

2069. HSIEH, Shu-nu. "Madness and Sextual [sic] Politics in Margaret Atwood's *Suffacing* [sic]." MA thesis. Tamkang University, 1997. 91 pp. For more see WorldCat.

2070. HUDGENS, Brenda. "Faded Photographs: The Elusive Male in Margaret Atwood's Fiction." *Publications of the Missouri Philological Association* 22 (1997): 47-56. *Cat's Eye* and *The Robber Bride*.

2071. JOHNSTON, Rita. "Memory as a Bridge to Self: A Narratological Study of Margaret Atwood's *Cat's Eye*." MA thesis. University of Wisconsin–Eau Claire, 1997. 63 pp.

2072. JUNEAU, Carol. "Through the Eyes of the Handmaid: A Dystopic Perspective of Fundamentalism in Atwood's *The Handmaid's Tale*." MA thesis. University of Houston–Clear Lake, 1997. 56 pp. Generally analyzed within the genres of feminist or utopian literatures, Margaret Atwood's *The Handmaid's Tale* is often overlooked as a novel with significant religious and philosophical connotations. For more see *MAI* 36.3 (June 1998): 682.

2073. JURAK, Mirko. "Northrop Frye in Margaret Atwood: Njun Odnos Do Kanadske Samobi-Nosti in Kulture." *Zbornik Ob Sedemdesetletnici Franceta Bernika.* Ed. Joze Faganel, Joze Pogacnik, and Matija Ogrin. Ljubljana: Znanstvenoraziskovalni center SAZU, Institut za slovensko literaturo in literarne vede, 1997. 227-240. Canadian national identity as reflected in Frye and Atwood. In Slovenian with English summary.

2074. KING, James. *The Life of Margaret Laurence.* Toronto: Knopf, 1997. Notes that Atwood's friendship with Laurence was ruptured because Laurence felt rivalry with the younger writer and resented that Atwood had phoned Laurence's daughter (Jocelyn) on the subject of her mother's drinking.

2075. KIZUK, R. Alexander. "A Rhetoric of Indeterminacy: The Poetry of Margaret Atwood and Robert Bly." *English Studies in Canada* 23.2 (June 1997): 141-158.

2076. KLAWITTER, Uwe. *The Theme of Totalitarianism in "English" Fiction: Koestler, Orwell, Vonnegut, Kosinski, Burgess, Atwood, Amis.* Frankfurt am Main; New York: P. Lang, 1997. See especially chapter 6 "Margaret Atwood: *The Handmaid's Tale* (1985) Speculating about a New Totalitarianism." 163-183. Originally presented as the author's thesis (doctoral)—Ruhr Universität, Bochum, 1996.

2077. KORTE, Barbara. *Body Language in Literature.* Toronto: University of Toronto Press, 1997. Examples from major works of literature, including novels and stories by Charles Dickens, J. D. Salinger, and Atwood.

2078. LAGA, Barry E. "Posthistory: Negating and Negotiating Representations of History." PhD thesis. Purdue University, 1997. 240 pp. Chapter 4 "reads *The Handmaid's Tale* as an historical compilation of fragments from the past rather than a dystopia or prophesy about the future...." For more see *DAI-A* 58.09 (March 1998): 3519.

2079. LECLAIRE, Jacques. "La deconstruction de la biographie dans *The Robber Bride* de Margaret Atwood." *La création biographique.* Ed. Marta Dvorak. Rennes: PU de Rennes, 1997. 153-150. Focus on Zenia.

2080. LI, Shuping. *Tu wei de ke neng xing: Xiao shuo....* Lanzhou, China: Lanzhou University, Foreign Language Department, 1997. 31. On *The Edible Woman.* Title in Chinese romanized; text in English only with some bibliographical references in Chinese.

2081. LIU, Kedong. "Narrative Situational Features in Margaret Atwood's Prose Fictions." MA thesis. Harbin Institute of Technology, 1997. 75 pp. Title romanized. Text in Chinese only; abstract and some bibliographical references in Chinese.

2083. LOUDERMILK, Kim A. "Fictional Feminism: Representing Feminism in American Bestsellers." PhD thesis. Emory University, 1997. 380 pp. "This study focuses on the fictional feminism developed by five bestselling novels and their film adaptations: *The Women's Room* and *The Bleeding Heart* by Marilyn French; *The World According to Garp* by John Irving; *The Witches of Eastwick* by John Updike; and *The Handmaid's Tale* by Margaret Atwood. Drawing on the work of cultural critics such as Stuart Hall, Frederic Jameson and Janice Radway, I argue that while these texts sometimes provide liberatory experiences for individual readers, on a societal level, they recuperate radical ideas and uphold dominant cultural norms. Fictional feminism has consequences that reach beyond the texts that create it, however; it also influences cultural politics. I argue that recent non-fiction books that address feminist politics tend to devalue second-wave feminism and to criticize it based on fictional feminism." (Author). For more see *DAI-A* 58.11 (May 1998): 4469.

2084. MacMURRAUGH-KAVANAGH, M. K. "'Through a Glass Darkly': Fields of Vision, Identity and Metaphor in Margaret Atwood's *Cat's Eye* and Shakespeare's *King Lear*." *British Journal of Canadian Studies* 12.1 (1997): 78-91.

2085. MANTEL, Hilary. "Is This Story True?" *Proceedings of the 20th International AEDEAN Conference*. Ed. P. Guardia and J. Stone. Barcelona: Universitat de Barcelona, 1997. 37-46. Hilary Mantel's novel *A Place of Greater Safety* (1992) is compared to Margaret Atwood's *Alias Grace* (1996).

2086. MARCH, Cristie. "Crimson Silks and New Potatoes: The Heteroglossic Power of the Object in Atwood's *Alias Grace*." *Studies in Canadian Literature* 22.2 (1997): 66-82.

2087. MATTHEWS, David R. "Ways of Understanding: Canada and the Concept of Canadian Studies." *Journal of Canadian Studies* 32.1 (Spring 1997): 28-43. Discusses Atwood's contribution to the debate through her book, *Survival*.

2088. McINTYRE, Susan Kathryn. "Angels and Sisters No More: Power among Women in Atwood's *The Handmaid's Tale, Cat's Eye*, and *The Robber Bride*." MA thesis. California State University, Fresno 1997. 71 pp. "Margaret Atwood's writing reveals her interest in the issue of power. In her earlier works, her female protagonists were engaged in power struggles with their male lovers or with patriarchal systems. In *The Handmaid's Tale* (1985), *Cat's Eye* (1988), and *The Robber Bride* (1992), however, Atwood focuses on the use and misuse of power in women's relationships with each other. Each consecutive novel portrays an increasingly powerful female figure who victimizes women, often with the help of other women. While this portrayal of women's treatment of each other is unsettling, it also debunks two myths of womanhood—the Victorian Angel in the House and the feminist Sister. Viewed in this light, the trio of books illustrates Atwood's belief that 'Equality (for women) means equally bad as well as equally good.'" (Author). For more see *MAI* 36.04 (August 1998): 912.

2089. MOREY, Ann-Janine. "Margaret Atwood and Toni Morrison: Reflections on Postmodernism and the Study of Religion and Literature." *Toni Morrison's Fiction: Contemporary Criticism*. Ed. David L. Middleton. New York: Garland, 1997. 247-268. Morrison's *Beloved* and Atwood's *Surfacing*.

2090. NELSON-BORN, Katherine A. "Trace of a Woman: Narrative Voice and Decentered Power in the Fiction of Toni Morrison, Margaret Atwood, and Louise Erdrich." *Literature Interpretation Theory* 7.1 (1997): 1-12. These authors "layer the voices and meanings in their texts, foregrounding the linguistic antagonism present in their pluralized worlds of discourse. They draw attention to the structure of their fiction to expose the limitations of a white male dominated literature and discourse and to warn against the dangerous repercussion of a totalizing monologic narrative. Foregrounding the heteroglossia present in their works, these writers reveal the multiple voices present in narrative discourse, thus enabling the reader to trace the way back to voices that have been previously marginalized and subverted." (Author).

2091. NISCHIK, R. M. "Nomenclatural Mutations: Forms of Address in Margaret Atwood's Novels." *Orbis Litterarum: International Review of Literary Studies* 52.5 (1997): 329-351.

2092. PALMER, Paulina. "Gender as Performance in the Fiction of Angela Carter and Margaret Atwood." *The Infernal Desires of Angela Carter: Fiction, Femininity, Feminism*. Ed. Joseph Bristow and Trev Lynn Broughton. London; New York: Longman, 1997. 24-42. See especially sections entitled: "Atwood: *The Hand-*

maid's Tale, The Edible Woman and *The Robber Bride*" and "Carter, Atwood and Lesbian Genre Fiction."

2093. PALUMBO, Alice Marie. "The Recasting of the Female Gothic in the Novels of Margaret Atwood." PhD thesis. University of Toronto, 1997. 272 pp. Also available on microfiche from Canadian Theses Service (2000) and in .pdf format: http://www.nlc-bnc.ca/obj/s4/f2/dsk2/ftp02/NQ41571.pdf. "Atwood's novels rewrite and re-vision aspects of the Female Gothic, the American Gothic, and the Canadian Gothic in their depiction of the problems of female identity and self-definition, human evil, and the demands and expectations placed on women and men by contemporary society....[After a short history of the Gothic] Chapters One through Seven will analyze each of Atwood's novels published to date in detail. In each, Atwood's use of the Gothic tropes of imprisonment, confinement, haunting, and surveillance will be examined. Atwood's use and rewriting of the Gothic canon will also be considered. In the conclusion, I will present a brief analysis of *Alias Grace*, Atwood's most recent novel, and show how Atwood has rewritten the Gothic form to depict female anxieties and contemporary political abuses, and to examine questions of human evil and the relations between space and time." (Author). For more see *DAI-A* 60.10 (April 2000): 3660.

2094. PAYNE, Lynn. *The NEAP Guide to* The Handmaid's Tale *(Margaret Atwood): NEAP Guide.* Carlton, Australia: NEAP [Novell Education Academic Partner], 1997. Guide for secondary school students.

2095. PELLIZZARI, Paul. "This Is Who I Am and Why: Codes, Will, Confession and Transformation in Atwood, Ricci, Salinger and Baldwin." MA thesis. Université de Montréal, 1997.

2096. PERRAKIS, Phyllis Sternberg. "Atwood's *Robber Bride*: The Vampire as Intersubjective Catalyst." *Mosaic: Journal for the Interdisciplinary Study of Literature* 30.3 (September 1997): 151-168. Drawing on the intersubjective theories of psychoanalysts Daniel Stern and Jessica Benjamin, Perrakis explores the paradoxical role that Zenia, the psychological vampire, plays in *The Robber Bride*.

2097. PHELPS, Henry C. "Atwood's *The Edible Woman* and *Surfacing*." *The Explicator* 55.2 (Winter 1997): 112-114. Similarities are observed between the two characters named "Joe" in both books. Both "Joes" have the same attitudes of concern and hostility towards women. The use of the two "Joes" in different books also illustrates the changes experienced by the first Joe in *The Edible Woman* during the 1960s, and the outcome of these changes as portrayed in *Surfacing*.

2098. PORTER-LADOUSSE, Gillian. "Gender and Language in Margaret Atwood's Poetry." *Commonwealth: Essays and Studies 20.1* (1997): 10-16.

2099. RAMASWAMY, S. "Time, Space and Place in Two Canadian Poems: An Indian View." *International Journal of Canadian Studies* 15 (Spring 1997): 121-133. Atwood's "You Want to Go Back" and Bliss Carmen's "Lord of My Heart's Elation."

2100. REPENTIGNY, Anik de. "Le cercle vicieux: Traduction de *The Circle Game* de Margaret Atwood. Suivi de la poésie de Margaret Atwood et la nontraduction." MA thesis. Université de Montréal, 1997. Translation of *The Circle Game*.

2101. RESTUCCIA, Frances. "Tales of Beauty: Aestheticizing Female Melancholia." *American Imago* 53.4 (Winter 1997): 353-384. Focuses on three women authors who produce melancholic writing including Anita Brookner, Margaret Drabble, and Atwood.

2102. RIEMAN, Janice Elizabeth. "Memory: The Mother of All Nine Muses: Remembrances of Childhood in Margaret Atwood's Fiction." PhD thesis. Georgia State

University, 1997. 234 pp. "Throughout Margaret Atwood's fiction are painful and unpleasant childhood stories. These narratives often remain imbedded in ostensible first stories wherein the characters encounter places or people that act as catalysts for remembering. Atwood's use of a dual narrative strategy to tell both the adult and childhood story shows the inevitable connections between the two tales being told. The childhood story itself, and even more important, the character's coming to terms with the story and somehow assimilating it into her present, remains paramount to her development and self-discovery....Atwood's novels all explore the issue of how we know ourselves through our life stories. How we use them and how we choose to tell them—even to ourselves—reveals a great deal about who we are. The truth of the life lies not only in the content, but in the telling.... Atwood uses the childhood stories of her characters to reinforce the importance of remembering and owning one's life story." (Author). For more see *DAI-A* 59.01 (July 1998): 179.

2103. ROBERTS, Nancy. *Schools of Sympathy: Gender and Identification through the Novel*. Montreal: McGill Queen's, 1997. See especially Chapter 6 "'Back Talk': The Work of Margaret Atwood and Angela Carter." 107-141.

2104. RUBIK, Margarete. "National Identity, International Life Styles and Cosmopolitan Culture in Margaret Atwood's 'Significant Moments in the Life of My Mother,' 'Hurricane Hazel' and 'Unearthing Suite.'" *Brno Studies in English* (issued as *Sbornik Praci Filozoficke Fakulty Brnenske Univerzity: Rada Anglisticka*) 23 (1997): 145-150.

2105. SADOWSKI, Marianne. "The Dystopian Novel: A Theory of Mass Culture." PhD thesis. University of Connecticut, 1997. 268 pp. Includes *The Handmaid's Tale*. For more see *DAI-A* 58.08 (February 1998): 3123.

2107. SHUGART, Helene A. "Counterhegemonic Acts: Appropriation as a Feminist Rhetorical Strategy." *Quarterly Journal of Speech* 83.2 (May 1997): 210-229. Shugart explores the rhetorical strategy of feminist appropriation in order to assess its function as a counter-hegemonic tactic. Two instances of feminist rhetorical appropriation are analyzed: the Australian film *Shame*, as an appropriation of the classical Western, *Shane*, and Margaret Atwood's poems "Orpheus" and "Eurydice," as a collective appropriation of the classical Greek myth.

2108. SHUPING, Li. "The Possibility of Breaking the Circle: An Analysis of Three Female Characters in *The Edible Woman*." PhD thesis. Lanzhou University, 1997. Text in English with some Chinese.

2109. SINCLAIR, Gail Ann D. "Rising to the Surface: Suicide as Narrative Strategy in Twentieth-Century Women's Fiction." PhD thesis. University of South Florida, 1997. Includes analysis of Atwood's *Surfacing*, which provides a protagonist who escapes society, takes an atavistic psychological journey towards selfhood, and re-emerges with resolve to move away from deadly response to personally confining prerogatives by taking charge of her life in a more proactive way. For more see *DAI-A* 58.11 (May 1998): 4266.

2110. SINHA, Krishna Kant. "Women in the World of Margaret Atwood and Kamala Markandaya: A Comparative Study." MA thesis. Ranchi University, 1997.

2111. SIZEMORE, Christine W. "Negotiating Between Ideologies: The Search for Identity in Tsitsi Dangarembga's *Nervous Conditions* and Margaret Atwood's *Cat's Eye*." *Women's Studies Quarterly* 25.3-4 (Fall 1997): 68-82. Explores the way two young girls negotiate their search for identity in two novels that speak to the long arm of British colonial ideology, simultaneously across racial and ethnic boundaries.

2112. STURGESS, Charlotte. "Manipulating Clichés: Margaret Atwood's Romance Narrative 'Bluebeard's Egg.'" *GRAAT Publication des Groupes de Recherches Anglo-Américaines de l'Université François Rabelais de Tours* 16 (1997): 143-148.

2113. SUÁREZ LAFUENTE, M. S. "Intertextualidad americana contemporánea delcuento 'El Novio Bandido.'" *Letras en el Espejo: Ensayos de literatura Americana comparada.* Ed. María José Alvarez Maurin, Manuel Broncano, and José Luis Chamosa. León, Spain: Universidad de León, 1997. 199-205. Includes discussion in Spanish of *Lady Oracle.*

2114. SUÁREZ LAFUENTE, M. S., and Urbano Viñuela ANGULO. "La ficción de la ficción." *Letras en el Espejo, II: Ensayos de literatura Americana comparada.* Ed. María José Alvarez Maurin, Manuel Broncano, and José Luis Chamosa. León, Spain: Universidad de León, 1997. 129-134. Eudora Welty's *The Robber Bridegroom* and Atwood's *The Robber Bride.*

2115. SUNAINI, Singh. *The Novels of Margaret Atwood and Anita Desai: A Comparative Study.* New Delhi: Creative, 1997.

2116. TELEKY, Richard. *Hungarian Rhapsodies: Essays on Ethnicity, Identity, and Culture.* Seattle: U of Washington P, 1997. 58-60. In one essay, "Without Words: Hungarians in North American Fiction," Teleky is particularly biting on the subject of a Margaret Atwood story, "Wilderness Tips," in which a main character is a sinister Hungarian immigrant.

2117. TEXTER, Douglas Walter. "Kissing the Shiny, Shiny Boot in Oceania and Gilead: George Orwell's *1984* and Margaret Atwood's *The Handmaid's Tale* as Sadomasochistic Discourse." MA thesis. Villanova University, 1997. 156 pp.

2118. THOMPSON, Lee Briscoe. *Scarlet Letters: Margaret Atwood's* The Handmaid's Tale. Toronto: ECW Press, 1997. (Canadian Fiction Studies).

2119. VAISHALI, K. S. *Prisoning Rhythms: A Study of Margaret Atwood's Poetry.* Bangalore: Focus Press, ©1997.

2120. VAN VUREN, Dalene. "The Seduction of Genre: A Study of Organic Narrative Techniques in the Novels of Margaret Atwood." Thesis (Doctor Litterarum). University of Pretoria, 1997. 375 pp.

2121. VANDERSLICE, Stephanie M. "Thin Air." PhD thesis. University of Southwestern Louisiana, 1997. 231 pp. *Thin Air* owes a great deal to *Cat's Eye*, especially in its treatment of time. For more see *DAI-A* 58.03 (September 1997): 876.

2122. VARBLE, Valery. "Tourists and Transients: (Re)Figuring Notions of Travel in Atwood's *Bodily Harm* and Varda's *Vagabond*." MA thesis. New Mexico State University, 1997. 95 pp.

2123. WALKER, Cheryl. "In Bluebeard's Closet: Women Who Write with the Wolves." *Literature Interpretation Theory* 7.1 (1997): 13-25. "The use of the tale of Bluebeard by certain women writers, including Rose Terry Cooke, Margaret Atwood, Angela Carter, and Edna St. Vincent Millay. These are women who would not themselves identify with either the innocent girl or the murdered wife of the myth; as they tell it, it may not be just a story about women's victimization but rather a story of confronting the dark side, or the dark Other of women's dreams." (Journal).

2124. WALL, Kathleen. "Representing the Other Body: Frame Narratives in Margaret Atwood's 'Giving Birth' and Alice Munro's 'Meneseteung.'" *Canadian Literature* 154 (Autumn 1997): 74-90. Both stories feature unique representations of the female body. An analysis of both works would show the authors' efforts to deromanticize that body. The interaction between the frame and the framed body is designed to attract the reader's attention to the margin and the marginal.

2125. WEAVER, Rosalie Mary. "Innovation within the Modern Short Story through the Interaction of Gender, Nationality, and Genre: Margaret Atwood's *Wilderness Tips* and Alice Munro's *Open Secrets.*" PhD thesis. University of Manitoba, 1997. 273 pp. "Through its review of the evolution of the short story and its application of feminist, postmodernist, Reader-response theory, and New Historicism to the recent short-story collections of Margaret Atwood and Alice Munro, this thesis asserts that both late twentieth-century writers are innovators within the short-story genre. Short-story critics' continuous disagreement over definition due to the hybrid nature of the short story is seen as analogous to Canadian women writers' ongoing concerns with issues of identity related specifically to gender and nationality. In *Wilderness Tips* and *Open Secrets*, Atwood's and Munro's problematization of gender and national identity correlates with their choice of genre. In their hands, the ensuing interaction of gender, nationality, and genre becomes a transformative force for innovation within the modern short story." (Author). For more see *DAI-A* 58.11 (May 1998): 4276.

2126. WECZERKA, Margrit. "'All of It Is a Reconstruction': Geschichte und Umgang mit Erinnerung in Margaret Atwoods Romanen *The Handmaid's Tale* und *The Robber Bride.*" *Literatur in Wissenschaft und Unterricht.* 30.2 (1997): 119-133.

2127. WEHMEYER, Paula J. "Universality and the Self-Discovery Narrative: Three Works by Contemporary Writers." MA thesis. South Dakota State University, 1997. 89 pp. *Cat's Eye* plus Alice Munro's *Lives of Girls & Women* and Lorrie Moore's *Who Will Run the Frog Hospital?*

2128. WEINER, Deborah. "Islands of Possibility: Gendered Workings of Power in the Lives and Texts of Shelley, Alcott, Woolf, Rhys, Laurie Anderson, Carter and Atwood." PhD thesis. University of Rochester, 1997. 357 pp. An investigation of the forces that have "enabled, facilitated, impeded, or blocked the work of [these] writers." Discusses *Cat's Eye* and several poems. For more see *DAI-A* 58.09 (March 1998): 3520.

2129. WHEELER, Kathleen. *A Critical Guide to Twentieth-Century Women Novelists.* Malden, MA: Blackwell, 1997. Includes short profile of Atwood, 267-271.

2130. WILKINS, Peter Duncan. "Finite Nations, Finite Selves: The Failure of Apocalypse in North American Fiction." PhD thesis. University of California, Irvine, 1997. Includes Atwood's *Surfacing* which deals with the external threat to Canada represented by the United States. For more see *DAI-A* 58.08 (February 1998): 3138.

2131. WÖRRLEIN, Andrea. "'The Female Body—It's a Hot Topic': Weibliche Korpererfahrung in Margaret Atwoods Romanen *The Edible Woman* und *Bodily Harm.*" *Zeitschrift für Anglistik und Amerikanistik* 45.2 (1997): 129-147.

2132. YAN, Qigang. "A Comparative Study of Contemporary Canadian and Chinese Women Writers." PhD thesis. University of Alberta, 1997. 241 pp. Canadians include Atwood, Gallant, Kogawa, and Munro. For more see *DAI-A* 58.09 (March 1998): 3516.

Reviews of Atwood's Works

2133. *Alias Grace*. Toronto: McClelland and Stewart, 1996. Also published by Blooms-
bury in the United Kingdom and by Nan A. Talese/Doubleday in the United States.
Alternative Law Journal 22.6 (December 1997): 315. By K.O.
Americas 49.6 (November-December 1997): 61-62. By Barbara MUJIKA.
(1204 w).
Buffalo News 19 January 1997 Secondary Book Reviews: 8F. By Janet KAYE.
(806 w).
Canadian Forum 75.856 (January 1997): 39-42. By Elspeth CAMERON.
Capital Times [Madison, WI] 25 April 1997 Section: Editorial: 17A. By Anita
WEIER. (560 w).
Chicago Tribune 19 January 1997 Section Books: 1. By Maureen McLANE.
(1829 w). (Compares *Alias Grace* with Anita Shreve's *The Weight of Water*.)
Christian Science Monitor 89.60 21 February 1997: 14. By Yvonne ZIPP.
Daily Yomiuri 23 March 1997: 15. By Linda Ghan. (817 w).
Denver Post 5 January 1997 Section: Asection: G12. By Cynthia PASQUALE.
(725 w).
Fiddlehead 191 (Spring 1997): 114-119. By Elizabeth E. ROSE. (2216 w).
Morning Call [Allentown, PA] 5 January 1997 Section: Arts and Travel: F1.
By Nicholas BASBANES. (998 w).
MPLS [St. Paul, MN] 25.3 (March 1997): 34. By William SWANSON.
(98 w).
MS 7.4 (January 1997): 79. By Victoria BROWNWORTH.
National Review 49.2 (10 February 1997): 58. By Mitt BEAUCHESNE.
(253 w).
New Straits Times [Malaysia] 26 November 1997 Section: Literary: 11.
By Wong Ming YOOK. (1338 w).
New York Law Journal 18 March 1997 Section: Lawyer's Bookshelf: 2.
By Alan MASS. (1373 w).
New Yorker 72.44 (27 January 1997): 76. ANON.
Orange County Register 19 January 1997 Section: Show: F36. By Rebecca
ALLEN. (905 w).
Partisan Review 64.1 (Winter 1997): 37-49. By Millicent BELL. (Group
review).
People Weekly 47.3 (27 January 1997): 34. By Kim HUBBARD. (265 w).
Roanoke Times & World News 16 March 1997 Section Books: 4. By Margaret
GRAYSON. (358 w).
School Library Journal 43.6 (June 1997): 151. By S. H. WOODCOCK.
Seattle Times 5 January 1997 Section Books: M2. By Melinda BARGREEN.
(812 w).
Sunday Gazette Mail [Charleston, SC] 19 January 1997 Section: News: 2E.
By Arline THOM. (695 w).
US Catholic 62.5 (May 1997): 46-49. By Patrick McCORMICK. (2192 w).
(Comparative review).
Waikato Times [Hamilton] 4 October 1997 Section: Features: Books: 7.
By Karin WARNAR. (375 w).
Western American Literature 32.2 (1997): 175. By Dana WILLIAMS.

Women's Review of Books 14.7 (April 1997): 1, 3. By Nina Auerbach. (1472 w).

The World and I 12 (February 1997): 262. By Roberta RUBENSTEIN.

World Literature Today 71.3 (Summer 1997): 587. By Mona KNAPP. (603 w).

2134. *Alias Grace* [Paperback]. London: Virago, 1997.

    Independent [London] 31 August 1997 Section: Books: 26. By Jenny TURNER. (149 w).

    Irish Times 16 August 1997 Section: Weekend: Paperback choice: 66. By Eileen BATTERSBY. (169 w).

    Sunday Times 31 August 1997 Section: Features. By Phil BAKER. (249 w).

    The Times 30 August 1997 Section: Features. Available from Lexis-Nexis.

2135. *Alias Grace* [Sound recording]. New York: Bantam-Books Audio, 1996. 4 cassettes. Abridged. Read by Elizabeth McGovern.

    Austin American-Statesman 13 April 1997 Section: Special: D6. By Joe STAFFORD. (428 w). (Group review).

    Booklist 93.21 (July 1997): 1830. By Scott WHITNEY. (Comparative review).

    Chatelaine 70.7 (July 1997): 12. By Gina MALLET.

    Dallas Morning News 12 January 1997: Section: Today: 2F. By David TARRANT.

2136. *Alias Grace* [Sound recording]. London: HarperCollins, 1997. Read by Diana Quick. 2 tapes, 3 hours.

    Irish Times 30 August 1997 Section: Weekend: Audiobooks: 76. By Arminta WALLACE. (Group review).

2137. *Cat's Eye*. New York: Bantam Doubleday Dell, 1996.

    Booklist 93.9-10 (1-15 January 1997): 882. By Stephanie ZVIRIN.

2138. *Deux sollicitudes: Entretiens*. Trois-Pistoles [QU]: Editions Trois-Pistoles, 1996.

    Nuit-blanche 68 (Autumn 1997): 7-8. By Renaud LONGCHAMPS.

2139. *The Edible Woman*. New York: Bantam, 1996.

    British Medical Journal 315.7123 (20-27 December 1997): 1714. By Brian HAYNES. (34 w).

2140. *The Journals of Susanna Moodie*. Toronto: Oxford UP, 1970.

    Malahat Review 32.1-2 (1997): 35-44. Group review. Reprint of original published in *Malahat Review* 5.2 (1970).

2141. *The Journals of Susanna Moodie*. Toronto: Macfarlane Walter & Ross, 1997.

    Globe and Mail 12 December 1997: D18. By Fraser SUTHERLAND.

    Toronto Sun 16 November 1997 Section: Comment/Books: C10. ANON. (238 w).

2142. *The Poetry of Gwendolyn MacEwen*. 2 vols. Toronto: Exile, 1993-1994.

    Canadian Literature 152-153 (Spring-Summer 1997): 244-247. By Diane STILES. (1988 w). (Comparative review).

2143. *Power Politics: Poems*. Concord [ON]: Anansi, 1996.

    Edmonton Journal 1 June 1997: C6. By Norm SACUTA. (799 w). (Compared to Pablo Neruda's *Ceremonial Songs*.)

    Vancouver Sun 1 March 1997: C8. By Susan MUSGRAVE. (943 w). (Compared to Al Purdy's *Rooms for Rent in the Outer Planets*.)

2144. *Princess Prunella and the Purple Peanut*. Toronto: Key Porter, 1995.

    Canadian Children's Literature 23.4 (1997): 81-83. By Jim GELLERT.

    Vancouver Sun 13 December 1997 Section: SatRev: K5. By Brenna TURVEY. (411 w).

2145. *The Robber Bride*. Toronto: McClelland and Stewart, 1993.
   Seventeen 56.9 (September 1997): 264, 202. By Menina BOYLE.
2146. *Strange Things: The Malevolent North in Canadian Literature*. Oxford: Oxford UP, 1996.
   Canadian Literature 154 (Autumn 1997): 111-113. By Sherrill GRACE.
2147. *Wilderness Tips*. Toronto: McClelland and Stewart, 1991. Also published London: Bloomsbury; New York: Talese/Doubleday.
   Toronto Sun 20 April 1997 Section: Comment/Books: C13. By Liz LANGLEY and Heather MALLICK. (636 w).

~ 1998 ~

Atwood's Works

2148. *Alias Grace*. Amsterdam: Ooievaar, 1998. Dutch translation by Gerda Baardman and Tjadine Stheeman.

2149. *Alias Grace*. Barcelona [Spain]: Ediciones B, 1998. Spanish translation by María Antonia Menini.

2150. *Alias Grace*. Oslo: Aschehoug, 1998. Norwegian translation by Inger Gjelsvik.

2151. *Alias Grace*. Zagreb: Fidas, 1998. Croatian translation by Nedeljka and Janko Paravic.

2152. *Alias Grace: Roman*. Munich: BTB, 1998. German translation by Brigitte Walitzek.

2153. "Animal Victims." *The Wild Animal Story*. Ed. Ralph H. Lutts. Philadelphia: Temple UP, 1998. 215-224. Reprinted from *Survival: A Thematic Guide to Canadian Literature*, ©1972.

2154. *Bie ming Geleisi Alias Grace*. [Computer file]. Nanjing: Yi lin chu ban she, 1998. Electronic reproduction.

2155. "Blackie in Antarctica." *Ontario Review* 48 (1998): 5-6. Poem.

2156. "Bluebeard's Egg." *The Penguin Anthology of Stories by Canadian Women*. Selected by Denise Chong. Toronto: Penguin Books, 1998. 211-243. Reprinted from *Bluebeard's Egg*.

2157. *Bluebeard's Egg*. New York: Anchor Books, 1998. Contents: "Significant Moments in the Life of My Mother," "Hurricane Hazel," "Loulou, or, The Domestic Life of the Language," "Uglypuss," "Betty," "Bluebeard's Egg," "Spring Song of the Frogs," "Scarlet Ibis," "The Salt Garden," "The Sin Eater," "The Sunrise," and "Unearthing Suite." Reprint of 1983 McClelland and Stewart edition.

2158. *Bluebeard's Egg and Other Stories*. Bath: Chivers, 1998. Large print edition.

2159. *Bodily Harm*. Toronto: McClelland and Stewart; New York: Doubleday 1998 ©1981.

2160. *Captive*. Paris: Laffont, 1998. French translation of *Alias Grace* by Michèle Albaret-Maatsch.

2161. *Cat's Eye*. New York: Anchor Books, 1998.

2162. *Cat's Eye*. Toronto: McClelland and Stewart, 1998. Paperback reissue of the 1997 Random House cloth edition.

2163. *Chicas bailerinas*. Barcelona: Editorial Lumen, 1998. Spanish translation of *Dancing Girls and Other Stories* by Víctor Pozanco. Contents: "El marciano," "Betty," "Polaridades," "Translúcida," "La tumba del famoso poeta," "Joyería capilar,"

"Cuando sucede," "Historia de un viaje," "El resplandeciente quetzal," "Aprendi-zaje," "Vidas de poetas," "Chicas bailerinas," "La comepecados," "Dar a luz."

2164. "A Christmas Lorac." *The Ark in the Garden: Fables for Our Times*. Ed. by Albert Manguel. Toronto: Macfarlane Walter & Ross, 1998. 7-13. In this story intended for children, with "profound apologies to Charles Dickens," Atwood offers a fable about Ebenezer Scrooge in Tory Ontario. Reprinted from *Globe and Mail* 23 December 1995: C1, C15.

2165. *The Circle Game*. Toronto: House of Anansi Press, 1998. Reprint of Anansi edition, ©1978. With an introduction by Sherrill Grace. Atwood's first collection of poetry, winner of the 1966 Governor General's Award.

2166. "Cricket." *Ontario Review* 49 (1998): 18-19. Poem.

2167. *Criminosa ou Inocente?* Lisbon: Livros do Brasil, 1998. Portuguese translation of *Alias Grace* by Clarisse Tavares.

2168. "Crosstalk." *Canadian Forum* 77.869 (1998): 18-21. Excerpt from *Two Solicitudes*. Margaret Atwood in conversation with Victor-Levy Beaulieu on tyranny, taboos, and making movies.

2169. *Dancing Girls and Other Stories*. Toronto: McClelland and Stewart, 1998 ©1977. Includes "The War in the Bathroom," "The Man from Mars," "Polarities," "Under Glass," "The Grave of the Famous Poet," "Rape Fantasies," "Hair Jewellery," "When It Happens," "A Travel Piece," "The Resplendent Quetzal," "Training," "Lives of the Poets," "Dancing Girls," "Giving Birth."

2170. *Dancing Girls and Other Stories*. New York: Anchor Books, 1998 ©1977. Short stories. The US edition substitutes "Betty" and "The Sin Eater," both of which were later published in the Canadian edition of *Bluebeard's Egg* (1983), for "The War in the Bathroom" and "Rape Fantasies."

2171. "Death by Landscape." *Mistresses of the Dark: 25 Macabre Tales by Master Storytellers*. Selected by Stefan R. Dziemianowicz, Denise Little, and Robert E. Weinberg. New York: Barnes & Noble, 1998. [1]-19. Reprinted from *Wilderness Tips*, ©1991.

2172. *Der lange traum*. Munich: BTB, 1998. German translation of *Surfacing*.

2173. *Der Report der Magd: Roman*. Hildesheim: Claassen, 1998. German translation of *The Handmaid's Tale* by Helga Pfetsch.

2174. "*Doctor Glas* by Hjalmar Söderberg." *Brick: A Literary Journal* 61 (1998): 17-18. In "Lost Classics" series.

2175. *Eating Fire: Selected Poetry, 1965-1995*. London: Virago, 1998. Includes selections reprinted from *Poems 1965-1975, Poems 1976-1986*, and *Morning in the Burned House*.

2176. *The Edible Woman*. Toronto: Seal Books, 1998. Reissue of 1978 Seal edition based on original edition published by McClelland and Stewart, 1969.

2177. *The Edible Woman*. New York: Anchor Books, 1998. Reprint of first US edition by Little, Brown, 1970.

2178. *The Edible Woman*. Toronto: Bantam; New York: Bantam-Dell-Doubleday, 1998. Reprint.

2179. "[Excerpt]." *100 Great Poems by Women: A Golden Ecco Anthology*. Ed. Carolyn Kizer. Hopewell: Ecco Press, 1998. 140-142. Reprint of 1995 edition. Twelve stanzas reprinted from "Circe/Mud Poems." Reprint from *Selected Poems*, 1976.

2180. "[Excerpt]." *Harmony: Photographic Journeys Across Our Cultural Boundaries / Harmonie: Voyages en photos à travers nos frontières culturelles*. Toronto: Harmony Movement; copublished by Macmillan Canada, 1998. 63. Reprinted from *The Robber Bride*.

2181. "[Excerpt]." *Texas Employment Law Letter* 9.4 (1998): s.p. From Atwood's *True Stories*, in the article by Clark, West, Keller, Bulter, and Ellis, entitled "The Truth Is Out There." Available from Lexis-Nexis.

2182. "A Failure." *Artes* 5 (1998): 93-[101].

2183. "The Female Body." *Style: A Pragmatic Approach.* Peter Richardson. Toronto; Boston; London: Allyn & Bacon, 1998. 70-73. With study questions, 73. Reprinted from *Good Bones and Simple Murders*, ©1994.

2184. "Fishing for Eel Totems." *Uncommon Waters: Women Write about Fishing.* 2nd ed. Ed. Holly Morris. Seattle, WA: Seal Press, 1998. 179. Poem.

2185. *Ha-Ishah ha-akhilah.* [Tel Aviv]: Kineret, 1998. Hebrew translation of *The Edible Woman* by Shelomit Hendelsman.

2186. *The Handmaid's Tale.* Toronto: Seal Books; New York: Anchor Books, 1998. Reprint of 1986 edition.

2187. *The Handmaid's Tale.* [Sound recording]. Read by Catherine Mead. Vancouver, BC: Crane Resource Centre, 1998. 7 tape reels.

2188. "Haunted by Their Nightmares." *Critical Essays on Toni Morrison's Beloved.* Ed. Barbara H. Solomon. New York: G. K. Hall, 1998. 39-42. A review of the book, reprinted from *The New York Times Book Review* 13 September 1987: 1, 49-50.

2189. "Heart." *Ontario Review* 49 (1998): 20. Poem.

2190. *Helenah mi-Troyah rokedet `al ha-dalpek.* Jerusalem: Karmel, 1998. English with Hebrew translation by Etan Miler on facing page of "Helen of Troy Does Countertop Dancing." Poem.

2191. "In Love with Raymond Chandler." *The New Oxford Book of English Prose.* Ed. John Gross. Oxford; New York: Oxford UP, 1998. 972-973. Also published in *Love Is Strange.* Ed. Richard Glyn Jones. London: Indigo, 1998. 103-104. Reprinted from *Good Bones*, ©1992.

2192. "In Search of *Alias Grace*: On Writing Canadian Historical Fiction." *American Historical Review* 105.5 (1998): 1503-1516. Essay originally delivered as the Bronfman Lecture, Ottawa, November 1996. It was published by and is available in volume form from the University of Ottawa Press, 1997.

2193. "Introduction." *Medea: A Modern Retelling.* By Christa Wolf. Translated from the German by John Cullen. New York: Nan A. Talese, 1998. ix-xvi.

2194. "Introduction." *Women Writers at Work: The Paris Interviews.* Ed. George Plimpton. Random House, 1998. ix-xviii.

2195. "It Is Dangerous to Read Newspapers." *From Both Sides Now: The Poetry of the Vietnam War and Its Aftermath.* Ed. Phillip Mahony. New York: Scribner Poetry, 1998. 141. Reprinted from *Selected Poems 1966-1984*, ©1990.

2196. *La donna che rubava i mariti.* Milan: Baldini & Castoldi, 1998. Italian translation of *The Robber Bride* by Margherita Giacobino.

2197. *Lady Oracle.* Toronto: McClelland and Stewart; New York: Anchor Books, 1998. Reprint of 1976 edition.

2198. *Lady Oracle.* New York: Bantam Books, 1998. Reprint.

2199. "Landcrab." *Perrine's Literature: Structure, Sound, and Sense.* 7th ed. [Ed.] Thomas R. Arp. Fort Worth, TX; Philadelphia: Harcourt Brace, 1998. 772. Poem, with study questions, 773. Reprinted from *True Stories*, ©1981.

2200. *Life Before Man.* Toronto: McClelland and Stewart, 1998 ©1979.

2201. "Late August." *Touching Fire: Erotic Writings by Women.* 4th ed. Ed. Louise Thornton, Jan Sturtevant, and Amber Coverdale Sumrall. New York: Carroll & Graf, 1998. 104. Reprint from *Selected Poems 1965-1975,* ©1976.

2202. *Li-te`anat Grais.* [Tel Aviv]: Kineret, 1998. Hebrew translation of *Alias Grace* by Yonatan Fridman.

2203. *Life Before Man.* Toronto: McClelland and Stewart, 1998. Reprint of 1979 edition. Also published New York: Anchor Books.

2204. *Life Before Man.* New York: Bantam Books, 1998. Reprint.

2205. "The Man from Mars." *The Norton Anthology of Contemporary Fiction.* 2nd ed. [Ed.] R. V. Cassill and Joyce Carol Oates. New York: Norton, 1998. 16-33. Reprinted from *Dancing Girls and Other Stories,* 1981 ©1977.

2206. "Masterpiece Theatre." *Los Angeles Times* 25 January 1998: Section: Book Review: 7. Atwood reviews Lewis Hyde's most recent book, *Trickster Makes This World: Mischief, Myth and Art* (Farrar, Straus & Giroux) and puts it in context of his earlier (1979) book: *The Gift: Imagination and the Erotic Life of Property* (Vintage). As usual, Atwood gives two enthusiastic thumbs up. Way up! (1746 w).

2207. *Mort en lisière.* Paris: Librairie générale française, 1998. French translation of *Wilderness Tips* by François Dupuigrenet-Desroussilles.

2208. "Mrs. Atwood's Calla Lilies." *The Real Dish: A Collection of Recipes from the Friends of Sisterling.* Toronto: Sisterling, 1998. 246. Reprinted from *The Canlit Foodbook,* ©1987.

2209. "The Nature of Gothic." *Ontario Review* 48 (1998): 8-9. Poem.

2210. *Nevesta zbojnícka.* Bratislava [Slovakia]: Aspekt, 1998. Slovak translation of *The Robber Bride* by Jana Juránová.

2211. "Of Souls as Birds." *Mirror, Mirror on the Wall: Women Writers Explore Their Favorite Fairy Tales.* Ed. Kate Bernheimer. New York: Anchor, 1998. 22-38. Atwood liked *The Complete Grimms' Fairy Tales.*

2212. *Opowiesc podrecznej.* Poznan: Zysk i S-ka, 1998. Polish translation of *The Handmaid's Tale* by Zofia Uhrynowsla-Hanasz.

2213. *Orjattaresi.* Helsinki: Kustannusosakeyhtiö Tammi, 1998. Finnish translation of *The Handmaid's Tale* by Matti Kannosto.

2214. *Pie ming K'ê-leisi.* Nanjing, China: Yilin ju ban she, 1998. Chinese translation of *Alias Grace* by Jianghai Mei. Title romanized.

2215. *Prinzessin Prunella und die purpurne Pflaume.* Hildesheim [Germany]: Gerstenberg Verlag, ©1998. German translation of *Princess Prunella and the Purple Peanut* by Edmund Jacoby.

2216. "Questioning the Dead." *Ontario Review* 48 (1998): 7. Poem.

2217. "Questions That Expect the Answer Yes." *Ontario Review* 49 (1998): 18-19. Poem.

2218. "Rape Fantasies." *Fiction: A Longman Pocket Anthology.* 2nd ed. [Ed.] R. S. Gwynn. New York: Longman, 1998. 244-252. Reprinted from *Dancing Girls and Other Stories,* ©1977.

2219. "Reading Blind." *Biblio* December 1998: 24. Atwood describes the criteria for writing successful short stories, focusing on the cadence and rhythm of language. Authors are advised to read their work aloud, as this provides a connection with the language's oral history and tradition. Narrative skill is considered not only vital to the telling of the story, but also to shape reader's perceptions.

2220. "A Red Shirt." *A Second Skin: Women Write about Clothes*. Ed. by Kirsty Dunseath. London: Women's Press, 1998. 144-148. Poem.

2221. "Resurrection." *Divine Inspiration: The Life of Jesus in World Poetry*. Ed. Robert Atwan, George Dardess, and Peggy Rosenthal. New York: Oxford UP, 1998. 121-122. Reprinted from *The Journals of Susanna Moodie*. Oxford, ©1970.

2222. *The Robber Bride*. Toronto: McClelland and Stewart; New York: Anchor Books, 1998. Reprint of 1993 edition.

2223. "Romantic." *Washington Post* 24 May 1998: X02. Poem reprinted from *Morning in the Burned House*, ©1995.

2224. "Siren Song." *Perrine's Literature: Structure, Sound, and Sense*. 7th ed. [Ed.] Thomas R. Arp. Fort Worth, TX; Philadelphia: Harcourt Brace, 1998. 829-830. Poem. Reprinted from *You Are Happy, Selected Poems 1965-1975*, ©1976.

2225. "Solicit." *Ethics and Behavior* 8.2 (1998): 123. Included in article by Anna C. Salter, "Silencing the Victim: The Politics of Discrediting Child Abuse Survivors," 125-140.

2226. "Sor Juana Works in the Garden." *Ontario Review* 48 (1998): 10. Poem.

2227. *Stories by Margaret Atwood*. Hong Kong: Longman; Tokyo: Distributed by Nan'undo Fenikkusu, 1998. Translation into Japanese of *Dancing Girls and Other Stories*. Japanese title romanized.

2228. "Strange Things." Read by Barbara Lyon. Toronto: CNIB, 1998. Originally presented as a Clarendon Lecture at Oxford University. Use restricted to persons with a print handicap.

2229. *Surfacing*. New York: Anchor Books, 1998. Reprint.

2230. "Survival." *Who Speaks for Canada? Words That Shape a Country*. Ed. Desmond Morton and Morton Weinfeld. Toronto: McClelland and Stewart, 1998. 237-239. Excerpt from book published in 1972.

2231. "This Is a Photograph of Me." *Harrod Lecture Series* 16 (1997-1998): 80-81. Poem ©1966. Included as part of lecture delivered by Irene Martyniuk (see 2355).

2232. *Tips om overlevelse*. Viborg: Lindhardt og Ringhof, 1998. Danish translation of *Wilderness Tips*.

2233. "Variation on the Word *Sleep*." *The Poetry Reader's Toolkit: A Guide to Reading and Understanding Poetry*. By Marc Polonsky. Lincolnwood, IL: NTC Publishing Group, 1998. 140-141.

2234. "When It Happens." *Perrine's Literature: Structure, Sound, and Sense*. 7th ed. [Ed.] Thomas R. Arp. Fort Worth, TX; Philadelphia: Harcourt Brace, 1998. [379]-386. Short story. From *Dancing Girls and Other Stories*, ©1977, 1982.

2235. *Wilderness Tips: Stories*. Toronto: Seal Books, 1998. Reissue of 1992 Seal edition based on original 1991 McClelland and Stewart edition. Contains "True Trash," "Hairball," "Isis in Darkness," "The Bog Man," "Death by Landscape," "Uncles," "The Age of Lead," "Weight," "Wilderness Tips," and "Hack Wednesday."

2236. *Wilderness Tips: Stories*. New York: Anchor, 1998. Reprint.

2237. *Wilderness Tips: Stories*. New York: Bantam, 1998. Reprint.

2238. *Wilderness Tips*. [Sound recording]. Read by Aileen Seaton. Toronto: CNIB, 1998.

2239. "Wisdom from the Deep Freeze." *Amphora* 110 (Winter 1997-98): 32-34.

2240. *Wynurzenie*. Katowice [Poland]: Videograf II, 1998. Polish translation of *Surfacing* by Jolanta Plakwicz and Teresa Poniatowska.

2241. *Zena k nakousnutí*. Prague: Sulc a spol., 1998. Czech translation of *The Edible Woman* by Drahomíra Hlínková.

2242. *Zhlubin*. Prague: Argo, 1998. Czech translation of *Surfacing* by Drahomíra Hlín-ková.

Adaptations of Atwood's Works

2243. *The Handmaid's Tale: An Opera in a Prologue, a Prelude, Two Acts and an Epi-logue*. [Copenhagen]: Edition Wilhem Hansen, 1998-2002? 75. Based on the novel by Margaret Atwood; libretto by Paul Bentley; [music by Poul Ruders].
2244. ESPIN, Barry, and Paul NEWMAN, saxophonist. *Albert and Other Stories* [Sound recording]. Toronto: Lead Chicken Publishing, 1998. 1 sound disc. Includes New-man's adaptation of Atwood's poem "Progressive Insanities of a Pioneer." (15:17).
2245. MOREHEAD, Patricia. *"The Handmaid's Tale*: For Two Pianos." [Musical score]. Chicago (600 South Dearborn St. #2016, Chicago, IL 60605): CUBE Contempo-rary Chamber Ensemble, 1998. Printed music 2 scores (31 each). Inspired by the novel of the same name by Margaret Atwood.

Quotations

2246. "[Quote]." *Atlantic Monthly* 1 August 1998: 37. Atwood on the Canadian tem-perament: "Canadian rebellions have never become revolutions precisely because they have never received popular support. 'Prophets' here don't get very far against the civil service."
2247. "[Quote]." *The Gazette* (Montreal) 30 January 1998: A1. *The Gazette's* "Quote of the Day": "An eye for an eye only leads to more blindness."
2248. "[Quote]." *Globe and Mail* 4 July 1998: D10. Atwood on receiving Doctorate of Letters (*honoris causa*) from Oxford University in June 1998: "There was an ele-ment of danger and suspense. We had to climb up some steep steps [to receive the degree]. I kept thinking, will the person fall? But I made it up and down okay"; "There were no drum majorettes, but there were trumpeters"; I was part of some-thing very old....I'm very honoured."
2249. "[Quote]." *Globe and Mail* 15 August 1998: D10. Atwood responding to question about what Canadian writers earn and what they ought to: "'Needs,' or 'would like'? If 'needs,' does the writer have a family to support? Where does the writer live? If it really is 'needs,' then the answer is: the cost of shelter, of adequate food and clothing, of writing materials and of free time in which to write. Free time. There lies the rub. You can't put a price on it. For instance, you've just winkled some of my own free time out of me, as I'm answering your questions instead of working on my novel. Are you willing to pay me what my time is actually worth, using current market values? If not, am I subsidizing you? I'd say so."
2250. "[Quote]." *Globe and Mail* 15 August 1998: D10. Atwood responding to question: "If a writer decides, or is compelled, to seek a second occupation, what do you think is the most suitable one?" "The most suitable 'second occupation' or day job, for a writer is the one that will not take up so much inner space that it crowds out the writing, and that will not exhaust the writer so much that he or she doesn't have the energy to lift a pencil. I used to think that being a waitress—now called 'food services professional'—would be dandy for me, until I tried it. Lost my ap-petite."

2251. "[Quote]." *Globe and Mail* 6 October 1998: C1. Atwood comparing Giller and Booker award dinners, after attending Booker dinners 3 times. Saying she did not anticipate anything quite so brutal in Toronto, remarking: "The Giller has managed to avoid those more sanguinary features....The English love a good brawl."

2252. "[Quote]." *Globe and Mail* 7 November 1998: D1. Atwood on motherhood and writing: "I waited until I had the money; I had the baby, and hired the help."

2253. "[Quote]." *Star Tribune* (Minneapolis, MN) 27 March 1998: 20A. Letter about violence against women quotes Atwood who once asked a male friend why men feel threatened by women. He replied, "They are afraid women will laugh at them." She then asked a group of women why they feel threatened by men. They answered, "We're afraid of being killed."

2254. "[Quote]." *The Times* 4 March 1998 Section: Features. On her beginnings: "The good thing to be said about announcing yourself as a writer in the colonial Canadian 1950s is that nobody told me I could not do it because I was a girl. They simply found the entire proposition ridiculous. Writers were dead and English, or else extremely elderly and American; they were not 16 years old and Canadian."

2255. "[Quote]." *Toronto Star* 30 March 1998: Section: Opinion: A16. Article arguing for a Canadian National Beaver Day quotes Atwood: "Canada was built on dead beavers."

2256. "[Quote]." *Vancouver Sun* 19 October 1998: A10. In connection with a forthcoming conference at York University focusing on former Prime Minister Trudeau's achievements, Atwood was quoted as saying that Canadians "had excellent baloney detectors built into their otherwise flabby analytical powers."

2257. "[Quote]." *Vancouver Sun* 14 November 1998: C8. A review by Susan Musgrave of Brian Brett's new book, *The Colour of Bones in a Stream*, referenced Atwood's introduction to the *CanLit Foodbook*. Referring to writers, their writing, and their cooking, Atwood remarked: "The relation between word and deed is not so simple as you think. That is, some write about it but don't do it, others do it but don't write about it. Sort of like sex."

2258. "[Quote]." *Women and Language* 21.1 (1998): s.p. "If I were going to convert to any religion, I would probably choose Catholicism because at least it has female saints and the Virgin Mary."

Interviews

2259. "Literary Honours." *The National* CBC-TV 19 November 1998. Transcript of brief interview with Atwood on occasion of her being selected as required reading in France for university students aspiring to teach English. Her remarks include: "It's something for them to have a living writer on the list. Usually the people on the list are books of a certain age and the authors are not living." Transcript available from *CBCA Current Events* (from Proquest).

2260. *Two Solicitudes*. With Victor-Levy Beaulieu. Translated from the French by Phyllis Aronoff. Toronto: McClelland and Stewart, 1998. Translation of 1996 book in which authors interviewed each other.

2261. CAMPION, Blandine. "Entretien avec Margaret Atwood." *Spirale* 161 (1998): 10-11. On *Captive (Alias Grace)* in French.

2262. GRACE, Judy. "Student Writer Shares Her Margaret Atwood Moment." *Toronto Star* 3 January 1998: Section: Arts: M6. Student interviews Atwood after 1997 convocation at the University of Ottawa. Asked what advice she would give a young writer, Atwood said: "Read and read and read and write and write and write. That's all."

2263. GRONDAHL, Paul. "The Appeal of Atwood Is Evident at Page Hall." *Times Union* (Albany, NY) 7 November 1998: Section: Life and Leisure: D5. Atwood lecturing to 800 students, mostly young women, at University of Albany.

When asked, "Where do your poems come from?" Atwood replied: "I don't know. Do you? I can guarantee you that if you put one hand on the earth and one hand in the sky and remain in that position for several hours, you will get a poem." She also claimed that her children's books were written "under duress." "I did it to answer pleas from my publishers."

She also noted that she had trouble convincing people that a writer's life is actual work. "My lawyer says I don't have a real job, that my novels flow like toothpaste from a tube....I wish that were true. It's bloody hard work, as Joan Sutherland used to say. My mom is 89 years old and still doesn't think I work. It still comes as a surprise to her when I say I'm working on a new book." Finally, she commented that literary fame was a two-edged sword: "When you're at my age and stage, if you write the telephone book, they'd publish it. I give my manuscripts to friends who are critical readers."

2264. KRULL, John. "Read, but Not over Her Shoulder: Margaret Atwood Wants Her Fiction and Poetry to Stand on Their Own and Resists Probes of Her Private Life." *Indianapolis Star* 26 April 1998: Section: Lifestyle: J01. Atwood interviewed before Marian McFadden Memorial Lecture. (1722 w). Atwood's reluctance to reveal too much about herself is defended by Mary Kirtz, an English professor at the University of Akron: "We sometimes forget that writers aren't like movie stars. They do not want to display themselves before us, and they shouldn't have to."

2265. LADOUSSE, Gillian Porter. "The Unicorn and the Booby Hatch." *Textes publiés sur Margaret Atwood dans Études canadiennes / Canadian Studies (1975-1997).* [Ed.] Jean-Michel Lacroix. Talence [France]: Association française d'études canadiennes (A.F.E.C.), 1998. 31-45. Original interview conducted in Paris on 4 February 1978. In it, Atwood reflects on growing presence of Canadian literature in the international market, as well as on herself as a feminist writer. Reprinted from *Études canadiennes / Canadian Studies* 5 (1978): 97-111.

2266. SNELL, Marilyn. "Power and Non-Power." *The Power to Bend Spoons: Interviews with Canadian Novelists.* Ed. Beverley Daurio. Toronto: Mercury Press, 1998. 20-24. Snell interviews Atwood.

2267. STIRLING, Claire. "Three Bits of Evidence Add to Novelist Atwood's Picture of the Historical Focus of *Alias Grace*: Margaret Atwood Worried She Might Have 'Got It All Wrong' in Her Novel about Grace Marks's Life." *Vancouver Sun* 17 June 1998: C7. Atwood interviewed in Thunder Bay when she was in town to collect one of the two honorary degrees she received in 1998. The interview includes Atwood's comments on new material which has emerged about Grace Marks, including a prison-release questionnaire signed by Marks uncovered by the archivist of the Kingston Penitentiary.

Atwood was amused by some of the questions. "It was a market research questionnaire about things like, 'How was the food?' On the verge of leaving, how are you going to answer? That it was terrible. Back in for you." One of the questions was "To what do you attribute your incarceration?'" Atwood: "Her answer was so perfect—I just loved it....She said 'To having been employed in the same household as a villain.' She didn't say, 'I killed somebody.' She didn't say 'I didn't kill somebody.'...Her handwriting was right there. It was a neat, controlled, self-contained signature, let me tell you. Not giving much away." In passing, Atwood also noted: "They taught [inmates] specifically to read and write in the penitentiary. It was so they could read the *Bible* and become improved. Thrashing and religion were the two things that were supposed to improve you in those days."

2268. VEVAINA, Coomi S. "Daring to Be Human: A Conversation with Margaret Atwood." *Margaret Atwood: The Shape Shifter*. Ed. Coomi S. Vevaina and Coral Ann Howells. New Delhi: Creative Books, 1998. [146]-156. Conversation took place at Atwood's residence in Toronto just before publication of *Cat's Eye* in 1988.

Scholarly Resources

2269. *"The Handmaid's Tale." Novels for Students*. Vol. 4. Ed. Marie Rose Napierkowski. Farmington Hills, MI: Gale, 1998. 114-136.

2270. ABITEBOUL, Maurice. " Le romanesque et le grotesque dans 'The Man from Mars' de Margaret Atwood ou le mythe démythifié." *Textes publiés sur Margaret Atwood dans Études canadiennes / Canadian Studies (1975-1997)*. [Ed.] Jean-Michel Lacroix. Talence [France]: Association française d'études canadiennes (A.F.E.C.), 1998. 81-92. Reprinted from *Études canadiennes / Canadian Studies* 24 (1988): 87-98.

2271. ADAMO, Laura Elizabeth. "The Imaginary Girlfriend: A Study of Margaret Atwood's *The Handmaid's Tale*, *Cat's Eye*, *The Robber Bride*, and *Alias Grace*." MA thesis. University of Calgary, 1998. 193 pp. Also available on microfiche from Canadian Theses Service (1998) and as .pdf file: http://www.nlc-bnc.ca/obj /s4/f2/dsk2/tape15/PQDD_0014/MQ31277.pdf. Shows how the feminist vision of harmonious relationships and politically effective alliances between and among women is frequently complicated and obscured by the multiple contradictions of power structures which form and inform women's relationships. For more see *MAI* 37.01 (February 1999): 67.

2272. BEER, Janet. "Doing It with Mirrors: History and Cultural Identity in *The Robber Bride*." *British Journal of Canadian Studies* 13.2 (1998): 306-316.

2273. BIGNELL, Jonathan. "Territories, Boundaries, Identities." *Margaret Atwood: The Shape Shifter*. Ed. Coomi S. Vevaina and Coral Ann Howells. New Delhi: Creative Books, 1998. 9-25. On *The Handmaid's Tale*.

2274. BONTATIBUS, Donna. "Reconnecting with the Past: Personal Hauntings in Margaret Atwood's *The Robber Bride*." *Papers on Language and Literature* 34.4 (1998): 357-371. Bontatibus argues that in the novel, Atwood draws from a specific folkloric tradition to give added meaning and depth to this contemporary ghost story.

2275. BRINK, André. *The Novel: Language and Narrative from Cervantes to Calvino*. London: Macmillan, 1998. See especially "Withdrawal and Return: Margaret Atwood, *Surfacing*." 253-268.

2276. BROWN, Lyn Mikel. "The Dangers of Time Travel: Revisioning the Landscape of Girls' Relationships in Margaret Atwood's *Cat's Eye*." *Analyzing the Different Voice: Feminist Psychological Theory and Literary Texts.* Ed. Jerilyn Fisher, Ellen S. Silber, and Carol Gilligan. Lanham, MD: Rowman & Littlefield, 1998. 27-43.

2277. BROWNLEY, Martine Watson. "Atwood on Women, War and History: 'The Loneliness of the Military Historian.'" *Lyrical Symbols and Narrative Transformations: Essays in Honor of Ralph Freedman.* Ed. Kathleen L. Komar and Ross Shideler. Columbia: Camden House, 1998. 186-203. Atwood as a recycler: Brownley contends that this dramatic monologue, first published in 1990, is by a character who is a prototype of Tony Fremont, the military historian who appeared three years later in *The Robber Bride.*

2278. BRUNET, Emmanuelle. "[Her] Genius Was Synthesis: L'Exogenèse de *The Handmaid's Tale*." *Margaret Atwood:* The Handmaid's Tale / Le Conte de la servante: *The Power Game.* Ed. Jean-Michel Lacroix and Jacques Leclaire. Paris: Presses de la Sorbonne Nouvelle, 1998. 17-34.

2279. BÜHLER ROTH, Verena. *Wilderness and the Natural Environment: Margaret Atwood's Recycling of a Canadian Theme.* Tübingen: Franke Verlag, 1998. Based on author's doctoral thesis (1997) at the University of Zürich.

2280. BUSCHINI, Marie-Pascale. "Idéologie et fonctionnement du pouvoir dans *The Handmaid's Tale*." The Handmaid's Tale: *Margaret Atwood.* Ed. Marta Dvorak. Paris: Ellipses, 1998. 41-50.

2281. CAREY, Gary, and Mary Ellen SNODGRASS. *A Multicultural Dictionary of Literary Terms.* Jefferson, NC: McFarland, 1998. Includes multiple Atwood references. For example, under "Absurdism," there is a reference to *The Handmaid's Tale.*

2282. CASTINO, Melissa. "Margaret Atwood and Northrop Frye: Voices of the Frontier." MA thesis. Bemidji State University, 1998. 74 pp.

2283. CHAKRAVARTY, Radha. "Mothers in Flight: The Space of the Maternal in Margaret Atwood's *Cat's Eye*." *Mapping Canadian Cultural Space: Essays on Canadian Literature.* Ed. Danielle Schaub. Jerusalem, Israel: Magnes, 1998. 104-121.

2284. CHUNG, Kathy K. Y. "Co-Editing Atwood Juvenilia: The Student Experience." *English Studies in Canada* 24.3 (1998): 309-318.

2285. COLES NOTES. *The Edible Woman.* Toronto: Coles Publishing, 1998. Student aid.

2286. ———. *Surfacing.* Toronto: Coles Publishing, 1998. Student aid.

2287. COLLETT, Anne. "Half Me and Half You: Voices of Real Ladies and Literary Grandmothers in the Poetry of Joan Crate and Margaret Atwood." *Margaret Atwood: The Shape Shifter.* Ed. Coomi S. Vevaina and Coral Ann Howells. New Delhi: Creative Books, 1998. [99]-113.

2288. COLVILE, Georgiana M. M. "Textualité et textilité du récit dans *The Handmaid's Tale*." The Handmaid's Tale: *Margaret Atwood.* Ed. Marta Dvorak. Paris: Ellipses, 1998. 156-161.

2289. COOKE, Nathalie. *Margaret Atwood: A Biography.* Toronto: ECW Press; Chicago: Distributed in the United States by LPCGroup-InBook, 1998.

2290. COSTA de BEAUREGARD, Raphaëlle. "Moving Photographic Images: Silent Movie and the Uncanny in Volker Schlöndorff's *The Handmaid's Tale*." *Lectures d'une oeuvre*: The Handmaid's Tale *de Margaret Atwood.* [Ed.] Jean-Paul Gabilliet and François Gallix. Paris: Éditions du temps, 1998. 123-134.

2291. DAWSON, Carrie. "Never Cry Fraud: Remembering Grey Owl, Rethinking Imposture." *Essays on Canadian Writing* 65 (1998): 120-140. Includes a discussion of Atwood's "The Grey Owl Syndrome," which was one of 4 essays collected in *Strange Things: The Malevolent North in Canadian Literature.*

2292. DELORD, Marie. "Margaret Atwood's *Alias Grace*: A Postmodernist Novel—Mémoire de maitrise." MA thesis. Université de Toulouse Le Miral UFR des études du monde, anglophone, 1998. 100 pp.

2293. DEMOS, John. "In Search of Reasons for Historians to Read Novels." *American Historical Review* 103.5 (1998): 1526-1529. Response to Atwood's Bronfman Lecture, reprinted in *AHR.*

2294. DETORE-NAKAMURA, Joanne. "From Victim to Victor: The Friendship Plot in Contemporary Women's Novels." PhD thesis. Southern Illinois University at Carbondale, 1998. 193 pp. "This dissertation argues that three contemporary North American women writers namely, Margaret Atwood, Louise Erdrich and Amy Tan, authored novels that reflect current feminist thinking in which the female protagonists complete both a spiritual and social quest that eventually ends with the female protagonist still adhering to ties with friends, family, and community. This friendship plot differs sharply from what has now been termed the feminine quest plot of woman-authored novels in which the female protagonist completes a spiritual quest and discovers her identity but is unable to complete a social quest and fit into society." (Author). The thesis features a chapter on *Cat's Eye* and *The Robber Bride.* For more see *DAI-A* 60.03 (September 1999): 737.

2295. DIOT, Rolande. "'Image du corps et stade du miroir': Un aspect de l'humour de Margaret Atwood dans *Lady Oracle.*" *Textes publiés sur Margaret Atwood dans Études canadiennes / Canadian Studies (1975-1997).* [Ed.] Jean-Michel Lacroix. Talence [France]: Association française d'études canadiennes (A.F.E.C.), 1998. 47-57. Reprinted from *Études canadiennes / Canadian Studies* 9 (1980): 51-61.

2296. DOLITSKY, Marlène. "Characterizing the Narrator: Narratee as Alter-Ego." *Margaret Atwood:* The Handmaid's Tale / Le Conte de la servante: *The Power Game.* Ed. Jean-Michel Lacroix and Jacques Leclaire. Paris: Presses de la Sorbonne Nouvelle, 1998. 101-116.

2297. ———. "The Meta-Narrative Invitation of Satire in *The Handmaid's Tale.*" The Handmaid's Tale: *Margaret Atwood.* Ed. Marta Dvorak. Paris: Ellipses. 112-124.

2298. DUBOIS, Dominique. "Appropriation et réappropriation du corps féminin dans *The Handmaid's Tale.*" The Handmaid's Tale: *Margaret Atwood.* Ed. Marta Dvorak. Paris: Ellipses, 1998. 77-87.

2299. DURAND, Régis. "L'individu et le politique: Notes sur les romans de Margaret Atwood et Leonard Cohen. " *Textes publiés sur Margaret Atwood dans Études canadiennes / Canadian Studies (1975-1997).* [Ed.] Jean-Michel Lacroix. Talence [France]: Association française d'études canadiennes (A.F.E.C.), 1998. 7-22. Reprinted from *Études canadiennes / Canadian Studies* 1 (1975): 63-72. Cohen's *Beautiful Losers* and Atwood's *Surfacing.*

2300. DVORAK, Marta. "What Is Real/Reel? Margaret Atwood's Rearrangement of Shapes on a Flat Surface, or Narrative as Collage." *Études anglaises; Grande-Bretagne—États-Unis* 51.4 (1998): 448-461. Primarily about *The Handmaid's Tale.*

2301. ———. "What's in a Name? Readers as Both Pawns and Partners or Margaret Atwood's Strategy of Control." *Margaret Atwood*: The Handmaid's Tale / Le

Conte de la servante: *The Power Game.* Ed. Jean-Michel Lacroix and Jacques Leclaire. Paris: Presses de la Sorbonne Nouvelle, 1998. 79-99.

2302. DVORAK, Marta, ed. The Handmaid's Tale: *Margaret Atwood.* Paris: Ellipses, 1998. Individual articles in this book are indexed in this section.

2303. DYMOKE, Sue. The Handmaid's Tale *by Margaret Atwood: A Post-16 Study Guide.* Sheffield: National Association for the Teaching of English, 1998.

2304. ELSLEY, Judy. "A Stitch in Crime: Quilt Detective Novels." *Uncoverings* 19 (1998): 137-153. Crime, detective, and mystery fiction in Atwood's *Alias Grace.*

2305. FEE, Margery, and Janice McALPINE. *Guide to English Canadian Usage.* Oxford UP, 1998. Looks at ways Canadians use language, relying on a variety of sources including Atwood's *Life Before Man,* ©1979, and S*econd Words: Selected Critical Prose,* 1982.

2306. FETHERLING, Douglas. *The Gentle Anarchist: A Life of George Woodcock.* Vancouver: Douglas & McIntyre, 1998. Book credits Atwood's poetry for giving Woodcock a new poetic self. He had left England as an "English poet of between the wars, for whom the most important figure to embrace or extricate oneself from was Auden, in terms of form." Then, all of a sudden in the 1970s, "he found a new self after discovering the poems of Margaret Atwood and became an imagist poet."

2307. FIAMENGO, Janice. "Under Whose Eye? Two Versions of the Disciplinary Society in *The Handmaid's Tale.*" *Lectures d'une oeuvre:* The Handmaid's Tale *de Margaret Atwood.* [Ed.] Jean-Paul Gabilliet and François Gallix. Paris: Éditions du temps, 1998. 27-42.

2308. GABILLIET, Jean-Paul. "Gilead, Canada, and the United States: Anti-Americanism and Colonial Critique in *The Handmaid's Tale.*" *Lectures d'une oeuvre:* The Handmaid's Tale *de Margaret Atwood.* [Ed.] Jean-Paul Gabilliet and François Gallix. Paris: Éditions du temps, 1998. 43-52.

2309. GABILLIET, Jean-Paul, and François GALLIX, eds. *Lectures d'une oeuvre:* The Handmaid's Tale *de Margaret Atwood.* Paris: Éditions du temps, 1998. Individual articles in this book are indexed in this section. The book also includes 3 appendixes: "Chronologie" (201-209), "Biblical References in *The Handmaid's Tale*" (210-212), and "Bibliographie: *The Handmaid's Tale* de Margaret Atwood." 213 ff.

2310. GABRIELE, Sandra. "Surveilled Women: Subjectivity, the Body and Modern Postopticism." MA thesis. St. Mary's University, 1998. 114 pp. Also available on microfiche from Canadian Theses Service (1999). Also available in .pdf: http://www.nlc-bnc.ca/obj/s4/f2/dsk2/tape15/PQDD_0001/MQ33842.pdf. This thesis "explores the ways in which surveillance enacts the power to limit the self definition and thus the subjectivity of the female subject. Understanding the body as being intimately connected to the development of an autonomous female subject, surveillance is examined as a means of maintaining social structures of gender, race, and class." (Author). *The Handmaid's Tale* is used as one of the author's sources. For more see *MAI* 37.03 (June 1999): 829.

2311. GALE, Marilyn Kravitz. "*Lilith's Garden:* A Novella and, a Contextual Essay on the Development of *Lilith's Garden.*" PhD thesis. Union Institute, 1998. 185 pp. *Lilith's Garden* is a novella written in the first person that describes the empowerment of a contemporary woman struggling through the divorce process and patriarchal legal system. The author reviews works by earlier revisionist feminist writers (Jean Rhys, Adrienne Rich, Susan Griffin, and Margaret Atwood) and reframes Biblical narratives to produce literary role models that are the foundation for *Lilith's Garden.* For more see *DAI-A* 59.8 (February 1999): 3243.

2312. GALLIX, François. "Dire et écrire l'évasion dans *The Handmaid's Tale*." *Lectures d'une oeuvre*: The Handmaid's Tale *de Margaret Atwood*. [Ed.] Jean-Paul Gabilliet and François Gallix. Paris: Éditions du temps, 1998. 187-200.

2313. GARNER, Lee. "Preface, Postface and Aporia: Telling Tales in *The Handmaid's Tale*." The Handmaid's Tale: *Margaret Atwood*. Ed. Marta Dvorak. Paris: Ellipses, 1998. 162ff.

2314. GENTY, Stéphanie. "Parodie et paradoxe: *The Handmaid's Tale* comme dystopie féministe." The Handmaid's Tale: *Margaret Atwood*. Ed. Marta Dvorak. Paris: Ellipses, 1998. 60-68.

2315. GOPALAN, Kamala. "Weaving New Patterns in *Alias Grace*." *Margaret Atwood: The Shape Shifter*. Ed. Coomi S. Vevaina and Coral Ann Howells. New Delhi: Creative Books, 1998. [75]-81.

2316. GRACE, Dominick M. "*The Handmaid's Tale:* 'Historical Notes' and Documentary Subversion." *Science Fiction Studies* 25.3 (1998): 481-494. Commentary on the "Historical Notes" that appear at the end of the book.

2317. GREENE, Michael. "'In Its Own Way Eloquent': Irony, History and *The Handmaid's Tale*." The Handmaid's Tale: *Margaret Atwood*. Ed. Marta Dvorak. Paris: Ellipses, 1998. 103-111.

2318. GREVEN-BORDE, Hélène. "L'espace dystopique: *The Handmaid's Tale* et la dialectique de l'inclusion." *Margaret Atwood: The* Handmaid's Tale / Le Conte de la servante: *The Power Game*. Ed. Jean-Michel Lacroix and Jacques Leclaire. Paris: Presses de la Sorbonne Nouvelle, 1998. 49-61.

2319. HAMMILL, Faye Louise. "Inspiration and Imitation: Responses to Canadian Literary Culture in the Work of Frances Brooke, Susanna Moodie, Sara Jeannette Duncan, L. M. Montgomery, Margaret Atwood and Carol Shields." PhD thesis. University of Birmingham, Department of American and Canadian Studies, School of Historical Studies, Faculty of Arts, 1998.

2320. HARISHANKAR, V. Bharathi. "Correlatives of Love: A Study of Atwood's *Power Politics* through the Rasa Theory." *Margaret Atwood: The Shape Shifter*. Ed. Coomi S. Vevaina and Coral Ann Howells. New Delhi: Creative Books, 1998. [126]-134. "The concept of rasa is one of the prominent theoretical ideas of Sanskrit poetics, and it dates back to Bharata's *Natyasastra*. Rasa may be defined as an emotion which is a 'permanent major instinct of man...capable of being developed and delineated to its climax with its attendant and accessory feelings...[and which evokes an] emotional sympathy at the presentation.' Thus, the basic assumption is that meanings cannot be generated without reference to some basic sentiments." (Author).

2321. HENGEN, Shannon. "Dialogic Time and *The Handmaid's Tale*." The Handmaid's Tale: *Margaret Atwood*. Ed. Marta Dvorak. Paris: Ellipses, 1998. 144-148.

2322. HERMANSSON, Casie Elizabeth. "Feminist Intertextuality and the Bluebeard Story." PhD thesis. University of Toronto, 1998. 286 pp. Also available on microfiche from Canadian Theses Service (1999) and as .pdf file: http://www.nlc-bnc.ca/obj/s4/f2/dsk2/tape15/PQDD_0004/NQ35183.pdf. Incorporates some aspects of *The Robber Bride*. For more see *DAI-A* 60.01 (July 1999): 139.

2323. HOWELLS, Coral Ann. "Dislocations in Dystopia." The Handmaid's Tale: *Margaret Atwood*. Ed. Marta Dvorak. Paris: Ellipses, 1998. 9-18.

2324. ———. *Margaret Atwood's* The Handmaid's Tale. Longman, 1998. 96 pp. Study notes.

2325. ———. "*Morning in the Burned House*: At Home in the Wilderness." *Margaret Atwood: The Shape Shifter*. Ed. Coomi S. Vevaina and Coral Ann Howells. New Delhi: Creative Books, 1998. [135]-145. Reprinted from *The Contact and the Culmination: Essays in Honour of Hena Maes-Jelinek*. Ed. Marc Delrez and Bénédicte Ledent. Liège: Liege Language and Literature, 1997. 69-78.

2326. ———. "Questions of Survival in *The Handmaid's Tale*." *Margaret Atwood*: The Handmaid's Tale / Le Conte de la servante: *The Power Game*. Ed. Jean-Michel Lacroix and Jacques Leclaire. Paris: Presses de la Sorbonne Nouvelle, 1998. 35-48.

2327. HULLEY, Kathleen. "Margaret Atwood and Leonard Cohen: The Feminine Voice." *Textes publiés sur Margaret Atwood dans Études canadiennes / Canadian Studies (1975-1997)*. [Ed.] Jean-Michel Lacroix. Talence [France]: Association française d'études canadiennes (A.F.E.C.), 1998. 17-22. More on Cohen's *Beautiful Losers* and Atwood's *Surfacing*. Reprinted from *Études canadiennes / Canadian Studies* 1 (1975): 73-78.

2328. HUNT, Lynn. "'No Longer an Evenly Flowing River': Time, History, and the Novel." *American Historical Review* 103.5 (1998): 1517-1521. Views on Atwood's thoughts about historical fiction.

2329. HUNTER, Lynette. "'That Will Never Do': Public History and Private Memory in *Nineteen Eighty-Four* and *The Handmaid's Tale*." The Handmaid's Tale: *Margaret Atwood*. Ed. Marta Dvorak. Paris: Ellipses, 1998. 19-29.

2330. INGERSOLL, Earl G. "Margaret Atwood's *The Handmaid's Tale* as a Self-Subverting Text." *Cultural Identities in Canadian Literature / Identités culturelles dans la littérature canadienne*. Ed. Marguiere Benedicte. New York: Peter Lang, 1998. 103-109. "The book problematizes the narrative desire by offering the reader a first-person narrative that suddenly stops with a historical note in a seemingly separate text. In essence, Atwood plays a narrative joke on her readers. This technique was reminiscent of George Orwell's Principle of Newspeak at the end of his novel, *1984*." (Journal).

2331. JACOB, Susan. "Woman, Ideology, Resistance: Margaret Atwood's *The Handmaid's Tale* and Third World Criticism." *Margaret Atwood: The Shape Shifter*. Ed. Coomi S. Vevaina and Coral Ann Howells. New Delhi: Creative Books, 1998. 26-43.

2332. JAMES, William Closson. *Locations of the Sacred: Essays on Religion, Literature, and Canadian Culture*. Waterloo, ON: Wilfrid Laurier UP, 1998. See especially Chapter 8: "Sacred Passages: Native Symbols in Atwood and Engel." 171-187. Study of *Surfacing* and Engel's *Bear*.

2333. JARRETT, Mary. "The Presentation of Montreal in Mavis Gallant's 'Between Zero and One' and of Toronto in Margaret Atwood's *Cat's Eye*." *Textes publiés sur Margaret Atwood dans Études canadiennes / Canadian Studies (1975-1997)*. [Ed.] Jean-Michel Lacroix. Talence [France]: Association française d'études canadiennes (A.F.E.C.), 1998. 93-101. Reprinted from *Études canadiennes / Canadian Studies* 29 (1990): 173-181.

2334. JONG, Nicole de. "Mirror Images in Margaret Atwood's *Cat's Eye*." *Nora: Nordic Journal of Women's Studies* 6.2 (1998): 97-107. "*Cat's Eye* is one of the many novels by Margaret Atwood which brings contemporary discussions concerning female subjectivity into focus. By concentrating on the complex mirror imagery in the novel, this article examines the way the female protagonist liberates herself from the gaze of her girlfriend, Cordelia. Referring to the work of Simone de

Beauvoir and Luce Irigaray, the many mirrors in *Cat's Eye* can be categorized as either flat or convex, each denoting a different type of perceiving the female self. Whereas flat mirrors frustrate the protagonist's attempts at defining herself, convex mirrors help her to come to a satisfactory definition." (Author).

2335. KOHLKE, M. L. "Imperfect Consummations: Aspects of Place and Time in the Short Stories of Anaïs Nin, Angela Carter, and Margaret Atwood." PhD thesis. University of Swansea (Wales), 1998.

2336. KRUK, Laurie. "Until We Are Like You: Reading Margaret Atwood's 'Statuary.'" *Newsletter of the Margaret Atwood Society* 21 (1998): 8, 15-16.

2337. KURJATTO-RENARD, Patrycja. "'I Am Like a Room Where Things Once Happened and Now Nothing Does': Houses and Interiors in Margaret Atwood's *The Handmaid's Tale*." The Handmaid's Tale: *Margaret Atwood*. Ed. Marta Dvorak. Paris: Ellipses, 1998. 88-102.

2338. LACROIX, Jean-Michel, [ed.]. *Textes publiés sur Margaret Atwood dans Études canadiennes / Canadian Studies (1975-1997)*. Talence [France]: Association française d'études canadiennes (A.F.E.C.), 1998. Individual entries indexed in this section.

2339. LACROIX, Jean-Michel, and Jacques LECLAIRE, eds. *Margaret Atwood*: The Handmaid's Tale / Le Conte de la servante: *The Power Game*. Paris: Presses de la Sorbonne Nouvelle, 1998. Individual articles are indexed in this section.

2340. LADOUSSE, Gillian. "Some Aspects of the Theme of Metamorphosis in Atwood's Poetry." *Textes publiés sur Margaret Atwood dans Études canadiennes / Canadian Studies (1975-1997)*. [Ed.] Jean-Michel Lacroix. Talence [France]: Association française d'études canadiennes (A.F.E.C.), 1998. 23-29. Reprinted from *Études canadiennes / Canadian Studies* 2 (1976): 71-77.

2341. LAMOUREUX, Cheryl Michelle Mary. "History as Hysterectomy: The Writing of Women's History in *The Handmaid's Tale* and *Ana Historic*." MA thesis. University of Manitoba, 1998. 73 pp. How the two novels represent phallogocentrism as a shaping force in Western society, most importantly in its history and language. For more see *MAI* 37.02 (April 1999): 437.

2342. LANGDON, Sandra. The Handmaid's Tale, *Margaret Atwood*. London: Letts Educational, 1998. 76 pp.

2343. LECLAIRE, Jacques. "De la dystopie à la métafiction dans *The Handmaid's Tale*." *Margaret Atwood:* The Handmaid's Tale / Le Conte de la servante: *The Power Game*. Ed. Jean-Michel Lacroix and Jacques Leclaire. Paris: Presses de la Sorbonne Nouvelle, 1998. 63-78.

2344. ———. "Féminisme et dystopie dans *The Handmaid's Tale* de Margaret Atwood." *Textes publiés sur Margaret Atwood dans Études canadiennes / Canadian Studies (1975-1997)*. [Ed.] Jean-Michel Lacroix. Talence [France]: Association française d'études canadiennes (A.F.E.C.), 1998. 71-80. Reprinted from *Études canadiennes / Canadian Studies* 21 (1986): 299-308.

2345. ———. "La metropole: Image du pouvoir dans les romans de Margaret Atwood." *Textes publiés sur Margaret Atwood dans Études canadiennes / Canadian Studies (1975-1997)*. [Ed.] Jean-Michel Lacroix. Talence [France]: Association française d'études canadiennes (A.F.E.C.), 1998. 103-110. Reprinted from *Études canadiennes / Canadian Studies* 30 (1991): 89-93.

2346. LEE, So-Hee. "A Study of *The Handmaid's Tale* Focused on the Representation of Sexuality and Intimacy." *Studies in Modern Fiction* 5.2 (1998): 183-204. In Korean; abstract in English.

214   ~ **1998** ~

2347. LIU, Cecilia H. C. "Folding the Time-Space Continuum: Atwood's *Cat's Eye* as Chronotopic Bildungsroman." *Canadian Culture and Literature and a Taiwan Perspective*. Ed. Steven Totosy-de-Zepetnek and Yiu-nam Leung. Edmonton: University of Alberta and the Department of Foreign Languages and Literature, National Tsing Hua University, 1998. 237-249.

2348. LLANTADA DÍAZ, María Francisca. "Language in Margaret Atwood's *Surfacing*." *Estudios de la mujer en el ámbito de los países de habla inglesa, III.* Ed. Ana Antón-Pacheco et al. Madrid, Spain: Universidad Complutense de Madrid, 1998. 107-116.

2349. LORRE, Christine. "The Interpolation of Narrative Sequences in *The Handmaid's Tale*." *Lectures d'une oeuvre*: The Handmaid's Tale *de Margaret Atwood*. [Ed.] Jean-Paul Gabilliet and François Gallix. Paris: Éditions du temps, 1998. 175-186.

2350. LOUVEL, Liliane. "Les Secrets de la servante." The Handmaid's Tale*: Margaret Atwood*. Ed. Marta Dvorak. Paris: Ellipses, 1998. 131-143.

2351. MacFARLANE, Karen. "'Fence-Climbing Sisterhood': Reading the 'Escaped Nun' Intertext of *The Handmaid's Tale*." *Q/W/E/R/T/Y/ 8* (1998): 181-188.

2352. ———. "The Politics of Self Narration: Contemporary Canadian Women Writers, Feminist Theory and Metafictional Strategies." PhD thesis. McGill University, 1998. 289 pp. Also available on microfiche from Canadian Theses Service (2000) and in .pdf format: http://www.nlc-bnc.ca/obj/s4/f2/dsk1/tape11/PQDD_0016/NQ44504.pdf. Emphasis on *Cat's Eye* and *The Handmaid's Tale*. For more see *DAI-A* 60.12 (June 2000): 4436.

2353. MacKEY, Melodie Anne. "The Female Hero." MA thesis. California State University, Dominguez Hills, 1998. 76 pp. "This thesis demonstrates the difference between the male monomyth as described by Joseph Campbell and the emerging female monomyth as put forward by Carol Christ, Annis Pratt, Maureen Murdock, and other feminist writers and critics....I applied my female monomyth model to two novels by women authors. In this comparison, I determined why one woman character's rebirth quest fails, as in *The Awakening* by Kate Chopin, and why another woman character's rebirth quest succeeds, as in *Surfacing* by Margaret Atwood. From this, I concluded that in order to complete their journeys, women characters must follow a quest pattern formulated specifically for female heroes based on their unique experiences as women." (Author). For more see *MAI* 36.05 (October 1988): 1287.

2354. MARI, Catherine. "Temps et dystopie dans *The Handmaid's Tale*." *Q/W/E/R/T/Y* 8 (1998): 189-194.

2355. MARTYNIUK, Irene. "The Role of Autobiography in Margaret Atwood's *Surfacing*." Harrod Lecture Series 16 (1997-1998): 79-97. This is a reprint of a lecture delivered 29 April 1998 at Fitchburg State College, MA.

2356. MASSOURA, Kiriaki. "'My Body ... a Desert Island ... Your Body ... Marred by War': The Female Body as Space and the Male Body as Time in Margaret Atwood's 'Circe/Mud' Poems." *Manuscript: Graduate Journal in English* 3.1 (1998): 5-23. Published by the University of Manchester.

2357. McLEAN, Barbara. "Women Writing, Women Teaching: Speculating on Domestic Space." *Canadian Woman Studies / Les cahiers de la femme* 17.4 (1998): 94-97. Includes discussion of *The Handmaid's Tale*.

2358. METZGER, Lore. "Atwood's *Robber Bride:* At the Borders of Feminist Narrative." *Lyrical Symbols and Narrative Transformations: Essays in Honor of Ralph*

Freedman. Ed. Kathleen L. Komar and Ross Shideler. Columbia: Camden House, 1998. 204-217.

2359. MOHR, Dunja. "The Split Self in Margaret Atwood's Female Dystopia *The Handmaid's Tale.*" *Selbst und Andere/s oder Von Begegnungen und Grenzziehungen.* Ed. Christina Strobel and Doris Eibl. Augsburg: Wißneer, 1998. 110-123.

2360. MORIN-OLLIER, Priscilla. "The Moral Government of God in Gilead." *Lectures d'une oeuvre:* The Handmaid's Tale *de Margaret Atwood.* [Ed.] Jean-Paul Gabilliet and François Gallix. Paris: Éditions du temps, 1998. 15-26.

2361. MOSS, Laura Frances Errington. "'An Infinity of Alternate Realities': Reconfiguring Realism in Postcolonial Theory and Fiction." PhD Queen's University, 1998. 198 pp. Also available on microfiche from Canadian Theses Service (1999) and as .pdf file: http://www.nlc-bnc.ca/obj/s4/f2/dsk2/tape15/PQDD_0004/NQ31944.pdf. Chapter Four looks at realism in Canada through an exploration of *Alias Grace* and Alice Munro's story "A Wilderness Station." For more see *DAI-A* 59.10 (April 1999): 3814.

2362. MUNDT, Hannelore. "Anpassung und Widerstand bei Doris Lessing, Margaret Atwood und Christa Wolf." *Orbis Litterarum: International Review of Literary Studies* 53.3 (1998): 191-211. In German. English title: "Adaptation and Resistance in the Works of Doris Lessing, Margaret Atwood and Christa Wolf." Includes discussion of Lessing's *Memoirs of a Survivor*, Atwood's *The Handmaid's Tale*, and Wolf's *Sommerstück*.

2363. MURRAY, Jennifer. "'The End of the World': Desire and Desolation in Margaret Atwood's 'The Grave of the Famous Poet.'" *Journal of the Short Story in English* 31 (1998): 23-35.

2364. ———. La vérité en question: Discours réflexif et subversion dans *The Handmaid's Tale.*" The Handmaid's Tale: *Margaret Atwood.* Ed. Marta Dvorak. Paris: Ellipses, 1998. 51-59.

2365. MYCAK, Sonia. "Psychoanalysis, Phenomenology, and the Novels of Margaret Atwood: A New Critical Approach." *Margaret Atwood*: The Handmaid's Tale / Le Conte de la servante: *The Power Game.* Ed. Jean-Michel Lacroix and Jacques Leclaire. Paris: Presses de la Sorbonne Nouvelle, 1998. 127-145.

2366. NADER, Elizabeth. "Walking Among Shadows." MA thesis. Northern Michigan University, 1998. 72 pp. Chiefly short stories influenced by Atwood and Alice Munro.

2367. NORRIS, Pamela. *The Story of Eve.* London: Picador, 1998. Draws on Atwood to show how ideas of the Biblical Eve have expressed themselves in literature.

2368. OLTARZEWSKA, Jagna. "Telling Stories: Resistance to World Reduction in *The Handmaid's Tale.*" The Handmaid's Tale: *Margaret Atwood.* Ed. Marta Dvorak. Paris: Ellipses, 1998. 30-39.

2369. ———. "Trauma and Testimony: The Status of Witnessing in Margaret Atwood's *The Handmaid's Tale.*" *Q/W/E/R/T/Y* 8 (1998): 195-202.

2370. OMHOVÈRE, Claire. "*The Handmaid's Tale* ou l'emprise des signes." *Lectures d'une oeuvre:* The Handmaid's Tale *de Margaret Atwood.* [Ed.] Jean-Paul Gabilliet and François Gallix. Paris: Éditions du temps, 1998. 89-102.

2371. OSBORNE, Brian S. "Some Thoughts on Landscape: Is It a Noun, a Metaphor, or a Verb?" *Canadian Social Studies* 32.3 (1998): 93-97. *Cat's Eye* used to make the case.

2372. OSBORNE, Carol Dale. "Visiting the Past: Narratives of Recovery." PhD thesis. University of Virginia, 1998. 221 pp. Analyses novels of Atwood, Stephen King,

Barbara Kingsolver, Dennis McFarland, and Jane Smiley in context of recovered memory syndrome. For more see *DAI-A* 59.07 (January 1999): 2508.

2373. PAINTER, Rebecca Miriam. "Attending to Evil: Fiction, Apperception, and the Growth of Consciousness." PhD thesis. New York University, 1998. 275 pp. Explores the subtleties and apperception of evil—by characters and readers—in novels by Iris Murdoch, Margaret Atwood, and Alice Walker. Focuses on *Cat's Eye* and *The Robber Bride*. For more see *DAI-A* 59.05 (November 1998): 1563.

2374. PAOLI, Marie-Lise. "Fécondité et stérilité dans *The Handmaid's Tale*: La terre gaste de Galaad." *Lectures d'une oeuvre*: The Handmaid's Tale *de Margaret Atwood*. [Ed.] Jean-Paul Gabilliet and François Gallix. Paris: Éditions du temps, 1998. 53-70.

2375. PAULS, Leina Marie. "[Not] Wanted in the Canon: A Study of the Impact of Literary Criticism upon Margaret Atwood's *The Handmaid's Tale* and Timothy Findley's *Not Wanted on the Voyage*." MA thesis. University of Arkansas–Fayetteville, 1998. 89 pp.

2376. PAVLISH, Catherine Ann. "The Uncertainty Principle and Certain Uncertain Writers: Melville, Dickinson, Woolf, Atwood and Others." PhD thesis. University of North Dakota, 1998. 589 pp. In 1927, Werner Heisenberg's Uncertainty Principle demonstrated that in any experiment, the observer always has some kind of effect upon the thing being observed; thus, Heisenberg complicated the boundaries that had been drawn between scientific objectivity and personal subjectivity, a position that has led to a more uncertain knowledge of the world. Within this context, part of this study examines the sexual uncertainty (and sex role uncertainty) in some contemporary heterosexual women in Atwood's works, among others. For more see *DAI-A* 59.05 (November 1998): 1586.

2377. PEEPRE, Mari. "Searching for Zenia: Time, Space, and the Mystery of *The Robber Bride*." *British Journal of Canadian Studies* 13.2 (1998): 317-326.

2378. PESSO-MIQUEL, Catherine. "See[ing] the World in Gasps: La Vision tronquée dans *The Handmaid's Tale*." *Lectures d'une oeuvre:* The Handmaid's Tale *de Margaret Atwood*. [Ed.] Jean-Paul Gabilliet and François Gallix. Paris: Éditions du temps, 1998. 103-122.

2379. PHELPS, Henry C. "Atwood's *Edible Woman* and *Surfacing*." *Explicator* 55.2 (1998): 112-114.

2380. PORTER-LADOUSSE, Gillian. "Time Past, Time Dystopian, Time Future." *Lectures d'une oeuvre:* The Handmaid's Tale *de Margaret Atwood*. [Ed.] Jean-Paul Gabilliet and François Gallix. Paris: Éditions du temps, 1998. 81-88.

2381. POTTS, Donna. "The White Goddess Displaced: National/Sexual Parallels in Atwood's *The Robber Bride*." *Literature of Region and Nation: Proceedings of the 6th International Literature of Region and Nation Conference University of New Brunswick in Saint John, Saint John New Brunswick, Canada, 2-7 August 1996*. Vol. 2. Ed. Winnifred M. Bogaards. Saint John: University of New Brunswick in Saint John, 1998. 230-238.

2382. POULAIN, Alexandra. "'Blessed Be the Silent': La communication dans *The Handmaid's Tale*." *Lectures d'une oeuvre*: The Handmaid's Tale *de Margaret Atwood*. [Ed.] Jean-Paul Gabilliet and François Gallix. Paris: Éditions du temps, 1998. 161-174.

2383. PROVENCAL, Vernon. "'Byzantine in the Extreme': Plato's Republic in *The Handmaid's Tale*." *Classical and Modern Literature: A Quarterly* 19.1 (1998): 53-76.

2384. RAMAIYA, Nita. "A Female Non-Being Emerging into a Being: A Feminist Approach to *The Journals of Susanna Moodie.*" *Margaret Atwood: The Shape Shifter.* Ed. Coomi S. Vevaina and Coral Ann Howells. New Delhi: Creative Books, 1998. [114]-125.

2385. RAO, Eleonora. "Language, Sexuality, Displacement: *Surfacing, Bluebeard's Egg, Life Before Man.*" *Margaret Atwood: The Shape Shifter.* Ed. Coomi S. Vevaina and Coral Ann Howells. New Delhi: Creative Books, 1998. [44]-55.

2386. RAVICHANDRA, C. P. "Memories of Resistance [sic]: Reading *Cat's Eye.*" *Margaret Atwood: The Shape Shifter.* Ed. Coomi S. Vevaina and Coral Ann Howells. New Delhi: Creative Books, 1998. [56]-63.

2387. REICHENBACHER, Helmut. "Reading Hidden Layers: A Genetic Analysis of the Drafts of Margaret Atwood's Novels *The Edible Woman* and *Bodily Harm.* PhD thesis. University of Toronto. 1998. 351 pp. Also available on microfiche from Canadian Theses Service (2000) and in .pdf format: http://www.nlc-bnc.ca /obj/s4/f2/dsk1/tape11/PQDD_0008/NQ41492.pdf. "Margaret Atwood's creative technique as a novelist is the subject of this thesis, which considers two of her novels, *The Edible Woman* (1969) and *Bodily Harm* (1981). The dissertation investigates Atwood's process of writing, from the earliest extant drafts of the novels to the final, published product. Genetic criticism, the methodology applied in analysing the manuscript material, studies textual versions without privileging a 'best' or definitive version." (Author). For more see *DAI-A* 60.10 (April 2000): 3661.

2388. ROGERSON, Margaret. "Reading the Patchworks in *Alias Grace.*" *Journal of Commonwealth Literature* 33.1 (1998): 5-22. A reading of the novel situating it within the cultural and literary history of patchwork.

2389. ROTH, Verena Bühler. *Wilderness and the Natural Environment: Margaret Atwood's Recycling of a Canadian Theme.* Tübingen; Basel: Francke Verlag, 1998. Originally a doctoral dissertation at the University of Zürich.

2390. SARBADHIKARY, Krishna. "Signifying Authority: The Short Stories of Margaret Atwood and Audrey Thomas." *Margaret Atwood: The Shape Shifter.* Ed. Coomi S. Vevaina and Coral Ann Howells. New Delhi: Creative Books, 1998. [82]-98.

2391. SCHAUB, Danielle. "'I Am a Place': Internalised Landscape and Female Subjectivity in Margaret Atwood's *Surfacing.*" *Mapping Canadian Cultural Space: Essays on Canadian Literature.* Ed. Danielle Schaub. Jerusalem: Magnes, 1998. 83-103.

2392. SMITH, Rowland. "Expected and Inverted Response: Righteousness and Fallibility in *The Handmaid's Tale.*" *Margaret Atwood*: The Handmaid's Tale / Le Conte de la servante: *The Power Game.* Ed. Jean-Michel Lacroix and Jacques Leclaire. Paris: Presses de la Sorbonne Nouvelle, 1998. 117-125.

2393. SOLECKI, Sam, ed. *Imagining Canadian Literature: The Selected Letters of Jack McClelland.* Toronto: Key Porter Books, 1998. Includes letters from McClelland to Atwood, in one of which he apologizes to Atwood for mislaying the manuscript to *The Edible Woman* for two years.

2394. SPENCE, Jonathan D. "Margaret Atwood and the Edges of History." *American Historical Review* 193.5 (1998): 1522-1525. Response to Atwood's Bronfman Lecture on Canadian historical fiction.

2395. SPRIET, Pierre. "L'homme de *Lady Oracle.*" *Textes publiés sur Margaret Atwood dans Études canadiennes / Canadian Studies (1975-1997).* [Ed.] Jean-Michel Lacroix. Talence [France]: Association française d'études canadiennes (A.F.E.C.),

1998. 59-69. Reprinted from *Études canadiennes / Canadian Studies* 9 (1980): 63-73.

2396. STABLEFORD, Brian. *Slaves of the Death Spider: Essays on Fantastic Literature*. San Bernardino, CA: Borgo Press, 1998. See especially Chapter 2, "Is There No Balm in Gilead? The Woeful Prophesies of *The Handmaid's Tale* (followed by a letter of comment by Gwyneth Jones)," 17-24.

2397. STAELS, Hilde. "The Eclipse of 'the Other Voice': Margaret Atwood's *The Handmaid's Tale*." *Q/W/E/R/T/Y* 8 (1998): 203-206.

2398. STAPLES, Joseph Perry. "'In the Hands of Nature': Remaking the Self in Novels by Marilynne Robinson, Margaret Atwood, and Linda Hogen." MA thesis. Utah State University, 1998. 100 pp. *Surfacing* is included in study which analyzes how contemporary women writers use landscape in their fiction. For more see *MAI* 37.01 (February 1999): 61.

2399. STILLMAN, Peter G. "Public and Private in Margaret Atwood's *The Handmaid's Tale* and *Bodily Harm*." *Q/W/E/R/T/Y* 8 (1998): 207-215.

2400. STURGESS, Charlotte. "The Female Body as Representation and Performance in Margaret Atwood's *The Handmaid's Tale*." The Handmaid's Tale: *Margaret Atwood*. Ed. Marta Dvorak. Paris: Ellipses, 1998. 69-76.

2401. ———. "Female Dystopia in *The Handmaid's Tale*: The Body, The Word and Transgressive Words." *Lectures d'une oeuvre:* The Handmaid's Tale *de Margaret Atwood*. [Ed.] Jean-Paul Gabilliet and François Gallix. Paris: Éditions du temps, 1998. 71-80.

2402. ———. "Text and Territory in Margaret Atwood's 'Unearthing Suite.'" *Textes publiés sur Margaret Atwood dans Études canadiennes / Canadian Studies (1975-1997)*. [Ed.] Jean-Michel Lacroix. Talence [France]: Association française d'études canadiennes (A.F.E.C.), 1998. 111-117. Reprinted from *Études canadiennes / Canadian Studies* 31 (1991): 81-87.

2403. SULLIVAN, Rosemary. "Alias Margaret: The Radcliffe Years." *Saturday Night* 113.5 (1998): 54-59. Excerpt from *The Red Shoes*.

2404. ———. *The Red Shoes: Margaret Atwood Starting Out*. Toronto: Harper-FlamingoCanada; New York: HarperCollins World; London: Hi Marketing, 1998.

2405. ———. "The Writer Bride." *Saturday Night* 113.6 (1998): 56-62. Excerpt from *The Red Shoes*.

2406. TUHKUNEN-COUZIC, Taïna. "Stratégies de scrabbleuse dans *The Handmaid's Tale*." The Handmaid's Tale: *Margaret Atwood*. Ed. Marta Dvorak. Paris: Ellipses, 1998. 149-155.

2407. TURCOTTE, Gerry. "Response: Venturing into Undiscoverable Countries: Reading Ondaatje, Malouf, Atwood and Jia in an Asia-Pacific Context." *Australian–Canadian Studies: A Journal for the Humanities & Social Sciences* 15, 16.2, 1 (1997-1998): 65-72.

2408. TYLER, Lisa. "'I Just Don't Understand It': Teaching Margaret Atwood's 'Rape Fantasies.'" *Teaching English in the Two-Year College* 25 (February 1998): 51-57.

2409. VALENTINE, Susan Elizabeth. "The Protagonist's Response to Power and Language in the Dystopian Novel." MA thesis. McMaster University, 1998. 85 pp. *The Handmaid's Tale* studied.

2410. VAN VUREN, Dalene. "The Seduction of Genre: A Study of Organic Narrative Techniques in the Novels of Margaret Atwood." PhD thesis. University of Pretoria, South Africa, 1998. "This thesis is a study of the organic narrative techniques used by Atwood to imbue her novels with a certain dynamism and originality. The study focuses on Atwood's manipulation of conventional form: on her 'seduction of genre.' Atwood employs traditional forms such as the thriller, the Gothic novel and science fiction which she then subverts to break their prescriptive moulds of stasis. Traditionally male dominated genres such as the thriller, science fiction or history are presented by Atwood from a female perspective which represents the unconscious. Atwood does not suggest that female perspectives are superior, but that a balance be achieved between the masculine conscious and feminine unconscious components of the self so that individuation results." (Author). For more see *DAI-A* 60.01 (July 1999): 137.

2411. VENTURA, Héliane. *Margaret Atwood*: The Handmaid's Tale. Paris: Éd. Messene, 1998. Texts in English and French.

2412. VEVAINA, Coomi S. "Quilting Selves: Interpreting Margaret Atwood's *Alias Grace*." *Margaret Atwood: The Shape Shifter*. Ed. Coomi S. Vevaina and Coral Ann Howells. New Delhi: Creative Books, 1998. [64]-74.

2413. ———. "So It Has Been Done: So It Shall Be Done—Archetypal Patterns in Margaret Atwood's *The Handmaid's Tale*." *Lectures d'une oeuvre:* The Handmaid's Tale *de Margaret Atwood*. [Ed.] Jean-Paul Gabilliet and François Gallix. Paris: Éditions du temps, 1998. 135-144.

2414. VEVAINA, Coomi S., and Coral Ann HOWELLS, eds. *Margaret Atwood: The Shape-Shifter*. New Delhi: Creative Books, 1998. Each article in this book has been indexed in this section.

2415. VINET, Dominique. "'Pen Is Envy' in Margaret Atwood's *The Handmaid's Tale*." *Lectures d'une oeuvre:* The Handmaid's Tale *de Margaret Atwood*. [Ed.] Jean-Paul Gabilliet and François Gallix. Paris: Éditions du temps, 1998. 145-160.

2416. ———. "La systémique du fantasme dans *The Handmaid's Tale*." *Margaret Atwood:* The Handmaid's Tale / Le Conte de la servante: *The Power Game*. Ed. Jean-Michel Lacroix and Jacques Leclaire. Paris: Presses de la Sorbonne Nouvelle, 1998. 147-167.

2417. WANG, Yiyan. "Language, Time and Introspection: Margaret Atwood and Jia Pingwa." *Australian–Canadian Studies: A Journal for the Humanities & Social Sciences* 15, 16.2, 1 (1997-1998): 13-41. Language's relationship to cultural identity in P'ing-wa and Atwood. [Ed. note: This journal has is a very unusual numbering system—but it is, as far as can be verified, accurate.]

2418. WHALEN-BRIDGE, John. *Political Fiction and the American Self*. Urbana: University of Illinois Press, 1998. Final chapter focuses on *The Handmaid's Tale*.

2419. WILKINS, Peter. "Defense of the Realm: Canada's Relationship to the United States in Margaret Atwood's *Surfacing*." *REAL: The Yearbook of Research in English and American Literature* 14 (1998): 205-222.

2420. WILSON, Sharon R. "Beyond Colonization: *The Handmaid's Tale* as a Postmodern and Postcolonial Metafiction." The Handmaid's Tale: *Margaret Atwood*. Ed. Marta Dvorak. Paris: Ellipses, 1998. 125-130.

2421. WYATT, Jean. "I Want to Be You: Envy, the Lacanian Double, and Feminist Community in Margaret Atwood's *The Robber Bride*." *Tulsa Studies in Women's Literature* 17.1 (1998): 37-64. The novel as a tale of envy.

2422. YORK NOTES. The Handmaid's Tale. Harlow: Longman, 1998. Study guide.

2423. ZIMMERMANN, Hannelore. *Erscheinungsformen der Macht in den Romanen Margaret Atwoods*. [Manifestations of Power in the Novels of Margaret Atwood]. Frankfurt am Main; New York: P. Lang, 1998. In German.

Reviews of Atwood's Works

2424. *Alias Grace*. Toronto: McClelland and Stewart, 1996.
  Booklist 94.9/10 (1998): 872. By Sue-Ellen BEAUREGARD.
  Canadian Literature 156 (Spring 1998): 110-112. By Aritha Van HERK.
  Hudson Review 50.4 (1998): 661-662. By W. H. PRITCHARD.

2425. *Captive.* Paris: Laffont, 1998. [*Alias Grace*]
  Chatelaine (Fr), 39.7 (1998): 20. *Nuit Blanche* 73 (Winter 1998-99): 10.
    By Jean-Paul BEAUMIER.
  Spirale 163 (November-December 1998): 17. By Francine BORDELEAU.

2426. *Deux Sollicitudes: Entretiens*. Trois-Pistoles, QC: Éditions Trois-Pistoles, 1996.
  University of Toronto Quarterly 67.1 (Winter 1997-98): 503-507. By André
    LAMONTAGNE.

2427. *Journals of Susanna Moodie*. Toronto: Macfarlane, Walter & Ross, 1997.
  Ottawa Citizen 24 January 1998: J3. By Charlotte GRAY.
  Virginia Quarterly Review 74.2 (Spring 1998): 66. ANON.

2428. *Morning in the Burned House*. London: Virago, 1995.
  Prairie Schooner 72.1 (Spring 1998): 183-185. By Dale JACOBS.

2429. *A Quiet Game and Other Early Works.* Ed. Kathy CHUNG and Sherrill GRACE.
  Edmonton: Juvenilia Press, 1997.
  Canadian Children's Literature 24.3/4 (1998): 158-160. By Elaine OSTRY.
    Review focuses on Juvenilia Press.
  Newsletter of the Margaret Atwood Society 21 (Fall-Winter 1998): 16-17.
    By Janice RIEMAN.

2430. *Strange Things: The Malevolent North in Canadian Literature*. Oxford: Oxford
  UP, 1996.
  Archiv fur das Studium der Neueren Sprachen und Literaturen 235.1 (1998):
    199-201. By W. PACHE.

2431. *Two Solicitudes: Conversations.* By Margaret Atwood and Victor-Lévy Beaulieu.
  Translated by Phyllis Aronoff and Howard Scott. Toronto: McClelland and Stew-
  art, 1998.
  The Gazette (Montreal) 27 June 1998: J5. By Bronwyn CHESTER.
  The Gazette (Montreal) 17 October 1998: J3. By Ian McGILLIS.
  Globe and Mail 11 July 1998: D10. By Ray CONLOGUE.
  Ottawa Citizen 17 May 1998: E4. By David HOMEL.
  Quill & Quire 64.5 (May 1998): 23. By Carolyne A. VAN DER MEER.
  Toronto Star 11 July 1998: K16. By Philip MARCHAND.
  Vancouver Sun 11 July 1998: G5. By Mark HARRIS.

~ 1999 ~

Atwood's Works

2432. "3 Moons." *Canada's Century: An Illustrated History of the People and Events That Shaped Our Identity.* Ed. Carl Mollins. Toronto: Key Porter Books, 1999. 284. Poem reprinted from *Maclean's,* 1969. Book contains several other references to Atwood's work.

2433. *Alias Grace.* Toronto: McClelland and Stewart, 1999. Trade paperback edition.

2434. *Alias Grace.* Hamburg: Petersen, 1999. In English.

2435. *Asesinato en la oscuridad.* Oviedo [Spain]: KRK, 1999. Spanish translation of stories from *Murder in the Dark* and other works by Isabel Carrera Suárez.

2436. "Asparagas." *How to Read a Poem ... and Start a Poetry Circle.* By Molly Peacock. Toronto: McClelland and Stewart; New York: Riverhead Books, 1999. 149-151. Reprinted from *Morning in the Burned House,* ©1995.

2437. "At First I Was Given Centuries." *Her War Story: Twentieth-Century Women Write about War.* Ed. Sayre P. Sheldon. Carbondale, IL: Southern Illinois UP, 1999. 297-298. Reprinted from *Selected Poems,* ©1976.

2438. "Best Utopia: God Is in the Details." *New York Times Magazine* 18 April 1999: Section 6: 94. Atwood comments on the utopian society of the Shakers in the 19th century.

2439. *Bluebeard's Egg.* Toronto: Seal Books, 1999.

2440. *Bluebeard's Egg.* Toronto: McClelland and Stewart, 1999. Trade paperback edition.

2441. "Bluebeard's Egg." *The Oxford Book of Stories by Canadian Women in English.* Ed. Rosemary Sullivan. Don Mills: Oxford UP, 1999. 269-291. Also in *The Classic Fairy Tales: Texts, Criticism.* Ed. Maria Tatar. New York: Norton, 1999. 156-178. Reprinted from the short story collection of same name (1983), McClelland and Stewart.

2442. "A Boat." *Evoluzioni: Poeti Anglofoni e Francofoni Del Canada.* Ed. Claudia Gasparini and Marina Zito. Naples: Libreria Dante & Descartes Universitaria, 1999. 118.

2443. *Bodily Harm.* Toronto: Seal Books, 1999.

2444. *Captive.* Paris: Laffont, 1999 ©1998. French translation of *Alias Grace* by Michèle Albaret-Maatsch. Paperback.

2445. *Cat's Eye.* Toronto: Seal Books, 1999 ©1988.

2446. *Cat's Eye.* [Sound recording]. Read by Doreen Odling. Vancouver, BC: Crane Resource Centre, 1999. 12 tape reels.

2447. *Dancing Girls and Other Stories.* Toronto: Seal Books, 1999.

2448. "Death by Landscape." *The Scribner Anthology of Contemporary Short Fiction: Fifty North American Stories since 1970.* Ed. Lex Williford and Michael Martone. New York: Scribner Paperback Fiction, 1999. 31-45.

2449. "Der Norden ist in unserem Kopf. Immer." *Kanadas Osten.* Hamburg: Merian, 1999. 30-46.

2450. *Die Giftmischer: Horror-Trips Und Happy-Ends.* Düsseldorf: Claassen, 1999. German translation of *Murder in the Dark* by Anna Kamp.

2451. *Die Unmöglichkeit Der Nähe.* Düsseldorf: Claassen, 1999. German translation of *Life Before Man* by Werner Waldhoff.

2452. *Eating Fire: Selected Poetry, 1965-1995.* London: Virago, 1999.

2453. *The Edible Woman.* Toronto: McClelland and Stewart, 1999. Trade paperback edition.

2454. "El Look Grunge / The Grunge Look." *Tameme: New Writing from North America / Nueva Literatura de Norteamérica.* Ed. C. M. Mayo. Los Altos, CA: Tameme, 1999. 70-87. Article appears both in Spanish and English. Reprinted from *Writing Away: The PEN Canada Travel Anthology,* ©1994.

2455. *El pene ha-mayim.* [Tel Aviv]: Kineret, 1999. Hebrew translation of *Surfacing* by Tamar Shtainits.

2456. "An Encyclopedia of Lost Practices: The Saturday Night Date." *New York Times* 6 December 1999: Section 6: 148. Dating in the 1950s explained. (426 w).

2457. "Euridyce." *Evoluzioni: Poeti Anglofoni e Francofoni Del Canada.* Ed. Claudia Gasparini and Marina Zito. Naples: Libreria Dante & Descartes Universitaria, 1999. 128.

2458. "[Excerpt]." *Architectural Digest* 56.4 (1999): 62. In the article entitled "Voices in the Twentieth Century: Writers on Subjects Close to Home," authors who had written previously for this publication are excerpted. Atwood's is from "Summers on Canada's Rideau Canal." *Architectural Digest* June 1988: 84, 88, 90-91.

2459. "[Excerpt]." *Baltimore Sun* 3 November 1999: Section: Today: 8E. Excerpt from *Princess Prunella and the Purple Peanut.* (816 w).

2460. "[Excerpt]." *Edmonton Journal* 8 August 1999: B1. An excerpt from stories published by Juvenilia Press: "The little boy went quietly to his room. He shut the door softly and moved with muffled steps across the thick grey carpet to his bed. He climbed up on the bed and with a strangly [sic] concentrated energy pounded the side of his head silently, furiously against the wooded bed-post. His face was set in the determination of habitual action. He could feel the pain increase and spread: it was a relief, a release." From *The Quiet Game* by Atwood as a teenager.

2461. "[Excerpt]." *Index on Censorship* 28.2 (1999): 157. From *The Handmaid's Tale.*

2462. "Foreword." *Flare Magazine Presents Made in Canada;* Photographs by Bryan Adams. Toronto: Key Porter, 1999. s.p. Black-and-white photographs of 89 Canadian women including Atwood taken by rock star Adams in support of the Canadian Breast Cancer Foundation. Volume unpaged.

2463. "Forgotten Treasures." *Los Angeles Times* 26 December 1999: Section: Book Review: 2. In a series in which writers are asked to share a "neglected classic," a book they love but which, for one reason or another has yet to find the readers it deserves, Atwood writes about *Doctor Glas,* a "short, astonishing novel by Hjalmar Soderberg, which was first published in Sweden in 1905 and caused a scandal because of its handling of sex and death, not to mention abortion and euthanasia."

2464. "Freeforall." *Northern Suns.* Ed. David G. Harwell and Glenn Grant. New York: Tor Books, 1999. 17-24. In this sci-fi collection, Atwood foresees another reactionary society not too far removed from that of *The Handmaid's Tale*—one in which rampant sexual disease leads to arranged matings and contract marriages brokered by post-feminist "house-mothers." "Reprinted from the *Toronto Star* and later in *Tesseracts* (1987. Ed. Douglas Barbour)."

2465. "Genesis of *The Handmaid's Tale* and Role of Historical Notes." The Handmaid's Tale, *Roman Protéen*. Textes réunis by Jean-Michel Lacroix, Jacques Leclaire, and Jack Warwick. Mont-Saint-Aignan: Publications de l'Université de Rouen, 1999. 7-14. Followed by a Roundtable, 15-24.

2466. "Good Housekeeping." *New York Times Magazine* 16 May 1999: Section 6: 164. Atwood discusses the history of advice books and women's magazine articles by such experts as Fannie Farmer, Betty Crocker, and Martha Stewart and traces their origin to the rise of a literate middle class in the 19th century and Isabella Beeton's *Beeton's Book of Household Management*. Reprinted as "Mrs. Beeton: The Original Martha Stewart" in *Ottawa Citizen* 18 May 1999: A12.

2467. *Grace i Grace*. Warsaw: Noir sur blanc, 1999. Polish translation of *Alias Grace* by Aldona Biala.

2468. *Greis*. Vilnius [Lithuania]: Tyto alba, 1999. Lithuanian translation of *Alias Grace* by Valdas V. Petrauskas.

2469. *The Handmaid's Tale*. Toronto: McClelland and Stewart, 1999. Trade paperback edition.

2470. "*The Handmaid's Tale*: A Feminist Dystopia." *Lire Margaret Atwood* The Handmaid's Tale. Ed. Marta Dvorak. Rennes, France: Presses universitaires de Rennes, 1999. 17-30. Address delivered in Rennes, 17 November 1998, followed by a question-and-answer period.

2471. "Haunted by Their Nightmares." *Toni Morrison's* Beloved: *Modern Critical Interpretations*. Ed. Harold Bloom. Philadelphia: Chelsea House, 1999. 5-9. Review reprinted from *The New York Times Book Review* 13 September 1987.

2472. "In Love with Raymond Chandler." *New Oxford Book of English Prose*. Ed. John Gross. Oxford; New York: Oxford UP, 1999. 972-973. Excerpt from *Good Bones*, ©1992.

2473. "In Praise of Shields: Hilarious Surfaces, Ominous Depths." *National Post* 22 October 1999: A19. Transcript of Atwood's comments during the "Salute to Carol Shields" held during the International Festival of Authors. (672 w). An excerpt from the speech is also available in the *Globe and Mail* 23 October 1999: D4.

2474. "Interlunar." *Evoluzioni: Poeti Anglofoni e Francofoni Del Canada*. Ed. Claudia Gasparini and Marina Zito. Naples: Libreria Dante & Descartes Universitaria, 1999. 124.

2475. "Islands of the Mind." *Women Travel: First-Hand Accounts of More Than 60 Countries*. Ed. Natania Jansz, Miranda Davies, Emma Drew, and Lori McDougall. 4th ed. London: Rough Guides, 1999. 169-180. Atwood travels around Ecuador's Galápagos Islands with her parents. Reprinted from *Without a Guide*, ©1994.

2476. *Ke yi chi de nu ren*. Shanghai: Shanghai yi wen chu ban she, 1999. Chinese translation of *The Edible Woman* by Liu Kai Fang Yi. Title romanized.

2477. *La petite poule rouge vide son coeur: Nouvelles*. Paris: Le Serpent à plumes, 1999. French translation of *Good Bones* by Hélène Filion. Based on the Quebec edition published as *La troisième main*. Lachine, QU: La Pleine lune, ©1995.

2478. "The Labrador Fiasco." *Turn of the Story: Canadian Short Fiction on the Eve of the Millennium*. Ed. Joan Thomas and Heidi Harms. Toronto: Anansi, 1999. 1-13.

2479. *Lady Oracle*. Toronto: Seal Books, 1999.

2480. *Lady Orakel: Roman.* Munich: BTB, 1999. German translation of *Lady Oracle* by Werner Waldhoff.

2481. *Le cercle vicieux.* Montréal: Éditions de Noroît; Sudbury: Prise de parole, 1999. French translation of *The Circle Game* by Anik de Repentigny.

2482. *Le uova di Barbablù.* Milan: Baldini & Castoldi, 1999. Italian translation of *Blue-beard's Egg* by Francesca Avanzini.

2483. *Luna nueva.* Barcelona: Icarus, 1999. Spanish translation of Atwood poetry by Luis Marigómez.

2484. *Margaret Atwood Omnibus.* London: Little, Brown, 1999. Contents: *Wilderness Tips* and *Cat's Eye.*

2485. *Modrobrada.* Zagreb [Croatia]: Znanje, 1999. Croatian translation of *The Robber Bride* by Giga Gracan.

2486. *New Oxford Book of Canadian Short Stories.* Toronto: CNIB, 1999. Braille ed., 8 v. (1207 pp.) of computer braille. Co-edited with Robert Weaver. Contains "Intro-duction" by Atwood and "True Trash." Originally published in *Wilderness Tips.* Based on 1995 title.

2487. *Okaleczenie ciala.* Poznan [Poland]: Zysk i S-ka, 1999. Polish translation of *Bod-ily Harm* by Maria Zborowska.

2488. "On 'Waking at 3 A.M.'" *Poets Reading: The FIELD Symposia.* Ed. David Walker. Oberlin, OH: Oberlin College Press, 1999. 517-520. About William Edgar Stafford's poem "Waking at 3 A.M." Reprinted from *Field* 41 (1989): 29-33.

2489. "[Photo]." *Toronto Life* 33.16 (1999): Cover and p. 101. Both photos, by Nigel Dickson, taken at Mount Pleasant Cemetery. All authors in shoot were promised they could use the photos on the dust jackets of their future books.

2490. *Pinnaletõus.* Tallinn [Estonia]: Eesti Raamat, 1999. Estonian translation of *Surfac-ing* by Karin Suursalu.

2491. "Préface de l'édition en langue anglaise (1976)." *Un Joualonais, sa Joualonie.* By Marie-Claire Blais. 2nd ed. [Montréal]: Boréal, 1999. 7-[16]. French translation by Christiane Teasdale.

2492. "Reflection Piece: Revisiting Anne." *L. M. Montgomery and Canadian Culture.* Ed. Irene Gammel and Elizabeth Epperly. Toronto: University of Toronto Press, 1999. 222-226.

2493. *The Robber Bride.* Toronto: Seal Books, 1999.

2494. "Scarlet Ibis." *Colonial and Postcolonial Fiction: An Anthology.* Ed. Robert Ross. New York: Garland, 1999. 399-416. Reprinted from *Bluebeard's Egg and Other Stories,* ©1983.

2495. "Screen: Why I Love *The Night of the Hunter.*" *The Guardian* (London) 19 March 1999: Section: Features: 12. Article (1372 w) begins: "I'm incapable of choosing my single favourite anything, so I picked *The Night of the Hunter* for other rea-sons...." Later, at the Everyman Cinema, Atwood introduced a new print of the film (which was originally released in 1955 just after she had begun dating).

2496. "The Small Cabin." *Evoluzioni: Poeti Anglofoni e Francofoni Del Canada.* Ed. Claudia Gasparini and Marina Zito. Naples: Libreria Dante & Descartes Universi-taria, 1999. 120.

2497. "Snake Woman." *Kalliope* 20.3 (1999): 59. Poem.

2498. *Surfacing.* Toronto: McClelland and Stewart, 1999. Trade paperback edition.

2499. "Survival, Then and Now." *Maclean's* 112.26 (1999): 54-58. "Canada's premier woman of letters takes a razor-sharp look at the state of Canadian literature." Re-printed in *World Press Review* 46.11 (November 1999): 6-7.

2500. "Testimonianze / Appreciations." *Pronuncia I nomi / Say the Names* [By] Al Purdy. Ravenna [Italy]: Longo Editore Ravenna, 1999. 6-9. Atwood's appreciation appears in English, with Italian translation opposite. Her comments are followed by appreciations from Anna Cascella, Dennis Lee, Sam Solecki, Frazer Sutherland, and Giuseppe Zigaina. Excerpt: "Purdy writes like a cross between Shakespeare and a Vaudeville comedian (so did Shakespeare)."

2501. "They Are My Friends." *Coming of Age: Literature about Youth and Adolescence.* 2nd ed. Vol. 1. Ed. Bruce Emra. Lincolnwood, IL: National Textbook Co., 1999. 92-96. Excerpt from *Cat's Eye*, ©1988. Includes study questions, 96-97. [Ed. note: Cover title of book: *Coming of Age Fiction about Youth and Adolescence.*]

2502. "Tips für die Wildnis." *Schwestern: Ein Frauenlesebuch.* Ed. Anne Rademacher. Munich: Goldman, 1999. 147.

2503. "Translation: Three Small Entries." *Literary Imagination: The Review of the Association of Literary Scholars and Critics* 1.1 (1999): 154-155.

2504. "The Trappers." *Crossing Boundaries: An International Anthology of Women's Experiences in Sport.* Ed. Susan J. Bandy and Anne S. Darden. Champaign, IL: Human Kinetics Press, 1999. 148-149. Poem. Reprinted from *Animals in That Country*, ©1968.

2505. "Under the Thumb: How I Became a Poet." *The Leap Years: Women Reflect on Change, Loss, and Love.* Ed. Mary Ann Maier and Joan Shaddox Isom. Boston: Beacon Press, 1999. 207-217. Reprint from *This Magazine*, March-April 1996.

2506. "Underneath All the Intelligence and Wit, There Was a Sweet Romantic: An Appreciation [of Matt Cohen, 1942-1999]." *Globe and Mail* 4 December 1999: R1, R13.

2507. "Variation on the Word *Sleep*." *Evoluzioni: Poeti Anglofoni e Francofoni Del Canada.* Ed. Claudia Gasparini and Marina Zito. Naples: Libreria Dante & Descartes Universitaria, 1999. 122.

2508. *Vera spazzatura: A altri racconti.* Milan: Baldini & Castoldi, 1999. Italian translation of *Wilderness Tips* by Francesca Avanzini.

2509. *Verletzungen: Roman.* [Munich]: BTB, 1999. German translation of *Bodily Harm* by Werner Waldhoff.

2510. *Wahre Geschichten.* Düsseldorf: Claassen, 1999. German translation of *True Stories* by Astrid Arz et al.

2511. *Wilderness Tips.* Toronto: McClelland and Stewart, 1999. Paperback edition.

2512. "Wilderness Tips." *The Art of the Story: An International Anthology of Contemporary Short Stories.* Ed. Daniel Halpern. New York: Viking, 1999. 42-57.

2513. "Woman Skating." *Crossing Boundaries: An International Anthology of Women's Experiences in Sport.* Ed. Susan J. Bandy and Anne S. Darden. Champaign, IL: Human Kinetics, 1999. 190-191. Reprinted from *Selected Poems 1966-1984*, ©1990.

2514. "A Woman's Issue." *Scanning the Century: The Penguin Book of the Twentieth Century in Poetry.* Ed. Peter Forbes. London: Viking, 1999. 229-230.

2515. "Yo, Ella y Eso." *Borges múltiple: Cuentos y ensayos de cuentistas.* Ed. Pablo Brescia and Lauro Zavala. México: Universidad Nacional Autónoma de Mexico, 1999. 29-30. Spanish translation of "Me, She, and It." *Antaeus* 73-74 (1994): 7 by Alfonso Montelongo. In this book, Atwood is noted as being from Los Estados Unidos.

Adaptations of Atwood's Works

2516. *Marrying the Hangman: Chamber Opera in One Act.* [Musical score]. Bryn Mawr, PA: Merion Music, 1999. 98. Text based on poem by Margaret Atwood, from *Eating Fire*, ©1999. Adapted by Ben Twist and Ronald Caltabiano; music by Ronald Caltabiano.
2517. *Oper und Musiktheater. Band 1.* [Sound recording]. Vienna: Vienna Modern Masters, 1999. 1 compact disc. Includes "Nacht in Royal Ontario Museum," adapted by Nancy Van de Vate from Atwood's poem, "Night in the Royal Ontario Museum."

Quotations

2518. "[Quote]." *Charleston Gazette* 9 April 1999: Section: Editorial: A4. Painful loss: "A divorce is like an amputation. You survive but there's less of you." Source: *Time* 19 March 1973.
2519. "[Quote]." *Columbus Dispatch* 26 December 1999: Section: Features: Accents and Arts: 1H. At the Columbus Metropolitan Library, Atwood described a scene in her novel, *Alias Grace*, in which a character "hurled blandishments." She paused, smiled and said: "I wish we still had blandishments. They seem quite useful."
2520. "[Quote]." *Denver Rocky Mountain News* 25 April 1999: Section: Books: 2E. On difficulties of writing: "It was like trying to stuff a dog with rigor mortis into two plastic bags."
2521. "[Quote]." *Flare* 21.9 (1999): 128. In an article entitled "20 Ways to Get Happy," Allan Hepburn quotes a series of writers, including Atwood. In her poem "You Are Happy," she writes: "To love is to let go / of those excuses, habits / we once used for our own safety." Happiness requires surrender.
2522. "[Quote]." *Milwaukee Journal Sentinel* 9 May 1999: Section: Lifestyle: 1. On motherhood: "Because I am a mother, I am incapable of being shocked as I never was when I was not one."
2523. "[Quote]." *National Post* 14 June 1999: D6. Atwood at Toronto's Harbourfront on lending [poet] Earle Birney her set of giant-bristle-filled hair rollers and doing him the favour of rolling his girlfriend's hair: "I've always been a soft touch for large men with no small-motor skills."
2524. "[Quote]." *National Post* 1 July 1999: A10. Atwood describing Vancouver: "It's the suicide capital of the country. You keep going west until you run out. You come to the edge. Then you jump off."
2525. "[Quote]." *National Post* 30 November 1999: C3. Atwood quoted from 1980s describing [appointed] Canadian Senate as "a featherbed for fallen Liberals."
2526. "[Quote]." *Sunday Star-Times* (Auckland) 18 July 1999: Section: Features: Books: 2. Story on how to become a writer quotes paper's book reviewer, Joy MacKenzie, who endorses Atwood's advice: "You learn by reading and writing, reading and writing. As a craft it is learnt through the apprentice system, but you chose your own teachers. Sometimes they are alive, sometimes dead."
2527. "[Quote]." *Tulsa World* 4 December 1999. Asked at an awards ceremony in Oklahoma about what constitutes Canadian literature, Atwood was unsure: "I don't think there is a Canadian perspective that you could sum up in a sentence, any

more than there is an Oklahoman perspective that you could sum up in a sentence."

2528. "[Quote]." *Tulsa World* 4 December 1999. Atwood remarks that she writes from a feminine perspective because she is a woman, but that she does not believe in women's issues: "Women are half the human race. There are actually no things that are women's issues; there are human issues which get ghetto-ized."

2529. "[Quote]." *Vancouver Sun* 1 July 1999: D1. "In this country you can say what you want because no one will listen to you anyway." (1981).

2530. "[Quotations]." *Oxford Dictionary of Quotations*. Ed. Elizabeth Knowles. 5th ed. Oxford; New York: Oxford UP, 1999. 32. Two listed.

Interviews

2531. "Atwood's Aria." *National Magazine (CBC)* 26 November 1999. Available from Lexis-Nexis. Interview by Leslie Mackinnon with Atwood concerning her commission by the Canadian Opera Company to write the libretto for an opera on life of Pauline Johnson.

2532. "A Passion for Poetry." *National Magazine (CBC)* 19 November 1999. Available from Lexis-Nexis. Atwood part of roundtable discussing Al Purdy's poetry. Atwood notes that the first time she met Al Purdy in 1964, he insulted her by calling her an academic—so she poured beer on his head.

2533. *The Power of Ideas.* [Videorecording]. Norman, OK: Power of Ideas, 1999. VHS tape, 1 videocassette (28 min., 40 sec.). Atwood discusses her work. First televised 13 December 1999.

2534. *Two Solicitudes: Conversations.* [Sound recording]. Toronto: CNIB, 1999. 2 cassettes (9 hrs. 44 min.). This book is based on 20 interviews with Atwood broadcast between 26 January and 7 June 1996 on the stereo (FM) network of Radio-Canada as well as interviews conducted with Victor-Levy Beaulieu. Based on 1996 title. Originally broadcast in French, the contents have been translated by Phyllis Aronoff and Howard Scott.

2535. BUTLER, Jeri. "Author Throws Book at Categories." *Palm Beach Post* 29 January 1999: ACCENT: 2F. Atwood interviewed in connection with her visit to Boca Raton [Florida] to speak about her life as a writer. Some comments from this short interview: "I had shown no particular promise when I was in school." Asked how she felt about her books being read in feminist literature classes she replied: "I don't like categories, but if we didn't have them, I guess some writers would never get read. When I was at Harvard taking American Studies, the only female authors we read were Emily Dickinson and Anne Bradstreet....Not even Edith Wharton."

2536. COOK, Eleanor. "Interview with Margaret Atwood." *Literary-Imagination* 1.1 (1999): 156-169. This is the premier issue of this journal, which is sponsored by the 2,150-member Association of Literary Scholars and Critics, founded in 1994.

2537. CREIGHTON, Judy. "Atwood's Mother Pivotal to Family." *London Free Press* 17 June 1999: Section: Lifestyle: C12. Interview with Atwood and her mother on occasion of the latter's 90th birthday.

2538. EICHENBERGER, Bill. "The Writer's Tale." *Columbus Dispatch* 30 September 1999: Section: Features: 8E. Atwood discusses writer's craft as well as popular culture such as movies and the Internet. "You've heard about the wonderful bug someone floated on the Internet—a grammar and punctuation bug where, if you tried to send a communication, it would block you until you improved your text. A bunch of stockbrokers got infected with it, and it drove them completely mad."

Scholarly Resources

2539. ALLEN, Paul Smith. *Metamorphosis and the Emergence of the Feminine: A Motif of "Difference" in Women's Writing.* New York; Washington: Peter Lang, 1999. See especially Chapter 4: "The Promethean Theft/Emergence." 89-129; more specifically Part 2 which discusses Atwood's *Surfacing.* 99-114.

2540. AMANO, Kyoka. "*The Robber Bride*: The Power and the Powerlessness." *Notes on Contemporary Literature* 29.5 (1999): 7-9.

2541. ARRÓSPIDE, Amparo. "Margaret Atwood en el corazón de las tinieblas." *Espéculo: Revista de Estudios Literarios* 13 (1999): s.p. Includes poems. http://www.ucm.es/info/especulo/numero13/atwood.html (1 May 2006).

2542. BECKER, Susanne. *Gothic Forms of Feminine Fictions.* Manchester, UK: Manchester UP, 1999. An analysis of *Lady Oracle* as well as Alice Munro's *Lives of Girls and Women* and Aritha Van Herk's *No Fixed Address.*

2543. BLOOM, Lynn Z., Donna Krolik HOLLENBERG, and Veronica MAKOWSKY. "Reading Together and Apart: Feminism and / Versus Ethnicity in Margaret Laurence and Margaret Atwood: A Conversation." *American Review of Canadian Studies* 29.1 (1999): 165-179.

2544. BRAMESHUBER-ZIEGLER, I. J. "Die weibliche Kuenstlerfigur in der nordamerikanischen Frauenfiktion = The Figure of Female Artists in North American Women's Fiction." Doctoral thesis. Universitaet Graz, 1999. 249 pp. "Several women writers have fictionalized the female artist's experience. The diversity of these accounts prevents a definition of the 'Kuenstlerinnenroman' as a genre. The critical approach of this dissertation is therefore pragmatic, allowing for a pluralistic investigation of the texts. The novels by and about women writers are discussed under the most prominent aspect for the particular female artist. Margaret Atwood's *Lady Oracle's* comedy 'spices' the account of creativity....While these aspects are particularly prominent in the respective novels, many of them are also thematized in other portraits of the female artist. The concluding cross-referencing projects a multi-faceted image of the female artist figure." (Author). In German.

2545. BROWNLEY, Martine Watson. "'The Muse as Fluffball': Margaret Atwood and the Poetry of the Intelligent Woman." *Women Poets of the Americas: Toward a Pan-American Gathering.* Ed. Jacqueline-Vaught Brogan and Cordelia Chavez Candelaria. Notre Dame, IN: University of Notre Dame Press, 1999. 34-50.

2546. BUSCHINI, Marie-Pascale. "Chenilles et papillons: La métamorphose dans *Lady Oracle* (1976) de Margaret Atwood." *Imaginaires: Revue du Centre de Recherche sur l'Imaginaire dans les Littératures de Langue Anglaise* 4 (1999): 187-199.

2547. COHEN, Mark. "Just Judgment: Censorship in and of Canadian Literature." PhD thesis. McGill University, 1999. 290 pp. Also available on microfiche from Canadian Theses Service (2001) and in .pdf format: http://www.nlc-bnc.ca/obj/s4/f2/dsk1/tape7/PQDD_0026/NQ50133.pdf. Includes a good chapter on the shift in Atwood's take on censorship between *Bodily Harm* and *The Handmaid's Tale*, as well as discussions of censorship in and of work by Margaret Laurence and Timothy Findley, among others. For more see *DAI-A* 61.06 (December 2000): 2307.

2548. COLVILE, Georgiana M. M. "The Workings of Regression in George Orwell's *Nineteen Eighty-Four* and Margaret Atwood's *The Handmaid's Tale*." The Hand-

maid's Tale, *Roman Protéen.* Textes réunis by Jean-Michel Lacroix, Jacques Leclaire, and Jack Warwick. Mont-Saint-Aignan: Publications de l'Université de
Rouen, 1999. 35-46.

2549. COOKE, Nathalie. "A Tribute to Ted Davidson." *Newsletter of the Margaret Atwood Society* 22-23 (1999): 1-2. An obituary of the noted Atwood scholar.

2550. COUTURIER-STOREY, Françoise. "L'Allegoire dans l'oeuvre de Margaret Atwood et d'Angela Carter." Université de Nice. Thèse microfichée 97 Nice 2019.

2551. ———. "Desire in *The Handmaid's Tale.*" The Handmaid's Tale, *Roman Protéen.*
Textes réunis by Jean-Michel Lacroix, Jacques Leclaire, and Jack Warwick. Mont-
Saint-Aignan: Publications de l'Université de Rouen, 1999. 63-70.

2552. DALE, Tina Louise. "The Emergence of the Narratee: Discovering Self Through
Confession in Margaret Atwood's *Lady Oracle.*" MA thesis. North Dakota State
University, 1999. 49 pp.

2553. DAVIES, Laurence. "At Play in the Fields of Our Lord: Utopian Dystopianism in
Atwood, Huxley, and Zamyatin." *Transformations of Utopia: Changing Views of
the Perfect Society.* Ed. George Slusser, Paul Alkon, Roger Gaillard, and Danielle
Chatelein. New York: AMS, 1999. 205-214. Discussion of *The Handmaid's Tale.*

2554. DAVIES, Robertson. *For Your Eyes Alone: Letters 1976-1995.* Toronto:
McClelland and Stewart, 1999. Davies comments to others on Atwood's works.
Book also contains a letter to Atwood herself, congratulating her on her 1983 con-
vocation address at the University of Toronto.

2555. DING, Linpeng. "Recurrent Themes in Margaret Atwood's Fiction." MA thesis.
Beijing University, 1999. Title translated and romanized.

2556. DELORD, Marie. "A Textual Quilt: Margaret Atwood's *Alias Grace.*" *Études
canadiennes / Canadian Studies* 46 (1999): 111-121.

2557. DOLITSKY, Marlene. "Irony in Offred's Tale." *Lire Margaret Atwood* The
Handmaid's Tale. Ed. Marta Dvorak. Rennes, France: Presses universitaires de
Rennes, 1999. 113-126.

2558. DUBOIS, Dominique. "Pouvoir, corruption, transgression et subversion dans *The
Handmaid's Tale.*" *Lire Margaret Atwood* The Handmaid's Tale. Ed. Marta Dvorak. Rennes, France: Presses universitaires de Rennes, 1999. 59-85.

2559. DUNCAN, Isla J. "Margaret Atwood's Reworking of the Wendigo myth in *The
Robber Bride.*" *British Journal of Canadian Studies* 14.1 (1999): 73-84.

2560. DUPLAY, Mathieu. "*The Handmaid's Tale,* New England, and the Puritan Tradition." The Handmaid's Tale, *Roman Protéen.* Textes réunis by Jean-Michel Lacroix, Jacques Leclaire, and Jack Warwick. Mont-Saint-Aignan: Publications de
l'Université de Rouen, 1999. 25-34.

2561. DVORAK, Marta. "Boundaries and Borders in the World of Margaret Atwood."
Études canadiennes / Canadian Studies 47 (1999): 13-44.

2562. ———. "Subverting Utopia: Ambiguity in *The Handmaid's Tale.*" *Lire Margaret
Atwood* The Handmaid's Tale. Ed. Marta Dvorak. Rennes, France: Presses universitaires de Rennes, 1999. 73-85.

2563. ———. "Writing Beyond the Beginning: Or, Margaret Atwood's Art of Storytelling." *Commonwealth: Essays and Studies* 21.1 (Autumn 1999): 29-35.

2564. DVORAK, Marta, ed. *Lire Margaret Atwood* The Handmaid's Tale. Rennes,
France: Presses universitaires de Rennes, 1999. Collection Interférences. Individual essays indexed in this section.

2565. FAND, Roxanne J. *The Dialogic Self: Reconstructing Subjectivity in Woolf, Lessing, and Atwood.* Selinsgrove, PA: Susquehanna UP, 1999. Focus on *Lady Oracle.*

2566. FIAMENGO, Janice. "Postcolonial Guilt in Margaret Atwood's *Surfacing*." *American Review of Canadian Studies* 29.1 (1999): 141-163.

2567. FOSTER, Malcolm. *Margaret Atwood's* The Handmaid's Tale. Piscataway, NJ: Research & Education Association, 1999. 131 pp. MAX notes. Includes bibliographical references.

2568. FURGE, Stefanie. "The Female Protagonist, Her Power, and the Circular Structure of Oppression in *Alias Grace* and *The Handmaid's Tale*, Two Works Written by Margaret Atwood." MA thesis. University of Indianapolis, 1999.

2569. GATENBY, Greg. *Toronto: A Literary Guide*. Toronto: McArthur, 1999. Twenty-five separate references in the index to Atwood's literary haunts.

2570. GERIG, Karin. "Ein Knick in der Optik: Visualität und Weibliche Identität in Margaret Atwoods *Cat's Eye*." *Geschlecht-Literatur-Geschichte, 1*. Ed. Gudrun Loster-Schneider. St. Ingbert, Germany: Röhrig, 1999. 213-234. *Cat's Eye.*

2571. GILBERT, Paula R., and Lorna M. IRVINE. "Pre- and Post-Modern: Regendering and Serial Killing in Rioux, Dandurand, Dé, and Atwood." *American Review of Canadian Studies* 29.1 (1999): 119-139.

2572. GLOVER, Douglas H. "Her Life Entire." *Notes Home from a Prodigal Son*. Ottawa: Oberon, 1999. 25-33. Includes a discussion of Atwood's *Cat's Eye*. Reprinted from *Books in Canada*, 1988.

2573. GOLDBLATT, Patricia F. "Reconstructing Margaret Atwood's Protagonists." *World Literature Today* 73.2 (1999): 275-282. Uses her novels and short stories to analyze Atwood's female characters and their relationship to survival.

2574. GOLDMAN, Marlene. "Margaret Atwood's *Wilderness Tips*: Apocalyptic Cannibal Fiction." *Études canadiennes / Canadian Studies* 46 (1999): 93-110.

2575. GREENE, Michael. "Body/Language in *The Handmaid's Tale*: Reading Notes." *Lire Margaret Atwood* The Handmaid's Tale. Ed. Marta Dvorak. Rennes, France: Presses universitaires de Rennes, 1999. 101-112.

2576. GREVEN-BORDE, Hélène. *Margaret Atwood:* The Handmaid's Tale. Paris: Didier Erudition, 1999. 107 pp.

2577. GROSSKURTH, Phyllis. *Elusive Subject: A Biographer's Life*. Toronto: Macfarlane Walter & Ross, 1999. According to Grosskurth, her father was used as a model for one of the characters in *Alias Grace* (7).

2578. GUERNALEC, Julie. "Memory in Margaret Atwood's Novels." Maîtrise LLCE Anglais. U.H.B. Rhennes II, 1999. 102 pp.

2579. HAMMILL, Faye. "Forest and 'Fairy Stuff': Margaret Atwood's *Wilderness Tips*." *49th Parallel: An Interdisciplinary Journal of North American Studies* 1 (1999): s.p. http://www.49thparallel.bham.ac.uk/back/issue1/hammill.htm (1 May 2006).

2580. ———. "Margaret Atwood, Carol Shields, and 'That Moodie Bitch.'" *American Review of Canadian Studies* 29.1 (1999): 67-91.

2581. HARMANSSON, Casie. "Canadian in the End?" *University of Toronto Quarterly* 68.4 (1999): 807-822. Reflections on Atwood's claim: "Yes, Virginia, there is a Canadian literature."

2582. HARRIS, Jocelyn. "*The Handmaid's Tale* as a Re-Visioning of *1984*." *Transformations of Utopia: Changing Views of the Perfect Society*. Ed. George Slusser et al. New York: AMS, 1999. 267-279.

2583. HENGEN, Shannon. "Margaret Atwood's Nature." The Handmaid's Tale, *Roman Protéen*. Textes réunis by Jean-Michel Lacroix, Jacques Leclaire, and Jack Warwick. Mont-Saint-Aignan: Publications de l'Université de Rouen, 1999. 77-84.

2584. INGRAM, Penelope Anne. "Becoming Women: 'Difference Feminism' and the Race for the 'Other.'" PhD thesis. University of New South Wales (Australia), 1999. "The thesis's main argument is that the project of sexual difference, which attempts to theorise a place for woman as the Other of the Other, is based on a prior assumption of the absolute alterity of the racial Other. In theories of sexual difference, the thesis contends, the racial Other represents the paradigm for un-colonisable otherness precisely because s/he is presumed to be, like Spivak's sub-altern, unsignifiable or unrepresentable....The thesis...examines a number of liter-ary works by white 'settler women,' [including] Margaret Atwood's *Surfacing*.... By reading feminist theorists of difference in dialogue with the work of post-colonial and race theorists who have revealed as illusory the concept of a native/racial Other who is 'pure' or 'uncontaminated' by the coloniser, I critique feminist projects of difference which would theorise the possibility of a similar alterity for woman and which, furthermore, would base their appeals to such alterity on the presumption of a racial Other who is wholly other." (Author). For more see *DAI-A* 60.08: (February 2000): 2917.

2585. JARMAN, Mark. "'Love Is All Around Us.'" *Canadian Fiction Magazine* 1999: 14-17. Atwood as a fictionalized character pops up all over.

2586. KENDALL, Kathleen. "Beyond Grace: Criminal Lunatic Women in Victorian Canada." *Canadian Women's Studies* 19.1/2 (1999): 110-115. Article inspired by *Alias Grace*, an excerpt from which appears at its head.

2587. KING, James. *Jack: A Life with Writers—The Story of Jack McClelland*. Toronto: Alfred A. Knopf, 1999. Lots on one of McClelland's favorite authors.

2588. KLOSS, Robert J. "The Problem of Who One Really Is: The Functions of Sexual Fantasy in Stories of Atwood, Lispector, and Munro." *Journal of Evolutionary Psychology* 20.3-4 (1999): 227-235. Focus on "Rape Fantasies."

2589. KNELMAN, Judith. "Can We Believe What the Newspapers Tell Us? Missing Links in *Alias Grace*." *University of Toronto Quarterly* 68.2 (1999): 677-686. "Atwood implies that the newspapers of the time failed Grace by sensationalizing and politicizing her case, and she also points out that the written accounts of the case were so contradictory that few facts emerged as unequivocally 'known.' However, it is unfair to impugn the reliability of newspapers as historical docu-ments because they did not tell one constant story. Stories and advertisements in old newspapers illuminate one another, pointing out paths that might be ap-proached through other forms of writing. They are valuable for the things they tell us incidentally and incrementally about past customs, attitudes, problems, and cop-ing tactics, thereby suggesting what constituted social and cultural reality at the time." (Author).

2590. KREY CATELLIER, Miriam. "A Study of Margaret Atwood's *The Handmaid's Tale*: From Novel to Film (*La servante écarlate* de Margaret Atwood: Du roman à l'adaptation cinématographique)." MA thesis. Université Laval, 1999. 96 pp. Also available on microfiche from Canadian Theses Service (2002) and as .pdf file: http://www.nlc-bnc.ca/obj/s4/f2/dsk1/tape9/PQDD_0018/MQ48934.pdf. Text in English. For more see *MAI* 38.06 (December 2000): 1452.

2591. KUHNERT, Matthias. "The Latest Area of Play: Postmodern Hats for Margaret Atwood's *The Robber Bride*." MA thesis. Acadia University, 1999. 109 pp. Also available on microfiche from Canadian Theses Service (2000) and in .pdf format: http://www.nlc-bnc.ca/obj/s4/f2/dsk1/tape9/PQDD_0004/MQ45371.pdf. "This thesis investigates Margaret Atwood's *The Robber Bride* by focusing on the novel's construction of postmodern centres. Informed by the postmodern theories

232   ~ 1999 ~

of Linda Hutcheon and Jean-François Lyotard, the thesis defines 'centre' as the combined value-systems of a particular society or individual. Postmodernism and modernism can be described as different reactions to the same cultural crisis: 'the loss of the centre,' the break-down of these established systems of belief. While modernist artists try to resolve the crisis by searching for the centre elsewhere, postmodernism gives up the belief in a single centre and recognizes that the world is multicentric....*The Robber Bride* is a postmodern novel." (Author). For more see *MAI* 38.03 (June 2000): 543.

2592. LACROIX, Jean-Michel, Jacques LECLAIRE, and Jack WARWICK, eds. The Handmaid's Tale, *Roman Protéen*. Mont-Saint-Aignan: Publications de l'Université de Rouen, 1999. Individual articles indexed in this section.

2593. LANE, Richard J. "Fractures: Written Displacements in Canadian/US Literary Relations." *Postcolonial Literatures: Expanding the Canon*. Ed. Deborah L. Madsen. London: Pluto, 1999. 45-57. Atwood's contribution.

2594. LECLAIRE, Jacques. "*The Handmaid's Tale*: A Feminist Dystopia." The Handmaid's Tale, *Roman Protéen*. Textes réunis by Jean-Michel Lacroix, Jacques Leclaire, and Jack Warwick. Mont-Saint-Aignan: Publications de l'Université de Rouen, 1999. 85-94.

2595. LEE, So-Hee. "A Study of Women's Speaking and Writing in *The Handmaid's Tale*: At the Intersection of Feminism and Postmodernism." *Journal of English Language and Literature* 45.1 (1999): 195-218. In Korean; abstract in English.

2596. LJUNGBERG, Christina [Stücklin]. "Re-enchanting Nature: Some Magic Links between Margaret Atwood and J. R. R. Tolkien." *Root and Branch: Approaches towards Understanding Tolkien*. Ed. Thomas Honegger. Zurich; Berne: Walking Tree Publishers, 1999. 151-162. "Although, at first sight, Margaret Atwood and J. R. R. Tolkien would seem to have little in common, a closer look reveals some intriguing affinities. Both writers use classical and popular mythologies to discuss issues of fundamental human concern; elements of the fantastic appear throughout their narratives, and both endow their characters with archetypal traits. Atwood's investigation of the metaphysical nature of *The Lord of the Rings* in her PhD thesis where she fits it into the English tradition of the metaphysical romance offers interesting inroads into the works of both authors." (Author).

2597. ———. *To Join, to Fit, and to Make: The Creative Craft of Margaret Atwood's Fiction*. New York: Peter Lang, 1999. Originally presented as author's PhD thesis. University of Zurich, 1999. Focus on *Cat's Eye* and *The Robber Bride*.

2598. LOSCHNIGG, M. "A Canadian Scheherezade: Narrative Technique and Identity of the Female Protagonist in Margaret Atwood's *Alias Grace*." *Germanisch-Romanische Monatsschrift* 49.4 (1999): 441-461. In German.

2599. LOVELADY, Stephanie. "I Am Telling This to No One but You: Private Voice, Passing, and the Private Sphere in Margaret Atwood's *Alias Grace*." *Studies in Canadian Literature* 24.2 (1999): 35-63.

2600. ———. "Inside Out: Immigration and Female Coming of Age in Willa Cather, Martha Ostenso, Margaret Atwood, Ana Castillo, Cristina Garcia, Barbara Kingsolver, and Julia Alvarez." PhD thesis. University of Maryland–College Park, 1999. 348 pp.

2601. MAISONNAT, Claude. "Amour, éthique et utopie dans *The Handmaid's Tale*." The Handmaid's Tale, *Roman Protéen*. Textes réunis by Jean-Michel Lacroix, Jacques Leclaire, and Jack Warwick. Mont-Saint-Aignan: Publications de l'Université de Rouen, 1999. 47-62.

2602. MOORE, Monica Leigh-Anne. "Coming and Going: The Effects of Displacement in Novels by Atwood, [Jacques] Poulin, [Jane] Urquhart, [Regine] Robin." MA thesis. University of Western Ontario, 1999. 119 pp. Also available on microfiche from Canadian Theses Service (2000) and in .pdf format: http://www.nlc-bnc.ca/obj/s4/f2/dsk1/tape9/PQDD_0005/MQ42179.pdf. "In the post-modern world, all nations, including Canada and Quebec, are cultural hybrids. Identities are also hybrid, as many different components contribute to their composition, including gender, class, race and nationality....Displacement often results in a broadening of one's perspective, providing insight into the 'Other's' point of view....Jacques Poulin's *Volkswagen Blues,* Margaret Atwood's *Bodily Harm*, Jane Urquhart's *The Underpainter*, and Regine Robin's *La Quebecoite* are four contemporary Canadian or Quebecois novels which explore personal displacement, each one illustrating how it affects both the process of identity formation and the individual's perception of Canada or Quebec." (Author). For more see *MAI* 38.01 (February 2000): 42.

2603. MORLEY, Patricia. "Atwood, Margaret." *Encyclopedia of World Literature in the 20th Century*. Steven R. Serafin, general editor. 3rd ed. Vol. 1 (A-D). Detroit, MI: St. James, 1999. 144-145.

2604. MORRA, Linda. "Articulating Madness: The Foucauldian Notion of Madness and Margaret Atwood's *Alias Grace*." *West Virginia Philological Papers* 45 (1999): 123-129.

2605. MORTON, Stephen. "Postcolonial Gothic and the New World Disorder: Crossing Borders of Space/Time in Margaret Atwood's *The Robber Bride*." *British Journal of Canadian Studies* 14.1 (1999): 99-114.

2606. MOSS, John. "To Criticize the Critics: Cooley, Rooke, Atwood and Lecker." *The Paradox of Meaning: Cultural Poetics and Critical Fictions*. Winnipeg: Turnstone Press, 1999. 26-49. Twenty of Moss's essays including one that is critical of Atwood's *Strange Things: The Malevolent North in Canadian Literature*, which he dismisses as "chatter," "platititudinous and banal."

2607. MYRSIADES, Linda. "Law, Medicine, and the Sex Slave in Margaret Atwood's *The Handmaid's Tale*." *Un-Disciplining Literature: Literature, Law, and Culture*. Ed. Kostas Myrsiades and Linda Myrsiades. New York: Peter Lang, 1999. 219-245.

2608. OLLIER-MORIN, Priscilla. "*The Handmaid's Tale* and American Protestant Fundamentalism: Discipline and Submission." *Lire Margaret Atwood* The Handmaid's Tale. Ed. Marta Dvorak. Rennes, France: Presses universitaires de Rennes, 1999. 33-45.

2609. OLTARZEWSKA, Jagna. "Reflections on the Concept of Territory in the Work of Margaret Atwood: Deconstructions and Reconstructions." *Études canadiennes / Canadian Studies* 47 (1999): 145-154.

2610. ———. "Strategies for Bearing Witness: Testimony as Construct in Margaret Atwood's *The Handmaid's Tale*." *Lire Margaret Atwood* The Handmaid's Tale. Ed. Marta Dvorak. Rennes, France: Presses universitaires de Rennes, 1999. 47-55.

2611. ———. "Témoignage, identité, survie stratégies féminines de lutte et d'émancipation dans l'oeuvre romanesque de Margaret Atwood." Doctoral dissertation. Université Paris X, 1999.

2612. PEACOCK, Molly. *How to Read a Poem .... and Start a Poetry Circle*. Toronto: McClelland and Stewart; New York: Riverhead Books, 1999. See especially Chapter 11: Taking a Bite," 150-163, which examines Atwood's "Asparagus."

2613. PELED, Nancy. "The Image of Women as Witch in Selected Novels of Fay Weldon and Margaret Atwood." MA thesis. University of Haifa, 1999.

2614. PONTUALE, Francesco. "Identità e luogo: Gli specchi nella poesia di Margaret Atwood." *Gioco di specchi: Saggi sull'uso letterario dell'immagine dello specchio*. Ed. Agostino Lombardo. Rome: Bulzoni, 1999. 661-673.

2615. POTTS, Donna L. "'The Old Maps Are Dissolving': Intertexuality and Identity in Margaret Atwood's *The Robber Bride*." *Tulsa Studies in Women's Literature* 18.2 (1999): 281-298.

2616. POZNAR, Susan. "The Totemic Image and the 'Bodies' of the Gothic in Margaret Atwood's *Cat's Eye*." *Yearbook of Comparative and General Literature* 47 (1999): 81-107.

2617. PRABHAKAR, M. *Feminism/Postmodernism: Margaret Atwood's Fiction*. New Delhi: Creative Books, 1999. Includes "*The Edible Woman*: Guide to Feminism," [37]-50; "*Lady Oracle*: Prophecy for a Brave New World," [51]-65; "*Bodily Harm*: Writing as Exposure," [66]-83; "*The Handmaid's Tale*: Language as Subversive-Weapon," [84]-98; "*Surfacing*: A Blue-Print of Revolt," [99]-112; "*Cat's Eye*: A Vision in the Dark," [113]-125; "*Life Before Man*: Negation of Marital Power Politics," [126]-138; "*The Robber Bride*: A Critique of 'the Battle of the Sexes,'" [139]-153. There is an introduction and conclusion, as well as a bibliography, [158]-176.

2618. PRESTON, Pasley Elizabeth. "Through a Glass Darkly: Gothic Intertexts in Margaret Atwood's *Cat's Eye*." MA thesis. Université de Montréal, 1999. Also available on microfiche from Canadian Theses Service (2000).

2619. RAO, Eleonora. "Immigrants and Other Aliens: Encounters in the 'Wild Zone' in Margaret Atwood's Recent Fiction." *Intersections: La Narrativa Canadese Tra Storia e Geografia*. Ed. Liana Nissim and Carlo Pagetti. Bologna: Cisalpino, 1999. 171-182. With emphasis on *The Robber Bride*.

2620. RATHJEN, Claudia. "Ökofeminismus in der Literatur: *Ein Vergleich* der Werke *Störfall* von Christa Wolf, *Die Wand* von Marlen Haushofer und Margaret Atwoods *Surfacing*." MA thesis. Université de Montréal, 1999. 101 pp. Also available on microfiche from Canadian Theses Service (1999). Study of *Surfacing* is part of master's thesis for the German Department.

2621. RIATT, Suzanne. "'Out of Shakespeare?' Cordelia in *Cat's Eye*." *Transforming Shakespeare: Contemporary Women's Re-Visions in Literature and Performance*. Ed. Marianne Novy. New York: St. Martin's, 1999. 181-197.

2622. RIGGIN, William. "Of Obstacles, Survival and Identity: On Contemporary Canadian Literature." *World Literature Today* 73.2 (1999): 229-230. Article highlights quotations from Atwood and Northrop Frye.

2623. ROGGIE, Kara. "A Feminist Critique of Margaret Atwood's 'Spelling.'" *Literary Criticism: An Introduction to Theory and Practice*. 2nd ed. Ed. Charles E. Bressler. Upper Saddle River, NJ: Prentice Hall, 1999. 193-195. Student essay which used psychoanalytic theories of Jacques Lacan in study of this poem to highlight feminist issues.

2624. SCHWARTZ, Meryl Fern. "The Political Awakening Novels of Margaret Atwood, Doris Lessing, and Michelle Cliff: Narrative Strategy, Reader Response, and Utopian Desire." PhD thesis. The University of Wisconsin–Madison, 1999. 235 pp. "This study analyzes late twentieth-century women's novels of political awakening through examination of three writers who have written multiple texts in the genre: Margaret Atwood, Doris Lessing, and Michelle Cliff. Political awakening novels chronicle a protagonists' evolving consciousness of her complicity with oppressive social structures and her responsibility to struggle against them....[T]heir narratives of awakening dramatize the interactions between gender relations and other arenas of struggle....The analysis of Margaret Atwood, titled 'Is the Reader Exempt?' analyzes the manipulation of the relationship between protagonist and reader in the novels *Bodily Harm* and *The Handmaid's Tale.* Both narratives struggle against strategies of containment that enable readers to experience themselves as exempt from complicity with systemic oppression." (Author). For more see *DAI-A* 60.9 (March 2000): 3355.

2625. SEEBER, Hans Ulrich. "Cultural Differences and Problems of Understanding in the Short Fiction of Margaret Atwood." *Intercultural Encounters-Studies in English Literatures.* Ed. Heinz Antor and Kevin L. Cope. Heidelberg: Carl Winter Universitatsverlag, 1999. 533-546. "Essays Presented to Rudiger Ahrens on the Occasion of His Sixtieth Birthday."

2626. SMITH, Kristine Leeann. "Sacrifice and the 'Other': Oppression, Torture and Death in *Alias Grace, Green Grass, Running Water,* and *News from a Foreign Country.*" MA thesis. University of Alberta, 1999. 90 pp. Also available on microfiche from Canadian Theses Service (2000) and in .pdf format: http://www.nlc-bnc.ca/obj/s4/f2/dsk2/ftp01/MQ40017.pdf. "Julia Kristeva's theories on sacrifice and the 'other' illuminate Margaret Atwood's *Alias Grace,* Thomas King's *Green Grass, Running Water,* and Alberto Manguel's *News from a Foreign Country Came.* Kristeva tells us that we often demonize others, projecting our negative qualities onto those we believe are different in the hope of eliminating these traits from our own psyches. The social contract which structures western society promotes the sacrifice—either physically, or through oppression—of this 'other.'... Kristeva believes that literature has the potential to guide us towards this reformed society, and each of these novels contributes to this process by helping the reader understand and embrace the 'other.'" (Author). For more see *MAI* 37.06 (December 1999): 1627.

2627. STAELS, Hilde. "The Social Construction of Identity and the Lost Female Imaginary in M. Atwood's *Surfacing.*" *Journal of Commonwealth and Postcolonial Studies* 6.2 (Fall 1999): 20-35.

2628. STEIN, Karen F. *Margaret Atwood Revisited.* New York: Twayne Publishers, 1999. Twayne's World Authors Series, 887. Contents: "Margaret Atwood, Storyteller," "Northern Gothic: The Early Poems, 1961-1975," "Home Ground, Foreign Territory: Atwood's Early Novels," "Lost Worlds: Three Novels," "Victims, Tricksters, and Scheherazades: The Later Novels," "Firestorms and Fireflies: The Later Poems, 1978-1995," "Scarlet Ibises and Frog Songs: Short Fiction," "Poets and Princesses: An Atwood Miscellany. Literary Criticism, Reviews and Children's Books."

2629. STURGESS, Charlotte. "The Handmaid as a Resource Heroine." The Handmaid's Tale, *Roman Protéen.* Textes réunis by Jean-Michel Lacroix, Jacques Leclaire, and Jack Warwick. Mont-Saint-Aignan: Publications de l'Université de Rouen, 1999. 71-76.

2630. SUGARS, Cynthia. "Noble Canadians, Ugly Americans: Anti-Americanism and the Canadian Ideal in British Readings of Canadian Literature." *American Review of Canadian Studies* 29.1 (1999): 93-118. Lots of Atwood references.

2631. THACKER, Robert. "A Scholar's Life Lived: Arnold E. 'Ted' Davidson." *American Review of Canadian Studies* 29.1 (1999): 6-9. Profile of scholar who, along with his many other accomplishments, was a founding member and officer of the Margaret Atwood Society.

2632. TRAHAIR, Richard C. S. *Utopias and Utopians: An Historical Dictionary*. West-port, CT: Greenwood, 1999. Entry on Atwood (21-22).

2633. TUHKUNEN-COUZIC, Taïna. "Amours et désamours en dystopie: *The Hand-maid's Tale*." *Lire Margaret Atwood* The Handmaid's Tale. Ed. Marta Dvorak. Rennes, France: Presses universitaires de Rennes, 1999. 89-99.

2634. VAN HERK, Aritha. "Scant Articulations of Time." *University of Toronto Quarterly* 68.4 (1999): 925-938. Analysis of the short-story format, with comments about Atwood.

2635. VILLEGAS LÓPEZ, Sonia. *Mujer y religión en la narrativa anglófona contemporánea*. Huelva: Universidad de Huelva, 1999. Atwood's *The Handmaid's Tale* discussed along with Jane Rogers's *Mr. Wroe's Virgins*.

2636. WECKERLE, Lisa Jeanne. "Revisioning Narratives: Feminist Adaptation Strategies on Stage and Screen." PhD thesis. University of Texas, Austin, 1999. 210 pp. "The dissertation focuses on discovering feminist strategies in the process of adapting fiction to stage and screen....The primary case studies are a screen adaptation of *The Handmaid's Tale* by Margaret Atwood and adaptations of *The Old Maid, The Age of Innocence*, and *The House of Mirth* by Edith Wharton. Some of the questions I am particularly interested in are: How can the feminist messages inherent in a text be preserved and/or heightened in an adaptation? How can women's subjectivity be preserved in the adaptation process? How do issues of fidelity and medium problematize the creation of feminist adaptations?" (Author). For more see *DAI*-A 61.1 (July 2000): 164.

2637. WHEELER, Kathleen M. "Constructions of Identity in Post-1970 Experimental Fiction." *An Introduction to Contemporary Fiction: International Writing in English since 1970*. Ed. Rod Mengham. Malden, MA: Polity-Blackwell, 1999. 15-31.

2638. WHITLOCK, Gillian. "Encounters with Canadian Women's Writing, Three Times." *Australian–Canadian Studies: A Journal for the Humanities & Social Sciences* 17.2 (1999): 43-53. Atwood plus Susanna Moodie and Audrey Callahan Thomas.

2639. WILSON, Jean. "Identity Politics in Atwood, Kogawa, and Wolf." *CLCWeb: Comparative Literature and Culture: A WWWeb Journal* 1.3 (1999): s.p. http://clcwebjournal.lib.purdue.edu/clcweb99-3/wilson99.html (1 May 2006). A comparative study of 3 texts published in the early 1980s: Atwood's "Significant Moments in the Life of My Mother," Kogawa's *Obasan*, and Wolf's *Cassandra*. Identity politics figure prominently in all 3 literary works, whose common poetic project is one of demythologization and of enabling at the same time the emergence of a new, liberating articulation, a language perhaps "never heard before."... All 3 works, albeit in different ways, challenge readers to consider identity interrogatively and to explore in new voices what it means to say "we," to say "they," to say "you," to say "I."

Reviews of Atwood's Works

2640. *The Handmaid's Tale*. Toronto: McClelland and Stewart, 1985.
    Globe and Mail 27 November 1999: D17. Reprint of 5 October 1985 review by William FRENCH.
2641. *In Search of Alias Grace: On Writing Canadian Historical Fiction*. Ottawa: University of Ottawa Press, 1997.
    Canadian Historical Review 80.2 (June 1999): 312-313. By David KIMMEL.
    University of Toronto Quarterly 69.1 (Winter 1999-2000): 348-349. By Judith KNELMAN.
2642. *Lady Oracle*. Toronto: McClelland and Stewart, 1976.
    Globe and Mail 30 October 1999: D30. By Judith FITZGERALD.
2643. *Two Solicitudes:* With Victor Levy Beaulieu. Translated from the French. Toronto: McClelland and Stewart, 1998.
    Iowa Review 29.3 (Winter 1999): 184. By Jennifer LeJEUNE.

Reviews of Adaptations of Atwood's Works

2644. "Good Bones." Directed by Urjo Kareda at Tarragon Extra Space Theatre in Toronto.
    National Post 21 January 1999: B13. By Robert CUSHMAN. (622 w).
    Toronto Star 20 January 1999: Section: Entertainment: s.p. By Vit WAGNER.
    Toronto Sun 21 January 1999: 64. By John COULBOURN.
    Variety 373.11 (1-7 February 1999): 71-72. By Mira FRIEDLANDER. (509 w).

~ 2000 ~

Atwood's Works

2645. *Aklais Slepkava*. Riga: Atena Klubs, 2000. Latvian translation of *The Blind Assassin* by Silvija Brice.

2646. "Al Purdy: The Awkward Sublime." *Border Crossings* 19.4 (2000): 46-51. Short reminiscence.

2647. *Alias Grace*. Toronto: Seal Books, 2000. Paperback reprint of 1996 title.

2648. *Alias Grace*. [Sound recording]. Vancouver, BC: Crane Resource Centre, 2000. 10 sound cassettes.

2649. "Animal Victims." *The Wild Animal Story*. Ed. Ralph H. Lutts. Philadelphia: Temple UP, 1998. 215-224. Reprinted from *Survival*, ©1972.

2650. "The Animals in That Country." *The Caedmon Poetry Collection*. [Sound recording]. New York: Caedmon, 2000. Compact disc, 3 sound discs (ca. 3-1/2 hr.). Atwood reads on disc 3.

2651. *The Blind Assassin*. Toronto: McClelland and Stewart; New York: Nan A. Talese; London: Bloomsbury, 2000.

2652. *The Blind Assassin*. London: Virago, 2000. Paperback edition.

2653. *The Blind Assassin*. New York: Random House; Leicester: Charnwood, 2000. Large print edition.

2654. *The Blind Assassin*. Charlesbourg, QU: Braille Jymico, 2000. Abridged Braille edition.

2655. *The Blind Assassin*. Bredbury, UK: National Library for the Blind, 2000. Braille ed., 12 v.

2656. *The Blind Assassin*. [Sound recording]. Read by Lorelei King. London: Harper-Collins, 2000. Abridged version.

2657. *The Blind Assassin*. [Sound recording]. Read by Margot Dionne. Prince Frederick, MD: Bantam Doubleday Dell Audio, 2000. Unabridged. 11 cassettes. 18 hours.

2658. *Bluebeard's Egg*. [Sound recording]. Read by Bonnie Hurren. Bath [UK]: Chivers, 2000. 9 hr., 8 cassettes.

2659. *Captive*. Paris: Pocket, 2000. French translation of *Alias Grace* by Michèle Albaret-Maatsch. Paperback version of hardcover edition originally published in 1998.

2660. "[Cartoons]." *The Brick* Fall 2000: 44, 90. Two sets of cartoons spoofing questions asked on book tours.

2661. "[Comment]." *Los Angeles Times* 13 August 2000: Section: Book Review: 2. On the eve of the Democratic Presidential Convention, Atwood was part of a symposium considering the following questions: Which novel (or novels) prompted (or deepened) your own political awakening? How old were you when you read it and what effect did it have on you? Do you think the novel today is able to embrace or sustain a deliberately political purpose consistent with a writer's aesthetic or artistic obligations? Which two or three political novels (past or present) do you regard as exemplary, and why?

2662. *Dama Parege*. Riga: Atena, 2000. Latvian translation of *Lady Oracle* by Silvija Brice. Incidentally, the Latvian translation of Margaret Atwood is Margareta Atvuda.

2663. *Dancing Girls and Other Stories*. [Sound recording]. Vancouver, BC: Crane Resource Centre, 2000. 6 sound cassettes. The book was originally published in 1977.

2664. *De Roofbruid*. Amsterdam: Ooievaar, 2000. Dutch translation of *The Robber Bride*. Paperback.

2665. "Dealing a Blank Card." *Globe and Mail* 1 November 2000: A15. The Canadian Alliance's Cultural Platform is naked as a jaybird, says Atwood. It ignores a multibillion dollar industry and a million workers. [Ed. note: The Canadian Alliance, formally the Canadian Reform Conservative Alliance, was a Canadian right-of-center conservative political party that existed between 2000 to 2003, serving as the Official Opposition in the House of Commons throughout its existence. The party supported policies that were both fiscally and socially conservative, seeking reduced government spending on social programs and reductions in taxation. In December 2003, the Canadian Alliance and the Progressive Conservative parties voted to disband and merge into the Conservative Party of Canada.]

2666. "Death by Landscape." *The Norton Anthology of Short Fiction*. 6th ed. Ed. R. V. Cassill and Richard Bausch. New York: Norton, 2000. [8]-20. Reprinted from *Wilderness Tips*, ©1991.

2667. *Den Blinde Mördaren*. Stockholm: Prisma, 2000. Swedish translation of *The Blind Assassin* by Ulla Danielsson. Also published by Pan.

2668. *Den spiselige kvinde*. [Copenhagen]: Lindhardt og Ringhof, 2000. Danish translation of *The Edible Woman* by Marit Lise Bøgh.

2669. *Der Blinde Mörder: Roman*. Berlin: Berlin Verlag, 2000. German translation of *The Blind Assassin* by Brigitte Walitzek.

2670. *Die Essbare Frau: Roman*. Berlin: BTB, 2000. German translation of *The Edible Woman* by Walter Waldhoff.

2671. *Die Giftmischer: Horror-Trips und Happy-Endings*. Munich: Claassen, 2000. German translation of *Murder in the Dark*, ©1983.

2672. "*Doctor Glas*: Hjalmar Söderberg." *Lost Classics*. Ed. Michael Ondaatje, Michael Redhill, Esta Spalding, and Linda Spalding. Toronto: Knopf, 2000. 1-4. On a forgotten novel; essay reprinted from *Brick: A Literary Journal*.

2673. "Dreams of the Animals." *Listener in the Snow: The Practice and Teaching of Poetry*. By Mark Statman. New York: Teachers and Writers Collaborative, 2000. 106.

2674. *Dzikosc zycia*. Wydawnictwo [Poland]: Zysk i S-ka, 2000. Polish translation of *Wilderness Tips* by Maria Zborowska.

2675. "The Elysium Lifestyle Mansions." *Ovid Metamorphosed*. Ed. Philip Terry. London: Chatto & Windus, 2000. 206-213. Story specially commissioned for this book. Also available as a sound recording. London: Watershed, 2000. Poem read by Maureen Lipman.

2676. "[Excerpt]." *Brilliant Careers: The Virago Book of Twentieth-Century Fiction.* Ed. Kasia Boddy, Ali Smith, and Sarah Wood. London: Virago, 2000. 450-455. Reprinted from *Cat's Eye,* ©1989.

2677. "[Excerpt]." *Educational Policy* 14.5 (November 2000): 564. Article by Sharon Keller titled "Religion and Normative Education in the Light of Current Law" begins with an excerpt from a 1995 Atwood poem: "...the sensed absence / of God and the sensed presence / amount to much the same thing, / only in reverse... / Several hundred years ago / This could have been mysticism / Or heresy. It isn't now."

2679. "[Excerpt]." *The Guardian* [London] 8 November 2000: Section: Guardian Home Pages: 8. The beginning of *The Blind Assassin.*

2680. "[Excerpt]." *Saturday Night* 115.17 (2 September 2000): 28-32. From *The Blind Assassin.*

2681. "[Excerpt]." *Toronto Star* 27 August 2000: Section: Entertainment. The beginning of *The Blind Assassin.*

2682. *Fantasie di Stupro: A Altri Racconti.* Milan: Baldini & Castoldi, 2000. Italian translation of *Dancing Girls and Other Stories* (1977) by Monica Nucera Mantelli.

2683. "Foreword." *Beyond Remembering: The Collected Poems of Al Purdy.* Ed. Al Purdy and Sam Solecki. Madeira Park, BC: Harbour Publishing, 2000. 17-18. Atwood's foreword reprinted from in *Pronuncia i nomi / Say the Names* (Ravenna, Italy: Longo Editore, 1999). Reprinted with her permission.

2684. "Foreword." *The Book Group Book: A Thoughtful Guide to Forming and Enjoying a Stimulating Book Discussion Group.* Ed. Ellen Slezak. 3rd ed. Chicago: Chicago Review Press, 2000. xi-xiii.

2685. "Frogless." *Cold Catches Fire: Essays, Poems and Stories Against Climate Catastrophe.* Ed. Sarah O'Gorman and Uche Nduka. Amsterdam: A SEED Europe, 2000. 101.

2686. "From an Italian Postcard Factory." *Audio Archive Anthology.* [Sound recording]. New York: Academy of American Poets, 2000. 2 compact discs. In a collection of historic recordings that spans 40 years of public readings sponsored by the Academy of American Poets, Atwood reading her poem appears on disc 2.

2687. *Giochi di Speechi = Tricks with Mirrors.* Ravenna [Italy]: Longo Editore, 2000. Selection of poems in English with Italian translation on facing page. Translations by Laura Forconi, Caterina Ricciardi, and Francesca Valente.

2688. "Giving Birth." *Mothers and Daughters in the Twentieth Century: A Literary Anthology.* Ed. Heather Ingman. Edinburgh: Edinburgh UP, 1999. 253-271. Reprinted from *Dancing Girls,* ©1977.

2689. "Going to the Wall for Toronto." *Globe and Mail* 29 January 2000: A21. The city doesn't get the respect or the arts funding it deserves, and the case in point is a new home for the Canadian Opera Company. See two letters in response in the *Globe and Mail* on 31 January 2000: A14.

2690. "Great Aunts." *Wrestling with the Angel: Women Reclaiming Their Lives.* Ed. Caterina Edwards and Kay Stewart. Calgary: Red Deer Press. 15-27. Autobiographical.

2691. "Habitation." *Pride and Prejudice and Related Readings.* New York: Glencoe/ McGraw-Hill, 2000. 306. Reprinted from *Selected Poems 1966-1984,* ©1990.

2692. "Hairball." *Bearing Life: Women's Writings on Childlessness.* Ed. Rochelle Ratner. New York: The Feminist Press at the City University of New York, 2000. 190-199. Reprinted from *Wilderness Tips,* ©1991.

2693. "If Our Society Wants to Have Art, Someone Will Have to Cough Up..." *Globe and Mail* 30 March 2000: A15. Based on a speech by Atwood celebrating the Rogers Communications Writers' Trust Fiction and Pearson Writers' Trust Non-Fiction prizes. The speech was originally delivered at a Canadian Club luncheon on Tuesday, 29 March, at Toronto's Royal York Hotel.

2694. *Juegos De Poder = Power Politics.* Madrid: Hiperión, 2000. Bilingual edition introduced, with notes, by Pilar Somacarrera Íñigo.

2695. "[Juvenilia]." *First Words.* Collected and ed. Paul Mandelbaum. Chapel Hill, NC: Algonquin Books, 2000. 3-15. Chapter includes introduction, five short pieces, with commentaries by the editor which reflect on the future appearance of some of Atwood's juvenile ideas in her mature work. Contains "A Representative" [4], a poem; "Three Cheers for Corona!" [4-6], a short essay arguing for a women's right to smoke cigars; "1956—and For Ever [6], poem; "The English Lesson" [7-9], short essay; "A Cliché for January" 10-[15], another short story. The latter is accompanied by a two-page photo of parts of Atwood's original manuscript.

2696. "The Landlady." *A Magical Clockwork: The Art of Writing the Poem.* Ed. Susan Ioannou. Toronto: Wordwrights Canada, 2000. 48-49.

2697. *Le tueur aveugle.* Paris: R. Laffont, 2000. French translation of *The Blind Assassin* by Michèle Albaret-Maatsch.

2698. "Let's Not Paint Artists into a Patronage Corner." *Globe and Mail* 19 January 2000: A17. Letting the wealthy choose our art does not enrich our culture.

2699. "Lichen and Reindeer Moss on Granite." [Port Townsend, WA]: Copper Canyon Press; [Seattle, WA]: Elliott Bay Books, 2000. Broadside poem. "Two hundred fifty copies designed and printed by Sam Hamill and Nellie Bridge, September, 2000."

2700. "Looking Backward 2100-2000." *Globe and Mail* 1 January 2000: M4. Short story.

2701. *Luna Nueva.* Barcelona: Icarus, 2000. Poetry translated into Spanish by Luis Marigómez.

2702. "Modrofúzovo Vajce." *Tichá Hudba: Antológia Ango-Kanadských Poviedok.* Bratislava: Branko Gorjup, 2000. 136.

2703. "My Life as a Bat." *In Our Nature: Stories of Wildness.* Selected and introduced by Donna Seaman. New York: Dorling Kindersley, 2000. 60-66. Reprinted with permission from *Good Bones and Simple Murders,* ©1994.

2704. *Nightingale.* Toronto: Harbourfront Reading Series Chapbook, 2000. Includes three stories: Bottle" (1-4), "It's Not Easy Being Half-Divine" (5-8), "Nightingale" (9-15). From the colophon: "This book is published in three editions totaling 556 copies. Thirty-one copies are printed on premium paper and are handbound in a quarter calf with cloth sides cover and marbled endpapers. This edition features a limited-edition print by the author. Twenty-six copies of this edition are signed and lettered from A to Z by the author and five are hors de commerce. Seventy-five copies are printed on premium paper and are handbound in full Japanese paper over board cover with marbled endpapers. Thirty-nine of these copies are signed and numbered in Roman numerals (from I to XXXIX) by the author and feature a limited-edition print by the author. Thirty-one copies of the book are signed and numbered in Roman numerals (from XL to LXX) by the author. Five are hors de commerce. Four hundred and fifty copies, of which 150 are signed and numbered by the author and fifty are hors de commerce, are printed on acid-free paper and staple-bound."

2705. *Nimeltään Grace*. Helsinki: Otava, 2000. Finnish translation of *Alias Grace* by Kristiina Drews.

2706. "Notes Towards a Poem That Can Never Be Written." *A Magical Clockwork: The Art of Writing the Poem*. Ed. Susan Ioannou. Toronto: Wordwrights Canada, 2000. 98.

2707. "Pinteresque." *Pinter Review: Annual Essays*, 2000: 5. Atwood looks at the relationship to the Old Testament in Harold Pinter's work.

2708. "Reminiscences of Robley Wilson: Editor, *North American Review* 1968-2000." *North American Review* 285.6 (2000): 4-7. Atwood and others remember the editor. Atwood worked with him when she was "just starting my job at St. Lawrence University as an Assistant Professor."

2709. *Second Words: Selected Critical Prose 1960-1982*. Toronto: Anansi, 2000. Reprint of 1982 edition.

2710. "[Selections]." *Hablar/Falar De Poesia: Revista Hispano/Portuguesa De Poesia* 3 (2000): 14. Reprinted from *Luna Nueva*. Includes "Las Palabras Siguen su Viaje," "La Luz," "La Casa Quemada," "La Taza Blanca," "Una Piedra."

2711. "Significant Moments in the Life of My Mother." *Snapshots: 20th Century Mother–Daughter Fiction*. Ed. Joyce Carol Oates and Janet Berliner. Boston: Godine, 2000. 24-38. Reprinted from *Bluebeard's Egg*, ©1993.

2712. *Sokea Surmaaja*. Helsinki: Otava, 2000. Finnish translation of *The Blind Assassin* by Hanna Tarkka.

2713. *Survival: A Thematic Guide to Canadian Literature*. Toronto: CNIB, 2000. Braille ed., 6 v. of title published in 1972.

2714. *Tichá hudba: Antológia anglo-kanadských poviedok*. Bratislava: Juga, 2000. 222. Slovak translations of several Atwood short stories by Alojz Keníz and Marián Gazdík.

2715. *Tornare a galla*. Milan: Baldini & Castoldi, 2000. Italian translation of *Surfacing* by Fausta Libardi.

2716. "Variation on the Word *Sleep*." *Americans' Favorite Poems: The Favorite Poem Project Anthology*. Ed. Robert Pinsky and Maggie Dietz. New York: Norton, 2000. 12-13. Reprinted from *Selected Poems II: Poems Selected and New 1976-1986*, ©1987.

2717. "'We Have Been Given Up as a Lost Cause.'" *Globe and Mail* 1 July 2000: A12-A13. Trapped in Quebec City as the English lay siege, Marie Payzant keeps a secret journal for her children. This story, an original work, is part of a series inspired by a pivotal moment in Canadian history.

2718. *Wilderness Tips*. [Sound recording]. Read by Denica Fairman. Sterling: Dist. by Chivers AudioBooks, 2000. 8-1/4 hours.

2719. "Yo, Ella y Eso." *Borges Múltiple: Cuentos y Ensayos de Cuentistas*. Comp. Pablo Brescia y Lauro Zavala. México: Universidad Nacional Autónoma de Mexico, 1999. 29-30. Spanish translation of "Me, She, and It" (which originally appeared in *Antaeus* 73.74 [1994]: 7) by Alfonso Montelongo.

Adaptations of Atwood's Works

2720. *The Handmaid's Tale*. [Sound recording]. London; Hampton, NH: BBC Worldwide, 2000. The novel dramatized by John Dryden. 2 sound cassettes (3 hours).

2721. RATHBUN, Andrew, composer. *True Stories*. [Sound recording]. [Barcelona]: Fresh Sound (New Talent), 2000. Compact disc, 1 sound disc. CD includes a testament to two of Atwood's lesser-known poems, "True Stories" and "Bluejays." Rathbun, in email conversation with Atwood, claimed "she was pleased with my choices and the subsequent CD."

2722. RUDERS, Poul, composer. "*Tjenerindens Fortælling* [Sound recording]." Copenhagen: Dacapo, 2000. Opera based on *The Handmaid's Tale*. Librettist, Paul Bentley. 2 sound discs in 1 container.

2723. VORES, Andy. "Six Songs on Poems of Margaret Atwood: For Mezzo-Soprano and Piano." [Musical score]. s.l.: s.n., 2000. score ([v], 49 pp.). Poems include "Circe," "They Eat Out," "Siren Song," "At First," "Owl Song," "Tricks with Mirrors."

Quotations

2724. "[Quote]." *Bath Chronicle* 6 March 2000: 19. "Fat women all look the same; they all look 42."

2725. "[Quote]." *Carnal Nation*. Ed. Camellia Brooks and Brett Josef Grubisic. Vancouver, BC: Arsenal Pulp Press, 2000. 7. Includes Atwood quote: "The question we must ask is why no Canadian writer has seen fit—or found it imaginable—to produce a Venus in Canada."

2726. "[Quote]." *Daily Mail* [London] 22 September 2000: 13. In article on Salman Rushdie, Christopher Hudson quotes Atwood declaring: "We should have a Tomb of the Unknown Writer, killed in the wars of the imagination."

2727. "[Quote]." *Daily Mail* [London] 19 October 2000: 26. Atwood quoted in article about women's sense of humor: "Women are putting off marriage for as long as they can because every wedding has to have a bridegroom."

2728. "[Quote]." *Essays on Canadian Writing* 70 (Spring 2000): 252. In article by Robert McGill, "The Sublime Simulacrum: Vancouver in Douglas Coupland's Geography of Apocalypse," the author quotes Atwood's remark on the city in *Cat's Eye*: "Vancouver is the suicide capital of the country. You keep going west until you run out. You come to the edge. Then you fall off."

2729. "[Quote]." *The Guardian* [Charlottetown, PEI] 9 November 2000: A6. Regarding the Booker Award which she won that year for *The Blind Assassin*: "It's a very deep honour and deeply gratifying but I also know having been there that one can not win the Booker and survive it and that life can go on."

2730. "[Quote]." *National Post* 15 December 2000: A20. When Atwood entered the front door of Chapters Books in Toronto for a book signing, Chris O'Keefe, a 20-year-old employee, mistook her for a customer. "I asked her if she was here for the book-signing," said Mr. O'Keefe. "And she dead-panned, 'I am the book-signing.'"

2731. "[Quote]." *Ottawa Citizen* 13 June 2000: A15. In letter arguing for support of culture, Shirley Thomson, Director of the Canada Council for the Arts, quotes Atwood: "The taxpayers' investment in me through this tiny $7,000 grant (in 1969) is probably the best investment they ever made. If I'd been a penny stock, I'd be written up in every financial journal on the planet."

2732. "[Quote]." *Ottawa Citizen* 9 September 2000: A16. Atwood, speaking at anti-free-trade rally in 1988, referred to Prime Minister Brian Mulroney: "He's the kid known as Brian, a name we know that's 'brain' with the letters scrambled." Article also quotes her from an earlier appearance before the Standing Committee on External Affairs and International Trade: "Canada as a separate but dominated country has done about as well under the US as women worldwide have done under men. About the only position they have ever adapted towards us, country to country, has been the missionary position, and we were not on top."

2733. "[Quote]." *Saturday Night* 115.4 (20 May 2000): 63-70. Article on Canadian designers quotes Atwood: "Not surprisingly in a country with such a high ratio of trees, lakes and rocks to people, images from Nature are almost everywhere. Added up, they depict a Nature that is often dead and unanswering or actively hostile to man; or, seen in its gentler spring and summer aspects, unreal." From *Survival*, ©1972.

2734. "[Quote]." *Toronto Life* 34.1 (January 2000): 55-61. Article on Toronto Dollars quotes Atwood, who spoke at a benefit for this charity on 4 June 1999: "We have all been brainwashed into believing that there is only one kind of money—one kind of wealth—and only one measure of human worth—how much money you have—and one kind of exchange—buying and selling. And only one motive to do so—the Siamese twins of consumer greed and the profit motive."

2735. "[Quote]." *Toronto Star* 22 April 2000: 1. Atwood quoted from a recent magazine article in which she told a joke about writers: "The devil appears to a writer and offers to make him a best-selling author and Nobel Prize laureate—he'll be critically acclaimed, world-famous and rich. Of course, he'll have to pay the price: 'There's your soul, of course,' the devil says. 'And then, let's see, I'll want your wife, your first-born child, your mother, your grandmother....' The writer grabs a pen and is about to sign on the dotted line when he pulls up short with a suspicious glint in his eye. 'Okay,' he says, 'what's the catch?'"

2736. "[Quote]." *Toronto Star* 5 November 2000: Section: Entertainment. Atwood on Booker: "An exercise in human sacrifice. The morning after the dinner, the winner gets massacred in the press for being unworthy, and the jurors get massacred for having made the wrong decision."

2737. "[Quote]." *Vancouver Sun* 8 April 2000: E7. In promo for National Poetry Month: "Poetry is the innermost core of language. It's where words are honed and reforged. That's why it's sharp and hot."

2738. "[Quotes]." *John Robert Colombo's Famous Lasting Words.* By John Robert Colombo. Vancouver, BC: Douglas & McIntyre, 2000. Atwood quoted 25 times.

Interviews

2739. "Light & Dark Margaret: Margaret Atwood Can Be, Um, Moody on the Road." *Ottawa Citizen* 29 October 2000: C16. Excerpts from Atwood's interviews with Mary McNamara (*Los Angeles Times*), Linda Matchan (*Boston Globe*), Susan Flockhart (*Sunday Herald*), Dan Cryer (*Newsday*), John Marshall (*Seattle Post Intelligencer*), and Jackie McGlone (*Scotland on Sunday*).

2740. "Literary Pulp." *Inside Borders* (September 2000): 8-9. Atwood interviewed about *The Blind Assassin* for the US bookstore's magazine.

2741. *Margaret Atwood.* [Videorecording]. Princeton, NJ: Films for the Humanities & Sciences, 2000. VHS tape, 1 videocassette (52 min.). In this interview, Atwood discusses topics such as how she became a writer and how the women's movement, World War II, and her home city of Toronto have influenced her writing. Excerpts from *The Robber Bride*—her recasting of the Grimms's tale "The Robber Bridegroom"—and *Cat's Eye* are read by actress Nadia Cameron.

2742. "Margaret Atwood Talks about Her Newest Novel." *Canada AM* (5 September 2000). Available from Lexis-Nexis. An interview with Valerie Pringle in which Atwood comments not only about *the Blind Assassin* but also upon the two biographies written about her, only one of whose titles she can remember. "I don't think you should write biographies of people who aren't dead. And it is my view that I am not dead."

2743. "Writer Margaret Atwood Talks about Her New Book." *Show: The National Magazine* 4 September 2000. Available from Lexis-Nexis. A feature interview with Carol Off;

2744. ABLEY, Mark. "Dire Things: Margaret Atwood." *Dream Elevators: Interviews with Canadian Poets.* Ed. Beverley Daurio. [Toronto]: Mercury Press, 2000. 9-26. Reprint of interview which appeared in *Poetry Canada Review* 15.2 (June 1995): 1, 3+.

2745. BATTERSBY, Eileen. "Unbuttoning Atwood." *Irish Times* 3 October 2000: Section: Arts: 11.

2746. BEMROSE, John. "Margaret's Museum." *Maclean's* 113.37 (2000): 54. Atwood on the writing of *The Blind Assassin* as well as on surviving book tours. Because the Canadian, American, British, Dutch, and German editions of the book came out simultaneously, Atwood talks about plans to do a Canadian tour, followed by an American one, and then a long stint in Europe.

2747. BIGSBY, Christopher. *Writers in Conversation.* Vol. 1. Norwich [UK]: Arthur Miller Centre for American Studies, 2000. See "In Conversation with Margaret Atwood," [45]-55. A nice overview of her career.

2748. CROOK, Barbara. "Atwood Shrugged." *Homemaker's Magazine* September 2000: 27-28.

2749. FICHTNER, Margaria. "Margaret Atwood: Cultivating the Wolves in Her Gothic Vision." *Miami Herald* 9 November 2000: Section: Entertainment News. Available from Lexis-Nexis. On *The Blind Assassin.* Reprinted in the *Milwaukee Journal Sentinel* 12 November 2000: Section: Cue: O6E under title "Margaret Atwood Calls Out the Wolves."

2750. FLOCKHART, Susan. "The Character Assassin: Margaret Atwood Tells Susan Flockhart That She Has the Right to Dislike Some People but Still Manages to Be a Gentle-Voiced Charmer." *Sunday Herald* [Scotland] 8 October 2000: 3. **Why does Atwood dwell so excruciatingly on pain?** "Let me tell you a story," she replies. "Yesterday, I had a wonderful breakfast, went for a beautiful walk in the sunshine, had an excellent lunch with my best friends. Now at what point in that story did your attention begin to wander? Pretty soon, I guess. Nobody would read a novel composed of nothing but wonderful experiences."

2751. FORTNEY, Valerie. "For the Love of the Game—Atwood the Tease: The Booker Prize Winner Is as Animated as the Characters in Her Novels, and Seems to Revel in Her Role of National Literary Icon." *Edmonton Journal* 12 November 2000: E13. Atwood on men: "I'm quite fond of men so long as they have a sense of humour. If they don't have a sense of humour, they're really just...they can be so difficult. I would say it's the guys without the sense of humour who do all this wife murdering."

2752. FRASER, John. "An Atwood Concordance: The Novelist as Ringmaster, Mentor and Reluctant Garage Sale Participant." *National Post* 26 August 2000: B1. The Master of Massey College profiles a Senior Fellow based on current and past interviews with her.

2753. FREEMAN, Alan. "Belle of the Booker." *Globe and Mail* 9 November 2000: Section: Globe Review: R1. Though thrilled to score the coveted Booker, Atwood says that nothing beats winning on her home turf.

2754. GERARD, Jasper. "The First Lady of Letters Is Smiling at Last." *Sunday Times* [London] 12 November 2000: Section: Features. Interviewer didn't like *The Blind Assassin* but would "cheerfully have given her the Booker on personality alone." One earlier interviewer asked Atwood if she were good at housework. Her response: "Check under the sofa." Another demanded to know if she liked men, and also if she were attractive to them. This is said to have elicited the response: "Are you attractive to women? You certainly aren't to me." Interview reprinted in the *Ottawa Citizen* 13 November 2000: A7.

2755. GESSELL, Paul. "I May Never Write Again." *Ottawa Citizen* 25 August 2000: E1. Atwood refuses to have a scripted, predictable life, and won't say what gives her a thrill. "You never know until they arrive. I saw my first grizzly bear last summer. That was a thrill. Luckily, it was going the other way." Atwood acknowledges earlier plans for an opera based on the life of Pauline Johnson have fallen through because "she's not mean enough for an opera."

2756. GORDON, Daphne. "Atwood, Crombie Chat." *Toronto Star* 29 October 2000: Section: Entertainment: D03. Report on interview with Atwood conducted by David Crombie, a former mayor of Toronto, during the International Festival of Authors. Crombie thanked Atwood for being "so nice." "I was so nice," agreed Atwood.

2757. GRAINGER, Brett. "Margaret Atwood." *Elm Street* October 2000: 26.

2758. GUSSOW, Mel. "An Inner Eye That Sheds Light on Life's Mysteries: Margaret Atwood on Vision, Sacrifice and Lyrical Complexities." *New York Times* 10 October 2000: E1. In the interview, Atwood describes herself as "an old crock," or rather, as she corrected herself, "an older crock."

   Asked if she planned to continue writing as long as she could: "Writing is not a necessity. It has been, but it need not continue to be. If I think I'm writing the telephone book, I'd stop....There's always this tug of war. If you're writing, you're not living, and if you're living, you're not writing. So which are you going to do?"

   Spotlight Question: **"You tend to keep the endings of your novels very open and ambiguous. Why not provide an absolute, concrete ending?"** Answer: "Well, partly because I live in the 21st century and we don't have a lot of faith anymore in 'This is the happy ending, and this is the only happy ending, and this is the only way the story can possibly end.' We tend to consider alternatives....We don't get closure in our society as much as we used to—things are just more open-ended, so it's partly for that reason. And the other reason is that I like the reader to feel that they can participate in the active imagination that is the novel."

2759. ———. "Margaret Atwood on Vision and Sacrifice." *International Herald Tribune* [Neuilly-Sur-Seine, France] 17 October 2000: Section: Feature: 24.

2760. HARVEY, Caroline. "Pop Goes the Writer: She Turned Down Gap, but in So Many Other Ways, Margaret Atwood Has Made Peace with Contemporary Culture." *Vancouver Sun* 11 November 2000: E5. Interview to coincide with Atwood's visit to town. [Atwood was asked to be in a Gap Inc. commercial, but turned it down. "I said no. I'm not a complete idiot. I know my limits."] Main thrust of interview is Atwood's acceptance of folks who don't like to read—you can't force them to. Other people's interests don't offend her; they amuse: "Ever seen Italian TV? A whole bunch of naked ladies with very little on bopping around in front of an announcer in a suit. Completely tasteless."

2761. HERBERT, Rosemary. "A Time for Vision: For Margaret Atwood, Author of the Book Club's Selection, *The Blind Assassin*, Writing Is a Revelation." *Boston Herald* 7 September 2000: Section: Arts & Life: O56. Based on telephone interview. Atwood notes that while she lives in an Edwardian home, built in 1911, she likes to "write anywhere, in places where the phone doesn't ring—park benches, airports, rented rooms."

2762. HUBBARD, Susan. "An Interview with Margaret Atwood." *Florida Review* 25.1 (2000): 28-36.

2763. JAY, Sian E. "The Hand-Made Tale." *Straits Times* (Singapore) 21 December 2000: Section: Life: 1, 4. Atwood discusses her life as a writer. When a documentary crew asked her Grade 11 teacher, Miss Medely, to talk about her, they were expecting her to say, "She was a genius, I saw it right away, she was brilliant and I recognized her talent." Miss Medely said, "She showed no particular aptitude in my class." Atwood: "I thought that was very honest of her, and she was right."

2764. MARSHALL, John. "Atwood's Newest Novel Can Be Tough Going, but Then, So Can the Writer." *Seattle Post-Intelligencer* 14 September 2000: Section: Life and Arts: E1. Interviewed when she was in Seattle, Atwood was not happy to be queried about the negative review of *The Blind Assassin* by Thomas Mallon in the *New York Times*.

2765. MARTIN, Sandra. "Atwood Interactive." *Globe and Mail* 28 August 2000: Section: Saturday: R1, 4.

2766. MATCHAN, Linda. "Nothing but the Book: Margaret Atwood Is Happy to Talk about Work, but Little Else." *Boston Globe* 4 October 2000: Section: Living: C1. Atwood not enjoying her book tour, perhaps because in Boston she suffered her "first book tour injury [she had dropped her heavy suitcase on her foot], perhaps because she was tired of 'tedious and uninformed questions' posed by reporters 'with bow ties and hair products, who follow me around like puppy dogs.'"

2767. McGLONE, Jackie. "Boxing Clever." *Scotland on Sunday* 15 October 2000: 12. Interviewer starts out stressed and ends up charmed.

2768. McNAMARA, Mary. "Canada's Sardonic Goddess of Dark Insightful Stories: Margaret Atwood Speaks of Her Ambitious New Novel and of Being a Successful Women in What Is Still a Man's World." *Los Angeles Times* 26 September 2000: Section: Southern California Living: E1. Story based on questions asked during the author's recent appearance at UCLA (University of California–Los Angeles). Her usual quirky comments:

On her early teaching career: "I taught grammar to engineering students in a Quonset hut at 8:30 in the morning. I made them read Kafka. I thought it would come in handy in their later lives."

On Canadian nationalism: "Canada is such a peculiar country that if you say 'Canada exists' people think you hate the United States." The next morning, at her hotel, she told the interviewer that, during book signings, people tend to present her with their entire Atwood libraries: "One dear sweet man had got a hold of an edition of my books for which I had done some watercolors. He wanted me to sign every one." And did she? "Of course not. Not one of my characters would have done such a thing. But I'm much nicer than any of my characters."

2769. METZLER, Gabriele. "Creativity: An Interview with Margaret Atwood." *Margaret Atwood: Works and Impact*. Ed. Reingard M. Nischik. Rochester, NY: Camden House, 2000. 277-286. Interview took place in March 1994. Chapter is a slightly shortened version of the interview first published in the *Zeitschrift für Kanada-Studien* 15.1 (1995): 143-150.

2770. MEYER, Carla. "Atwood as Complex as Her Latest Novel." *San Francisco Chronicle* 20 September 2000: Section: Daily Datebook: C1. In interview Atwood notes she pulled the idea of incorporating the '30s adventure-fantasy pulp genre into *The Blind Assassin* from "the huge filing cabinet" of historical and literary tidbits that is her brain. She says, "The stuff is all in there. I'm just not thinking about it all the time." She laughs, adding, "I'm a walking footnote." She also didn't like the "feminist author" tag. "I'm too old to be formed by that (feminist) school....I started writing in 1956, and it wasn't even on the horizon." "Do I write about women? Sure, so did Tolstoy." In the interview, she wondered why she isn't referred to as "the environmentalist author." "Think what progress could be made if the feminists and the environmentalists could get together and make all the women buy more energy-efficient washing machines."

2771. MILNE, Kirsty. "More to Tom Kitten and Jemima Puddle-Duck Than Meets the Eye." *The Scotsman* 10 November 2000: 17. In a cryptic press conference after the Booker ceremony, Atwood explains why her biggest literary influence was the tales of Beatrix Potter, "especially her dark period."

2772. REHM, Diane. [*Margaret*] *Atwood* The Blind Assassin. [Sound recording]. Washington, DC: WAMU, American University, 2000. Cassette tape, 1 sound cassette (ca. 60 min.). Interview originally broadcast 27 September 2000.

2773. ROSS, Val. "The Elusive Margaret Atwood: 'Canada's Foremost Literary Star Talks about Fame, Politics and the Nature of Buttons." *Quill & Quire* 66.9 (September 2000): 18-19.

2774. ROSTON, Elana. "Canadian Author Margaret Atwood Answers Questions and Discusses Her New Novel within a Novel." *New Times* [Los Angeles] 14 September 2000: Section: Calendar. A short interview that also promotes Atwood's appearance at UCLA's Royce Hall on 15 September.

2775. SMULDERS, Marilyn. "Our Margaret: Don't Believe the Negative Hype." *Halifax Daily News* 10 September 2000: 23. Atwood doesn't claim *The Blind Assassin* is her best novel. "There's a dance in the old dame yet....Just remember, Robertson Davies was just getting wound up at my age. I can only hope I won't have a great big white beard shortly."

2776. STEINBERG, Sybil. "*PW* Talks to Margaret Atwood." *Publishers Weekly* 247.30 (2000): 68. An interview about her writings, her response regarding the formats she uses, and an explanation of the secret elements in her writings.

2777. STRUCKEL, Katie. "The Human Nature of Margaret Atwood." *Writer's Digest* 80.10 (2000): 34-35.

2778. TILLOTSON, Kristin. "Blind Faith." *Star Tribune* (Minneapolis) 29 November 2000: Section: Variety: 1E. Atwood interviewed before her appearance in the city. When asked to explain the differences between Canadians and US residents, she said: "We have to think about you. You don't have to think about us. That about sums it up." Tweaking her involuntary status as a Canadian icon, she remarked "Icons inspire iconoclasm. I can always count on a few people in my native land to throw horse buns."

2779. Van LUVEN, Lynne. "Blind Assassin's Illusions." *Edmonton Journal* 27 August 2000: E13. Pre-publication interview.

2780. VINER, Katherine. "Double Bluff: Atwood Can Enter the Mind of a Murderer or a Child Bully with Ease...." *The Guardian* [London] 16 September 2000: 18. An extensive personal interview.

2781. WERTHEIM, Margaret. "Northern Exposer." *LA Weekly* 17 November 2000: Section: Features: 49. Atwood as a fantasy writer.

2782. WILLIAMSON, Dave. *Author! Author! Encounters with Famous Writers*. Winnipeg: Great Plains, 2000. Includes "Margaret Atwood and Graeme Gibson: A Provencal Lunch." 190-195.

2783. WITTMAN, Juliet. "Time Pieces: Acclaimed Author Margaret Atwood Delves into the Past to Make Her Stories Stick." *Denver Rocky Mountain News* 1 October 2000: Section: Books: 1E. Atwood on the importance of memory: "A man goes to the doctor. The doctor says, 'I've got two pieces of bad news.' The man says, 'Oh dear. That's awful. What are they?' The doctor says, 'First of all, you're just riddled with cancer.' The man says, 'That's horrifying. What is the second piece of bad news?' The doctor says, 'The second piece of really bad news in that you're in the terminal stages of Alzheimer's disease.' And the man says, 'At least I don't have cancer.'"

2784. WONG, Jan. *Lunch with Jan Wong*. Toronto: Doubleday, 2000. 11-15. Atwood started off the series on 7 September 1996 and, after publication in the *Globe and Mail*, Atwood tried to get the interview zapped from the newspaper's electronic database, apparently because it mentioned the name of her daughter.

Scholarly Resources

2785. ALAIMO, Stacy. *Undomesticated Ground: Recasting Nature as Feminist Space*. Ithaca, NY; London: Cornell UP, 2000. See especially Chapter 6, "Playing Nature: Postmodern Natures in Contemporary Fiction," 133-170, which includes some discussion of *Surfacing*.

2786. ANDREWS, Jennifer. "Humouring the Border at the End of the Millennium: Constructing an English Canadian Humour Tradition for the Twentieth Century and Beyond." *Essays on Canadian Writing* 71 (2000): 140-149. In the works of Margaret Atwood, Stephen Leacock, Thomas King, and Lionel Stevenson, Andrews examines the question "Where is here?" through critical treatments of the 49th parallel by Canadian literary scholars. Shows how comic writers reveal their critical biases shaping conceptions of humor and nation and how they anticipate some important directions for this area of study in the 21st century.

2787. ARMITT, Lucie. *Contemporary Women's Fiction and the Fantastic*. New York: St. Martin's Press, 2000. See especially "Vampires and the Unconscious: Marge Piercy, Margaret Atwood, Toni Morrison and Bessie Head," 66-101, and especially the subsection: "Freud, Dora and *Alias Grace*," 91-101, plus "Ghosts and (Narrative) Ghosting: Margaret Atwood, Jeanette Winterson and Toni Morrison," 102-129, and especially the subsection: "Apparitional Geometries: *The Robber Bride* (1993)," 107-115.

2788. BACCHILEGA, Cristina. "Atwood, Margaret." *The Oxford Companion to Fairy Tales*. Ed. Jack Zipes. New York: Oxford UP, 2000. 29. Entry includes some bibliographical citations.

2789. ———. *Postmodern Fairy Tales: Gender and Narrative Strategies*. Philadelphia: U of Pennsylvania P, 1997. Reference to Atwood in discussion of "Bluebeard Plot." 133ff.

2790. BACCOLINI, Raffaella. "Gender and Genre in the Feminist Critical Dystopias of Katharine Burdekin, Margaret Atwood, and Octavia Butler." *Future Females, the Next Generation: New Voices and Velocities in Feminist Science Fiction Criticism.*

Ed. Marleen S. Barr. Lanham, MD: Rowman & Littlefield, 2000. 13-34. *The Handmaid's Tale*.

2791. BARZILAI, Shuli. "Accountable Malignity: Three Kitchen Scenes in Atwood's Fiction." *Newsletter of the Margaret Atwood Society* 24 (Fall 2000): 1-5.

2792. ———. "'Say That I Had a Lovely Face': The Grimms's 'Rapunzel,' Tennyson's 'Lady of Shalott' and Atwood's *Lady Oracle*." *Tulsa Studies in Women's Literature* 19.2 (Fall 2000): 231-254.

2793. ———. "Who Is He? The Missing Persons behind the Pronoun in Atwood's *Surfacing*." *Canadian Literature* 164 (2000): 57-79.

2794. BECKER, Susanne. "Celebrity or a Disneyland of the Soul: Margaret Atwood and the Media." *Margaret Atwood: Works and Impact.* Ed. Reingard M. Nischik. Rochester, NY: Camden House, 2000. 28-40.

2795. BEYER, Charlotte. "Feminist Revisionist Mythology and Female Identity in Margaret Atwood's Recent Poetry." *Literature and Theology: An International Journal of Theory, Criticism and Culture* 14.3 (2000): 276-296. Focuses on *Interlunar* (1984) and *Morning in the Burned House* (1995). Winner of the Atwood Society's award for best article of 2000.

2796. BLOOM, Harold, ed. *Margaret Atwood*. Philadelphia: Chelsea House, 2000. Individual articles, all reprints, indexed in this section.

2797. BONHEIM, Helmut. "Models of Canadianness." *New Worlds: Discovering and Constructing the Unknown in Anglophone Literature.* Ed. Martin Kuester, Gabriele Christ, and Rudolf Beck. Munich: Vögel, 2000. 51-71. Irving Layton's poem, "Butterfly on a Rock," set against Atwood's "Progressive Insanities of a Pioneer" and George Johnston's "War on the Periphery."

2798. BOUSON, J. Brooks. "*The Edible Woman's* Refusal to Consent to Femininity." *Margaret Atwood*. Ed. Harold Bloom. Philadelphia: Chelsea House, 2000. 71-91. Reprinted from *Brutal Choreographies: Oppositional Strategies and Narrative Design in the Novels of Margaret Atwood* (1993).

2799. BRIN, David. "Our Favorite Cliché: A World Filled with Idiots...Or Why Fiction Routinely Depicts Society and Its Citizens as Fools." *Extrapolation* 41.1 (Spring 2000): 7-20. Atwood's *The Handmaid's Tale* used as an example: "When Margaret Atwood posits a world dominated by screeching misogynists, in *The Handmaid's Tale*, she sets up a glorious straw man to protest male oppression. Never mind that 80 percent of the men and the great percent of the women in North America would have fought to their dying breath to prevent Atwood's scenario from ever coming about in the first place. Likelihood is not an issue in the art of polemic, which is useless at persuading your opponents but provides a self-righteous rush to the already committed. (Can you name one person whose pre-established opinions were changed by Atwood's book?)" (Author).

2800. BROWNLEY, Martine Watson. *Deferrals of Domain: Contemporary Women Novelists and the State*. New York: St. Martin's Press, 2000. See especially Chapter 3: "Fantasies of Power, Margaret Atwood's *Bodily Harm*." 67-96.

2801. CAVALCANTI, Idlney. "Utopias of/f Language in Contemporary Feminist Dystopias." *Utopian Studies: Journal of the Society for Utopian Studies* 11.2 (2000): 152-180. Atwood *The Handmaid's Tale* compared to Lisa Tuttle's "The Cure" and Suzette Haden Elgin's *Native Tongue*.

2802. COHEN, M. "A Dystopia of Silence: Atwood's Anti-Censorship Arguments in *The Handmaid's Tale." Zeitschrift für Kanada-Studien* 37 (2000): 113-135.

2803. COHEN, Matt. *Typing: A Life in 26 Keys*. Toronto: Random House, 2000. Autobiography includes snapshots of friends such as Atwood.

2804. COOKE, Nathalie. "Lions, Tigers, and Pussycats: Margaret Atwood (Auto)Bio-graphically." *Margaret Atwood: Works and Impact.* Ed. Reingard M. Nischik. Rochester, NY: Camden House, 2000. 15-27.

2805. DAVIDSON, Arnold E. "Future Tense: Making History in *The Handmaid's Tale.*" *Margaret Atwood.* Ed. Harold Bloom. Philadelphia: Chelsea House, 2000. 21-28. Reprinted from *Margaret Atwood: Vision and Forms,* ©1988.

2806. De ZORDO, Ornella. "Larger Than Life: Women Writing the Excessive Female Body." *Textus: English Studies in Italy* 13.2 (2000): 427-448. *Lady Oracle* compared to Angela Carter's *The Passion of New Eve* (1977) and Jeanette Winterson's *Sexing the Cherry* (1989).

2807. DEER, Glenn. "*The Handmaid's Tale:* Dystopia and the Paradoxes of Power." *Margaret Atwood.* Ed. Harold Bloom. Philadelphia: Chelsea House, 2000. 93-112. Reprinted from *Postmodern Canadian Fiction and the Rhetoric of Authority,* ©1994.

2808. DEERY, June. "Science for Feminists: Margaret Atwood's Body of Knowledge." *Margaret Atwood.* Ed. Harold Bloom. Philadelphia: Chelsea House, 2000. 223-236. Reprinted from *Twentieth Century Literature* 43.4 (Winter 1997): 470-483.

2809. DEYOUNG-PATRIE, Bettie Jo. "Unpopular Gals, a Murderess, and a Bitch: Margaret Atwood's Wicked and Ambiguous Feminism." MA thesis. Northern Michigan University, 2000. 66 pp.

2810. DJWA, Sandra. "'Here I Am': Atwood, Paper Houses, and a Parodic Tradition." *Essays on Canadian Writing* 71 (2000): 169-185. On *Surfacing.*

2811. ———. "'Nothing by Halves': F. R. Scott." *Journal of Canadian Studies* 34.4 (1999-2000): 52-69. Notes that poetry of F. R. Scott (from Montreal) has had "an acknowledged influence on the later work...of Atwood" and that as early as 1950s, Scott isolated "survival" as a Canadian paradigm, two decades before Atwood emphasized this quality in Canadian political life and writing.

2812. DUGAN, Stephen M. "Spectacle versus Surveillance: Panopticism in *One Flew over the Cuckoo's Nest* and *The Handmaid's Tale.*" MA thesis. University of North Carolina at Wilmington, 2000. 37 pp.

2813. FIAMENGO, Janice. "'A Last Time for This Also': Margaret Atwood's Texts of Mourning." *Canadian Literature* 166 (2000): 145-164. Atwood's poetry, focusing on *Morning in the Burned House,* ©1995.

2814. FORSTER, Russell. *A Student's Guide to* Cat's Eye *by Margaret Atwood.* Ballarat, Australia: Wizard Books, 2000. 48 pp.

2815. FOWLER, Karen Joy. "Margaret Atwood." *The Salon.Com Reader's Guide to Contemporary Authors.* Ed. Laura Miller with Adam Begley. New York: Penguin, 2000. 16-19.

2816. FU, Xinyu. "Magelite Aitewude de zuo pin 'Fu xian' zhu ti fen xi = Analysis of the themes in Margaet [sic] Atwood's *Surfacing.*" MA thesis. Lanzhou da xue, 2000. 64 pp. Title in Chinese and English; text in English only with bibliographical references in English and Chinese. Chinese title romanized.

2817. GERIG, Karin. *Fragmentarität: Identität und Textualität bei Margaret Atwood, Iris Murdoch und Doris Lessing.* Tübingen: Narr, 2000.

2818. GHOSH, Nabanita. "The Unbreakable Bond: Absent/Present Mothers and Daughters in the Fiction of Margaret Atwood, Toni Morrison, Amy Tan and Daphne Merkin." PhD thesis. State University of New York at Binghamton, 2000. 225 pp. "My analysis is feminist in nature; it aims to uncover the complexity and ambiguity in the mother-daughter bond through the motif of absence and presence. The mothers I examine are complex, contradictory and vulnerable, like their daughters.

The troubles between absent and present mothers and daughters in these novels ironically reinforce the continuity and connection between these women; this intricate link continues to animate the contours of their lives in intricate ways. Margaret Atwood's *Cat's Eye* and Daphne Merkin's *Enchantment* are written primarily from the daughter's point of view; Toni Morrison's *Beloved* and Amy Tan's *The Kitchen God's Wife* foreground the voice of the mother." (Author). For more see *DAI-A* 61.05 (November 2000): 1834.

2819. GIACOPPE, Monika Frances. "Creating a Usable Past: History in Contemporary Inter-American Women's Fiction." PhD thesis. Pennsylvania State University, 2000. 220 pp. Includes discussion of *Alias Grace*. "Due to the violent establishment of 'New World' nations and the exclusion of women from most written histories, women in the Americas have inherited a doubly ruptured past. Through the use of historiographic metafictions (in Linda Hutcheon's terms), writers such as Margaret Atwood (English Canada), Maryse Conde (Guadeloupe), Rosario Ferre (Puerto Rico), Anne Hebert (Quebec), Nelida Piñon (Brazil), and Leslie Marmon Silko (US Native American) combat this cultural amnesia and work toward establishing a sense of tradition and continuity for Inter-American women." (Author). For more see *DAI-A* 61.08 (February 2001): 3129.

2820. GOETSCH, Paul. "Margaret Atwood: A Canadian Nationalist." *Margaret Atwood: Works and Impact*. Ed. Reingard M. Nischik. Rochester, NY: Camden House, 2000. 166-179.

2821. GRIBBLE, Jill. "Motifs of Transformation in Four Novels of Margaret Atwood" MA thesis. University of Cape Town, 2000.

2822. HAAG, Stefan. "Ecological Aurality and Silence in Margaret Atwood." *Canadian Poetry: Studies, Documents, Reviews* 47 (2000): 14-39.

2823. HARGER-GRINLING, Virginia, and Tony CHADWICK. "Anne Hébert's *Kamouraska* and Margaret Atwood's *Alias Grace*: Individuals in History." *Etudes canadiennes / Canadian Studies: Revue interdisciplinaire des études canadiennes en France* 49 (2000): 51-57.

2824. HATCH, Ronald B. "Margaret Atwood, the Land, and Ecology." *Margaret Atwood: Works and Impact*. Ed. Reingard M. Nischik. Rochester, NY: Camden House, 2000. 180-201.

2825. HENDERSON, Margaret Kathryn. "Mothering the Nation [Manuscript]: Representations of [The] Mother in the Poetry of Judith Wright and Margaret Atwood." PhD thesis. Monash University, 2000. 251 pp. Available in microfiche format (5 microfiches: negative).

2826. HERST, B. "Quiet Apocalypses: The Textual Theatre of Clare Coulter in Margaret Atwood's 'Good Bones.'" *PAJ: A Journal of Performance and Art* 64 (2000): 65-71.

2827. HITE, Molly. "Optics and Autobiography in Margaret Atwood's *Cat's Eye*." *Margaret Atwood*. Ed. Harold Bloom. Philadelphia: Chelsea House, 2000. 131-150. Reprinted from *Twentieth Century Literature* 41.2 (Summer 1995): 135-155.

2828. HÖNNIGHAUSEN, Lothar. "Margaret Atwood's Poetry 1966-1995." *Margaret Atwood: Works and Impact*. Ed. Reingard M. Nischik. Rochester, NY: Camden House, 2000. 97-119.

2829. HORVITZ, Deborah M. *Literary Trauma: Sadism, Memory, and Sexual Violence in American Women's Fiction*. Albany: State University of New York Press, 2000. This book examines portrayals of political and psychological trauma, particularly sexual trauma, in the work of seven American women writers. See especially "Intertexuality and Poststructural Realism in Margaret Atwood's *Alias Grace* and Charlotte Perkins Gilman's 'The Yellow Wallpaper.'" 99-129.

2830. HORWOOD, Harold. *Among the Lions: A Lamb in the Literary Jungle*. St. John's [NF]: Killick Press, 2000. The co-founder of the Writers' Union of Canada comments on his colleagues, including Atwood: "Compassionate, working for human liberation, not tough, cruel, or 'going for the jugular' as some critics liked to say." No index.

2831. HOSSNE, Andrea Saad. *Bovarismo e romance: Madame Bovary e Lady Oracle*. Cotia: Ateliê Editorial, 2000. 300. In Portuguese.

2832. HOWELLS, Coral Ann. "*Cat's Eye*: Creating a Symbolic Space out of Lost Time." *Margaret Atwood*. Ed. Harold Bloom. Philadelphia: Chelsea House, 2000. 173-189. Reprinted from *Modern Novelists: Margaret Atwood* (1996). [Ed. note: Those who check Bloom's book will discover that this reference has been transcribed correctly. The problem is that Bloom himself failed to correctly transcribe his sources. The book title is correctly attributed to Howells, but the article is incorrect (the Howells article is attributed to Staels [see 2886], and the Staels article is attributed to Howells). Equally disturbing, Bloom did not receive permission from either author to reproduce their work.]

2833. ———. "Transgressing Genre: A Generic Approach to Margaret Atwood's Novels." *Margaret Atwood: Works and Impact*. Ed. Reingard M. Nischik. Rochester, NY: Camden House, 2000. 139-156.

2834. IRVINE, Lorna. "Recycling Culture: Kitsch, Camp, and Trash in Margaret Atwood's Fiction." *Margaret Atwood: Works and Impact*. Ed. Reingard M. Nischik. Rochester, NY: Camden House, 2000. 202-214.

2835. JAIDKA, Manju. *From Slant to Straight: Recent Trends in Women's Poetry—Anne Sexton (America), Margaret Atwood (Canada), Stevie Smith (England), Kamala Das (India), Anna Akhmatova (Russia)*. New Delhi: Prestige Books, 2000. See especially "Imperialist Designs and Gender Wars: Margaret Atwood's *Power Politics*." [47]-65.

2836. JONES, Raymond E., and Jon C. STOTT. *Canadian Children's Books: A Critical Guide to Authors and Illustrators*. Don Mills [ON]: Oxford UP, 2000. Entry on Atwood (8-10) lists works for children, citations to some reviews of each, followed by a short essay commenting on each of the titles.

2837. KAARTO, Tomi, and Lasse KEKKI. *Subjektia rakentamassa: Tutkielmia minuudesta teksteissä*. [Turku, Finland]: Turun yliopisto, 2000. Includes discussion of *The Edible Woman*.

2838. KING, Nicola. *Memory, Narrative, Identity: Remembering the Self*. Edinburgh: Edinburgh UP, 2000. See especially Chapter 3: "'A Life Entire': Narrative Reconstruction in Sylvia Fraser's *My Father's House* and Margaret Atwood's *Cat's Eye*." 61-92.

2839. KIRTZ, Mary K. "English-Canadian Literary Cultures Observed: Shields's *Small Ceremonies* and Atwood's *Lady Oracle*." *Canada Observed: Perspectives from Abroad and from Within*. Ed. Jurgen Kleist and Shawn Huffman. New York: Lang, 2000. 175-183.

2840. KNIGHT, Brenda. *Women Who Love Books Too Much: Bibliophiles, Bluestockings & Prolific Pens from the Algonquin Hotel to The Ya-Ya Sisterhood*. Berkeley: Conari Press, 2000. See especially 153-154. Book on women writers...and women readers.

2841. KNOWLES, Nancy Anne. "From Protest to Process: Pacifism and Post-1970 Women's Novels Written in English." PhD thesis. University of Connecticut,

2000. 275 pp. "Battlefront novels are frequently pacifist, teaching pacifism by showing war's horrors. However, another approach to pacifism occurs in novels that invite inductive analysis of the causes of and solutions to war. These novels can be classified as pacifist based on feminist pacifism, which recognizes violence not only at the battlefront but also in otherwise peaceful oppressive relationships. Such pacifist novels posit a reciprocal relationship between battlefront violence and homefront oppression by reversing the setting typical to war literature." (Author). Atwood's *Surfacing* used as an example. For more see *DAI-A* 61.08 (February 2001): 3166.

2842. KOLODNY, Annette. "Margaret Atwood and the Politics of Narrative." *Margaret Atwood*. Ed. Harold Bloom. Philadelphia: Chelsea House, 2000. 29-48. Reprinted from *Studies on Canadian Literature: Introductory and Critical Essays* (1990).

2843. KREUITER, Allyson. "The Representation of Madness in Margaret Atwood's *Alias Grace*." MA thesis. University of South Africa, 2000.

2844. LILBURN, Jeffrey M. *Margaret Atwood's* The Edible Woman. Piscataway, NJ: Research and Education Association, 2000. 110 pp. Study notes.

2845. LJUNGBERG, Christina. "Iconic Dimensions in Margaret Atwood's Poetry and Prose." *The Motivated Sign: Iconicity in Language and Literature*. Ed. Olga Fischer and Max Nanny. Amsterdam: Benjamins, 2000. 351-366.

2846. MacCANNELL, Juliet Flower. *The Hysteric's Guide to the Future Female Subject*. Minneapolis: University of Minnesota Press, 2000. Discussion on *The Handmaid's Tale*, 191-216.

2847. MacKEY, Eva. "'Death by Landscape': Race, Nature, and Gender in Canadian Nationalist Mythology." *Canadian Women's Studies* 20.2 (Summer 2000): 125-130. Examines the cultural politics of race, gender, and nature in the nationalist ideas of the Canada First Movement, the Group of Seven, Margaret Atwood, and Northrop Frye.

2848. MacMURRAUGH-KAVANAGH, M. K. (Madeleine K.) Cat's Eye, *Margaret Atwood*. Harlow: Longman, 2000. 128 pp. York notes.

2849. MacPHERSON, Heidi Slettedahl. *Women's Movement: Escape as Transgression in North American Feminist Fiction*. Amsterdam: Rodopi, 2000. "The author analyzes key feminist and postfeminist novels of the last three decades, focusing on escape as transgression and the essential differences between male and female escape narratives. She argues that escape narratives by women writers reflect the changing face of feminism. She analyzes works by Canadian and US writers, including Marian Engel, Marilynne Robinson, Joan Barfoot, Margaret Atwood, Anne Tyler, and Erica Jong, among others. She finds that the most common escape in feminist fiction is the flight from restrictive gender roles; she also suggests that a woman may escape via physical flight, excessive daydreaming, or emotional paralysis. Although escape has traditionally been viewed as a negative, cowardly reaction, feminist literature reconfigures it as resistance or revolt and, therefore, a positive action." (Publisher).

2850. MANGUEL, Alberto, and Gianni GUADALUPI, eds. *The Dictionary of Imaginary Places*. New York: Harcourt Brace, 2000. Includes "Jaguar Throne, Realm of" from *Murder in the Dark*, 327.

2851. MARINHEIRO, Ana Cristina Barbosa de. "Margaret Atwood [Texto policopiado]: A busca do ser em *Surfacing*." MA thesis. Universidade do Minho [Portugal], 2000. 160 pp.

2852. MARTIN, Frédéric. "L'enfer en ce jardin." *Lettres Québécoises* 100 (2000): 31-32. French translations of Atwood set against translations of Trevor Ferguson and Mordecai Richler.

2853. MATTES, Kimberly. "Margaret Atwood's Warning to Surrogate Mothers: Beware Becoming the Handmaids of the Millennium." MA thesis. University of West Florida, 2000. 48 pp.

2854. McCARTHY, E. "'Great Unexpectations': A Study of Margaret Atwood's *The Edible Woman* and *Lady Oracle* as Bildungsromane." MA thesis. University College, Cork, 2000.

2855. McCOMBS, Judith. "Atwood's Haunted Sequences: *The Circle Game, The Journals of Susanna Moodie,* and *Power Politics.*" *Margaret Atwood.* Ed. Harold Bloom. Philadelphia: Chelsea House, 2000. 3-20. Reprinted from *The Art of Margaret Atwood,* ©1981.

2856. McDERMOTT, Sinead. "Putting Myself in Her Place: Identity, Identification and Irishness in Nuala O'Faolain's *Are You Somebody?* and Margaret Atwood's *Alias Grace.*" *Developing Identities: Feminist Readings in Home and Belonging.* Ed. Lynne Pearce. Aldershot, UK; Burlington, VT: Ashgate, 2000. 110-127.

2857. METZLER, G. "Margaret Atwood and Her Festschrift: A Photo Essay." *Zeitschrift fur Kanada Studien* 20.2 (2000): 7-9.

2858. MILLER, Ryan Edward. "The Gospel According to Grace: Gnostic Heresy as a Narrative Strategy in Margaret Atwood's *Alias Grace.*" MA thesis. Simon Fraser University, 2000. 108 pp. Also available on microfiche from Canadian Theses Service (2002) and as .pdf file: http://www.nlc-bnc.ca/obj/s4/f2/dsk2 /ftp01 /MQ61470.pdf. "Offering her novel as a parodic response to the wild-eyed 'murderesses' of Victorian fiction, Atwood explores Grace's crime and confinement through a lens of Biblical/historical construction, imagining how an incarcerated woman might respond to those processes, while communicating also the privatization of 'self' as conceptualized by Gnostic symbol and myth. Atwood's use of Gnostic myth brilliantly locates the potential for feminist licence in a historical crisis of faith. My reading proposes that she is using this understanding of 'gnosis'— or self-knowledge—as a playful attempt to localize in Grace Marks the alienation and suffering of the divine feminine." (Author). For more see *MAI* 40.02 (April 2002): 309.

2859. MOGFORD, Sheilagh A. "The Murder of the Goddess in Everywomen: Mary Daly's Sado-Ritual Syndrome and Margaret Atwood's *The Handmaid's Tale.*" *Feminist Interpretations of Mary Daly.* Ed. Sarah Lucia Hoagland and Marilyn Frye. University Park: Pennsylvania State UP, 2000. 132-163.

2860. MOREY, Ann-Janine. "Margaret Atwood and Toni Morrison: Reflections on Postmodernism and the Study of Religion and Literature." *Toni Morrison's Fiction: Contemporary Criticism.* Ed. David L. Middleton. New York; London: Garland, 2000. 247-268. *Surfacing* and *Beloved.* Reprinted from *Journal of the American Academy of Religion* 60.3 (1992): 493-513.

2861. MORRISON, Sarah R. "Mothering Desire: A Romance Plot in Margaret Atwood's *The Handmaid's Tale* and Susan Fromberg Schaeffer's *The Madness of a Seduced Women.*" *Tulsa Studies in Women's Literature* 19.2 (2000): 315-356.

2862. MOYLAN, T. *Scraps of the Untainted Sky.* Boulder, CO: Westview Press, 2000. See especially Chapter 5, "The Dystopian Turn," 147-182. About science fiction and dystopias in various works, including Atwood's *The Handmaid's Tale.*

2863. MÜLLER, Klaus Peter. "Re-Constructions of Reality in Margaret Atwood's Literature: A Constructionalist Approach." *Margaret Atwood: Works and Impact.* Ed. Reingard M. Nischik. Rochester, NY: Camden House, 2000. 229-258.

2864. MURRAY, Jennifer. "Perspectives paradoxales: Le sens de l'histoire chez Margaret Atwood." These de doctorat. Université de Franche-Comté, 2000. 454 pp. *The Journals of Susanna Moodie, The Robber Bride,* and *Alias Grace* are examined.

2865. NIEDERHOFF, Burkhard. "How to Do Things with History: Researching Lives in Carol Shields's *Swann* and Margaret Atwood's *Alias Grace.*" *Journal of Commonwealth Literature* 35.2 (2000): 71-85. Examines the literary approach to the reconstruction of the past in both books.

2866. NIKOLAI, Jennifer. "Dance/Theatre Performance: Text, Object, Voice and Movement: 'Half-Hanged Mary.'" MFA thesis. Simon Fraser University, 2000. Thesis inspired by Atwood poem.

2867. NISCHIK, Reingard M., ed. *Margaret Atwood: Works and Impact.* Rochester, NY: Camden House, 2000. Individual articles indexed in this section. Also includes photographs of Atwood (59-70), statements about her from fellow writers (305-310), cartoons by and of the author (313-318), as well as bibliographies of books (only) by and on Atwood. Winner of the Atwood Society's award for best book, 2000.

2868. PACHE, Walter. "'A Certain Frivolity': Margaret Atwood's Literary Criticism." *Margaret Atwood: Works and Impact.* Ed. Reingard M. Nischik. Rochester, NY: Camden House, 2000. 120-135.

2869. PALUMBO, Alice M. "On the Border: Margaret Atwood's Novels." *Margaret Atwood: Works and Impact.* Ed. Reingard M. Nischik. Rochester, NY: Camden House, 2000. 73-85.

2870. PARKER, Emma. "You Are What You Eat: The Politics of Eating in the Novels of Margaret Atwood." *Margaret Atwood.* Ed. Harold Bloom. Philadelphia: Chelsea House, 2000. 113-130. Reprinted from *Twentieth Century Literature* 41.3 (Fall 1995): 349-367.

2871. PARKER, Janice. *Writers.* Calgary: Weigl, 2000. Intended for younger readers, Chapter 1 (6-11) is on Atwood.

2872. PERRAKIS, Phyllis Sternberg. "Atwood's *The Robber Bride*: The Vampire as Intersubjective Catalyst." *Margaret Atwood.* Ed. Harold Bloom. Philadelphia: Chelsea House, 2000. 205-221. Reprinted from *Mosaic* 30.3 (September 1997): 151-168.

2873. REICHENBÄCHER, Helmut. "Challenging the Reader: An Analysis of Margaret Atwood's Creative Technique in Her First Published Novel." *Margaret Atwood: Works and Impact.* Ed. Reingard M. Nischik. Rochester, NY: Camden House, 2000. 261-276. The origins of *The Edible Woman.*

2874. RESTUCCIA, Frances L. *Melancholics in Love: Representing Women's Depression and Domestic Abuse.* Lanham, MD; New York; Oxford: Rowman & Littlefield, 2001. See especially Chapter 3, "Tales of Beauty: Brookner's, Atwood's, and Drabble's 'Feminine Symbolic,'" 35-56. Includes analysis of *Lady Oracle.* "This chapter is a reprint of Frances L. Restuccia, 'Tales of Beauty: Aestheticizing Female Melancholia,' *American Imago,* vol. 53, no. 4 (Winter 1996), 353-383."

2875. RIDER, Janine. "*Alias Grace.*" *Masterplots II: Modern Fiction Series.* Rev. ed. Ed. Steven G. Kellman. Vol. 1. Pasadena, CA: Salem Press, 2000. 29-33. Main characters; summary of novel plus comments on characters, themes, and meanings, and the critical context. Short, non-specialist bibliography.

2876. RIDOUT, Alice. "Temporality and Margaret Atwood." *University of Toronto Quarterly* 69.4 (2000): 849-870. Atwood's attempt to define "What's Canadian about Canadian Literature" in *Survival* is a helpful starting point for considering the way the stories in *Dancing Girls, Bluebeard's Egg*, and *Wilderness Tips* relate to the short-story genre and Canadian literature as broad, limiting categories.

2877. RIGELHOF, T. F. *This Is Our Writing*. Erin: Porcupine's Quill, 2000. While Atwood is not profiled directly, *Life Before Man* is tagged as her best novel, followed by *Alias Grace*.

2878. RIGNEY, Barbara Hill. "Alias Atwood: Narrative Games and Gender Politics." *Margaret Atwood: Works and Impact*. Ed. Reingard M. Nischik. Rochester, NY: Camden House, 2000. 157-165.

2879. ROJAS, Adena. "Maids in Their-Land: A Study of the Effects of the Cult of True Womanhood on Charlotte Perkins Gilman's *Herland* (1915) and Margaret Atwood's *The Handmaid's Tale* (1986)." MA thesis. Southwest Texas State University, 2000.

2880. ROSENTHAL, Caroline. "Canonizing Atwood: Her Impact on Teaching in the US, Canada, and Europe." *Margaret Atwood: Works and Impact*. Ed. Reingard M. Nischik. Rochester, NY: Camden House, 2000. 41-56.

2881. ROWLAND, Susan. "Imaginal Bodies and Feminine Spirits: Performing Gender in Jungian Theory and Atwood's *Alias Grace*." *Body Matters: Feminism, Texuality, Corporeality*. Ed. Avril Horner and Angela Keane. Manchester: Manchester UP, 2000. 244-254.

2882. RUTHERFORD, Lisa Jane. "Objectification, Fragmentation, and Consumption: A Consideration of Feminist Themes in Margaret Atwood's *The Edible Woman*." MA thesis. Carleton University, 2000. Also available on microfiche from Canadian Theses Service (2001) and in .pdf format: http://www.nlc-bnc.ca/obj/s4/f2/dsk2/ftp03/MQ57683.pdf. "This paper examines [the manner in which] Margaret Atwood's *The Edible Woman* plays out the objectification, fragmentation, and consumption of female desire in contemporary Western society." (Author). For more see *MAI 39.5* (October 2001): 1294.

2883. SCEATS, Sarah. *Food, Consumption and the Body in Contemporary Women's Fiction*. Cambridge: Cambridge UP, 2000. Atwood compared to Angela Carter, Anna Margaret Haycraft, Doris Lessing, and Michele B. Roberts. See especially Chapter 4, "Sharp Appetites: Margaret Atwood's Consuming Politics," 94-124.

2884. SOMACARRERA, Pilar. "'Barometer Couple': Balance and Parallelism in Margaret Atwood's *Power Politics*." *Language and Literature* (Journal of the Poetics and Linguistics Association) 9.2 (May 2000): 135-149.

2885. ———. *Margaret Atwood: Poder y Feminismo*. Madrid: Editiones del Orto, 2000.

2886. STAELS, Hilde. "Atwoodian Gothic: From *Lady Oracle* to *The Robber Bride*." *Margaret Atwood*. Ed. Harold Bloom. Philadelphia: Chelsea House, 2000. 151-172. Reprinted from *Margaret Atwood's Novels: A Study of Narrative Discourse* (1995). [Ed. note: Those who check Bloom's book will discover that this reference has been transcribed correctly. The problem is that Bloom himself failed to correctly transcribe his sources. The book title is correctly attributed to Staels, but the article is incorrect (the Staels article is attributed to Howells [see 2832], and the Howells article is attributed to Staels). Equally disturbing, Bloom did not receive permission from either author to reproduce their work.]

2887. ———. "Intertexts of Margaret Atwood's *Alias Grace*." *Modern Fiction Studies* 46.2 (2000): 427-450. Comments on the fictionalization of life of Irish immigrant Grace Marks.

2888. STEIN, Karen. "Margaret Atwood's Modest Proposal: *The Handmaid's Tale*." *Margaret Atwood*. Ed. Harold Bloom. Philadelphia: Chelsea House, 2000. 191-204. Reprinted from *Canadian Literature* 148 (Spring 1996): 57-71.

2889. STREHLE, Susan. "To the Beat of a Different Conundrum: Postmodern Science and Literature." *Postmodern Times: A Critical Guide to the Contemporary*. Ed. Thomas Carmichael and Alison Lee. DeKalb: Northern Illinois UP, 2000. 209-228. Atwood's short-story "Age of Lead" jump-starts analysis.

2890. STURGESS, Charlotte. "Body, Text and Subjectivity in Margaret Atwood's *The Handmaid's Tale* and Nicole Brossard's *Mauve Desert*." *Études canadiennes / Canadian Studies* 49 (2000): 59-66.

2891. ———. "Margaret Atwood's Short Fiction." *Margaret Atwood: Works and Impact*. Ed. Reingard M. Nischik. Rochester, NY: Camden House, 2000. 87-96.

2892. SULLIVAN, Rosemary. *De Röda Skorna: Den Tidiga Margaret Atwood*. Stockholm: Prisma, 2000. Swedish translation of *The Red Shoes* by Ulla Danielsson.

2893. ———. *The Red Shoes: Margaret Atwood Starting Out*. [Sound recording]. Toronto: CNIB, 2000. 9 sound cassettes (13 hr., 28 min.). Recorded from Harper-Collins 1998 title.

2894. TAROZZI, Bianca. "Le divinità vendicative e Margaret Atwood." *Giochi di specchi*. Ed. B. Gorjup and F. Valente. Ravenna [Italy]: Longo, 2000. 26-27.

2895. THOMPSON, Dawn. *Writing a Politics of Perception: Memory, Holography and Women Writers in Canada*. Toronto: University of Toronto Press, 2000. See especially Chapter 2, "Re*Surfacing*: Quantum Visions of Shamanic Transformations," 43-61.

2896. WARE, Tracy. "Where Was Here?" *Essays on Canadian Writing* 71 (2000): 203-214. Discusses the impact of authors Northrop Frye and Margaret Atwood on other Canadian writers' work.

2897. WARNER, Lionel. "Raising Paranoia: Child-Theft in Three 1980s Novels." *Use of English* 52.1 (2000): 49-55. The abduction of children in Graham Swift's *Waterland* set against Atwood's *The Handmaid's Tale* and Ian McEwan's *The Child in Time*.

2898. WEST, Robert Malvern. "Contemporary Portraits of the Fragmented Self." PhD thesis. University of North Carolina at Chapel Hill, 2000. 193 pp. "A recurrent figure in late twentieth-century Anglo-American literature is the fragmented self. In prose fiction and drama, it may take the form of a character who experiences a splitting or a multiple fracturing of consciousness; in poetry, such a figure may be the subject under consideration and/or the poetic persona itself speaking. Although the notion of such a self is hardly original with the current period, it does appear in contemporary writing with remarkable frequency. In chapter three, West discusses novels and short stories by Thomas Pynchon and Margaret Atwood and explores the ways they use fragmentation as a device for characterization." (Author). For more see *DAI-A* 60.04 (October 2000): 1396.

2899. WILSON, Sharon Rose. "The Artist's Marriage to Death in *Bodily Harm*." *Margaret Atwood*. Ed. Harold Bloom. Philadelphia: Chelsea House, 2000. 49-70. Reprinted from *Margaret Atwood's Fairy-Tale Sexual Politics* (1993).

2900. ———. "Mythological Intertexts in Margaret Atwood's Works." *Margaret Atwood: Works and Impact*. Ed. Reingard M. Nischik. Rochester, NY: Camden House, 2000. 215-228.

2901. WISKER, Gina. *Post-Colonial and African American Women's Writing: A Critical Introduction*. New York: St. Martin's Press, 2000. "Provides a critical introduction to well established women writers: Toni Morrison, Alice Walker, Margaret Atwood, Suniti Namjoshi, Bessie Head, and others from the US, India, Africa, Britain, Australia, New Zealand, and introduces emergent women writers from South East Asia, Cyprus, and Oceania." (Publisher).

2902. WORKMAN, Nancy. "Vulnerability in Margaret Atwood's 'Rape Fantasies': A Game of Cards about Life." *Studies in Canadian Literature* 25.2 (2000): 131-144.

2903. YORK, Lorraine. "'He Should Do Well on the American Talk Shows': Celebrity, Publishing, and the Future of Canadian Literature." *Essays on Canadian Writing* 71 (Fall 2000): 96-105. "Three writers with ambiguous relationships to the celebrity world: Margaret Atwood, Michael Ondaatje, and Carol Shields. They have each offered caustic critiques of star systems and yet been caught up in the Canadian celebrity marketing game. The prize-driven literary economy means that writers like these operate in an arena in which literary production is shaped as literary performance." (Journal).

Reviews of Atwood's Works

2904. *Alias Grace*. Toronto: McClelland and Stewart, 1996.
   Journal of Modern Literature 23.3-4 (Summer 2000): 565-573. By W. H. New. Book among several reviewed.
   Law Now 25.3 (December-January 2000-2001): 38-39. By Rob NORMEY.

2905. *The Blind Assassin*. New York: Doubleday, 2000.
   Albuquerque Journal 13 October 2000: 5. By Bay ANAPOL. (725 w).
   Atlanta Journal and Constitution 27 August 2000: 3D. By Diane ROBERTS. (745 w).
   Boston Globe 19 October 2000: Section: Living: D3. By Monica L. WILlIAMS. (913 w).
   Boston Herald 28 September 2000: Section: Arts and Life: 50. By Reeve LINDBERG. (422 w).
   Bulletin with Newsweek 118.6247 (24 October 2000): 103. By Anne SUSSKIND.
   Calgary Herald 2 September 2000: G6. By Catherine FORD.
   Charlotte Observer 28 September 2000: Section: Entertainment News: s.p. By Polly Paddock GOSSETT. Available from Lexis-Nexis. (695 w).
   Chatelaine 73.10 (October 2000): 18. By Bonnie SHIEDAL.
   Chicago Sun-Times 10 September 2000: Section: Show: 18. By Wendy SMITH. (886 w).
   Christian Science Monitor 92.196 (31 August 2000): 16. By Ron CHARLES. (853 w).
   Christian Science Monitor 92.249 (15 November 2000): 19. By Marilyn GARDNER. (617 w).
   Columbus Dispatch 5 November 2000: Section: Features: 7F. By Margaret QUAMME. (738 w).
   Daily News [New York] 10 September 2000: Section: Showtime: 15. By Sherryl CONNELLY. (492 w).
   Daily Telegraph 16 September 2000: 03. By Allison PEARSON.
   Daily Yomiuri [Tokyo] 19 November 2000: 15. By Linda GHAN. (741w).
   Denver Post 3 September 2000: H-04. By Dorman T. SHINDLER.
   Desert News [Salt Lake City] 12 November 2000: Section: Arts: E08. By Susan WHITNEY.

Detroit Free Press 7 September 2000: Section: Entertainment News: s.p. By Susan HALL-BALDUF. Available from Lexis-Nexis. (903w).

Economist 356.8189 (23 September 2000): 101-102. ANON. (752 w).

Edmonton Journal 3 September 2000: E15. By Marc HORTON.

Elle 16.1 (September 2000): 212. By Vince PASSARO.

Entertainment Weekly 558 (8 September 2000): 83. By Megan HARLAN.

Essays on Canadian Writing. Winter 2000: 131-137. By Allan HEPBURN. (2637 w).

Evening Standard [London] 25 September 2000: 61. By Kate CHISHOLM. (630 w).

Financial Mail [South Africa] 1 December 2000: Section: Arts & Leisure: 126. By Itumeleng MAHABANE. (710 w).

Financial Times (London) 16 September 2000: Section: Books: 4. By Michele ROBERTS. (709 w).

Florida Times-Union 1 October 2000: Section: Insight: G4. By Polly Paddock GOSSETT. (665 w).

Fortune 142.9 (16 October 2000): 446. ANON.

Fresh Air 12 September 2000: s.p. By Terry GROSS. Available from Lexis-Nexis. (797w).

The Gazette [Montreal] 2 September 2000: J1. By Donna Bailey NURSE.

Globe and Mail 2 September 2000: D8-D9. By Marina WARNER.

The Guardian 30 September 2000: Section: Guardian Saturday Pages: 10. By Alex CLARK. (1154 w).

Hamilton Spectator 2 September 2000: Section: Books: W04. ANON. (909 w).

Harper's Bazaar 3466 (September 2000): 406. By Melanie REHAK.

Hartford Courant 1 October 2000: Section: Arts: G3. By Susan DUNNE. (619 w).

The Herald [Glasgow] 14 October 2000: 20. By Graeme WOOLASTON. (403 w).

Houston Chronicle 24 September 2000: Section: Zest: 21. By Sharan GIBSON: "Atwood Doesn't Succeed with Complex Novel." (934w).

The Independent [London] 23 September 2000: Section: Features: 11. By Lisa APPIGNANESI. (934 w).

International Herald-Tribune 7 September 2000: Section: Feature: 4. By Michael DIRDA. (Reprint of *Washington Post* review).

Irish Times 16 September 2000: Section: Weekend: 69. By Eileen BAT-TERSBY. (1357w).

Jerusalem Post 29 September 2000: Section: Books: 16B. By Nan GOLD-BERG. (591 w).

Library Journal 125.13 (August 2000): 151. By Beth E. ANDERSEN.

London Free Press 2 September 2000: C7. By Nancy SCHIEFER. (1082 w).

Los Angeles Times 22 October 2000: Section: Book Review: 7. By Merle RUBIN. (1152 w).

Maclean's 113.37 (11 September 2000): 54. By John BEMROSE. (1846 w).

Mail on Sunday 15 October 2000: 66. By Katie OWEN.

Milwaukee Journal Sentinel 3 September 2000: 06E. By Robert Allen PAPIN-CHAK. (604 w).

Nation 271.19 (11 December 2000): 58. By Brenda WINEAPPLE.

National Post 2 September 2000: B7. By Noah RICHLER.

New Statesman 129.4506 (2 October 2000): 53. By Elaine SHOWALTER. (710 w).

New York Times 8 September 2000: E43. By Michiko KAKUTANI. (788 w).

New York Times Book Review 149.51500 (3 September 2000): 7. By Thomas MALLON. (1444 w).

New Yorker 76.27 (18 September 2000): 142. By John UPDIKE. (2625 w).

Newsweek 136.12 (18 September 2000): 85. By Catherine McGUIGAN.

The Observer 17 September 2000: Section: Review Pages: 13. By Adam MARS-JONES. (707 w).

Ottawa Citizen 3 September 2000: C16. By Rosalind MILES.

People 54.14 (2 October 2000): 64. By Jean REYNOLDS.

Plain Dealer 24 September 2000: Section: Sunday Arts: 111. By Ron ANTO-NUCCI. (501 w).

The Press [Christchurch, NZ] 14 October 2000: Section: Features: 13. By Margaret QUINCY. (508 w).

Press Journal [Vero Beach, FL] 24 September 2000 : Section: Indian River Country: C6. By Marilyn CHENAULT.

The Province [Vancouver, BC] 24 Septemer 2000: D17. By Glen SCHAEFER.

Publishers Weekly 247.30 (24 July 2000): 67. By Sybil S. STEINBERG.

Quill & Quire 66.8 (August 2000): 21. By Stephen SMITH. (1051 w).

The Record [Bergen County, NJ] 17 September 2000: Section: Your Times: Y3. By Susan HALL-BALDUF. (546 w).

St. Petersburg Times 3 September 2000: Section: Perspective: 5D. By Samantha PLUCKETT. (549 w).

San Diego Union Tribune 3 September 2000: Section: Books: 1. By Jennifer De POYEN. (1703 w).

Scotland on Sunday 8 October 2000: 13. By Margaret MONTGOMERY.

The Scotsman 7 October 2000: 10. By Michael FABER. (703 w).

Seattle Times 10 September 2000: Section: Books: O12. By Robert Allen PAPINCHAK.

The Spectator 7 October 2000: 50. By Anita BOOKNER.

Star Tribune [Minneapolis] 3 September 2000: Section: Entertainment: 14F. By Joyce SLATER.

Straits Times [Singapore] 4 November 2000: Section: Life: 18-19. By Jeremy SAMUEL.

Sunday Oregonian 10 September 2000: Section: Arts and Living: E10. By Angie JABINE. (958 w).

Sunday Telegraph [London] 17 September 2000: 14. By Kathryn HUGHES.

Sunday Times [London] 24 September 2000: Section: Features: s.p. By Peter KEMP. (855 w).

The Telegram [St. John's, NF] 17 September 2000: 19. By Anne Marie TOBIN.

Time 156.11 (11 September 2000): 118. By Paul GRAY.

The Times [London] 20 September 2000: Section: Features: s.p. By Erica WAGNER. (786 w).

Times-Colonist [Victoria] 8 September 2000: D8. By Anne Marie TOBIN.

Times-Picayune 13 September 2000: Section: Living: 01. By Susan LARSON. (969 w).

TLS 5087 (29 September 2000): 24. By Lorna SAGE.

Toronto Star 27 August 2000: Section: Entertainment: s.p. By Philip MARCHAND.

Toronto Sun 10 September 2000: Section: Comment: C12. By Nancy
    SCHIEFER. (786 w).

US Weekly 293 (25 September 2000): 56. By Katherine DIECKMANN.

Vancouver Sun 26 August 2000: E1. By Annabel LYON.

Vogue 190.9 (September 2000): 466. By Chloe BLAND.

Wall Street Journal 1 September 2000: W 9. By Laura MILLER.

Washington Post 3 September 2000: Section: Book World: X15. By Michael
    DIRDA. (1843 w).

Washington Times 24 September 2000: Section: Books: B7. By Julie HYMAN.
    (1098 w).

2906. *The Blind Assassin*. [Sound recording]. Read by Lorelei King. London: Harper-
Collins, 2000.

The Independent [London] 18 November 2000: Section: Features: 11. By Chris-
    tina HARDYMENT. (569 w).

The Observer 19 November 2000: Section: *Observer* Review Pages: 14. By Kim
    BUNCE. (249 w).

Sunday Times [London] 19 November 2000: Section: Features: s.p. By Karen
    ROBINSON. (155 w).

2907. *The Blind Assassin*. [Sound recording]. Read by Margot Dionne. Prince Frederick,
MD: Bantam-Doubleday Dell Audio, 2000.

Calgary Herald 23 December 2000: G14. By Sandy BAUERS.

Library Journal 1 December 2000: s.p. By D. L. SELWYN.

Los Angeles Times 15 October 2000: Section: Southern California Living: E2.
    By Rochelle O'GORMAN. (797 w).

Philadelphia Inquirer 17 December 2000: Section: Entertainment News: s.p.
    By Sandy BAUERS.

University of Toronto Quarterly 69.1 (Winter 1999-2000): 348. By Judith
    KNELMAN.

2908. *The Labrador Fiasco*. London: Bloomsbury, 1996.

Canadian Children's Literature 26.4-27.1 (Winter-Spring 2000): 157-159.
    By Jim GELLERT.

2909. *A Quiet Game and Other Early Works*. Ed. Kathy Chung and Sherrill Grace. Edmonton: Juvenilia Press, 1997.

English Studies in Canada 26.3 (2000): 366-369. By Barbara PELL.

2910. *Two Solicitudes*. Toronto: McClelland and Stewart, 1998.

Iowa Review 29.3 (Winter 2000): 184-187. By Jennifer LEJEUNE.

2911. *Wilderness Tips*. [Sound recording]. Read by Denica Fairman. Sterling: Dist. by
Chivers AudioBooks, 2000. 8-1/4 hours.

Booklist 97.2 (15 September 2000): 262-263. By Leah SPARKS.

Library Journal 125.16 (1 October 2000): 167. By Laurie SELWYN.

~ 2001 ~

Atwood's Works

2912. "[Afterword]." *We Wasn't Pals: Canadian Poetry and Prose of the First World War*. Ed. Barry Callaghan and Bruce Meyer. Toronto: Exile Editions, 2001. 207-212. Reflections on "In Flanders Fields."

2913. *Alias Grace* [Electronic resource]. Toronto: CNIB, 2001. Computer data (6 files: 130, 119, 129, 128, 103, 119 kilobytes). Braille formatted file.

2914. "The Animals in That Country." *15 Canadian Poets X3*. 4th ed. Ed. Gary Geddes. Don Mills, ON: Oxford UP, 2001. 286. Reprinted from *Selected Poems 1966-1984*, ©1990.

2915. "Betty." *Coming of Age: Short Stories about Youth and Adolescence.* [Sound recording]. [Ed.] Bruce Emra. Burnaby, BC: Library Services Branch, Province of British Columbia, 2001. 11 sound cassettes. Based on 1994 title.

2916. *The Blind Assassin*. Leicester: Charnwood, 2001. Large print edition.

2917. *The Blind Assassin*. Toronto: Seal Books; New York: Anchor Books. Random House; London: Virago, 2001. Paperback.

2918. *The Blind Assassin*. [Sound recording]. Read by Aileen Seaton. Toronto: Canadian National Institute for the Blind, 2001. 1 CD-ROM (21 hr., 45 min.). Also available as 15 cassettes (22 hr., 20 min.).

2919. "[Blurb]." *People You'd Trust Your Life To: Stories*. By Bronwen Wallace. Paperback. Toronto: McClelland and Stewart, 2001. Atwood's well-known dislike of blurbs is set aside for this reprint. Her comments: "These are real stories about people so real you'd think they live next door. All the textures of life are here—the grime, the dailyness, the intricacies, the pain, and then, like small but devastating miracles, moments of intense joy that will take your breath away."

2920. "The Bombardment Continues (Translated from the French)." *Story of a Nation: Defining Moments in Our History*. Toronto: Doubleday, 2001. 5-23. One of several original stories by Canadian writers focusing on great events in Canada's past. Atwood's story captures the journal entries of a frightened French woman, trapped in Quebec City as the English attack in 1759.

2921. *Boven Water*. Amsterdam: Ooievaar, 2001. Dutch translation of *Surfacing* (1979) by Atis J. van Braam.

2922. "[Cartoon]." *Globe and Mail* 8 September 2001: R5. Entitled "Survivalwoman," Atwood supplied this original cartoon in support of *This Magazine*, a periodical for which she had written in the 1970s (in its earlier incarnation as *This Magazine*

Is about Schools). The caption has Survivalwoman, the non-flying, snow-shoed non-heroine of *ThisMag* saying: "Sheesh...I turn my back for a mere 25 years and the whole place goes to rodent excrement!" A little mouse at the bottom responds: "Never any shortage, pal..."

2923. "Crickets." *Landfall* 201 (Autumn 2001): 132.

2924. *De Blinde Huurmoordenaar*. Amsterdam: B. Bakker, 2001. Dutch translation of *The Blind Assassin* by Paul van den Hout.

2925. "Death of a Young Son by Drowning." *15 Canadian Poets X3*. 4th ed. Ed. Gary Geddes. Don Mills, ON: Oxford UP, 2001. 291-292. Reprinted from *Selected Poems 1966-1984*, ©1990.

2926. *Den Blinde Morderen*. Oslo: Aschehoug, 2001. Norwegian translation of *The Blind Assassin* by Inger Gjelsvik.

2927. *Den Spiselige Kvinde*. Copenhagen: Lindhardt og Ringhof, 2001. Danish translation of *The Edible Woman* (1969) by Marit Lise Bogn.

2928. "Diogenes of Montreal." *Globe and Mail* 4 July 2001: R1, R7. Atwood's obituary of Mordecai Richler, 1931–2001.

2929. *Doña oráculo*. Barcelona: Muchnik Editores, 2001. Spanish translation of *Lady Oracle* by Sofía Carlota Noguera.

2930. *The Edible Woman*. London: Virago, 2001.

2931. *The Edible Woman*. [Sound recording]. Read by Barbara Byers. Toronto: Canadian National Institute for the Blind, 2001. 1 CD-ROM (10 hr., 41 min.). "Restricted to use by people with documented print impairment."

2932. *The Edible Woman*. [Sound recording]. Read by Paula Bennett. Vancouver, BC: Crane Resource Centre, 2001. 7 tape reels.

2933. *El Asesino Ciego*. Barcelona: Ediciones B, 2001. 627 pp. Spanish translation of *The Blind Assassin* by Dolors Udina.

2934. *El Cuento de la Criada*. Barcelona: Ediciones B, 2001. Spanish translation of *The Handmaid's Tale* by Elsa Mateo Blanco.

2935. "Eurydice." *Gods and Mortals: Modern Poems on Classical Myths*. Ed. Nina Kossman. New York: Oxford UP, 2001. 102. Reprinted from *Selected Poems 1966-1987*.

2936. "[Excerpt]." *Books in Canada* 30.4 (November-December 2001): 32-33. From Atwood poem "Explorers."

2937. "[Excerpt]." *Hand Luggage: A Personal Anthology*. [Ed.] John Bayley. New York: Continuum, 2001. 139-140. On Raymond Chandler. Reprinted from *Good Bones*, ©1992.

2938. "[Excerpt]." *Toronto Sun* 7 January 2001: C13. From *The Blind Assassin*: "The temptation is to stay inside; to subside into the kind of recluse whom neighborhood children regard with derision and a little awe; to let the hedges and weeds grow up, to allow the doors to rust shut, to lie on my bed in some gown-shaped garment and allow my hair to lengthen and spread out over the pillow and my fingernails to spread into claws, while candle wax drips onto the carpet. But long ago I made a choice between classicism and romanticism. I prefer to be upright and contained—an urn in daylight."

2939. "[Excerpt]." *University of Toronto* [Magazine] 28.3 (Spring 2001): 20. From *The Robber Bride*. Excerpt set in article in U of T alumni magazine entitled "Writes of Passage" which is designed to illustrate how alumni authors have incorporated various university settings into their novels.

2940. *Fru Orakel*. Copenhagen: Lindhardt og Ringhof, 2001. 309 pp. Danish translation of *Lady Oracle* by Lisbeth Møller-Madsen.

2941. "Game after Supper." *15 Canadian Poets X3*. 4th ed. Ed. Gary Geddes. Don Mills, ON: Oxford UP, 2001. 292-293. Reprinted from *Selected Poems 1966-1984*, ©1990.

2942. "Gertrude Talks Back." *Literary Cavalcade* 53.6 (March 2001): 20. Also in *Literature and Its Writers: An Introduction to Fiction, Poetry and Drama*. 2nd ed. Ed. Ann and Samuel Charters. Boston: Bedford / St. Martin's, 2001. 77. In *Hamlet*, Gertrude never had the chance to defend herself against her son's outrage. In this piece, Atwood gives Hamlet's much-maligned mother the chance to "talk back."

2943. "Giving Birth." *Mother Reader: Essential Writings on Motherhood*. Ed. Moyra Davey. New York: Seven Stories Press, 2001. 311-323. Reprinted with permission from *Dancing Girls*, ©1977.

2944. *Good Bones and Simple Murders*. Toronto: McClelland and Stewart, 2001. Reprint of 1994 title. Short stores, including "Murder in the Dark," "Bad News," "Unpopular Girls," "The Little Red Hen Tells All," "Gertrude Talks Back," "There Was Once," Women's Novels," "The Boys' Own Annual, 1911," "Stump Hunting," "Making a Man," "Men at Sea," "Simmering," "Happy Endings," "Let Us Now Praise Stupid Women," "The Victory Burlesk," "She," "The Female Body," "Cold-Blooded," "Liking Men," "In Love with Raymond Chandler," "Simple Murders," "Iconography," "Alien Territory," "My Life as a Bat," "Hardball," "Bread," "Poppies: Three Variations," "Homelanding," "The Page," "An Angel," "Third Handed," "Death Scenes," "We Want It All," "Dance of the Lepers," "Good Bones."

2945. *The Handmaid's Tale*. [Sound recording]. Read by Mauralea Austin. Toronto: Canadian National Institute for the Blind, 2001. 1 CD-ROM (10 hr., 25 min.). "Restricted to use by people with documented print impairment."

2946. "Happy Endings." *40 Short Stories: A Portable Anthology*. Ed. Beverly Lawn. Boston: Bedford / St. Martin's, 2001. 434-437. Reprinted from *Good Bones and Simple Murders*, ©1983.

2947. "Haunted by *The Night of the Hunter*." *Globe and Mail* 24 November 2001: 1. "Rife with sexuality and images of good versus innocence, *The Night of the Hunter*, is a gripping, quintessentially American movie that has stayed with Atwood since she was a teenager." Written on the occasion of the film's screening by Cinematique Ontario.

2948. *Ho typhlos dolophonos*. Athens: Okeanida, 2001. Greek translation of *The Blind Assassin* by Poly Moschopoulou. Title romanized.

2949. "Horatio's Version." *Sunday Herald* 9 December 2001: 9. This short story was commissioned by the *Sunday Herald* to promote Writing Wrongs, a short-story competition held jointly by Amnesty International and Canongate Publishing. The Canongate Prize is an annual competition for unpublished writing with £30,000 spread equally among 15 writers whose pieces are then published.

2950. "If You Can't Say Something Nice, Don't Say Anything at All." *Saturday Night* 6, 13 January 2001: 27-29, 32-33. Essay later published in *Dropped Threads: What We Aren't Told*. Ed. Carol Shields and Marjorie Anderson. Toronto: Vintage Canada, 2001. 133-148.

2951. "Introducción / Introduction." *Parables: Selected Poems / Parábolas: Poemas*. By Pablo Armando Fernández. Oakville: Mosaic Press, 2001. x-xi. Excerpt from Atwood's one-page introduction also appears on the back cover of book in the form of a blurb: "The poetry of Fernández, if it were music, would be a duet for flute and cello. From this tension, between intensely-loved life and intensely-felt death, come [sic] poems that manage to be at one and the same time elegies and songs of praise." The poet lives in Havana, Cuba.

2952. *Jijo No Monogatari*. Tokyo: Hayakawa Shobo, 2001. 573. Japanese translation of *The Handmaid's Tale* by Eiji Saito. Title romanized.

2953. "Ka-Ching!" *New Yorker* 23 (30 April 2001): 72. Essay by Atwood on her first job.

2954. *Katzenauge: Roman*. Frankfurt am Main: Fischer Taschenbuch, 2001. German translation of of *Cat's Eye* by Charlotte Franke.

2955. *Kör Suikastçi*. Istanbul: Oglak, 2001. 656 pp. Turkish translation of *The Blind Assassin* by Canan Silay.

2956. *L'Assassí Cec*. Barcelona: Proa Beta 2001. 652 pp. Catalan translation of *The Blind Assassin* by Mercé Lopez Arnabat and Albert Subirats.

2957. *L'Assassino Cieco: Romanza*. Milan: Ponte Alle Grazie, 2001. Italian translation of *The Blind Assassin* by Raffaella Belletto.

2958. *Le tueur aveugle: Roman*. Paris: R. Laffont, 2001. French translation of *The Blind Assassin* by Michèle Albaret-Maatsch.

2959. "Margaret Atwood on Joy Kogawa and the Toronto Dollar." *Catholic New Times* 25.7 (April 2001): 6. From a speech given 4 June 1999.

2960. "Morning in the Burned House." *15 Canadian Poets X3*. 4th ed. Ed. Gary Geddes. Don Mills, ON: Oxford UP, 2001. 298-299. Reprinted from *Morning in the Burned House*, ©1995.

2961. *Myös Sinun Nimesi*. Helsinki: Werner Söderström Osakeyhtiö, 2001. 115. Finnish translation of some selected poems from *Interlunar; Poems: 1976-1986* and *Eating Fire, Selected Poetry, 1965-1995* by Tero Valkonen.

2962. *Narichakha Ia Greis*. Sofia: Luchezar Minchev, 2001. Bulgarian translation of *Alias Grace* by Mariana Melnishka.

2963. *Netoru Onna*. Tokyo: Sairyusha, 2001. Japanese translation of *The Robber Bride* by Ayako Sato and Hiromi Nakajima. Title romanized.

2964. "A Night at the Royal Ontario Museum." *15 Canadian Poets X3*. 4th ed. Ed. Gary Geddes. Don Mills, ON: Oxford UP, 2001. 287-288. Reprinted from *Animals in That Country*, ©1968.

2965. "Notes Towards a Poem That Can Never Be Written: *For Carolyn Forché*." *15 Canadian Poets X3*. 4th ed. Ed. Gary Geddes. Don Mills, ON: Oxford UP, 2001. 294-296. Reprinted from *Selected Poems 1966-1984*, ©1990.

2966. "A Novel Worthy of a Queen(Ey)." *Globe and Mail* 4 August 2001: D2. Review of Beryl Bainbridge's *According to Queeney*.

2967. *O Assassino Cego*. Lisbon: Édição Livros do Brasil, 2001. Portuguese translation of *The Blind Assassin* by Elsa T. S. Vieira.

2968. *O Assassino Cego*. Rio de Janeiro: Rocco, 2001. Portuguese translation of *The Blind Assassin* by Léa Viveiros de Castro.

2969. "Orpheus (2)." *Gods and Mortals: Modern Poems on Classical Myths*. Ed. Nina Kossman. New York: Oxford UP, 2001. 119. Reprinted from *Selected Poems 1966-1987*.

2970. "The Ottawa River by Night." *Wading through Deep Water: The Parkinson's Anthology*. Ed. Tony Curtis. Coychurch: Coychurch Press, 2001. 64-65. Available from The Parkinson's Disease Society, 215 Vauxhill Bridge Road, London, UK, SWIV IEJ.

2971. "P. K. Page as a Non-Snow Angel." *P. K. Page: Essays on Her Works*. Ed. Linda Rogers and Barbara Colebrook Peace. Toronto: Guernica, 2001. [12]-13. Poem.

2972. "[Photo]." *First Chapter: The Canadian Writers Photography Project.* Don Denton. Banff: Banff Center Press, 2001. 12-13. Beside photo, Atwood answers question: How do you write? ("Read and write and read and write") and supplies some advice to her younger self, starting out as a writer: "...Toss things out. Get back on the horse that threw you. Develop a good set of back exercises—you'll need them. Get a thick skin, because you'll need that too."

2973. *Pime Palgamõrvar.* Tallinn: Eesti Raamat, 2001. Estonian translation of *The Blind Assassin* by Karin Suursalu.

2974. "Poppies: Three Variations." *And Other Stories.* Ed. George Bowering. Vancouver, BC: Talonbooks, 2001. 53-59. "Reprinted from *Good Bones*, ©1992."

2975. *Príbeh Sluzobnícky.* Ruzomberok: Epos, 2001. Slovak translation of *The Handmaid's Tale* by Marián Gazdik.

2976. *Prinsesse Prunella og den Purpurfarvede Pebernod.* Copenhagen: Lindhardt og Ringhof, 2001. Danish translation of *Princess Prunella and the Purple Peanut* (1995) by Lisbeth Moller-Madsen.

2977. "Progressive Insanities of a Pioneer." *15 Canadian Poets X3.* 4th ed. Ed. Gary Geddes. Don Mills, ON: Oxford UP, 2001. 288-291. Reprinted from *Selected Poems 1966-1984*, ©1990.

2978. "Questioning the Dead." *Landfall* 201 (Autumn 2001): 130.

2979. "Remembering Marian Engel." *The Vintage Book of Canadian Memoirs.* Ed. George Fetherling. Toronto: Vintage Canada, 2001. 571-576. Originally published *Saturday Night*, 1985.

2980. *Shi Nu Nde Gu Shi* [Chinese]. Nanjing: Yi lin chu ban she, 2001. 350 pp. Chinese translation of *The Handmaid's Tale* by Chen Xiao Wei yi. Title romanized.

2981. "Siren Song." *New Straits Times* [Malaysia] 25 July 2001: Section: Literary: 4. Atwood poem taken from *An Introduction to Poetry. 8th ed.* By X. J. Kennedy and Dana Gioia. (New York: HarperCollins, 1994). Piece includes commentary on the same page by Susan Philip. Also in *Gods and Mortals: Modern Poems on Classical Myths.* Ed. Nina Kossman. New York: Oxford UP, 2001, 265, and in *Literature and Its Writers: An Introduction to Fiction, Poetry and Drama.* Ed. Ann and Samuel Charters. 2nd ed. Boston: Bedford / St. Martin's, 2001. 914. Reprinted from *Selected Poems, 1966-1984*, ©1990.

2982. *Slepý Vrah.* Prague: BB art, 2001. 398 pp. Czech translation of *The Blind Assassin* by Sona Nová and Ondrej Poduska.

2983. *Sokea surmaaja.* [Helsinki]: Otava, 2001. 709. Finnish translation of *The Blind Assassin* by Hanna Tarkka.

2984. "Sor Juana Works in the Garden." *Landfall* 201 (Autumn 2001): 131. Volume titled: Shelter.

2985. "Spotty-Handed Villainesses: Problems of Female Bad Behavior in the Creation of Literature." *Uncommon Voices: The Best from Rochester Arts & Lectures' Stage.* Ed. Susan Herman and Susan Chekow Lusignan. Rochester, NY: Rochester Arts and Lecturers, Inc., 2001. 71-84. Speech delivered in 1994.

2986. "Squaw Lilies: Some Notes." *Flora Poetica: The Chatto Book of Botanical Verse.* Ed. Sarah Maguire. London: Chatto & Windus, 2001. 27. Reprinted from *Poems 1976-1986* (Virago, 1992).

2987. *Surfacing.* [Sound recording]. Read by Aileen Seaton. Toronto: Canadian National Institute for the Blind, 2001. 1 CD-ROM (7 hours). "Restricted to use by people with documented print impairment."

2988. "[Synthesia: An Operetta in One Set]." *Globe and Mail* 29 December 2001: D2. The opening act of the first draft of Atwood's home economics opera presented in 1956. Excerpt is part of a broader story called "Writerly Beginnings."

2989. "They Are My Friends." *Coming of Age: Literature about Youth and Adolescence* 2nd ed. Vol. 1. Ed. Bruce Emra. Regina: Saskatchewan Education, 2001. Braille edition. Excerpt from *Cat's Eye*, ©1988. Based on 1999 title.

2990. "They Eat Out." *15 Canadian Poets X3*. 4th ed. Ed. Gary Geddes. Don Mills, ON: Oxford UP, 2001. 293-294. Reprinted from *Power Politics*, ©1971.

2991. "This Is a Photograph of Me." *Working with Texts: A Core Introduction to Language Analysis*. By R. Carter et al. 2nd ed. New York: Routledge, 2001. 148. Poem. Reprinted from *The Circle Game*, ©1966. Commentary: 148-150.

2992. *Tipps für die Wildnis: Zwei Storys*. Frankfurt am Main: Fischer Taschenbuch, 2001. 94. German translation of two stories from *Wilderness Tips* by Charlotte Franke: "Isis in der Dunkelheit" and "Tipps für die Wildnis."

2993. "The Two Fires." *The Spirit of Canada*. Ed. Barbara Hehner. Toronto: Stoddart, 2001. 84-85. Poem. Reprinted from *The Journals of Susanna Moodie*, ©1970.

2994. "Una Camissia Rossa." *33 Scrittrici Raccontano: Seconda Pelle: Quando le Donne Si Vestono / A Second Skin: Women Write about Clothes*. Ed. Kirsty Dunseath. Milan: Feltrinelli, 2001. 176.

2995. *Unter Glas*. Berlin: BTB, 2001. German translation of *Dancing Girls and Other Stories* by Helga Pfetsch.

2996. "Variation on the Word *Sleep*." *The Dominion of Love: An Anthology of Canadian Love Poems*. Ed. Tom Wayman. Madeira Park, BC: Harbour Publishing, 2001. 73-74. Originally published *Selected Poems II 1976-1986* (Toronto: Oxford UP, ©1986).

2997. "The War in the Bathroom." *First Fiction: An Anthology of the First Published Stories by Famous Writers*. [Sound recording]. Los Angeles: Braille Institute of America, 2001 ©1994. This edition consists of 3 sound cassettes and includes Atwood's piece and many others.

2998. "When Afghanistan Was at Peace." *New York Times* 28 October 2001: Section: 6: 82. Recollection of a trip made to Afghanistan in 1978 by Atwood and her family.

2999. *Wilderness Tips*. London: Virago, 2001 ©1991.

3000. "A Women's Issue." *15 Canadian Poets X3*. 4th ed. Ed. Gary Geddes. Don Mills, ON: Oxford UP, 2001. 297-298. Reprinted from *Selected Poems 1966-1984*, ©1990.

3001. "You Fit into Me." *The Seagull Reader: Poems*. Ed. Joseph Kelly. New York, London: Norton, 2001. 14. Reprinted from *Power Politics*, ©1971.

Adaptations of Atwood's Works

3002. *The Handmaid's Tale*. Santa Monica: MGM Home Entertainment, 2001. Re-issue on DVD of 1990 motion picture; screenplay by Harold Pinter.

Quotations

3003. "[Quote]." CBC TV [Sunday Report]. 28 January 2001. Available from Lexis-Nexis. Supporting a Cornwall teen facing 4 charges of uttering death threats, Atwood comments: "One reason childhood can be hell is that, as a child, you can have no power and you can have no recourse and you can have nobody who will actually believe you."

3004. "[Quote]." *The Guardian* (London) 16 August 2001: 19. Atwood quoted in letter to the editor on relations between men and women: "Men fear being laughed at by women. Women fear being killed by men."

3005. "[Quote]." *Halifax Daily News* 4 July 2001: 21. Atwood's comments in statement released after death of novelist Mordecai Richler: "Mordecai Richler was a fine novelist, a brilliant satirist, and an invaluable commentator on the absurdities of national life....He was a consummate professional; he was also a decent and generous man, loved by his friends and respected by his fellow writers. He will be very much missed."

3006. "[Quote]." *The Independent* (London) 1 November 2001: 4. When asked by Canongate, a British publisher, to contribute a comment for the cover of one of its books, Atwood replied as follows: "In my youth," said Ms. Atwood, "I blurbed with the best;

I practically worked with a stencil!
I strewed quotes about with the greatest largesse,
And the phrases flowed from my pencil."

The poem continues in this vein before hitting a more downbeat note:

"But now I am ageing; my brain is all shrunk,
And my adjective store is depleted:
My hair's getting stringy; I walk as though drunk;
As a quotester I'm nigh-on defeated."

Atwood advises Canongate to ask a younger, hungrier author to endorse the book, concluding:

"I wish you Good Luck, and your author, and book,
Which I do hope to read later, with glee.
Long may you publish, and search out the blurbs,
Though you will not get any from me."

3007. "[Quote]." *The National* [CBC] 3 July 2001. Available from Lexis-Nexis. Atwood commenting on Mordecai Richler who had just passed: "He was out to skewer the hot air balloons, and anybody who does that is perceived as being, you know, mean, sharp, et cetera. But unless you have a side of you that is interested in common human decency, you wouldn't be bothered skewering hot air balloons."

3008. "[Quotes]." *The Quotable Gardener: Words of Wisdom from Walt Whitman, Jane Austen, Robert Frost, Martha Stewart, The Farmer's Almanac, and More.* Compiled by Kathy Ishizuka. New York: McGraw-Hill, 2001. 48, 110. Includes two Atwood quotes: "In the spring, at the end of the day, you should smell like dirt" (48) and "Gardening is not a rational act" (110).

3009. "[Quotes]." *The Quotable Woman: The First 5,000 Years.* Compiled and ed. Elaine T. Partnow. New York: Checkmark Books, 2001. 639-640. Includes 28 choice Atwood quotes, almost all from her novels, such as this line from *Cat's Eye*: "If a stranger taps you on the ass and says, "How's the little lady today!" you will probably cringe. But if he's an American, he's only being friendly."

3010. "[Quotes]." *Speaking of Success: Collected Wisdom, Insights and Reflections.* By Pamela Walin. Toronto: Key Porter Books, 2001. 78, 172, 200, 245. Includes various pieces of advice from Atwood.

Interviews

3011. "Atwood Happy to Cross Choppy Sea to Readers." *Sydney Morning Herald* 8 March 2001: s.p. Available from Lexis-Nexis. There are advantages to being short-listed for a literary award 3 times before actually winning it. For starters, says Atwood, "you get better at deciding what to wear...."

3012. BARNETT, Nick. "Write of Passage." *The Dominion* [Wellington, NZ] 6 March 2001: 9. Why Atwood dislikes being labeled a feminist and why she loves surprises: "If my main reason for being on earth was to support women, I wouldn't be a writer. I'd be working in legal aid."

3013. CLARK, Lucy. "Write Again." *Daily Telegraph* [Sydney] 24 February 2001: G08. Interview in advance of Atwood's trip to Australia, a place she likes to visit. Her husband's mother was an Australian from Brisbane and they have "rellies" there. Focus on her as writer.

3014. ELLIOTT, Helen. "The Good Witch: The Sting in the Tale." *Weekend Australian* 3 March 2001: R01. Atwood, daughter of an entomologist, does not like to be pinned down. Lots of new quotes on such topics as "What's Marian [*The Edible Woman*] doing now?" Atwood also complains about lazy journalists: "We get endless faxes and telephone calls [from journalists] wanting to flesh out their Valentine's Day pieces asking what qualities you most value in men, what's your favorite kind of chocolate, if Valentine's Day weren't red, what color would you prefer it to be? Blah, blah blah..."

3015. FIELD, Thalia S. "Author Atwood Visits Harvard, Offers Wilderness Tips." *University Wire* 30 November 2001: s.p. Available from Lexis-Nexis. Atwood interviewed by *Harvard Crimson* on 19 November when she was in town to deliver a speech as part of the Radcliffe Institute's Dean's Lecture Series.

3016. FOCAMP, Paul. "High Priestess of Literature." *Southland Times* [NZ] 3 March 2001: 35. Atwood interviewed in Dunedin. On Toronto in the 1950s: "If you saw a writer's name in the paper it was probably because the old ladies were giving him a tea." In the interview, she discusses her early literary influences from Orwell to Huxley to T. S. Eliot. She also said that as a specialist in Victorian literature she had read *Middlemarch* (George Eliot) at least 5 times.

3017. GOULD, Alan. "Write on! Margaret Atwood." *Good Times* 12.3 March 2001: 10-13.

3018. HEILMANN, Ann, and Debbie TAYLOR. "Interview with Margaret Atwood, Hay-on-Wye, 27 May 2001." *European Journal of American Culture* 20.3 (2001): 132-147. "This interview took place during the 2001 literature festival in Hay-on-Wye in which Margaret Atwood featured prominently. Here she talks about her work as a writer, with particular reference to her latest, Booker Prizewinning novel, *The Blind Assassin*, which was also nominated for the Orange Prize and which won the International Crime Writers' Association's Dashiell Hammett Award." (Author).

3019. HILLER, Susanne. "Atwood's Town: How Toronto Figures in the Author's Novels, and in Her Life." *National Post* 15 September 2001: E1. Atwood interviewed over Sunday breakfast at People's Restaurant on Dupont Street. (Her meal: brown toast and coffee, followed by a "big tip.")

3020. IRVINE, Denise. "Word Perfect." *Waikato Times* [Hamilton, NZ] 5 March 2001: 8. On the origins of *The Blind Assassin* and related topics.

3021. JACOBSON, Michael. "The Sights of the Assassin." *Gold Coast Bulletin* 24 March 2001: W14. Interviewer in awe of Atwood and manages to survive a few darts. Jacobson: "I float across the Queen Street Bridge, not so much chuffed that writer extraordinaire Margaret Atwood has remembered me but thrilled that she could even be bothered....And the privilege of being in her company is as deep as the relief of being out of it."

3022. LAFLAMME, Lisa. "Canadian Author's Book to Become Four-Part Miniseries." *Canada AM* 10 September 2001. Available from Lexis-Nexis. Atwood explains why *The Blind Assassin* was optioned as a mini-series rather than a movie.

3023. LANGDON, Julia. "All the Glittering Prizes." *The Herald* [Glasgow] 8 August 2001: 2. Atwood pooh-poohs literary prizes. In the interview, she also discusses her forthcoming title, *Negotiating with the Dead*, which is based on a series of six lectures she gave in Cambridge: "It's not how to write, it's not why I write, it's not my brilliant career, but it is what is this thing called writing and what do people think they're doing when they do it?" **Does she come up with an answer?** "Well I came up with six lectures, so obviously it's not a short answer."

Atwood also said she has been interested in Scotland for a very long time. Her father's mother, one Florence McGowan, was a Scot who left for Nova Scotia in the Clearances. Margaret and Graeme lived in Edinburgh for a year when he was the first Canadian–Scottish exchange writer and she was writing *Life Before Man*; they made a journey all round the outside of the country, exploring its extremities, and they hiked in Orkney. Her most enduring memory of Edinburgh, however, is of technological problems to do with writing, 22 years ago. Their apartment had two electrical outlets and she had an electric typewriter. This means that she could only ever have any two of light, heat, or electrical power for the typewriter. She had to write in the dark, or the cold, or not write at all. She also had a small child to keep warm. Surely she could have found an adaptor? "If you plugged them all in at once, everything blew."

3024. LAYMAN, Margaret. "Atwood Reveals the Labor of Her Craft." *Daily Yomiuri* [Tokyo] 22 April 2001: 18. Atwood, in Tokyo to speak at Canadian embassy, speaks on the genesis of *The Blind Assassin*, etc. Some comments: "You can never read your own books because, having written them, you already know what happens." When asked about people attributing a political agenda to her work, she responded with a story about her visit to a Japanese monastery. "There was a picture on the wall of a bunch of Jizo figures, and they looked to me quite happy. They were in a sort of cave and they had a candle, so I asked the young monk what this picture meant and he was quite evasive about it. I said it seemed these figures are quite happy and he said, 'Perhaps that is because you are happy.' Then I looked again and there was a quite different way of reading the picture. Some of them looked maybe sort of sleepy, some looked self-satisfied. You could read a number of different things into it," she said.

3025. MOORE, Christopher. "Defying Definition." *The Press* [Christchurch, NZ] 24 February 2001: 4. Interview on eve of Atwood's New Zealand tour.

3026. NICHOL, Ruth. "Taking the Biscuit." *Evening Post* [Wellington, NZ] 10 March 2001: 30. Atwood talks about strange coincidences, [Girl] Guide biscuits, and the perils of wearing plaid. Who is the Blind Assassin? "Some people think the blind assassin is time....There's a little bit in the book that says there are two blind dogs, one is love and the other is justice. You could have Iris, you could even have Laura, and you could have the obvious suspect which is the blind assassin in the story."

3027. O'REILLY, Finbarr. "Atwood on Awards and Almost Dying." *National Post* 13 June 2001: A13. An amusing interview in which Atwood is asked what the best award she ever won was. Answer: "Well, I'd never pick and choose, but who would have ever guessed I'd win the Swedish humour award? My publishers went to accept it and the prize was a crystal ball or bowl—I never did find out because they took it back to their office and someone stole it."

3028. SCHULTZ, Judy. "Her Life, Her Times: Margaret Atwood." *Edmonton Journal* 12 February 2001: C1. Phone interview in advance of Atwood's opening lecture in the Unique Lives and Experiences Series.

3029. SHARP, Iain. "Atwood at Large." *Sunday Star-Times* [Auckland] 25 February 2001: 3. Interview before Atwood headed off to New Zealand for book-signings "and a spot of bird watching." In interview, Atwood claims to love travel. "I'm a nomad by temperament. Things haven't really changed that much since my early days when I'd travel the length and breadth of Canada promoting my poetry...."

3030. SHEPHERD, Rose. "Drama Queen: Booker Prize-Winning Novelist Margaret Atwood Is Fascinated by Fear." *Mail on Sunday* 18 November 2001: 23. In wide-ranging interview Atwood reveals for the first time how she protects herself from germs: "You travel around in planes that are filled with germs," she says. "And if you do something such as the Frankfurt Book Fair, you are infected by germs from all over the world. You're jammed up against other people, they're all talking and laughing all over you, and it's quite a battle to fend off illness....[If] you would like to know how I do it, I will tell you. Firstly I put a gel called Zicam up my nose. Secondly, I swallow a zinc lozenge. Thirdly, I take some Echinacea. And lastly, I take two 1,000 mg vitamin Cs. That usually does the trick."

3031. SIBREE, Bron. "Held Hostage by a Master StoryTeller." *Canberra Times* 3 March 2001: A2. Atwood on her writing career. Example: As a child, she became interested in the writer Susanna Moodie, "because the two Os in her name are the same as the two Os in mine."

3032. TURNBALL, Barbara. "Last Minute Margaret." *Toronto Star* 29 January 2001: Section: Entertainment: C:01. Atwood interviewed in connection with pinch hitting for Margaret Turnball in the kick-off lecture of the Unique Lives and Experiences Series. "Last minute is my specialty," she said. "People come into the world with different capabilities and I was a language person....And I was a language person from the Year One. Like a lot of children, I talked to myself all the time when I was two, and writers probably just keep on doing that." When asked about her devotion to social causes, she commented, "I don't have a day job. No one's going to fire me for saying things that will get other people fired."

3033. WALKER, Susan. "Atwood at Work Again." *Toronto Star* 9 September 2001: D11. A review of Atwood's activities in 2001 in an interview which takes place in Arlequin Restaurant, her local dining spot and interview location of choice [134 Avenue Road, Toronto. Phone: 416-928-9521 for reservations]. Atwood arrives at interview bearing gifts—*The Blind Assassin* bookmarks. They're an item in the point-of-sale merchandise about to flood bookstores on both sides of the Atlantic as the paperback of her Booker Prizewinning novel is released. There's a full-size, cardboard female—the flapper from the much-reproduced cover of *The Blind Assassin*, dump bins, little book ends. "And there's a banner that I plan to turn into a cocktail dress," she jokes.

3034. WIGOD, Rebecca. "Margaret Atwood: A Simple Tale of Herself." *Vancouver Sun* 17 February 2001: B1. Interview with author before her appearance in the Unique

Lives and Experiences Series, Vancouver version. "My whole message is that I don't have a message. I'm a writer. I don't have the secret of life."

Scholarly Resources

3035. "Happy Endings." *Short Stories for Students: Presenting Analysis, Context, and Criticism on Commonly Studied Short Stories*. Vol. 13. Ed. Jennifer Smith. Detroit, MI: Gale, 2001. 149-161.

3036. ABBAS, Herawaty. "The Notion of Power as It Is Reflected in *The Edible Woman* and *Karmila*: A Comparative Study (Margaret Atwood, Marga T., Indonesia)." MA thesis. St. Mary's University, 2001. 99 pp. Also available on microfiche from Canadian Theses Service (2002). "It is found that the major protagonists of the two novels are similar in the effort to free themselves from other people's control, especially from male domination. However, viewed from a cultural point of view, the way each novel asserts their [sic] power is different. This is because the two novels come from different cultural backgrounds. Or in other words, in terms of asserting power, something perhaps is 'small' if it is viewed from one culture, but it is 'big' if it is viewed from another culture. This work is done not to generalize how Canadian and Indonesian women assert their power, but to show how literary works can teach women to empower themselves and to take advantage of each other's culture." (Author). For more see *MAI* 40.05 (October 2002): 1166.

3037. ADHIKARI, Madhumalati. "The Game of Power: Margaret Atwood's *The Handmaid's Tale*, Anita Desai's *Clear Light of Day* and Shobha De's *Snapshots*." *The Feminist Mode in Commonwealth Literature*. Ed. R. A. Singh. Bara Bazar: Prakash Book Depot, 2001. 26-36.

3038. AGUIAR, Sarah Appleton. *The Bitch Is Back: Wicked Women in Literature*. Carbondale and Edwardsville: Southern Illinois UP, 2001. Extensive discussion of wicked women in *Cat's Eye* and *The Robber Bride*.

3039. AMOURA-PATTERSON, Sana. "Using Short Fiction to Explore Definitions of Rape." *Eureka Studies in Teaching Short Fiction* 2.1 (Fall 2001): 76-84. Teaching approaches to rape using Atwood's "Rape Fantasies" and Lessing's "One off the Short List."

3040. BACCOLINI, Raffaella. "Viaggi in distopia: Memoria e immaginazione nell'opera di K. Burdekin, G. Orwell, M. Atwood e M. Piercy." *El Viaje y la Utopia*. Ed. V. Fortunati and O. Steimberg. Buenos Aires: ATUEL, 2001. 157-177.

3041. BARAT, Urbashi. "Feminine Awareness and Feminine Selfhood: Jean Rhys's *Wide Sargasso Sea*, Margaret Atwood's *Cat's Eye*, Bapsi Sidwa's *An American Brat* and Shobha De's *Socialite Evenings*." *The Feminist Mode in Commonwealth Literature*. Ed. R. A. Singh. Bara Bazar: Prakash Book Depot, 2001. 37-48.

3042. BLOOM, Harold, ed. *Margaret Atwood's* The Handmaid's Tale. Philadelphia: Chelsea House Publishers, 2001. Reprints key articles; each indexed in this section.

3043. BLUE, Sarah Jane. "Selfhood and the Art of the Found Object: Self Creation in Three Novels by Margaret Atwood, Colette, and Monique Wittig." PhD thesis. University of Georgia, 2001. "This study examines the problematic of selfhood in three novels by women authors: *Cat's Eye* by Margaret Atwood; *La Maison de Claudine* by Colette; and *L'Opoponax* by Monique Wittig. It views the project of selfhood as an essentially artistic undertaking when read through the lens of object relations theories developed by D. W. Winnicott, Marion Milner, and Jessica Benjamin." (Author). For more see *DAI-A* 62.08 (February 2002): 2750.

3044. BOUSON, J. Brooks. "The Misogyny of Patriarchal Culture in *The Handmaid's Tale.*" *Margaret Atwood's* The Handmaid's Tale. Ed. Harold Bloom. Philadelphia: Chelsea House Publishers, 2001. 21-62. Reprinted from *Brutal Choreographies: Oppositional Strategies and Narrative Design in the Novels of Margaret Atwood,* ©1993.

3045. BROWN, Russell M. "The Practice and Theory of Canadian Thematic Criticism: A Reconsideration." *University of Toronto Quarterly* 70.2 (Spring 2001): 653-689. Includes discussion of *Survival.*

3046. BRUNET-ARVANITAKIS, Emmanuelle. "Les éléments visuels dans les romans de Margaret Atwood de 1969 à 1993." Doctoral thesis. Université Paris III, 2001.

3047. COAD, David. "Hymens, Lips and Masks: The Veil in Margaret Atwood's *The Handmaid's Tale.*" *Literature and Psychology* 47.1 (2001): 54-67.

3048. COCOUAL, Ifiq. "'I'm Sorry It's in Fragments': Poétique du fragment, spécularité, jeux rhétoriques et narratifs dans un passage de *The Handmaid's Tale.*" *Études canadiennes / Canadian Studies: Revue interdisciplinaire des études canadiennes en France* 51 (December 2001): 145-155.

3049. COFFELT, Jamie Roberta. "She 'Too Much of Water Hast': Drownings and Near-Drownings in Twentieth-Century North American Literature by Women (Kate Chopin, Zora Neale Hurston, Eudory Welty, Margaret Atwood, Pam Houston)." PhD thesis. University of North Texas, 2001. 170 pp. "Drowning is a frequent mode of death for female literary characters because of the strong symbolic relationship between female sexuality and water. Drowning has long been a punishment for sexually transgressive women in literature....Chapter 5 analyzes a set of works by Margaret Atwood. *Lady Oracle* includes another faked drowning, while "The Whirlpool Rapids" and "Walking on Water" feature a protagonist who feels invulnerable after her near-drowning. *The Blind Assassin* includes substantial drowning imagery." (Author). For more see *DAI-A* 63.12 (June 2003): 4307.

3050. COHEN, Mark. *Censorship in Canadian Literature.* Montreal: McGill-Queen's, 2001. See especially Chapter 3, "The Ambivalent Artist: Margaret Atwood," 49-87. Extensive discussion of *Bodily Harm* and *The Handmaid's Tale.* Based on author's 1999 PhD thesis.

3051. COUTURIER-STOREY, Françoise. "Subversive Corporeal Discourse in Margaret Atwood's 'The Female Body.'" *Telling Stories: Postcolonial Short Fiction in English.* Ed. Jacqueline Bardolph. Amsterdam: Rodopi, 2001. 35-43.

3052. DEER, Glenn. "*The Handmaid's Tale*: Dystopia and the Paradoxes of Power." *Margaret Atwood's* The Handmaid's Tale. Ed. Harold Bloom. Philadelphia: Chelsea House Publishers, 2001. 93-112. Reprinted from *Postmodern Canadian Fiction and the Rise of Rhetoric,* 1994.

3053. DiMARCO, Danette. "'A Woman Was a Kind / of Joke': Humor as Strategy in *Morning in the Burned House.*" *Newsletter of the Margaret Atwood Society* 26-27 (Fall-Winter 2001): 12, 35.

3054. DVORAK, Marta. "Margaret Atwood's *Cat's Eye*: Or the Trembling Canvas." *Études Anglaises: Grande Bretagne, États-Unis* 54.3 (2001): 299-310.

3055. ———. "What Is Real/Reel? Margaret Atwood's 'Rearrangement of Shapes on a Flat Surface,' or Narrative as Collage." *Margaret Atwood's* The Handmaid's Tale. Ed. Harold Bloom. Philadelphia: Chelsea House Publishers, 2001. 141-153. Reprinted from *Études anglaises* 51.4 (October-December 1998).

3056. FISHER, Susan. "Animalia." *Canadian Literature* 170-171 (Fall-Winter 2001): 256-261. Article discusses several publications that feature animal imagery and specifically Canadian concern for the animal kingdom. Atwood's *Survival* among books analyzed.

3057. FONTAINE, Dorothy-Ann. "'Going Native' in the Twentieth Century (Grey Owl, Margaret Atwood, Dian Fossey, Randy Borman)." PhD thesis. Rice University, 2001. 170 pp. "Originally a pejorative label assigned to someone who has left a structured, civilized, sophisticated society for one (presumably) less responsible, less structured, and less industrious than the original, going native seems deceptively simple to define in its implications. However, it raises critical questions about one's sense of self within a group or nationality, opening up new categories within old oppositions. As the term's pejorative nature seems to continue to moderate, this text seeks to find the spaces in which the term 'going native' places itself in the writing and film of the 1900's....The final chapter looks at an extreme of going native—going feral—(where the new native joins another species rather than another culture) through Margaret Atwood's *Surfacing* and the story of Dian Fossey." (Author). For more see *DAI-A* 62.07 (January 2002): 2416.

3058. GODARD, Barbara. "My (m)Other, My Self: Strategies for Subversion in Atwood and Hébert." *The Art and Genius of Anne Hébert: Essays on Her Works: Night and Day Are One.* Ed. Janis L. Pallister. Madison: Fairleigh Dickinson UP, 2001. 316-334.

3059. GOLDMAN, Marlene. "Margaret Atwood's *Wilderness Tips*: Apocalyptic Cannibal Fiction." *Eating Their Words: Cannibalism and The Boundaries of Cultural Identity.* Ed. Kristen Guest. Albany: State University of New York Press, 2001. 167-185.

3060. GOTTLIEB, Erika. *Dystopian Fiction East and West: Universe of Terror and Trial.* Montreal; Kingston, ON; London; Ithaca, NY: McGill-Queen's UP, 2001. See especially Chapter 4, "Dictatorship without a Mask: Bradbury's *Fahrenheit 451*, Vonnegut's *Player Piano*, and Atwood's *The Handmaid's Tale*," 88-112, and more, particularly, 103-111.

3061. GRACE, Dominick M. "*The Handmaid's Tale:* 'Historical Notes' and Documentary Subversion." *Margaret Atwood's* The Handmaid's Tale. Ed. Harold Bloom. Philadelphia: Chelsea House Publishers, 2001. 155-166. Reprinted from "*Science-Fiction Studies* 25 part 3 (November 1998)."

3062. HERMANSSON, Casie. *Reading Feminist Intertextuality through Bluebeard Stories.* Lewiston, NY: Edwin Mellen Press, ©2001. Based on author's 1998 thesis. Incorporates some references to *The Robber Bride.*

3063. HOLZNER, Judith. "The Taboo against Female Aggression in *Moll Flanders, Lady Audrey's Secret*, and *Alias Grace*." MA thesis. University of Alabama in Huntsville, 2001. "In her book *When She Was Bad: How Women Get Away with Murder*, Patricia Pearson describes the tendency of society to only ascribe men with aggression....Using this theory, it is interesting to look at Daniel Defoe's *Moll Flanders* (1722), Mary Elizabeth Braddon's *Lady Audley's Secret* (1861), and Margaret Atwood's *Alias Grace* (1996)....Each of the three female criminals is not seen as the individual person that she is, but it is attempted to force her into the ideal image of a woman. Since the women who do not conform to society's rules pose a threat to the patriarchy, they need to be controlled." (Author). For more see *MAI* 39.04 (August 2001): 996. [Ed. note: *Lady Audrey's Secret*, by Mary Elizabeth Braddon (1837–1913), was originally published by S. H. Goetzel in Mobile, AL, in 1864, not 1861.]

3064. HUGGAN, Graham. *The Postcolonial Exotic: Marketing the Margins.* New York: Routledge, 2001. See especially Chapter 8, "Margaret Atwood, Inc. or, Some Thoughts on Literary Celebrity," 209-227.
3065. INGERSOLL, Earl G. "Engendering Metafiction: Textuality and Closure in Margaret Atwood's *Alias Grace.*" *American Review of Canadian Studies* 31.3 (2001): 385-401. Examines the gender issues in the history of women's crime and punishment in mid-19th-century Canada.
3066. JAMIESON, Sara. "Mourning in the Burned House: Margaret Atwood and the Modern Elegy." *Canadian Poetry* 48 (Spring-Summer 2001): 38-68.
3067. JOANNOU, Maroula. "'Finding New Words and Creating New Methods': *Three Guineas* and *The Handmaid's Tale.*" *Virginia Woolf and Fascism: Resisting the Dictators' Seduction.* Ed. Merry M. Pawlowski and Jane Marcus. Basingstoke, UK: Palgrave, 2001. 139-155.
3068. KACZVINSKY, Donald P. "*Surfacing* and The Kyklopes: Atwood's Odyssean Escape." *Notes on Contemporary Literature* 31.4 (September 2001): 8-10.
3069. KIM, Bong Eun. "Simulations of America in Mark Twain's *Extract from Captain Stormfield's Visit to Heaven.*" *Journal of English Language and Literature / Yongo Yongmunhak* 47.4 (Winter 2001): 1211-1225. Twain's treatment of America compared to Atwood's *Surfacing.* Korean summary.
3070. KROLL, Jeri. "'I Am a Desert Island': Postmodern Landscapes in Margaret Atwood's 'Circe/Mud Poems.'" *AUMLA: Journals of the Australasian Universities Language and Literature Association* 96 (November 2001): 114-134.
3071. KUHN, Cynthia Guerrera. "Style and Textile: The Performance of Dress in Margaret Atwood's Fiction." PhD thesis. University of Denver, 2001. 236 pp. "Clothing is inherently linked to voice and narrative—we say someone makes a fashion 'statement' or we discuss the 'lines' of a dress. Dressing and storytelling both provide a means for creating identities, and in Margaret Atwood's work, this association is made explicit....The clothed body often becomes a battleground in Atwood's fiction as female protagonists respond to divisive cultural scripts through self fashioning; thus, styling the self becomes a survivalist act. Atwood also seems to collapse the opposition between the material and the spiritual through clothing, to consider dress a fitting metaphor for the space between the natural and the supernatural. While the connections among dress, body, and story are visible from Atwood's earliest novel forward, I contend that they achieve their most unified and powerful effect in *The Robber Bride* (1993) and *Alias Grace* (1996), where Atwood's reconception of the classical idea that the body clothes the soul creates a postmodern frame for the complex relationships among subjectivity, representation, voice, gender, and culture." (Author). For more see *DAI-A* 62.11 (May 2002): 3780.
3072. LEVY, Patricia. *A Guide to* The Handmaid's Tale. London: Hodder & Stoughton, 2001. 105 pp. Teach yourself guides. Advanced.
3073. LJUNGBERG, Christina. "Iconic Dimensions in Margaret Atwood's Poetry and Prose." *The Motivated Sign: Iconicity in Language and Literature 2.* Ed. Olga Fischer and Max Nänny. Amsterdam; Philadelphia: John Benjamins Publishing Company, 2001. [351]-366.
3074. LOSCHNIGG, Maria, and Christina LJUNGBERG. "Buchbesprechungen: To Join, To Fit, and To Make: The Creative Art of Margaret Atwood's Fiction." *Arbeiten aus Anglistik und Amerikanistik* 26.2 (2001): 251-255.
3075. LOWERY, Adrien Jeanette. "The Unconvincing Truth: The Diabolical Politics of Identity Creation in the Novels of Atwood, Munro, and Gilchrist (Alice Munro,

Ellen Gilchrist)." PhD thesis. University of Southern California, 2001. 262 pp. "Specific novels of Margaret Atwood, Alice Munro, and Ellen Gilchrist feature narrator/protagonists who, in their development as artists, discover their own dialogically constructed identities. As children during World War II who come of age as women during the feminist revolution of the '60s/'70s, these women are caught in the dialogical dyad between traditionally modeled feminine roles and their developing career paths as artists. Social interactionist theory uncovers their social communities' influences on them. These daughters become aware of the behavioral and linguistic constructs formed in relationship with their families, their lovers, and their peers—constructs which they have allowed to shape their self images." (Author). For more see *DAI-A* 63.09 (March 2003): 3195.

3076. MacFARLANE, Karen. "Through the Glass Darkly: Humor in Margaret Atwood's Essays." *Newsletter of the Margaret Atwood Society* 26-27 (Fall-Winter 2001): 11-12.

3077. MAK, Elaine Ngah Lam. "Eugenics in Dystopian Novels." MPhil thesis. University of Hong Kong, 2001.

3078. MALAK, Amin. "Margaret Atwood's *The Handmaid's Tale* and the Dystopian Tradition." *Margaret Atwood's* The Handmaid's Tale. Ed. Harold Bloom. Philadelphia: Chelsea House Publishers, 2001. 3-10. Reprinted from *Canadian Literature* 112 (Spring 1987).

3079. MARSHALL, Ian. "Forget The Phallic Symbolism, Consider the Snake: Biocentrism and Language in Margaret Atwood's 'Snake Poems.'" *Mapping the Ethical Turn: A Reader in Ethics, Culture, and Literary Theory*. Ed. Todd F. Davis and Kenneth Womack. Charlottesville: UP of Virginia, 2001. 195-208.

3080. MASSOURA, Kiriaki. "The Politics of Body and Language in the Writing of Margaret Atwood." PhD thesis. University of York [UK], 2001. "This dissertation explores the themes of body and language in relation to male and female power politics throughout Atwood's poetry, short stories and novels. Other issues related to body and language such as pregnancy, maternity, disease, pornography and split personality are also discussed and analysed." (Author).

3081. McDOWELL, John N. "Naturalism, Canadian Literature, and Atwood's 'Polarities.'" *Excavatio: Nouvelle revue Emile Zola et le naturalisme international* 15.3-4 (2001): 253-264. Study of Atwood's well-known short story.

3082. MEYERS, Helene. *Femicidal Fears: Narratives of the Female Gothic Experience*. Albany, NY: State University of New York Press, 2001. See especially Chapter 7, "Beyond Postfeminism: Revaluing the Female Body and the Body Politic," 133-152, which contains an extensive analysis of *Bodily Harm*.

3083. MICHAEL, Magali Cornier. "Rethinking History as Patchwork: The Case of Atwood's *Alias Grace*." *MFS: Modern Fiction Studies* 47.2 (Summer 2001): 421-447.

3084. MILFULL, Alison. "Songs of the Siren: Women Writers and the Femme Fatale." PhD thesis. University of New South Wales (Australia), 2001. "I became interested in foregrounding the responses of women writers to this particular representation of femininity and examining the reception, analysis and attempted resignification of the figure in their work. Drawing upon various theoretical matrices—including feminist theory, psychoanalysis and post-structuralism—I discuss the themes and issues raised by these women writers in regard to conventional representations of the *femme fatale*, explore the varied techniques deployed by these authors in responding to such a prevalent stereotype of femininity, and consider the implications of revisionary feminist mythopoesis. Whilst clear differences arise between their treatments of the myth, the work of Rachilde, [Vernon] Lee, [Angela] Carter, Atwood and [Alina] Reyes will indicate a common interest within English, French and North American feminisms spanning two centuries. The representation of the femme fatale, moreover, emerges as a fascinating field of enquiry which raises critical questions about subjectivity, power, desire, male masochism and sexual difference." (Author). For more see *DAI-A* 64.02 (August 2003): 493.

3085. MINER, Madonne. "'Trust Me': Reading the Romance Plot in Margaret Atwood's *The Handmaid's Tale.*" *Margaret Atwood's* The Handmaid's Tale. Ed. Harold Bloom. Philadelphia: Chelsea House Publishers, 2001. 21-39. Reprinted from *Twentieth Century Literature* 37, no. 2 (Summer 1991).

3086. MINGAY, Philip Frederick James. "Vivisectors and the Vivisected: The Painter Figure in the Postcolonial Novel (Margaret Atwood, George Lamming, V. S. Naipal, Patrick White)." PhD thesis. University of Alberta, 2001. Also available on microfiche from Canadian Theses Service (2002) and as .pdf file: http://www.nlc-bnc.ca/obj/s4/f2/dsk3/ftp04/NQ60328.pdf. *Cat's Eye* plus George Lamming's *Water with Berries*, V. S. Naipaul's *Enigma of Arrival*, and Patrick White's *Vivisector*. See especially Chapter Three, "A Career Not Exactly Real: Margaret Atwood's *Cat's Eye*," which examines the history of the terms "artist" and "painter" and this history's role in the formation of the asocial painter figure. It also explores the effects of education and landscape on painter Elaine Risley's struggle to create "authentic" art. For more see *DAI-A* 62.05 (November 2001): 1826.

3087. MURRAY, Jennifer. "Historical Figures and Paradoxical Patterns: The Quilting Metaphor in Margaret Atwood's *Alias Grace.*" *Studies in Canadian Literature* 26.1 (March 2001): 65-83.

3088. ———. "'The Past, Its Density and Drowned Events': La rivière Moira dans 'Death of a Young Son by Drowning,' poème de Margaret Atwood." *Études canadiennes / Canadian Studies: Revue interdisciplinaire des études canadiennes en France* 50 (June 2001): 211-219.

3089. NEALE, Emma. "Touchpapers: The Poetics of the House Fire." *Landfall [New Zealand Arts and Letters]* 201 (2001): 134-142. Treatment of fire in the poetry of Louise Glück, Atwood, and Cilla McQueen.

3090. PAPINCHAK, Robert Allan. "Judgement Calls." *Writer* 114.4 (April 2001): 40-42. Author discusses the requirements for writing a book review and uses as an example his own review of Atwood's *The Blind Assassin* originally published in *Seattle Times*.

3091. PORDZIK, Ralph. *The Quest for Postcolonial Utopia: A Comparative Introduction to the Utopian Novel in the New English Literatures.* New York; Frankfurt am Main: Peter Lang, 2001. See especially Chapter 5, "Women of the Future: Feminist Issues in Postcolonial Utopia," 89-106. Includes study of *The Handmaid's Tale*, which is set against other contemporary novels.

3092. POSH, Dorothy Ellen Kimock. "Struggling to Survive: The Violent Bildungsroman of Atwood, Kosinski and McCabe (Jerzy Kosinski, Patrick McCabe)." PhD thesis. Lehigh University, 2001. "The three novels in this study—Margaret Atwood's *Cat's Eye*, Jerzy Kosinski's *The Painted Bird*, and Patrick McCabe's *The Butcher Boy*—seem an unlikely trio, but the similarities among the protagonists Elaine Risley, the Boy, and Francie Brady and situations depicted in the three novels far exceed differences in time, place, or gender. Each protagonist endures the same harrowing experience of growing up in a violent world....The characters struggle to remain connected with their humanity; they do this primarily by using language to tell their own stories and to try to make meaning of their experience. This study considers the role of violence; the child's reaction to it; the family, especially the mother, whose relationship with the child is a crucial to well-being; the role of animals, who act as mirrors for the child in the continuum of violence; and the ways in which characters and authors use language to create and convey meaning." (Author). For more see *DAI-A* 62.12 (June 2002): 4146.

3093. ROGERS, Jane, ed. *Good Fiction Guide*. New York: Oxford UP, 2001. Atwood biography (151) plus references to her in articles on Canada (19-22), science fiction (90-93), sexual politics (98-101), and short stories (102-105).

3094. RUBENSTEIN, Roberta. "Nature and Nurture in Dystopia: *The Handmaid's Tale.*" *Margaret Atwood's* The Handmaid's Tale. Ed. Harold Bloom. Philadelphia: Chelsea House Publishers, 2001. 11-20. Reprinted from *Margaret Atwood: Vision and Forms*, 1988.

3095. SAJIC, Emma Louise. "Critical Readings of the Female Body in the Novels of Margaret Atwood: Feminist, Postmodern and Postmodern Feminine Perspectives." MPhil thesis. University of Birmingham, 2001.

3096. SATO, Ayako. "Akuju Wa Toritkusta: Magareto Atouddo Ga Kataru Akujo No Hanashi." *Eigo Seinen / Rising Generation* 147.7 (October 2001): 430-434. In Japanese; titles romanized. Women as villains in *The Robber Bride*.

3097. SHAFFER, C. Lyon. "Scrapbook (Original Writing: Toni Morrison, Margaret Atwood)." PhD thesis. University of Cincinnati, 2001. 90 pp. Dissertation, largely a collection of original poetry by Shaffer, also includes a critical essay about biblical and apocryphal revision in Morrison's *Jazz* and Atwood's *Alias Grace*. For more see *DAI-A* 63.01 (July 2002): 191.

3098. SHECKELS, Theodore F., and Kathleen M. SWEENEY. "Scene, Symbol, Subversion: The Evolving Uses of Mapping in Margaret Atwood's Fiction." *American Review of Canadian Studies* 31.3 (2001): 403-421. Atwood's literal—and metaphorical—use of mapped places in *The Edible Woman* (1969), *Lady Oracle* (1976), *Life Before Man* (1979), *Cat's Eye* (1989), and *The Robber Bride* (1989).

3099. SIEMERLING, Winfried. "Other Canons: Margaret Atwood and the Québecois Reception of English Canadian Literature." *Journal of Indo-American Studies* 1.1 (January 2001): 48-59.

3100. SOKOLOV, Rachel Anne. "Confession, Power and Gender in *The French Lieutenant's Women* and *Alias Grace* (John Fowles, Margaret Atwood)." MA thesis. Truman State University, 2001. 91 pp. "Margaret Atwood's *Alias Grace* and John Fowles's *The French Lieutenant's Woman* are modern novels that highlight the dynamics between two fictional 19th-century working class female social pariahs and their scientific gentleman saviors. The power differences between these 'mad' women and the men authorized to cure them illustrate that their cross-talk is what allows these 'powerless' women to subvert the traditional hierarchy of the therapeutic relationship...In Atwood's novel, accused murderess Grace Marks controls her confession to Dr. Simon Jordan in a way that brings into question the ways we construct our personalities and see the world." (Author). For more see *MAI* 39.05 (October 2001): 1292.

3101. STAELS, Hilde. "Margaret Atwood's *The Handmaid's Tale*: Resistance through Narrating." *Margaret Atwood's* The Handmaid's Tale. Ed. Harold Bloom. Philadelphia: Chelsea House Publishers, 2001. 113-126. Reprinted from "English Studies 76.5 (September 1995)."

3102. STEIN, Karen. "Margaret Atwood's Modest Proposal: *The Handmaid's Tale.*" *Margaret Atwood's* The Handmaid's Tale. Ed. Harold Bloom. Philadelphia: Chelsea House Publishers, 2001. 127-140. Reprinted from *Canadian Literature* 148 (Spring 1996): 57-71.

3103. STRAUBEL, Linda H., and Gayle ELLIOTT. "Margaret Eleanor Atwood." *A Reader's Companion to the Short Story in English*. Ed. Erin Fallon et al. Westport, CT: Greenwood Press, for Society for the Study of the Short Story, 2001. 29-37.

3104. STRINGER, K. "Changing the Story: Authenticity and Identity in the Poetry of Margaret Atwood and Eavan Boland." PhD thesis. University of Dundee, 2001. "I examine the differences in the poet's interpretations of mythic and literary texts and the extent to which postcolonial and feminist discourses inform their poetry... The first chapter focuses on Atwood's rewriting of the Circe, Orpheus and Eurydice myths in her *You Are Happy* and *Interlunar*...The second chapter examines Atwood's rewriting of the accounts of Susanna Moodie in her sequence, *The Journals of Susanna Moodie*, as she addresses the gaps in Susanna Moodie's original texts and uses Moodie's accounts as a focus for her exploration of her own personal poetic mythology of Canadian identity. Nature, and the culture/nature dualism, feature prominently in these poems." (Author).

3105. SULLIVAN, Rosemary. *Memory-Making: Selected Essays*. Windsor [ON]: Black Moss Press, 2001. See especially "Alias Margaret: The Radcliffe Years." 38-52. Reprint of 1998 essay.

3106. SVERRISDÓTTIR, Halla. "Í krafti orðsins: Um *The Blind Assassin* eftir Margaret Atwood." *Tímarit Máls og Menningar* 62.1 (2001) 54-55. Translation of German title: "In the Power of the Word: On *The Blind Assassin* by Margaret Atwood."

3107. SZALAY, Edina. "The Gothic as Maternal Legacy in Margaret Atwood's *Lady Oracle*." *Neohelicon* 28.1 (2001): 216-236.

3108. TEMPLIN, Charlotte. "Margaret Atwood's Comedy: The Trickster, the Fat Lady, and the Gendered Body in *Lady Oracle*." *Newsletter of the Margaret Atwood Society* 26-27 (Fall-Winter 2001): 11.

3109. TIEDEMANN, Heidi Janean. "After the Fact: Contemporary Feminist Fiction and Historical Trauma (Margaret Atwood, Nora Okja Keller, Joy Kogawa, Edwidge Danticat, Julia Alvarez)." PhD thesis. University of Toronto, 2001. Also available on microfiche from Canadian Theses Service (2002) and as .pdf file: http://www .nlc-bnc.ca/obj/s4/f2/dsk3/ftp04/NQ63656.pdf. "Many trauma novels take the form of historical fiction, narrated in the first-person by fictional or fictionalized survivors whose accounts bear witness to the need for violent actions to be admitted into public consciousness. This dissertation proposes that concerns about the construction of identities, chiefly in terms of gender, race, and sexuality, have been grafted onto past events, creating a testimonial and explicitly feminist form of fiction authored by women writers from a range of cultural backgrounds. These novels frequently deal with women survivors, highlighting the relationships between narration, gender, and trauma. The works I examine—Margaret Atwood's *Alias Grace*, Nora Okja Keller's *Comfort Woman*, Joy Kogawa's *Obasan*, Edwidge Danticat's *The Farming of Bones* and Julia Alvarez's *In the Time of the Butterflies*—stress that both trauma and recovery have collective as well as individual dimensions...They make claims on readers to function as the receivers of painful and complicated stories, in order to assist in the creation of historical memory." (Author). For more see *DAI-A* 62.11 (May 2002): 3963.

3110. TOMC, Sandra. "'The Missionary Position': Feminism and Nationalism in Margaret Atwood's *The Handmaid's Tale*." *Margaret Atwood's* The Handmaid's Tale.

Ed. Harold Bloom. Philadelphia: Chelsea House Publishers, 2001. 81-91. Reprinted from *Canadian Literature* 138-139 (Fall-Winter 1993).

3111. WILSON, Sharon Rose. "Off the Path to Grandma's House in *The Handmaid's Tale*." *Margaret Atwood's* The Handmaid's Tale. Ed. Harold Bloom. Philadelphia: Chelsea House Publishers, 2001. 63-79. Reprinted from *Margaret Atwood's Fairy-Tale Sexual Politics*, ©1993.

3112. WITTKE, Petra. "Of 'Heres' and 'Theres' and 'Wheres' and 'Whats': Die literarische Kartographie einer nationalen Identität." *Literatur in Wissenschaft und Unterricht* 34.1 (2001): 41-48. A look at national identity in fiction by Margaret Atwood and Alice Munro.

3113. YÜCEL, Sükran. "Margaret Atwood: Sanatçinin Bir Kadin Olarak Portresi." *E: Aylik Kültür ve Edebiyat Dergisi* 23 (2001): 69-71. Turkish article on Atwood.

Reviews of Atwood's Works

3114. "Margaret Atwood." *Short Story Criticism: Criticism of the Works of Short Fiction Writers.* Vol. 46. Ed. Justin Carr. Detroit, MI; New York: Gale, 2001. 24-101.
A compendium of excerpts from critics and reviewers.

3115. *The Blind Assassin.* New York: Doubleday, 2000. Also published in New York by Nan A. Talese and in London by Bloomsbury.
Americas 53.1 (January-February 2001): 61-62. By Barbara MUJICA.
Birmingham Evening Mail 13 January 2001: 39. By Z.C. (179 w).
Border Crossings 20.1 (February 2001): 77-79. By Wayne TEFS.
Capital Times [Madison, WI] 5 January 2001: 7A. By Anita WEIER.
(720 w).
Christian Century 118.17 (28 February 2001): 28. By Ann-Janine MOREY.
The Herald [Glasgow] 6 January 2001: 10. By Pamela TIMMS. Opinions of a book club. (1258 w).
Herizons 14.4 (Spring 2001): 30. By Irene D'SOUZA.
Lancet 357.9262 (7 April 2001): 1138. By Rebecca J. DAVIES. (1039 w).
Library Journal 126.13 (1 August 2001): 196. By Nancy PEARL. 1 of 4 books reviewed.
Missouri Review 24.2 (2001): 202-203. By Melissa SOLIS.
Resource Links (Canadian Council for Learning Resources) 7.1 (October 2001): 56-57. By Margaret MACKEY.
Room of One's Own 23.3 (2001): 101-102. By Virginia AULIN.
Southland Times [NZ] 27 January 2001: 34. By Paul FOCAMP.
Sunday Age [Melbourne] 25 February 2001: Section: Books: 11. Reader comments.
Sunday Times [London] 26 August 2001: Section: Features: s.p. By Trevor LEWIS. (271 w). Available from Lexis-Nexis.
Yale Review 89.2 (April 2001): 159-169. By Diana POSTLETHWAITE. ("This story is not nearly worthy of its author's talents.")
Women's Review of Books 18.6 (March 2001): 1-2. By Molly HITE.
World and I 16.1 (January 2001): 234. By Roberta RUBENSTEIN.

3116. *The Blind Assassin.* London: Virago, 2001.
Birmingham Post 29 September 2001: 53. By Charlie HILL. (473 w).
New Straits Times (Malaysia) 3 October 2001: Section: Books: 5. By Sharon TOH. (817 w).

3117. *The Blind Assassin* [Sound recording]. Read by Lorelei King. London: Harper-Collins, 2000. Abridged version.
    Irish Times 20 January 2001: 73. By Arminta WALLACE. (128 w).
3118. *The Blind Assassin* [Sound recording]. Read by Margot Dionne. Prince Frederick, MD: Bantam Doubleday, 2000.
    Booklist 97.12 (15 February 2001): 1164. By Mary Frances WILKENS.
    Roanoke Times & World News 11 February 2001: Section Books: 6. By Mary Ann JOHNSON.
    San Antonio Express-News 7 January 2001: 6G. By Sanda BAURS.
3119. *Bluebeard's Egg* [Sound recording]. Read by Bonnie Hurren. Bath [UK]: Chivers, 2000. 9 hr., 8 cassettes.
    Booklist 97.12 (15 February 2001): 1166.
3120. *Good Bones and Simple Murders*. New York: Nan A. Talese, 2001?
    Buffalo News 18 November 2001: F5. By Charity VOGEL. (521 w).
3121. *A Quiet Game and Other Early Works*. Edmonton: Juvenilia Press, 1997.
    Canadian Literature 168 (Spring 2001): 120-121. By Pilar SOMACARRERA.
3122. *Two Solicitudes: Conversations*. Toronto: McClelland and Stewart, 1998.
    Canadian Literature 168 (Spring 2001): 120-121. By Pilar SOMACARRERA.

Reviews of Adaptations of Atwood's Works

3123. RUDERS, Poul, composer. "*Tjenerindens Fortælling* [Sound recording]." Dacapo, 2000. Opera based on *The Handmaid's Tale*. Librettist, Paul Bentley. 2 sound discs in 1 container.
    Daily Telegraph [London] 17 February 2001: 11. By Matthew RYE. (217 w).
    Globe and Mail 1 March 2001: R6. By Robert EVERETT-GREEN.
    The Guardian (London) 19 January 2001: 15. By Tim ASHLEY. (134 w).
    The Independent (London) 19 January 2001: 16. By Rob COWEN. (611 w).
    St. Petersburg Times 5 August 2001: 8F. By John FLEMING. (1294 w).

~ 2002 ~

Atwood's Works

3124. *A mulher comestível.* Lisbon: Editora Livros do Brasil, 2002. Portuguese translation of *The Edible Woman* by Paulo Moreira.

3125. *Alias Grace.* Halifax, NS: Atlantic Provinces Special Education Authority Resources Centre for the Visually Impaired, 2002. Large print ed., 2 v.

3126. *The Blind Assassin.* [Sound recording]. Read by Johanne Marshall. Vancouver, BC: Crane Resource Centre, 2002. 14 tape reels.

3127. *Bodily Harm.* Thorndike, ME: Center Point Publishing, 2002 ©1982. Large print edition.

3128. *Bodily Harm.* [Sound recording]. Read by Bonnie Hurren. Bath [UK]: Chivers Audio Books; Hampton, NH: Chivers North America, 2002. Cassette tape, 8 sound cassettes (ca. 10 hr., 8 min.).

3129. *Cat's Eye.* [Sound recording]. Multiple readers. Vancouver, BC: Crane Resource Centre, 2002. 11 sound cassettes.

3130. "Comment je suis devenue écrivaine." *Châtelaine* 43.2 (February 2002): 40-45

3131. "Cryogenics: A Symposium." *When the World Comes Leaping Up: Personal Encounters with Nature.* Ed. David T. Suzuki. Vancouver, BC; New York: Greystone Books, 2002. 143-148.

3132. *Den blinde morder.* Copenhagen: Lindhardt og Ringhof, 2002. Danish translation of *The Blind Assassin* by Lisbeth Møller-Madsen.

3133. *El cuenta de la criada.* Madrid: Suma de Letras, 2002. Spanish translation of *The Handmaid's Tale* by Elsa Mateo Blanco.

3134. "End Economic Sanctions against Iraq." *Morning Star* 20 March 2002: 20. Atwood is one of a number of signatories on this open letter.

3135. "[Excerpt]." Chronicle of Higher Education 48.23 (15 February 2002): B6. From *Negotiating with the Dead: A Writer on Writing.*

3136. "[Excerpt]." *National Review* 3 July 2002: s.p. Available from Lexis-Nexis. Excerpt from Atwood's poem "The Loneliness of the Military Historian" in an article by Victor David Hanson entitled "The Return of Military History?"

3137. "[Excerpt]." *Vancouver Sun* 9 March 2002: D15. From *Negotiating with the Dead.*

3138. "[Excerpt]." *Women of Words: A Personal Introduction to More Than Forty Important Writers.* 2nd ed. Ed. Janet Bukovinsky Teacher. Philadelphia: Running Press, 2002. 207-209. From *The Robber Bride.*

3139. "First Job." *The Broadview Anthology of Expository Prose*. Ed. Tammy Roberts et al. Peterborough, ON: Broadview Press, 2002. 626-628. First published as "Ka-Ching!" *New Yorker* 23, 30 April 2001: 72.

3140. *Good Bones*. [Electronic resource]. Toronto: CNIB, 2002. 1 computer laser optical disc (2 hr., 36 min.). Based on 1992 edition.

3141. "The Great God Pan: Images of the Writer as Priestess and Femme Fatale." *TLS: Times Literary Supplement* 22 February 2002: 12-14. Problems faced by female artists, particularly in regard to money.

3142. "Green Gifts." *Globe and Mail* 30 November 2002: L5. Atwood shares her eco-picks for the holiday. These include: 1) The French or cotton shopping bag; 2) The garden rake; 3) A hemp product; 4) The organic cotton T-shirt; 5) A set of Nature Clean cleaning products; 6) The light, self-sharpening push mower from Lee Valley; 7) The Caroma double-flush toilet; 8) The four-stoke outboard motor; 9) The Prius hybrid car; and 10) The Arise all-solar-powered house. She comments briefly on each product, and then the *Globe* thoughtfully tells readers where to obtain each one.

3143. "Hairball." *To Come to Light: Perspectives on Chronic Illness in Modern Literature*. Ed. Amy Bonomi. Seattle, WA: Whit Press, 2002. 21. A limited edition anthology published primarily for attendees of the Congress on Improving Chronic Care, 23-24 September 2002 in Seattle. Reprinted with permission from *Wilderness Tips*, ©1990.

3144. *The Handmaid's Tale*. Toronto: Emblem Editions, 2002. Reprint.

3145. *The Handmaid's Tale*. Korea: Goldenberg, 2002. Korean translation edition is published by arrangement with O.W. Toad, c/o Curtis Brown, London. Title romanized.

3146. *The Handmaid's Tale*. [Sound recording]. Read by Geneviève Pelletier. Winnipeg: Manitoba Education and Training, 2002. 13 sound cassettes (12 hr., 30 min.).

3147. "Happy Endings." *The Longman Masters of Short Fiction*. [Ed.] Dana Gioia and R. S. Gwynn. New York: Longman, 2002. 22-24. Reprinted from *Good Bones and Simple Murders*, ©1983.

3148. "How I Became a Writer." [Videorecording]. [Chicago]: Northeastern Illinois University, 2002. VHS tape, 1 videocassette (ca. 80 min.). Atwood speaks about how she became a writer and the life experiences which influenced her over the past 4-1/2 decades. At the end of the lecture some questions were taken from the audience. Videotaped for the Presidential Lecture Series, Northeastern Illinois University, 17 January 2002.

3149. "The Indelible Woman." *The Guardian* (London) 7 September 2002: 37. Atwood wonders how she could have been so wrong about *To the Lighthouse*.

3150. "Introduction." *Doctor Glas*. Hjalmar Söderberg. New York: Anchor Books, 2002. [5]-10. This edition has been translated from the original Swedish by Paul Britten Austin.

3151. "Introduction." *Ground Works: Avant-Garde for Thee*. Ed. Christian Bök. Toronto: Anansi, 2002. ix-xv. Atwood confesses to being "the instigator of this book."

3152. "Introduction." *High Latitudes: A Northern Journey*. By Farley Mowat. Toronto: Key Porter, 2002. ix-xi.

3153. "Introduction." *She*. By H. Rider Haggard. New York: Modern Library, 2002. xvii-xxiv.

3154. "Jay Macpherson: Poems Told Twice." *American and Canadian Women Poets 1930–Present*. Ed. Harold Bloom. Philadephia: Chelsea House, 2002. 175-178. Reprinted from *Second Words*, ©1982.

3155. *Kakacs*. Riga: Atena Klubs, 2002. Latvian translation of *Cat's Eye* by Silvija Brice.

3156. *La donna da mangiare: Romanzo*. Milan: Corbaccio, 2002. Italian translation of *The Edible Woman* by Mario Manzari.

3157. *Le tueur aveugle*. Paris: Éditions Robert Laffont, 2002. French translation of *The Blind Assassin* by Michèle Albaret-Maatsch.

3158. *Mang Yan Ci Ke*. Taipei: Tian pei wen hua you xian gong si, 2002. Chinese translation of *The Blind Assassin* by Liang Yong'an yi. Title romanized.

3159. *Mao yan*. Nanking: Yilin Press, 2002. Chinese translation of *Cat's Eye* by Haocheng Yang. Title romanized.

3160. *Modrovousovo vejce*. Prague: Volvox Globator, 2002. Czech translation of *Bluebeard's Egg* by Martina Kotrbová.

3161. "Muerte Pos Paisaje." *Dónde Es Aquí? 25 Cuentos Canadienses*. Ed. by Claudia Lucotti. Mexico: Fondo de Cultura Económica, 2002. 223-245. Excerpt from *Wilderness Tips* (1991); translated into Spanish by Monica Mansour.

3162. *Muzeum zkamenelin*. Prague: Odeon, 2002. Czech translation of *Life Before Man* by Viktor Janiš.

3163. "Mystery Man: *The Selected Letters of Dashiell Hammett, Dashiell Hammett* [and] *Crime Stories and Other Writings*." *New York Review of Books* 49.2 (14 February 2002): 19-21. Book reviews of Hammett's letters, of his daughter Jo's memoirs, and of his crime stories.

3164. *Negotiating with the Dead: A Writer on Writing*. New York; Cambridge: Cambridge UP, 2002. "What is the role of the writer? Prophet? High Priest of Art? Court Jester? Or witness to the real world? Looking back on her own childhood and the development of her writing career, Margaret Atwood examines the metaphors which writers of fiction and poetry have used to explain—or excuse!—their activities, looking at what costumes they have seen fit to assume, what roles they have chosen to play. In her final chapter she takes up the challenge of the book's title: if a writer is to be seen as 'gifted,' who is doing the giving and what are the terms of the gift?" (Publisher).

3165. *Negoziando con le ombre*. Milan: Ponte alle Grazie, 2002. Italian translation of *Negotiating with the Dead* by Massimo Birattari and Riccardo Cravero.

3166. *Nimeltään Grace*. Helsinki: Otava, 2002. Finnish translation of *Alias Grace* by Kristiina Drews.

3167. "Nostalgia." *Vogue* 192.12 (December 2002): 78, 80. Atwood discusses how she designed and made her own clothes when she was a teenager.

3168. *Occhio di gatto*. Milan: Ponte alle Grazie, 2002. Italian translation of *Cat's Eye* by Marco Papi.

3169. "Of Myths and Men." *Globe and Mail* 13 April 2002: R10. The first time Atwood saw the Inuit epic, *Atanarjuat: The Fast Runner*, she was on an ice-breaker in the Arctic; it was an unusual but perfect way to experience this breathtaking new movie.

3170. *Ojo de gato*. Barcelona: Ediciones B, 2002. Spanish translation of *Cat's Eye* by Jordi Mustieles.

3171. "On the Canadian Identity." *The Longman Masters of Short Fiction*. [Ed.] Dana Gioia and R. S. Gwynn. New York: Longman, 2002. 24-25. Reprinted from *Strange Things*, ©1995.

3172. "On the Trail of Dashiell Hammett." *Globe and Mail* 28 February 2002: R1, R7. A longer version of this article appeared in the *New York Review of Books*. See 3163.

3173. *Oryx and Crake: A Novel*. New York: Random House Large Print, 2002. 571 pp.

3174. "The Owl and the Pussycat, Some Years Later." *Pretext* 5 (2002): 167-172. Poem concludes this volume of writing published by Pen & Inc. Press, which began in the School of English and American Studies at the University of East Anglia.

3175. "A Path Taken, with All the Certainty of Youth." *New York Times* 11 March 2002: E1. Excerpt from *Negotiating with the Dead* reflects on Atwood's decision to become a writer.

3176. *Princess Prunella and the Purple Peanut*. Toronto: Key Porter, 2002. Paper reprint.

3177. "Pump Twin." *April Witch: A Novel*. By Majgull Axelsson. New York: Villard, 2002. [97]. Excerpt from "A Sad Child" published in *Morning in the Burned House*, ©1995. *April Witch* was originally published in Swedish in 1997.

3178. "The Queen of Quinkdom." *New York Review of Books* 49.14 (26 September 2002): 23-25. Review of Ursula K. Le Guin's *Birthday of the World and Other Stories* (New York: Harper Collins, 2002).

3179. "Quick. Name 10 Prominent Canadians Who Are Against Kyoto ... (...You Can't, Can You? Nobody Can)." *Globe and Mail* 7 November 2002: s.p. Also available as .pdf file http://www.caw.ca/campaigns&issues/ongoingcampaigns/pdf/Sierra_ad.pdf. Atwood is one of about 100 well-known Canadians to sign this open letter in favor of the Kyoto agreement.

3180. "Rereadings: Death and the Maiden." *The Guardian* (London) 26 October 2002: 36. An edited extract of Atwood's Introduction to Hjalmar Soderberg's *Doktor Glas* published by Harvil Press.

3181. *The Robber Bride*. [Electronic resource]. Toronto: CNIB, 2002. 5 computer laser optical discs (20 hr., 56 min.).

3182. *Rüs faribkar*. Tehran [Iran]: Ququnüs, 2002. Persian translation of *The Robber Bride* by Shahin Asayash.

3183. *Selected poems 1966-1984*. [Sound recording]. Winnipeg: CNIB, 2002. 7 sound cassettes (7 h). Based on 1990 edition.

3184. *Shi nu de gu shi = The Handmaid's Tale*. Taipei: Ten Points, 2002. Chinese translation by Xiaowei Chen. Title in Chinese and English; text in Chinese only. Title romanized.

3185. "Silence Is Not the Answer." *Globe and Mail* 17 December 2002: A21. Atwood, along with more than 100 others, calls for tolerance at Canadian universities in the midst of bitter tensions between Palestinians and Jews, which have particularly affected Jews.

3186. *Ślepy zabójca*. Poznan: Zysk i S-ka, 2002. Polish translation of *The Blind Assassin* by Małgorzata Hesko-Kołodzińska.

3187. *Surfacing*. [Sound recording]. Read by Karen DeVito. Vancouver, BC: Crane Resource Centre, 2002. 5 sound cassettes. Based on 1994 New Canadian Library edition.

3188. "Taking *Everyman* by the Hand; Noticing the Impact of Impacts." *Chronicle of Higher Education* 48.23 (15 February 2002): B6. Atwood reflects on some university reading.

3189. "A Tasty Slice of Pi and Ships." *Sunday Times* (London) 5 May 2002: Section: Features. Review of Yann Martel's *Life of Pi*. (858 w).

3190. *Telesna Povreda*. Belgrade: Filip Viðnjic, 2002. Serbian translation of *Bodily Harm* by David Albahari.

3191. "They Eat Out." *Off the Wall*. Ed. Niall MacMonagle. Dublin: Marino, 2002. 132-133. Poem.

3192. "Three Chronicles." *Ms.* 12.3 (Summer 2002): 30-34. Short story.

3193. "Tiff: A Tribute." *Globe and Mail* 22 June 2002: R1, R11. From a speech by Atwood at a tribute evening to Timothy Findley at the International Authors' Festival in Toronto, October 2001.

3194. "Tiff and the Animals." *Brick: A Literary Journal* 70 (Winter 2002): [157]-159. In the piece Atwood discusses Timothy Findley's relationship with Beatrix Potter's *The Tale of Peter Rabbit* on the occasion of the Timothy Findley Memorial Evening, Convocation Hall, University of Toronto, 29 September 2002. Title in the table of contents of this journal: "A Tribute to Timothy Findley."

3195. "*Tishomingo Blues*." *New York Review of Books* 49.9 (23 May 2002): 21-23. Review of Elmore Leonard's 37th novel.

3196. "Variation on the Word *Sleep*." *Poetry in Motion from Coast to Coast: One Hundred and Twenty Poems from the Subways and Buses*. Ed. Elise Paschen and Brian Fletcher Lauer. New York; London: Norton, 2002. 140. An excerpt from this poem (the last 4 lines). Reprinted from *Selected Poems II: Poems Selected and New 1976-1986*, ©1987.

3197. "Who Do You Think You Are?" *Globe and Mail* 2 Mar. 2002: D8-D9, D12. Excerpt from *Negotiating with the Dead*.

3198. "The Wrong Box: Matt Cohen, Fabulism and Critical Taxonomy." *Uncommon Ground: A Celebration of Matt Cohen*. Ed. Graeme Gibson et al. Toronto: Alfred A. Knopf Canada, 2002. 66-82.

3199. *Yami no satsujin gemu: Tanpen shosetsu to sanbunshi = Murder in the Dark: Short Fictions and Prose Poems*. Tokyo: Hokuseidō Shoten, 2002. Japanese translation by Keiko Nakajima. Title romanized.

3200. "You Begin." *Gifts: Poems for Parents*. Ed. Rhea Tregebov. Toronto: Sumach Press, 2002. 27-28. Reprinted from *Two Headed Poems* (Toronto: Oxford UP, 1978).

3201. "You Fit into Me." *To Hell with Love: Poems to Mend a Broken Heart*. Ed. Mary D. Esselman and Elizabeth Ash Vélez. New York: Warner, 2002. 9.

Adaptations of Atwood's Works

3202. *The Atwood Stories*. [Videorecording]. Kelowna, BC: Shaftesbury Films, 2002. A dramatic anthology of stories based on Atwood's short stories. The series pairs award-winning writers and directors in the exploration of themes contained in Atwood's work. Each title is available on a single tape. Titles include: "Polarities," "Man from Mars," "Betty," "Death by Landscape," "Isis in Darkness," "The Sunrise," Originally broadcast on the W Network.

3203. *The Handmaid's Tale*. Santa Monica: MGM Home Entertainment, 2002. Videocassette (109 min.). Originally released as motion picture in 1990.

3204. CARLEY, Dave. *The Edible Woman*. Winnipeg: Scirocco Drama, 2002. Play based on the novel.

3205. PENNYCOOK, Bruce. *Selected Compositions*. [Sound recording]. Lakeway, TX: Penntech Records, 2002. Compact disc, 1 sound disc. Includes adaptation of Atwood's poem "Speeches for Dr. Frankenstein."

Quotations

3206. "[[Mis]Quote]." *Catholic New Times* 28 (10 October 2002): 2. "Powerlessness and silence go together. We should use our privileged positions not as a shelter from the world's reality, but as a platform from which to speak. A voice is a gift. It should be cherished and used." From an address to Amnesty International in *Second Words: Selected Critical Prose* (Toronto: Anansi, 1982): 396, which is quite different from this version. The original reads: "We in this country should use our privileged position not as a shelter from the world's realities but as a platform from which to speak. Many are denied their voices; we are not. A voice is a gift; it should be cherished and used, to fully utter human speech if possible. Powerlessness and silence go together; one of the first efforts made in any totalitarian takeover is to suppress the writers, the singers, the journalists, those who are the collective voice. Get rid of the union leaders and pervert the legal system and what you are left with is a reign of terror."

3207. "[Quote]." *Canadian Speeches* 16.2 (May-June 2002): 56-60. Ballerina Karen Kain quotes Atwood, who once said of Canada: "You really have to choose this country, because it's so easy to leave."

3208. "[Quote]." *Charlottetown Guardian* 11 May 2002: C1. Article by Sandra Devlin on motherhood, quotes Atwood: "Who gives birth? And to whom is it given? Certainly it doesn't feel like giving, which implies a flow, a gentle handing over, no coercion....Maybe the phrase was made by someone viewing the result only."

3209. "[Quote]." *Evening Standard* (London) 9 April 2002: 18. "Wanting to meet an author because you like his work is like wanting to meet a duck because you like pâté."

3210. "[Quote]." *Hill Times* (Ottawa) 28 January 2002: s.p. Available from Lexis-Nexis. Article on Canadian Senate by Bill Curry quotes Atwood, who once called the Senate "a feather bed for fallen Liberals."

3211. "[Quote]." *Korea Herald* 8 March 2002: s.p. Available from Lexis-Nexis. "An eye for an eye only leads to more blindness."

3212. "[Quote]." *Melus* (Los Angeles) 27.4 (Winter 2002): 137-154. In an interview with poet Luz Maria Umpierre, author quotes Atwood on food: "Eating is our earliest metaphor, preceding our consciousness of gender difference, race, nationalism and language" and then asks for comment. Maria DiFrancesco, "Poetic Dissonance: An Interview with Luz Maria Umpierre."

3213. "[Quote]." *The National* (CBC) 25 January 2002. Available from Lexis-Nexis. A CBC news broadcast quotes Atwood, among others, discussing Peter Gzowski's significance on the occasion of his death: "I think he opened up a lot of Canada to the rest of Canada because our problem has always been that we are a very large country geographically and very spread out."

3214. "[Quote]." *Ottawa Citizen* 21 April 2002: C6. Atwood on Carol Shields: "Because she's a comic writer and genuinely funny, early on, she was put in the 'sweet' box, where she does not belong....The fact is, there's a dark thread in everything she writes." From article on Shields by Maria Russo.

3215. "[Quote]." *The Times* (London) 25 September 2002: Section: Features: 23. "If the national mental illness of the United States is megalomania, then that of Canada is paranoid schizophrenia." Atwood quoted in connection with commentary about Canadians short-listed for Booker.

Interviews

3216. "Looking Back at the Life of Peter Gzowski." *The National* (CBC) 24 January 2002: s.p. Available from Lexis-Nexis. On occasion of Gzowski's death, CBC replayed a number of the interviews he conducted as a CBC host, including one with Atwood in the late 1970s or early '80s. "GZOWSKI: **Do you think you frighten people? Do you ever get that sense?** ATWOOD: Oh, yeah, sure, I frighten people. G: **Have you any idea why?** A: I'll frighten them less as I get older. G: **Why?** A: People are more frightened of young women who do things than they are of old women who do things. Don't ask me why. It's not my problem."

3217. *Margaret Atwood.* [Videorecording]. Princeton: Films for the Humanities & Sciences, 2002. 1 videodisc (52 min.). In this interview, Atwood discusses topics such as how she became a writer and how the women's movement, World War II, and her home city of Toronto have influenced her writing. Excerpts from *The Robber Bride* and *Cat's Eye* are read by actress Nadia Cameron. Originally broadcast in 1993 as an episode of the television program *The South Bank Show.*

3218. BROWN, DeNeen L. "Split Personality: In Margaret Atwood Reside Both the 'Ordinary' Person and the Extraordinary Writer." *Washington Post* 6 April 2002: C01.

3219. DONNELLY, Pat. "Atwood to Appear at Salon du Livre: Guest of Honour—Lady of Letters Has Proven Popular in Translation." *Montreal Gazette* 9 November 2002: H1. Interview prior to her visit. Atwood was the only English-language author in the Salon's 9-member "invités d'honneur" list. She contrasted the Salon to the Frankfurt Book Fair: "Everybody always says they hate Frankfurt and they always go. I think the main thing is getting through it." Vitamins help, she added. "I always got through it (Frankfurt) because I took massive doses of Vitamin C." Any such event is not "fun." "It's like saying to an actor, 'Is it fun?' No. Actually, it's my job. I suppose if it wasn't fun in some way, I wouldn't do it. But the criteria isn't, are you going to have fun? The criteria is, are you going to get there on time?"

   In the interview, Atwood announced she will be contributing to a volume prepared by a colleague in England on authors' accounts of their most humiliating experiences in public and that her new novel (*Oryx and Crake*) was just finished and would appear the following April.

   Atwood also commented on being translated. She has had the same French (from France) translator, Michèle Albaret-Maatsch, for her last two books. "It has been very difficult because *Alias Grace* had a lot of archaic words and *Blind Assassin* had this bizarre, newspaper style. You had to get the equivalent in French. So it really requires a mastery. It's not literal, word by word. She's wonderful. We confer a lot and work on it to get the right thing."

   Does she feel alienated from her work when she reads it in French? "No. I feel that I have several different personalities and that's one of them." Atwood's books have been translated into about 35 languages. With other languages, she's not as hands-on. "I'd like to say I was, but, you know, Serbo-Croatian, I don't have a handle on." In those circumstances, "You just have to trust the publisher. There's nothing else you can do. And you never know."

3220. DUNN, Sharon. "The Great Ones Are Always Unflappable: Margaret Atwood Discusses Canada's 'Strange' Literary Past." *National Post* 21 October 2002:

AL2. Dunn catches up with Atwood and partner Graeme Gibson at the Art Gallery of Ontario during the opening of the Gauguin to Matisse Exhibition. The interview focuses on *Ground Works*, a collection of experimental fiction written between 1965 and 1985 and edited by Christian Bök. Atwood wrote the introduction.

3221. GEORGE, Lianne. "Roughing It in the Bush League: With *Ground Works*, a New Anthology of Avant-Garde Canadian Writing, Margaret Atwood Wanted to Remind Readers of the Pioneering Work Created Before There Was Such a Thing as CanLit." *National Post* 7 October 2002: AL3. Atwood reflects on what it was like to write before the age of big literary prizes and huge book sales. Atwood interviewed at book launch held at The Mockingbird on King Street West in Toronto.

3222. GZOWSKI, Peter. *A Celebration of Peter Gzowski*. [Sound recording]. [Toronto]: CBC Audio, 2002. Compact disc, 2 sound discs (ca. 2 hr.). Collection of interviews from Peter Gzowski's radio programs and excerpts from tributes to him broadcast after his death. Participants: Peter Gzowski; others include Atwood, along with Shelagh Rogers, Margaret Visser, Joe Ghiz, Stuart McLean, John Diefenbaker, Jean Chretien, Pierre Trudeau, Natalie McMaster, Dan Aykroyd, Sylvia Tyson, Rick Mercer, Wayne Gretzky, W. O. Mitchell, and Robertson Davies.

3223. HEER, Jeet. "Literary Gathering Intended to Be a Celebration of Carol Shields: Atwood, Ondaatje and Urquhart among Speakers at Tonight's Event." *National Post* 2 April 2002: B6. Atwood interviewed in connection with an event celebrating Carol Shields. Commenting about the dark thread in Shields's work, Atwood notes that it is frequently missed although "obviously not [by] moi." Ultimately, Atwood believes, Shields is not taken seriously "because she's cute, short and a blond. If she were tall, brunette with a pointy nose, nobody would have missed it. I'm a blend. I'm short, dark with a pointy nose, so I can swing either way."

3224. JACOB, Didier. "Margaret et les extraterrestres: Elle publie *Le Tueur aveugle*." *Le Nouvel Observateur* 1953 (11 April 2002): 66. Interview (in French) with Atwood who talks about her childhood and her book *The Blind Assassin*.

3225. MARTIN, Sandra. "When a Good Idea Goes Bad." *Globe and Mail* 29 June 2002: R9. Short piece, part of a series of other pieces, in which writers such as Atwood are interviewed about on "roads not taken." In the article, Atwood reflects on the origins of *The Blind Assassin* and *Alias Grace.*

3226. O'DOWD, Nora. "Margaret Atwood: A Writer on Writing." *Newshouse News Service* 12 April 2002: Entertainment. Atwood's reflections on writing, sparked by appearance of *Negotiating with the Dead*. Atwood notes she is "at work on a new book" and she expects it to be published "in about a year."

3227. POLANYI, Margaret. "Atwood on Atwood: One of Canada's Most Famous Authors Talks about Her Upbringing, Celebrity and Fears as a Writer." *Reader's Digest* (Canadian edition) (April 2002): 58-67.

3228. REHM, Diane. [*Margaret*] *Atwood* The Handmaid's Tale. [Sound recording]. Washington, DC: WAMU, American University, 2002. Cassette tape, 1 sound cassette (ca. 60 min.). Interview with Atwood originally broadcast 18 January 2002.

3229. ———. *Margaret Atwood* Negotiating with the Dead. [Sound recording]. Washington, DC: WAMU, American University, 2002. Cassette tape, 1 sound cassette (ca. 60 min.). Interview with Atwood originally broadcast 9 April 2002.

3230. REYNOLDS, Margaret. "Interview with Margaret Atwood." *Margaret Atwood: The Essential Guide:* The Handmaid's Tale, Bluebeard's Egg, The Blind Assassin. By Margaret Reynolds and Jonathan Noakes. London: Vintage, 2002. 11-25. Originally conducted at the Hay-on-Wye Book Festival, 26 May 2001.

3231. SACUTA, Norm. "The Messenger Never Arrives." *Where the Words Come Reprinted from Canadian Poets in Conversation*. Ed. Tim Bowling. Roberts Creek, BC: Nightwood Editions. 2002. 213-224.

Scholarly Resources

3232. BARRY, Peter. "Contemporary Poetry and Ekphrasis." *Cambridge Quarterly* 31.2 (2002): 155-165. Extensive discussion of Atwood's poem, "This Is a Photograph of Me."

3233. BENNETT, Donna. "Nation and Its Discontents: Atwood's *Survival* and After." *Canadística Canaria (1991-2000): Ensayos Literarios Anglocanadienses*. Ed. Juan Ignacio Oliva et al. La Laguna, Spain: Universidad de La Laguna, 2002. 13-29.

3234. BERARD, Nicole Julia. "Wandering Women: The Emergence of the Picaresque in Postmodern, Feminist Canadian Literature (Margaret Atwood, Susan Swan, Aritha Van Herk)." MA thesis. Acadia University, 2002. 115 pp. Also available on microfiche from Canadian Theses Service (2002). "The picaresque genre developed as a result of class disparity in Spain during the sixteenth century. Successive generations of authors have adapted the defining characteristics of the picaresque genre in order to subvert the social structures most pressing during their eras and the latest generation of authors to take up the tenets of the picaresque are postmodern feminist Canadian authors writing in the late twentieth century. Margaret Atwood's *Lady Oracle* and *The Robber Bride*, Susan Swan's *The Biggest Modern Woman of the World* and Aritha van Herk's *No Fixed Address: An Amorous Journey* are all examples of this new transformation of the picaresque tradition." (Author). For more see *MAI* 41.02 (April 2003): 385.

3235. BETTS, Lenore. "*Puffball* and *The Handmaid's Tale*: The Influence of Pregnancy on the Construction of Female Identity." MA thesis. University of Stellenbosch, 2002. 84 pp. *Puffball* was written by Fay Weldon.

3236. BIRDEN, Lorene M. "'Sortir de l'auberge': Strategies of (False) Narration in Atwood and Triolet." *Comparative Literature Studies* 39.2 (2002): 120-145. A comparative study of the narrative strategies of Atwood and Elsa Triolet. Western European feminist movements argue that a commonality of origins in feminist opposition to patriarchy exists on some level. This philosophy suggests that a commonality of approaches and devices seems to exist within feminist discourse across national and cultural boundaries. This implies that a transcendence of cultural or social differences is attainable, that literary comparisons can be made between texts from different cultural traditions. In the context of modernist and postmodernist writing, the writer demonstrates the similarity of writing strategies employed by Atwood and Triolet, two women from different sides of the Atlantic, and writing at different times.

3237. BOYNTON, Victoria. "The Sex-Cited Body in Margaret Atwood." *Studies in Canadian Literature / Études en littérature canadienne* 27.2 (2002): 51-70. Focus on *Lady Oracle*.

3238. BRADY, Lenore Lillian. "With Clear Epistolary Intent: A Cross-Cultural Study of Unsent Letters in Contemporary Women's Fiction." PhD thesis. University of Arizona, 2002. 153 pp. "While many contemporary scholars have examined the function and trajectory of the epistolary novel, most have paid little or no attention to letters in works of fiction that are written but not sent. Existing within the framework of the epistolary genre, the unsent letter is a site of complex self-disclosure closely associated with the categories of autobiography, diary, confession, memoir and testimony. Unsent letter or letter-like communications in Ama Ata Aidoo's *Our Sister Killjoy*, Margaret Atwood's *The Handmaid's Tale*, Edwidge Danticat's *Children of the Sea*, Christina Garcia's *Dreaming in Cuban*, Sylvia Molloy's *Certificate of Absence*, and Toni Morrison's *Beloved* are potent discursive forces in the production, exploration and assertion of identity within the cross-cultural universes of these texts." (Author). For more see *DAI-A* 63.11 (May 2003): 3941.

3239. BRANDON, Paul, and Robert DINSMORE. *Margaret Atwood:* The Handmaid's Tale. Toronto: Coles, 2002. vi, 144 pp. Coles notes.

3240. COLLINGWOOD, Laura Emma. "Masculine Gender Performances in Margaret Atwood's *The Edible Woman*." MPhil thesis. University of Birmingham, 2002. 106 pp.

3241. CONDÉ, Mary. "The Royal Family in Contemporary Women's Fiction." *Études canadiennes / Canadian Studies* 53 (2002): 75-85. Includes some discussion of *Cat's Eye*.

3242. COSTANTINI, Marie-Louise. "[The] Influence of Fairy Tales and Religion on Margaret Atwood's Novel, *The Handmaid's Tale*." Mémoire de Maîtrise d'Anglais. Université de Corse, 2002. 180 pp.

3243. COUTURIER-STOREY, Françoise. "Law, the Word of God and Subversion in Margaret Atwood's *The Handmaid's Tale*." *Cycnos* 19.2 (2002): 135-145.

3244. DAVISON, Carol. "Margaret Atwood (1939–)." *Gothic Writers: A Critical and Bibliographical Guide*. Ed. Douglass H. Thomson, Jack G. Voller, and Frederick S. Frank. Westport, CT: Greenwood Press, 2002. 24-32.

3245. DELLAMORA, Richard. "Isabella Valancy Crawford and an English-Canadian Sodom." *Canadian Literature* 173 (Summer 2002): 16-32. Dellamora focuses on a short story, "Extradited" by Isabella Valancy Crawford, that Margaret Atwood chose to open *The Oxford Book of Canadian Short Stories in English*. By selecting the story as the point of departure for this collection, Atwood implies that it has something important to say about the emergence of modern Canada. The story suggests that Crawford and some of her readers envisaged the possibility of opening Canadian literature and history to an incarnate "fierce joy" that would find in life not only a "stormy place" and "cloud of mist" but also a spiral towards the light.

3246. DOUTHAT, Ross, and Selena WARD. The Handmaid's Tale, *Margaret Atwood*. New York: Spark Publishing, ©2002. 88 pp. Sparknotes.

3247. DVORAK, Marta. "The Right Hand Writing and the Left Hand Erasing in Margaret Atwood's *The Blind Assassin*." *Commonwealth Essays and Studies* 25.1 (2002): 59-68.

3248. ECONOMOU-BAILEY, Mary. "Triumphant Survivors: Margaret Atwood's Heroines." *Canadian Identity through Literature*. Ed. Mary Koutsoudaki. Athens: Savalas, 2002. 35-49.

3249. EVAIN, Christine. "Compromising with the Market Economy." *Newsletter of the Margaret Atwood Society* 29 (2002): 3-10, 18, 19. Is, as Atwood contends in *Negotiating with the Dead*, a writer's artistic value unrelated to the "money factor"?

3250. GARBETT, Ann D. "Margaret Atwood." *Great American Writers: Twentieth Century*. Vol. 1. Ed. R. Baird Shuman. New York: Marshall Cavendish, 2002. 81-100.

3251. GARY, Lara Karine. "Motherlands: Re-Imagining Maternal Function in Contemporary Women's Fiction." PhD thesis. University of California, Davis, 2002. 218 pp. "This study examines substitute mother-child relationships that inform the narrative strategies of contemporary women writing in English. Works by Margaret Atwood, Shirley Jackson, Marilynne Robinson, and Doris Lessing are the focus of discussions. Feminist readings of Freudian psychoanalytic theory, as well as object-relations theory, intersubjectivity, trauma studies, and theories of women's autobiography guide the reading of these works. These approaches reveal how some women writers are using the model of substitute mother-child, particularly mother-daughter, relationships to suggest an alternative form of self-making.... Chapter Two explores *Alias Grace* as a response to Freud's *Dora*." (Author). For more see *DAI-A* 63.08 (February 2003): 2867.

3252. GEIS, Deborah R. "Deconstructing (A Streetcar Named) Desire: Gender Re-Citation in *Belle Reprieve*." *American Drama* 11.2 (2002): 21-31. Includes analysis of *The Handmaid's Tale.*

3253. GRACE, Sherrill E. *Canada and the Idea of North.* Montreal: McGill-Queen's UP, 2002. Includes multiple references to Atwood's ideas, as well as specific comments on *Strange Things, Surfacing,* and *Wilderness Tips.*

3254. GREENWOOD, R. "Amazing Grace." *English Review* 12.4 (April 2002): 24-25. Teaching *Alias Grace* to high school students.

3255. HAMILTON, Nicholas Alexander. "An Ecoclinical Analysis of Margaret Atwood's *Surfacing*." MA thesis. Trent University, 2002. 165 pp. Also available on microfiche from Canadian Theses Service (2004). "An ecological, interdisciplinary analysis of the novel draws out some interesting relationships between humans, other animals, flora, and the land. The novel's Narrator explores herself and her past in order to find a point of balance, an understanding of her niche in her environment. This understanding leads her to reject the dominative power relationships which lead to her own and her environment's exploitation by the power-crazed 'Americans.'" (Author). For more see *MAI* 42.01 (February 2004): 59.

3256. HEILMANN, Ann. "The Devil Herself? Fantasy, Female Identity and the Villainess Fatale in *The Robber Bride*." *The Devil Himself: Villainy in Detective Fiction and Film.* Ed. Stacy Gillis and Philippa Gates. Westport, CT: Greenwood Press, 2002. 171-182.

3257. HENGEN, Shannon. "Atwood, Margaret." *Encyclopedia of Literature in Canada.* Ed. William H. New. Toronto: University of Toronto Press, 2002. 48-51.

3258. HENIGHAN, Stephen. *When Words Deny the World: The Reshaping of Canadian Writing.* Erin: Porcupine's Quill, 2002. Argues that Canadian writers, including Atwood, now write for a more universal audience. This had led to an evaporation of anything distinctly Canadian in their work. The book has no index so the references to Atwood are scattered hither and yon.

3259. HIGA, Lisa S. "'I'm What's Left Over': The Genealogy of History in Margaret Atwood's *Cat's Eye* and *The Robber Bride*." MA thesis. Arizona State University, 2002. 59 pp.

3260. HOBGOOD, Jennifer. "Anti-Edibles: Capitalism and Schizophrenia in Margaret Atwood's *The Edible Woman*." *Style* (Northern Illinois University) 36.1 (Spring 2002): 146-168. "Typically, critics have read Margaret Atwood's *The Edible Woman* as either an optimistic celebration of female 'liberation' or a materialist feminist protest. But Atwood's style, primarily her manipulation of a shifting narrative point of view and her use of an unbalanced, tripartite structure, reflects a more complex picture of capitalism and female subjectivity in the 1960s. By varying structural and narrative form within the novel and by using anorexia as a discursive technique, Atwood constructs states of paranoia, decomposition, and schizophrenia to emphasize the dynamic nature of the capitalist system, its exploitative disposition as well as its potential to release female desire from systemic constraint." (Author).

3261. HORNER, Avril, and Sue ZLOSNIK. "Agriculture, Body Sculpture, Gothic Culture: Gothic Parody in Gibbons, Atwood and Weldon." *Gothic Studies* 4.2 (November 2002): 167-177. Focus on *Lady Oracle.*

3262. HOWELLS, Coral Ann. "Margaret Atwood: Twenty-Five Years of Gothic Tales." *Littcrit* 28.1 (June 2002): 10-27. [Ed. note: *Littcrit* published Kariavattom, Trivandrum, Kerala: Institute of Correspondence Courses, University of Kerala (India).]

3263. ———. "Margaret Atwood's Discourse of Nation and National Identity in the 1990s." *The Rhetoric of Canadian Writing.* Ed. Conny Steenman-Marcusse. Amsterdam: Rodopi, 2002. 199-216.

3264. HUMPHREYS, Emyr. "Negotiating with the Living." *New Welsh Review: Wales's Literary Magazine in English* 58 (2002): 28-34. A look at the creative process in *Negotiating with the Dead.*

3265. HUNT, Richard. "How to Love This World: The Transpersonal Wild in Margaret Atwood's Ecological Poetry." *Ecopoetry: A Critical Introduction.* Ed. J. Scott Byron. Salt Lake City: University of Utah Press, 2002. 232-244.

3266. JAMIESON, Sara Louise. "'There Is No Sadness / I Can't Enter': Four Canadian Women Poets and the Contemporary Elegy." PhD thesis. Queen's University, 2002. 198 pp. Also available on microfiche from Canadian Theses Service (2003). "In recent poetry collections by Margaret Atwood, P. K. Page, Margaret Avison, and Lorna Crozier, elegiac themes of death, loss, and consolation have become increasingly prominent. This thesis examines how these poets both reproduce and revise the conventions of a long and varied tradition of elegiac poetry. It participates in an ongoing critical discussion of how contemporary poets preserve and interrogate the conventions of poetic mourning....Each chapter focuses not only on the elegies of a particular poet, but also addresses specific issues arising from a particular type of elegy prominent in that poet's work [for example] Margaret Atwood's family elegies....Overall, this study shows women poets engaged in a productive and enabling dialogue with the traditional elegiac canon, and reveals the persistence of elegiac motifs in poems which may initially seem very far removed from elegiac tradition." (Author). For more see *DAI-A* 63.10 (April 2003): 3558.

3267. JONES, Anne G. "Margaret Atwood: Songs of the Transformer, 'Songs of the Transformed.'" *Twayne Companion to Contemporary Literature in English, I: Ammons-Lurie; II: Macleod-Williams.* Ed. R. H. W. Dillard and Amanda Cockrell. New York: Twayne; Thomson Gale, 2002. 55-67.

3268. JURAK, Mirko. "Northrop Frye and Margaret Atwood: On National Identity in Canadian Literature." *Missions of Interdependence: A Literary Directory.* Ed. Gerhard Stilz. Amsterdam: Rodopi, 2002. 23-34.

3269. LENK, Uta. "Konzeptuelle Metaphern Zu Sprache in Literarischen Texten: Möglichkeiten Einer Interdisziplinären Anglistik." *Arbeiten aus Anglistik und Amerikanistik* 27.1 (2002): 51-68. Discusses *The Handmaid's Tale* (and a few other titles) in connection with teaching of literature in Germany.

3270. LI, Tsui Yan. "The Female Self, Body and Food: Strategies of Resistance in Doris Lessing, Margaret Atwood, Zhang Jie and Xi Xi." PhD thesis. Chinese University of Hong Kong, 2002. 239 pp. "Since numerous ideologies exist in society, women are subjected to the influence of many ideologies, such as feminism and individualism, and not just patriarchal culture. The conflicting beliefs among the ideologies open up the possibilities for women to resist the patriarchal rule so as to assert the female self. In...Margaret Atwood's *The Edible Woman* and *Lady* Oracle...the female protagonists seek to assert the female self by adopting different strategies to resist the biased assumptions hidden in traditional representations of the female self encoded in body and food. There is a necessity of women's strategies of resistance against the stereotyping of femininity in order to construct an independent self that is liberated from the patriarchal rule." (Author). For more see *DAI-A* 63.10 (April 2003): 3549.

3271. LOVELL-SMITH, Rose. "Anti-Housewives and Ogres' Housekeepers: The Roles of Bluebeard's Female Helper." *Folklore* 113.2 (October 2002): 197-214. While not directly about Atwood's "Bluebeard's Egg," this article makes some reference to it.

3272. LUCOTTI, Claudia. "La voz que nos ocupa: Cuatro lecturas de la poesía de Margaret Atwood." MA thesis. Universidad Nacional Autónoma de México, 2002. 174 pp.

3273. MacPHERSON, Heidi Slettedahl. "'What Is the Narrative of Us?' Teaching Canadian Texts as North American Literature." *Journal of Commonwealth and Postcolonial Studies* 9.1 (2002): 7-22. Atwood is the prime example.

3274. MAK, Elaine, Ngah Lam. "Eugenics in Dystopian Novels." MPhil thesis. University of Hong Kong, 2002. 147 pp. A study of *The Handmaid's Tale* as well as Charlotte Franken Haldane's *Man's World*, Aldous Huxley's *Brave New World*, and Anthony Burgess's *The Wanting Deed*. Full text available from Hong Kong Theses Online: http://sunzi1.lib.hku.hk/hkuto/index.jsp.

3275. MASSOURA, Kiriaki. "The Relationship of Food to Body and Language in Margaret Atwood's *The Edible Woman*." *Passages to Canada: Eighteen Essayistic Routes / Passages vers Le Canada: Dix huit routes essaylistique*. Proceedings of the European Student Seminars on Graduate Work in Canadian Studies. Ed. Markus Müller, Robert Chr. Thomsen, and David Parris. Brno [Czech Republic]: Masaryk UP, 2002. 63-73.

3276. McCLENAGAN, Cindy Marlow. "The Postmodern End for the Violent Victorian Female." PhD thesis. Texas Tech University, 2002. 164 pp. "Recent media attention on the trial and conviction of Andrea Yates, the Texas woman convicted of drowning her five children, as well as on female suicide bombers in Israel, indicates not only 'a morbid curiosity in the United States relating to mothers killing their children'...but also a special, intense fascination with women who involve themselves in 'masculine' acts of violence, especially murder. Since contemporary examples of violent women abound, why do authors—and the public—continue to turn to the past, to nineteenth-century cases of female aggression, for inspiration? Perhaps it is as Margaret Atwood suggests [in *Alias* Grace], that in turning to the past we hope to explore and then expose the possible misconstruction of that past, thereby infusing it with multi-layered meanings for present and future generations." (Author). For more see *DAI-A* 63.10 (April 2003): 3550.

3277. McELROY, Ruth. "Whose Body, Whose Nation? Surrogate Motherhood and Its Representation." *European Journal of Cultural Studies* 5.3 (2002): 325-342. In *The Handmaid's Tale.*

3278. MICHEL, Anthony J. "Cultural Rhetorics: Writing and Disciplinarity at the Intersection of British Cultural Studies and Rhetoric." PhD thesis. Michigan State University. Program in American Studies, 2002. 161 pp. "This project reads scholarship on the intersections of cultural studies and composition to argue that the counterdisciplinary emphasis of British cultural studies has been eliminated in US composition and rhetoric studies. In response to the de-politicization of cultural studies that results from the elimination of concerns over disciplinarity, this project advocates a strategic recovery of British cultural studies and demonstrates how the counterdisciplinary focus of cultural studies helps intervene in contemporary scholarship in composition and rhetoric. This project then demonstrates the uses of cultural rhetorics, for composition scholarship and pedagogy, through critical readings of Margaret Atwood's novel *Alias Grace* and Julie Dash's film, *Daughters of the Dust.*" For more see *DAI-A* 63.09 (March 2003): 3175.

3279. MILLER, Ryan. "The Gospel According to Grace: Gnostic Heresy as Narrative Strategy in Margaret Atwood's *Alias Grace.*" *Literature and Theology* 16.2 (2002): 172-187.

3280. MOORE, Emily Ruth. "Plots, Paradoxes and Parodies: Women Writers Rewriting 'Bluebeard.'" PhD thesis. City University of New York, 2002. 244 pp. "In this study, I examine the plots, paradoxes and parodies in re-visions of one fairy tale— 'Bluebeard,' written by Charles Perrault in 1697—in selected works written mainly by women in the nineteenth and twentieth centuries: Charlotte Brontë, Anne Thackeray Ritchie, Edna St. Vincent Millay, Shirley Jackson, Angela Carter, Suniti Namjoshi, Joyce Carol Oates, and Margaret Atwood." (Author). For more see *DAI-A* 62.12 (June 2002): 4146.

3282. MURRAY, Jennifer. "Questioning the Triple Goddess: Myth and Meaning in Margaret Atwood's *The Robber Bride.*" *Canadian Literature* 173 (Summer 2002): 72-90. "Atwood's *The Robber Bride* calls upon mythological intertexts in two different ways: first of all, by echoing preexisting texts, mythical references make actions, characters, themes and structures pleasantly recognizable to the reader. The second function of myth is to frame meaning within boundaries as well as to set it up as something that is not limited in possibilities. This use of mythical intertext, Murray argues, is the restriction which prevents the novel from opening up to the reader a range of potentially radical positions." (Author).

3283. NISCHIK, Reingard M. "Von Guten Knochen und Mord im Dunklen: Margaret Atwoods inverse Poetik intertextueller Winzigkeit." *Germanisch-Romanische Monatsschrift* 52.3 (2002): 401-416.

3284. NISCHIK, Reingard M., ed. *Margaret Atwood: Works and Impact.* Toronto: Anansi; Rochester, NY; Columbia, SC: Camden House; Woodbridge: Boydell & Brewer, 2002. Reprint of 2000 edition.

3285. PAILLOT, Patricia. "To Bind or Not to Bind: Irony in *The Blind Assassin* by Margaret Atwood." *Études canadiennes / Canadian Studies: Revue interdisciplinaire des études canadiennes en France* 53 (2002): 117-126.

3286. POOLE, Ralph J. *Delikate Damen: Zur Symptomatik des weiblichen Körpers im Werk Margaret Atwoods.* Frankfurt am Main: Hänsel-Hohenhausen, 2002. On eating disorders in Atwood's writing.

3287. PURDY, Anthony. "Unearthing the Past: The Archaeology of Bog Bodies in Glob, Atwood, Hébert and Drabble." *Textual Practice* 16.3 (Winter 2002): 443-458. Atwood's short story, "The Bog Man," compared to Anne Hébert's *Kamouraska*, Margaret Drabble's *A Natural Curiosity*, and Peter Vilhelm Glob's *Mosefolket.*

3288. RAO, Eleonora. *Heart of a Stranger: Contemporary Women Writers and the Metaphor of Exile.* Naples: Liguori, 2002. See especially Chapter 5, "Margaret Atwood's Later Fiction," [107]-119. In spite of the title, this chapter focuses on *Cat's Eye* and *The Robber Bride.*

3289. REESE, James D. "Learning for Understanding: The Role of World Literature." *English Journal* 91.5 (May 2002): 63-69. "Units of work that use world literature to improve high school students' global understanding in an International Baccalaureate English course are presented. The units require students to study *Alias*

Grace, by Margaret Atwood; *If This Is a Man*, by Primo Levi; and *The God of Small Things*, by Arundhati Roy. The three units address the overarching goals that concern how and why students should develop their critical reading and thinking ability, how literature can open their minds to new ways of seeing the world, and how learning about different cultures and eras can help them to understand their own world. Specific goals for understanding for each unit focus on the book being studied and also refer to the three overarching goals." (Journal).

3290. REYNOLDS, Margaret, and Jonathan NOAKES. *Margaret Atwood: The Essential Guide:* The Handmaid's Tale, Bluebeard's Egg, The Blind Assassin [*and Other Stories*]. London: Vintage, 2002. iv, 163 pp. Student study guide. Includes interview with Atwood (see Interview section) and bibliographical references 158-163. [Ed. note: Cover title adds "*and Other Stories.*"]

3291. RIMSTEAD, Roxanne. "Working-Class Intruders: Female Domestics in *Kamouraska* and *Alias Grace*." *Canadian Literature* 175 (Winter 2002): 44-67.

3292. ROBINSON, Laura M. "'Acts of Self-Exposure': Closeted Desire in Margaret Atwood's *Cat's Eye*." *English Studies in Canada* 28.2 (June 2002): 223-246.

3293. SARRAZIN, Timothy M. C. "Reading *The Handmaid's Tale*." MA thesis. University of Hong Kong, 2002. ii, 39 pp. Contents and abstract viewable at http://sunzi1 .lib.hku.hk/hkuto/index.jsp.

3294. SENECAL, Nikole Alexa. "(Mis)Representations of Violent Women." PhD thesis. University of Southern California, 2002. 225 pp. "My dissertation reexamines the issue of women's violence from a feminist perspective that is open to the idea of such aggression redefining 'femininity' in helpful ways. Rejecting the positions of both conservative forces and those feminists who believe that a woman is naturally non-violent, I undertake a more nuanced reading of the violent woman. I argue that opening and continuing discussions of women's violence allows scholars to critique fully the ideals of womanhood and to explore all options for women's equality. This study focuses on works by contemporary North American women writers Margaret Atwood, Toni Morrison, and Joyce Carol Oates." (Author). For more see *DAI-A* 64.06 (December 2003): 2087.

3295. SIMMONS, Rachel. *Odd Girl Out: The Hidden Culture of Aggression in Girls*. New York: Harcourt, 2002. Includes discussion of *Cat's Eye*, pages 21-22.

3296. SIZEMORE, Christine Wick. *Negotiating Identities in Women's Lives: Eight Postcolonial and Contemporary British Novels*. Westport, CT: Greenwood Press, 2002. See especially Chapter 1, "Girlhood Identities: The Search for Adulthood in Tsitsi Dangarembga's *Nervous Conditions* and Margaret Atwood's *Cat's Eye*," [21]-35.

3297. STILL, Judith. "Bluebeards and Bodies: Margaret Atwood's Men." *Ilha do Desterro: A Journal of Language and Literature* 42 (2002): 165-180. Focus on *The Blind Assassin*. Portuguese summary.

3298. STOTT, Belinda. "The Cinderella Syndrome: Margaret Atwood's Fairy Tale Imagery and the Deeper Implications of its Appeal to the Contemporary Women." *Passages to Canada: Eighteen Essayistic Routes / Passages vers Le Canada: Dix huit routes essaylistique.* Proceedings of the European Student Seminars on Graduate Work in Canadian Studies. Ed. Markus Müller, Robert Chr. Thomsen, and David Parris. Brno [Czech Republic]: Masaryk UP, 2002. 54-62. "The Cinderella Syndrome refers to a behavioural pattern which involves denying responsibility for one's situation in life by adhering to the role of a passive victim, and that victim ostensibly awaits salvation from an external other." (Author).

3299. STRINGER, Kim. "Shared Experiences: Susanna Moodie Relived in Margaret Atwood's *The Journals of Susanna Moodie.*" *British Journal of Canadian Studies* 15.1-2 (2002): 170-181.

3300. SWEENEY, Megan Louise. "Doing Time, Reading Crime: Rethinking 'The Female Criminal.'" PhD thesis. Duke University, 2002. 400 pp. "[This thesis] combines ethnographic and interpretive work in order to theorize how individuals reading literary texts, and literary texts reading the social world, can help to wrest prisons from their normalized status as the primary means of addressing social problems. My ethnographic archive consists of interviews and group conversations with seventeen women imprisoned in the North Carolina Correctional Institution for Women. My literary archive consists of fiction featuring criminalized women—by Margaret Atwood, Toni Cade Bambara, Carole Maso, Gayl Jones, Pearl Cleage, and Toni Morrison—and a variety of true crime books. In exploring how the featured readers and texts reproduce, resist, and/or retheorize dominant conceptions of 'the female criminal,' I shuttle between literary analysis, readers' responses, discussions of issues such as the criminalization of drug use during pregnancy, and engagements with feminist legal theory, political theory, critical race theory, literary criticism, and criminology." (Author). For more see *DAI-A* 64.01 (July 2003): 195.

3301. TRIGG, Susan. "Mermaids and Sirens as Myth Fragments in Contemporary Literature." MA thesis. Deakin University, Victoria, 2002. 97 pp. "[This thesis] examines novels by Margaret Atwood and Angela Carter that contain myth fragments of mermaids and sirens. It postulates the origin of the myths as stemming from the ambivalent relationship that male infants form with the mother, and discusses how these authors deconstruct the binary oppositions that disadvantage women." (Author).

3302. WAGNER-LAWLOR, Jennifer A. "The Play of Irony: Theatricality and Utopian Transformation in Contemporary Women's Speculative Fiction." *Utopian Studies* 13.1 (2002): 114-134. "Presents an essay that explored the trope of performance, theatricality and utopian potentialities that pervades a number of 20th-century works of speculative fiction by women. *The Female Man* by Joanna Russ, *The Handmaid's Tale* by Margaret Atwood, *The Gate to Women's Country* by Sheri S. Tepper." (Author abstract).

3303. WILSON, Sharon R. "Margaret Atwood and Popular Culture: *The Blind Assassin* and Other Novels." *Journal of American and Comparative Cultures* 26.3-4 (Fall-Winter 2002): 270-275.

3304. WISKER, Gina. *Margaret Atwood's* Alias Grace: *A Reader's Guide.* New York; London: Continuum, 2002. 96 pp. Series: Continuum Contemporaries.

3305. WOOD, Ruth. "Called to be a Handmaid: Defending Margaret Atwood." *Censored Books, II: Critical Viewpoints, 1985-2000.* Ed. Nicholas J. Karolides and Nat Hentoff. Lanham, MD: Scarecrow, 2002. 199-205.

3306. ZIRKER, Herbert. *Selected Essays in English Literatures: British and Canadian—Jonathan Swift, Margaret Laurence, Margaret Atwood, Di Brandt and Dennis Cooley.* Berlin: Peter Lang, 2002. See especially Chapter 6, "Margaret Atwood, *The Handmaid's Tale:* A 'Variety of Literary Utopias,'" 117-130.

Reviews of Atwood's Works

3307. *The Blind Assassin*. Toronto; New York: McClelland and Stewart; Doubleday, 2000.
> *Atlanta Journal and Constitution* 27 January 2002: 5D. By Greg CHANGNON. (676 w). Reprinted by the *Cox News Service.*
> *Canadian Literature / Littérature canadienne* 173 (Summer 2002): 114-116. By Coral Ann HOWELLS.
> *Southern Humanities Review* 36.1 (Winter 2002): 91-93. By E. TEMPLEMAN.
> *World Literature Today* 76.1 (Winter 2002): 110. By B. A. St. ANDREWS.

3308. *The Blind Assassin*. [Sound recording]. Read by Margaret Dionne. Prince Frederick, MD: Bantam Doubleday, 2000.
> *The Virginian-Pilot* (Norfolk, VA) 3 February 2002: E3. By Peggy EARLE. (132 w).

3309. *The Edible Woman*. New York: Anchor Books, 1998.
> *Chicago Sun-Times* 9 July 2002: Section: Features: 20. By Carol SLEZAK.

3310. *Good Bones and Simple Murders*. New York: Nan A. Talese / Doubleday, 2001.
> *Boston Globe* 20 January 2002: G3. By Amanda HELLER. (716 w).

3311. *Good Bones and Simple Murders*. Toronto: McClelland and Stewart, 2001.
> *Books in Canada* 31.1 (February 2002): 10. By Kathryn KUITENBROUWER. (564 w).

3312. *The Journals of Susanna Moodie*. Toronto: Macfarlane Walter & Ross, 1997. Originally published in 1980 in a limited edition as a livre d'artiste. Includes a memoir by Charles Pachter and a foreword by David Staines.
> *Canadian Literature* 175 (Winter 2002): 118-120. By Jon KERTZER.

3313. *Negotiating with the Dead: A Writer on Writing*. Cambridge: Cambridge UP, 2002.
> *Atlanta Journal and Constitution* 17 March 2002: 5D. By Steven G. KELLMAN. (541 w).
> *Baltimore Sun* 3 March 2002: 10E. By Michael PAKENHAM. (1074 w).
> *Books in Canada* 31.4 (June-July 2002): 5-6. By T. F. RIGELHOF.
> *Boston Globe* 7 July 2002: D4. By James SALLIS. (797 w).
> *Calgary Herald* 9 March 2002: ES09. By Gordon MORASH.
> *Canberra Times* 29 June 2002: A16. ANON.
> *Charlotte Observer* 6 June 2002: Section: Entertainment News. By Jean Blish SIERS. (271 w).
> *Choice* 40.2 (October 2002): 275-276. By E.R. BAER.
> *Columbus Dispatch* 14 April 2002: 07F. By Kassie ROSE.
> *Contemporary Review* June 2002: 383-384. ANON (i.e., P.P.F.).
> *Courier Mail* [Queensland, Australia] 23 March 2002: M05. By Phillip DEAN. (922 w).
> *Cox News Service* 14 March 2002: Section: Entertainment, Television and Culture. By Steven G. KELLMAN. (540 w).
> *Daily Telegraph* (London) 9 March 2002: 04. By Sam LEITH. (687 w).
> *Edmonton Journal* 10 March 2002: D12. By Todd BABIAK.
> *Globe and Mail* 23 March 2002: D5. By J. S. PORTER.
> *The Herald* (Glasgow) 9 March 2002: 12. ANON. (670 w).
> *Herald Sun* (Melbourne) 6 April 2002: W28. By Sarah HUDSON. (87 w).

The Independent (London) 19 July 2002: Section: Features: 17. By Ruth PADEL. (536 w).

Irish Times 15 June 2002: Section: Weekend: 58. By Eilis ni DHUIBHNE. (675 w).

Library Journal 127.5 (15 March 2002): 80. By Mary Paumier JONES.

London Free Press (Ontario) 9 March 2002: D7. By Nancy SCHIEFER. (800 w).

London Review of Books 24.8 (25 April 2002): 14. ANON.

Los Angeles Times 18 March 2002: Section: Southern California Living: Part 5: 3. By Merle RUBIN. (922 w).

Magill Book Reviews 1 November 2002: s.l. By Rosemary M. Canfield REISMAN. (277 w). "Not an easy read...." Available from Ebsco's Academic Search Premier.

Montreal Gazette 18 May 2002: G3. By Pat DONNELLY.

National Post 9 March 2002: SP1. By Joan BODGER.

New Zealand Herald 28 July 2002: Section: Entertainment; Books; Reviews. By Jane WESTAWAY. (518 w).

Ottawa Citizen 17 March 2002: C11. By Reamy JANSEN.

Richmond Times Dispatch 26 May 2002: E4. By Jeff LODGE.

The Scotsman 2 March 2002: 7. By Allan MASSIE. (805 w).

Scotsman on Sunday 17 March 2002: 4. By Andrew CRUMEY. (517 w).

Seattle Times 24 March 2002: I11. By Irene WANNER.

South China Morning Post (Hong Kong) 4 May 2002: Section: Feature: 4. By Doug NAIRNE. (449 w).

The Spectator 9 March 2002: 44-45. By Anita BROOKNER. (1069 w).

Sunday Telegraph (London) 10 March 2002: 13. By Christopher TAYLOR. (638 w).

Sunday Times (London) 7 April 2002: Section: Features.

The Times (London) 13 March 2002: Section: Features. By Iain FINLAYSON. (171 w).

Times Colonist (Victoria) 21 April 2002: C9. By Reamy JANSEN.

Times Union (Albany, NY) 24 March 2002: J4. By Steven G. KELLMAN. (250 w).

TLS: Times Literary Supplement 5174 (31 May 2002): 24. By Margaret STEAD.

Toronto Star 24 March 2002: D15. ANON (1549 w).

Tulsa World 20 June 2002: Section: Books. By Jean Blish SIERS.

Vancouver Sun 9 March 2002: D15. By Lynn COADY.

Washington Post 17 March 2002: T08. By Craig NOVA. (837 w).

Women's Review of Books 19.8 (May 2002): 10-11. By Susan BALEE.

Reviews of Adaptations of Atwood's Works

3314. *The Edible Woman*. Adapted by Dave CARLEY. Winnipeg: Scirocco Drama, 2002. Play based on the novel.
    Globe and Mail 23 February 2002: R19. ANON.
    Hamilton Spectator 6 March 2002: D04. By Gary SMITH. (859 w).
    National Post 25 February 2002: B15. ANON.
    Toronto Sun 1 March 2002: E12. By John COULBOURN. (492 w).
3315. *The Handmaid's Tale*. Santa Monica, CA: MGM Home Entertainment, 2002. Videocassette (109 min.). Originally released as motion picture in 1990.
    Daily Record 29 June 2002: Section: Television: 27. (Review of [then] upcoming TV broadcast.)

~ 2003 ~

Atwood's Works

3316. *Adam'kush-i kur*. Tehran: Ququnus, 2003. Persian translation of *The Blind Assassin* by Shahin Asayish.

3317. *Aklasis zudikas*. Vilnius: Alma Littera, 2003. Lithuanian translation of *The Blind Assassin* by Valdas V. Petrauskas.

3318. *Alias Grace*. [Electronic resource]. Toronto: CNIB, 2003. Computer data (21 files: 213.15 mb).

3319. *Alias Grace*. [Internet resource]. New York: RosettaBooks, 2003. Accessible at http://www.contentreserve.com/TitleInfo.asp?ID={A3CE95B0-3BDD-496E-FB7-78832FE3D2B9}&Format=150 [Palm Reader version].

3320. "Amazement." *Prize Writing: The 10th Anniversary Collection*. Ed. Gary Stephen Ross. Toronto: The Giller Prize Foundation in association with Coach House Books, 2003. 39-46. Focus on *Alias Grace*, which won the prize in 1996.

3321. "Apple Jelly." *Stories from Where We Live: The Great Lakes*. Ed. Sara St. Antoine. Minneapolis: Milkweed Editions, 2003. 139. Poem.

3322. "Arguing Against Ice Cream." *New York Review of Books* 50.10 (2003): 6-8. Review of Bill McKibben's *Enough: Staying Human in an Engineered Age*.

3323. "At Home among the Bluenosers." *New York Times Magazine* 16 November 2003: Section: 6: Pt. 2: 52. Lunenburg, NS; a travel piece (1541 w).

3324. *Att förhandla med de döda: En författare om skrivandet*. Stockholm: Prisma, 2003. Swedish translation of *Negotiating with the Dead: A Writer on Writing* by Ulla Danielsson.

3325. *The Blind Assassin*. Toronto: Emblem Editions, 2003. Paperback.

3326. *The Blind Assassin*. [Electronic resource]. Toronto: CNIB, 2003. Computer data (138 files: 593 mb).

3327. *The Blind Assassin*. [Internet resource]. New York: RosettaBooks, 2003. Electronic book accessible at http://www.contentreserve.com/TitleInfo.asp?ID = {0E5F54C4-76DA-43B8-9E23-9BF27F235750}&Format = 50 [Abobe acrobat version]; http://www.contentreserve.com/TitleInfo.asp?ID = {0E5F54C4-76DA-43B8-9E23-9BF27F235750}&Format = 150 [Palm Reader version].

3328. *Bodily Harm*. [Sound recording]. Read by Bonnie Hurren. Bath [UK]: BBC Audiobooks; Hampton, NH: BBC Audiobooks America, 2003. Unabridged. 8 CD-ROMS; ca. 10 hours.

3329. *Bodily Harm.* [Sound recording]. Read by Sandy McNeil. Vancouver, BC: Crane Library, 2003. 7 tape reels.

3330. "Bonaparte to Bush: You'll Be Sorry" *Globe & Mail* 1 March 2003: A17. Lessons from Napoleon that Bush might have paid attention to. (958 w). Also published as "Why the 1812 Overture Should Be Ringing Some Bells Today." *Daily Telegraph* (London) 5 March 2003: 24; "Napoleon's Blunders: A Tale of Preemptive Strikes Gone Wrong." *Los Angeles Times* 16 March 2003: M1; "Tchaikovsky's Overture and the Risk of Preemption." *The Record* (Bergen County, NJ) 20 March 2003: Section: Opinion: L11; "Napoleon's Blunders." *Standard* (St. Catharines, ON) 21 March 2003: A7; "Liberators Aren't Always Welcome." *Vancouver Sun* 21 March 2003: A10; "Pre-emptive Strikes Gone Wrong: Napoleon's Blunder." *Edmonton Journal* 23 March 2003: D8. Commenting in the *Los Angeles Times* on 19 March (Section: California Metro: 12), Frank O. Clark noted: "To suggest that universal truths emanate through the nexus of Atwood's point of view in this whimsical history lesson is farfetched and misguided. I do, however, believe her successful career as a writer of fiction is secure."

3331. "The Book Lover's Tale: Using Literature to Stay Afloat in a Fundamentalist Sea." *Literary Review of Canada* September 2003: 5-6. A review of *Reading* Lolita *in Tehran: A Memoir in Books* by Azar Nafisi.

3332. *Captive.* Paris: Laffont, 2003 ©1998. French translation of *Alias Grace* by Michèle Albaret-Maatsch.

3333. "Carol Shields: 2 June 1935-16 July 2003." *Entertainment Weekly* 743 (26 December 2003): 103. Short obituary of Shields (135 w).

3334. "Castle of the Imagination." *New York Review of Books* 50.1 (16 January 2003): 27-28. Review of Alice McDermott's *Child of My Heart.*

3335. *Cat's Eye.* [Internet resource]. New York: RosettaBooks, 2003. Accessible at http://www.contentreserve.com/TitleInfo.asp?ID={02F2B82B-AE78-4105-83A3-B09B36DAFD05}&Format=50 [Adobe Acrobat version].

3336. *Dançarinas e outras histórias.* Rio de Janeiro: Rocco, 2003. Portuguese translation of *Dancing Girls and Other Stories* by Lia Wyler.

3337. "The Dark Side of Perfection." *The Times* (London) 18 June 2003: Section: Features: 18. Review of Bill McKibben's *Enough: Genetic Engineering and the End of Human Nature* (London: Bloomsbury, 2003). An earlier version of this article appeared in the *New York Review of Books.*

3338. "Democracy: Use It or Lose It." *Harvard Magazine* 105.6 (July-August 2003): 65. Reprint of luncheon address. Also available at http://www.harvardmagazine.com/on-line/070300.html (1 May-June 2006).

3339. *Den blinde morderen.* Oslo: Aschehoug Moderne, 2003. Norwegian translation of *The Blind Assassin* by Inger Gjelsvik.

3340. "Der Lesende by Kathe Kollwitz." *Paris Review* 45.167 (2003): 100-101. Presents the interpretation of the charcoal drawing on butten paper "Der Lesende" by Kathe Kollwitz.

3341. *The Edible Woman.* [Electronic resource]. Toronto: CNIB, 2003. Computer data (44 files: 146 mb).

3342. *El Asesino Ciego.* 3rd ed. Barcelona: Ediciones B, 2003. Spanish translation of *The Blind Assassin* by Dolors Udina.

3343. "Elegy for the Giant Tortoises." *Intersections: The Human Impact on the Global Environment—A Course for All First-Year Students.* Designed by Intersections Council Members. Lincoln, MA: Tapestry Press, 2003. 1. Reprinted from *The Animals in That Country,* ©1969 and *Selected Poems 1965-1975,* ©1976.

3344. *Entering the Labyrinth: Writing* The Blind Assassin. Wollongong: University of Wollongong Press, 2003. Volume includes Atwood's address, with the same title as the volume, 15-30, plus two essays also indexed here, one by Coral Ann Howells, "Sites of Desolation" (31-46), and the other by Dorothy Jones, "Narrative Enclosures" (47-67). Atwood's Nortel Networks Canadian Studies Address was presented on 9 March 2001. This is the second in a series edited by Gerry Turcotte.

3345. "[Excerpt]." *Albuquerque Journal* (NM) 6 April 2003: Section: Final: B8. From Atwood's "Letter to America" on the Iraq War (see 3376).

3346. "[Excerpt]." *Almost to Freedom*. By Vaunda Micheaux Nelson and Colin Bootman. Minneapolis: Carolrhoda Books, 2003. Frontispiece. Excerpt from Atwood poem ("A doll is a witness who cannot die, with a doll you are never alone") included on frontispiece of a book telling the story of a young girl's dramatic escape from slavery via the Underground Railroad, from the perspective of her beloved rag doll.

3347. "[Excerpt]." *Globe & Mail* 24 May 2003: Section: Focus: F5. Article on celebrities who earn honorary doctorates from various Canadian universities includes excerpt from Atwood's convocation address at McMaster University on 4 June 1996: "I shall open with a resounding quote from Charles Dickens: 'It is the best of times, it is the worst of times.' Let me revise that. It is the best of times. For those who think a cut in their income tax will improve their golf game, cure their arthritis, and make them generally overjoyed. And it is the worst of times for those who don't have any income in the first place, being unemployed. Now comes the part of the speech where I tell you how different everything was when I was younger. So here goes: When I was younger, the main problem was not world or local hunger, but merely how to avoid becoming a lawyer, or else marrying one. When I graduated it was 1961."

3348. "[Excerpt]." *The Guardian* (London) 11 October 2003: Section: *Guardian* Weekend: 16. Stories of 3 mortifications past (autographing in the underwear section in Edmonton, the interview on a TV talk show which followed the Colostomy Association, and a new one dating from 2003 on another TV show in Mexico in which was asked whether she was feminine). Reprinted from *Mortification: Writers' Stories of Their Public Shame*. Ed. Robin Robertson. London: Fourth Estate, 2003.

3349. "[Excerpt]." *South China Morning Post* (Hong Kong) 1 March 2003: Section: Feature: 4. Reprinted from "Charivari," in Margaret Atwood's *Selected Poems, 1966-1984*, ©1990: "They capped their heads with feathers, masked / their faces, wore their clothes backwards, howled / with torches through the midnight winter / and dragged the black man from his house / to the jolting music of broken / instruments, pretending to each other / it was a joke, until / they killed him. I don't know / what happened to the white bride." Article recommends Atwood's overlooked poetry.

3350. "[Excerpt]." *Star Tribune* (MN) 13 April 2003: Section: Variety: 1E. From *The Handmaid's Tale* (234 w).

3351. "[Excerpt]." *Weekend Australian* 26 April 2003: Section: Review: B14. From *Oryx and Crake*, chapter one. (1313 w).

3352. "[Excerpts]." *The Book Lover's Cookbook: Recipes Inspired by Celebrated Works of Literature and the Passages That Feature Them.* By Shaunda Kennedy Wenger and Janet Kay Jensen. New York: Ballantine Books, ©2003. 36, 78, 299. All from *Cat's Eye*.

3353. "[Excerpts]." *Margaret Atwood: Reading.* [Videorecording]. Georgetown, TX: Southwestern University, 2003. 1 videocassette (82 min.). Atwood reads excerpts from *Oryx and Crake.* Filmed at Southwestern University on 6 November 2003 in the Alma Thomas Theater.

3354. "Foreword." *A Breath of Fresh Air: Celebrating Nature and School Gardens.* By Elise Houghton. Toronto: The Learnxs Foundation and Sumach Press in co-operation with the Toronto District School Board, 2003. 13-19.

3355. "Foreword." *Inspiring Women: A Celebration of Herstory.* By Mona Holmlund and Gail Youngberg. Regina, SK: Coteau Books, 2003. [i-ii]. There is also a pro-file of Atwood, 234, indexed under secondary sources.

3356. *Gazela i Kosac.* Zagreb: Profil, 2003. Croatian translation of *Oryx and Crake* by Marko Maras.

3357. *Good Bones.* [Electronic resource]. Toronto: CNIB, 2003. Computer data (35 files: 35.8 mb).

3358. *The Handmaid's Tale.* Charlesbourg, QU: Braille Jymico, 2003. Braille ed., 4 v.

3359. *The Handmaid's Tale.* [Electronic resource]. Toronto: CNIB, 2003. Computer data (70 files: 141 mb).

3360. "Happy Endings." *The Longman Masters of Short Fiction.* [Sound recording]. Princeton, NJ: Recording for the Blind & Dyslexic, 2003. 1 sound disc. Atwood story included in this collection. "Distribution is restricted to RFB & D members who have a documented print disability such as a visual impairment, learning dis-ability or other physical disability."

3361. "Happy Endings." *The Story and Its Writer: An Introduction to Short Fiction.* By Ann Charters. 6th ed. Boston; New York: Bedford / St. Martin's, 2003. 69-71.

3362. "He Springs Eternal." *New York Review of Books* 50.17 (2003): 78-80. Review of Studs Terkel's *Hope Dies Last: Keeping the Faith in Difficult Times.*

3363. "I Bit My Fingers as I Do When Tense." *Globe & Mail* 3 April 2003: Section: *Globe* Review: R1, 7. On the origins of *The Handmaid's Tale.* Also published as "For God and Gilead," *The Guardian* (London) 22 March 2003: s.l. Available at http://books.guardian.co.uk/departments/generalfiction/story/0,6000,918519,00. html (1 May 2006).

3364. "Inside Story: Orwell and Me." *The Guardian* (London) 16 June 2003: Section: Features: 4. Also published as "Why *Animal Farm* Changed My Life." *The Age* (Melbourne) 12 July 2003: Section: Review: 1. Some comments on the occasion of the 100th anniversary of Orwell's birth, originally broadcast on BBC Radio 3.

3365. "Introduction." *The Complete Stories, Volume 4.* By Morley Callaghan. Toronto: Exile Editions, 2003. ix-xix.

3366. "Introduction." *Cuba: Grace under Pressure.* By Rosemary Sullivan. Toronto: McArthur, 2003. ix-xi. Introduction to a book of photography by Malcolm David Batty, with text by Rosemary Sullivan.

3367. "Just Think 'What If.'" *Western Mail Magazine* 24 May 2003: 153-155. On the origins of *Oryx and Crake.*

3368. *Kocie Oko.* Poznan: Zysk i S-ka, 2003. Polish translation of *Cat's Eye* by Magda-lena Konikowska.

3369. *Kuraki me no ansatsusha.* Tokyo: Hayakawa Shobo, 2003. Japanese translation of *The Blind Assassin* by Yukiko Kounosu. Title romanized.

3370. *L'assassi cec.* Barcelona: Punt de Lectura, 2003. Catalan translation of *The Blind Assassin* by Mercè López Arnabat.

3371. *L'assassino cieco: Romanzo.* Milan: TEA, 2003. Italian translation of *The Blind Assassin* by Raffaella Belletti.

3372. *L'ultimo degli uomini.* Milan: Ponte Alle Grazie, 2003. Italian translation of *Oryx and Crake* by Raffaella Belletti.

3373. *La mujer comestible.* Barcelona: Ediciones B, 2003. Spanish translation of *The Edible Woman* by Juanjo Estrella.

3374. *Lady Oracle.* London: Virago, 2003 ©1976. (Virago Modern Classics).

3375. *Lady Oracle.* [Electronic resource]. Toronto: CNIB, 2003. Computer data (92 files: 480 mb).

3376. "Letter to America." *Globe & Mail* 28 March 2003: A17. Atwood expresses concerns about various directions in which America is heading. Also in *The Nation* 276.14 (14 April 2003): 22.

3377. *Life Before Man.* [Electronic resource]. Toronto: CNIB, 2003. 1 computer laser optical disc (11 hr., 26 min.).

3378. *Life Before Man.* [Sound recording]. Read by Lorelei King. Bath [UK]: Chivers Audio Books; Hampton, NH: Chivers North America, 2003. Unabridged. 10 cassettes; ca. 12 hours.

3379. *Macje oko.* Belgrade: Laguna, 2003. Serbian translation of *Cat's Eye* by Maja Kaluderovic.

3380. *Madame Oráculo.* Rio de Janeiro: Rocco, 2003. Portuguese translation of *Lady Oracle* by Léa Viveiros de Castro.

3381. *Mang ci ke.* Shanghai: Shanghai yi wen chu ban she, 2003. Chinese translation of *The Blind Assassin* by Han Zhong Hua. Title romanized.

3382. "Margaret Atwood." *Mortification: Writers' Stories of Their Public Shame.* Ed. Robin Robertson. London: Fourth Estate, 2003. 1-4. Three of Atwood's most embarrassing moments.

3383. *Moondatute Laulud.* Tallinn: Eesti Keele Sihtasutus, 2003. Estonian translation by Ene-Reet Soovik of poems from *Selected Poems 1966-1984*, ©1990 and *Morning in the Burned House*, ©1995.

3384. *Negotiating with the Dead: A Writer on Writing.* Toronto; New York: Anchor Books; London: Virago, 2003. Paperback of 2002 book.

3385. *The New Oxford Book of Canadian Short Stories.* [Electronic resource]. Toronto: CNIB, 2003. Computer data (100 files: 352.7 mb). Co-edited with Robert Weaver. Contains "Introduction" by Atwood and "True Trash," originally published in *Wilderness Tips*, ©1991.

3386. *Oriksa un Kreiks.* Riga, Latvia: Atenas Bilioteka III, 2003. Latvian translation of *Oryx and Crake* by Silvija Brice.

3387. *Oryx and Crake.* Toronto: McClelland and Stewart; New York: Nan A. Talese; London: Bloomsbury, 2003. "The narrator of Atwood's riveting novel calls himself Snowman. When the story opens, he is sleeping in a tree, wearing an old bedsheet, mourning the loss of his beloved Oryx and his best friend Crake, and slowly starving to death. He searches for supplies in a wasteland where insects proliferate and pigoons and wolvogs ravage the pleeblands, where ordinary people once lived, and the Compounds that sheltered the extraordinary. As he tries to piece together what has taken place, the narrative shifts to decades earlier. How did everything fall apart so quickly? Why is he left with nothing but his haunting memories? Alone except for the green-eyed Children of Crake, who think of him as a kind of monster, he explores the answers to these questions in the double journey he takes —into his own past, and back to Crake's high-tech bubble-dome, where the Paradice Project unfolded and the world came to grief." (Publisher).

3388. *Oryx and Crake.* Toronto: McClelland and Stewart, 2003. Braille edition.

3389. *Oryx and Crake: A Novel.* New York: Anchor Books, 2003. Paperback.

3390. *Oryx and Crake.* [Sound recording]. Princeton, NJ: Recording for the Blind & Dyslexic, 2003. 1 sound disc. Distribution is restricted to RFB&D members who have a documented print disability such as a visual impairment, learning disability, or other physical disability. Contents: "Mango," "Flotsam," "Voice," "Bonfire," "Organic Farms," "Lunch," "Nooners," "Downpour," "Rakunk," "Hammer," "Crake," "Brainfizz," "HottTotts," "Toast," "Fish," "Bottle," "Oryx," "Birdcall," "Roses," "Pixieland Jazz," "Sveltana," "Purring," "Blue," "SoYummie," "Happicuppa," "Applied Rhetoric," "Asperger's U.," "Wolvogs," "Hypothetical," "Extinctathon," "Hike," "RejoovanEsense," "Twister," "Vulturizing," "AnnoYou," "Garage," "Gripless," "Pigoons," "Radio," "Rampart," "Pleebcrawl," "BlyssPluss," "MaddAddam," "Paradice," "Crake in Love," "Takeout," "Airlock," "Bubble," "Scribble," "Remnant," "Idol," "Sermon," "Footprint."

3391. *Oryx and Crake.* [Sound recording]. Read by Alex Jennings. [London]: Bloomsbury, 2003.

3392. *Oryx and Crake.* [Sound recording]. Read by Brenda Berck. Vancouver, BC: Crane Resource Centre, 2003. 8 sound cassettes.

3393. *Oryx and Crake.* [Sound recording]. Read by Campbell Scott. Santa Ana, CA: Books on Tape, 2003. Unabridged ed.; 9 CD-ROMS; ca. 10.5 hours.

3394. *Oryx and Crake.* [Sound recording]. Read by Campbell Scott. New York: Random House Audio, 2003. Unabridged ed.; 7 cassettes; ca. 10.5 hours.

3395. *Oryx en Crake.* Amsterdam: B. Bakker, 2003. Dutch translation by Tinke Davids.

3396. *Oryx ja Crake.* Helsinki: Kustannusosakeyhtiö Otava, 2003. Finnish translation by Kristiina Drews.

3397. *Oryx och Crake.* Stockholm: Prisma, 2003. Swedish translation by Birgitta Gahrton.

3398. *Oryx og Crake.* Oslo: Aschehoug, 2003. Norwegian translation by Inger Gjelsvik.

3399. *Oryx og Crake: Roman.* Copenhagen: Lindhardt og Ringhof, 2003. Danish translation by Lisbeth Møller-Madsen.

3400. *Oryx und Crake.* Berlin: Berlin Verlag. German translation by Barbara Lüdemann.

3401. "A Path Taken, with All the Certainty of Youth." *Writers on Writing: Vol. II— More Collected Essays from the* New York Times. Ed. Jane Smiley. New York: Henry Holt and Company, 2003. 9-12.

3402. "Rape Fantasies." *The Story and Its Writer: An Introduction to Short Fiction.* By Ann Charters. 6th ed. Boston; New York: Bedford / St. Martin's, 2003. 71-78.

3403. "Reading Blind." *The Story and Its Writer: An Introduction to Short Fiction.* By Ann Charters. 6th ed. Boston; New York: Bedford / St. Martin's, 2003. 1456-1459. Originally published as the Introduction to *The Best American Short Stories, 1989.* Atwood's job was to pick 20 out of 2,000 stories published that year. This essay is an attempt to answer the questions: "What would be my criteria, if any? How would I be able to tell the best from the merely better? How would I know?"

3404. *Realitātes šovs.* Riga: Atena, 2003. Latvian translation of *Wilderness Tips* by Silvija Brice.

3405. "Resisting the Veil: Reports from a Revolution." *The Walrus* 1.1 (October 2003): 86-89. Review of the following books: *Persepolis: The Story of a Childhood*, by Marjane Satrapi, translated by Mattias Ripa and Blake Ferris (Pantheon Books, 2003); *Reading* Lolita *in Tehran: A Memoir in Books*, by Azar Nafisi (Random House, 2003); *The Bathhouse*, by Farnoosh Moshiri (Beacon Press, 2003); *Shah of Shahs*, by Ryszard Kapuscinski, translated by William R. Brand and Katarzyna Mroczkowska-Brand (Vintage Books, 1992); *The Crisis of Islam: Holy War and Unholy Terror*, by Bernard Lewis (The Modern Library, 2003); *The Crusades*

Through Arab Eyes, by Amin Maalouf, translated by Jon Rothschild (Al Saqi Books, 1984).

3406. *The Robber Bride*. [Electronic resource]. Toronto: CNIB, 2003. Computer data. 287 mb.

3407. "The Rise and Fall of Imperial Dreams." *Globe & Mail* 8 February 2003: Section: Books: D15. Atwood review of *A History of Warfare* by John Keegan (Knopf, 1993); *Guns, Germs and Steel* by Jared Diamond (Norton, 1997); and *A Green History of the World* by Clive Ponting (St. Martin's Press, 1992).

3408. *Rude Ramsay and the Roaring Radishes*. Toronto: Key Porter Kids, 2003. 29 pp. Juvenile.

3409. *Slepi ubica*. Belgrade: Laguna, 2003. Serbian translation of *The Blind Assassin* by Goran Kapetanovic.

3410. *Slepoj ubijitsa*. Moscow: Eksmo, 2003. Russian translation of *The Blind Assassin*.

3411. *Slepy zabójca*. Warsaw: Swiat Ksiazki, 2003. Polish translation of *The Blind Assassin* by Malgorzata Hesko-Kolodzinska .

3412. *Surfacing*. [Electronic resource]. Toronto: CNIB, 2003. Computer data (8 files: 96.4 mb).

3413. "Survival Then and Now." *The Canadian Distinctiveness into the XXIst Century / La dictinction canadienne au tournant du XXIe siècle*. Ed. Chad Gaffield and Karen L. Gould. Ottawa: University of Ottawa Press, 2003. 47-55. "Elements of this presentation appeared in the article published in 1 July 1999 issue of *Maclean's*, entitled "Survival, Now and Then."

3414. *Tipps für die Wildnis*. Berlin: Berliner Taschenbuch Verlag, 2003. German translation of *Wilderness Tips*.

3415. "To the Light House: Carol Shields Who Died Last Week, Wrote Books That Were Full of Delights." *The Guardian* (London) 26 July 2003: Section: Saturday Pages: 28. Obituary of Canadian writer. Excerpt: "She knew about the darkness, but—both as an author and as a person—she held on to the light." (1263 w).

3416. "Tribute." *Arc* 50 (Summer 2003): 55. To Don Coles, for making "sad, wise, and complex music for three decades and for his literary works of poetry."

3417. "[Verse]." *Sunday Telegraph* (London) 8 June 2003: 14. Atwood, in honor of the 30th birthday of Virago, her British publisher, wrote and recited some comic verse that recalled her paperback publisher's humble origins in a seedy office in Soho:

> They stormed the land of spangles and garters—
> One room on Wardour Street they hired, for starters.
> Up dimly lit stairways they bravely groped,
> While men in macintoshes leered and hoped.
> They had leather satchels and sensible shoosies,
> Though some mistook them for upmarket floozies.
> Not any more.

3418. *Wilderness Tips*. [Electronic resource]. Toronto: CNIB, 2003. Computer data (30 files: 455 mb).

3419. "You Fit into Me." *Washington Post* 10 February 2003: C10. Story by Mary Esselman and Elizabeth Velez entitled "The Extraordinary Measure of Love" includes Atwood poem: "You fit into me / like a hook into an eye / a fish hook / an open eye."

Adaptations of Atwood's Works

3420. *The Atwood Stories* [DVD]. Kelowna, BC: Shaftesbury Films, 2003. DVD titles include: v.1. "Polarities," "Man from Mars." v.2. "Betty," "Death by Landscape." v.3. "Isis in Darkness," "The Sunrise." Bonus feature: Complete shooting scripts for each program in .pdf format. Available from Filmwest Associates www.filmwest.com (1 May 2006).

3421. *John Beckwith.* [Sound recording]. Toronto: Centrediscs, 2003 ©1969. Compact disc, 2 sound discs. Atwood's "The Trumpets of Summer" basis of first work on disc 2. Originally recorded at Hallmark Studios, Toronto, 20-22 February 1969.

Quotations

3422. "[Quote]." *The Express* 18 October 2003: Section: Columns: 51. "My most intoxicating honour was having a 236-ton sewer tunnelling machine in Hull [Quebec] named after me."

3423. "[Quote]." *Hamilton Spectator* (ON) 31 December 2003: G8. "The beginning of Canadian nationalism was not 'Am I really that oppressed?' but 'Am I really that boring?'" In year-end review of events.

3424. "[Quote]." *Houston Chronicle* 5 October 2003: Section: Travel: 6. In a visit to the Watercolor Inn, in Watercolor, Florida, Harry Shattuck noted an Atwood quote on the body lotion container: "For years I wanted to be older, and now I am." The Inn is surrounded by quotes. On the shampoo tube for example, Dinah Shore remarks: "Bing Crosby sings like everyone else thinks they sing in the shower." Ann Landers is quoted as saying, "Don't accept your dog's admiration as conclusive evidence that you are wonderful," and the editors of the *Farmer's Digest* advise, "If you can't get people to listen to you, tell them it is confidential."

3425. "[Quote]." *Lawyer's Weekly* 23.30 (5 December 2003): s.p. Available from Lexis-Nexis. Article entitled "Telecommunications Raise Privacy and Ethics Issues" by David Bilinsky starts off with following quote: "A voice is a human gift; it should be cherished and used, to utter fully human speech as possible. Powerlessness and silence go together."

3426. "[Quote]." *The Record* (Bergen County, NJ) 25 June 2003: Section: Opinion: L11. Article on George Orwell disputes Atwood's comment: "With the fall of the Berlin Wall in 1989, it seemed for a time that…henceforth state control would be minimal and all we would have to do is go shopping and smile a lot, and wallow in pleasures, popping a pill or two when depression set in."

3427. "[Quote]." *The Record* (Bergen County, NJ) 11 September 2003: Section: Religion & Values: L05. "God is not the voice in the whirlwind. God is the whirlwind." Atwood quoted by Mary A. Jacobs within her story about the website of the World Pantheist Movement. This quote, along with Atwood's smiling face, also appears on the site: http://www.pantheism.net (1 May 2006).

3428. "[Quote]." *The Record* (Kitchener-Waterloo) 17 May 2003: Section News: D16. With the publication of *Oryx and Crake* Atwood's out with a series of cleverly worded refrigerator magnets: "I think therefore I spam," "No brain no pain," and the curious "Life experiments like a rakunk at play."

3429. "[Quote]." *Salon.com* 27 November 2003: s.p. Available from Lexis-Nexis. Atwood commenting on Studs Terkel's *Working*: It contained "raw material for 1,000 novels in one medium-sized book."

Interviews

3430. "Atwood Pushes for Forest-Friendly Paper." *Daily Herald-Tribune* (Alberta) 10 October 2003: Section: Entertainment: 39. Atwood was interviewed by phone from Frankfurt where she was attending the book fair as part of a Canadian-led effort to persuade the industry to use so-called Ancient Forest Friendly paper, which is 100% post-consumer recycled, chlorine-free paper and fiber. "It's nice to be a world leader in something," Atwood said with a wry tone. Two years earlier, Canadian publishers McClelland and Stewart and Raincoast Books signed onto a campaign by a Tofino, BC, environmentalist and began sourcing the costly paper.

3431. "Books Find Their Readers." *Maclean's* 20 October 2003: 56. Atwood answers questions about *Rude Ramsay and the Roaring Radishes.* Some examples:

Where did the idea for *Rude Ramsay* come from? The same place *Princess Prunella and the Purple Peanut* [1995] came from. I did it partly because Anna Porter, the publisher, is an old friend of mine and was saying, "Help me!" I had this story that I used to amuse my child with when I was trying to comb her hair after having washed it. Her hair being somewhat like mine, it would take a long time, so I used to tell her the story about Princess Prunella. I just wrote some of it down for Anna. *Rude Ramsay and the Roaring Radishes* was generated partly because Anna was saying "Help me!" again, due to the Stoddart fiasco.

How long does it take you to write a children's book? A few days, for the first draft. It's like poetry. You have to do it all in one go, and then you can twiddle with it.

Working on children's stories, is there something in particular that you like? I'm exploring my inner nitwit. Inside every take-me-serious person, there's a silly person just dying to get out.

3432. "Margaret Atwood." *Gardening Life* 7.5 (August-September 2003): 104. Atwood interviewed about her gardening interests.

3433. "Margaret Atwood." *National Post* 30 August 2003: Section: Books: 6. Email interview with Atwood about *Rude Ramsay and the Roaring Radishes.*

3434. "Margaret Atwood Pens New Children's Book." *Canada AM* 9 September 2003: s.l. Available from Lexis-Nexis. Interview with Marci Ien covered *Rude Ramsay and the Roaring Radishes* as well as *Oryx and Crake.* When asked, "What is next for you, Ms. Atwood?" she replied: "What is next? Well, you can never second-guess the future. So, I don't know. And if I knew I wouldn't tell, because I have a superstition about it. But in the children's-book line, let us say I've got my eye on the letter S."

3435. BETHUNE, Brian. "Atwood Apocalyptic." *Maclean's* 28 April 2003: Section: Books: 44. Speaking of genetically modified corn and other crops, and the law of unintended consequences, Atwood paused. "You know," she smiled, "there are studies that indicate corn-based stuff tells the body to put on more fat. And about 70 percent of the US is somewhat overweight. I'm thinking of writing a new scary dystopia called 'Waddle,' about fast-running alien predators and people who can't get away from them."

3436. CASE, Eleanor, and Maggie McDONALD. "Life After Man." *New Scientist* 178.2393 (3 May 2003): 40-43. Interview with Atwood about *Oryx and Crake* when she was in London for the premiere of the opera *The Handmaid's Tale.*

3437. CAULFIELD RYBAK, Deborah. "Future Shock." *Star Tribune* (Minneapolis) 14 April 2003: Section: Variety: 1E. Extensive interview in anticipation of the arrival of *The Handmaid's Tale* at the Minnesota Opera. The book "had a different reception from different countries," she recalled. "The English said, 'Jolly good yarn!' They'd done all this under Oliver Cromwell and they're not about to do it again. The Canadians, in their anxious way, said: 'Could it happen here?' which is what they always say about everything. The Americans said, 'How long have we got?'"

3438. CHAMBERLAIN, Adrian. "Back to the Future." *Times-Colonist* (Victoria) 24 April 2003: Section: GO: D7. Atwood in Victoria to read and field questions for a sold-out crowd at Alix Goolden Hall, having ferried over after attending the Vancouver International Writers and Readers Festival. In Victoria, she planned to visit her writer friends Carol Shields and Audrey Thomas.

Did the essential plot-line of *Oryx and Crake* come to her in one flash of insight? "It did come in a flash. And then you have to work out the flash," Atwood said. "Like all flash experiences, it's built on a huge mountain of non-flash. The eureka experience, as anyone will tell you, comes out of long times of thinking about a problem."

The interviewer also observed that Atwood certainly was no ogre. She was sharp, amusing, and intelligent. Yet there was a sense that she didn't suffer fools gladly. A week earlier a *Globe and Mail* reporter had written: "Talking with Atwood is like playing an interactive video game with a highly competitive and wily opponent." "Famously prickly and formidable," wrote another journalist. When the interviewer asked Atwood about the latter quote, she said that such a reputation may have been forged in the 1970s, when fiction writers—especially female fiction writers—were routinely asked rude and hostile questions. These included (Atwood dispatched them in the voice of an obnoxious radio hot-liner): I haven't read your book. And I'm not going to! But why don't you tell us in about 25 words what it's about. ■ What's the book about and why should anybody read it? ■ Do men like you? ■ When do you find time to do the housework? Said Atwood: "It was like, 'Who do you think you are, writing these books? Eh?'" She laughed. "This doesn't happen today, of course." But she believed it could well happen to another, younger writer.

3439. COFFEY, Edel. "Alias a Chronicler of a Future Dystopia." *Sunday Tribune* 8 June 2003: 2. On the difference between science fiction and speculative fiction: "Science fiction to me means way out there, other planets or intelligent beings with eight legs, or things we have thought about theoretically but nobody has any idea of how to do, such as going from one dimension to another or 'Beam me up, Scotty,'" she said, indulging in her low laugh, a kind of half-hearted but good-humored chuckle. "Speculative to me means that we could actually do it, we've done it somewhere on the planet of Earth, we have the tools."

Coffey notes that *Oryx and Crake* is her first novel that has a male narrator the whole way through. "Somebody said, 'why a boy narrator'? And I said, how many girls do you know who spend endless hours playing video games? I actually clipped a piece from the paper yesterday where they were trying to study whether video games improved your visual acuity, and they could only find one girl; the rest were all boys. Girls go for things that involve relationships much more, which is why they will not relentlessly watch cricket, except as an accompaniment to husband." Atwood added that she could understand the male point of view having grown up in "an all-male household—my dad was a boy, my brother was a boy and my mom was also a boy."

Coffey also remarks that if there is one thing Atwood is good at, it's getting it right. She had one of her early books, which featured paleontologists, proofread by paleontologists, just to be sure. "Even my daughter gave me a piece of advice on a certain bit of swearing. I think it was supposed to be 'what the fuck' rather than 'what in the fuck.' A minor point."

3440. COMBS, Marianne. "Minnesota Opera Premiers *The Handmaid's Tale*." *All Things Considered* (National Public Radio) 12 May 2003. Available from Lexis-Nexis. Atwood one of several interviewed in connection with opera's North American debut.

3441. ———. "*The Handmaid's Tale*: A Cautionary Opera." *Voice of America News* 19 May 2003. Available from Lexis-Nexis. Transcript of story about opera presented by Minnesota opera, which includes comments by Atwood.

3442. COULSON, Sandra. "Atwood an Eclectic Interview." *London Free Press* (ON) 18 June 2003: Section: Entertainment: D7. Interview in connection with Atwood's upcoming visit to the city.

3443. ECKLER, Rebecca. "How Can I Tell Her How I Feel: Meeting My Idol Gives Me First-Date Butterflies." *National Post* 16 April 2003: Section: Arts & Life: AL: 2. Eckler and a friend meet Atwood at launch party for *Oryx and Crake* at Toronto's Gladstone Hotel. Conversation goes as follows: "'Hi, Ms. Atwood?' I say. 'My name is Rebecca Eckler. I'm a reporter with the *National Post*. I just wanted to tell you you're the reason I wanted to become a writer.' Phew. 'Oh,' says Atwood, staring at me with her ice-blue eyes, smiling thinly. Then...silence. This is why Atwood is the only person in the city who scares me. I'm not scared simply because I want to be her (or rather, that I want her talent) but because I've seen her interviewed many times and you just never know how she's going to respond. I wouldn't have been surprised if she'd walked away without saying anything.

"Instead, she said, 'Oh.' 'Yep,' I continue. 'I just, uh, wanted to let you know that.' 'Are you writing a novel now?' she inquires. Asking an aspiring novelist if she's writing a novel is like asking an aspiring mother who has no partner whether she is pregnant yet—a bit of pressure, a lot of regret, a feeling of 'I have to get moving on that.' I knew it would be wrong to tell her the truth—that I believed I was well on my way to winning the Giller Prize because I have recently purchased a new computer, a good first step toward writing a novel. Instead, I answer, 'Well, no, I have this full-time job at the paper and everything.' 'So what do you write?' she asks. Apparently, my hero has never read a word I've written. How could this be? Maybe I should get her a *Post* subscription. 'Girl stuff,' I answer, at the same moment my friend answers, 'She writes about her sex life.' Which isn't exactly true. 'That's good,' says Atwood. 'If you have a sex life.' This is also why I love Atwood. She is funny."

3444. ———. "Read Us a Story, Aunt Peggy." *National Post* 10 September 2003: Section: AL: 5. Atwood comes over to Eckler's apartment to read *Rude Ramsay and the Roaring Radishes* to the pregnant Eckler and her dog Bogie. "'Shut up now, dog,' she says to Bogey. 'I'm about to read here.' (God, how can you not love a woman who tells a dog to shut up?) She begins. 'Rude Ramsay resided in a ramshackle rectangular residence with a roof garden, a root cellar and a revolving door.' She reads the book in its entirety, laughing when she stumbles on a couple of sentences. (You try saying, 'Ramsay emerged into a resplendent realm. A ranch-sized garden with a river rippling through it revealed itself to his regard, rendering Ramsay rhapsodic.') 'I've never read to anyone's stomach,' she tells me afterward, 'except my own when I was pregnant.' I ask her if she enjoyed being a mother. 'I loved it. Your life will never be the same again. You'll get your brain back in about two years.'"

3445. EICHLER, Leah. "Imperfect Timing." *CairnsPost / Cairns Sun* (Australia) 24 May 2003: Section: Weekend Extra: 48. Coincidence of SARS events in *Oryx and Crake*.

3446. EVERETT-GREEN, Robert. "Words into Music: Novelist Margaret Atwood and the Art of an Opera Librettist." *Opera Canada* 44.2 (Summer 2003): 18-21.

3447. FORTNEY, Valerie. "Apocalyptic Atwood: Author Takes on End of the World with Humour." *Calgary Herald* 23 September 2003: B9. Interview in connection with *Oryx and Crake*.

3448. GESSELL, Paul. "Atwood Takes a 'Realistic' Look at the Future in Chilling Novel." *Standard* (St. Catharines, ON) 24 May 2003: E6. (832 w).

3449. GOODLIFFE, Kim. "In Search of a Saving Grace." *Vancouver Sun* 19 April 2003: Section: Mix: D7. On 11 September 2001, Margaret Atwood was working on Part Eight of her new novel, *Oryx and Crake*, while waiting for a flight to New York at the Toronto airport. Her response? "I stopped writing for a number of weeks. It's deeply unsettling when you're writing about a fictional catastrophe and then a real one happens. I thought maybe I should turn to gardening books, something more cheerful. But then I started writing again, because what use would gardening books be in a world without gardens, without books?"

What motivated her to keep writing, after her first (and still unpublished) novel, *Up in the Air So Blue*, was simply this: She had another idea. "By the time that first [novel] was completely rejected by everybody, I'd already started a second one. In fact, the first one was rejected definitively in the restaurant at the top of Hotel Vancouver when I was living [in BC] in 1964 and 1965. The man there said, very nicely, 'Do you think you could change the ending?' And I very nicely said no. And he reached across the table and patted my hand and said, 'Is there anything we can do?' I said, 'No, I'm fine.'" Her vision of the novel was already very firm.

When asked if her perspective has changed as her awareness of aging changes, she didn't hesitate: "Absolutely," she said. "It's the only point of aging. You get a new view....[W]hat you know is an accumulation of knowing lots of people, making mistakes, having successes, eating ethnic food. It's why prophets and seers are depicted as old: They know the plot."

3450. JONES, Adrienne. "Margaret Atwood." *Australian Financial Review* 5 December 2003: Section: Boss: 28. Questions focus on Atwood's ideas about organizations and business. (2185 w).

3451. KEENAN, Catherine. "She Who Laughs Last." *Sydney Morning Herald* 3 May 2003: Section: Spectrum: 6. Phone interview with Atwood in Toronto about *Oryx and Crake*. "This engaging woman with the wicked sense of humour is not the Margaret Atwood of legend: stern, intimidating, giving short shrift to fools. I didn't find her like that when I met her in person, either. Other journalists have also found her generous, helpful, and this is a constant, very smart. I suspect the latter is why she is sometimes depicted negatively, as she has answers for everything. In conversation she flits from the war in Iraq, to George Orwell, to Napoleon and to gene-splicing without missing a beat and she expects people to try to keep up, at least."

3452. KEMP, Peter. "Future Shock." *Sunday Star Times* (Auckland) 4 May 2003: 27. Atwood interviewed in her Toronto home about the origins of *Oryx and Crake*. Originally published in *Sunday Times* (London) 20 April 2003: Section: Features: 5. (1749 w).

3453. LANPHER, Katherine. "Talking Volumes: Margaret Atwood." Minnesota Public Radio 9 May 2003. One-hour interview with Atwood, focusing on *The Handmaid's Tale* is available at http://news.minnesota.publicradio.org/programs /midmorning/listings/mm20030505.shtml (1 May 2006).

3454. LINLEY, Boniface. "Our Fate in Her Hands." *Dominion Post* (Wellington, NZ) 8 November 2003: Section: Features: 8. Report of discussion about *Oryx and Crake* on occasion of her book tour. "My book is quite cheery, because, first of all, it's just a book," she says. "You can choose to say, oh, it hasn't happened yet. You can be like Scrooge—he wakes up, discovers it was all a dream and goes out and buys everyone turkeys. The other thing about my book is that at least it doesn't tell you everyone's happy. A book that tells you everyone's happy—throw that against the wall!"

3455. MADDOCKS, Fiona. "A Twist in the Tale: Margaret Atwood Is Dreading the UK Premier of Her Novel *The Handmaid's Tale*—It Will Be a Shocking Theatrical Experience." *Evening Standard* (London) 3 April 2003: 45. Interviewed in London before opening, Atwood remarked that *The Handmaid's Tale* lends itself surprisingly well to operatic setting. "Because so much of it uses internal monologue, it actually works better as opera than as film. In cinema, unless you use voiceover, it's hard to convey that what someone is saying may not be what they are thinking. In opera you can have soliloquies. Characters can come forward on stage and say things the rest of the cast can't hear. And a sextet or trio, even when you can't hear all the words, is an accepted way of allowing you into the minds of the characters. Ruders and Bentley have found a very effective way of disentangling the different layers of the book. Someone asked me the other day how they ended the opera and do you know I've completely forgotten."

3456. MARTIN, Deborah. "For Writer Atwood, 'Stories Appear': Man Booker Prize Winner to Speak, Read from Latest Chiller in S.A." *San-Antonio Express News* 12 October 2003: Section: Culturas: 1J. Atwood interviewed before appearance in town. Commenting on *Oryx and Crake*, she noted that as disturbing as the book is, it's also darkly funny, something she expects Texans to pick up on. "Texan people have a robust sense of humor; it's hard to avoid," she said. "That's why I gave you a republic all your own in *The Handmaid's Tale*." Atwood has said that the story sprang into her mind so forcefully that she immediately started writing. That's pretty much how it happens for everything she writes, she said: "Stories appear; there's no other way of describing where they come from. Those are the only ones you write if you are an indolent person such as myself. Otherwise, it's right to the hammock." She also noted that she writes out her stories longhand, sometimes on spiral notepads, then transcribes them—not a simple task. She edits as she transcribes, then re-writes. When she can't take the story any further, she knows she's at the end. "You keep going until you don't know what's going to happen next, you don't know which way the cat would jump. If you can't go on, you can't go on."

3457. MARTIN, Sandra. "Beyond Here Be Crakes." *Globe & Mail* 19 April 2003: Section: Weekend Review: R1, 16. Interview in the Royal Ontario Museum.

3458. McGLONE, Jackie. "Hand Made Tails from a Gene Genie." *Scotland on Sunday* 27 April 2003: 3. On the occasion of the publication of *Oryx and Crake*. (1398 w).

3459. O'HARA, Delia. "Global Warning." *Chicago Sun-Times* 5 June 2003: Section: Features: 45. Interview conducted with Atwood by phone from England in anticipation of her visit to Chicago.

3460. O'REGAN, Nadine. "Atwood's Apocalypse." *Sunday Business Post* 8 June 2003: s.l. Available from Lexis-Nexis. The author interviewed on the mezzanine floor of the Shelbourne Hotel in Dublin.

Atwood on awards: "Everyone should have some. Awards for all! Do you know that joke about the genie? A woman has been walking along a beach; she finds a bottle, rubs it, and the genie comes out. He says to the woman, 'You can have any one wish you want.' She says, 'Oh good, in that case, I'll wish for thin thighs.' He says, 'What? You could have wished for world peace, an end to famine, and you ask for thin thighs?' She says, 'Alright, let me think. I know, thin thighs for everyone!' So, awards for everyone."

Atwood on Graeme Gibson, her partner: They never read each other's work before it appears in published form. "What you want from your partner is tea and sympathy," Atwood explains. "You want them to understand that the process is often difficult and makes you crabby, but I don't think they should be in the position of having to say, 'This is a real stinker!' That should be your agent." While Atwood is a Canadian national icon, Gibson, though well-known, has not succeeded on this scale.

Has there ever been any jealousy or competitiveness between them? "No," Atwood grins. "Why? Because this person is six foot four and gets the tops off jars." Good answer. And, by all accounts, Atwood and Gibson are devoted to each other. When one American female novelist declared that "every woman writer should be married to Graeme Gibson," Atwood delightedly wore the compliment on her tee shirt.

3461. POTTS, Robert. "Light in the Wilderness: Margaret Atwood." *The Guardian* (London) 26 April 2003: Section: *Guardian* Saturday Pages: 20. A profile of Atwood, largely biographical.

3462. REHM, Diane. [*Margaret*] *Atwood: Oryx and Crake*. Washington, DC: WAMU, American University, 2003. 1 sound cassette (ca. 60 min.). Interview with Atwood originally broadcast on 13 May 2003 as part of the Diane Rehm Show.

3463. RICHLER, Noah. "Atwood's Ground Zero." *National Post* 26 April 2003: Section: Spring Books: BK1, BK4. When asked what rules she set herself when writing a "speculative" fiction, Atwood replied: "You have to be able to back everything up with facts....I have a big, brown box in the cellar that is constantly being filled, except that I am collecting [these materials] even while I am writing.... Everything is filed....The genetic decoding of the SARS corona virus and the discovery of the autism gene. The nanotechnology that allows water to be extracted from air."

3464. ROBERTSON, Lloyd [anchor]. "The Race for Mayor in Toronto." CTV News 6 November 2003. Available from Lexis-Nexis. Atwood and others interviewed about the race. A supporter of the eventual winner, David Miller who promised change, Atwood commented: "Things have been a little murky and grubby around the city for a while."

3465. RYAN, Laura T. "Defining Atwood." *The Post-Standard* (Syracuse) 6 April 2003: Section: Stars: 21. Atwood interviewed by phone before her reading in Syracuse's Rosamond Gifford Lecture Series.

3466. ST. GERMAIN, Pat. "Peg Can't Be Pegged: Atwood Defies Expectations." *Winnipeg Sun* 24 September 2003: Section: Entertainment: 19. Atwood interviewed when in town for International Writers Festival.

3467. STOFFMAN, Judy. "This Book Is Brought to You by the Letter R." *Toronto Star* 13 September 2003: Section: Arts: J13. Interview with Atwood about *Rude Ramsay and the Roaring Radishes.* "If Margaret Atwood's mighty novels give you morbid migraines, don't miss her mesmerizing manuscript for mini-readers, in which her mission is mainly mayhem and mischief. Also to massage the mood of her publisher Anna Porter by maybe making her millions."

3468. SULLIVAN, Jane. "Atwood's Way with Words." *The Age* (Melbourne) 29 November 2003: Section: Review: 3. Lots of stories, little lectures and jokes (2106 w). "Here's one for you," she says. "The devil agrees to show an author writers' heaven and writers' hell. He opens a door and there's a huge room full of desks with computers. At each desk sits a writer, writing, knocking back coffee and wine, smoking, having writer's block, nervous breakdowns. 'Oh,' says the author, 'this must be writers' hell.' Then the devil shows him another room, full of desks with computers: 'This is writers' heaven.' At each desk sits a writer, writing, knocking back coffee and wine, smoking, having writer's block, nervous breakdowns....'What's the difference?' screams the author. 'Ah,' says the devil, 'these are the published writers.'" Atwood allows herself a brief, fiendish chuckle.

Scholarly Resources

3469. ADAMS, Robert. *A Love of Reading: The Second Collection—More Reviews of Contemporary Fiction.* Toronto: McClelland and Stewart, 2003. Chapter 1 (1-17) is an analysis of *Alias Grace.*

3470. ALMEIDA, Léila. "As meninas más na literatura de Margaret Atwood e Lucía Etxebarría." *Espéculo: Revista de Estudios Literarios* 25 (2003). Available at http://www.ucm.es/info/especulo/ (1 May 2006). (Universidad Complutense de Madrid).

3471. ALMONTE, Richard. "Posthumous Praise: Biographical Influence in Canadian Literature (Susanna Moodie, Gwendolyn MacEwen, Pat Lowther, Carol Shields, Margaret Atwood)." PhD thesis. McMaster University, 2003. 250 pp. Also available on microfiche from Canadian Theses Service (2004). This dissertation explores the phenomenon whereby a number of deceased Canadian women writers have had their lives utilized in subsequent works of fiction, drama, poetry, film, and biography. Includes study of *The Blind Assassin.* For more see *DAI-A* 65.01 (July 2004): 148.

3472. ARBOR, Joy. "Margaret Atwood 1939– ." *American Writers—A Collection of Literary Biographies, Supplement XIII: Edward Abbey to William Jay Smith.* Ed. Jay Parini. New York: Scribner's, 2003. 19-39.

3473. BARNARD, Anette. "Margaret Atwood: Challenging the Unity of the Body and the Text." MA thesis. Potchefstroom University of Christian Higher Education [South Africa], 2003. 120 pp.

3474. BERAN, Carol L. "Strangers within the Gates: Margaret Atwood's *Wilderness Tips*." *Margaret Atwood's Textual Assassinations: Recent Poetry and Fiction.* Ed. Sharon R. Wilson. Columbus: Ohio State UP, 2003. 74-87. "Examines how Atwood's strangers in *Wilderness Tips* push readers toward becoming the creative nonvictims of *Survival*...." from Introduction, xiv.

3475. BORK, Carol Denise. "The Narrative in Suspense: Women at the Intersection of Feminism and Postmodernism in the Late-Twentieth-Century Novel." PhD thesis. Rutgers, the State University of New Jersey–New Brunswick, 2003. "This project identifies and explores 'the narrative in suspense—a postmodernist feminist fictional form that dismantles the conventional 'marriage or death' formula of Anglo-American novelistic discourse to posit new, less constraining structural and thematic roles for women in the novel. While some novelists and theorists respond to what Jean-François Lyotard calls the 'postmodern…incredulity toward metanarratives' with a sense of despair or meaninglessness, I contend that we can also find optimism in the plurality of provisional narratives that characterize the 'postmodern condition.'…My reading of Margaret Atwood's *Lady Oracle* demonstrates that narrative itself—the stories we tell about ourselves, and the stories that are told about us—informs perceptions of self and reality, and thus the postmodern local narrative can be deployed to reconfigure women's experiences." (Author). For more see *DAI-A* 64.06 (December 2003): 2092.

3476. BOUSON, J. Brooks. "A Commemoration of Wounds Endured and Resented: Margaret Atwood's *The Blind Assassin* as Feminist Memoir." *Critique* 44.3 (2003): 251-271.

3477. BUSBY, Brian John. *Character Parts: Who's Really Who in CanLit*. Toronto: A. A. Knopf Canada, 2003. Includes top half of Atwood's face on its dust jacket (along with bottom half of Mordecai Richler's). The real-life persons behind characters in *Cat's Eye, The Edible Woman, Lady Oracle, Life Before Man, Negotiating with the Dead, The Robber Bride,* as well as in shorter pieces "In Search of Rattlesnake Plantain," "Isis in Darkness," and finally "Uncles."

3478. CHARRERON, Elodie. "Resistance in Volker Schlondorff's Adaptation of Margaret Atwood's *The Handmaid's Tale*." MS thesis. Université de Poitiers. 2003. 132 pp.

3479. CHILTON, Myles. "Atwood's *Cat's Eye* and Toronto as the Urban Non-Place." *The Image of the City in Literature, Media, and Society*. Ed. Will Wright and Steven Kaplan. Pueblo, CO: Society for the Interdisciplinary Study of Social Imagery, University of Southern Colorado, 2003. 154-160.

3480. CUDER, Pilar. *Margaret Atwood: A Beginner's Guide*. London: Hodder & Stoughton, 2003. 86 pp.

3481. DANIELS, Margaret J., and Heather E. BOWEN. "Feminist Implications of Anti-Leisure in Dystopia Fiction." *Journal of Leisure Research* 35.4 (2003): 423-440. "This essay provides a feminist perspective on dystopian anti-leisure. Dystopias are futuristic anti-utopias where leisure is distorted and individuals are manipulated to further the agenda of the politically powerful.…The purpose of this essay is to illustrate how women in dystopian societies are subjected to anti-leisure as evidenced by the devaluation of their personal leisure spaces. A feminist definition of leisure is used to guide a poststructuralist feminist analysis of four dystopian novels: Margaret Atwood's *The Handmaid's Tale*, Aldous Huxley's *Brave New World*, Kurt Vonnegut's *Player Piano* and George Orwell's *1984*. Synopsis and discussion are then employed to demonstrate how two binary oppositions of female disempowerment are evidenced in the novels and to consider how these same forces operate in reality to jeopardize women's personal leisure spaces." (Author).

3482. DYMOND, Erica Joan. "Atwood's *The Handmaid's Tale*." *The Explicator* 61.3 (2003): 181-183.

3483. FAND, Roxanne J. "Margaret Atwood's *The Robber Bride*: The Dialogic Novel of a Nietzschean Fairy Tale." *Critique* 45.1 (Fall 2003): 65-81.

3484. FORD, Susan Allen. "Teaching Contemporary Female Gothic: Murdoch, Carter, Atwood." *Approaches to Teaching Gothic Fiction: The British and American Traditions.* Ed. Diane Long Hoeveler and Tamar Heller. New York: Modern Language Association of America, 2003. 177-183. Iris Murdoch's *The Unicorn*, Angela Carter's *The Bloody Chamber*, and Atwood's *Lady Oracle.*

3485. FU, Jun. *Magelite Atewude yan jiu = Margaret Atwood and Her Writing.* Nanjing Shi: Yi lin chu ban she, 2003. 440 pp. In Chinese. Title romanized.

3486. GARCIA, Jennifer Renee. "Popularizing Feminist Politics: Margaret Atwood's *The Handmaid's Tale*, Feminism, and Popular Culture. MA thesis. University of Texas at El Paso, 2003. 109 pp. For more see *MAI* 43.02 (April 2005): 401.

3487. GAULT, Cinda. "Female and National Identities: Laurence, Atwood, and Engel, 1965-1980." PhD thesis. York University (ON), 2003. 325 pp. Also available on microfiche from Canadian Theses Service (2004). "[In examining Atwood, I note] that her fiction sparked controversy among critics, who were confused about whether or not her endings were to be understood as happy. The predominant conclusion among her contemporaries was that they were to be read this way, thus extending hope that female and national identities might eventually be workable. I explore a consistently realist interpretation to ascertain what other meanings might be possible if these characters and plots are seen as displaced from mythic narrative patterns to the point where meaning shifts from successful identity quests to explanations of characters and events in terms of social forces. Attempts to resolve social contradictions can be understood not only through utopian pictures of resolved identity, as would be expected in romance, but also through realist portrayals of the historical forces producing particular people in particular circumstances. Mythic story patterns suggest more optimistic expectations of identity success than do those narrative conventions that give a sense of verisimilitude. In the latter instance, realist solutions contribute to a vision of what an individual character needs to do to resolve a social contradiction." (Author). For more see *DAI-A* 65.01 (July 2004): 149.

3488. GREGERSDOTTER, Katarina. "Watching Women, Falling Women: Power and Dialog in Three Novels by Margaret Atwood." PhD thesis. Umeå universitet, Institutionen för moderna språk, 2003. 190 pp. On *Alias Grace*, *Cat's Eye*, and *The Robber Bride*.

3489. HAMMILL, Faye. "'Death by Nature': Margaret Atwood and Wilderness Gothic." *Gothic Studies* 5.2 November (2003): 47-63. "Recent criticism has increasingly asserted the centrality of gothic in the Canadian canon, and explicitly gothic conceptions of the forested and frozen North inform several of Margaret Atwood's novels, poems, essays and short stories. Her haunted wilderness settings are sites for the negotiation of identity and power relationships. This essay focuses on her 1970 poem sequence *The Journals of Susanna Moodie* and her short story 'Death by Landscape' (from her 1991 *Wilderness Tips* collection), considering them in relation to critical models of postcolonial gothic." (Author).

3490. ———. *Literary Culture and Female Authorship in Canada 1760-2000.* New York; Amsterdam: Rodopi, 2003. See especially Chapter 6, "Forest and 'Fairy Stuff': Margaret Atwood's *Wilderness Tips*," 135-166, and Chapter 7, "Margaret Atwood, Carol Shields and 'That Moodie Bitch,'" 167-203. Chapter 7 is based on an article with the same title published in *American Review of Canadian Studies* 29 (1999): 67-91.

3491. HENGEN, Shannon. "Strange Visions: Atwood's *Interlunar* and Technopoetics." *Margaret Atwood's Textual Assassinations: Recent Poetry and Fiction.* Ed.

Sharon R. Wilson. Columbus: Ohio State UP, 2003. 42-53. "Suggests that *Interlunar* marks a conclusion to the poetry volumes preceding it but still presents a changed perspective, a 'stranger vision.'..." from Introduction, xiv.

3492. HOLMLUND Mona, and Gail YOUNGBERG. *Inspiring Women: A Celebration of Herstory.* Regina, SK: Coteau Books, 2003. See especially "Margaret Atwood." 234. An inaccurate profile. By 2003, Atwood had, for example, published more than "two novels."

3493. HOWELLS, Carol [sic] Ann. "*The Robber Bride*; or Who Is a True Canadian?" *Margaret Atwood's Textual Assassinations: Recent Poetry and Fiction.* Ed. Sharon R. Wilson. Columbus: Ohio State UP, 2003. 88-101. "Reading *The Robber Bride* as a postcolonial novel, Coral Ann Howells suggests...that the novel is part of Atwood's ongoing inquiry into Canadian identity, a means of 'narrating the nation.'..." from Introduction, xiv.

3494. HOWELLS, Coral Ann. *Contemporary Canadian Women's Fiction: Refiguring Identities.* New York; Basingstoke [UK]: Palgrave Macmillan, 2003. See especially Chapter 2, "'Don't Ever Ask for the True Story': Margaret Atwood, *Alias Grace*, and *The Blind Assassin*," 25-52.

3495. ———. The Handmaid's Tale, *Margaret Atwood.* Harlow: Longman, 2003. 136 pp. York notes.

3496. ———. "Sites of Desolation." *Entering the Labyrinth: Writing* The Blind Assassin. Ed. Gerry Turcotte. Wollongong: University of Wollongong Press, 2003. 31-46.

3497. HUDGINS, Christopher C. "Harold Pinter's *The Handmaid's Tale:* Freedom, Prison, and a Hijacked Script." *Captive Audience: Prison and Captivity in Contemporary Theater.* Ed. Thomas Fahy and Kimball King. New York: Routledge, 2003. 81-108.

3498. HUTCHISON, Lorna. "The Book Reads Well: Atwood's *Alias Grace* and the Middle Voice." *Pacific Coast Philology* 38 (2003): 40-59.

3499. INGERSOLL, Earl. "Waiting for the End: Closure in Margaret Atwood's *The Blind Assassin*." *Studies in the Novel* 35.4 (2003): 543-559.

3500. JENAINATI, Cathia. "Narrating the Self: Memory as Narrative Strategy in the Fiction of Margaret Atwood." PhD thesis. University of Warwick, 2003. "The dissertation investigates the utilisation of memory as a narrative strategy in the fiction of Margaret Atwood. It is structured in four chapters. The Introduction provides the rationale for my research and establishes the critical framework within which I intend to analyse Atwood's novels. The subsequent chapters build up an overall argument demonstrating that Atwood utilises memory as a narrative strategy in order to illustrate the female protagonist's quest for individuation." (Author).

3501. JONES, Dorothy. "Narrative Enclosures." *Entering the Labyrinth: Writing* The Blind Assassin. Ed. Gerry Turcotte. Wollongong: University of Wollongong Press, 2003. 47-67. Imprisonment as an Atwood theme, especially in *The Blind Assassin.*

3502. KIM, Youngmin. "The Experimental Spirit in Canadian Poetry: Margaret Atwood, Eli Mandel, George Bowering, and the Experimental Poets Thereafter." *Journal of English Language and Literature / Yomgo Yongmunhak* 49.4 (Winter 2003): 755-780.

3503. KIRTZ, Mary K. "(Dis)Unified Field Theories: The Clarendon Lectures Seen Through (a) *Cat's Eye.*" *Margaret Atwood's Textual Assassinations: Recent Poetry and Fiction.* Ed. Sharon R. Wilson. Columbus: Ohio State UP, 2003. 54-73. "Examines both Atwood's representation and transformation of the myth of the malevolent north...." from Introduction, xiv.

3504. KLICK, Donna M. "Open Endings and Questionable Liberation in Margaret Atwood's *Alias Grace, Cat's Eye* and *The Handmaid's Tale*." MA thesis. State University of New York–Brockport, 2003. 83 pp.

3505. LAWN, Jenny. "Born Under the Sign of Joan: Margaret Atwood's *Lady Oracle,
Mommie Dearest*, and the Uses of Maternal Ambivalence." *Journal of the Association for Research on Mothering* 5.1 (Spring-Summer 2003): 33-44.

3506. LINTON, Michael. "The Bigot's Opera." *First Things: A Monthly Journal of Religion & Public Life* 137 (November 2003): 14-17. Comments on the moral questions about *The Handmaid's Tale*, an opera by Danish composer Poul Ruders
based on Atwood's novel.

3507. LONG, Maureen Eleanor. "Food, Sex, Death, and Quest: The Literary Legacy of
Sir John Franklin." MA thesis. University of Alaska, 2003. Examines Franklin's
influence on a variety of authors, including Atwood as reflected in her short story
"The Age of Lead."

3508. MacFARLANE, Susan. "Living on: *Survival*." *Open Letter* (Canada) (11th series)
8 (2003): 73-86.

3510. MAUS, Jessica Rene. "The Role of Text in the Metaphysical Detective Story."
MA thesis. University of Alaska Anchorage, 2003. 107 pp. The metaphysical detective story may be defined as a text that raises profound ontological and epistemological questions, and this thesis will elaborate on its characteristics and
themes, particularly as those themes relate to the role, definition and use of texts.
More specifically, the role of texts and how the use of real events and historical
documents alter the ontological and epistemological questions these novels raise
are examined….Chapter Two analyzes the relationship between literary and historical documents in Margaret Atwood's *Alias Grace*." (Author). For more see
MAI 41.06 (December 2003): 1587.

3511. MÉNDEZ DÍAZ, Luisa Cristina. "Dos poemas, dos poetas, un encuentro: Margaret Atwood y Wislawa Szymborska." *Espéculo: Revista de Estudios Literarios* 24
(July-October 2003): s.p. Available at http://www.ucm.es/info/especulo (1 May
2006). (Universidad Complutense de Madrid).

3512. MICHAEL, Magali Cornier. "Freedom Reconsidered: Margaret Atwood's *The
Handmaid's Tale* (1985)." *Women in Literature: Reading through the Lens of
Gender*. Ed. Jerilyn Fisher, Ellen S. Silber, and David Sadker. Westport, CT:
Greenwood Press, 2003. 134-136.

3513. MILLER, Tanya J. "Rewriting History: New Historical Criticism of Margaret Atwood's *Alias Grace*." MA thesis. Bemidji State University, 2003. 99 pp.

3514. MURRAY, Jennifer. "History as Poetic Indetermination: The Murder Scene in
Margaret Atwood's *Alias Grace*." *Études anglaises* 56.3 (2003): 310-323.

3515. NISCHIK, Reingard M. "*Murder in the Dark:* Margaret Atwood's Inverse Poetics
of Intertextual Minuteness." *Margaret Atwood's Textual Assassinations: Recent
Poetry and Fiction*. Ed. Sharon R. Wilson. Columbus: Ohio State UP, 2003. 1-17.
"Uses some of Atwood's published and unpublished cartoons, including cultural
implications of their dichotomy of *large* and *small*, to trace this size motif
throughout Atwood's work and approach aspects of the brevity, generic hybridity,
and intertextual impact of *Murder in the* Dark." from Introduction, xiii.

3516. ÖZDEMIR, Erinç. "Power, Madness, and Gender Identity in Margaret Atwood's
Surfacing: A Feminist Reading." *English Studies* 84.1 (2003): 57-80.

3517. PADOLSKY, Enoch. "'The Old Country in Your Blood': Italy and Canada in Frank Paci's *Black Madonna* and Margaret Atwood's *Lady Oracle*." *F. G. Paci: Essays on His Works*. Ed. Joseph Pivato. Toronto; Buffalo, NY: Guernica Editions, 2003. 37-38.

3518. POTVIN, Liza. "Voodooism and Female Quest Patterns in Margaret Atwood's *Cat's Eye*." *Journal of Popular Culture* 36.3 (2003): 636-650.

3519. REESE, Kelly S. "Surviving Women: A Study of Margaret Atwood's Protagonists." [Internet resource]. MA thesis. Central Connecticut State University, 2003. 139 pp. Access: http://www.consuls.org/record=b2646395 (1 May 2006). "Atwood argues that survival is the main theme commonly found in Canadian literature. The purpose of this thesis is to examine this theory of 'survival' in Margaret Atwood's own work. Atwood states in her thematic guide to Canadian literature entitled *Survival* that 'literature is not only a mirror; it is also a map, a geography of the mind. For the members of a country or a culture, shared knowledge of their place, their here, is not a luxury but a necessity. Without that knowledge we will not survive' (*Survival* 19). A close study of *Surfacing, Cat's Eye, Bodily Harm,* and *The Handmaid's Tale* proves this theory to be true." (Author).

3520. SHECKELS, Theodore F. *The Island Motif in the Fiction of L. M. Montgomery, Margaret Laurence, Margaret Atwood, and Other Canadian Women Novelists*. New York: Peter Lang, 2003. (Studies on Themes and Motifs in Literature; Vol. 68) See especially Chapter 7, "Dangerous Idylls: Gabrielle Roy's *The Tin Flute*; Margaret Atwood's *Bodily Harm*; Marie-Claire Blais's *These Festive Nights*," 149-180.

3521. STAMBOVSKY, Phillip. "Mythemic Figuration and the Limits of Reason in Philosophy and Literature." MA thesis. Boston College, 2003. 161 pp. "This study explores how modernists in philosophy and literature have used the depictive rationality of mythemic figuration to delineate, in self-reflexive ways, the limits of discursive sense-making in religious, national-cultural, psychosocial, and psychobiological domains of experience. It illustrates four widely diverse examples of this critical species of mythical depiction in works by Sören Kierkegaard, Miguel de Unamuno, Henry James, and Margaret Atwood." (Author). For more see *MAI* 42.05 (October 2004): 1499.

3522. STANLEY, Sandra Kumanoto. "The Eroticism of Class and the Enigma of Margaret Atwood's *Alias Grace*." *Tulsa Studies in Women's Literature* 22.2 (2003): 371-386.

3523. STEELE, James. "Margaret Atwood's *Cat's Eye:* New Feminism or Old Comedy." *Northrop Frye: Eastern and Western Perspectives*. Ed. Jean O'Grady and Wang Ning. Toronto: University of Toronto Press, 2003. 121-135.

3524. STEIN, Karen F. "A Left-Handed Story: *The Blind Assassin*." *Margaret Atwood's Textual Assassinations: Recent Poetry and Fiction*. Ed. Sharon R. Wilson. Columbus: Ohio State UP, 2003. 135-153. "Reads Atwood's . . . novel as a Gothic text, with the central theme of hiding and revealing." from Introduction, xv.

3525. ———. "Talking Back to *Bluebeard*: Atwood's Fictional Storytellers." *Margaret Atwood's Textual Assassinations: Recent Poetry and Fiction*. Ed. Sharon R. Wilson. Columbus: Ohio State UP, 2003. 154-171. Examines how storytelling contributes to the power that Atwood's female protagonists gain in *Bluebeard's Egg* and throughout her work...." from Introduction, xv.

3526. SZALAY, Edina. "Quilting Her Story: The Resisting Female Subject in Margaret Atwood's *Alias Grace*." *Hungarian Journal of English and American Studies* 9.1 (2003): 173-180.

3527. TENNANT, Colette. *Reading the Gothic in the First Seven Novels of Margaret Atwood.* Lewiston, NY: Edwin Mellen, 2003. (Studies in Comparative Literature; Vol. 55). "This study contains a thorough reading of Margaret Atwood's works (*The Edible Woman; Survival; Surfacing; Lady Oracle; Selected Poems; Life Before Man; Second Words; Bluebeard's Egg; Bodily Harm; Murder in the Dark; The Handmaid's Tale; Selected Poems II;* and *Cat's Eye*) through both a Gothic lens and a feminist perspective." (Publisher).

3528. TIEDEMANN, Mark W. "Inclusions." *New York Review of Science Fiction* 15.12 [180] (2003): 1, 4-6. *The Handmaid's Tale* and *Oryx and Crake* compared to the work of H. G. Wells and Henry James Jr.

3529. TRIGG, Tina. "Casting Shadows: A Study of Madness in Margaret Atwood's Novels." PhD thesis. University of Ottawa, 2003. Also available on microfiche from Canadian Theses Service (2004). "Madness is a recurrent aspect of Margaret Atwood's novels to date and represents perhaps her most discomforting challenge to the reader who is implicated as co-creator, interpreter, and participant of the fiction. Her novels question the binary of normality and madness by situating madness both in the margins and foreground, thereby exposing 'normality' as a tendentious construct designed to obscure contemporary Western society's psychic imbalance caused by fear of the unknown within the self." (Author). For more see *DAI-A* 64.10 (April 2004): 3692-3693.

3530. TSUJIMOTO, Yasuko. "Yohaku No Shokkaku: Kono Taeko No Sekai." *Eigo Seinen / Rising Generation* 149.2 (May 2003): 88-89. Female villains in *The Robber Bride.* Journal published out of Tokyo contains articles on English language and literature in both Japanese and English.

3531. VanSPANCKEREN, Kathryn. "Humanizing the Fox: Atwood's Poetic Tricksters and *Morning in the Burned House.*" *Margaret Atwood's Textual Assassinations: Recent Poetry and Fiction.* Ed. Sharon R. Wilson. Columbus: Ohio State UP, 2003. 102-120. "Offers a meditation on death in this most recent poetry volume, suggesting that the book moves from a foxlike cynical vision of survival in the body through imaginative experiences of death to a transformed appreciation of life and vulnerability...." from Introduction, xiv-xv.

3532. VINET, Dominique. *Romanesque britannique et psyché: Étude du signifiant dans le roman anglais.* Paris: L'Harmattan; Budapest: L'Harmattan Hongrie; Turin: L'Harmattan Italia, 2003. See especially "L'élaboration du fantasme dans *The Handmaid's Tale* de Margaret Atwood." 209-232.

3533. VOGLER, Heini. "Der Letzte Homo Sapiens." *Reformatio* 52.3 (2003): 235-238. On *Oryx and Crake.*

3534. WAGNER-LAWLOR, Jennifer A. "From Irony to Affiliation in Margaret Atwood's *The Handmaid's Tale.*" *Critique* 45.1 (Fall 2003): 89-96.

3535. WILSON, Sharon R. "*The Blind Assassin.*" *The Literary Encyclopedia: Literature in English around the World.* Founding editors Robert Clark, Emory Elliott, and Janet Todd. [2003] http://www.litencyc.com (1 May 2006).

3536. ———. "Fiction Flashes: Genre and Intertexts in *Good Bones.*" *Margaret Atwood's Textual Assassinations: Recent Poetry and Fiction.* Ed. Sharon R. Wilson. Columbus: Ohio State UP, 2003. 18-41. "Maintains that apart from the differences of genre, style, tone, and a growing use of postmodern techniques and postcolonial theses, Atwood uses some of the same myths and other folklore intertexts, particularly goddess and trickster ones, in fairly consistent ways throughout her career...." from Introduction, xii.

3537. ———. "Quilting as Narrative Art: Metafictional Construction in *Alias Grace*." *Margaret Atwood's Textual Assassinations: Recent Poetry and Fiction*. Ed. Sharon R. Wilson. Columbus: Ohio State UP, 2003. 121-134. "Argues that, like many of Atwood's previous novels, *Alias Grace* is again a feminist, postmodern, and postcolonial metafiction, exposing all of our 'truths' as theories or speculations, constructions over the abyss...." from Introduction, xv.

3538. WILSON, Sharon Rose, ed. *Margaret Atwood's Textual Assassinations: Recent Poetry and Fiction*. Columbus: Ohio State UP, 2003. Individual chapters in this book are indexed in this section. Book comes complete with an introduction by the editor (xi-xv), a list of works cited (173-186), and notes on contributors (187-188).

3540. ZORZI, Rosella Mamoli. "Margaret Atwood's Use of the Folk and Fairy Tales." *Annali di Ca'Foscari: Rivista della Facoltà di Lingue e Letterature Straniere dell'Università di Venezia* 42.4 (2003): 223-238.

Reviews of Atwood's Works

3541. *The Blind Assassin*. London: Bloomsbury, 2000.
  The Guardian (London) 29 November 2003: 32. By John MULLAN. (67w).

3542. *Bodily Harm*. [Sound recording]. Read by Bonnie Hurren. Chivers: BBC Audiobooks America, 2002. 8 cassettes, 10 hours.
  Library Journal 128.5 (15 March 2003): 131. By Laurie SELWYN. (162 w).

3543. *Deux Sollicitudes*, with Victor-Lévy Beaulieu. Trois-Pistoles: Éditions Trois-Pistoles, 1996.
  Canadian Literature 177 (Summer 2003): 170-171. By Nathalie COOKE.

3544. *Life Before Man*. [Sound recording]. Read by Lorelei King. Chivers: BBC Audiobooks America, 2003.
  Library Journal 128.17 (15 October 2003): 114. By Laurie SELWYN. (191 w).

3545. *Negotiating with the Dead: A Writer on Writing*. New York: Cambridge UP, 2002.
  American Review of Canadian Studies 33.3 (Autumn 2003): 433-435. By Lorna IRVINE.
  Ariel 34.2-3 (April-July 2003): 268-270. By Shannon Catherine MacRAE.
  Canadian Women's Studies 22 (Spring-Summer 2003): 222-223. By Sherrill CHEDA.
  Contemporary Literature 44.4 (Winter 2003): 737-743. By Susan STREHLE.
  Études anglaises 56.3 (2993): 392-393. By Marta DVORAK.
  Gothic Studies 5.1 (May 2003): 132-133. By David SEED.
  University of Toronto Quarterly 73.1 (Winter 2003-2004): 348-350. By Sherrill GRACE.
  World Literature Today 77.3-4 (October-December 2003): 99-101. By B. A. St. ANDREWS.

3546. *Negotiating with the Dead: A Writer on Writing*. London: Virago, 2003. Paperback.
  The Guardian (London) 1 November 2003: Section: Saturday Pages: 21. By John DUGDALE. (151 w).
  Irish Times 1 November 2003: Section: Weekend: Paperbacks: 62. By Kate BATEMAN. (150 w).
  New Straits Times (Malaysia) 8 October 2003: Section: Books: 7. By U-En NG. (70 w).

3547. *Oryx and Crake.* Toronto: McClelland and Stewart, 2003. Also published: London: Bloomsbury; New York: Nan A. Talese.

> *The Advertiser* 24 May 2003: Section: Magazine: W13. By Katharine ENGLAND. (648 w.)
>
> *The Age* (Melbourne) 3 May 2003: Section: Review: 5. By Michelle DE KRETSER. (913 w.)
>
> *America* 189.4 (18 August 2003): 24-25. By John B. BRESLIN. (728 w.)
>
> *Americas* 55.1 (September-October 2003): 55-57. By Barbara MUJICA. (2297 w.)
>
> *Atlanta Journal-Constitution* 4 May 2003 Section: Issue: 5C. By Donna SEAMAN. (716 w.)
>
> *Australian Financial Review* 13 June 2003: Section: Weekend Review: 4. By Peter CRAVEN. (2129 w.)
>
> *Belfast News Letter* 17 May 2003: Section: Features: 35. By Lindesay IRVINE. (299 w.)
>
> *Birmingham Post* 17 May 2003: Section: Features: 49. By Lindesay IRVINE. (811 w.)
>
> *BMC* [Book of the Month Club] *News* June 2003: [3].
>
> *Booklist* 99.14 (15 March 2003): 1251. By Donna SEAMAN. (233 w.)
>
> *Books in Canada* 32.7 (October 2003): 18-19. By Cindy McKENZIE. (1637 w.)
>
> *Boston Globe* 11 May 2003: Section: Books: H6. By Gail CALDWELL. (1129 w.)
>
> *Buffalo News* 4 May 2003: Section: Book Reviews: F5. By Pat YORK. (393 w.)
>
> *Calgary Herald* 26 April 2003: Section: Books: ES11. By Catherine FORD. (1136 w.)
>
> *Chatelaine* 76.6 (June 2003): 32. ANON.
>
> *Chicago Sun-Times* 4 May 2003: Section: Show: 14. By Thomas M. DISCH. (874 w.)
>
> *Christian Science Monitor* 8 May 2003: 18. By Ron CHARLES. (920 w.)
>
> *Columbus Dispatch* 11 May 2003: Section: Features: 07G. By Jeb PHILLIPS. (614 w.)
>
> *Costco Connection* 16.3 (May-June 2003): 59. By Valerie RYAN.
>
> *Courier-Mail* (Queensland, Australia) 10 May 2003: Section: BAM: M07. By Glyn DAVIS. (992 w.)
>
> *Courier-Post* (Cherry Hill, NJ) 3 May 2003: 6X. By Kevin RIORDAN. (449 w.)
>
> *Daily Mail* (London) 9 May 2003: 58. By Hephzibah ANDERSON. (449 w.)
>
> *Daily News* (New Plymouth, NZ) 28 June 2003: Section: Features: 18. By John WHELAN. (466 w.)
>
> *Daily News* (New York) 11 May 2003: Section: Showtime: 16. By Sherryl CONNELLY. (561 w.)
>
> *Daily Telegraph* (London) 10 May 2003: 08. By Helen BROWN. (729 w.)
>
> *Denver Post* 18 May 2003: Section Books: EE-02. By Dorman T. SHINDLER. (694 w.)
>
> *Deseret Morning News* (Salt Lake City) 20 July 2003: Section: Arts: E08. By Susan WHITNEY. (468 w.)
>
> *Ecologist* 33.6 (July 2003): 60. By Jeremy SMITH.
>
> *The Economist* (US) 367.8322 (3 May 2003): 76. (722 w.)
>
> *The Express* 10 May 2003: Section: Features: 65. By Clare HEAL. (535 w.)
>
> *Entertainment Weekly* 709 (9 May 2003): 79. By Oliver MORTON. (755 w.)
>
> *Evening Standard* (London) 6 May 2003: 46. By Jane SHILLING. (469 w.)

Financial Times 24 May 2003: 36. By Katherine SALE. (626 w).

Financial Times 5 July 2003: 2. By Rachel CUSK. (939 w).

The Gazette (Montreal) 26 April 2003: Section: Books and Visual Arts: 1. By Donna Bailey NURSE. (909 w).

Globe & Mail 26 April 2003: Section: Books: D22-D23. By Aritha VAN HERK.

The Guardian (London) 10 May 2003: Section: *Guardian* Saturday Pages: 26. By Natasha WALTER. (1110 w).

Guelph Mercury 26 April 2003: Section: Books: C4. By Robert REID. (770 w).

Habitat Australia 31.5 (October 2003): 28. ANON. (87 w).

Hamilton Spectator (ON) 26 April 2003: Section: Magazine: M03. By Murray TONG. (922 w).

Hartford Courant (CT) 25 May 2003: Section: Arts: G3. By John FREEMAN. (648 w).

The Herald (Glasgow) 26 April 2003: 12. By Rosemary GORING. (1193 w).

Herald Sun (Melbourne) 17 May 2003: Section: Weekend: W28. By Denise CIVELLI. (331 w).

Houston Chronicle 15 June 2003: Section: Zest: 19. By Victoria BROWN-WORTH. (606 w).

Houston Chronicle 12 October 2003: Section: Special: 2. By Fritz LANHAM. (1299 w).

The Independent 26 April 2003: Section: Features: 22. By Lisa APPIGNANESI. (1134 w).

Independent on Sunday (London) 1 June 2003: Section: Features: 16. By Catherine PEPINSTER. (739 w).

International Herald Tribune 1 July 2003: Section: Feature: 18. By Mel GUSSOW. (1255 w).

Irish Times 3 May 2003: Section: Weekend: 60. By Mary MORRISSY. (868 w).

January Magazine June 2003. By Linda RICHARDS. Available at http://www.januarymagazine.com/fiction/oryxandcrake.html (1 May 2006).

Kirkus Reviews 71.6 (15 March 2003): 408. ANON. (332 w).

Library Journal 128.8 (1 May 2003): 152. By Caroline HALLSWORTH. (225 w).

London Free Press 3 May 2003: Section: Lifestyles: D10. By Nancy SCHIEFER. (903 w).

London Review of Books 25.14 (24 July 2003): 35. By Elaine SHOWALTER.

Los Angeles Times 11 May 2003: R-3. By Michael HARRIS. (925 w).

Maclean's 28 April 2003: 48. By Robert J. SAWYER. (711 w).

Milwaukee Journal Sentinel 25 May 2003: Section: Cue: 06E. By Robert Allen PAPINCHAK. (659 w).

National Post 26 April 2003: BK1. By Ronald WRIGHT. (1063 w).

New Republic 22 September 2003: 31. By Richard A. POSNER. (4103 w).

New Statesman 132.4638 (19 May 2003): 50. By Hugo BARNACLE. (733 w).

New York Review of Books 50.11 (3 July 2003): 43-45. By Daniel MENDELSOHN.

New York Review of Science Fiction 180 (August 2003): 1, 4-6. By Mark TIEDEMANN.

New York Times 13 May 2003: E9. By Michiko KAKUTANI. (557 w).

New York Times Book Review 18 May 2003: 12. By Sven BIRKERTS.

New Yorker 79.12 (19 May 2003): 88. By Lorrie MOORE. (1827 w).

New Zealand Herald 11 May 2003: Section: Entertainment: s.l. ANON. Available from Lexis-Nexis.

The Observer 11 May 2003: Section: *Observer* Review Pages: 15. By Joan SMITH. (976 w).

Newsweek International 14 July 2003: 49. By Tara PEPPER. (758 w).

Orlando Sentinel 14 May 2003: K1838. By Mary Ann HORNE. (689 w).

Ottawa Citizen 27 April 2003: C8. By Robert J. SAWYER. (1121 w).

Palm Beach Post 20 July 2003: Section: Arts and Entertainment: 7J. By Tess FELDER. (685 w).

People 59.19 (19 May 2003): 59. By Lee AITKEN.

Pittsburgh Post-Gazette 8 June 2003: Section: Arts and Entertainment: B4. By John FREEMAN. (624 w).

Plain Dealer (Cleveland, OH) 18 May 2003: Section: Sunday Arts: J10. By Karen SANDSTROM. (947 w).

Publishers Weekly 7 April 2003: 44. ANON. (366 w).

The Record (Bergen County, NJ) Section: Entertainment: E03. By Mary Ann HORNE. (506 w).

The Record (Kitchener-Waterloo, ON) 26 April 2003: Section: Books: C8. By Robert REID. (775 w).

Resource Links 9.1 (October 2003): 57. By Ingrid JOHNSTON. (228 w).

Richmond Times Dispatch (VA) 25 May 2003: Section: Commentary: E4. By Judi GOLDENBERG. (360 w).

Roanoke Times & World News 29 June 2003: Section: Books: 6. By Margaret GRAYSON. (662 w).

Rocky Mountain News (Denver, CO) 23 May 2003: Section: Entertainment: 24D. By Juliet WITTMAN. (877 w).

Salon.com 27 May 2003: s.p. By Laura MILLER. (885 w). Available from Lexis-Nexis.

San Diego Union-Tribune 11 May 2003: Section: Books: 1. By Julie BRICK-MAN. (1684 w).

San Francisco Chronicle 27 April 2003: Section: Sunday Review: M1. By David KAPLAN. (1003 w).

Science 302.5648 (14 November 2003): 1154-1155. By Susan M. SQUIER.

Science Fiction Weekly 9.28 (14 July 2003): s.p. By John CLUTE. Available at http://www.scifi.com/sfw/issue325/excess.html (1 May 2006).

The Scotsman 10 May 2003: 7. By Jane SHILLING. (421 w).

Scripps Howard News Service Section: Entertainment: s.l. By Clay EVANS. (840 w). Available from Lexis-Nexis.

Shenandoah 53.4 (Winter 2003): 179-182. By Lesley WHEELER.

Spectator 291.9116 (26 April 2003): 35. By Philip HENSHER. (1112 w).

St. Louis Post Dispatch 11 May 2003: Section: A&E: F13. By John FREEMAN. (621 w).

St. Petersburg Times 4 May 2003: Section: Perspective: 4D. By Colette BAN-CROFT. (635 w).

Sunday Business Post 22 June 2003: By Nadine O'REGAN. (720 w). Available from Lexis-Nexis.

Sunday Oregonian 6 July 2003: Section: Arts and Living: G09. By Monica DRAKE. (835 w).

Sunday Tasmanian 16 November 2003: s.p. By Christopher BANTICK. (662 w). Available from Lexis-Nexis.

Sunday Times (London) 27 April 2003: Section: Features: 35. By Peter KEMP. (1305 w).

Sunday Times (South Africa) 7 September 2003: Section: Lifestyle & Leisure: 12. By Leon de KOCK. (926 w).

Sunday Telegraph (London) 4 May 2003: 12. By David ROBSON. (408 w).

Sunday Tribune 18 May 2003: 9. By Lisa APPIGNANESI. (1103 w).

Sydney Morning Herald 10 May 2003: Section: Spectrum: 14. By Andrew RIEMER. (1196 w).

Telegram (St. John's, NF) 1 June 2003: B4. By Robin MCGRATH. (856 w).

Time 161.20 (19 May 2003): 72. By Richard LACAYO. (473 w).

Time Canada 28 April 2003: 55. ANON.

Time International 28 April 2003: 55. By Richard LACAYO. (891 w).

Time Out 21 May 2003: 62. By John FREEMAN. (317 w).

The Times (London) 23 April 2003: Section: Features: 13. By Erica WAGNER. (840 w).

Times Colonist (Victoria, BC) 27 April 2003: D8. By Joe WEIBE. (589 w).

Times Union (Albany, NY) 8 June 2003: Section: Books: J5. By John FREEMAN. (578 w).

TLS 5224 (16 May 2003): 19-20. By Ronald WRIGHT.

Toronto Star 27 April 2003: Section: Entertainment: D12. By Philip MARCHAND. (1630 w).

Toronto Sun 11 May 2003: Section: Showcase: S22. By Jane VAN DER VOORT. (901 w).

Townsville Bulletin (Australia) 17 May 2003: Section: Weekender: 56. By Mary VERNON. (444 w).

Tulsa World 22 June 2003: Section: Living: H9. By Victoria BROWNWORTH. (654 w).

University Wire 15 October 2003: Section: Book Review: s.p. By Lisa RUDDEN. (837 w). Available from Lexis-Nexis.

USA Today 27 May 2003: Section: Life: 05d. By Jackie PRAY.

Village Voice 8 July 2003: Section: Books: 52. By Dennis LIM. (177 w).

Virginia-Pilot (Norfolk, VA) 29 June 2003: Section: Daily Break: E5. By Rosemary ARMAO. (654 w).

Washington Post 27 April 2003: Section: Book World: T03. By Thomas M. DISCH. (837 w).

Weekend Australian 3 May 2003: Section: Review: B08. By Helen ELLIOTT. (753 w).

Windsor Star (ON) 10 May 2003: F7. By Anne-Marie TOBIN. (496 w).

Wired 11.5 (May 2003): 78. By Allison WILLMORE.

3548. *Oryx and Crake.* [Sound recording]. Books on Tape, 2003. 7 cassettes. Unabridged.

    Library Journal 128.20 (December 2003): 184. By Laurie SELWYN.

    Science 303.5648 (14 November 2003): 1154-1155. By Susan SQUIER.

3549. *Oryx and Crake.* [Sound recording]. Read by Alex Jennings. [London]: Bloomsbury, 2003.

    The Guardian (London) 2 August 2003: Section: Saturday Pages: 18. By Sue ARNOLD. (413 w).

The Observer 10 August 2003: Section: *Observer* Review Pages: 18. By Rachel REDFORD. (271 w).

Sunday Times 3 August 2003: Section: Features: 47. By Karen ROBINSON. (135 w).

3550. *Oryx and Crake.* [Sound recording]. Read by Campbell Scott. Random House Audio, 2003. 9 cassettes, 10.5 hours.

Booklist 100.4 (15 October 2003): 443. By Whitney SCOTT. (145 w).

Kliatt 37.6 (November 2003): 51. By Nancy C. CHAPLIN. (159 w).

Milwaukee Journal Sentinel 3 August 2003: Section: Cue: 07E. By Rochelle O'GORMAN. (285 w).

3551. *Rude Ramsay and the Roaring Radishes.* Toronto: Key Porter Kids, 2003.

Chatelaine 76.12 (December 2003): 36. ANON.

Globe & Mail 13 September 2003: D13. By Kevin BOLGER.

London Free Press (ON) 27 September 2003: Section: Lifestyles: D10. By Bob BISHOP. (106 w).

Resource Links 9.1 (December 2003): 1. By Denise PARROTT. (192 w).

Toronto Star 28 September 2003: Section: Entertainment: D15. By Deirdre BAKER. (292 w).

Toronto Sun 21 September 2003: Section: Showcase: S23. By Bob BISHOP. (106 w).

Reviews of Adaptations of Atwood's Works

3552. RUDERS, Poul. *The Handmaid's Tale.* Copenhagen: Edition Wilhelm Hansen, 1998-2002? Based on Atwood's novel; libretto by Paul Bentley.

First Things: A Monthly Journal of Religion & Public Life 137 (November 2003): 14-17. By Michael LINTON.

Performance in London reviewed:

Brockville Record & Times (ON) 5 April 2003: Section: Entertainment: D10. By Sharon LINDORES. (622 w).

Daily Telegraph (London) 5 April 2003: 18. By Rupert CHRISTIANSEN. (591 w).

Edmonton Journal 5 April 2003: Section: Entertainment: E2. By Sharon LINDORES. (526 w).

Evening Standard (London) 4 April 2003: 34. By Brian HUNT. (417 w).

Financial Times 7 April 2003: Section: Arts: 17. By Andrew CLARK. (1033 w).

The Guardian (London) 5 April 2003: Section: Guardian Leader Pages: 18. By Andrew CLEMENTS. (427 w).

The Independent 8 April 2003: s.l. By Keith POTTER. (501 w). Available from Lexis-Nexis.

Morning Star 9 April 2003: 9. By David NICHOLSON. (610 w).

Scotland on Sunday 13 April 2003: 9. By Louise RIMMER. (1013 w).

The Stage 17 April 2003: 17. By George HALL. (264 w).

Sunday Express 13 April 2003: Section: Features: 63. By David FINGLETON. (507 w).

Sunday Telegraph (London) 6 April 2003: 05. By Michael KENNEDY. (1210 w).

The Times (London) 5 April 2003: Section: Features: 27. By Robert THICK-NESSE. (500 w).

TLS 11 April 2003: 20. By Andrew POTTER.

Performance by Minnesota Opera reviewed:

Edmonton Journal 16 May 2003: E18. By Anthony TOMMASINI. (547 w).

Opera News 68.2 (August 2003): 64-65. By Joshua ROSENBLUM.

Star-Tribune (Minneapolis) 12 May 2003: Section: News: 2B. By Michael ANTHONY. (759 w).

St. Petersburg Times 8 June 2003: Section: Floridian: 10F. By John FLEMING. (1135 w).

USA Today 5 May 2003: Section: Life: 04d. By Thomas MAY. (601 w).

~ 2004 ~

Atwood's Works

3553. *Adam Küsh Kür*. Tehran [Iran]: Ququnüs, 2004. Persian translation of *The Blind Assassin* by Shahin Asayash.

3554. "The Age of Lead." *Telling Tales*. Ed. Nadine Gordimer. New York: Picador (Farrar, Straus & Giroux), 2004. 87-104. Short story reprinted from *Wilderness Tips*, ©1991.

3555. "Amazement." *Prize Writing: The 10th Anniversary Collection*. Ed. Gary Stephen Ross. Toronto: Giller Prize Foundation in association with Coach House Press, 2004. 39-48. Atwood reminisces about the writing of *Alias Grace* which won the Giller Prize in 1996.

3557. "Anger Management." *National Post* 24 June 2004: A18. In comment piece, co-written with Jack Rabinovitch (of Giller Prize fame), Atwood remarks on the current crop of Canadian political leaders.

3558. "The Art of the Matter: Science Is a Tool—The Arts Express Those Dreams for Which We Want to Use Our Tools." *Globe and Mail* 24 January 2004: A19. Excerpt from "Scientific Romancing," the 2004 Kesterton Lecture, delivered 22 January by Atwood at the Carleton University School of Journalism (Ottawa).

3559. "The Arts Go Marching One by One: Which Candidates Are Serving Up Nourishing Cultural Policies? Voters Should Look Before They Bite." *Globe and Mail* 9 June 2004: A23. Column written in connection with the 2004 federal election. See also Terrence Corcoran, "Canadian Culture Safe with Canadians." *National Post* 12 June 2004: Section: Financial Post Comment: FP11.

3560. "At Brute Point." *TLS [Times Literary Supplement]* 5299 (22 October 2004): 27. Poem.

3561. *Atutai Andhu*. Dhaka [Bangladesh]: Shundash Bui Phura, 2004. Bengali translation of *The Blind Assassin* by Muhammad Shafi'nl'alam.

3562. *Bashful Bob and Doleful Dorinda*. Toronto: Key Porter, 2004. "Bashful Bob and Doleful Dorinda is a boisterous and delightful dissertation on discovering the uncharted depths of one's personality. Abandoned by his bubble-headed mum and raised by a bunch of dogs, Bob is understandably bashful around humans. Deprived of her parents while still in diapers, Dorinda endures a dreadful existence with distant relatives. On a dark and drizzly December…." (Publisher).

3563. *The Blind Assassin*. London: Virago, 2004. Originally published London: Bloomsbury, 2000.

3564. *The Blind Assassin*. [Electronic resource]. Toronto: CNIB, 2004. 1 CD-ROM. "Suitable for use with adaptive technology for the print disabled."

3565. *Bottle*. Hay, UK: Hay Festival Press, 2004. Short stories. Contents: "Bottle," 7-11; "It's Not Easy Being Half-Divine," 13-17; "King Log in Exile," 19-23; "Take Charge," 25-29; "Thylacine Ragout," 31-34; "Post-Colonial," 35-39; "Faster," 41-42; "Nightingale," 43-49; "Bottle II," 51-54.

3566. *Cat's Eye*. London: Virago, 2004. Reprint.

3567. *Cat's Eye*. [Electronic resource]. Toronto: CNIB, 2004. Computer data (202 files: 558 mb). Audio and text.

3568. "Death by Landscape." *Contemporary Fiction: 50 Short Stories since 1970*. Ed. Lex Williford and Michael Martone. New York: Simon & Schuster for Borders Books, 2004. 31-45. Reprinted from *Wilderness Tips*, ©1991.

3569. "[Excerpt]." *Air Fare: Stories, Poems & Essays on Flight*. Ed. Nickole Brown and Judith Taylor. Louisville, KY: Sarabande Books, 2004. 149-155. From *Cat's Eye* (Chapter 68), ©1988.

3570. "[Excerpt]." *Globe and Mail* 14 August 2004: Section: Weekend Review: R1. Atwood not alone among novelists writing lyrics for One Ring Zero's new album. Article by Carl Wilson entitled "Lit Rock Is on a Roll" excerpts some of Atwood's lyrics from "Frankenstein Monster Song": "Doctor, doctor, / You're the one to blame. / You put me together, / You forgot the name. / Sew me a lady, / Sew me a lady, / Sew me a monster lady / just like me." The author recently donated her lyrics to One Ring Zero—a quirky two-man Brooklyn band with a klezmer-meets-indie-rock sound.

3571. "[Excerpt]." *Globe and Mail* 2 October 2004: D9. From "A Double-Bladed Knife" in *Moving Targets*.

3572. "[Excerpt]." *Maclean's* 24 May 2004: Section: Closing: 94. From Atwood's Frankenstein Monster Song: "Doctor, doctor, / You're the one to blame. / You put me together, / You forgot the name. / Sew me a lady, / Sew me a lady, / Sew me a monster lady / Just like me. / I've got a dead man's heart and a dead man's brain / I look in the mirror and it's pure pain."

3573. "[Excerpt]." *National Post* 27 March 2004: Section: Books: RB7. Atwood's Edmonton story excerpted from *Mortification: Writers' Stories of Their Public Shame*. Ed. Robin Robertson. New York: Fourth Estate, 2003.

3574. "[Excerpt]." *Unhomely States: Theorizing English-Canadian Postcolonialism*. Ed. Cynthia Sugars. Peterborough, ON: Broadview Press, 2004. 20-26. Reprinted *from Survival: A Thematic Guide to Canadian Literature*, ©1972.

3575. "Hairball." *More Stories We Tell: The Best Contemporary Short Stories by North American Women*. Ed. Wendy Martin. New York: Pantheon, 2004. 99-114. Reprinted from *Wilderness Tips*, ©1991.

3576. *The Handmaid's Tale*. [Toronto]: Seal Books, 2004. Paperback ©1985.

3577. *The Handmaid's Tale*. [Electronic resource]. Vancouver, BC: Provincial Resource Centre for the Visually Impaired, 2004. 1 CD-ROM. "Suitable for use with adaptive technology for the print disabled."

3578. *The Handmaid's Tale*. [Sound recording]. Read by Michael O'Brien. Fredericton, NB: BTC Audio Books, 2004. Unabridged. 2 CD-ROMS (ca. 2 hours).

3579. "*The Handmaid's Tale* and *Oryx and Crake* in Context." *PMLA: Publications of the Modern Language Association of America* 119.3 (May 2004): 513-517. Essay on science v. speculative fiction that originated as a keynote address at the 5th Academic Conference on Canadian Science Fiction and Fantasy, held in August 2003 in Toronto.

3580. "Handmaids' Tales." *The Times* (London) 21 August 2004: Section: Features: Weekend Review: 8. Atwood reviews *From Eve to Dawn*, Marilyn French's 3-volume history of women. (1661 w).

3581. "Haunted by a Face." *National Post* 2 October 2004: RB1. Reprint of Atwood's introduction to *Frozen in Time: The Fate of the Franklin Expedition* by Owen Beattie and John Geiger.

3582. "Headscarves to Die For." *New York Times* 15 August 2004: Section: 7: 1. Atwood reviews *Snow*, Turkish writer Orthan Pamuk's 7th novel. (1378 w).

3583. "I Left Ottawa in a Packsack." *Globe and Mail* 7 February 2004: R14. Atwood writes about her early life experiences after delivering Carleton University's Kesterton Lecture in January.

3584. *Il racconto dell'ancella*. Milan: Editore Ponte alle Grazie, 2004. Italian translation of *The Handmaid's Tale* by Camillo Pennati.

3585. "Introduction." *Carol Shields: Collected Stories*. New York: HarperCollins, 2004. [xiii]-xvii.

3586. "Introduction." *Frozen in Time: The Fate of the Franklin Expedition*. Owen Beattie and John Geiger. Rev. edition. Vancouver, BC: Greystone Books (Douglas & McIntyre), 2004. 1-8. On occasion of reissue of title originally published in 1987.

3587. "It Is Dangerous to Read Newspapers." *An Invitation to Poetry*. Ed. Robert Pinsky and Maggie Dietz. New York: Norton, 2004. 12-13. Reprinted from *Selected Poems 1965-1975*, ©1976.

3588. *Kobieta Go Zjedzenia*. Poznan: Zyski S-ka Wydawn, 2004. Paperback. Polish translation of *The Edible Woman* by Malgorzata Golewska-Stafiej.

3589. *La mujer comestible*. Barcelona: Ediciones B, 2004. Spanish translation of *The Edible Woman*.

3590. "A Little Light Musing." *Globe and Mail* 22 May 2004: D7. Review of *Acquainted with the Night: Excursion Through the World After Dark* by Christopher Dewdney (HarperCollins). Dewdney's father was a "canoe tripping pal" of Atwood's father and Dewdney himself attended Atwood's mother's 90th birthday.

3591. "Lusus Naturae." *McSweeney's Enchanted Chamber of Astonishing Stories*. Ed. Michael Chabon. New York: Vintage Books, 2004. 3-9.

3592. *Margaret Atwood Presents Stories by Canada's Best New Women Writers*. [Sound recording]. Fredericton, NB: BTC Audiobooks, 2004. 2 CD-ROMS (ca. 2 hours). Stories by Nancy Lee, Caroline Anderson, Annabel Lyon, Elise Levine, Lisa Moore, Kristi-Ly Green, and Sheila Heti selected and introduced by Atwood. First broadcast on CBC Radio, 6 April-11 May 2003.

3593. *Matin dans la maison incendiée*. Trois-Rivières: Écrits des Forges, 2004. French translation of *Morning in the Burned House* by Marie Évangeline Arsenault.

3594. "The Mays of Vetadorn." *American Poetry Review* 33.3 (May-June 2004): 29. A review of W. S. Merwin's *The Mays of Ventadorn*. Washington, DC: National Geographic Directions, 2002.

3595. *Mo Shi Nan Nü*. [Taipei]: Tian pei wen hua you xian gong si, 2004. Chinese translation of *Oryx and Crake*. Title romanized.

3596. *Morning in the Burned House*. [Sound recording]. Read by Renate Preuss. Vancouver, BC: Crane Resource Centre, 2004. 1 compact disc in MP3 audio format. "Restricted to use by people with documented print impairment."

3597. *Moving Targets: Writing with Intent, 1982-2004*. Toronto: Anansi, 2004. Includes 51 short pieces penned by Atwood since 1982; a companion volume to *Second Words: Selected Critical Prose* (Toronto: Anansi, 1982). Includes "Dennis Revisited," 13-16, on poet Dennis Lee. Originally published: *Descant* 39 (Winter 1982): 13-15.—"Wondering What It's Like to Be a Woman. [Review of] *The Witches of Eastwick* by John Updike," 17-22. Originally published: *New York Times Book Review* 13 May 1984: 1, 40.—"The Sorcerer as Apprentice. [Review of] *Difficult Loves* by Italo Calvino," 23-25. Originally published: *New York Times Book Review* 1 October 1984: 13.—"Margaret Atwood Remembers Marian Engel," 26-33. Originally published: *Saturday Night* 11.8 (August 1985): 38-40.—"Introduction [to] *Roughing It in the Bush, Or, Life in Canada*," 34-42. Originally published: London: Virago, 1986. vii-xiv.—"True North," 43-58. Originally published: *Saturday Night* 102.1 (January 1987): 141-144, 146, 148.—"Haunted by Their Nightmares. [Review of] *Beloved* by Toni Morrison," 59-64. Originally published: *New York Times Book Review* 13 September 1987: 1, 49-50.—"Afterword [to] *A Jest of God* by Margaret Laurence," 65-69. Originally published: Toronto: McClelland and Stewart, 1988. 211-215.—"Preface [to] *the Canadian Green Consumer Guide*," 70-71. Originally published: Toronto: McClelland and Stewart, 1989: 2-3.—"Great Aunts," 72-84. Reprinted from *Family Portraits: Remembrances by Twenty Distinguished Writers*. Ed. Carolyn Anthony. New York: Doubleday, 1989. 3-16.—"Introduction: Reading Blind." (Atwood's introduction to *The Best American Short Stories, 1989*. Ed. Margaret Atwood and Shannon Ravenel), 85-98. Originally published: New York: Houghton, 1989. xi-xxiii.—"The Public Woman as Honorary Man. [Review of] *The Warrior Queens* by Antonia Fraser," 99-101. Originally published: *Los Angeles Times Book Review* 2 April 1989: 3.—"Writing Utopia" (on the origins of *The Handmaid's Tale*), 102-111. Unpublished speech, 1989.—"A Double-Bladed Knife: Subversive Laughter in Two Stories by Thomas King," 119-129. Originally published: *Native Writers and Canadian Writing*. Ed. W. H. New. Vancouver, BC: UBC Press, 1990. 243-250.— "Nine Beginnings," 130-136. Originally published: *The Writer on Her Work*, Vol. 2. Ed. Janet Sternberg. New York: Norton: 1990, 2000. 150-156.—"A Slave to His Own Liberation. [Review of] *The General in His Labyrinth* by Gabriel García Marquez," 137-140. Originally published: *New York Times Book Review* 16 September 1990: 1, 30.—"Afterword [to] *Anne of Green Gables* by Lucy Maud Montgomery," 141-146. Originally published: Toronto: McClelland and Stewart, 1992. 331-336.—"Introduction: Early Years" [Introduction to] *The Poetry of Gwendolyn MacEwen: The Early Years*. Ed. Margaret Atwood and Barry Callaghan, 147-151. Originally published: Toronto: Exile Editions, 1993. vii-xii.— "Why I Love *The Night of the Hunter*," 152-156. (Review of *The Night of the Hunter*, dir. Charles Laughton, 1955). Originally published: *The Guardian* 19 March 1999: 12.—"Spotty-Handed Villainesses: Problems of Female Bad Behaviour in the Creation of Literature," 157-172. An address delivered in the Cheltenham Lecture Series, University of Gloucester, 8 October 1993.—"The Grunge Look," 173-182. Originally published: *Writing Away: The PEN Canada Travel Anthology*. Ed. Constance Rooke. Toronto: McClelland and Stewart, 1994. 1-11.— "Not So Grimm: The Staying Power of Fairy Tales. [Review of] *From the Beast to the Blond: On Fairy Tales and Their Tellers* by Marina Warner," 183-187. Originally published: *Los Angeles Times Book Review* 29 October 1995: 1.—"Rich Dessert from a Saucy Carter. [Review of] *Burning Your Boats: The Collected Short Stories* by Angela Carter," 188-190. Originally published: *Globe and Mail* 6 May 1996: C18.—"[Review of] *An Experiment in Love* by Hilary Mantel," 191-195. Originally published: *New York Times Book Review* 2 June 1996: 11.—"In Search of *Alias Grace*: On Writing Canadian Historical Fiction," 196-217. An address given at Bronfman Lecture Series (Ottawa: November 1996), Smithsonian Institute (Washington, DC: 11 December 1996), Chicago Library Foundations (6 January 1997), Oberlin College Friends of the Library (8 February 1997), City Arts & Lectures (San Francisco: 5 March 1997). Reprinted in *American Historical Review* 103.5 (December 1998): 1503-[1516].—"Masterpiece Theatre. [Review of] *Trickster Makes This World: Mischief, Myth and Art* [and] *The Gift: Imagination and the Erotic Life of Property* by Lewis Hyde," 218-223. Originally published: *Los Angeles Times Book Review* 25 January 1998: 7.—"The Awkward Sublime," 224-225, on Al Purdy's poetry. Originally published: *BorderCrossings* 19.4 (November 2000): 46-51.—"Mordecai Richler, 1931–2001: Diogenes of Montreal," 232-233. Originally published: *Globe and Mail* 4 July 2001: R1, R7.— "Introduction [to] *She* by H. Rider Haggard," 234-241. Originally published: New York: Random House, 2002. xvii-xxiv.—"When Afghanistan Was at Peace," 242-244. Originally published: *New York Times Magazine* 28 October 2001: 82.— "Mystery Man: Some Clues to Dashiell Hammett," 245-258. Review of *The Selected Letters of Dashiell Hammett, 1921-1960*. Ed. Richard Layman with Julie Rivett; *Dashiell Hammett: A Daughter Remembers*, by Jo Hammett. Ed. Richard Layman with Julie Rivett; *Dashiell Hammett: Crime Stories & Other Writings*. Selected and ed. Steven Marcus. Originally published: *New York Review of Books* 49.2 (14 February 2002): 19-21.—"Of Myths and Men. [Review of] *Atanarjuat: The Fast Runner*," 259-262. (Dir. Zacharias Kunuk, 2001). Originally published: *Globe and Mail* 13 April 2002: R10.—"Cops and Robbers. [Review of] *Tishomingo Blues* by Elmore Leonard," 263-274. Originally published: *New York Review of Books* 49.9 (23 May 2002): 21-23.—"Tiff and the Animals (On the Occasion of the Timothy Findley Memorial Evening, Convocation Hall, University of Toronto, September 29, 2002)," 275-280. Unpublished address.—"The Indelible Woman. [Comment on] *To the Lighthouse* by Virginia Woolf," 278-280. Originally published: *The Guardian* 7 September 2002: [7].—"The Queen of Quinkdom. [Review of] *The Birthday of the World and Other Stories* by Ursula K. Le Guin," 281-292. Originally published: *New York Review of Books* 49.14 (26 September 2002): [23-25].—"Introduction [to] *Ground Works*. Ed. Christian Bök," 293-299. Originally published: Toronto: Anansi, 2002. ix-xv.—"The Wrong Box: Matt Cohen, Fabulism and Critical Taxonomy," 300-314. Originally published: *From Common Ground: A Celebration of Matt Cohen*. Ed. Graeme Gibson, Wayne Grady, Dennis Lee, and Priscila Uppal. Toronto: Knopf, 2002. 66-82.— "Introduction [to] *Dr. Glas* by Hjalmar Söderberg," 315-319. Originally published: New York: Anchor, 2002: 5-10.—"Napoleon's Two Biggest Mistakes," 320-323. Originally published: *Globe and Mail* 1 March 2003: A17.—"Letter to America," 324-327. Originally published: *The Nation* 14 April 2003: 22-23.—"Writing *Oryx and Crake*," 328-330. Originally published *Book-of-the-Month Club / Bookspan.* January 2003.—"George Orwell: Some Personal Connections," 331-338. An address broadcast on BBC Radio, 3 and 13 June 2003. Reprinted as "Orwell and Me." *The Guardian* 16 June 2003: [4].—"Arguing Against Ice Cream. [Review of] *Enough: Staying Human in an Engineered Age* by Bill McKibben," 339-350. Originally published: *New York Review of Books* 12 June 2003: 6, 8, 10.— "Victory Gardens. [Foreword to] *A Breath of Fresh Air* by Elise Houghton," 351-359. Originally published: Toronto: Sumach Press, 2003. 13-19.—"Carol Shields, Who Died Last Week, Wrote Books That Were Full of Delights," 360-363. Originally published: *The Guardian* 26 July 2003: 28.—"Resisting the Veil: Reports from a Revolution," 364-371. Review of the following books: *Persepolis: The*

Story of a Childhood by Marjane Satrapi; *Reading* Lolita *in Tehran: A Memoir in Books* by Azar Nafisi; *The Bathhouse* by Farnoosh Moshiri; *Shah of Shahs* by Ryszard Kapuściński; *The Crisis of Islam: Holy War and Unholy Terror* by Bernard Lewis; *The Crusades Through Arab Eyes* by Amin Maalouf. Originally published: *The Walrus* 1.1 (October 2003): ix-xix.—"Introduction [to] *The Complete Stories, Volume 4* by Morley Callaghan," 372-381. Originally published: Toronto: Exile Editions, 2003. ix-xix.—"He Springs Eternal. [Review of] *Hope Dies Last: Keeping the Faith in Difficult Times* by Studs Terkel," 382-394. Originally published: *New York Review of Books* 6 November 2003: 78-80.—"To Beechy Island," 395-405. Originally published: *Solo: Writers on Pilgrimage.* Ed. Katherine Govier. Toronto: McClelland and Stewart, 2004. 201-216.—"Mortification," 406-409. Originally published: *Mortification: Writers' Stories of Their Public Shame.* Ed. Robin Robertson. London: Fourth Estate, 2003. 1-4.

3598. *Murder in the Dark.* [Electronic resource]. Toronto: CNIB, 2004. Computer data (74 files: 92.1 mb). Audio and text.

3599. "My First Book." *The Times* (London) 11 December 2004: Section: Features: Weekend Review: 8. Atwood, along with Antony Beevor and Ian Rankin, reflect on publishing their first books; in Atwood's case, *Double Persephone.*

3600. "On Writing Poetry." *Word: On Being a [Woman] Writer.* Ed. Jocelyn Burrell. New York: Feminist Press, 2004. 138-147. Originally delivered as a lecture in Hay on Wye, Wales. (1995). Autobiographical.

3601. *Oryks i derkacz.* Poznan: Zyski S-ka, 2004. Polish translation of *Oryx and Crake* by Malgorzata Hesko-Kolodzinska.

3602. *Oryx and Crake.* Charlesbourg, QU: Braille Jymico Inc., 2004. Braille ed., 8 v.

3603. *Oryx and Crake.* Toronto: Seal; London: Virago, 2004.

3604. *Oryx and Crake.* Leicester [UK]: Charnwood, 2004 ©2003. Large print edition.

3605. *Oryx and Crake.* [Electronic resource]. Toronto: CNIB, 2004. Computer data (169 files: 611 mb). Audio and text.

3606. *Oryx and Crake.* [Sound recording]. Toronto: CNIB, 2004. 2 cassettes (11 hr., 9 min.).

3607. *Oryx and Crake: A Novel.* New York: Anchor Books, 2004.

3608. *Oryx e Crake.* Rio de Janeiro: Editora Rocco, 2004. Portuguese translation by Léa Viveiros de Castro.

3609. *Oryx y Crake.* Barcelona: Ediciones B, 2004. Spanish translation by Juanjo Estrella.

3610. "Reading Blind." *The Story and Its Writer* [CD-ROM]. Ann Charters. Princeton, NJ: Recording for the Blind & Dyslexic, 2004. A commentary by Atwood on the practice and theory of writing short fiction. Originally published: Boston: St. Martin's, 2003 (6th ed.). Distribution is restricted to RFB&D members who have a documented print disability such as visual impairment, learning disability or other physical disability. (Since 1995, RFB&D = Recording for the Blind and Dyslexic.)

3611. *Resurgir.* Madrid: Alianza Editorial, 2004. Spanish translation of *Surfacing* by Gabriela Bustelo.

3612. *Rude Ramsay and the Roaring Radishes.* New York: Bloomsbury Children's Books, 2004. "Atwood offers a deliciously ridiculous tale about the virtues of resisting restrictions. Rude Ramsay has reached the end of his rope! Sick of eating rock-hard rice, wrinkled ravioli, and raw rhinoceros, Ramsay and Ralph the red-nosed rat resolve to leave their rectangular residence in a quest for more refreshing repast and to prove that the grass really is greener on the other side of the fence. With lots of 'r's' to help the story roll along, Margaret Atwood's rollicking text, combined with Dusan Petricic's lively art, make this book a real treat for Margaret Atwood fans, old and new." (Publisher).

3613. "Siren Song." *Prentice Hall Literature: Timeless Voices, Timeless Themes*. [Sound recording]. Princeton, NJ: Recording for the Blind & Dyslexic, 2004. Sound disc originally published: Upper Saddle River, NJ: Prentice-Pearson, 2003. Distribution restricted to RFB&D members.

3614. *Slepoi Ubiitsa*. Moscow: Eksmo, 2004. Russian translation of *The Blind Assassin* by V. Bernatskoi.

3615. *Strange Things: The Malevolent North in Canadian Literature*. London: Virago, 2004. Originally published in 1995 by Oxford UP.

3616. *Survival: A Thematic Guide to Canadian Literature*. Toronto: McClelland and Stewart, 2004. Reprint of 1972 edition.

3617. "Three Novels I Won't Write Soon." *The Times* (London) 18 December 2004: Section: Features: 10. Novels include *Worm Zero*, *Spongedeath*, and *Beetleplunge.* (1169 w).

3618. "To Beechy Island." *Solo: Writers on Pilgrimage*. Ed. Katherine Govier. Toronto: McClelland and Stewart, 1994. [201]-216. Arctic journey.

3619. "Uncovered: An American Iliad." *The Times* (London) 28 February 2004: Section: Features: 10. Review of the 3-volume series, Masterworks of the Classical Haida Mythtellers: v.1: *A Story as Sharp as a Knife: The Classical Haida Mythtellers and Their World* by Robert Bringhurst (Vancouver, BC: Douglas & McIntyre, 1999); v.2: *Nine Visits to the Mythworld* by Gandl and Robert Bringhurst (Vancouver, BC: Douglas & McIntyre, 2002); v.3: *Being in Being: The Collected Works of Skaay of the Qquuna Qiighawaay* by Skaay and Robert Bringhurst (Vancouver, BC: Douglas & McIntyre, 2001). (1867 w).

3620. *Writing* Oryx and Crake *and* The Handmaid's Tale. [Toronto]: Canadian Opera Company, 2004. Booklet distributed by COC on occasion of its production of *The Handmaid's Tale*, 23,26,29 September and 1,5,9 October 2004, at the Hummingbird Centre for the Performing Arts, Toronto.

3621. *Wynurzenie*. Poznan: Zyski S-ka, 2004. Polish translation of *Surfacing* by Jolanta Plakwicz and Teresa Poniatowska.

3622. *Yu Si Zhe Xie Shang: Ma Ge Li Te. Ai Te Wu Tan Xie Zuo*. Taipei: Mai tian chu ban: Cheng bang wen hua fa hang, 2004. Chinese translation of *Negotiating with the Dead: A Writer on Writing* by Ai wu de. Title romanized.

Adaptations of Atwood's Works

3623. "Frankenstein Monster Song." *As Smart as We Are*. One Ring Zero. Brooklyn: Soft Skull Press [2004]. Track 9. Atwood poem set to music and recorded by One Ring Zero.

3624. VORES, Andy et al. *Six Songs on Poems of Margaret Atwood / American Folk Songs [Book 1] / The Little Box* [CD-ROM]. s.l.: s.n., 2004. CD is 66 minutes; Atwood section, 28:28. Source: WorldCat.

Quotations

3625. "[Quote]." *The Advertiser* 9 September 2004: Section: Opinion: 19. "We still think of a powerful man as a born leader and a powerful woman as an anomaly." In an article by Marty Smith.

3626. "[Quote]." *The Guardian* (London) 29 December 2004: 9. Atwood on death of Susan Sontag: "She was a unique and courageous woman. Even if you didn't agree with her, she was always courageous and always a unique thinker. She always made you think. What made her unique? She wasn't like anyone else....Whatever she set her mind to—whatever she'd come up with—it wasn't going to be the received opinion. She ran received opinion through the shredder and looked at things again. She was a grown-up emperor's-new-clothes child. When kids say the emperor's naked, you tell them they shouldn't say those things in public. When adults say it, they get in a lot of trouble—and she didn't mind getting into trouble."

3627. "[Quote]." *Ottawa Citizen* 11 April 2004: C2. In an article by Janice Kennedy about Toronto, Atwood is quoted as saying that it is "the city that really justifies the country."

3628. "[Quote]." *School Libraries in Canada* 23.4 (2004): 37. In article entitled "Inspiring Quotes about the Importance of Libraries in Society," Atwood is quoted: "A word after a word after a word is power." (From *True Stories*).

3629. "[Quote]." *The Tennessean* 28 July 2004: 7M. "A divorce is like an amputation. You survive it, but there's less of you." Atwood quoted by Henry Piarrot in story about a teacher turned divorce-mediator.

3630. "[Quote]." *Toronto Star* 25 July 2004: Section: News: A09. Atwood is quoted in article by Olivia Ward on evolution's next stage: "'The argument for the perfectibility of mankind rests on a logical fallacy,' writes Margaret Atwood in the *New York Review of Books*. 'Thus man is by definition imperfect, say those who would perfect him. But those who would perfect him are themselves, by their own definition, imperfect. And imperfect beings cannot make perfect decisions. If we can extend life by 30 years, we'll have done more or less all we need to do.'"

3631. "[Quote]." *Toronto Sun* 13 August 2004: Section: Lifestyle: 59. "The Eskimos had 52 names for snow because it is important to them; there ought to be as many for love."

Interviews

3632. "Atwood's Latest Alliteration-Filled Children's Book." *Canada AM* 29 November 2004. Available from Lexis-Nexis. An interview with Seamus O'Regan about her "sixth" book for children written on the train to Windsor, "which lasts about three hours. So you can see. But then of course you polish them up afterwards. They're not very long." Atwood admitted she didn't have a dictionary on the trip "but I augmented my story afterwards." In the interview Atwood also discussed her upcoming collection of essays (*Moving Targets*), her second collection, after *Second Words*, published in 1982. "I probably do about 20 of them a year. So, you can see we had to go through a great wad of stuff to pick out what we were going to put into the book."

3633. "Margaret Atwood on the Creation of *The Handmaid's Tale*." *Margaret Atwood's The Handmaid's Tale*. Ed. Harold Bloom. Philadelphia: Chelsea House, 2004. 77-78. Excerpt from Marvyn Rothstein's "No Balm in Gilead for Margaret Atwood." *New York Times* 17 February 1986: C11. Interview.

3634. "Whither CanLit: Atwood Answers Readers' Mail." *Ottawa Citizen* 13 June 2004: C10. Excerpt from a story in the *Daily Telegraph* in which Atwood responded to readers' questions. Examples:

Dylan / Edinburgh: How hard would you find it to write a novel with, for example, Arnold Schwarzenegger as the protagonist? **Atwood:** Now that's a challenge. Arnold the governor might be a little boring; Arnold the Terminator—well, it's been done. Maybe Arnold could wake up one morning and find that he's changed into a gerbil. A Kafkaesque take, as it were. This would allow for some inner monologues of interest. Possibly.

Kelly / Washington, DC: Is the golden age of Canadian literature over? **Atwood:** When was that golden age? Golden ages have a way of being fantasy times that never existed. Usually a "golden age" is the time just before yours, or so you think. It comes from not being allowed to stay up for the adult parties when you were a child.

Tazim Kassam / New York: Assuming that President Bush had the sense to request your advice on how to secure humanity and Earth a better future, what would you say to him? **Atwood:** Well, that's a big assumption. My advice would tend to come out sounding like grannies everywhere: Look before you leap, don't bite off more than you can chew, for want of a nail the shoe was lost, all war and no peace makes George a dull boy, etc.—and maybe a bit like J. Christ—before condemning the mote in your neighbour's eye, deal with the beam in your own; insofar as you do it unto the least of these prisoners, you do it unto me, etc. But on a practical level, I'd say, Get America off the oil addiction. Develop new sources of energy that are less destructive, both to the country and to the world. They do exist! Return America to its higher self and its former prestige by embodying its best values rather than merely quoting them. Hands up all who think such advice would be taken.

3635. "You Ask the Questions: So, Margaret Atwood, Your Latest Novel Foretells the End of the Human Race: How Long Have We Got Left? And Where Do You Keep Your Booker Prize?" *The Independent* 20 April 2004: s.p. Available from Lexis-Nexis. Atwood responds to various questions submitted by readers: Examples:

Michael Jones (email): Will you write an autobiography, or do you prefer to keep us guessing? **Atwood:** I lead an uneventful and boringly virtuous life. But then, I would say that, wouldn't I?

Clare Shannon (email): Among the reams written about you and your work by academics and students, have you found anything insightful or interesting? **Atwood:** Such material is the Medusa's head. Look at it and you turn to stone. I'm glad it keeps people busily employed and off the streets, but I don't have to read it.

Jules Mason / London: Are you nostalgic for your early days as a writer? I understand you used to recite your poetry in bohemian coffeehouses. It sounds very romantic. **Atwood:** It does sound romantic, doesn't it? Actually, it was kind of smoky. Also, every time you came to your most plangent line, someone would flush the toilet or turn on the espresso machine. No, I'm not too nostalgic. I was consumed with anxiety. Young people have a lot of stresses on them. They don't know how the plot is likely to turn out.

Jo Stella / Leeds: Would the world be a better place without literary critics? **Atwood:** Actually, no. Think of them as the town criers or the village gossips. "Love the shoes, hated the hat, and did you get a load of that metaphor...." But at least they let people know that an event has taken place, so you can go and see for yourself. I write literary criticism myself from time to time. But I'm not chained to a desk in the cellar, lashed by an editor who demands controversy, so I can write about books I like.

Owen Hey / Reading: Do you have any entirely trivial pastimes? **Atwood:** I watch peculiar science-fiction films. Also—when unobserved—puffball comedies such as *Legally Blonde.*

Bonnie Mayers (email): Where do you keep your Booker prize? **Atwood:** It has a happy home on a shelf near "The Horrible Head," which is a plaster cast of a sculpture made of my head.

3636. BROCKES, Emma. "Do Keep It Up: She Is Famously Abrasive, Sardonic and Intellectually Rigorous. Does It All Stem from Margaret Atwood's Upbringing in a Family of Self-Sufficient Scientists, Or Is She Just a Natural Nit Picker?" *The Guardian* (London) 12 April 2004: Section: Guardian features: 4. Atwood in feisty interview responds to questions about her.

Is she a feminist? "First of all, what is feminism? Second, which branch of it? Am I against women having rights? Actually, no. Am I really a puppet of the women's movement? No, I'm too old for that. I've been writing since 1956 and there was no women's movement in sight at the time. Was I interested in Germaine Greer and Betty Friedan? Yes. Do I have a large library of stuff about women? Actually, I do. I also have a large library about war. I used to have them side by side. Does that mean I'm a militarist? Actually not."

Is she competitive? No, awards don't excite her. "It's an inert position; you're a pumpkin at the fair. However, I did get second prize in the dolls' dress competition in grade three."

Her proudest moment? "No, I was quite pissed off. I wanted first. Although I had a friend who was Miss Wool USA and she had to carry around a lamb which peed on her. So there's a downside to winning."

3637. CALDWELL, Rebecca. "Atwood Finds Opera 'Powerful.'" *Globe and Mail* 18 September 2004: Section: Weekend Review: R9. Atwood's relationship to opera, especially *The Handmaid's Tale*, references her interest as a child when she read librettos to accompany the epics piped over the radio into her television-less home.

Asked whether her other famous futuristic dystopia, *Oryx and Crake*, might be given the operatic treatment? "I'm quite keen on doing *Oryx and Crake* as an opera. I think that would be quite bizarre. You'd have to have a number of uninhibited people willing to scamper around with parts of them painted blue, but that aside, I think it would make a really good opera," she said. First, however, she said she is waiting for a chance to hear her libretto about Sumerian goddess Inanna set to Winnipegger Randolph Peters's nearly completed score. *Inanna's Journey*, commissioned by the COC, is slated to be staged in 2006.

She added that she was not about to give up writing novels or poetry for libretto-writing any time soon, however. "It's not really what I do, I'm a novelist," she said. "I'm happy to help and it's fun, but it's not something I'm likely to devote my entire life to."

3638. D'SOUZA, Irene. "Margaret Atwood: Is This the Patch We Want to Be On?" *Herizons* 17.4 (Spring 2004): 16-20, 45. Focuses on Atwood as a woman. Some unusual insights about her past.

3639. DOHERTY, Mike. "A Supportive Message in a Bottle." *Globe and Mail* 5 June 2004: Section: Weekend Review: R1, R7. Atwood interviewed in connection with *Bottle*, a short book she prepared for the Hay-on-Wye festival in Wales that she could not attend that year because she was in Toronto celebrating her mother's 95th birthday.

3640. FICHTNER, Margaria. "Atwood's Bleak Worlds Start in Nature." *Milwaukee Journal Sentinel* 11 April 2004: Section: Cue: 08E. Atwood interviewed in Los Angeles at 8:30 a.m., after staggering off a flight from Japan only hours earlier.

OK, so why the Jimmy/Snowman character as a protagonist instead of someone more Atwoodian, someone named, oh, Shirley/Snow Woman? I think if you write about Shirley/Snow Woman, it becomes a book about the woman question, and a lot of women's concerns would get into it. She probably would have been much more upset about the deaths of small children, not that Jimmy isn't upset, but I think the kind of upset would have been different. So that's one reason why. The other reason was that I got very tired of people always saying to me, "Why do you always write about women?" So I would point laboriously out that I didn't always write about women, and I would tell them which men I had written about, but there's no question about this one. It's a guy. Therefore, it was also a challenge to do, but as with all my books with anything in them that needs research, I got it checked out. I felt that it should be read by a couple of young men to see how accurate it was, and they gave me a couple of swearing tips, but on the whole they said, "Uuuuu-uuuu, how did you know all this?"

How have readers taken to the switch? I thought the readers might have shifted away from women, but women have always been able to read everything. It's men who get squirrelly about being caught in public with a book by a woman who isn't dead. Brown paper covers on *Sense and Sensibility*. But men, especially younger sci-fi fans, who tend to be male anyway, seem to be reading this book. As well as women, who will read anything.

3641. FLATOW, Ira. "Margaret Atwood Discusses Science Concepts Used in the Various Novels She's Authored." *Talk of the Nation*: 30 April 2004. Available from Lexis-Nexis. Interview on National Public Radio (5393 w). Program may be heard at http://www.sciencefriday.com/kids/sfk©20040430-2.html#hear (1 May 2006). (RealPlayer required).

3642. FOX, Matthew. "Are You There, God? It's Me, Margaret Atwood: Margaret Atwood Discusses Writing, the Flu and Her New Book of Essays." *Maisonneuve: Arts, Opinions, Ideas* 11.4 October-November (2004): 11.

3643. GEORGE, Lianne. "On Opera, Pop and Politics." *Maclean's* 27 September 2004: Section: Music: 21. Atwood interviewed in connection with impending launch of the opera based on *The Handmaid's Tale* in Canada.

3644. GODSEY, Kristin D. "Unlocking the Door." *Novel Writing* August 2004: 18-21. Margaret Atwood expounds on finding your voice, the beauty of multi-tasking and what "chick lit" may have in common with Dracula and Frankenstein.

3645. IKENBERG, Tamara. "Atwood Looks to the Future at Author Forum." *Courier-Journal* (Louisville, KY) 8 April 2004: Section: Features: 1C. Atwood interviewed while in Salt Lake City. Interviewer notes that amidst all her other honors, Atwood "even has a club created by her devotees: The Margaret Atwood Society." Interview focuses on *Oryx and Crake*.

3646. KARRAS, Christy. "Atwood's World: Author of *Oryx and Crake* Which Casts a Wary Eye on Science to Visit SLC [Salt Lake City]." *Salt Lake Tribune* 28 March 2004: Section: Sports: D1. In town at the invitation of Betsy Burton, owner of the King's English bookstore. Twice-told tales about the origins and writing of the book.

3647. KNELMAN, Martin. "The Handmaid's Homecoming." *Toronto Star* 18 September 2004: Section: Arts: J01. On Atwood and opera.

3648. LIBEDINSKY, Juana. "Margaret Atwood: El Poder Del Odio y Del Deseo." *Suplemento Cultura La Nación (Buenos Aires)* 16 May 2004: 1-2. Interview in Spanish.

3649. MARTIN, Valerie. "Interview with Margaret Atwood." 1 December 2004. Available at http://www.lannan.org/lf/rc/event/margaret-atwood (ca. 24 min.) (1 May 2006). Part of Lannan Foundation's Readings and Conversations series.

3650. MELNYK, Olenka. "Stick Shifting Margaret Atwood Makes for Uneasy Ride." *The Standard* (St. Catharines, ON) 2 October 2004: E3. Focuses on *Moving Targets*. Excerpt: "Since the publication of her first novel 35 years ago, Atwood's output has been prolific, formidably so. But she has run aground with two other novels that never got completed and with a number of short stories as well. When you find yourself reading trashy romances rather than working on your book, then you think to yourself, 'This is obviously not interesting me anymore.' 'Facing a blank page doesn't get any easier with time, but it doesn't necessarily get any harder,' says Atwood, who describes writing as wrestling with a greased pig in the dark. Atwood turns 65 in November, but she has no plans of retiring or slowing down. Sixty-five is not the same kind of milestone for writers as it is for people who hold down salaried day jobs. 'The thing about writers is that they're basically self-employed,' she says. 'As long as they can stagger around at the keyboard, there they are.'"

3651. O'CONNOR, Shaunagh. "Method in Madness." *Herald Sun* (Melbourne) 3 July 2004: Section: Weekend: W29. O'Connor asks Atwood if she believes in the notion of love at first sight, considering her father saw her mother slide down a bannister when the two were at college together and declared that was the woman he would marry. "It's not a question of whether I believe in it or not. Science has shown that it actually exists," she says.

O'Connor tries a "fun question" for her, then: If you could live as a woman in any other era which would it be? She is told that, to rid herself of such romantic notions, "you should probably read Marilyn French's three-volume history of women, *From Eve to Dawn*....So if I was going to be anything I would be a hunter-gatherer...[for] after they invented agriculture and land ownership one of the first commodities that got traded were women. It was probably the template for slavery."

In short, O'Connor concludes, Atwood, 65, intellectualizes everything she speaks about. Perhaps asking if she has grandchildren will have her pulling out photos of chubby babies: the soft side of Margaret Atwood? "I have two step-grandchildren," she says. "I used to have two cats, but they are dead, I used to have dogs but they're dead, too. I also had sheep that are dead, and had horses—also dead. I also had chickens which we ate....What else do you want to know about my extended family?"

3652. RYAN, Laura T. "A Fun-Filled Warning: Author Margaret Atwood Comes to Syracuse to Talk about Her Work." *Post-Standard* (Syracuse, NY) 11 April 2004: Section: Stars: 22. A few days earlier, the Booker Prize-winning novelist flew from Australia to Japan to Los Angeles to Denver to Salt Lake City to Dallas to Boston. She was on tour to promote her latest novel, *Oryx and Crake* (Anchor Books), now out in paperback. Atwood would spend a week in Syracuse as a visiting professor at Syracuse University and that would be her second trip to the Salt City in a little over a year (the preceding April, she spoke in the Rosamond Gifford Lecture Series).

Is it bizarre to travel around and answer questions out loud about worlds you invented quietly in your head? Yeah, it is bizarre, quite frankly. But the celebrity interview, that has been around since the end of the 19th century. Henry James writes about it in some of his short stories. It's when newspapers got the idea they didn't have to put in just news. So it is not a completely new phenomenon, but let us say that Mr. Proust probably never had to do it.

Are you envious of Mr. Proust? No, he was too ill. You can't be envious of him, because he was really quite ill most of the time. But I do sometimes amuse myself by imagining him on a book tour: "I'm now going to read you 50 pages composed of only one sentence."

3653. SANTIAGO, Soledad. "Margaret Atwood: Future Shocker." *Santa Fe New Mexican* 26 November 2004: P36. Atwood interviewed by phone in anticipation of visit to Santa Fe as part of the Lannan Foundation's Readings and Conversations series.

3654. WHITNEY, Susan. "Margaret Atwood Complex in Writing and in Conversation." *Deseret Morning News* (Salt Lake City) 28 March 2005: s.p. Available from Lexis-Nexis. Reporter phoned Atwood in Toronto one hour late—and Atwood interviewed reporter as to the reasons, saying this stuff of real life is where she gets her ideas for fiction.

In the interview, she was willing to describe **a normal working day**. "When I'm working, the phone rings. I can't turn it off. My mum's almost 95. I suppose I could turn it off and be cold about it....But I grew up subject to interruptions." In her family, she said, "I'm the person with the sign on the door, 'Do not disturb,' to which nobody pays the least bit of attention." Atwood has written most of her novels with a cat on her lap. Sometimes the cat would even try to sit on her hands while she typed. "They know where the attention is focused."

She can't describe **the process of writing**. "When you are writing, you are not actually thinking, 'How am I doing this?' It's like skiing," she said. "If you think about it, you'll fall down. When you are writing you are either in a state of flow or you are not in a state of flow....When the flow goes away, you think it will never return," she said. "When that happens, I redirect myself." She stands up and does something else.

3655. WITTMAN, Juliet. "Notes from the Underworld: Playing Shaman, Atwood Brings Back Word of a Bleak Future." *Rocky Mountain News* (Denver, CO) 2 April 2004: Section: Entertainment: Weekend Spotlight: 28D. Atwood interviewed by phone from Toronto prior to her visit to Denver. "All our creations, good and bad, come from a human wish list of desires and fears," says Atwood. "We have wanted some things for a very long time. In the past, we could want them without having to suffer the consequences of actually getting them." She began listing these desires: "Endless youth and beauty; a guaranteed supply of delicious food objects that would appear whenever we wanted them and be cleared up by invisible hands and servants we would never have to pay. The closest we've come to that is fast food chains....We desired cloaks of invisibility so that we could spy on people without them knowing we were there—and we have the Secret Service. We've always wanted invincible weapons. A purse that would be filled with gold whenever we opened it....Spouses who are faithful to us and love us very much, and at the same time large supplies of sexually attractive partners and no consequences. We've wanted wonderful children who will do exactly what they're told, but never gotten them. Maybe that's why we're working on robots."

Scholarly Resources

3657. BARR, Marleen S. "Introduction: Textism—An Emancipation Proclamation." *PMLA: Publications of the Modern Language Association of America* 119.3 (May 2004): 429-442. A critique of the review of Margaret Atwood's science fiction *Oryx and Crake* by Sven Birkerts (*New York Times Book Review* 18 May 2003: 12).

3658. BARTLETT, Sally A. "The Female Phantasmagoria: Fantasy and Third Force Psychology in Four Feminist Fictions (Toni Morrison, Charlotte Perkins Gilman, Margaret Atwood, Virginia Woolf)." PhD thesis. University of South Florida, 2004. 164 pp. This dissertation illuminates the ways in which both fantasy and mimesis combine in 20th-century feminist representations of reality including Atwood's *Lady Oracle*. For more see *DAI-A* 65.02 (August 2004): 501.

3659. BENET-GOODMAN, Helen Charisse. "Forgiving Friends: Feminist Ethics and Fiction by Toni Morrison and Margaret Atwood." PhD thesis. University of Virginia, 2004. This dissertation uses the representations of women's friendship found in *Sula* by Toni Morrison and *Cat's Eye* by Margaret Atwood to frame an interrogation of contemporary ideas about friendship. For more see *DAI-A* 65.01 (July 2004): 169.

3660. BJØRHOVDE, Gerd. "When Foreignness and Familiarity Become One: Defamiliarization in Some Canadian Short Stories." *The Art of Brevity: Excursions in Short Fiction Theory and Analysis*. Ed. Per Winther, Jakob Lothe, and Hans H. Skei. Columbia: U of South Carolina P, 2004. 128-137. Includes discussion of Atwood's "A Travel Piece."

3661. BJORNSON, Kathryn. "Pink Tickets and Feathered Frocks: Sexual Politics in Yevgeny Zamyatin's *We* and Margaret Atwood's *The Handmaid's Tale*. MA thesis. Dalhousie University, 2004. 151 pp. Also available on microfiche from Canadian Theses Service (2005). "Dystopian novels generally depict totalitarian or oligarchic societies that undertake to control the individual through the manipulation of sexuality, procreation, family life, and gender roles. This thesis compares the sexual motifs and gender implications of Yevgeny Zamyatin's *We* and Margaret Atwood's *The Handmaid's Tale*, two dystopian novels written near the beginning and the end of the twentieth century, respectively." (Author). For more see *MAI* 43.06 (December 2005): 1935.

3662. BLANC, Marie Therese. "Another Face of Justice: Interpretative Debates within the Canadian Trial Novel after 1970." PhD thesis. McGill University, 2004. 264 pp. This study examines Canadian works of fiction that contain historical trial narratives and that enact an adversarial trial of their own for an implied reader who acts as appellate judge. Included are four Canadian novels published after 1970 that fictionalize the circumstances leading to notorious criminal trials: Margaret Atwood's *Alias Grace* (1996), Lynn Crosbie's *Paul's Case: The Kingston Letters* (1997), and Rudy Wiebe's *The Temptations of Big Bear* (1973), and *The Scorched-Wood People* (1977). For more see *DAI-A* 66.01 (July 2005): 183.

3663. BLODGETT, Harriet. "Mimesis and Metaphor: Food Imagery in International Twentieth-Century Women's Writing." *Papers on Language & Literature* 43.3 (Summer 2004): 260-295. Blodgett examines how 20th-century women's novels, short stories, and poems use food imagery. She argues that women writers use such imagery to address, among other things, psychological problems, sex, and domesticity. Among the works she discusses for their references to food are *The Bone People* by Keri Hulme, *The Edible Woman* by Margaret Atwood, and *The God of Small Things* by Arundhati Roy.

3664. BLOOM, Harold, ed. *Margaret Atwood's* The Handmaid's Tale. Philadelphia: Chelsea House, 2004. Includes a Biographical Sketch of Margaret Atwood, The Story Behind the Story, Summary/Analysis, and a Descriptive List of Characters. Individual chapters indexed in this section.

3665. BOUSON, J. Brooks. "'It's Game over Forever': Atwood's Satiric Vision of a Bioengineered Posthuman Future in *Oryx and Crake.*" *Journal of Commonwealth Literature* 39.3 (September 2004): 139-156.

3666. BRUHN, Mark J. "Margaret Atwood's Lucy Poem: The Postmodern Art of Otherness in *Death by Landscape.*" *European Romantic Review* 15.3 (2004): 450-461.

3667. CAMINERO-SANTANGELO, Marta. "Marta Caminero-Santangelo on Resistent Postmodernism." *Margaret Atwood's* The Handmaid's Tale. Ed. Harold Bloom. Philadelphia: Chelsea House, 2004. 88-89. Excerpt from "Moving Beyond 'The Blank White Spaces': Atwood's Gilead, Postmodernism, and Strategic Resistance." *Studies in Canadian Literature* 19.1 (1994): 20-42.

3668. CHEN, Qiuhua. "The Analysis of Atwood's Novels from an Ecological Perspective." *Foreign Literature Studies* 106 (2004): 56-62. In Chinese.

3669. COOKE, Nathalie, ed. *Margaret Atwood: A Critical Companion.* Westport, CT: Greenwood Press, 2004. In a text that can be read by serious high school students, Cooke, the author of *Margaret Atwood: A Biography* (Toronto: ECW Press, 1998), covers Atwood in 8 chapters. In the 1st she supplies a short biography (1-18); in the 2nd she discusses her Canadian nationalist/feminist/post-modern literary heritage (19-29); in the 3rd *The Edible Women* (31-52); in the 4th *Surfacing* (53-78); in the 5th *Lady Oracle* (79-95); in the 6th *Cat's Eye* (97-112); in the 7th *The Handmaid's Tale* (113-135); and in the 8th *The Blind Assassin* (137-155). There is also an extensive bibliography, not all of which is on Atwood directly (157-167).

3670. COOPER, Pamela. "Pamala [sic] Cooper on Voyeurism and the Filming of *The Handmaid's Tale.*" *Margaret Atwood's* The Handmaid's Tale. Ed. Harold Bloom. Philadelphia: Chelsea House, 2004. 93-95. Excerpt from "Sexual Surveillance and Medical Authority in Two Versions of *The Handmaid's Tale.*" *Journal of Popular Culture* 28.4 (Spring 1995): 49-61.

3671. DARROCH, Heidi. "Hysteria and Dramatic Testimony: Margaret Atwood's *Alias Grace.*" *Essays on Canadian Writing* 81 (2004): 103-121. Atwood's first historical novel, *Alias Grace*, is concerned in part with the relationship between trauma and confessional discourse. The novel's depiction of a convicted "murderess" as a trauma survivor with a complex and painful story to tell allows Atwood a means to investigate both 19th-century and 20th-century theories of traumatic memory and amnesia. In the process, Atwood raises questions about the reliability of both autobiographical memories and historical narratives.

3672. DAVIDSON, Arnold E. "Arnold Davidson on 'Historical Notes'": *Margaret Atwood's* The Handmaid's Tale. Ed. Harold Bloom. Philadelphia: Chelsea House, 2004. 85-88. Excerpt from "Future Tense: Making History in *The Handmaid's Tale.*" *Margaret Atwood: Vision and Forms.* Ed. Kathryn VanSpanckeren and Jan Garden Castro. Carbondale: Southern Illinois UP, 1988. 114-115, 120-121.

3673. DEER, Glenn. "Glenn Deer on Sanctioned Narrative Authority." *Margaret Atwood's* The Handmaid's Tale. Ed. Harold Bloom. Philadelphia: Chelsea House, 2004. 90-91. Excerpt from "*The Handmaid's Tale*: Dystopia and the Paradoxes of Power." *Margaret Atwood.* Ed. Harold Bloom. Philadelphia: Chelsea House, 2004.

93-112. Reprinted from *Post-Modern Canadian Fiction and the Rhetoric of Authority*. Montreal: McGill-Queens UP, 1994.

3674. DJWA, Sandra. "P. K. Page: A Portrait of the Artist as a Young Woman." *Journal of Canadian Studies / Revue d'études canadiennes* 38.1 (2004): 9-22. Includes an analysis of how Page's early poetry and prose influenced later writers such as Margaret Atwood.

3675. DOPP, Jamie. "Jamie Dopp on Limited Perspective." *Margaret Atwood's* The Handmaid's Tale. Ed. Harold Bloom. Philadelphia: Chelsea House, 2004. 92-93. Excerpt from "Subject-Position as Victim-Position in *The Handmaid's Tale.*" *Studies in Canadian Literature* 19.1 (1994): 43-57.

3676. EHRENREICH, Barbara. "On Feminist Dystopia." *Margaret Atwood's* The Handmaid's Tale. Ed. Harold Bloom. Philadelphia: Chelsea House, 2004. 78-80. Excerpt from "Feminism's Phantoms: *The Handmaid's Tale* by Margaret Atwood." *New Republic* 17 March 1986: 33-35.

3677. FEUER, Lois. "Lois Feuer on *The Handmaid's Tale* and *1984.*" *Margaret Atwood's* The Handmaid's Tale. Ed. Harold Bloom. Philadelphia: Chelsea House, 2004. 97-100. Excerpt from "The Calculus of Love and Nightmare: *The Handmaid's Tale* and the Dystopian Tradition." *Critique: Studies in Contemporary Fiction* 38.2 (1997): 83-95.

3678. GARDINER, Anne Barbeau. "The Interrelated Defense of Abortion and Pornography in Margaret Atwood's *The Handmaid's Tale.*" *Life and Learning XIII: Proceedings of the Thirteenth University Faculty for Life Conference at Georgetown University 2003*. Ed. Joseph W. Koterski, S.J. Washington, DC: University Faculty for Life [Georgetown University], 2004. 87-101.

3680. GRABENHORST, Tina. "A Mitten of Bird (with Original Writing, Poetry)." MA thesis. University of Windsor, 2004. 108 pp. Also available on microfiche from Canadian Theses Service (2005). This thesis project consists of two sections: the first is a collection of the author's own poetry, chiefly lyric, but also narrative and confessional, written for this project; the second is a paper on her poetics, in which she explores ecopoetry, with a focus on how her work fits within the genre both stylistically and thematically, and on her own writing in relation to other poets on the subject of nature, including Margaret Atwood. For more see *MAI* 43.01 (February 2005): 58.

3681. GRACE, Sherrill. *Inventing Tom Thomson: From Biographical Fictions to Fictional Autobiographies and Reproductions*. Montreal; Kingston: McGill-Queens, 2004. Includes numerous references to Atwood.

3682. GRIFFITHS, Anthony. "Genetics According to *Oryx and Crake.*" *Canadian Literature / Littérature canadienne* 181 (2004): 192-195.

3683. GRONEWOLD, Laura. "Margaret Atwood's Evil Women in *Lady Oracle, Cat's Eye*, and *The Robber Bride.*" MA thesis. University of Montana–Missoula, 2004.

3684. HEILAND, Donna. *Gothic & Gender*. Malden, MA: Blackwell, 2004. See especially Chapter 8, "Feminist, Postmodern, Postcolonial: Margaret Atwood and Ann-Marie MacDonald Respond to the Gothic," 156-179. Published in a different form as "Postmodern Gothic: Lady Oracle and its Eighteenth Century Antecedents." *RSSI (Recherches sémiotiques / Semiotic Inquiry)* 12.1-2 (1992): 115-136. This chapter also includes a discussion of *The Blind Assassin*.

3685. HILL, Colin. "Atwood, Margaret Eleanor (1939–)." *Dictionary of Literary Influences: The Twentieth Century, 1914-2000*. Ed. John Powell. Westport, CT: Greenwood Press, 2004. 24-25. Enumerates without proof the authors who have influenced Atwood.

3686. HILTON, Lisa. "From the Lilac House." MALS thesis. State University of New York–Empire State College, 2004. "The journey theme is explored through the creation of a poetry manuscript, *From the Lilac House.* This is accomplished through research of the way this theme is carried out in particular mythological tales, historical texts, and travel essays. The poetry of Margaret Atwood, Basho, Elizabeth Bishop, Gwendolyn Brooks, and Pablo Neruda is also considered with attention to how the poets create a sense of place. The creative process is discussed in terms of a journey, tracing the development of poems through inspiration and revision to the final version." (Author). For more see *MAI* 42.06 (December 2004): 1969.

3687. HORLACHER, Stefan. "Daniel Martin, America, Faith in Fakes / Travels in Hyperreality und das Verschwinden der Realität-Überlegungen zum Antizipatorischen Potential von Literatur." *Beyond Extremes: Repräsentation und Reflexion von Modernisierungsprozessen im Zeitgenössischen Britischen Roman.* Ed. Stefan Glomb and Stefan Horlacher. Tübingen: Narr, 2004. 291-329. John Fowles's *Daniel Martin* set off against Atwood's *The Edible Woman,* both within their cultural context.

3688. HOWELLS, Coral Ann. "Margaret Atwood: *Alias Grace.*" *Where Are the Voices Coming From? Canadian Culture and the Legacies of History.* Ed. Coral Ann Howells. Amsterdam: Rodopi, 2004. 29-37.

3689. INGERSOLL, Earl G. "Survival in Margaret Atwood's *Oryx and Crake.*" *Extrapolation: A Journal of Science Fiction and Fantasy* 45.2 (2004): 162-175.

3690. KETTERER, David. "'Another Dimension of Space': Canadian Science Fiction and Fantasy and Atwood's *Blind Assassin.*" *Worlds of Wonder: Readings in Canadian Science Fiction and Fantasy Literature.* Ed. Jean-François Leroux and Camille R. La Bossière. Ottawa: University of Ottawa Press, 2004. 8-34.

3691. KOROLCZUK, Elizabeth. "One Woman Leads to Another: Female Identity in the Works of Margaret Atwood." *American Studies* (Warsaw) 21 (2004): 35-51.

3692. KU, Chung-hao. "Eating, Cleaning, and Writing: Female Abjection and Subjectivity in Margaret Atwood's *The Blind Assassin.*" *Concentric: Literary and Cultural Studies* 30.1 (January 2004): 93-129.

3693. KYSER, Kristina. "Reading Canada Biblically: A Study of Biblical Allusion and the Construction of Nation in Contemporary Canadian Writing." PhD thesis. University of Toronto, 2004. 229 pp. "This is a study of the use of biblical allusion by Canadian thematic critics of the 1960s and '70s and by Canadian novelists writing in the 1990s and following. It examines the manner in which Canada has been constructed through such allusions over the last four decades. In doing this it addresses, from a new perspective, several issues that have long been relevant to the study of literature in Canada, including the definition of 'Canadian' and the related importance of nationalism. The argument is ordered around four central biblical events (Creation, the Deluge, the Incarnation, and the Crucifixion)." (Author). The texts considered include writings of critics such as Atwood. For more see *DAI-A* 65.10 (April 2005): 3812.

3694. LOUDERMILK, Kim A. *Fictional Feminism: How American Bestsellers Affect the Movement for Women's Equality.* New York: Routledge, 2004. See especially Chapter 5, "'Consider the Alternatives': Feminism and Ambivalence in Margaret Atwood's *The Handmaid's Tale,*" 123-148. Argues that the book betrays a profound ambivalence towards certain tendencies in feminist theory and practice.

3695. MacPHERSON, Heidi Slettedahl. "Prison, Passion, and the Female Gaze: Twentieth-Century Representations of Nineteenth-Century Panopticons." *In the Grip of the Law: Trials, Prisons and the Space Between.* Ed. Monica Fluderniok and Greta Olson. Frankfurt: Peter Lang, 2004. 205-221. References to *Alias Grace.*

3696. MALAK, Amin. "Amin Malak on Atwood in the Dystopian Tradition." *Margaret Atwood's* The Handmaid's Tale. Ed. Harold Bloom. Philadelphia: Chelsea House, 2004. 82-84. Excerpt from "Margaret Atwood's *The Handmaid's Tale* and the Dystopian Tradition." *Canadian Literature* 112 (Spring 1987): 9-11, 15.

3697. MANGUEL, Alberto. *A Reading Diary.* New York: Farrar, Straus & Giroux, 2004. Includes Atwood's *Surfacing,* which was read during April 2003. 175-188.

3698. MASSOURA, Kiriaki. "'I Look at It and See My Life Entire': Language, Third-Eye Vision and Painting in Margaret Atwood's *Cat's Eye.*" *British Journal of Canadian Studies* 17:2 (2004): 210-223.

3699. ———. "Margaret Atwood: Ena Psifidoto Erotismou, Ponou Kai Epiviosis." (Margaret Atwood: A Mosaic of Eroticism, Pain, and Survival). *Diavazo* 450 (2004): 96-102.

3700. McCARTHY, E. "Margaret Atwood and the Female Bildungsroman." PhD thesis. Bristol University, 2004. "This thesis examines Margaret Atwood's work in the context of the complex history of the Bildungsroman, or novel of personal development....[It] demonstrates that Atwood's early work, her own 'coming of age' fiction *The Edible Woman* (1969), *Lady Oracle* (1976), and her collection of short stories, *Dancing Girls* (1977), both engage with and work against the ideas of unity of identity which are traditionally associated with the genre....It examines the ways in which Atwood's later novels, namely *Cat's Eye* (1988), *The Robber Bride* (1993), and *The Blind Assassin* (2000) revisit and develop the formulations of selfhood and identity put forward in her early fiction. It goes on to survey the Canadian female Bildungsroman in English since the late 1970s, considering Atwood's influence on these later developments." (Author).

3701. MUNDLER, Helen E. "Heritage, Pseudo-Heritage and Survival in a Spurious Wor(l)d: *Oryx and Crake* by Margaret Atwood." *Commonwealth Essays and Studies* 27.1 (2004): 89-98.

3702. NEWLAND, Nancy. "Journeys of Self-Transformation in Contemporary Literature." MALS thesis. State University of New York–Empire State College, 2004. 72 pp. "This study's objective is to follow the development and maturation of three characters in contemporary literature in order to gain insight into the process of self-development using Quoyle from *The Shipping News* by Annie Proulx, Iris Chase Griffen from Margaret Atwood's *The Blind Assassin,* and Sister John from *Lying Awake* by Mark Salzman. It presents a discussion of how literature reflects life and why fictional characters can be considered real people. The tools of interpretation used to analyze the characters' life journeys include concepts of the psychology of being by Abraham Maslow and John Welwood, the tale of Cupid and Psyche and its implications in the development of conscious relationship, insights into literature by Carolyn Heilbrun and Ian Watt, and the role of mysticism and epilepsy in contemplative life." (Author). For more see *MAI* 42.05 (October 2004): 1484.

3703. OATES-INDRUCHOVÁ, Libora. "Initiation Motives in Margaret Atwood's *The Robber Bride.*" *Theory and Practice in English Studies.* Ed. Pavel Drábek and Jan Chovanec. Brno: Masaryk University, 2004. 127-134.

3704. PARKIN-GOUNELAS, Ruth. "'What Isn't There' in Margaret Atwood's *The Blind Assassin:* The Psychoanalysis of Duplicity." *Modern Fiction Studies* 50.3 Fall (2004): [681]-700. Atwood's *The Blind Assassin* has to do with memory as retrospection, temporality being figured spatio-materially, with the emphasis on vision. In attempting to "fix" time through an obsessive elaboration of material objects, the novel foregrounds the lure and deception of the visual, the way images, like symbols, function, to stand in for what isn't there. Images of duplicity or doubling, encapsulated in the photo of the two often indistinguishable sisters, torn in half, suggest a return to that moment of simultaneous self-identity and self-alienation in the mirror, described by Lacan as a violent "tearing" between self and other, a perpetual (self-) assassination.

3705. RIDOUT, Alice Rachel. "'To Be and Not to Be': The Politics of Parody in Toni Morrison, Margaret Atwood, and Doris Lessing (Zimbabwe)." PhD thesis. University of Toronto, 2004. 259 pp. Also available on microfiche from Canadian Theses Service (2005). "Parody enables these writers to position themselves simultaneously inside and outside discourse, a position Carolyn Heilbrun identifies particularly with women and captures in the image of the threshold. Toni Morrison, Margaret Atwood, and Doris Lessing are all on the threshold or margin of their national cultures....In my thesis, I show how Margaret Atwood uses parody to negotiate contradictory contemporary models of subjectivity. In *Lady Oracle*, Joan succeeds in telling her life story through self-parody....Parody emphasizes process as it takes finished texts and turns them into part of the process of creating a new text. Atwood's and Lessing's highly self-reflexive novels, *The Blind Assassin* and *The Golden Notebook*, exploit this aspect of parody to reflect the incessant process of writing a woman's life." (Author). For more see *DAI-A* 65.05 (November 2004): 1776.

3706. ROUSSELOT, E. "Re-writing Women into Canadian History: Margaret Atwood and Anne Hébert." PhD thesis. University of Kent, 2004. *The Journals of Susanna Moodie* as well as *Alias Grace* among works examined.

3707. SHURBUTT, Sylvia Bailey. "Margaret Atwood, 1939– ." *World Writers in English, Vol. 1: Chinua Achebe to V. S. Naipaul*. Ed. Jay Parini. New York: Scribner's, 2004. 59-80.

3708. SIDDALL, Gillian. "'This Is What I Told Dr. Jordan...' Public Constructions and Private Disruptions in Margaret Atwood's *Alias Grace*." *Essays on Canadian Writing* 81 (2004): 84-102. Atwood's historical novel *Alias Grace* includes a number of excerpts from the public media of the day in which Grace Marks is discursively constructed not just as a murderer but also as someone who strays from normative femininity—as a violent deviant who fails to live up to her feminine role as purveyor of moral values and keeper of the domestic realm. This article explores the ways in which Atwood's Grace critiques these ideologies and disrupts public discourses of class and gender.

3709. SOLECKI, Sam, ed. *Yours, Al: The Collected Letters of Al Purdy*. Madeira Park, BC: Harbour: 2004. Includes correspondence by and about Atwood.

3710. STAELS, Hilde. "Atwood's Specular Narrative: *The Blind Assassin*." *English Studies: A Journal of English Language and Literature* 85.2 April (2004): 147-160.

3711. STEIN, Karen. "Karen Stein on Frame and Discourse." *Margaret Atwood's* The Handmaid's Tale. Ed. Harold Bloom. Philadelphia: Chelsea House, 2004. 95-97. Excerpt from "Margaret Atwood's Modest Proposal: *The Handmaid's Tale*." *Canadian Literature* 148 (Spring 1996): 69-70.

3712. STEVENSON, Sharon. "The Nature of 'Outsider Dystopias': Atwood, Starhhawk, and Abbey." *The Utopian Fantastic: Selected Essays from the Twentieth International Conference on the Fantastic in the Arts*. Ed. Martha A. Bartter. Westport, CT: Praeger, 2004. 129-136. Paper originally delivered in 1999.

3713. STIMPSON, Catharine R. "On 'Atwood Woman.'" *Margaret Atwood's* The Handmaid's Tale. Ed. Harold Bloom. Philadelphia: Chelsea House, 2004. 80-81. Excerpt from "Atwood Woman." *The Nation* 31 May 1986: 764-765.

3714. TOLAN, Fiona. "Connecting Theory and Fiction: Margaret Atwood's Novels and Second Wave Feminism." PhD thesis. University of Durham, 2004. 307 pp. "This thesis undertakes an examination of the manner in which a novelist interacts with a contemporary theoretical discourse. I argue that the novelist and the theoretical discourse enter into a symbiotic relationship in which each influences and is influenced by the other. This process, I suggest, is simultaneous and complex. The thesis demonstrates how the prevailing theoretical discourse is absorbed by the contemporary author, is developed and redefined in conjunction with alternative concerns, and comes to permeate the narrative in an altered state. The novelist's new perspectives, frequently problematising theoretical claims, are then disseminated by the novel, promoting further discussion and development of the theoretical discourse." (Author).

3715. TRIGG, Tina. "Casting Shadows: A Study of Madness in Margaret Atwood's Novels." PhD thesis. University of Ottawa, 2004. 432 pp. "Madness is a recurrent aspect of Margaret Atwood's novels to date and represents perhaps her most discomforting challenge to the reader who is implicated as co-creator, interpreter, and participant of the fiction....The particular areas of investigation include: Atwood's comical representation of psychology as a prominent undercurrent of popular culture in *The Edible Woman*, and her contrasting serious—even threatening—portrayal of normative limits as social constructs in *Bodily Harm*. With regard to the individual, *Lady Oracle* exhibits the role of fantasy in psychic balance and posits the protagonist as an unlikely manifestation of 'normality.' Although still focused on the individual, *Life Before Man* represents the converse: the capacity for fantasy is lost in the dissociated condition of 'normalized' characters. The Jungian process of individuation is studied through the projection of one's shadow figure in *The Robber Bride*. Finally, Atwood's most direct and strategic implication of the reader in determining the variable boundaries of (in)sanity is examined in *Alias Grace*." (Author). For more see *DAI-AI* 64.10 (April 2004): 3692-3693.

3716. UPPAL, Priscila. "Recovering the Past through Language and Landscape: The Contemporary English-Canadian Elegy." PhD thesis. York University (ON), 2004. 393 pp. Also available on microfiche from Canadian Theses Service (2005). "The dissertation explores how the consolatory sites of landscape and language provide contemporary English-Canadian elegists with a means for reconnection between the living and the dead, thereby diverging from their conventional roles in the traditional English elegy and in conventional mourning practices. Whereas successful mourning in psychological (Freud), anthropological (Van Gennep), and literary (Orphic elegy) models has previously been determined by the achievement of separation between the mourner and the dead, these elegies reorient the focus of mourning as an inclusive and dialectic process of creative exchange. The work of mourning, therefore, is understood as an active and repeated process of connection and invention." (Author). Atwood among poets discussed. For more see *DAI-A* 66.01 (July 2005): 184.

3717. VERDUYN, Christl, and Kathleen GARAY, eds. *Marian Engel: Life in Letters*. Toronto: University of Toronto Press, 2004. Includes letters both to and from Atwood, as well as a number of references to Atwood in Engel's letters to others.

3718. VERWAAYEN, Kimberly J. "Fiction Alices: Through the Looking-Glass of Poststructuralist AutoBYography, and, Four (Eight? Fifteen?) Canadian Women's

Texts (Daphne Marlatt, Anne Michaels, Margaret Atwood, Joan Crate)." PhD thesis. University of Western Ontario, 2004. 311 pp. Also available on microfiche from Canadian Theses Service (2004). "This thesis explores issues of authorial property and voice in relation to textual identities in / and gendered bodies, informed by proliferating autobiographical theories and poststructuralist understanding of ambulatory subjectivities. Always-already tenuous distinctions between self and other, fact and fiction, autobiography and biography are exploded along 'fault' lines triggered by writers whose work in 'fiction/theory' / 'fictionalysis' blows up the field of representation / representability itself." (Author). Atwood among writers examined. For more see *DAI-A* 65/11: 4205 (May 2005).

3719. WALLACK, Karen M. "The Question of Power: Margaret Atwood's *Cat's Eye* through a Foucauldian Optic." MA thesis. Bowling Green State University, 2004.

3720. WHIDDEN, Abra Lynn. "Feminist Fallen Women: Rewriting Interwar Patriarchy in Margaret Atwood's *The Blind Assassin*, Ann-Marie MacDonald's *Fall on Your Knees*, and Gail Anderson-Dargatz's *A Recipe for Bees*.'" MA thesis. Acadia University, 2004. 146 pp. Also available on microfiche from Canadian Theses Service (2004). "In *The Blind Assassin*, *Fall on Your Knees*, and *A Recipe for Bees*, Margaret Atwood, Ann-Marie MacDonald, and Gail Anderson-Dargatz provide a contemporary Canadian contrast to the Fallen Woman trope by daring to let their fallen heroines live. Although their protagonists commit adultery, prostitute themselves, or have illegitimate children, the three authors allow their protagonists to live and to pass down their stories to future generations. While the authors end their novels with different degrees of hope and integration for their fallen protagonists, they all subvert patriarchy in three ways: first, they reveal the flaws in and the complexity of patriarchy; second, they create protagonists who undermine patriarchy by deliberately becoming fallen women; and third, they broaden the scope of feminist action beyond individual acts of resistance to the larger theme of female communication and community." (Author). For more see *MAI* 43.02 (April 2005): 401.

3721. WHITSON, Kathy J. *Encyclopedia of Feminist Literature* Westport, CT; London: Greenwood Press, 2004. See especially "Margaret Atwood." 20-24. Almost exclusive reference to *The Handmaid's Tale.*

3722. WYATT, Jean. *Risking Difference: Identification, Race, and Community in Contemporary Fiction and Feminism.* Albany: State University of New York Press, ©2004. See especially Chapter 1, "The Politics of Envy in Academic Feminist Communities and in Margaret Atwood's *The Robber Bride*," 20-41.

Reviews of Atwood's Works

3723. *Bashful Bob and Doleful Dorinda.* Toronto: Key Porter, 2004.
   Globe and Mail 11 December 2004: D18. By Bill RICHARDSON.
   London Free Press 18 December 2004: Section: Lifestyles: C10. By Barbara TAYLOR.

3724. *Moving Targets: Writing with Intent.* Toronto: Anansi, 2004.
   Globe and Mail 2 October 2004: D8. By J. S. PORTER.
   Guelph Mercury 6 November 2004: Section: Books: D4. By Robert REID. (877 w).
   Hamilton Spectator 25 September 2004: Section: G0: G15. By Moira L. MacKINNON. (655 w).

London Free Press 25 September 2004: Section: Lifestyles: D8. By Nancy
   SCHIEFFER. (948 w).
National Post 16 October 2004: RB7. By David GILMOUR.
The Record (Kitchener-Waterloo) 6 November 2004: Section: Books: P3.
   By Robert REID. (877 w).
The Telegram (St. John's, NF) 24 October 2004: B4. By Robin McGRATH.
Toronto Life 34.10 (October 2004): 90. Atwood's book compared to Margaret
   Wente's *An Accidental Canadian.*
3725. *Negotiating with the Dead.* New York: Cambridge UP, 2002.
   Cambridge Quarterly 33:2 (2004): 184-187. By Sarah SAVITT.
   Canadian Literature 183 (Winter 2004): 90-92. By Janice FIAMENGO. "At-
      wood deserves respect for her willingness to engage a wide readership in dis-
      cussing the social meaning of literature, and she has undoubtedly created an
      accessible volume that will enable interested readers to follow up on the mag-
      nificent sources she has brought together. Still, it is hard to escape the conclu-
      sion that she has put less than she is capable of into these essays. In recycling
      old material and emphasizing humour over complexity, she has not done jus-
      tice to her subject."
   Contemporary Literature 44.4 (Winter 2004): 737-743. By Susan STREHLE.
   Letters in Canada 73.1 (Winter 2003-2004): 348-350. By Sherrill GRACE.
   Studies in the Novel 36.1 (Spring 2004): 126-128. By Earl INGERSOLL.
      Correction by publisher in *Studies in the Novel* 36.2 (Summer 2004): 233.
3726. *Oryx and Crake.* Toronto: Seal; London: Virago, 2004.
   Canadian Literature 183 (Winter 2004): 92-93. By Coral Ann HOWELLS.
3727. *Oryx and Crake.* New York: Anchor Books, 2004.
   Canadian Literature 181 (Summer 2004): 192-196. By Anthony GRIFFITHS.
   Eigo Seinen / Rising Generation 150.5 (August 2004): 298. By Ayako SATO.
      In Japanese.
   Environmental Politics 13.2 (Autumn 2004): 642-650. By Andrew DOBSON.
   The Guardian (London) 10 April 2004: Section: Guardian Saturday Pages: 31.
      By Isobel MONTGOMERY. (144 w).
   Hudson Review 57.1 (Spring 2004): 133-140. By Tom WILHELMUS.
      Also reviewed: *Platform* by Michael Houllebecq; *The Namesake* by Jhumpa
      Lahiri; *The Great Fire* by Shirley Hazzard.
   Irish Times 24 April 2004: Section: Weekend: Paperbacks: 62. By Eileen BAT-
      TERSBY. (166 w). "There are moments of pathos, but ultimately the novel is
      too ironic, too farcically bleak and far too knowingly clever. Atwood's heav-
      ily satiric tone consistently overpowers her post-apocalyptic narrative, leaving
      it contrived and a bit laboured."
   Leonardo 37.5 (2004): 416-417. By G. GESSERT.
   Organization & Environment 17.4 (December 2004): 549-551.
      By G. R. BERRY.
   South China Morning Post 28 March 2004: Section: Paperbacks: 8. ANON.
      (150 w). "It's a novel of ideas rather than plot and she finishes her tale by
      coming to an abrupt end."
   Sunday News (Lancaster, PA) 11 January 2004: Section: P: 5. Helen Colwell
      ADAMS. (267w).
   Sunday Times (London) 4 April 2004: Section: Features: 54. By Trevor LEWIS.
      (237 w).

The Times (London) 20 March 2004: Section: Features: 16. By Chris POWER. (159 w).

Washington Post 2 May 2004: Section: Book World: T11. ANON. (207 w).

3728. *Oryx and Crake.* [Sound recording]. Read by Alex Jennings. [London]: Bloomsbury, 2003.

Irish Times 17 January 2004. ANON. (126 w). "Each of the tracks on this 'CD audiobook' is 15 minutes long. So what do you do when you're eight minutes into a track and are forced to switch it off for some reason? Go back and listen to the eight minutes again? Or skip to the next track and miss something crucial? Remember good old stop/start audiotape? Did somebody say the future just got worse?"

3729. *Oryx and Crake.* [Sound recording]. Read by Campbell Scott. Santa Ana, CA: Books on Tape, 2003.

Library Journal 128.20 (15 December 2004): 184. By Laurie SELWYN.

3730. *Rude Ramsay and the Roaring Radishes.* Toronto, Key Porter.

Kirkus Reviews 72.16 (15 August 2004): 802.

Publishers Weekly 23 August 2004: Section: PW Forecasts: 54. ANON. (293 w).

School Library Journal 50.11 (November 2004): 90. By Caroline WARD. "A rather wretched effort."

Sunday Telegram (MA) 5 September 2004: Section: Insight: G5. By Nicholas BASBANES. (127 w).

Washington Post 7 November 2004: Section: Book World: T11. By Elizabeth WARD. (138 w).

3731. *Strange Things: The Malevolent North in Canadian Literature.* London: Virago, 2004. Originally published in 1995 by Oxford UP.

Independent on Sunday 28 March 2004 Section: Features: 31. By Murrough O'BRIEN. (220 w).

3732. *Survival: A Thematic Guide to Canadian Literature.* Toronto: McClelland and Stewart, 2004.

Canadian Literature 183 (Winter 2004): 191-193. By Janice FIAMENGO.

Reviews of Adaptations of Atwood's Works

3733. *The Edible Woman.* Adapted by Dave CARLEY. Winnipeg: Scirocco Drame, 2002. Play based on the novel.

Calgary Herald 17 April 2004: Section: Entertainment: C6. By Bob CLARK. (502 w).

Columbus Dispatch 20 March 2004: Section: Features: 4B. By Michael ROSSBERG. (507 w).

3734. RUDERS, Poul. *The Handmaid's Tale.* Copenhagen: Edition Wilhelm Hansen, 1998-2002?

Performance in Toronto (2004) reviewed:

Buffalo News 4 October 2004: Section: Entertainment: C7. By Herman TROTTER. (542 w).

Globe and Mail 24 September 2004: A10. By Robert EVERETT-GREEN.

Maclean's 20 September 2004: Section: Film/Television/Music/Books/ Performing Arts/Games: 62. By Lianne GEORGE. (444 w).

Toronto Star 24 September 2004: Section: Entertainment: C11. By William LITTLER. (673 w).

Toronto Sun 25 September 2004: Section: Entertainment: 43. By John COULBOURN. (590 w).

Variety 18-24 October 2004: Section: Legit Reviews: B47. By Richard OUZOUNIAN. (1084 w).

~ 2005 ~

Atwood's Works

3735. "After the Last Battle." *New York Review Books* 52.6 (2005): 38-39. Review of *Visa for Avalon* by Bryher.

3736. *Alias Grace.* Toronto: Emblem; London: Virago, 2005. Paperback reprint.

3737. "Aliens Have Taken the Place of Angels." *The Guardian* 17 June 2005: Section: *Guardian* Friday Pages: 5. On the difference between science fiction and speculative fiction. (845 w).

3738. "And Who Told You to Pull My Strings?" *The Times* (London) 25 June 2005: Section: Features: 12. Review of Eileen Blumenthal's *Puppetry and Puppets*. (1184 w). Excerpt: "Among my own first literary efforts was a puppet show, performed by me at the age of 6, using a cardboard box for a stage. In it, a morally reprehensible giant got squashed by the Moon, a fate I have since longed to visit on various world leaders. As an adolescent, I went on to a hand-puppet troupe with a repertoire of cannibalistic crowd-pleasers—The Three Little Pigs, Little Red Riding Hood—performed to audiences of bloodthirsty 5-year-olds. Children of that age are not surprised by talking simulacra, but it really bothers them when the backdrop falls down and the whole thing is revealed as a fraud."

3739. "The Arctic." *Granta* 91 (Fall 2005): 225-226. Atwood discusses the shrinking of the ice cap around the Arctic and reflects on the possible consequences for humanity, which include the inundation of countries by rising seawater and the release of huge quantities of methane from organic matter due to the melting of the permafrost under the tundra.

3740. "The Art of Cooking and Serving: A Short Story." *Toronto Life* 39.8 (August 2005): 44-49. "The story is from a collection of stories by Margaret Atwood entitled *Moral Disorder*, which will be published by Bloomsbury in September 2006."

3741. "Autobiography." *Open Field: 30 Contemporary Canadian Poets.* Ed. Sina Queyras. New York: Persea Books, ©2005. 6. Short fiction. Reprinted from *Murder in the Dark*, ©1983.

3742. "Baumbaby." *Ein neuer Anfang.* Berlin: Berliner Taschenbuch Verlag, 2005. 11-14.

3743. *The Blind Assassin.* [Sound recording]. Read by Margot Dionne. New York: Random House; Prince Frederick, MD: Recorded Books, 2005. Compact disc, 15 sound discs (ca. 18 hr.).

3744. *The Blind Assassin.* [Sound recording]. Read by Michael O'Brien. Fredericton, NB: BTC Audiobooks, 2005. 3 compact discs (ca. 3 hr.).

3745. "Brave New World: Kazuo Ishiguro's Novel Really *Is* Chilling." *Slate Magazine* [www.slate.com] Posted 1 April 2005. Also available from Lexis-Nexis. A review of "*Never Let Me Go…*the 6th novel by Kazuo Ishiguro, who won the Booker Prize in 1989 for his chilling rendition of a bootlickingly devoted but morally blank English butler, *The Remains of the Day.*"

3746. "But It Still Could Still." *New Beginnings*. London; New York: Bloomsbury; Vancouver, BC: Raincoast, 2005. 5-6. Short fiction.

3747. "Chicken Little Goes Too Far." *Harper's Magazine* 311.1865 (October 2005): 78-79. Short story. [Ed. note: Atwood also converted this story into an original 15-page handwritten and illustrated book which was put up for bid on eBay as a fund-raising tool for the Canadian chapter of the World Wildlife Fund. See *Globe and Mail* 30 March 2005: R2.]

3748. "A Conversation." *Washington Post* 16 October 2005: Section: Book World: T10. Atwood interviews writer Patrick Lane on the occasion of the publication of his memoir, *What the Stones Remember*. (1089 w). Excerpt from her Introduction: "I was more than delighted to read *What the Stones Remember* when it came out, although I was also astonished by it. I had no idea that Pat's early life had been so vicious and abusive; nor did I know about his multiple addictions and the periods of total blackout he'd gone through. Perhaps the biggest surprise for me though was his love of nature, and especially of gardens and their healing pleasures, that the book revealed. It was almost as if a world previously viewed as dead or hostile had come benevolently to life. *What the Stones Remember* is a tough, lovely book and it shows the person that was in there through all the desperate times—a person who had now, finally, grown into his real skin."

3749. "Culture: 'She's Left Holding the Fort': Margaret Atwood Makes Her Acting Debut Tonight in Her Update of *The Odyssey*—Told from the Viewpoint of Odysseus's Wife. She and Phyllida Lloyd Explain Why." *The Guardian* 26 October 2005: Section: *Guardian* Features Page: 22. (1090 w). The two performers alternate in the explanation. Excerpt: "The book is in essence theatrical. It's a lot like the structure of a Greek tragedy, in that the central characters' stories are told in quite long monologues, then the chorus comment on the action. The book has the chorus line; the 12 women were hanged—pretty maids all in a row—with their feet twitching, which brings to mind the chorus line, except with a different kind of twitching feet. The singing and dancing in the court of Odysseus and Penelope would have been performed by slaves. Then the guests would be allowed to help themselves to the maids—they were entertainment, servants and sex toys all in one. Some of their numbers are written as songs, some dance numbers, some chanting."

3750. *Curious Pursuits: Occasional Writing 1970-2005*. London: Virago, 2005. Includes 47 short pieces penned by Atwood since 1973. Although the titles Atwood uses may vary, note that a number overlap with those published in *MT* [*Moving Targets: Writing with Intent, 1982-2004*. Toronto: Anansi, 2004 (see *MT* for sources or original publication)]. Includes "Introduction 1970-1989" 3-6.—"Travels Back" 7-13. Originally published: *Maclean's* 86 (January 1973): 28, 31, 49.—"Review of *Diving into the Wreck: Poems 1971-1972* by Adrienne Rich" 15-18. Originally published: *New York Times Book Review* 30 December 1973: 1-2.—"Review of *Anne Sexton: A Self-Portrait in Letters*" 19-21. Originally published: *New York Times Book Review* 6 November 1977: 15.—"The Curse of Eve—Or, What I Learned in School" 23-35. Originally published: *Women on Women*. Ed. Ann B. Shteir. Toronto: York University, Gerstein Lecture Series, 1978. 13-26.—

"Northrop Frye Observed" 37-45. Originally published: *Second Words: Selected Critical Prose 1960-1982* by Margaret Atwood. Toronto: Anansi, 1982. 398-406.—"Writing the Male Character" 47-63. Originally published: *This Magazine* 16.4 (September 1982): 4-10. A somewhat different version of this paper was delivered as the Hagey Lecture at Waterloo University, February 1982.— "Wondering What It's Like to Be a Woman" 65-70. [*MT*] (Review of *The Witches of* Eastwick by John Updike).—"Introduction to *Roughing It in the Bush* [*Or, Life in Canada*]" 71-78. [*MT*]. —"Haunted by Their Nightmares" 79-84. [*MT*] (Review of *Beloved* by Toni Morrison). —"Writing Utopia" 85-94. [*MT*].—"Great Aunts" 95-107. [*MT*].—"Introduction: Reading Blind." *The Best American Short Stories*. Ed. Margaret Atwood and Shannon Ravenel. 109-122. [*MT*].—"The Public Woman as Honorary Man" 123-125. [*MT*]. (Review of *The Warrior Queens* by Antonia Fraser).—"A Double-Bladed Knife: Subversive Laughter in Two Stories by Thomas King" 131-141. [*MT*].—"Nine Beginnings" 143-149. [*MT*].—"A Slave to His Own Liberation" 151-154. [*MT*] (Review of the *General in His Labyrinth* by Gabriel García Márquez).—"Angela Carter: 1940-1992" 155-157. Originally published: No source.—"Afterword to *Anne of Green Gables* by Lucy Maud Montgomery" 159-164. [*MT*]. —"Introduction: *The Early Years* [*The Poetry of Gwendolyn MacEwen*. Ed. Margaret Atwood and Barry Callaghan]" 165-169. [*MT*].—"Spotty-Handed Villainesses: Problems of Female Bad Behaviour in the Creation of Literature" 171-186. [*MT*].—"The Grunge Look" 187-196. [*MT*].— "Not So Grimm: The Staying Power of Fairy Tales" 197-201. [*MT*]. (Review of *From the Beast to the Blonde: On Fairy Tales and Their Writers* by Marina Warner).—"'Little Chappies with Breasts'" 203-207. [*MT*] (Review of *An Experiment in Love* by Hilary Mantel).—"In Search of *Alias Grace*: On Writing Canadian Historical Fiction" 209-229. [*MT*].—"Pinteresque" 241-242. Originally published: *Pinter Review: Annual Essays*, 2000: 5.—"Mordecai Richler, 1931–2001: Diogenes of Montreal" 243-244. [*MT*].—"When Afghanistan Was at Peace," 245-247. [*MT*].—"Introduction to *She* by Rider Haggard" 249-256. [*MT*].—"Introduction to *Doctor Glas* by Hjalmar Söderberg" 257-261. [*MT*].—"Mystery Man: Some Clues to Dashiell Hammett" 263-276. [*MT*]. (Review of *The Selected Letters of Dashiell Hammett, 1921-1960*, ed. Richard Layman and Julie Rivett; *Dashiell Hammett: A Daughter Remembers* by Jo Hammett, ed. Richard Layman and Julie Rivett; and *Dashiell Hammett: Crime Stories and Other Writings*, ed. Steven Marcus).—"Of Myths and Men" 277-280. [*MT*]. (Review of *Atanarjuat: The Fast Runner*, dir. Zacharias Kunuk, 2001).—"Cops and Robbers" 281-291. [*MT*]. (Review of *Tishomingo Blues* by Elmore Leonard).—"The Indelible Woman" 293-295. [*MT*]. (Comment on *To the Lighthouse* by Virginia Woolf).—"The Queen of Quinkdom" 297-308. [*MT*]. (Review of *The Birthday of the World and Other Stories* by Ursula K. Le Guin).—"'Victory Gardens' [Foreword] to *A Breath of Fresh Air: Celebrating Nature and School Gardens* by Elise Houghton" 309-316. [*MT*].— "Mortification" 317-320. [*MT*].—"Writing *Oryx and Crake*" 321-323. [*MT*].— "Letter to America" 325-328. [*MT*].—"Edinburgh and Its Festival" 329-332. Originally published: *Edinburgh Festival Magazine* May 2003: s.p.—"George Orwell: Some Personal Connections" 333-340. [*MT*].—"Carol Shields Who Died Last Week, Wrote Books That Were Full of Delights" 341-344. [*MT*].—"He Springs Eternal" 345-357. [*MT*]. (Review of *Hope Dies Last: Keeping the Faith in Difficult Times* by Studs Terkel).—"To Beechey Island" 359-368. [*MT*]. [Ed. note: In *Moving Targets* as well as *Writing with Intent*, Beechey is spelled without the "e"; the "y" remains.]—"Uncovered: An American *Iliad*" 369-375. (Review of the

3-volume series, Masterworks of the Classical Haida Mythtellers. v.1: *A Story as Sharp as a Knife: The Classical Haida Mythtellers and Their World* / Robert Bringhurst [Vancouver, BC: Douglas & McIntyre, 1999].—v.2: *Nine Visits to the Mythworld* / Gandl, Robert Bringhurst [Vancouver, BC: Douglas & McIntyre, 2002].—v.3: *Being in Being: The Collected Works of Skaay of the Qquuna Qiighawaay* / Skaay, Robert Bringhurst [Vancouver, BC: Douglas & McIntyre, 2001]). Originally published: *The Times* (London) 28 February 2004: Section: Features: 10.—"Headscarves to Die For" 377-381. (Review of *Snow*, Turkish writer Orthan Pamuk's 7th novel). Originally published: *New York Times* 15 August 2004: Section: 7: 1.—"Ten Ways of Looking at *The Island of Doctor Moreau*" 383-395. Originally published as the Introduction to *The Island of Doctor Moreau*. London: Penguin, 2005. xxiii-xxvii.

3751. *Dancing Girls and Other Stories.* [Sound recording]. Read by Aileen Seaton. Toronto: CNIB, 2005. Computer data (38 files: 456 mb).

3752. "Death by Landscape." *Sleepaway: Writings on Summer Camp.* Ed. Eric Simonoff. New York: Riverhead Books, 2005. 3-27. Reprinted from *Wilderness Tips*, ©1991.

3753. *Die Penelopiade: Der Mythos von Penelope und Odysseus.* Berlin: Berlin Verlag, 2005. German translation of *The Penelopiad* by Malte Friedrich.

3754. "Don, Still Roaming Four Centuries after His Creation: Cervantes' Hero Lives on in a Host of Artistic Reincarnations." *Financial Times* (London) 16 April 2005: Section: Weekend Magazine: 37. Atwood celebrates the 400th anniversary of "the wonderful Don Quixote." (902 w). "An edited extract of a speech Margaret Atwood will give at the PEN Literary Festival in New York this weekend to mark the 400th anniversary of the publication of *Don Quixote* in 1605."

3755. "Don't Ghettoize Women's Rights." *Globe and Mail* 10 September 2005: A23. By Atwood et al. An open letter to Ontario Premier Dalton McGuinty on the legalization of religious arbitration in Ontario.

3756. *The Edible Woman.* London: Virago, 2005 ©1969.

3757. "Foreword." *Toronto Tree Portraits: 2006 Calendar.* [Toronto]: Toronto Parks and Trees Foundation, 2005. [i].

3758. "Four Short Pieces: King Log in Exile, Post-Colonial, Salome Was a Dancer and Take Charge." *Daedalus* 134.2 (Spring 2005) 119-123. "King Log," 119-120. "Post-Colonial," 120-121. "Salome Was a Dancer," 121-122. "Take Charge," 122-123.

3759. "Frankenstein Monster Song." *New York Spleen: As Smart as We Are.* Paris: Naïve, 2005. 34.

3760. *The Handmaid's Tale.* London: Vintage, 2005. Paperback. (Vintage future classics).

3761. "Happy Endings." *3 x 33: Short Fiction by 33 Writers.* [Comp.] Mark Winegardner. Boston: Thomson Wadsworth, 2005. 26-28. Also in *Literature: An Introduction to Fiction, Poetry, and Drama.* Ed. X. J. Kennedy and Dana Gioia. 9th ed. New York: Pearson Longman, 2005. 497-501. Reprinted from *Good Bones and Simple Murders*, ©1983.

3762. "Haunted by Their Nightmares." *Toni Morrison.* Ed. Harold Bloom. Philadelphia: Chelsea House Publishers, 2005. 143-147. "Selected" reprint of book review that appeared in *New York Times Book Review* 13 September 1987.

3763. *Il Canto di Penelope.* Milan: Rizzoli, 2005. Italian translation of *The Penelopiad.*

3764. "Introduction." *The Island of Dr. Moreau.* H. G. Wells. London: Penguin, 2005. xxiii-xxvii.

3765. *L'odyssée de Pénélope*. Montréal: Boréal, 2005. French translation of *The Penelopead* by Lori Saint-Martin and Paul Gagné.

3766. "La chanson du monstre de Frankenstein." *New York Spleen: As Smart as We Are.* Paris: Naïve, 2005. 36-37.

3767. *La femme comestible*. [Sound recording]. Read by Michele Rivest. Toronto: CNIB, 2005. Computer data (11 files: 150 mb). French translation of *The Edible Woman* by Hélène Filion.

3768. *Le dernier homme*. Paris: R. Laffont, 2005. French translation of *Oryx and Crake* by Michèle Albaret-Maatsch.

3769. "A Letter from Margaret Atwood: The Novelist Answers Your Most Intimate Questions about Her Unotchit Remote Book-Signing Device, Starting with the Rumour That It's Nothing but a Hoax." *Globe and Mail* 12 February 2005: R12. (851 w).

3770. "The Loneliness of the Military Historian." *Open Field: 30 Contemporary Canadian Poets*. Ed. Sina Queyras. New York: Persea Books, ©2005. 8-11. Poem. Reprinted from *Morning in the Burned House*, ©1995.

3771. "Me and My Monster Hand: Some People Wondered If Her Invention of a Remote Book-Signing Device Wasn't a Bit Creepy. Margaret Atwood Insists That Her Intentions Are Purely Benevolent." *Globe and Mail* 22 January 2005: R9. (851 w).

3772. "The Moment." *Open Field: 30 Contemporary Canadian Poets*. Ed. Sina Queyras. New York: Persea Books, ©2005. 12. Poem. Reprinted from *Morning in the Burned House*, ©1995.

3773. *Morning in the Burned House*. [Sound recording]. Read by Kathleen Miller. Toronto: CNIB, 2005. Computer data (98 files: 23.9 mb).

3774. "Mother Atwood's Molasses Cookies." *A Fair Feast: 70 Celebrity Recipes for a Fairer World*. Comp. Vicky Bhogal. London: Simon and Schuster, 2005. 47. The actual recipe. "In memory of my grandmother, Mrs. Florence McGowan Atwood, of Nova Scotia, Canada." See 3792.

3775. *Muzhchina i zhenshchina v epokhu dinozavrov*. Moscow: Eksmo, 2005. Russian translation of *Life Before Man*. Title romanized.

3776. "My Life in Science Fiction / Ma vie et la science-fiction." *Cycnos* 22.2 (2005): 155-176.

3777. "The Myths Series and Me: Rewriting a Classic Is Its Own Epic Journey." *Publishers Weekly* 28 November 2005: Section: Soapbox: 58. (723 w).

3778. "The Myths Series and Me." *Read: Life with Books* 6.1 (2005): 35-38. [Ed. note: *Read: Life with Books* is a house organ of Random House of Canada also available at http://www.readmagazine.ca. (1 May 2006).]

3779. "Nightingale." *The Crucifix Is Down: Contemporary Short Fiction*. Ed. Kate Gale and Mark E. Cull. [Los Angeles]: Red Hen Press, 2005. 7-9. Reprinted from *Nightingale*. Toronto: Harbourfront Reading Series Chapbook, 2000. 9-15. Also available at http://www.redhen.org/files/pdf/188899634x.pdf.

3781. "On Flogging Poets and Catching Fish: At a Recent Writers' Festival in Iceland, Margaret Atwood Spoke Out about the Orhan Pamuk Case. Here's What She Had to Say." *Globe and Mail* 8 October 2005: R13. An excerpt from her address in defense of the writer about to stand trial in Turkey for having spoken about the deaths of Armenians and Kurds in that country at the time of the First World War. (775 w). [Ed. note: In the event, Turkey, in the spotlight because of its interest in joining the European Union, dropped the case. See Ercan Ersoy, "Writer Has Charges Dropped." *The Irish Times* 24 January 2006: Section: World: 9.]

3782. *Oryx and Crake*. Toronto: Emblem, 2005. Paperback.

3783. *Oryx y Crake*. Barcelona: Ediciones B, 2005. Spanish translation.

3784. *P`enellop`iadu: Odiseusu wa P`enellop`e*. Paju, South Korea: Munhak Tongne, 2005. Korean translation of *The Penelopiad* by Kim Chin-jun omgim. Title romanized.

3785. *Penélope y las doce criadas*. Barcelona: Salamandra, 2005. Spanish translation of *The Penelopiad*.

3786. *The Penelopiad*. Toronto: Knopf; New York; Edinburgh: Canongate, 2005. "I've chosen to give the telling of the story to Penelope and to the twelve hanged maids. The maids form a chanting and singing Chorus which focuses on two questions that must pose themselves after any close reading of *The Odyssey*: what led to the hanging of the maids, and what was Penelope really up to? The story as told in *The Odyssey* doesn't hold water: there are too many inconsistencies. I've always been haunted by the hanged maids; and, in *The Penelopiad*, so is Penelope herself." (From introduction).

3787. *The Penelopiad*. [Sound recording]. Read by Laural Merlington. Grand Haven, MI: Brilliance, 2005. Compact disc, 3 sound discs (3 hr.). Also available on cassette tape, 2 sound cassettes (3 hr.).

3788. *Pēnelopiāde: Mīts par Pēnelopi un Odiseju*. Rīga: Jāna Rozes apg., ©2005. Latvian translation by Ingūna Beķere.

3789. *Pozhiratel'nitsa grekhov*. Moscow: Eksmo, 2005. Russian translation of *Dancing Girls and Other Stories*, ©1982. Title romanized.

3790. *Pšrešzívá nejsmutnšejší*. Prague: Mladá Fronta, 2005. Czech translation of *Oryx and Crake* by Jana Housarová.

3792. "[Recipe]." *The Guardian* 7 September 2005: Section: *Guardian* Features Pages: 8. An excerpt from a new cookbook, *A Fair Feast: 70 Celebrity Recipes for a Fairer World*, compiled by Vicky Bhogal featuring fair-trade ingredients includes: Mother Atwood's Molasses Cookies "In memory of my grandmother, Mrs. Florence McGowan Atwood, of Nova Scotia, Canada."

> 1/2 cup Fairtrade sugar
> cup shortening (butter)
> 1/2 teaspoon salt
> 1 teaspoon ground ginger
> 1 cup molasses
> 1 teaspoon bicarbonate of soda, dissolved in 1/4 cup hot water
> 3 cups of white flour, plus flour for rolling
> 1. Cream the sugar and shortening together in a bowl.
> 2. Add the salt, ginger, and molasses, and mix well. Add the bicarbonate of soda and then the flour. Mix and knead well into a dough.
> 3. Roll out the dough and cut out with a cookie cutter. Place them on a greased baking tray.
> 4. Bake the cookies at 180C for 8 to 9 minutes. Place them on a wire rack to cool.

3793. "[Recommended reading]." *Washington Post* 4 December 2005: Section: Book World: T08. Atwood is one of 14 writers who were asked what book they would recommend to a friend craving a little escape from the world's cares. Her answer: "A book for a friend craving escape from the cares of the world? In a shameless act of cronyism, I will recommend *The Bedside Book of Birds* by Graeme Gibson—despite the fact that he's been my dear companion for 32 years—because it fills the bill perfectly. Your friend will be freed from those cares of the world in an instant, on wings of song and with the aid of 180 stunning images of bird-related artworks that Graeme collected from many times and places. The world your friend will escape into is the world of birds, but not just that—it's the world of humankind's imagining of birds. This miscellany—poems, bits of novels, myths, recipes and more—covers the whole range. By the time your friend gets to the last chapter, the one about Hope, that friend will be out of this world."

3794. "Romantic." *Sweeping Beauty: Contemporary Women Poets Do Housework.* Iowa City: University of Iowa Press, 2005. 6. Also in *Literature: An Introduction to Fiction, Poetry, and Drama.* Ed. X. J. Kennedy and Dana Gioia. 9th ed. New York: Pearson Longman, 2005. 1143. Reprinted from *Morning in the Burned House,* ©1995.

3795. *Rotznase Ramsay und die röhrenden Radieschen.* Berlin: Bloomsbury, 2005. German translation of *Rude Ramsay and the Roaring Radishes* by Malte Friedrich.

3796. *Rude Ramsay and the Roaring Radishes.* London: Bloomsbury Children's, 2005 ©2004.

3797. "A Sad Child." *I Just Hope It's Lethal: Poems of Sadness, Madness, and Joy.* Collected by Liz Rosenberg and Deena November. Boston: Graphia/Houghton Mifflin, 2005. 3-4. Reprinted from *Morning in the Burned House,* ©1995.

3798. *Slepoi ubiitsa.* Moscow: Eksmo, 2005. Russian translation of *The Blind Assassin.* Title romanized.

3799. "Small Cabin." *World Literature.* [Sound recording]. Princeton, NJ: Recording for the Blind & Dyslexic, 2005. Poem, originally published *Selected Poems 1965-1975.* Distribution is restricted to RFB&D members who have a documented print disability such as a visual impairment, learning disability, or other physical disability.

3800. "A Soap Bubble Hovering over the Void: A Tribute to Carol Shields." *Virginia Quarterly Review* 81.1 (2005): 139-142.

3801. "Something Has Happened." *New Beginnings.* London; New York: Bloomsbury; Vancouver, BC: Raincoast, 2005. 3. Short fiction.

3802. *Strange Things: The Malevolent North in Canadian Literature.* [Sound recording]. Read by Barbara Lyon. Toronto: CNIB, 2005 ©1995. Computer data (20 files: 70.3 mb).

3803. "Strawberries." *Open Field: 30 Contemporary Canadian Poets.* Ed. Sina Queyras. New York: Persea Books, ©2005. 7. Short fiction. Reprinted from *Murder in the Dark,* ©1983.

3804. "The Tent." *Harper's Magazine* 311.1865 (October 2005): 80.

3805. "Through the One-Way Mirror." [Sound recording]. *Language of Literature: The Interactive Reader.* [Ed.] Arthur N. Applebee. Princeton, NJ: Recording for the Blind & Dyslexic, 2005. Compact disc, 1 sound disc.

3806. "[Tip]." *New Scientist* 29 October 2005: Section: Creative Minds: 54. Atwood, one of 11 novelists, artists, and scientists who were asked for their top tips on how to be creative, wrote: "I have a great big cupboard stuffed with ideas and when I want one I open the door and take the first one that falls out. Alternatively, if you want an idea, do the following. Close your eyes, put your left hand on the ground, raise your right hand into the air. You are now a conductor. The ideas will pass through you. Sooner or later one will pass through your brain. It never fails, though the waiting times vary and sometimes lunch intervenes."

3807. "Travelling Through the Body." *Three Rivers: The Yukon's Great Boreal Wilderness.* Ed. Juri Peepre. Madeira Park, BC: Harbour Publishing, 2005. 11-17. Atwood's Introduction to this book.

3808. "Tree Baby." *New Beginnings*. London; New York: Bloomsbury; Vancouver, BC: Raincoast, 2005. 1-2. Short story.

3809. "True Trash." *3 x 33: Short Fiction by 33 Writers*. [Comp.] Mark Winegardner. Boston: Thomson Wadsworth, 2005. 43-59. Reprinted from *Wilderness Tips*, ©1991.

3810. "Variation on the Word *Sleep*." *Your Drive Me Crazy: Love Poems for Real Life*. Ed. Mary D. Esselman and Elizabeth Ash Vélez. New York: Warner Books, 2005. 15-16. Reprinted from *Selected Poems II: Poems Selected and New 1976-1986*, ©1987.

3811. "Voice." *Walrus* 2.6 (July-August 2005): 79. Short fiction; one of "Seven Love Letters: Meditations on Desire" from Atwood and 6 others.

3812. "Vultures." *The Bedside Book of Birds: An Avian Miscellany*. By Graeme Gibson. London: Bloomsbury, 2005. 204-205. Poem. From *True Stories*, ©1981.

3813. "Warlords." *Walrus* 2.2 (March 2005): 50. Short fiction.

3814. "What a Tangled Web She Wove." *The Times* (London) 22 October 2005: Section: Features: 12. (1029 w). An article triggered by her appearance on stage as Penelope: "On October 26, I may swing from a rope. Or I may be wrapped in a piece of fishnet, or I may rise sepulchrally from a darkened pulpit—all in St James's Church, Piccadilly, during a staged reading of *The Penelopiad*. I'll be impersonating Penelope, or such is the plan...."

3815. "Wilderness Tips." *3 x 33: Short Fiction by 33 Writers*. [Comp.] Mark Winegardner. Boston: Thomson Wadsworth, 2005. 29-42. Reprinted from *Wilderness Tips*, ©1991.

3816. *Writing with Intent: Essays, Reviews, Personal Prose, 1983-2005*. New York: Carroll & Graf Publishers, 2005. Includes 58 short pieces penned by Atwood since 1983. Although the titles Atwood uses may vary, note that a number overlap with those published in [*CP*] *Curious Pursuits: Occasional Writing 1970-2005*. London: Virago, 2005, or [*MT*] *Moving Targets: Writing with Intent, 1982-2004*. Toronto: Anansi, 2004 (see *CP* and/or *MT* for sources of original publication). Includes "Review: *The Witches of Eastwick* by John Updike" 6-11. [*MT, CP*].— "Laughter vs. Death" 12-18. Originally published: "Atwood on Pornography" *Chatelaine* 56 (September 1993): 61, 118+.—"Review: *Difficult Loves* by Italo Calvino" 19-21. [*MT*].—"That Certain Thing Called the Girlfriend" 22-30. (Women's friendships in novels by women). Originally published New *York Times Book Review* 91 (11 May 1986): 1+.—"True North" 31-45. [*MT*].—"Review: *Beloved* by Toni Morrison" 46-51. [*CP, MT*].—"Afterword: *A Jest of God* by Margaret Laurence" 52-55. [*MT*].—"Great Aunts" 56-67. [*CP, MT*].—"Introduction: Reading Blind: The Best American Short Stories 1989" 68-79. [*CP, MT*].— "Introduction: Women Writers at Work: *The Paris Review Interviews*, George Plimpton, editor" 80-88. Originally published: New York: Penguin, 1989. xi-xviii.—"Review: *The Warrior Queens* by Antonia Fraser" 89-91. [*CP, MT*].— "Writing Utopia" 92-100. [*CP, MT*].—"Nine Beginnings" 105-110. [*CP, MT*].— "Review: *The General in His Labyrinth* by Gabriel García Márquez" 111-114. [*CP, MT*].—"Afterword: *Anne of Green Gables* by Lucy Maud Montgomery" 115-120. [*CP, MT*].—"Why I Love *The Night of the Hunter*, a film by Charles Laughton" 121-124. [*CP, MT*]—"Spotty-Handed Villainesses: Problems of Female Bad Behaviour in the Creation of Literature" 125-138. [*CP, MT*].—"The Grunge Look" 139-146. [*CP, MT*].—"Review*: From the Beast to the Blonde: On Fairy Tales and Their Tellers* by Marina Warner" 147-150. [*CP, MT*].—"Review: *Burning Your Boats: The Collected Short Stories* by Angela Carter" 151-153. [*MT*].—"Review:

An Experiment in Love by Hilary Mantel" 154-157. [*CP, MT*].—"In Search of *Alias Grace*: On Writing Canadian Historical Fiction" 158-176. [*CP, MT*].— "Review: *Trickster Makes This World: Mischief, Myth, [and] Art* and *The Gift: Imagination and the Erotic Life of Property* by Lewis Hyde" 177-181. [*MT*].— "First Job, Waitressing" 189-191. Originally published as "Ka-Ching!" *New Yorker* 23, 30 April 2001: 72.—"Eulogy: Mordecai Richler, 1931–2001: Diogenes of Montréal" 192-193. [*CP, MT*].—Review: *According to Queeney* by Beryl Bainbridge" 194-197. Originally published as "A Novel Worthy of a Queen(Ey)." *Globe and Mail* 4 August 2001: D2.—"Introduction: *She* by H. Rider Haggard" 198-204. [*CP, MT*].—"When Afghanistan Was at Peace" 205-207. [*CP, MT*].— "Review: *The Selected Letters of Dashiell Hammett, 1921-1960*, ed. Richard Layman with Julie Rivett; *Dashiell Hammett: A Daughter Remembers* by Jo Hammett, ed. Richard Layman with Julie Rivett; and *Dashiell Hammett: Crime Stories and Other Writings*, ed. Steven Marcus" 208-219. [*CP, MT*].—"Review: *Atanarjuat: The Fast Runner*, a film by Zacharias Kunuk" 220-223. [*CP, MT*].—"Review: *Life of Pi* by Yann Martel" 224-226. Originally published as: "A Tasty Slice of Pi and Ships." *Sunday Times* (London) 5 May 2002: Section: Features.—"Review: *Tishomingo Blues* by Elmore Leonard" 227-236. [*MT*].—"Eulogy: Tiff and the Animals" 237-239. [*MT*].—"*To the Lighthouse* by Virginia Woolf" 240-242. [*CP, MT*].—"Review: *The Birthday of the World and Other Stories* by Ursula K. Le Guin" 243-253. [*CP, MT*].—"Introduction: *Ground Works*, Christian Bök, editor" 254-259. (*MT*).—"Introduction: *Doctor Glas* by Hjalmar Söderberg" 260-264. [*CP, MT*].—"Introduction: *High Latitudes* by Farley Mowat" 265-267. Originally published North Royalton, VT: Steerforth, 2002.—"Review: *Child of My Heart* by Alice McDermott" 268-276. Originally published as "Castle of the Imagination." *New York Review of Books* 50.1 (16 January 2003): 27-28.—"Napoleon's Two Biggest Mistakes" 277-279. [*MT*].—"Letter to America" 280-283. [*CP, MT*].— "Writing *Oryx and Crake*" 284-286. [*CP, MT*].—"George Orwell: Some Personnel Connections" 287-293. [*CP, MT*].— "Review: *Enough: Staying Human in an Engineered Age* by Bill McKibben" 294-304. [*MT*].—"Foreword: *Victory Gardens: A Breath of Fresh Air* by Elise Houghton" 305-312. [*CP, MT*].—"Eulogy: Carol Shields, Who Died Last Week, Wrote Books That Were Full of Delight" 312-316. [*CP, MT*].—"Review: *Reading* Lolita *in Tehran: A Memoir in Books* by Azar Nafisi" 317-321. Originally published as "The Book Lover's Tale: Using Literature to Stay Afloat in a Fundamentalist Sea." *Literary Review of Canada* September 2003: 5-6. [Ed. note. *Moving Targets* contains "Resisting the Veil: Reports from a Revolution," 364-371, which was originally published in *Walrus* and contains an essay reviewing the Nafisi book as well as *Persepolis: The Story of a Childhood* by Marjane Satrapi; *The Bathhouse* by Farnoosh Moshiri; *Shah of Shahs* by Ryszard Kapuściński; *The Crisis of Islam: Holy War and Unholy Terror* by Bernard Lewis; and *The Crusades Through Arab Eyes* by Amin Maalouf.]—"Introduction: *The Complete Stories, Volume 4* by Morley Callaghan" 322-330. [*MT*].—"Review: *Hope Dies Last: Keeping the Faith in Difficult Times* by Studs Terkel" 331-342. [*CP, MT*].—"Mortifications" 343-345. [*MT*].—"Review: *A Story as Sharp as a Knife: The Classical Haida Mythtellers and Their World* by Robert Bringhurst" 346-351.—"Review: *The Mays of Ventadorn* by W. S. Merwin" 352-355. Originally published: *American Poetry Review* 33.3 (May-June 2004): 29.—"Review: *Snow* by Orhan Pamuk" 356-359. [*CP*].—"Review: From *Eve to Dawn* by Marilyn French" 360-364. Originally published as "Handmaids' Tales." *The Times* (London) 21 August 2004: Section: Features: Weekend Review: 8.—"To Beechy Island" 365-374. [*CP. MT*].—"Introduction: *Frozen in Time: The Fate of the Franklin Expedition* [rev. ed.] by Owen Beattie and John Geiger" 375-381. Originally published Vancouver, BC: Greystone Books (Douglas & McIntyre), 2004. 1-8.— "Review: *Acquainted with the Night: Excursions Through the World After Dark* by Christopher Dewdney" 382-385. Originally published "A Little Light Musing." *Globe and Mail* 22 May 2004: D7. [Ed. note. *Writing with Intent* gives no source for this review (cf.405).]—"Introduction: Ten Ways of Looking at *The Island of Doctor Moreau* by H. G. Wells" 386-398. [*CP*].

3817. *Writing with Intent: Essays, Reviews, Personal Prose, 1983-2005.* [Sound recording]. Princeton, NJ: Recording for the Blind & Dyslexic, 2005. 1 sound disc. Distribution is restricted to RFB&D members who have a documented print disability such as a visual impairment, learning disability, or other physical disability.

3818. "You Fit into Me." *In Fine Form: The Canadian Book of Form Poetry.* Ed. Kate Braid and Sandy Shreve. Vancouver, BC: Polestar, an Imprint of Raincoast Books, 2005. 66. Also in *Literature: An Introduction to Fiction, Poetry, and Drama.* Ed. X. J. Kennedy and Dana Gioia. 9th ed. New York: Pearson Longman, 2005. 828. Reprinted from *Power Politics*, ©1973.

3819. "You Fit into Me." *The Seagull Reader: Poems.* [Sound recording]. Ed. Joseph Kelly. Princeton, NJ: Recording for the Blind & Dyslexic, 2005. 1 compact disc. Originally published: New York: W.W. Norton, ©2001. "Distribution is restricted to RFB&D members who have a documented print disability such as a visual impairment, learning disability or other physical disability."

Quotations

3821. "[Quote]." *Books in Canada* 34.7 (1 October 2005): 19. In a review of Orhan Pamuk's two recent books, Michael Harris, the reviewer, quotes Atwood, who, in an essay on duplicity, posited that every writer has two selves: "I mean," she explains, "the person who exists when no writing is going forward—the one who walks the dog, eats bran for regularity, takes the car to be washed, and so forth— and that other, more shadowy and altogether more equivocal personage who shares the same body, and who, when no one is looking, takes it over and uses it to commit the actual writing."

3822. "[Quote]." *Briar Patch* 34.7 (1 November 2005): 30. Theresa Green, in discussing new book about Ken Sprague, *The People's Artist*, quotes Atwood: "Creativity is an act of defying death."

3823. "[Quote]." *Daily Telegraph* (London) 3 December 2005: Section: Books: 1. In an article entitled "The Stuff of Life: We've Had a Taste for Cookbooks Since Before Printing Was Invented, Yet Most Recipes Get No Further Than the Page," Kate Colquhoun writes: "As Margaret Atwood said in 1987, 'One man's cookbook is another woman's soft porn: there is a certain sybaritic voyeurism involved, an indulgency by proxy.'"

3824. "[Quote]." *The Gazette* (Montreal) 5 March 2005: Section: News: A1. "Canada must be the only country in the world where a policeman is used as a national symbol."

3825. "[Quote]." *Maclean's* 10 October 2005: Section: Reflection: 7. Peter Newman, reviewing the history of *Maclean's*, noted that "when we published an article by Margaret Atwood and allowed a few errors to creep in, she sent me a pointed note: 'There's a wonderful invention kicking around. It's called the telephone. Some magazines use it for a process called checking. That's because they like the material they publish to be as accurate as possible. Sincerely, Margaret Atwood.'"

3826. "[Quote]." *Ottawa Citizen* 16 January 2005: Section: Citizen's Weekly: C13. Margaret Atwood on her last book tour and the inspiration behind her plans to create a remote autographing device: "I thought, there has to be a better way of doing this. I am now an old-age pensioner, I cannot keep doing this. I can't keep eating Pringles (from the hotel minibar) and keep getting on the plane at four in the morning."

3827. "[Quote]." *The Scotsman* 29 August 2005: 30. Report of an Atwood appearance at the Edinburgh Book Festival by Susan Mansfield notes that at one point she told her audience: "I write more than I publish. With some people it's the other way around."

3828. "[Quote]." *Sunday Herald* 22 May 2005: Section: 7 Days: 18. An article by Alan Taylor, in which author Ali Smith is interviewed about her new novel, quotes Atwood: "You are only as good as your last book sells."

3829. "[Quote]." *Toronto Star* 27 October 2005: Section: Editorial: A24. In writing about the importance of funding to the arts, James Fleck quotes Atwood: "If the teeny Canada Council arts grant I got in 1969 were to be viewed as an investment, dollar for dollar, it is certainly one of the better investments anyone ever made."

3830. "[Quote]." *Toronto Star* 8 November 2005: Section: Entertainment: C06. In Chicago to accept the 2005 *Chicago Tribune* Literary Prize, Atwood noted that Chicago "is a lot like Toronto...but with Studs Terkel, more Art Deco, and a better waterfront."

Interviews

3831. BEHE, Regis. "Dark Topics Find, Inspire Writer." *Pittsburgh Tribune Review* 22 January 2005: s.p. Available from Lexis-Nexis. Atwood interviewed by phone prior to her visit to Pittsburgh.

3832. BETHUNE, Brian. "Pretty Maids Hanging in a Row." *Maclean's* 31 October 2005: Section: BackTalk: 74. Bethune notes that there's never any shortage of things to talk about with Atwood. She may have sat down to discuss *The Penelopiad*, but she's just as happy to talk about the latest historical thinking on the Black Death—"apparently a Marburg-Ebola variant, not the bubonic plague at all," she says. Or 13th-century Mongol raids, even getting up from her chair to demonstrate the different bowshots mastered by Genghis Khan's cavalry. Atwood is a voracious reader as well as a dedicated researcher, but her interest in two key medieval events raises the suspicion her next novel will feature disease-ridden horsemen from hell. As to *The Penelopiad*, Atwood's imaginative version offers a convincing explanation and a nasty punishment for Odysseus: "I'm willing, like everybody else, to let him off for killing the suitors, but not the girls."

3833. DESMEULES, Christian. "Margaret Atwood: Visions du futur." *Le Devoir* 16 April 2005: F3. Interviewed in the offices of her Quebec publisher about *Le dernier homme*. (689 w).

3834. DIXON, Guy. "A Desperate Housewife in Ancient Greece: The Man Is Gone. The Kid Is Lippy. And Who Killed the Maids? Margaret Atwood Reimagines Penelope." *Globe and Mail* 22 October 2005: R12. Atwood interviewed about her new book. (1015 w).

3835. EAST, Louise. "Looking Beyond Version A." *Irish Times* 29 October 2005: Section: Weekend: 10. Interview in advance of reading at Dublin's Liberty Hall. Atwood began to write the book working with North American mythology, but after several failed attempts, she gave up. "You look beyond the story you're presented with, 'version A' you could call it, because version A is never the whole story," Atwood says simply. "I almost backed out of the contract," she added. "Cue frosty silence from my agent. So I said I'd give it three weeks." During those three weeks, the poor dead maids kicked the way into her consciousness. "It just comes to you in the bath, that eureka moment," she says. "Everyone will tell you the same thing….You're working on the wrong thing, you give it up and then the right thing presents itself. I don't know how that works." The silenced maids finally get to speak in *The Penelopiad* in the form of sea shanties, skipping rhymes and ballads (not for nothing has Atwood written 13 volumes of verse as well as novels, criticism, and children's writing), each of which are interspersed with Penelope's dispatches from the brilliantly dreary underworld.

3836. EBERHART, John Mark. "Margaret Atwood Cautions America, Like a Good Neighbor." *Herald News* (Passaic County, NJ) 19 June 2005: Section: Life: C03. Also available in *Courier Mail* (Queensland, Australia) 4 June 2005: Section: Bam: M08; *Kansas City Star* 25 May 2005: Section: Entertainment News: s.p. Available from Lexis-Nexis. Atwood interviewed in Era Ora, a restaurant near her home whose kitchen was being renovated, on occasion of the publication of *Writing with Intent* (one of whose essays is reflected in this article's headline). Eberhart comments that "it is, in fact, simple to sum up Atwood for neophytes: This writer imagines bad things happening but hopes for the best." (1759 w).

3837. ENRIGHT, Michael. *Great Conversations with Michael Enright. Vol. One, Talking to Writers.* [Toronto]: CBC Audio, 2005. Disc 1: Atwood interviewed on Sunday Edition on the connection between writer, book, and reader. (29 April 2002).

3838. GODSEY, Kristin D. "Margaret Atwood: Unlocking the Door to Creativity by Multitasking." *Writer's Market 2006*. Ed. Kathryn S. Brogan. Cincinnati, OH: Writer's Digest Books, 2005. 39-42.

3839. GOODLIFFE, Kim. "Mythmaking on a New Level: Margaret Atwood Launches Ambitious New Global Series." *Ottawa Citizen* 31 October 2005: C1. Also in: *Vancouver Sun* 22 October 2005: Section: Books: D17. Atwood interviewed in the lounge of Vancouver's Four Seasons Hotel about *The Penelopiad*. Excerpt: "When we say 'myth,' we don't mean something that's untrue. Nor do we mean any old story. Jokes are stories; they're not myths. Fables—fox and grapes—they're stories; they're not myths. Certain folktales are stories but not myths. What do we mean by 'myth'? We mean a story that is the foundation stone of a cultural system. So, Noah and the Ark, Adam and Eve, the Trojan War all count as myths."

3840. GORING, Rosemary. "The Hard Lady of Literature." *The Herald* (Glasgow) 18 June 2005: Section: Magazine: 21. Report of an afternoon spent with Atwood and Graeme Gibson in which both were interviewed about their relationship and writing. (3958 w).

3841. HAMMOND, Margo. "The Joys of Small." *St. Petersburg Times* (FL) 30 January 2005: Section: Perspective: 4P. Atwood caught by Hammond having just returned from an ice rink where she was taping a comedy show [as a goalie] that aired on CBC Television's *Rick Mercer Report*. A wide-ranging interview before her upcoming visit to the Florida Seacoast Writers' Conference. Some excerpts: "Canadians know everything about America, but Americans know very little about Canada. We have to know those things. We're a small country, a trading country. We have to be aware of global situations. We have to be aware of things outside our own borders. Is it a liability or an asset to be a writer from a small country? The li-

ability of being small? People can shove you around. The liability of being big?
You don't watch where you're going and that can lead you to bad errors, such as
falling into holes. The asset of being small? Being small makes you very aware of
other people. You're very aware of where their feet are at all times. I am small in
stature as an individual, and I'm from a relatively small country. Being small,
you're just more aware. You don't take it for granted that you are bigger than everybody, because you're not. It makes you nimble."

**Do you think these differences in size affect what Canadian writers and
American writers are concerned about?** "Alistair McLeod, the Canadian writer,
says that writers write about what worries them. There are a lot of things that
worry writers in the United States. But if we were going to make a list of worries,
our worries (in Canada) would be different."

What would be at the top of your list? "You. We worry about you. We worry
about America. We worry about it from several different angles. What's it going to
do to us next? What's it going to do next? If it falls down a hole, a whole lot of
other people are going to go with it. So actually you don't want it to fall down a
hole."

Do you like the label Canadian writer? "I don't actually care. But I don't see
why you can't be more than one thing. I'm a short, 65-year-old female, white,
straight, Toronto, Ontario, Canada, North America, the world writer who believes
women are human beings. Plus I have curly hair. Plus I have blue eyes."

Here's another label. Politically, you call yourself a red Tory. What is that?
"That's a common term here. You don't have those, so it's very hard to describe to
you. You've got Republicans or Democrats. You've got liberals or conservatives.
We don't slice that way. Partly because Canada is a far more socially conservative
country than you. We have a way lower murder rate, a lower divorce rate, but we
have more tolerant attitudes. Put those together."

What is the role of a writer? "We've never found that out. We know that they
make people in power very nervous. And the closer to totalitarianism a government becomes, the more nervous artists make them. They're likely to blurt out
things that people in power find unpalatable and disagreeable."

So they are a kind of watchdog? A prophet? "Well, you can't tell writers
what to be. As soon as you tell them they're supposed to be, they'll do the opposite."

3842. HILLER, Susanne. "A Weaver's Tale." *National Post* 22 October 2005: Section:
Weekend Post: WP4. Atwood on *The Penelopiad* and life as a blond. Some excerpts:

What intrigued you about the project...? "Well, I grew up with this kind of
thing. You remember Andrew Lang? I used to get those books out of the public library as a child. I had all of these folklore books. I read Grimm's fairy tales very
early on, and the Greek myths. Then in school we had *The Iliad* and *The Odyssey*,
which we had to translate. Then I went to Victoria College, at U. of T., where I
met Northrop Frye, who was interested in mythology. Myths are old and an oral
tradition and really the building block of storytelling."

**A lot of people would say it is classic Atwood to do a feminist reclamation of
the myth.** "I wouldn't even call it feminist. Every time you write something from
the point of view of a woman, people say that it's feminist, and when you write
something from the point of view of a man, they say, 'Why did you write it from
the point of view of a man?' You actually can't win on those gender issues."

How did you research? "I had the primary text. I enjoyed rereading it. It made me realize how cleverly it was put together. It cuts back and forth like a movie. And all the information about Penelope's ancestry came from Robert Graves's *The Greek Myths*."

On a totally different note, we hear that you dyed your hair blond. "What is this word 'dyed'? I'm helping nature. It's called blending in the grey."

So do blonds have more fun? "For comparative purposes, I would have had to be blond at an earlier age. Let me put it this way: It's better to look at the back of your head in a mirror and see light with dark roots, than see dark with light roots."

3843. HOOVER, Bob. "Atwood Sounds Off on American Reality." *Pittsburgh Post-Gazette* 22 January 2005: Section: Arts & Entertainment: C6. Atwood interviewed prior to her visit to Pittsburgh. In the interview, she emphasized the growing differences between Canada and the United States and the importance of writers keeping their independence from authorities.

3844. HUY, Minh Tran. "Les mondes perdus de Margaret Atwood." *Magazine Littéraire* 441 (April 2005): 92-92. An interview focussing on *Le dernier homme* (*Oryx and Crake*).

3845. LITTLE, Melanie. "Mythic Revisions: Margaret Atwood Rewrites the Story of Penelope." *Calgary Herald* 22 October 2005: Section: Books & The Arts: K1. Atwood interviewed when visiting Calgary's Wordfest Festival about *The Penelopiad*.

3846. MacDONALD, Marianne. "Sweet Subversive." *National Post* 4 June 2005: Section: Weekend Post: WP5. Atwood interviewed in Dublin on her boyish early years in the bush, feminism (whatever that is), marriage, and the writing life.

3847. PETROWSKI, Nathalie. "Margaret Atwood: La fin du monde est à quelle heure?" *La Presse* 17 April 2005: Section: Arts spectacles: 1. An interview conducted in English but reported in French. Atwood didn't like the translation of *Oryx and Crake* into French as *Le dernier homme* but claimed no expertise in translation. If she had been left to translate *Surfacing* into German, speakers of that language would have thought the book dealt with submarines. Atwood also participated in the interviewer's quick quiz: **Last film:** *Finding Neverland*, with Johnny Depp; **last CD:** The new Martha Wainwright album; **last book:** *The History of Attila the Hun*; **most disturbing work:** *Vera Drake*, a film by Mike Leigh about an abortionist in Britain during the 1950s; **most inspiring artist:** Mozart or Kafka; **who would she be if she were a city:** London, which she loves, or Aix-en-Provence, a bourgeois city which she resembles; **if she lived in another era, where would it be:** Ancient Egypt; **who would she be if she could be a fictional character:** Elizabeth Bennett, from Jane Austen's classic *Pride and Prejudice*. (1275 w).

3848. ROBINSON, David. "The Truth about Myths." *The Scotsman* 29 October 2005: 6. Atwood interviewed at the Frankfurt Book Fair.

On getting involved with the Myths series: "With me, it was...at the [Edinburgh] Book Festival, at Channings, the hotel I was staying in—and before breakfast, when I say yes to everything. But I'd known of Canongate when we'd lived in Edinburgh in 1978-79, and I liked the books like *The Assassin's Cloak* that Jamie'd [Byng] been publishing, and in any case with my own background in Canada I was conditioned to support small publishers. Then he won the Booker with *Life of Pi* and I wondered why I'd bothered!"

On why she wanted to write about *The Odyssey* from the point of view of Odysseus's wife Penelope—and particularly that of her 12 maids, who were all hanged when the conquering hero returned to Ithaca. There were, she suggests, a few possible reasons—their deaths might have been honor killings, or to prevent them revealing Penelope's infidelities with the suitors occupying Odysseus's palace at Ithaca, or the whole story might have had a wider, mythic meaning. Atwood: "When I read about the hanged maids, I thought, there's something wrong here. Those maids were left dangling at the end of *The Odyssey* in such an unjust way. Even when I was 15, I thought that. I noticed that even when the BBC read *The Odyssey* on the radio, they left out the story of the maids. James Joyce didn't put them into *Ulysses* either. It's because there's this guy in the story that we've quite liked up to now and then he hangs the maids...."

On the creative process: "In a book I wrote called *Negotiating with the Dead*, I wanted to write about writing and what writers think they are doing when they're doing it. I started by giving all the motives I'd ever come across and by asking other writers for theirs, and looking at prologues from the past. There was no common factor. So I said to novelists, 'What does it feel like when you're going into a book?' And they all said, it's dark, like going into a dark room—as Virginia Woolf said, going there with a lamp and lighting up the furniture—but they all mentioned darkness followed by light, every single one. You have to go into the dark and muck around in there. Maybe you will succeed, maybe you won't, but unless you go into the dark, you're not going to find what you're looking for. My version of that is going to sleep and often—and many people will say this—in the morning it will be there. That's all I can tell you. With this book, I woke up and it was there, the first sentence in the book. And you think 'Who am I hearing here?' Well, I knew who it was, so writing the book afterwards was like skiing downhill. But there's a lot of false starts in the labyrinth. Creative people usually can't tell you where they get their ideas from— they're not working with logos."

3849. SEAMAN, Donna. *Writers on the Air: Conversations about Books*. Philadelphia: Paul Dry, 2005. See especially "Margaret Atwood." 93-106. From an interview conducted in 2003, the focus of which was *Oryx and Crake*.

3850. TONKIN, Brad. "Old Myths, New Truths." *The Independent* 28 October 2005: Section: Features: 2-4. With a focus on *The Penelopiad*. Evidently Atwood "made two false starts on other legendary yarns before settling on Penelope—one a native American story, the other the Norse myth about the creation of humanity out of two logs of wood. 'But I couldn't get the logs of wood animated.'"

3851. TURPIN, Adrian. "Nothing Darker Than the Truth." *Sunday Times* 21 August 2005: Section: Features: 5. Atwood interviewed by phone in Toronto before coming to Edinburgh Book Festival and after arriving from an Arctic trip. Some excerpts: "You can tell a lot about a writer's state of mind by what they're reading. On Atwood's bedside table is *The Return of the Black Death*, which argues that the illness that swept Europe in the 14th century was not bubonic plague, but a haemorrhagic virus, more like ebola. ('It could so easily happen again,' Atwood says, almost breezily.) Before that she has finished books about William the Conqueror, Attila the Hun, and Genghis Khan. Atwood seems to thrive on the idea of civilisations threatened by forces barely within their control."

Would she describe herself as a pessimist? "'No pessimist is a pessimist,' she replies. 'They all say what I'm about to say. I'm a realist. If I was a pessimist, why would I write? Graeme is much more pessimistic than I am. Besides him, I'm little Mary Sunshine....' The voice on the phone line from Toronto is a low, warm, almost sleepy drawl. I was expecting to be intimidated, I say."

What went wrong? "Sometimes I do the 'Oh she's so scary' thing in interviews, and sometimes it's the 'Margaret Atwood, she's not so scary after all.' It keeps the variety," she adds dryly. [She also noted] "I'm working on poetry at the moment....What I'm really trying to do, though, is talk myself out of the next berserk novel."

3852. VAN HERK, Aritha. "A Practical Sibyl: Margaret Atwood Is Eerily Adept at Predicting the Future." *Calgary Herald* 15 October 2005: Section: Books & The Arts: F1. Interview before Atwood accepted the Banff Centre National Arts Award. Some examples of the topics covered:

On Canadian literature: "I don't like speaking for a whole generation, but I have witnessed enormous changes in Canadian books....All of the things we writers once wished for, we now have. Book tours, readings in bookstores, lots of publicity. It started in coffee houses, the beatnik era, candles in Chianti bottles, and black walls. It wasn't romantic—but grotty. And now, I am inclined to say be careful what you wish for. Those book tours and readings aren't always fun."

On academics: "One of the beautiful things about scholarship is that it is interested in knowledge for the sake of knowledge. It's not going to help you build a better mousetrap, although it may have a lot to say about the history of the mousetrap. I like watching somebody's well-wrought argument twitching on the page."

On quotidian advice: "Don't build on flood plains. Use a low-energy washing machine."

On sorting her clothing by color: "Then you can find things easily and things match. Blacks go on the left and pinks and whites on the right. I like that rainbow arrangement. People ought to wear colour. It gives the rest of us something to look at. People should be visually varied to entertain the random eye of the passerby."

Scholarly Resources

3853. ARIAS DOBLAS, Rosario. "Talking with the Dead: Revisiting the Victorian Past and the Occult in Margaret Atwood's *Alias Grace* and Sarah Waters's *Affinity*." *Estudios Ingleses de la Universidad Complutense (EIUC)* 13 (2005): 85-105.

3854. AZAR-LUXTON, Grizéll. "Margaret Atwood: Prize-Winning Novelist." *Cape Librarian* 49.6 (November-December 2005): 23-26. An introduction to Atwood and her work.

3855. BARZILAI, Shuli. "The Bluebeard Syndrome in Atwood's *Lady Oracle*: Fear and Femininity." *Marvels & Tales* 19.2 (16 November 2005): 249-273. "The multiple identities of Joan Foster in *Lady Oracle* are the by-products of many literary and social models. Joan exists partly as a central narrative agent and partly as a nexus or repository of language and culture. At stake, however, is something more than an authorial display of postmodernist temperament and virtuosity. The intricate weave of the Bluebeard syndrome into the heterogeneous narratives that constitute *Lady Oracle* dramatizes the complex exchanges between popular culture and the reality of women's lives. Atwood explores the unsettling transpositions between literary and literal romance, on the one hand, and between imagined and experienced aggression against women, on the other." (Author).

3856. BIDIVILLE, Annick. "Margaret Atwood's *The Edible Woman:* From Body Representations to Feminist Theories." *Newsletter of the Margaret Atwood Society* 34 (Fall 2005): 4-15.

3857. BLACKFORD, Holly. "Haunted Housekeeping: Fatal Attractions of Servant and Mistress in Twentieth-Century Female Gothic Literature." *Literature Interpretation Theory* 16.2 (April-June 2005): 233-261. "In 20th-century female gothic stories, women of different backgrounds struggle for possession of households. This possession is vital to female authenticity and desire. Houses, signifying domestic function, are substitutes for uncaring or persecuting husbands, whose attentions both mistress and servant seek. The intimacy and competition between mistress and servant represents the degree to which protagonists and gothic authors articulate ambiguity about awakening sexual desire in young women. In their struggles with servants, young protagonists struggle with themselves and the question of whether domestic ideology truly makes female desire productive and palatable. In this context, the following works are examined: Edith Wharton's ghost stories, Daphne Du Maurier's novel *Rebecca*, Shirley Jackson's novel *Hill House*, and Margaret Atwood's novel *Alias Grace*." (Author).

3858. BOWERING, George. *Left Hook: A Sideways Look at Canadian Writing*. Vancouver, BC: Raincoast Books, 2005. See especially Chapter [15], "Atwood's Hook," 157-172. On the short Atwood poem "You Fit into Me like a Hook," according to Bowering: "You belong; you hurt like hell."

3859. DiMARCO, Danette. "Paradice Lost, Paradise Regained: *Homo Faber* and the Makings of a New Beginning in *Oryx and Crake*." *Papers on Language and Literature: A Journal for Scholars and Critics of Language and Literature* 41.2 (Spring 2005): 170-195. "Margaret Atwood's novel *Oryx and Crake* (2003) critiques modernity's commitment to *homo faber*—he who labors to use every instrument as a means to achieve a particular end in building a world, even when the fabrication of that world necessarily demands a repeated violation of its materiality, including its people. Atwood propels her novel through the memories of the main character, Snowman, a survivor of a deadly viral pathogen created and unleashed by his best friend, Crake. Too much a product of a profit-driven world who mirrors its economy of self-interest, Crake emerges as the quintessential *homo faber*, making it unlikely that any kind of positive social change will happen directly through him." (Author).

3860. DUNNING, Stephen. "Margaret Atwood's *Oryx and Crake*." *Canadian Literature* 186 (2005): 86-101. "The article examines how the novel…warns against pursuing a purportedly therapeutic scientific project and insists that sacred narrative cannot be excised without the loss of humanity. Atwood is able to capture modernity's ethos and portray its potential for disaster as depicted in the novel." (Journal).

3861. EVANS, Shari Michelle. "Navigating Exile: Contemporary Women Writers Discover an Ethics of Home." PhD thesis. University of New Mexico, 2005. 266 pp. "This dissertation examines the reformulation of home-spaces in recent novels by Margaret Atwood, Toni Morrison, and Octavia Butler. My work conceives of home as an active, dynamic space where multiple ideologies, imaginations and material realities engage one another. Because women have historically been controlled and condemned by the tyrannies of domestic space and of racial and gendered constructions, women writers have turned to exile as a site of freedom. Against the conventions of domestic space, Atwood, Morrison and Butler construct home in an ethics that creates and practices amorphous, inclusive, and changing community….In *Oryx and Crake*, Atwood investigates the possibility that we are already exiled because we have destroyed both imagination and community leaving us with the hope that we still have enough imagination to respond to aesthetic pleasure and invent ethical practices." (Author). For more see *DAI-A* 66.06 (December 2005): 2209.

3862. FLEITZ, Elizabeth J. "Troubling Gender: Bodies, Subversion, and the Mediation of Discourse in Atwood's *The Edible Woman*." MA thesis. Bowling Green State

University, 2005. 66 pp. Available as .pdf file from Electronic Theses and Dissertations from OhioLINK member universities: http://www.ohiolink.edu/etd/.

3863. GOLDMAN, Marlene. *Rewriting Apocalypse in Canadian Fiction.* Montreal: McGill-Queen's UP, ©2005. See especially Chapter 3, "Margaret Atwood's 'Hairball': Apocalyptic Cannibal Fiction," 83-100.

3864. HAMMILL, Faye. "Margaret Atwood: *The Handmaid's Tale.*" *A Companion to Science Fiction.* Ed. David Seed. Oxford: Blackwell, 2005. 522-533.

3865. HAROLD, James. "Narrative Engagement with *Atonement* and *The Blind Assassin.*" *Philosophy & Literature* 29.1 (April 2005): 130-145. "Two recent novels, Ian McEwan's *Atonement* and Margaret Atwood's *The Blind Assassin*, are philosophically instructive. These books are interesting, I argue, because they reveal something about understanding and appreciating narrative. They show us that audience's participation in narrative is much more subtle and complex than philosophers generally acknowledge. An analysis of these books reveals that narrative imagining is not static or unified, but dynamic and multipolar. I argue that once the complexity of narrative engagement is better understood, some prominent philosophical problems and debates concerning narrative dissolve." (Author).

3866. HORNER, Avril, and Sue ZLOSNIK. *Gothic and the Comic Turn.* Houndmills; Basingstoke; Hampshire; New York: Palgrave Macmillan, 2005. See especially Chapter 5, "Women Writing Women," 116-135, which includes some discussion of the gothic in *Lady Oracle, Surfacing*, and *The Robber Bride.*

3867. HOWELLS, Coral Ann. *Margaret Atwood.* 2nd ed. New York: Palgrave Macmillan, 2005. "The second edition is thoroughly revised and updated and includes four new chapters covering Atwood's recent novels, *Alias Grace* and *The Blind Assassin*, her 2002 book on writing, *Negotiating with the Dead*, and her latest novel, *Oryx and Crake*, published in 2003." (Publisher).

3868. JOHNSON, Kristyn. "Othering the Woman's War." MA thesis. St. Bonaventure University, 2005. 85 pp. A study of *The Edible Woman*, as well as Sylvia Plath's *The Bell Jar* plus the work of Simone de Beauvoir and Ursula K. Le Guin.

3869. KELLY, Sarah M. "Tracing the Transition to Empire in Feminist Fiction." MA thesis. Villanova University, 2005. 64 pp. Atwood's *Surfacing* set against Zadie Smith's *White Teeth* and Karen Tei's *Yamashita's Tropic of Orange.*

3870. KUHN, Cynthia G. *Self-Fashioning in Margaret Atwood's Fiction: Dress, Culture, and Identity.* New York: Peter Lang, 2005. Contents: "'Clothed in Words': Margaret Atwood and Dress." "Border Crossing: Dress as Performative Boundary and Margin." "Toxic Chic: Dress and Dreams in *The Robber Bride.*" "Amazing Space: Veils and Vogues in *Alias Grace.*" "Style and Text(ile): A Conclusion."

3871. LABUDOVÁ, Katarína. "From Retrospective to Reconstruction of the 'Auto/Biographical' Subject in *Cat's Eye* by Margaret Atwood." *Theory and Practice in English Studies: Proceedings from the Eighth Conference of English, American and Canadian Studies.* Vol. 4. Ed. Jan Chovanec. Brno: Masaryk University, 2005. 109-114.

3872. LIN, Michelle Hoefahn. "'Only the Blind Are Free': Sight and Blindness in Margaret Atwood's *The Blind Assassin.*" MA thesis. North Carolina State University, 2005. 92 pp. Available in .pdf from http://www.lib.ncsu.edu/theses/available/etd-03292005-142653/unrestricted/etd.pdf.

3873. MacDONALD, Tanis Louise. "The Daughter's Consolation: Melancholia and Subjectivity in Canadian Women's Paternal Elegies." PhD thesis. University of Victoria (Canada), 2005. 249 pp. "This study investigates the redefinition of female filial piety and the negotiations of female subjectivity in paternal elegies written by Canadian women. It sets Freud's theory of the work of mourning against the potential for a 'work of melancholia' in order to read the elegies as inquiries into the rhetoric of mourning as it is complicated by father-daughter kinship. Examining poetic texts by P. K. Page, Jay MacPherson, Margaret Atwood, Lola Lemire Tostevin, Anne Carson, and Erin Mouré, this study considers these 'daughterly elegies' as literary artifacts that adopt politicized subjectivities that grow from the poets' investigation into the function and limitations of elegiac convention." (Author). For more see *DAI-A* 66.10 (April 2006).

3874. MASSOURA, Kiriaki, and Mark GARNER. "A Language Is Everything You Do: The Reflective Self in an Autobiographical Narrative." *Journal of Language and Literature* 4 (2005): 1-19. Available online: http://www.jllonline.net. "On Atwood's *Surfacing* analysed through the social-psychological concept of Reflective Self Function." (Author).

3875. McKAY, Robert. "'Identifying with the Animals': Language, Subjectivity, and the Animal Politics of Margaret Atwood's *Surfacing*." *Figuring Animals: Essays on Animal Images in Art, Literature, Philosophy, and Popular Culture*. Ed. Mary S. Pollock and Catherine Rainwater. Basingstoke [UK]; New York: Palgrave Macmillan, 2005. 207-227.

3876. MESKOVA, Sandra. "Metaliteraturas elementi Margaretas Atvudas un Gundegas Repses proza." *Latvijas Universitates raksti 681.sej: Literaturzinatne un folkloristika*. Riga, Latvia: Latvijas Universitate, 2005. 77-82. In Latvian.

3877. MOHR, Dunja M. *Worlds Apart: Dualism and Transgression in Contemporary Female Dystopias*. Jefferson, NC: McFarland, 2005. See especially Chapter 5, "The Poetic Discourse of the Split Self: Margaret Atwood's *The Handmaid's Tale*," 229-269. "Suzette Haden Elgin's *Native Tongue* trilogy, Suzy McKee Charna's *Holdfast* series, and Margaret Atwood's *The Handmaid's Tale* are analyzed within the context of this subgenre of 'transgressive utopian dystopias.' The analysis focuses particularly on how these works cover the interrelated categories of gender, race and class, along with their relationship to classic literary dualism and the dystopian narrative." (Publisher).

3878. PYRHÖNEN, Heta. "Bluebeard's Accomplice: Rebecca as a Masochistic Fantasy." *Mosaic: A Journal for the Interdisciplinary Study of Literature* 38.3 (September 2005): 149-165. "This article focuses on the Bluebeard Gothic, which is a specific variant of the Gothic romance that uses the Bluebeard fairy tale as its key intertext. Many women authors have used it in order to explore patriarchal power structures. Examples include Margaret Atwood's *Lady Oracle*, Angela Carter's *The Bloody Chamber*, Charlotte Perkins Gilman's *The Yellow Wallpaper*, and Jean Rhys's *Wide Sargasso Sea*, to name a few. For author Michelle Massé the Gothic romance is about female masochism, as it portrays suffering women whose painful initiations provide some vague pleasure for women authors, characters, and readers." (Author).

3879. SNODGRASS, Mary Ellen. *Encyclopedia of Gothic Literature*. New York: Facts on File, 2005. See especially "Atwood, Margaret (1939–)," 16-17, and "*The Handmaid's Tale* Margaret Atwood (1985)," 168-169.

3880. SPENCER, Guylaine. "The Allure of Atwood's Toronto." *Americas* 57.6 (November-December 2005): 14-21. "Presents information on destinations in the city of Toronto in Ontario used as a setting for novels by Atwood such as the Park Hyatt Hotel [i.e., Park Plaza] in *Cat's Eye*; Royal Ontario Museum in *Life Before Man*; Queen's Park in *Lady Oracle*." (Author).

3881. SRISERMBHOK, Amporn. "Approaches to Margaret Atwood's *The Edible Woman.*" *How Far Is America from Here? Selected Proceedings of The First World Congress of The International American Studies Association, 22-24 May 2003*. Ed. Theo d' Haen et al. Amsterdam; New York: Rodopi, 2005. 247-261.

3882. STOREY, Françoise, and Jeff STOREY. "History and Allegory in Margaret Atwood's *Oryx and Crake.*" *Cycnos* 22.2 (2005): 129-138.

3883. STORROW, Richard F. "The Handmaid's Tale of Fertility Tourism: Passports and Third Parties in the Religious Regulation of Assisted Conception." *Texas Wesleyan Law Review* 12.1 (Fall 2005): 189-211. "Infertility is a devastating global malady triggering worldwide demand for a vast array of reproduction assisting technologies. Infertility is particularly devastating in 'pronatalist' societies marked by high rates of infertility and large disparities in access to medical services. Poverty in particular impedes large segments of the population in pronatalist Third World countries from gaining access even to very basic techniques of infertility treatment and consigns them to ineffective traditional remedies. In this Article drawing on both ethnographic work on infertility in the Third World and on Margaret Atwood's *The Handmaid's Tale*, Professor Storrow examines two starkly class-stratified societies where reproduction is regulated by means of rigid adherence to religious doctrine." (Journal).

3884. THACKER, Robert. *Alice Munro: Writing Her Lives*. Toronto: McClelland and Stewart, 2005. Includes a number of references to Atwood, showing the relationship between the two writers. Atwood was, for example, crucial in finding Munro an agent.

3885. TOLAN, Fiona. "Feminist Utopias and Questions of Liberty: Margaret Atwood's *The Handmaid's Tale* as Critique of Second Wave Feminism." *Women* 16.1 (Spring 2005): 18-32. "*The Handmaid's Tale* appeared during a period of heightened interest in utopian literature, particularly feminist utopias. Against a backdrop of postmodernist debate, the mid-1980s became a period of evaluation and reinvention for feminism, as a second generation of feminists inherited the second wave. The book uses this moment of transition to evaluate the motives and means of what was becoming an increasingly theorized feminism. To a certain extent, postmodernism can be understood to have grown out of, or at least alongside, anti-utopianism." (Journal).

3886. ———. "Situating Canada: The Shifting Perspective of the Postcolonial Other in Margaret Atwood's *The Robber Bride.*" *American Review of Canadian Studies* 25.3 (Autumn 2005): 453-470. "This article examines Canada's dual power position in *The Robber Bride*. Post-colonialism in this book is largely read through the experiences of white women. The author demonstrates that Atwood's examination of women's power is frequently employed as a metaphor for Canada's experience as a postcolonial nation. Atwood articulates a common late-twentieth-century interest in postcolonial discourse, but she translates prevalent postcolonial ideas of difference and otherness to fit her own understanding." (Journal).

3887. TU, Shu-shu. "Reinventing Female Subjectivity: The Impulse of Postmodern and Feminist Writing in Margaret Atwood's *The Robber Bride.*" MA thesis. Tamkang University, 2005.

3888. TURNER, Kate, and Bill FREEDMAN. "Nature as a Theme in Canadian Literature." *Environmental Reviews* 13.4 (2005): 169-198. Includes analysis of Atwood's views on the significance of nature in Canadian literature (*Survival*) as well as the role of nature in her poetry and some other writing.

3889. VICKROY, Laurie. "Seeking Symbolic Immortality: Visualizing Trauma in *Cat's Eye*." *Mosaic: A Journal for the Interdisciplinary Study of Literature* 38.2 (June 2005): 129-143. "The article investigates how *Cat's Eye*, a...novel about an artist's development, explores the complex interrelationship between trauma, identity, and culture, and specifically, how trauma shapes the construction of the protagonist's gendered identity and visual sense while her artistic discipline mediates trauma and helps her decipher fantasies perpetuating her emotional stasis." (Author).

3890. WELLINGHOFF, Lisa Ann. "Detecting the Author: Narrative Perspective in Paul Auster's *The New York Trilogy*, V. S. Naipaul's *The Enigma of Arrival*, Margaret Atwood's *Alias Grace*." PhD thesis. University of Tulsa, 2005. 195 pp. "Writers are constantly asked to elaborate on their status as writers. Paul Auster, V. S. Naipaul, and Margaret Atwood all respond to the mystery of that status by asserting their role as authors within their fiction and nonfiction. They extend the mystery of the author by explaining authorship as a game run by the author and played on the reader....Margaret Atwood has publicly explained her role as a writer and the purpose of her novel *Alias Grace*. Atwood extends the authorship game by presenting the story of Grace, a historical woman accused of murder and a representation of the writer. The writer is a murderess, a con-artist, and an alias." (Author). For more see *DAI-A* 66.3 (September 2005): 987.

3891. WHITE, Roberta. *A Studio of One's Own: Fictional Women Painters and the Art of Fiction*. Madison [NJ]: Fairleigh Dickinson UP, ©2005. See especially Chapter 6, "Northern Light: Margaret Atwood's *Cat's Eye*," 152-173.

3892. WILLIAMS, Ian. "The Poetics of Tone and Voice in the Poetry of Anne Sexton." PhD thesis. University of Toronto, 2005. 288 pp. "In literary criticism, the terms tone and voice are used loosely; the first translates generally as mood, and the second as author or style. This dissertation develops a more precise poetics of tone and voice through a study of the work of the American confessional poet, Anne Sexton. Because the terms originate in the contexts of orality and music, I emphasize the oral, performative cues which are imbedded in poetic diction, and the identity, or presence that is constructed from language. Consequently, in this discussion, language is inseparable from the social context that shapes interpretation and performance." (Author). To demonstrate the wide applicability of the poetics of tone and voice. Sexton is paired with 4 contemporary poets, including Atwood. For more see *DAI-A* 66.10 (April 2006).

3893. WITTKE-RÜDIGER, Petra. *Literarische Kartographien des kanadischen Nordens*. Würzburg [Germany]: Königshausen & Neumann, ©2005. See Chapter 6, "'Of Mapbreakers and Mapmakers': Literarische Kartographien des kanadischen Nordens bei Margaret Atwood, Marian Engel und Ann B. Tracy," 128-261, and especially 6.1, "'Imitating the Map': Die öko-feministische Besinnung auf präkoloniale Mythen in Margaret Atwoods Roman *Surfacing*," 129-176.

3894. WRIGHT, Laura. "National Photographic: Images of Sensibility and the Nation in Margaret Atwood's *Surfacing* and Nadine Gordimer's *July's People*." *Mosaic: A Journal for the Interdisciplinary Study of Literature* 38.1 (March 2005): 75-92. "Psychological frameworks for both a national and sensible 'imagined community' are socially transmitted via photographic images and illustrations to the female protagonists of Atwood's *Surfacing* and Gordimer's *July's People*. This essay examines the protagonists' disruption of such visually instilled sensible and colonizing behaviour." (Journal).

Reviews of Atwood's Works

3895. *Bashful Bob and Doleful Dorinda.* Toronto: Key Porter, 2004.
  CM: Canadian Review of Materials 21 January 2005: s.p. By Sylvia PAN-
    TELEO. (453 w).
  Resource Links 10.4 (April 2005): 1-2. By Adriane PETTIT. (279 w).
3896. *The Blind Assassin.* [Sound recording]. Read by Michael O'Brien. Fredericton,
  NB: BTC Audiobooks, 2005.
  Publishers Weekly 252.39 (3 October 2005): 54. ANON.
3897. *Curious Pursuits*: Occasional Writing 1970-2005. London: Virago, 2005.
  Daily Telegraph (Sydney) 23 July 2005: Section: Features: 110. By Anita PUN-
    TON. (71 w). "It's interesting to see how Atwood's feminism became less of
    a concern as the 20th century rolled on. Fans will find it an engaging read."
  The Guardian (London): Section: *Guardian* Saturday Pages: 13. By Natasha
    WALTER. (973 w).
  The Herald (Glasgow) 7 May 2005: Section: ABC: 5. By Rosemary GORING.
    (782 w).
  The Independent on Sunday 1 May 2005: Section: Features: 28. By Lesley
    McDOWELL. (688 w).
  The Observer 8 May 2005: Section: *Observer* Review Pages: 16. By Stephanie
    MERRITT. (685 w).
  Scotland on Sunday 1 May 2006: 6. By Anna MILLAR. (498 w).
  The Spectator 14 May 2005: 61. By Caroline MOORE. (1032 w).
  Sunday Business Post 8 May 2005: s.p. By Joanne HAYDEN. (622 w).
    Available from Lexis-Nexis.
  Sunday Herald 8 May 2005: Section: Seven Days: 35. By Alan TAYLOR.
    (867 w).
  Sunday Times 15 May 2005: Section: Features: 50. By Peter KEMP. (714 w).
  The Times (London) 23 April 2005: Section: Features: 10. By Joan SMITH.
    (499 w).
3898. *The Edible Woman.* London: Virago, 2005.
  Derby Evening Telegraph 30 September 2005: Section: Features: 38. ANON.
    (187 w).
  Herizons 18.4 (Spring 2005): 40. By Stacy KAUDER. (257 w).
3899. *The Handmaid's Tale.* [Sound recording]. BBC Audiobooks America, 2004.
  3 CDs; 2 cassettes. Unabridged.
  Library Journal 130.10 (1 June 2005): 188. By Laurie SELWYN.
3900. *Le dernier homme.* Paris: R. Laffont, 2005. [*Oryx and Crake*].
  Le Droit 26 March 2005: A20. By Caroline Barrière. (502 w).
  La Presse 1 May 2005: Section: Arts spectacles: 4. By Gilbert GRAND.
    (111 w).
3901. *Moving Targets: Writing with Intent, 1982-2004.* Toronto: Anansi, 2004.
  Malahat Review 150 (Spring 2005): 105-107. By Kitty HOFFMAN.
3902. *Oryx and Crake.* Toronto: Emblem, 2005.
  Chronicle of Higher Education 51.36 (13 May 2005): B6-B8. By Martha
    MONTELLO. Group review.
  Globe and Mail 12 November 2005: D21. By H. J. KIRCHHOFF.

3903. *The Penelopiad*. Toronto: Knopf; New York; Edinburgh: Canongate, 2005.

Bookseller 5202 (28 October 2005): 38. Group review. [Ed. note: By the end of 2005, the series included *A Short History of Myth* by Karen Armstrong, *The Penelopiad* by Margaret Atwood, and *Weight* by Jeanette Winterson.]

Daily Mail (London) 28 October 2005: Section: 04: 64. By Michael ARDITTI. Includes review of other published titles. Excerpt: "Atwood offers a conventionally feminist slant on the tale of Penelope, the faithful wife who is harassed by a horde of importunate suitors during her husband's absence at the Trojan War. To outwit them, she promises to make a choice of one of them when she has woven a shroud for her father-in-law, which she then unravels every night. Despite displaying the occasional felicitous phrase, Atwood is writing way below par. The choruses for Penelope's maids rarely rise above doggerel. Far from revivifying an ancient myth, this is an arch and empty literary conceit."

Daily Telegraph (London) 22 October 2005: Section: Books: 006. By David FLUSFEDER. (962 w). A review of the series.

Edmonton Journal 30 October 2005: E10. By Douglas BARBOUR.

The Expositor (Brantford, ON) 29 October 2005: D8. By Pat DONNELLY.

Financial Times (London) 29 October 2005: Section: Weekend Magazine: 30. By Angel GURRIA-QUINTANA. (1320 w). Includes review of *Weight* by Jeanette Winterson.

The Gazette (Montreal) 22 October 2005: Section: Arts & Books: H1. By Pat DONNELLY. A review of the series.

Globe and Mail 22 October 2005: D4. By Donald Harman AKENSON. A review of the series. (2524 w).

The Guardian (London) 29 October 2005: Section: Guardian Review Pages: 8. By Mary BEARD. (2127 w). One of 4 books reviewed.

Herald Sun (Melbourne) 5 November 2005: Section: Weekend: W31. By Blanche CLARK. Includes review of *Weight* by Jeanette Winterson.

Independent on Sunday 27 November 2005: Section: Features: 20. By Catherine TAYLOR. Includes review of *Weight* by Jeanette Winterson.

Korea Herald 8 November 2005: s.p. By Yang SUNG-JIN. Includes review of *Weight* by Jeanette Winterson. Available from Lexis-Nexis.

London Review of Books 27.22 (17 November 2005): 23. By Thomas JONES.

Maclean's 118.44 (31 October 2005): 74. By Brian BETHUNE.

National Post 22 October 2005: Section: Weekend Post: WP4. By Gerald Owen.

National Public Radio 25 November 2005: Show: All Things Considered. By Alan CHEUSE. (376 w). Available from Lexis-Nexis.

New Statesman 134.4764 (31 October 2005): 48-50. By Simon GOLDHILL. (1073 w). A review of the series.

New York Times 11 December 2005: Section: 7: 16. By Caroline ALEXANDER. Includes a review of *Weight* by Jeanette Winterson.

The Observer 23 October 2005: Section: Observer Review Pages: 17. By Peter CONRAD. (1156 w). A review of the series.

Ottawa Citizen 23 October 2005: Section: Arts & Books: C5. By Albert WIERSEMA.

The Province (Vancouver, BC) 30 October 2005: B16. ANON.

San Diego Union-Tribune 13 November 2005: Section: Books: 5. By Gregory MILLER. Includes review of *Weight* by Jeanette Winterson.

The Spectator 22 October 2005: 43-44. By Sam LEITH. (1420 w). A review of the series.

Sunday Times (London) 23 October 2005: Section: Features: 52. By Lucy HUGHES-HALLETT. (811 w). A review of the series.

Times Educational Supplement 28 October 2005: Section: Books: 17. By Adele GERAS. (770 w). A review of the series.

Times-Colonist (Victoria, BC) 30 October 2005: D11. By Pat DONNELLY.

TLS 5355 (18 November 2005): 23. By Carolyne LARRINGTON. A review of the series.

Vancouver Sun 22 October 2005: Section: Books: D17. By Sara O'LEARY.

Washington Post 25 December 2005: Section: Book World: T13. By Elizabeth HAND. Includes a review of *Weight* by Jeanette Winterson.

Washington Times 20 November 2005: Section: Books: B08. By Merle RUBIN. Includes a review of *Weight* by Jeanette Winterson.

3904. *Writing with Intent. Essays, Reviews, Personal Prose, 1983-2005*. New York: Carroll & Graf Publishers, 2005.

Arkansas Democrat-Gazette (Little Rock) 3 July 2005: Section: Travel: s.p. By John FREEMAN. (864 w). Available from Lexis-Nexis.

Booklist 101.13 (1 March 2005): 1130-1131. By Donna SEAMAN.

Columbus Dispatch (OH) 5 June 2005: Section: Features: 07. By Margaret QUAMME. (612 w).

Kirkus Reviews 73.2 (15 January 2005): 91-92. ANON.

Library Journal 130.5 (15 March 2005): 84. By Nancy R. IVES.

Publishers Weekly 252.9 (28 February 2005): 56. ANON. (237 w).

Seattle Times 8 May 2005: Section: Books: J10. By Kimberly Marlowe HARNETT. (471 w).

Times Union (Albany, NY) 17 July 2005: Section: Travel-Books: J4. By John FREEMAN. (822 w).

Reviews of Adaptations of Atwood's Works

3905. *Alias Grace*. Directed Laurence Strangio. Performed in Melbourne.

Herald Sun (Melbourne) 14 June 2005: Section: Arts: 70. By Chris Boyd. (299 w).

Margaret Atwood on the Web
Alain Lamothe

Margaret Atwood is, without a doubt, a popular and prolific author. Throughout the course of her career she has published a plethora of literary works: poems, stories, plays, and novels. Her works have been cited hundreds of times, and she has been the subject of many publications and research projects. This is not to mention the countless awards she has won, as well as the multitude of presentations, speeches, and recitals she has given.

The level of literature available to her effect can be easily illustrated if one performs a keyword search for the word "Atwood" in the *MLA International Bibliography* (http://www.mla.org/)—one of the most important informational resources for languages and literature throughout the years (Hysell, 472). Such a search has produced a total of 1,006 citations. If searching for "Margaret Atwood" rather than simply "Atwood," it reduced the results to 892. This remains an enormous number of citations to browse through. A similar search performed in another useful database for the literary arts, *Literature Online* (http://lion.chadwyck.com), has yielded more than 850 citations. Furthermore, information detailing Atwood's life and works can also be found in other electronic products such as *Contemporary Authors* (http://www.gale.com). Unfortunately, these online databases and services are available by subscription only and at considerable cost, with access typically provided by academic or highly funded public libraries.

Fortunately there exists an alternative, although the results of a search for Margaret Atwood would not be as pristine. This alternative is the Internet. There does exist some limited information on freely available web-based encyclopedias such as *Wikipedia* (http://wikipedia.org) or *Answers.com* (http://www.answers.com) but, to date, the information they provide is restricted to short biographies and bibliographies. For anyone needing more than barebones facts, it is unlikely that either will satisfy.

An alternative is to search for "Atwood" using either *Google, Yahoo!Search, Altavista*, or some other web search engine. For this chapter, a simple search was performed on *Google* (http://www.google.com), since it has become the most popular of all web search engines (Bloom, 18-21; Jacso, 28-29; McGarvey, 108-113; Mossberg and Boehret, D1-D6). On 25 April 2006, the following terms or sequence of terms were searched to produce an astonishing number of hits (Fig. 1). Even with the quotations marks to narrow the search, an amazing 2.3 million hits were obtained. Links point to everything from relevant sources, to various booksellers wishing to sell copies of her books, to irrelevant pages with information on some other Margaret Atwood.

Atwood	=	13,900,000 hits
Margaret Atwood	=	4,330,000 hits
"Margaret Atwood"	=	2,330,000 hits

Fig. 1: Google search results for Margaret Atwood.

This leads to the purpose of this chapter: to simplify cumbersome results and extract what can be considered a site of value. This is not to say that *Google* or any other such search engine is not entirely useless in information gathering. They certainly have their worth. For example, if someone wishes to locate material on a specific work, this might prove to be the more practical strategy. One can enter the string "'Margaret Atwood' and 'Handmaid's Tale'" and immediately bring up sites specific to this topic. But, in the case of someone searching for information of a more global nature, *Google* might not be the best approach.

Four main websites dealing comprehensively with Margaret Atwood are presented and discussed: *O.W. Toad*; *Luminarium Margaret Atwood Page*; *The Margaret Atwood Society*; *Margaret Atwood WWW Resources*. Such comprehensive sites, as the names imply, contain a wide variety of information ranging from biographies, bibliographies, awards, discussions and critiques, as well as links leading to important external websites.

Following this, additional websites containing specific resources will be listed. Typically these sites provide a single but useful piece of information relating to Margaret Atwood. For instance, one such site would have an interview with Margaret Atwood, a critical analysis of one of her works, or even an audio file in which she reads one of her poems.

Comprehensive Websites

O.W. Toad: Margaret Atwood Reference Site
http://www.owtoad.com/; Atwood, 2005

This site has been quoted as being the official Margaret Atwood information site (Goodman, 2004) and is the first and best place for any newcomer to Margaret Atwood to begin his or her studies. *O.W. Toad* is an extensive website presenting a wide variety of information. For those interested, *O.W. Toad* is an anagram of "Atwood" that she not only uses as her domain name but also as the copyright name for her books (Gussow, 9).

The concise biography gives her birth date, education, employment, places of residence from 1939, as well as a list of associations in which she has participated. Details are somewhat brief—they appear essentially in point form—but they are quite complete.

Her literary works are presented in categories: poetry, short fiction, novels, children's stories, nonfiction, and so forth. Everything is included, from her major literary efforts, to her "small press editions," to her radio and television scripts. Not only are her English language works provided but also those written in French. In addition, the reader can find a detailed bibliography of critical writings on her efforts (http://www.owtoad .com/critical.html and http://www.owtoad.com/morebooksabout.html). This information is available as a PDF (portable document format) to anyone wishing to download and print.

Other items found include newspaper clippings; an important list of external links allowing access to secondary sources; a section devoted to her husband, Graeme Gibson; and an inventory of awards and honorary degrees. For those who have studied or researched Margaret Atwood, it comes as no surprise that this list is lengthy.

What I have found to be the most valuable and fun information on this site is the *What's New* section, which appears to be frequently updated. In simple terms, it provides the particulars of upcoming events in which Margaret Atwood will be participating. These events include lectures, readings, and book signings, all for the current and following year. Dates, places, contact addresses, and outside links are always available for anyone wishing to retrieve additional details. Other events are not so traditional. For instance, on 7–9 August 2006, one could have enjoyed a three-day kayaking tour with Margaret Atwood, among other renowned Canadian authors. This is a fascinating, dynamic, and informative section of *O.W. Toad*.

From the Desk of Margaret Atwood is another very interesting, albeit image-intensive, section of the site. It is not recommended to those using a slow Internet connection. Here, the researcher will first be greeted by the clear image of a typical working desk complete with drawers, papers, books, boxes, and other stationery. When the cursor is moved over a drawer it opens, revealing its content of papers and documents. Clicking on a particular opened drawer allows the user to access various images and sound clips. Included are reproductions of her book covers, comic strips, and poetry readings. Most impressive is a photo album portraying Atwood through the decades. The photographs are black and white as well as color. Oddly, one drawer is labeled "Worst Reviews Ever," but is empty. When clicking on the opened drawer, the user is presented with a "coming soon" message. Now, could this be an attempt at humor?

The section entitled *On Writing* provides the researcher, as much as the aspiring writer, with helpful hints, suggestions, and strategies to follow when becoming involved in the world of publishing. Such comments and advice are extremely useful.

One must not forget the *Frequently Asked Questions* page which has been written by Margaret Atwood's assistants, both past (Sarah Cooper) and current (Jennifer Osti). Here, inquiries by prospective writers are answered. Osti's work address is provided for those wishing to contact either her or Atwood.

From a technical standpoint, *O.W. Toad* could use some improvement. When first entering the site, the user is faced with a simple and nearly blank title page consisting of only the site's name and the word "ENTER" to be clicked on before proceeding. That, in itself, is no different from many other websites in existence. Unfortunately, this empty page remains loaded and persists in the background. Instead of the page changing into what should be the introduction to the site, another much smaller window opens at the center of the screen. This new window displays that introduction. The title page should not persist throughout the visit to the website. Once the user has clicked on "ENTER," this page provides no added value.

Overall, this is an impressive website. There has obviously been a tremendous amount of work spent in its creation and the site is a must-see for the Margaret Atwood enthusiast and novice alike.

Luminarium Margaret Atwood Page

http://www.luminarium.org/contemporary/atwood/; Jokinen, 2007

Here is another extensive website that offers both biographical and bibliographical material. Unlike *O.W. Toad*, the biography section contains a great deal more information, including details on her father, her education, her previous marriage to Jim Polk, and her publications. It is presented in flowing paragraphs rather than a simple point list.

Mimicking *O.W. Toad*, her literary works are categorized by form: novels, short stories, poems, children's books, and nonfiction books. The similarity ends here, however. First, this inventory appears immediately on the main page to the right of Atwood's biography. I was very pleased to see all important content immediately upon entering the site; there was no need for second-guessing.

Another important feature: Atwood's works are hyperlinked to corresponding companion and study guides. Each guide will supply the researcher with access to an enormous and extremely valuable amount of information specific to an individual work. For example, clicking on *The Penelopiad* leads to a description of her novel as well as actual excerpts, book reviews, and interviews. The type of information varies from work to work and can include not only brief descriptions but also lead the user to plot synopses and links to essays on a particular book, short story, or poem. It is clear that Jokinen has expended a significant amount of time and effort gathering and compiling so much information onto a single site.

The external link section located at the very bottom of the main web page is rather brief yet incorporates links to major sites such as *O.W. Toad* and that of the *Margaret Atwood Society*. Also available are links to articles, speeches, and audio and video files.

The site is well designed and intuitive with its clear and always present navigation menu. The text font is large and crisp, even at resolutions of 1280 x 1024 pixels. As in many websites, going to the main URL (http://www.luminarium.org/contemporary /atwood/) will bring the user to a splash page which is nothing more than a blank page with an image centered within and a link to the actual site. I would much rather be brought directly into the site itself and avoid this extra click.

The Margaret Atwood Society Website
http://margaretatwoodsociety.org/; Margaret Atwood Society, 2007

This is a very useful site packed with an enormous amount of material freely available to any visitor, and the information presented has a different focus from that which appears on *O.W. Toad*. Instead of treating Margaret Atwood as the main subject of discussion, this is an information page about the Margaret Atwood Society. This society is an international association of scholars, teachers, and students sharing an interest in her works, and includes exchange of views and ideas about them (T. Friedman and The Margaret Atwood Society, 2005). This site is, however, currently in the process of changing from one domain to another.

The original site can still be found at http://www.cariboo.bc.ca/atwood/. Since this changeover is not yet complete, caribou.bc.ca should not be discounted from this discussion as there remains some useful material. Compared to the new site, the original website is very cumbersome to use. The text is extremely large; its font certainly not one I prefer to view on a web browser. Tables are blocky and visually unappealing. Additionally, some sections do not function very well with all browsers.

For instance, at the time that this chapter was written, links within the bibliography of Margaret Atwood did not work with Internet Explorer (v. 6) for Windows (98 or XP). When clicking on any of the links, Internet Explorer did not connect to or load any of the indicated web pages. Instead, an error message was generated stating that the particular page had not been found. The results are very different when using other web browsers (e.g., Mozilla, Netscape). In these cases, the web page functioned normally. The same can be said for those who would rather use a Mac. Both Safari and Internet Explorer for Mac worked well. It seemed to be a problem only for IE (v. 6) for Windows.

On what is now the official website for the Margaret Atwood Society (http:/ /margaretatwoodsociety.org), there is a detailed description of the Society. There is also a form to fill out to become a member of the Society (http://www.margaretatwoodsociety .org/membershipform.doc). Officers come from a variety of North American, European, and Australasian nations. Emails are available for all officers: president and vice-president, treasurer and secretary, as well as the various bibliographers and the webmistress. The inclusion of such information is of great importance for anyone wishing to contact the Society. If one does not find what he or she is seeking, it is thus possible to communicate with someone who might have the answer or, at least, know where to find it.

A *Call for Papers* is posted. Any scholar wishing to contribute to the analysis of Margaret Atwood's works is free to do so. The focus and publication requirements are stated as well as the appropriate people or organization to contact. Conferences and conventions are given with dates and locations. Conference panels are described in detail.

The Society awards prizes to those who write about Margaret Atwood. Deadlines are provided along with a list of judges for each category: best book on Atwood; best article in a scholarly journal; best graduate essay, thesis, or dissertation; and best undergraduate essay. This is important information to provide to the public as it encourages both students and scholars to contribute to the field.

The new Margaret Atwood Society site has a much better presentation with clean text font as well as a clear and logical informational order. This is, without a doubt, a major improvement over its predecessor.

Margaret Atwood: WWW Resources
http://www.mnstate.edu/goodman/atwood.htm; Goodman, 2004

Compiled by Brittney Goodman—Director, Instructional Resources at Minnesota State University (http://www.mnstate.edu/goodman/index.htm)—this is strictly a compilation of links. It is, however, an amazing and extensive collection that deserves to be mentioned. Present are not only links to the two sites previously discussed but also to a variety of discussion pages, interviews, and other resources. The researcher will find links to critical analyses on *The Handmaid's Tale*, *The Robber Bride*, *Alias Grace*, *The Blind Assassin*, *Oryx and Crake*, various poems, and much more.

Unpretentious, the *Margaret Atwood WWW Resources* page is a quirky and colorful site that was found to be relaxing of sorts. Although it may not contain the details that a scholar might seek, it can perfectly suit the needs of the high school student or teacher in a search for quick information or a shortcut to reviews and analyses of some of Atwood's most famous works.

The site is straightforward and easy to use. Every bit of data Goodman has found is included in a single, though lengthy, web page. As opposed to many existing web pages, there is no second-guessing involved when browsing through this one.

Specific Resources

Information in this section has been presented differently from that above. Instead of recording and describing each website individually, sites have been categorized by resource type, such as interviews, speeches, and study guides. Since these sites typically include a single piece of information, this approach is thought to be clearer.

Interviews

There is literally an overabundance of web pages giving access to interviews with Margaret Atwood. Just as an example, on 7 June 2006, a combined search for "margaret atwood" and "interview" was performed on *Google* that resulted in an astounding 213,000 hits. Some provide the transcript of the interview while others supply an actual recording. The length of the interview can vary, but what is important is the fact that Atwood's actual words can be read or heard (provided the researcher has the necessary software to operate these sound files). Furthermore, these interviews vary in date, ranging from the late 1960s to the present. Researchers will be able to experience for themselves the evolution of Atwood's thoughts.

There is a most impressive collection of ten radio and television interviews found at the Canadian Broadcasting Corporation (CBC) website (http://archives.cbc.ca/IDD-1-68-1494/arts_entertainment/margaret_atwood/). These have been taken throughout the course of her career. The interviews are available as sound or video clips that can be listened to or viewed directly from the web browser. Atwood can be heard talking about puppetry, opera, television appearances, her novels, her awards, and much more. Similar French-language interviews are available at the Radio-Canada website (http://archives .radio-canada.ca/IDD-0-72-1397/arts_culture/margaret_atwood/). As with the CBC interviews, these represent a collection of ten interviews.

Next is a 2003 interview with Katherine Lanpher of Minnesota Public Radio in which Atwood discusses her work *The Handmaid's Tale* (http://www.publicradio.org/tools/media/player/news/midmorning/2003/05/09_midmorn2.ram). As with the CBC and Radio-Canada interviews, it is also strictly available as a sound clip. Unfortunately, this clip is of the ".ram" format, making the installation of RealPlayer® (http://www.real .com/player) necessary.

The 2000 interview with Linda Richards of *January Magazine* (http://www .januarymagazine.com/profiles/atwood.html) is not only lengthy but also provides a list of Atwood's works. Here, the author discusses her career, her role models and influences, her works and successes, as well as her future projects.

In a 1997 interview with Laura Miller of *Salon Magazine* (http://www.salon .com/jan97/interview970120.html), Victorian murderesses and Atwood's claim to Connecticut are the focus. A second 1997 interview with Marilyn Snell of *Mother Jones* (http://www.motherjones.com/arts/qa/1997/07/visions.html) answers questions relating to Atwood's political and creative involvement, as well as more personal matters about herself, money, and feminism.

In 1996 Atwood was interviewed by Harriet Gilber of the BBC (http://www.bbc.co .uk/bbcfour/audiointerviews/profilepages/atwoodm1.shtml). This interview is freely available as sound clips in which Atwood talks about realism, tragedy and comedy, and her novels *Surfacing*, *The Handmaid's Tale*, and *Cat's Eye*. As with other sound clips, these recordings are also in ".ram" format.

The questions asked during the 1991 interview with Raymond H. Thompson (http://www.lib.rochester.edu/camelot/intrvws/atwood.htm) pertain to her interest in the Arthurian legend. And, even earlier, in 1986 she spoke with Don Swaim of CBS to discuss her novels, Canada, her thoughts on religion and human rights, and her decision to not major in journalism (http://wiredforbooks.org/margaretatwood/). This is another interview that is only available in ".ram" format.

Sound Clips

The following are sound clippings and poetry readings in which Margaret Atwood can be heard reading her own words:

A special collection includes readings from *A Sad Child*; *All Bread*; *Flowers*; *King Lear in Respite Care*; *The Loneliness of the Military Historian*; *The Moment*; *This Is a Photograph of Me*; *Variation on the Word* Sleep; *Werewolf Movies*; and *You Begin*. Fortunately, all clippings are located at the same site: http://www.owtoad.com/sound.html.

All clippings are in ".mp3" format and all readings are clear and crisp. The researcher will definitely feel Margaret Atwood's presence.

Additional poetry readings can be found at http://www.poetryarchive.org/poetry-archive/singlePoet.do?poetId=96. In this case, the text of each poem has been conveniently provided along with the sound clipping. The researcher can read the poem while listening to Atwood's voice. Available are *The Immigrants*, *King Lear in Respite Care*, *The Moment*, and *Siren Song*.

Speeches and Lectures

The Waterstone's Poetry Lecture (http://www.owtoad.com/writingpoetry.html) was delivered at Hay on Wye, Wales, in June 1995. In it Atwood discusses her life as a poet. In another speech given in 1994 and entitled *Spotty-Handed Villainesses* (http://www.owtoad.com/villainesses.html), she discusses female bad behavior in various literary genres.

Study Guides

There is Paul Brians's (1995a) work, "Study Guide to Margaret Atwood: *The Handmaid's Tale*," which is a chapter-by-chapter analysis of the book (http://www.wsu.edu:8000/~brians/science_fiction/handmaid.html). Brians is a professor in the department of English, Washington State University, and has produced this guide to aid his students with their learning experience (Brians, 1995b).

Also available is Gabriele Twohig' lengthy thesis (http://www.linse.uni-essen.de/esel/atwood.htm). Her emphasis is on the creativity and power through language as it relates to the presentation and contents of *The Handmaid's Tale* (Twohig, 1998).

Finally, there is Random House's *Book Group Corner* (http://www.randomhouse.com/resources/bookgroup). With such a name, one would expect to find this site classified among discussion groups. This is not the case. *Book Group Corner* provides companions to various literary works published by many authors. In the case of Margaret Atwood, information on nine of her novels has been incorporated: *Alias Grace*, *Bodily Harm*, *Cat's Eye*, *The Edible Woman*, *The Handmaid's Tale*, *Lady Oracle*, *Life Before Man*, *The Robber Bride*, and *Surfacing*.

Typically, these companions are comprised of summaries, letters, and suggested readings from Atwood herself, reviews, and personal comments from interested readers as well as thought-provoking questions and topics that interested parties can discuss. Such proposed questions may prove extremely useful to the student writing a school paper, as they may give rise to new ideas and lead to new directions in thinking.

Discussion Groups

Discussion groups are always interesting. They allow people to exchange views while using the Internet as the medium.

The *Margaret Atwood Group* is a discussion group in which Margaret Atwood enthusiasts can freely participate. To sign up, one needs only to go to http://groups.yahoo.com/group/Margaret_Atwood/. Anyone is welcome to join and instructions on how to sign up and post messages are supplied at the site.

Another discussion group exists at *Atwood-L*. It is sponsored by the Margaret Atwood Society. To subscribe, send your mail to mailserv@cariboo.bc.ca. Leave the subject line empty but enter "subscribe atwood-l [yourfirstname yourlastname]" in the message content.

LongPen

It would not be appropriate to close a chapter on Internet resources concerning Margaret Atwood without the special mention of a new and amazing product: LongPen. This is a remote signing device, the idea of which came to Atwood at 4:00 in the morning during one of her stays at the Drake Hotel in Toronto (Atwood, 2006).

This portable device enables a person in, say, a bookstore, to make a specific autograph request to a writer while having a conversation with that writer via a two-way screen and camera system. In other words, both Atwood and the reader can watch and talk to each other; she from the comfort of her home and the reader from another location. Margaret Atwood would then write the requested autograph on an electronic tablet. The result would simultaneously be observed by the person making the request. If corrections are necessary, they can be done before printing begins. When the autograph is satisfactory, the requester places a book underneath a remotely operated mechanical arm and the print job is initiated. The robotic arm writes the signature and autograph in Margaret Atwood's handwriting, exactly how she had scribed it from her home. As of now, this innovative and fascinating invention can sign books, CDs, hockey sticks, contracts, and agreements.

For more information, a visit to http://www.unotchit.com/index.html will reveal the full capability of this device. Here, anyone can watch video recordings in which Margaret Atwood explains how this invention came to be, as well as its variety of uses. The videos are available in both QuickTime and Windows Media formats (http://www.unotchit.com /watch-the-videos.html).

References

Atwood, M. "On Writing Poetry: Waterstone' Poetry Lecture." O.W. Toad, Inc.
    1995. 25 May 2006. <http://www.owtoad.com/writingpoetry.html>
Atwood, M. "O.W. Toad: Margaret Atwood Reference Site." O.W. Toad, Inc. 2005.
    7 June 2006. <http://www.owtoad.com>
Atwood, M. "Spotty-Handed Villainesses: Problems of Female Bad Behaviour in the
    Creation of Literature." O.W.Toad, Inc. 1994. 25 May 2006.
    <http://gos.sbc.edu/a/atwood.html>
Atwood, M. "What Is LongPen?" Unotchit, Inc. 2006. 26 June 2006.
    <http://www.unotchit.com/watch-the-videos.html>
Bloom, M. "Internet Research Made Easy." *Writing* 27.3 (2004): 18-21.
Brians, P. "Study Guide to Margaret Atwood: *The Handmaid's Tale*." Washington State
    University. 1995a. 21 May 2006.
    <http://www.wsu.edu:8000/~brians/science_fiction /handmaid.html>
Brians, P. "About These Guides." Washington State University. 1995b. 26 June 2006.
    <http://www.wsu.edu :8000/~brians/about_guides.html>
Friedman, T., and The Margaret Atwood Society. "The Margaret Atwood Society." The
    Margaret Atwood Society. 2005. 30 May 2006.
    <http://www.cariboo.bc.ca /atwood/>
Goodman, B. "Margaret Atwood: WWW Resources." Minnesota State University. 2004.
    5 June 2006. <http://www.mnstate.edu/goodman/atwood.htm>

Gussow, M. "The Alternate Personalities in an Author's Life and Art." *New York Times.* 30 December 1996: Section C: Page 9: C2.

Hysell, S. G. "MLA International Bibliography of Books and Articles on the Modern Languages and Literature." *ARBA* 33 (2002): 472.

Jacso, P. "Rating the Metasearch Engines." *Information Today* 18.11 (2001): 28-29.

Jokinen, A. "Luminarium Margaret Atwood Page" *Luminarium* 20 February 2007. <http://www.luminarium.org/contemporary/atwood/>

Lanpher, K. "Talking Volumes, Margaret Atwood." Midmorning on Minnesota Public Radio. 9 May 2003. Twin Cities, MN. 15 May 2006. <http://www.publicradio.org/tools/media/player/news/midmorning/2003/05/09_midmorn2.ram>

Margaret Atwood Society. "The Margaret Atwood Society." The Margaret Atwood Society. 20 February 2007. <http://www.mscd.edu/~atwoodso/>

McGarvey, R. "Search Us, Says Google." *Technology Review* 103.6 (2000): 108-113.

Miller, L. "Margaret Atwood on Famous Victorian Murderesses, Her Claim to Connecticut, and the Deep Satisfaction of a Clean, Folded Towel." *Salon* January 1997. 25 May 2006. <http://www.salon.com/jan97/interview970120.html>

Mossberg, W. S., and K. Boehret. "What You Should Know about Web Searches." *Wall Street Journal—Eastern Edition* 246.140 (2005): D1-D6.

O.W. Toad Ltd. "O.W. Toad: Margaret Atwood Reference Site." O.W. Toad, Inc. 2006. 15 May 2006. <http://www.owtoad.com>

Richards, L. "Margaret Atwood." *January Magazine* November 2000. 25 May 2006. <http://www.januarymagazine.com/profiles/atwood.html>

Snell, M. "Margaret Atwood." *Mother Jones* 7 July 1997. 25 May 2006. <http://www.motherjones.com/arts/qa/1997/07/visions.html>

Swain, D. "Audio Interview with Margaret Atwood." *Wired for Books* 10 February 1986. 10 April 2007.

Thompson. R. H. "Interview with Margaret Atwood." *Interviews with Authors of Modern Arthurian Literature.* Ed. R. H. Thompson. Rochester, NY: University of Rochester, 1991. 15 May 2006. <http://www.lib.rochester.edu/camelot/intrvws/atwood.htm>

Twohig, G. "The Politics of Language: A Device of Creativity and Power in Margaret Atwood's Novel *The Handmaid's Tale.*" Universitat GH Essen, 1998. 25 May 2006. <http://www.linse.uni-essen.de/esel/atwood.htm>

Unotchit, Inc. "LongPen: Writing Around the World." Unotchit, Inc. 2006. 26 June 2006. <http://www.unotchit.com/index.html>

Author Index

Note: This is an index to the authors of Interviews and Scholarly Resources, referenced to entry numbers.

Abbas, Herawaty, 3036
Abiteboul, Maurice, 74, 2270
Abley, Mark, 1566, 1806, 2744
Adamo, Laura Elizabeth, 2271
Adams, Alice E., 1311
Adams, Carol J., 292
Adams, Robert, 3469
Adhikari, Madhumalati, 1580, 3037
Aguiar, Sarah Appleton, 1091, 2034, 3038
Ahearn, Catherine, 1092
Ahern, Stephen, 1093
Aisenberg, Nadya, 1312
Alaimo, Stacy, 1313, 2785
Allen, Beverly, 1581
Allen, Lisa F., 1314
Allen, Paul Smith, 2539
Allison, Alida Louise, 468
Almeida, Léila, 3470
Almonte, Richard, 3471
Amano, Kyoka, 2540
Amende, Coral, 1315
Amoura-Patterson, Sana, 3039
Anderson, Jon, 277
Anderson, Michele E., 469
Andraszek, Katharine, 2035
Andre, Alestine, 853
Andrews, Jennifer, 2786
Andriano, Joseph, 1094
Angulo, Urbano Viñuela, 2114
Apter, Terri, 1582
Arbor, Joy, 3472
Arias Doblas, Rosario, 3853
Arias-Beautell, Eva, 1818
Armbruster, Jane, 470

Armitt, Lucie, 2787
Arnold, David Scott, 471
Arróspide, Amparo, 2541
Ash, Susan, 667
Atherton, Stanley S., 472
Atrops, Lorene A., 1819
Augier, Valérie, 293
Azar-Luxton, Grizéll, 3854

Bacchilega, Cristina, 2788-2789
Baccolini, Raffaella, 855, 1095, 1820, 2790, 3040
Bach, Susanne, 1316
Bachinger, Katrina, 294, 473
Bader, Rudolf, 1567
Baer, Elizabeth R., 75
Baer, Susan, 455
Balcom, Ted, 856
Baldwin, Dean, 1317
Balestra, Gianfranca, 1318
Bancroft, Colette M., 1069
Banerjee, Chinmoy, 474-475
Barat, Urbashi, 1583, 3041
Barbour, Douglas, 76
Bargreen, Melinda, 1287
Barnard, Anette, 3473
Barnett, Nick, 3012
Barr, Marleen S., 77, 857, 1096, 3657
Barry, Peter, 3232
Bartkowski, Frances, 295
Bartlett, Sally A., 3658
Barzilai, Shuli, 1821-1822, 2791-2793, 3855
Basbanes, Nicholas A., 1568
Batstone, Kathleen Loren, 1319

Battersby, Eileen, 1807, 2745
Baughman, Cynthia, 476
Bazin, Nancy Topping, 668
Beard, William, 1320
Becker, Susanne, 2542, 2794
Beddoes, Julie, 1097
Beer, Janet, 2272
Behe, Regis, 3831
Behuniak-Long, Susan, 669
Bell, Virginia Ellen, 2036
Bellis, Miriam Hamilton, 1823
Bemrose, John, 2746
Benatar, Giselle, 278
Benet-Goodman, Helen Charisse, 3659
Benn Jones, Yvonne P., 2037
Bennett, Donna, 1321, 1824, 3233
Benson, Stephen, 1825
Bentley, D. M. R., 1322
Benton, Carol L., 78, 1826
Beran, Carol L., 477-478, 670, 858, 1098,
    1827, 3474
Berard, Nicole Julia, 3234
Berg, Temma F., 1323
Bergmann, Harriet F., 296
Bessner, Neil, 859
Bethune, Brian, 3435, 3832
Betts, Lenore, 3235
Beyer, Charlotte, 1584-1586, 2795
Bharathi, V., 1587
Bidiville, Annick, 3856
Bieber, David Charles, 1099
Biese, Eivor, 1828
Bignell, Jonathan, 1100, 2273
Bigsby, Christopher, 2747
Billi, Mirella, 297
Birden, Lorene M., 3236
Bishop, M. G. H., 1325
Bjerring, Nancy, 1829
Bjørhovde, Gerd, 3660
Bjornson, Kathryn, 3661
Black, J. L., 1588
Black, Joseph, 1588
Blackford, Holly, 3857
Blaise, Clark, 479
Blake, Marjorie Rose, 860
Blanc, Marie Therese, 3662
Blaze, Margaret K., 1589
Blodgett, E. D., 79, 1101
Blodgett, Harriet, 3663
Bloom, Harold, 2796, 3042, 3664
Bloom, Lynn Z., 1590, 2543
Blott, Anne, 80
Blue, Sarah Jane, 3043
Bohner, Jennifer Anne, 2038

Boily, Lisa, 1102
Bök, Christian, 861
Bone, James, 1808
Bonheim, Helmut, 2797
Bontatibus, Donna, 2274
Booker, M. Keith, 1326, 1830
Bork, Carol Denise, 3475
Borstad, Louise Marie, 671
Bossert, Rex Thomas, 81
Bouchard, Guy, 480
Bouson, J. Brooks, 298, 481, 1103, 1591, 1831,
    2798, 3044, 3476, 3665
Boutelle, Ann Edwards, 82
Bowen, Deborah, 482
Bowen, Heather E., 3481
Bower, Martha Gilman, 862
Bowering, George, 83, 863, 3858
Boynton, Victoria Anne, 1592, 3237
Bradford, Kelly Jean, 1104
Brady, Lenore Lillian, 3238
Brain, Tracy Eileen, 864, 1593
Brameshuber-Ziegler, I. J., 2544
Brampton, Sally, 279
Brandon, Paul, 3239
Brans, Jo, 64
Brewster, Elizabeth, 84, 865
Brin, David, 2799
Brink, André, 2275
Britton, Krista M., 866
Brockes, Emma, 3636
Bromberg, Pamela S., 85
Brown, DeNeen, L., 3218
Brown, Jane, 1594
Brown, Julie, 672
Brown, Lyn Mikel, 1595, 2276
Brown, Russell, 86, 483
Brown, Russell M., 3045
Brownley, Martine Watson, 2277, 2545, 2800
Bruhn, Mark J., 3666
Brunet, Emmanuelle, 2278
Brunet-Arvanitakis, Emmanuelle, 3046
Brunton, Rosanne D., 484
Brydon, Diana, 1596, 1832
Buchbinder, David, 87
Buck, M. Laurel, 485
Bühler Roth, Verena, 2279
Burack, Cynthia, 299
Burdette, Martha, 486
Burnham, Julie E., 867
Busby, Brian John, 3477
Buschini, Marie-Pascale, 2280, 2546
Buss, Helen, 300
Butler, Jeri, 2535
Butt, William, 88

Caenepeel, Mimo, 89
Cakebread, Caroline Marcus, 2039
Caldwell, Larry W., 868
Caldwell, Rebecca, 3637
Call, Nancy J., 2040
Callwood, June, 1288
Calvert, Michelle, 673
Cameron, Elspeth, 90
Caminero-Santangelo, Marta, 1327, 3667
Campbell, Elizabeth A., 301, 1597
Campbell, Josie P., 91
Campbell-Furtick, Cristy, 869
Campion, Blandine, 2261
Cannon, Elizabeth Monroe, 2041
Canty, Joan F., 1598
Caporale Bizzini, Silvia, 1599
Carey, Gary, 2281
Carley, Dave, 3204
Carpenter, Sherida Hughes, 870
Carrera Suarez, Isabel, 302, 1328
Carriker, Kitti, 487
Carrington, Ildikó de Papp, 92, 674, 1105
Casciato, Paul, 2024
Case, Eleanor, 3436
Castino, Melissa, 2282
Castro, Jan Garden, 65, 172
Caulfield Rybak, Deborah, 3437
Cavalcanti, Idlney, 2801
Cecil, Lynn Anne, 1834
Chadwick, Tony, 2823
Chakovsky, Sergei, 871
Chakravarty, Radha, 2283
Chamberlain, Adrian, 3438
Chandler, Joel C., 1106
Chandra, Suresh, 1107
Chapman, Suzette, 1835
Charreron, Elodie, 3478
Cheever, Leonard A., 1600
Chen, Qiuhua, 3668
Chen, Zhongming, 1330
Chilton, Myles, 3479
Choe, Okyoung, 1331
Christ, Carol P., 1601
Christy, Marian, 280
Chung, Kathy K. Y., 2284
Clark, Lucy, 3013
Clark, Miriam Marty, 1108
Clarke, Elizabeth, 1602
Clayton, Jay, 1109
Close, Ajay, 1070
Coad, David, 3047
Cocoual, Ifiq, 3048
Coffelt, Jamie Roberta, 3049
Coffey, Edel, 3439
Cohen, Mark, 2547, 3050

Cohen, Matt, 2802-2803
Coles Editorial Board, 872, 1110, 1332, 2285-
    2286
Collett, Anne, 2287
Collingwood, Laura Emma, 3240
Coltrera, Francesca, 281
Colvile, Georgiana M. M., 2288, 2548
Combs, Marianne, 3440-3441
Comellini, Carla, 1603
Comiskey, B., 2043
Comiskey, Barbara Anne, 1604
Commire, Anne, 62
Conboy, Sheila C., 1111
Condé, Mary, 1112-1113, 3241
Conrad, Peter, 1605
Continelli, Louise, 1289
Cook, Eleanor, 2536
Cooke, John, 1836
Cooke, Nathalie, 873, 1606, 1824, 2289, 2549,
    2804, 3669
Cooley, Dennis, 1333
Cooper, Pamela, 1607, 2044, 3670
Costa de Beauregard, Raphaëlle, 2290
Costantini, Marie-Louise, 3242
Coulson, Sandra, 3442
Coupe, Laurence, 2045
Couturier-Storey, Françoise, 2550-2551, 3051,
    3243
Cowan, Amy, 1837
Cowart, David, 303, 874
Cox, Michele Lee, 875
Craig, Paul, 1071
Creighton, Judy, 2537
Crook, Barbara, 2748
Crosbie, Lynn, 1114
Crowder, Diane Griffin, 1115
Cuder, Pilar, 3480
Cuder-Dominguez, Pilar, 675, 1116
Culpeper, Richard, 304

Dale, Tina Louise, 2552
Daniels, Margaret J., 3481
Daniels, Steven Robert, 876
Dañobeitia, María Luisa, 488
D'Arcy, Chantal Cornut-Gentille, 1838
Darroch, Heidi, 3671
Davey, Frank, 93-96, 877, 1117, 1334-1336
David, Jack, 339, 528-530
Davidson, Arnold E., 97-98, 676, 1337, 1839,
    2046, 2805, 3672
Davies, Laurence, 2553
Davies, Linda, 1290
Davies, Robertson, 2554
Davison, Carol, 3244
Dawson, Carrie, 2291

De Angelis, Valerio Massimo, 1338
De Voogd, Peter J., 99
De Zordo, Ornella, 2806
DeBoer, Ron B., 1118
Deconcini, Barbara, 489
Deer, Glenn, 878, 1339, 2807, 3052, 3673
Deery, June, 2047, 2808
Delbaere-Garant, Jeanne, 305
Dellamora, Richard, 3245
Delord, Marie, 2292, 2556
Delville, Michel, 2048
DeMarco, Donald, 677
Demos, John, 2293
Denison, D. C., 1072
DeRocco, David, 2049
Desjardins, Louise, 490, 879
Desmeules, Christian, 3833
Detore-Nakamura, Joanne, 2294
Detweiler, Robert, 306, 491
Dev, Jai, 492
Devaney, Sheila Ann, 1340
Devi, N. Rama, 1608
Devine, Maureen, 880
Deyoung-Patrie, Bettie Jo, 2809
Dhar, T. N., 678
DiBenedetto, Tamra Elizabeth, 881
Dijck, José van, 953
DiMarco, Danette, 1609, 3053, 3859
Ding, Linpeng, 2555
Dinsmore, Robert, 3239
Diot, Rolande, 2295
Divasson Cilveti, Lourdes, 307-308, 493
Dixon, Guy, 3834
Djwa, Sandra, 1610, 1840, 2810-2811, 3674
Dobris, Catherine Aileen, 309
Dodson, Danita Joan, 1341, 2025, 2050
Doherty, Mike, 3639
Dolitsky, Marlène, 2296-2297, 2557
Donaldson-Tosh, Kathy, 882
Donawerth, Jane L., 1342
Donelson, Ken, 2051
Donnelly, Pat, 3219
Dopp, Jamie, 883, 1343, 3675
Dorfman, Ariel, 1569
Doss, Michelle M., 2052
Doty, William G., 491, 494
Douthat, Ross, 3246
Downey, Mike, 495
Dreifus, Claudia, 838
D'Souza, Irene, 3638
Dubois, Dominique, 2298, 2558
Dugan, Stephen M., 2812
Duncan, Isla J., 2053, 2559
Duncker, Patricia, 1119
Dunn, Sharon, 3220

Dunning, Stephen, 3860
Duplay, Mathieu, 2560
Dupriez, Bernard, 679
Durand, Régis, 2299
Durix, Carole, 1120
Durix, Jean-Pierre, 1120
Dvorak, Marta, 2300-2302, 2561-2564, 3054-
    3055, 3247
Dymoke, Sue, 2303
Dymond, Erica Joan, 3482

Eagleton, Mary, 2054
East, Louise, 3835
Easun, Sue, 2055
Eberhart, John Mark, 3836
Eckler, Rebecca, 3443-3444
Economou-Bailey, Mary, 3248
Edgecombe, Rodney Stenning, 1611
Edwards, Jannie, 310
Ehrenreich, Barbara, 3676
Eichenberger, Bill, 2538
Eichler, Leah, 3445
Elliott, Gayle, 3103
Elliott, Helen, 3014
Elliott, Marilyn O. Mercer, 680
Elsley, Judy, 2304
Emberley, Julia, 681
Eng, Monica, 2026
Engeler, Beth, 1291
Enos, Jennifer, 1612
Enright, Michael, 3837
Ens, Kelly Linda, 311
Epstein, Grace Ann, 496, 1121-1122
Epstein, Hugh, 682
Evain, Christine, 3249
Evans, F. E. M. See Evans, Francis Eric Mark
Evans, Francis Eric Mark, 884
Evans, Gillian M., 1841
Evans, Mark, 1344
Evans, Shari Michelle, 3861
Evenson, Laura, 2027
Everett-Green, Robert, 3446

Fand, Roxanne Joyce, 1613, 2565, 3483
Farrell, Kirby, 1842
Farwell, Marilyn R., 1123
Fawcett, Brian, 683
Feay, Suzi, 1570
Fee, Margery, 1124, 2305
Fenwick, Julie, 885
Ferns, Chris, 312
Fetherling, Douglas, 2306
Feuer, Lois, 2056, 3677
Fiamengo, Janice, 2307, 2566, 2813
Fiand. See Quigley

Fichtner, Margaria, 2749, 3640
Field, Thalia S., 3015
Figueira, Dorothy, 497
Filipczak, Dorota, 1125, 1614
Findley, Timothy, 1345
Finnell, Susanna, 1126
Fisher, Susan, 3056
Fitting, Peter, 313, 498
Fitz, Earl E., 684
Flatow, Ira, 3641
Fleitz, Elizabeth J., 3862
Flockhart, Susan, 2750
Florén, Celia, 1843
Focamp, Paul, 3016
Foertsch, Jacqueline, 2057
Foley, Michael, 314, 499
Fontaine, Dorothy-Ann, 3057
Ford, Susan Allen, 3484
Forsberg, Myra, 282
Forster, Russell, 2814
Forth, Sarah S., 1346
Fortney, Valerie, 2751, 3447
Foster, John Wilson, 100
Foster, Malcolm, 2567
Fowler, Karen Joy, 2815
Fox, Matthew, 3642
Fox, Sue, 1292
Fox-Genovese, Elizabeth, 886
Franzke, Anne Disney, 1846
Fraser, John, 2752
Fraser, Matthew, 655
Fraser, Wayne, 685
Freedman, Bill, 3888
Freeman, Alan, 2753
Freibert, Lucy M., 101
Friedman, Thomas B., 1844-1845, 1917
Frye, Northrop, 1127
Fu, Jun, 3485
Fu, Xinyu, 2816
Fulford, Robert, 102
Fullbrook, Kate, 500
Furge, Stefanie, 2568

Gabilliet, Jean-Paul, 2308-2309
Gabriele, Sandra, 2310
Gadpaille, Michelle, 103, 1128
Gale, Marilyn Kravitz, 2311
Gallix, François, 2309, 2312
Garay, Kathleen, 3717
Garbett, Ann D., 3250
García, Ana María, 2058
Garcia, Jennifer Renee, 3486
Gardiner, Anne Barbeau, 3678
Gardiner, Heather, 2059
Gardner, Laurel J., 1347

Garlick, Barbara, 887
Garner, Lee, 2313
Garner, Mark, 3874
Garrett-Petts, W. F., 104, 888
Garron, Rebecca, 1293, 1571
Gary, Lara Karine, 3251
Gasparotti, Alessandra, 686
Gatenby, Greg, 2569
Gatz, Diana M., 2060
Gault, Cinda, 3487
Gebbia, Alessandro, 1348
Geddes, Gary, 105
Geis, Deborah R., 3252
Genty, Stéphanie, 2314
George, Jacqueline A., 315
George, Lianne, 3221, 3643
Geracimos, Ann, 283
Gerard, Jasper, 2754
Gerig, Karin, 2570, 2817
Germain, Guy C., 525
Gernes, Sonia, 687, 1129
Gerry, Thomas M. F., 1130
Gerstenberger, Donna, 106
Gessell, Paul, 2755, 3448
Ghosh, Nabanita, 2818
Giacoppe, Monika Frances, 2819
Gilbert, Emily, 1349, 2061
Gilbert, Paula R., 2571
Gilbert, Sandra M., 688, 1350
Gilbert-Maceda, Ma Teresa, 501, 1351
Gillen, Francis X., 66
Gillespie, Tracey, 502
Ginsberg, Robert, 1615
Gioia, Dana, 889
Givner, Jessie, 316, 890
Glasberg, Ronald P., 1352
Glickman, Susan, 689
Glover, Douglas H., 107, 2572
Godard, Barbara, 317, 891, 1353, 3058
Goddard, Peter, 456
Godsey, Kristin D., 3644, 3838
Goetsch, Paul, 2820
Goldblatt, Patricia F., 2573
Goldensohn, Barry, 1354
Goldman, Marlene, 2574, 3059, 3863
Gomez, Christine, 1355, 1616
Gooch, Brad, 1073
Goodliffe, Kim, 3449, 3839
Goodwin, Ken, 503
Gopalan, Kamala, 2315
Gordon, Daphne, 2756
Goring, Rosemary, 1356, 3840
Gorjup, Branko, 1847
Gorlier, Claudio, 2062
Gotsch-Thomson, Susan, 504

Gottleib, Erika, 3060
Gould, Alan, 3017
Gould, Allan M., 67
Grabenhorst, Tina, 3680
Grace, Dominick M., 2063, 2316, 3061
Grace, Judy, 2262
Grace, Sherrill E., 108, 1357-1359, 1617, 3253, 3681
Graeber, Laurel, 1074
Grainger, Brett, 2757
Granofsky, Ronald, 505, 1618
Grant, Cynthia, 1360
Gray, Francine du Plessix, 109
Greene, Gayle, 110, 506, 690-691, 1131
Greene, Michael, 2317, 2575
Greene, Sharon Elaine, 111
Greenwood, Gillian, 1294
Greenwood, R., 3254
Gregersdotter, Katarina, 3488
Gregory, Eileen, 1361
Greven-Borde, Hélène, 2318, 2576
Gribble, Jill, 2821
Griesinger, Emily Ann, 318
Griffin, Gabriele, 1132
Griffiths, Anthony, 3682
Groening, Laura Smith, 1133
Grondahl, Paul, 2263
Gronewold, Laura, 3683
Grosskurth, Phyllis, 112, 2577
Guadalupi, Gianni, 2850
Gubar, Susan, 688, 1350
Guernalec, Julie, 2578
Gulick, Angela Michelle, 692
Gussow, Mel, 1809, 2028, 2758-2759
Guttridge, Peter, 839
Gzowski, Peter, 2029, 3222

Haag, Ed, 68
Haag, Stefan, 2822
Habib, Marlene, 1572
Hales, Lesley Ann, 507
Hamilton, Nicholas Alexander, 3255
Hammer, Stephanie Barbé, 508, 1848
Hammill, Faye, 2064, 2319, 2579-2580, 3489-3490, 3864
Hammond, Margo, 3841
Hansen, Elaine Tuttle, 693, 2065
Hansot, Elisabeth, 1362
Harger-Grinling, Virginia, 2823
Hariprasanna, A., 1619
Harishankar, V. Bharathi, 2320
Harker, John W., 1363
Harkness, David L, 319
Harmansson, Casie, 2581
Harold, James, 3865

Harris, Jocelyn, 2582
Harting, Heike, 1849
Harvey, Caroline, 2760
Hatch, Ronald B., 2824
Haughton, Rosemary, 694
Hawkins, Harriett, 509
Hayes, Becci, 556
Heer, Jeet, 3223
Heidenreich, Rosmarin, 320
Heiland, Donna, 892, 3684
Heilmann, Ann, 3018, 3256
Heinimann, David, 893, 2066
Heller, Arno, 113, 1850
Heller, Daniel, 2032
Hellman, Mary, 1295
Helwig, David, 114, 894
Henderson, Jennifer, 695, 895
Henderson, Margaret Kathryn, 2825
Hengen, Shannon Eileen, 115, 696, 1134, 1620, 1845, 1917, 2321, 2583, 3257, 3491
Henighan, Stephen, 3258
Henneberger, Sandra, 510
Herbert, Rosemary, 2761
Hermansson, Casie Elizabeth, 2322, 3062
Hermes, Liesel, 1135
Herndl, Diane Price, 1136
Herrick, Jim, 511
Herst, B., 2826
Herzig-Danielson, Viola Angela, 1621
Hewitt, Pamela, 1851
Higa, Lisa S., 3259
Hill, Colin, 3685
Hiller, Susanne, 3019, 3842
Hilton, Lisa, 3686
Hinz, Evelyn J., 116
Hirsch, Marianne, 321
Hite, Molly, 117, 322, 896, 1622-1623, 2827
Hjartarson, Paul, 118
Hobgood, Jennifer, 3260
Hoeppner, Kenneth, 323
Hogsette, David S., 2067
Hollenberg, Donna Krolik, 2543
Hollinger, Veronica, 1364
Hollis, Hilda, 1624
Hollister, Michael, 1625
Holmlund, Mona, 3492
Holtze, Elizabeth A., 1137
Holzner, Judith, 3063
Hönnighausen, Lothar, 2828
Hooper, Brad, 897
Hoover, Bob, 1296, 3843
Hope, Joan, 1852
Horikawa, Tetsushi, 898
Horlacher, Stefan, 3687
Horne, Helen Marion, 1138, 1365

Horner, Avril, 512, 3261, 3866
Horvitz, Deborah M., 2829
Horwood, Harold, 2830
Hossne, Andrea Saad, 2831
Howard, Philip, 840
Howells, Coral Ann, 324, 697, 1139, 1366-
    1367, 1626-1628, 1853, 2068, 2323-2326,
    2414, 2832-2833, 3262-3263, 3493-3496,
    3688, 3867
Howlett, Jeffrey Winslow, 1629
Hsieh, Shu-nu, 2069
Hubbard, Kim, 284
Hubbard, Susan, 2762
Hudgens, Brenda, 2070
Hudgins, Christopher C., 3497
Hufnagel, Jill, 1854-1855
Huggan, Graham, 325-326, 1368, 3064
Hulley, Kathleen, 2327
Humm, Maggie, 698
Humphreys, Emyr, 3264
Hung, Mei-hwa, 1369
Hunt, Lynn, 2328
Hunt, Richard, 3265
Hunter, Lynette, 2329
Hutcheon, Linda, 119, 327, 699, 899, 1140
Hutchison, Beth, 700
Hutchison, Lorna, 3498
Huy, Minh Tran, 3844

Ikenberg, Tamara, 3645
Inge, M. Thomas, 871
Ingersoll, Earl G., 458-459, 701, 840, 900,
    1141, 1856, 2330, 3065, 3499, 3689
Ingram, Penelope Anne, 2584
Irvine, Denise, 3020
Irvine, Lorna M., 120-121, 1142, 2571, 2834
Italie, Hillel, 1075

Jackson, Kevin, 1143
Jacob, Didier, 3224
Jacob, Susan, 2331
Jacobsen, Sally A., 1857
Jacobsohn, Rachel W., 1370
Jacobson, Michael, 3021
Jaidev, 513
Jaidka, Manju, 2835
James, William Closson, 2332
Jamieson, Sara Louise, 3066, 3266
Jarman, Mark, 2585
Jarrett, Mary, 514, 2333
Jay, Sian E., 2763
Jeffries, Lesley, 1144
Jena, Seema, 515
Jenainati, Cathia, 3500
Jennings, Rosalind Maria, 1858

Joannou, Maroula, 3067
Johnson, Anne S., 1435
Johnson, Brian, 1859-1860
Johnson, Constance Hochstein, 1371
Johnson, Jeri, 656
Johnson, Kristyn, 3868
Johnston, Rita, 2071
Johnston, Sheila, 460
Johnston, Susan, 901
Jones, Adrienne, 3450
Jones, Ann Rosalind, 1131
Jones, Anne G., 3267
Jones, Dorothy, 328, 3501
Jones, Michelle Lynne, 902
Jones, Raymond E., 2836
Jong, Nicole de, 2334
Jorgensen, Mary Crew, 1145
Jump, Harriet Devine, 702
Juneau, Carol, 2072
Juneja, Om P., 516
Jurak, Mirko, 2073, 3268

Kaarto, Tomi, 2837
Kaczvinsky, Donald P., 3068
Kadar, Marlene, 1861
Kalb, John Douglas, 329
Kaler, Anne K., 330
Kamboureli, Smaro, 703
Kammler, Heike, 704
Kanaar, Kay, 1146
Kane, Patricia, 122
Kaplan, E. Ann, 903
Karras, Christy, 3646
Karrasch, Anke, 1630
Kauffman, Linda S., 331, 517, 904, 1131
Kaur, Iqbal, 1372
Keefer, Janice Kulyk, 1373
Keenan, Catherine, 3451
Keith, Cassandra M., 1631
Keith, W. J., 332-333, 705, 905, 1374, 1632
Kekki, Lasse, 2837
Kellaway, Kate, 1076
Kelly, Darlene, 1633
Kelly, Karen, 1810
Kelly, M. T., 1297
Kelly, Sarah M., 3869
Kemp, Mark Alexander Riach, 1862
Kemp, Peter, 3452
Kendall, Kathleen, 2586
Kennedy, Marjorie, 1634
Kenyon, Olga, 841
Kertzer, J. M., 706
Ketterer, David, 334, 906, 3690
Keulen, Maggi, 1635
Kim, Bong Eun, 3069

Kim, Youngmin, 3502
King, Bruce, 1147
King, James, 2074, 2587
King, Nicola, 2838
Kingden, Elizabeth, 123
Kirtz, Mary K., 907, 1863, 2839, 3503
Kitch, Sally L., 518
Kizuk, A. R., 335
Kizuk, R. Alexander, 2075
Klappert, Peter, 519
Klarer, Mario, 520-521, 1636
Klawitter, Uwe, 2076
Klick, Donna M., 3504
Kloss, Robert J., 2588
Knelman, Judith, 2589
Knelman, Martin, 3647
Knight, Brenda, 2840
Knowles, Nancy Anne, 2841
Kohlke, M. L., 2335
Kolmerton, Carol A., 1342
Kolodny, Annette, 522, 707, 2842
Kormali, Sema, 1864
Korolczuk, Elizabeth, 3691
Korte, Barbara, 523-524, 2077
Kreuiter, Allyson, 2843
Krey Catellier, Miriam, 2590
Kroll, Jeri, 3070
Kröller, Eva-Marie, 908
Krótki, Karol Jósef, 525
Kruk, Laurie Ann, 909, 2336
Krull, John, 2264
Krywalski, Diether, 910
Ku, Chung-hao, 3692
Kuester, Martin Herbert, 526, 911
Kuhn, Cynthia Guerrera, 3071, 3870
Kuhnert, Matthias, 2591
Kuribayashi, Tomoko, 124
Kurjatto-Renard, Patrycja, 2337
Kurtz, Roman, 1865
Kyser, Kristina, 3693

Labudová, Katarína, 3871
Lacroix, Jean-Michel, 2338-2339, 2592
Ladousse, Gillian Porter. See Porter-Ladousse,
  Gillian
Laflamme, Lisa, 3022
Laga, Barry E., 2078
Lahaie, Christiane, 1375
Laine-Wille, Ilona, 1637
Lal, Malashri, 1376, 1638
Lamb, Martha Moss, 1377
Lamoureux, Cheryl Michelle Mary, 2341
Lancashire, Ian, 1148
Landa, José Ángel García, 1838
Landis, Kathleen M., 912

Lane, Patrick, 336, 1639
Lane, R. D., 1149
Lane, Richard, 1150
Lane, Richard J., 2593
Langdon, Julia, 1811, 3023
Langdon, Sandra, 2342
Langer, Beryl Donaldson, 69, 125
Langer-Devine, Maureen C., 527
Lanpher, Katherine, 3453
Lappas, Catherine, 1640, 1866
Larkin, Joan, 126
Larson, Janet L., 337
Laurence, Margaret, 127, 1641
Laurent, Delphine, 1378
Lauret, Maria Laetitia Josephine, 913, 1379
Lawn, Jennifer. See Lawn, Jenny
Lawn, Jenny, 1642, 3505
Layman, Margaret, 3024
Laz, C., 1867
LeBihan, Jill, 708, 1151
Lecker, Robert, 339, 528-530, 709, 1152
Leclaire, Jacques, 338, 531, 710, 2079, 2339,
  2343-2345, 2592, 2594
Lecy, Maren, 1868
Ledyard, M. D., 1380
Lee, Hermione, 285
Lee, Jerrine Emma, 532
Lee, So-Hee, 1869, 2346, 2595
Lenk, Uta, 3269
Leonard, Garry, 1870
Letcher, Bettina Havens, 711
Levesque, John, 1077
Levine-Keating, Helane, 1871
Levy, Patricia, 3072
Lewochko, Mary, 340
Li, Shuping, 2080
Li, Tsui Yan, 3270
Libedinsky, Juana, 3648
Lilburn, Jeffrey M., 2844
Lilienfeld, Jane, 128
Lin, Michelle Hoefahn, 3872
Linley, Boniface, 3454
Linton, Michael, 3506
Little, Judy, 1381
Little, Melanie, 3845
Little, Philippa Susan, 712
Liu, Cecilia H. C., 2347
Liu, Kedong, 2081
Ljungberg, Christina Stücklin, 2596-2597,
  2845, 3073, 3074
Llantada Díaz, María Francisca, 2348
Lockett, Jacqueline Rose, 713
Lombardi, Giancarlo, 1382, 1872
Long, Maureen Eleanor, 3507
Long, Michael, 1383

Longo, Maria Luisa, 1153
Lopez, Barbara Leaman, 1154
Lorre, Christine, 2349
Loschnigg, Maria, 2598, 3074
Lott, Lisa, 1873
Loudermilk, Kim A., 2083, 3694
Louvel, Liliane, 2350
Lovelady, Stephanie, 2599-2600
Lovell-Smith, Rose, 3271
Lowe, Julia, 714
Lowery, Adrien Jeanette, 3075
Lozar, Tom, 129
Lucas, Linda E., 341
Lucking, David, 533
Lucotti, Claudia, 3272
Lutwack, Leonard, 1384
Lyall, Sarah, 1078
Lyden, Jack, 1298
Lyke, M. L., 1299
Lynch, Denise E., 130

MacCannell, Juliet Flower, 2846
MacDonald, Marianne, 3846
MacDonald, Tanis Louise, 3873
MacFarlane, Karen, 2351-2352, 3076
MacFarlane, Susan Elizabeth Wilson, 1874,
    3508
MacKey, Eva, 2847
MacKey, Melodie Anne, 2353
Macklin, Lisa A., 1155
MacLaren, Sherrill, 657
MacLennan, Jennifer Margaret, 1156
MacLulich, T. D., 131
MacMurraugh-Kavanagh, M. K., 2084, 2848
MacPherson, Heidi Slettedahl, 2849, 3273,
    3695
Maddocks, Fiona, 3455
Mahoney, Elisabeth, 1875
Maisonnat, Claude, 2601
Mak, Elaine Ngah Lam, 3077, 3274
Makowsky, Veronica, 1590, 2543
Malak, Amin, 1876, 3078, 3696
Malcolm, Andrew H., 461
Mallick, Heather, 1812
Mallinson, Jean, 132, 1157
Mandel, Ann, 133
Mandel, Eli, 134
Manderson, Jill, 342
Manguel, Alberto, 914, 2850, 3697
Manley, Kathleen E. B., 1877
Mansnerus, Laura, 286
Mantel, Hilary, 2085
Manuel, Katrina, 1878
March, Cristie, 2086
Marchand, Philip, 658, 842, 1079, 1573

Mari, Catherine, 2354
Marinheiro, Ana Cristina Barbosa de, 2851
Marinovich, Sarolta, 1385
Marra, Giulio, 1386
Marshall, Ian, 3079
Marshall, John, 2764
Marshall, Tom, 915
Martin, Deborah, 3456
Martin, Frédéric, 2852
Martin, Sandra, 2765, 3225, 3457
Martin, Shannon, 1643
Martin, Valerie, 3649
Martinez-Zalce, Graciela, 1387
Martyniuk, Irene, 2355
Mascaro, Patricia Ellen, 1388
Masel, C., 1158
Mason, Carol Ann, 1879
Massé, Michelle A., 916
Massoura, Kiriaki, 2356, 3080, 3275, 3698-
    3699, 3874
Matchan, Linda, 2766
Mattes, Kimberly, 2853
Matthews, David R., 2087
Matthews, Patricia Shaw, 1389
Maus, Jessica Rene, 3510
Mayo, Kathleen A., 917
Mays, Lynda Graham, 715
McAlpine, Janice, 2305
McCarthy, E., 2854, 3700
McClenagan, Cindy Marlow, 3276
McCombs, Judith, 135-137, 343-344, 716-717,
    1390, 1880, 2855
McDermott, Sinead, 2856
McDonald, Christie, 718
McDonald, Maggie, 3436
McDowell, John N., 3081
McElroy, James, 1080
McElroy, Ruth, 3277
McGlone, Jackie, 2767, 3458
McGuire, Ann, 534
McIntyre, Susan Kathryn, 2088
McKay, George, 918
McKay, Robert, 3875
McLean, Barbara, 2357
McLean, Sandy, 1813
McMahon, Daniel Jordan, 1881
McMillan, Ann, 138
McNamara, Mary, 2768
McVann, Mark, 535
Meindl, Dieter, 345, 1159, 1391
Melley, Timothy Daniel, 1644, 1882
Melnyk, Olenka, 3650
Méndez Díaz, Luisa Cristina, 3511
Merivale, Patricia, 1645, 1883
Meskova, Sandra, 3876

Metzger, Lore, 2358
Metzler, Gabriele, 2769, 2857
Meyer, Bruce, 843
Meyer, Carla, 2770
Meyers, Helene, 719, 3082
Michael, Magali Cornier, 536, 1884, 3083, 3512
Michel, Anthony J., 3278
Mildon, Denis Albert, 919
Milfull, Alison, 3084
Milinder, Le'Ann, 1160
Miller, Jane, 720
Miller, Kathy, 1885
Miller, Lauri, 1300
Miller, Ryan Edward, 2858, 3279
Miller, Tanya J., 3513
Milne, Kirsty, 2771
Miner, Madonne, 721, 3085
Miner, Valerie, 920
Mingay, Philip Frederick James, 3086
Mishler, Barbara Ensor, 921
Mitchell, E., 1392
Mogford, Sheilagh A., 1393, 2859
Mohan, Chandra, 516
Mohr, Dunja M., 1646-1647, 2359, 3877
Molnár, Judith, 722
Montelaro, Janet J., 1161, 1648
Montigny, Denise de, 139
Montresor, Jaye Berman, 1162
Moody, Gayle Lawson, 1163
Moore, Christopher, 3025
Moore, Emily Ruth, 3280
Moore, Micki, 462
Moore, Monica Leigh-Anne, 2602
Moos, Patricia Danelle, 723
Morey, Ann-Janine, 537, 922-923, 2089, 2860
Morin-Ollier, Priscilla, 2360
Morley, Patricia, 2603
Morra, Linda, 2604
Morris, Diana Marlene, 1886
Morris, Gregory L., 1317
Morris, Mary, 463
Morrison, Sarah R., 2861
Morton, Stephen, 2605
Moss, John, 2606
Moss, Laura Frances Errington, 2361
Mourier, P. F., 1649
Moyes, Lianne, 924
Moylan, T., 2862
Müller, Klaus Peter, 2863
Mundler, Helen E., 3701
Mundt, Hannelore, 2362
Murphy, Patrick D., 538
Murray, Heather, 539

Murray, Jennifer, 2363-2364, 2864, 3087-3088, 3282, 3514
Murray, Shauna, 540
Muzychka, Martha Deborah, 1394
Mycak, Sonia, 1164, 1650, 1887, 2365
Myhal, Bob, 1651
Myrsiades, Linda, 2607

Nabar, Vrinda, 140
Nader, Elizabeth, 2366
Nagy, Erzsébet, 346
Naulty, Patricia Mary, 141
Navarro, Emilia, 1653
Neale, Emma, 3089
Neidorf, Robin M., 1301
Nelson, Sandra, 925
Nelson-Born, Katherine A., 1888, 2090
Nestor, Theo Pauline, 541
New, W. H., 347, 724
Newland, Nancy, 3702
Newman, Christina, 142
Newman, J., 1654
Nichol, Ruth, 3026
Nicholson, Colin, 1395-1396
Niederhoff, Burkhard, 2865
Nikolai, Jennifer, 2866
Nilsen, Helge Normann, 1397-1398
Nischik, Reingard M., 725-726, 1165, 1399, 2091, 2867, 3283-3284, 3515
Nixon, Lois Lacivita, 1449
Noakes, Jonathan, 3290
Norris, Ken, 542
Norris, Pamela, 2367
Novy, Marianne, 1166, 1400

Oates-Indruchová, Libora, 3703
O'Briant, Don, 1574
O'Brien, Peter, 1167
O'Connor, Shaunagh, 3651
O'Dowd, Nora, 3226
O'Hara, Delia, 3459
O'Keefe, Bernard, 1168
Ollier-Morin, Priscilla, 2608
Oltarzewska, Jagna, 2368-2369, 2609-2611
Omhovère, Claire, 2370
Ondaatje, Michael, 143
Onley, Gloria, 144
Oravits, June Rapp, 1655
O'Regan, Nadine, 3460
O'Reilly, Finbarr, 3027
O'Riordan, Brian, 843
Osadnik, Waclaw M., 145-146
Osborne, Brian S., 2371
Osborne, Carol Dale, 1401, 1656, 2372

Ousby, Ian, 1169
Özdemir, Erinç, 3516

Pache, Walter, 926, 2868
Paddon, David, 1575
Padolsky, Enoch, 1889, 3517
Paget, Elsie, 543
Paillot, Patricia, 1890, 3285
Painter, Rebecca Miriam, 2373
Palecanda, Uma Devi Vaneeta K., 1891
Paletta, Anna, 544
Palmer, Carole L, 717
Palmer, Paulina, 348, 1657, 2092
Palumbo, Alice Marie, 1402-1403, 2093, 2869
Paoli, Marie-Lise, 2374
Papinchak, Robert Allan, 3090
Parker, Emma, 1658, 1892, 2870
Parker, Janice, 2871
Parker, Peter, 1404
Parkin-Gounelas, Ruth, 3704
Parry, Sally E., 545
Pate, Nancy, 1814
Patterson, Helen Jayne, 349
Patton, Marilyn, 350, 727, 927
Pauls, Leina Marie, 2375
Pavlish, Catherine Ann, 2376
Payant, Katherine B., 1170
Payne, Lynn, 2094
Peacock, Molly, 2612
Pearce, Lynne, 1405
Pearlman, Mickey, 1406
Peck, Elizabeth G., 546
Peel, Ellen, 351
Peepre, Mari, 2377
Peled, Nancy, 2613
Pellauer, David, 547
Pellizzari, Paul, 2095
Pennycook, Bruce, 3205
Pepinster, Catherine, 1815
Peri, Camille, 287
Perkin-McFarland, Anne Louise, 928
Perrakis, Phyllis Sternberg, 1659, 2096, 2872
Perry, Gerald, 464
Perry, Susan, 1893
Pesso-Miquel, Catherine, 2378
Peterson, Nancy Jean, 728
Petrowski, Nathalie, 3847
Phelps, Henry C., 2097, 2379
Picheca, Donna M., 929
Piercy, Marge, 147
Pintarich, Paul, 1302
Piré, Luciana, 1407
Piusinska-Wozniak, Maria, 548
Poehls, Alice O'Toole, 352
Polanyi, Margaret, 3227

Pollvogt, Lieselotte, 1408
Pontuale, Francesco, 1409, 2614
Poole, Ralph J., 930, 3286
Pordzik, Ralph, 3091
Portelli, Alessandro, 1410
Porter-Ladousse, Gillian, 1411, 2098, 2265, 2340, 2380
Posh, Dorothy Ellen Kimock, 3092
Post, Stephen G., 931
Potter, Nick, 1412
Potts, Donna L., 2381, 2615
Potts, Robert, 3461
Potvin, Liza, 3518
Poulain, Alexandra, 2382
Powers, Meredith A., 729
Poznar, Susan, 2616
Prabhakar, M., 1413, 1660-1662, 2617
Preston, Pasley Elizabeth, 2618
Pringle, Mary M., 1414
Provencal, Vernon, 2383
Pullinger, Kate, 288
Purdy, Alfred W., 148, 1171
Purdy, Anthony, 3287
Pylvainen, Tina Tammy, 1894
Pyrhönen, Heta, 3878

Quartermaine, Peter, 1415
Quental, Cheryl Mary, 1895
Quigley, Ellen, 339, 528-530
Quigley, Theresia Maria, 549, 730
Quinn, Antoinette, 353

Raglon, Rebecca, 1896
Ramaiya, Nita P., 1172, 1663, 2384
Ramakrishnan, E. V., 1416
Ramaswamy, S., 2099
Rao, Eleonora, 354, 731, 1173-1174, 1417, 2385, 2619, 3288
Rao, T. Nageshwara, 1418
Rao, Vimala Rama, 1664
Raschke, Deborah, 1665
Rathbun, Frances Margaret, 1419
Rathjen, Claudia, 2620
Ravichandra, C. P., 2386
Redekop, Magdalene, 149
Reese, James D., 3289
Reese, Kelly S., 3519
Reesman, Jeanne Campbell, 732
Regier, Ami M., 1666
Reginald, Robert, 1897
Rehm, Diane, 2772, 3228-3229, 3462
Reichenbächer, Helmut, 1175, 2387, 2873
Reitinger, Douglas W., 1898
Relke, Diana M. A., 932
Repentigny, Anik de, 2100

Restuccia, Frances L., 1900, 2101, 2874
Reynolds, Margaret, 3230, 3290
Riatt, Suzanne, 2621
Ribeiro, Ofelia, 550, 733
Ricciardi, Caterina, 1420
Richards, Bernard, 659
Richards, Beth, 1082
Richards, Mary Elizabeth, 551
Richler, Noah, 3463
Rider, Janine, 2875
Ridout, Alice Rachel, 2876, 3705
Rieman, Janice Elizabeth, 2102
Rigelhof, T. F., 2877
Riggin, William, 2622
Rigney, Barbara Hill, 2878
Riley, Ruby J., 150
Rimstead, Roxanne, 3291
Rindisbacher, Hans J., 933
Ritchie, Harry, 1083
Roberts, Claudette M., 355
Roberts, Nancy, 1176, 2103
Robertson, Lloyd, 3464
Robinson, David, 3848
Robinson, Laura M., 3292
Robinson, Sally, 151
Rocard, Marcienne, 734, 1901
Rockburn, Ken, 1576
Rodríguez, Ileana, 735
Rogers, Jane, 3093
Rogers, Jaqueline Eleanor McLeod, 152
Rogerson, Margaret, 2388
Roggie, Kara, 2623
Rojas, Adena, 2879
Rooke, Constance, 356-357
Rose, Ellen Cronan, 1177
Rosenberg, Jerome H., 1667, 1902
Rosenfelt, Deborah Silverton, 736
Rosenthal, Caroline, 2880
Rosowski, Susan J., 153
Ross, Catherine, 934
Ross, Jean W., 70
Ross, Robert L., 1421
Ross, Val, 660, 1084, 2773
Roston, Elana, 2774
Roth, Verena Bühler, 2389
Rousselot, E., 3706
Rowland, Susan, 2881
Rowlands, Helen Caroline Anne, 552
Rubbo, Michael, 71, 661
Rubenstein, Roberta, 154-155, 358, 3094
Rubik, Margarete, 2104
Russotto, Márgara, 1422
Rutherford, Lisa Jane, 2882
Ryan, Bryan, 737
Ryan, Laura T., 3465, 3652

Sackville-West, Sophia, 662
Sacuta, Norm, 3231
Sadowski, Marianne, 2105
Sage, Lorna, 935
Saint-Jacques, Bernard, 1903
Sajic, Emma Louise, 3095
Salat, M. F., 1423
Saline, Carol, 2030
Salyer, Gregory, 937
Sample, Peggy, 1360
San, Shusmita, 156
Sandin, Maria, 553
Sands, Melissa, 289
Sanfilippo, Matteo, 1424
Santiago, Soledad, 3653
Sarbadhikary, Krishna, 2390
Sarrazin, Timothy M. C., 3293
Sato, Ayako, 3096
Scacchi, Anna, 1425
Scannavini, Anna, 1426
Sceats, Sarah, 2883
Schall, Birgitta, 1427, 1668
Schaub, Danielle, 2391
Schenk, Susan Jean, 359
Schissel, Wendy L., 738
Schlueter, June, 157
Scholtmeijer, Marian, 1178
Schultz, Judy, 3028
Schultz, Susy, 1816
Schwartz, Meryl Fern, 2624
Scobie, Stephen, 360
Seagrove, Susan, 1360
Seaman, Donna, 1303, 3849
Seeber, Hans Ulrich, 2625
Senecal, Nikole Alexa, 3294
Senkpiel, Aron, 938
Sexton, Melanie, 1179
Shaffer, C. Lyon, 3097
Shands, Kerstin W., 1428
Sharp, Iain, 2031, 3029
Sharpe, Martha, 1180-1181
Shaw, Monica Leigh, 1429
Sheckels, Theodore F., Jr., 1904, 3098, 3520
Shelton, Robert, 1182
Shepherd, Rose, 3030
Shepherd, Valerie, 1669
Shinn, Thelma J., 1905
Shoemaker, Adam, 939
Shojania, Moti Gharib, 1670
Shugart, Helene A., 2107
Shuping, Li, 2108
Shurbutt, Sylvia Bailey, 3707
Sibree, Bron, 3031
Siddall, Gillian, 3708
Siemerling, Winfried, 3099

Simmons, Jes, 1183
Simmons, Rachel, 3295
Simpson-Housley, P., 2061
Sinclair, Gail Ann D., 2109
Singh, Sunaina, 554, 1430
Sinha, Krishna Kant, 2110
Sisk, David Warner, 1431
Sizemore, Christine Wick, 2111, 3296
Skelton, Robin, 158-159
Slopen, Beverley, 844
Smith, Bonnie Lynne, 1432
Smith, Erin, 1184
Smith, James Gregory, 1671
Smith, Kristine Leeann, 2626
Smith, Rowland, 2392
Smith, Stephen, 1085
Smulders, Marilyn, 2775
Smyth, Donna, 1672
Smyth, Jacqui, 940
Snell, Marilyn, 2032, 2266
Snodgrass, Mary Ellen, 1433, 2281, 3879
Snyder, Karyn, 1673
Snyder, Sharon Lynn, 1674
Söderlind, Sylvia, 739
Sokolov, Rachel Anne, 3100
Solecki, Sam, 2393, 3709
Somacarrera, Pilar, 2884-2885
Sparrow, Fiona, 555
Spector, Judith Ann, 1185
Spence, Jonathan D., 2394
Spencer, Guylaine, 3880
Spivak, Gayatri Chakravorty, 1186
Spriet, Pierre, 361, 2395
Srisermbhok, Amporn, 3881
St. Germain, Pat, 3466
St. Peter, Christine, 936
Stableford, Brian, 2396
Stacey, Wendy, 663
Staels, Hilde, 160, 740, 941, 1434, 1675-1676,
    2397, 2627, 2886-2887, 3101, 3710
Stahlman, Susan Jane, 741
Staines, David, 1677
Stambovsky, Phillip, 1906, 3521
Stanley, Sandra Kumanoto, 3522
Staples, Joseph Perry, 2398
Steele, James, 3523
Stein, Karen F., 942, 1907, 2628, 2888, 3102,
    3524-3525, 3711
Steinberg, Sybil, 2776
Stephenson, Anne, 1086
Steven, Laurence, 161
Stevens, Peter, 162
Stevenson, Sharon, 3712
Stewart, Bruce, 1908
Stewart, Margaret, 742

Still, Judith, 3297
Stillman, Peter G., 163, 1435, 2399
Stimpson, Catharine R., 3713
Stirling, Claire, 2267
Stocks, Anthony G., 743
Stoffman, Judy, 3467
Stone, John, 1577
Storey, Françoise, 3882
Storey, Jeff, 3882
Storrow, Richard F., 3883
Stosky, Sandra, 1678
Stott, Belinda, 3298
Stott, Jon C., 2836
Stouck, David, 164
Stow, Glenys, 165
Straubel, Linda H., 3103
Strehle, Susan, 943, 2889
Streitfeld, David, 290
Stringer, Kim, 3104, 3299
Strobel, Christina, 944
Strong, Amy L., 1436
Struckel, Katie, 2777
Stummer, Peter O., 945
Sturgess, Charlotte Jane, 362, 744, 1187, 2112,
    2400-2402, 2629, 2890-2891
Suárez Lafuente, M. S., 2113-2114
Sugars, Cynthia, 1188, 2630
Sujan, Deehra, 1304
Sullivan, Jane, 3468
Sullivan, Rosemary, 166, 2403-2405, 2892-
    2893, 3105
Sunaini, Singh, 2115
Sutherland, Katherine, 1189
Sverrisdóttir, Halla, 3106
Swearingen, C. Jan, 745
Sweeney, Kathleen M., 3098
Sweeney, Megan Louise, 3300
Szalay, Edina, 3107, 3526

Tantakis, Penny, 1437
Tarozzi, Bianca, 2894
Taylor, Debbie, 3018
Taylor, Donna Joyce, 946
Taylor, Judith, 1679
Taylor, Linda Anne, 1190
Teeuwen, Ruud, 1909
Teleky, Richard, 2116
Templin, Charlotte, 746, 1191, 1910, 3108
Tennant, Colette Giles, 747, 3527
Texter, Douglas Walter, 2117
Thacker, Robert, 2631, 3884
Thieme, John, 947
Thomas, Sue, 167
Thompson, Dawn, 1438, 2895
Thompson, Lars, 556

Thompson, Lee Briscoe, 948, 2118
Tidmarsh, Andrew, 845
Tiedemann, Heidi Janean, 3109
Tiedemann, Mark W., 3528
Tiger, Virginia, 557
Tillotson, Kristin, 2778
Tolan, Fiona, 3714, 3885-3886
Tomc, Sandra, 1192, 3110
Tompkins, Cynthia Margarita, 363
Tonkin, Brad, 3850
Trabattoni, Grazia, 1439
Tracy, Laura, 748
Trahair, Richard C. S., 2632
Trapani, Hilary Jane, 1440
Trigg, Susan, 3301
Trigg, Tina, 3529, 3715
Trouard, Dawn, 1441
Truman, James C. W., 1442
Tschachler, Heinz, 168, 558, 949
Tsujimoto, Yasuko, 3530
Tu, Shu-shu, 3887
Tucker, Lindsey, 1443
Tuhkunen-Couzic, Taïna, 2406, 2633
Turcotte, Gerry, 2407
Turnball, Barbara, 3032
Turner, Alden R., 169
Turner, Kate, 3888
Turpin, Adrian, 3851
Twigg, Alan, 72
Tyler, Lisa, 2408

Unes, Diana L., 1680
Uppal, Priscila, 3716

Vaishali, K. S., 2119
Valentine, Susan Elizabeth, 2409
Van Berkel, Elizabeth Christine, 559
Van Herk, Aritha, 1444, 2634, 3852
Van Luven, Lynne, 2779
Van Vuren, Dalene, 2120, 2410
Vanderslice, Stephanie M., 2121
VanSpanckeren, Kathryn, 170-172, 1911, 3531
Varble, Valery, 2122
Ventura, Héliane, 2411
Verduyn, Christl, 3717
Verwaayen, Kimberly J., 1681, 3718
Vespermann, Susanne, 1682
Vevaina, Coomi S., 73, 560, 749, 1912, 2268, 2412-2414
Viacava, Anna, 2062
Vickroy, Laurie, 3889
Villegas López, Sonia, 2635
Viner, Katherine, 2780
Vinet, Dominique, 2415-2416, 3532
Vipond, Dianne, 1683

Vitale, Ronald M., 1913
Vogler, Heini, 3533
Vogt, Kathleen, 173
Vokey, Krista R., 1445
Vores, Andy, 3624
Voros, Joseph John, 1446

Wachtel, Eleanor, 1087
Wagener, Christel, 561
Wagner, Monika, 1684
Wagner-Lawlor, Jennifer A., 3302, 3534
Wagner-Martin, Linda, 1447, 1685
Walker, Cheryl, 2123
Walker, Nancy A., 174, 562, 1686
Walker, Susan, 3033
Walker Fields, Ingrid, 950
Wall, Kathleen, 175, 563, 2124
Wallack, Karen M., 3719
Wang, Yiyan, 2417
Ward, David, 1448
Ward, Selena, 3246
Ware, Tracy, 2896
Warner, Lionel, 2897
Warwick, Jack, 2592
Waugh, Patricia, 364
Wear, Delese, 1449
Weaver, Rosalie Mary, 2125
Webb, Janeen, 951
Weber, Jean Jacques, 952
Weckerle, Lisa Jeanne, 2636
Weczerka, Margrit, 1450, 2126
Wehmeyer, Paula J., 2127
Wein, Toni, 1687
Weiner, Deborah, 365, 2128
Weinhouse-Richmond, Linda, 1914
Weinstein, Sheri M., 1688
Weiss, Allan, 1451
Welby, Sharon Kay, 1915
Wellinghoff, Lisa Ann, 3890
Wertheim, Margaret, 2781
Wertheimer, Linda, 1578
Wesseling, Lies, 953
West, Robert Malvern, 2898
Whalen, Terence, 954
Whalen-Bridge, John, 955, 2418
Wheeler, Kathleen, 2129
Wheeler, Kathleen M., 1452, 2637
Whidden, Abra Lynn, 3720
White, Lesley, 846
White, Roberta, 1193, 3891
Whitlock, Gillian, 2638
Whitney, Susan, 3654
Whitson, Kathy J., 3721
Widmer, Kingsley, 176
Wiede-Behrendt, Ingrid, 177

Wigod, Rebecca, 3034
Wild-Bicanic, Sonia, 178
Wilkins, Peter Duncan, 2130, 2419
Willard, Thomas, 1689-1690
Williams, David, 750
Williams, Ian, 3892
Williamson, Dave, 2782
Willmott, Glenn, 1691
Wills, Deborah, 1453
Wiloch, Thomas, 179
Wilson, Jean, 2639
Wilson, Rob, 751, 1454
Wilson, Sharon Rose, 180, 366, 564-565, 752-
    753, 1194-1195, 1916-1917, 2420, 2899-
    2900, 3111, 3303, 3535-3538
Wilt, Judith, 566
Winegar, Karin, 1088
Wisker, Gina, 2901, 3304
Withim, Philip, 567
Wittke, Petra, 3112
Wittke-Rüdiger, Petra, 3893
Wittman, Juliet, 2783, 3655
Wohlmuth, Sharon J., 2030
Wolmark, Jenny, 1455
Wong, Jan, 1817, 2784
Wood, Diane S., 956
Wood, Ruth, 3305
Woodcock, George, 181, 568, 754, 1196, 1456
Woodward, Calvin, 465
Workman, Nancy V., 367, 2902
Wörrlein, Andrea, 2131
Worthington, Kim L., 1918
Wright, Laura, 3894
Wright, Terence R., 569
Wurst, Gayle, 182
Wyatt, Jean, 570, 2421, 3722

Yan, Qigang, 2132
Yarnall, Judith H., 368
York, Lorraine M., 183, 571, 957, 1457-1458,
    1692-1693, 1919, 2903
York Notes, 2422
Yost, Barbara, 1305
Youngberg, Gail, 3492
Yücel, Sükran, 3113

Zaman, Sobia, 1694
Zamost, Julie, 184
Zeuge, Paula, 1695
Zimmerman, Barbara, 1696
Zimmerman, Hannalore, 2423
Zimmermann, Juta, 1920
Zirker, Herbert, 1197, 3306
Zlosnik, Sue, 512, 3261, 3866
Zondervan, Jean Marie, 1198
Zorzi, Rosella Mamoli, 1697, 3540
Zuo, Qiang-hua, 572
Zupancic, Metka, 1698

Subject   Index

abjection, female, 3692
abortion
  in *The Handmaid's Tale*, 1879, 3678
  in *Surfacing*, 566, 931
Acorn, Milton, 158
adaptation, cultural, 488
African Americans, 2050; *see also* race
"Age of Lead, The," 2889, 3507
  translations of
    French, 585
    Spanish, 792
aggression, female, 3063, 3295
aging, 1582, 2058
  women's, 1589
Aidoo, Ama Ata, 3238
Akhmatova, Anna, 2835
Alcott, Louisa May, 2128
Alford, Edna, 909, 1603
Alias Grace, 2085-2086, 2315, 2877, 3469,
  3494, 3867
  adaptation, dramatic, review of, 3905
  approaches to
    Foucault, Michel, 2604, 3695
    Freud, Sigmund, 2787, 3251
    Kristeva, Julia, 2626
    New Historicism, 3513
  biblical revision in, 3097
  the body in, 2881
  Canada in, 3688
  class in, 3522, 3708
    domestic workers, 3291
    servant-mistress relationship, 3857
  closure in, 3504
  clothes in, 3071, 3870
  confession in, 3100, 3671
  crime in, 2586, 2626, 3065, 3695
    detective fiction, 2304
    murder, 3063, 3514
  cultural rhetoric in, 3278
  as fantasy, 2787
  female progatonist in, 2568, 2598

friendship in, 2271
gender in, 3100, 3708
ghosts in, 2787
goddess in, 2858
as gothic, 3857
as historiography, 2823, 2864, 3083, 3513,
  3706
  trauma and, 3109
  Victorian, 3853
  women's, 2819
insanity in, 2586, 2604, 2843
as Inter-American fiction, 2819
interviews about, 1810, 2024, 2267, 3225
  French translation *Captive*, 2261
Irish in, 2856, 2887
law in, 3695
  reader as judge, 3662
middle voice in, 3498
models for characters, 2577
newspapers in, 2589
occult in, 3853
oppression in, 2626
postmodernism, 2292
power in, 3488
  and gender, 2271, 3100
public vs. private in, 2599, 3708
punishment in, 3065
quilts in, 2304, 2388, 2412, 2556, 3087
  as narrative, 3537
reader
  as judge, 3662
  and the Other, 2626
realism in, 2361
religion in, 3279
  gnosticism, 2858, 3279
resistance in, 3526
reviews of, 1921, 2133-2134, 2424, 2641,
  2904
reviews of audiobook, 2135-2136
study guide, 2874, 3304

suffering and violence in, 2858, 3276
  murder, 3063, 3514
  and the Other, 2626
teaching, 3254, 3289
translations of
  Bulgarian, 2962
  Chinese, 2214
  Croatian, 2151
  Danish, 1935
  Dutch, 1714, 2148
  Finnish, 1984, 2705, 3166
  French, 2160, 2444, 2659, 3332
    reviewed, 2425
  German, 1715, 2152
  Hebrew, 2202
  Italian, 1971
  Lithuanian, 2468
  Norwegian, 2150
  Polish, 2467
  Portuguese, 1999, 2167
  Spanish, 2149
  Swedish, 1936
  Turkish, 1981
trauma in, 2829
  confession and, 3671
writer as alias in, 3890
alienation, 749, 1912
allegory, 2550, 3882
allusion
  biblical; *see* Bible
  classical, 87
Alvarez, Julia, 2600, 3109
ambivalence and ambiguity, 516
  in *The Edible Woman*, 1608
  in *The Handmaid's Tale*, 732, 2562, 3694
  in *Surfacing*, 1822
American literature
  Atwood and, 950, 1678, 3250
  postmodern, 950, 1108
  women and nature in, 1313
Anderson, Laurie, 2128
Anderson-Dargatz, Gail, 3720
Angelou, Maya, 913
animals, 339
  Canadian concern for, 3056
  in fiction
    The Edible Woman, 292
    Surfacing, 3875
  in poetry, 173
  in *Survival*, 1178, 3056
The Animals in That Country, 114, 166, 181,
  1457
  as gothic, 134
anorexia, 141, 671, 930, 1593; *see also*
  body; food

anti-Americanism, 2630
  in *The Handmaid's Tale*, 2308
  in *Lady Oracle*, 685
  in *Surfacing*, 129
  in *Survival*, 129
anti-feminism, 1379, 1686, 2798
"Any Resemblance Is Purely Coincidental"
  set to music, 653
apocalypse
  in *The Handmaid's Tale*, 2057
  in *Surfacing*, 2130
  in *Wilderness Tips*, 2574, 3059
archetypes, 2413
art and the artist
  death and, 2899
  female, 2544, 3075, 3086, 3891
    in *Bodily Harm*, 570
    in *Cat's Eye*, 1180, 1583, 3891
    in *The Handmaid's Tale*, 559
    in *Surfacing*, 734
  literature and, 355, 1836
  love and, 509, 570
  in *Negotiating with the Dead*, 3249
  in novels, 2544, 3074-3075, 3891
    Bodily Harm, 570, 2899
    Cat's Eye, 509, 531, 753, 874, 1180,
      1583, 1880, 3086, 3698, 3891
    The Handmaid's Tale, 559
    Lady Oracle, 509, 750
    Surfacing, 682, 734, 750, 944
  society and, 682, 3086
art, visual, by Atwood, 301, 1194-1195
  Bodily Harm and, 565
  sexual politics in, 180
artificiality, 2060
"Asparagus," 2612
Astley, Thea, 503
"At First"
  set to music, 2723
Atwood, Margaret, 849, 1133, 1315, 2840,
  3113; *see also* critical reception
  according to other writers, 1167, 1171,
    1345, 1639, 2587, 3709
  adaptations of; *see* individual titles
  on animals, 339
  as anthologist, 751
  approaches to
    as American writer, 950, 1678, 3250
    as Asia-Pacific writer, 2407
    constructionalist, 2863
    as feminist writer, 1170
    as gothic writer, 3244
    as popular fiction writer, 1170
    as settler writer, 2584
    as world author, 1678, 3707

archival papers, 927
autobiography, 2804
bibliography, 291, 743, 753-754, 851,
    1130, 1306, 1310, 1421, 1456, 2567,
    2617
    primary sources, 160, 179, 666, 737,
        849, 1579, 2867, 2875; children's
        literature, 2836
    secondary sources, 160, 717, 2309
biography
    biocritical, 160, 291, 466, 665, 737, 743,
        753-754, 1310, 1902, 2289, 3257,
        3472
    book, 2289
    general reference work, 850, 1307, 1690,
        3492
    interview, 3217
    literary reference work, 179, 666, 676,
        752, 848, 851, 910, 1105, 1157, 1169,
        1306, 1308-1309, 1345, 1357, 1421,
        1456, 2033, 2129, 2603, 2815, 3093,
        3721, 3879
    newspaper article, 1292
Bronfman Lecture, 2293, 2394
on Canada, 1649, 3093
as Canadian writer, 347, 360, 528-530,
    664, 676, 709, 847, 859, 914, 1120,
    1367, 1631
as canonical author, 1824
celebrity and, 2903, 3064
censorship and, 3305
civil rights movement and, 913
Clarendon lectures, 3503
creative process, 680, 877, 927, 1390,
    3654
    Bodily Harm, 1142, 1175, 2387
    Cat's Eye, 2597
    The Edible Woman, 2387
    Lady Oracle, 1124
    Life Before Man, 1098
    The Robber Bride, 2597
as critic, 705, 924, 1187, 1584, 1631,
    2606, 2868
    of Canadian literature, 932, 1628, 2581
    influence on Canadian literature, 1874
critical reception, 1170, 1402, 1447, 1604
    book reviewers, 1910
critical studies of, 332, 737, 743, 752, 754,
    915, 1153, 1399, 1422, 1427, 1439,
    1586, 1630, 1667, 1846, 2062, 2628,
    2796, 2901, 3284, 3485, 3538, 3876
    introductory, 3854
    poetry, 1167, 1310
    for young readers, 2871
cultural nationalism and, 724

early works and career, 136, 534, 1610
    editing of, 2284
    graduate work, 696
    Radcliffe years, 2403, 3105
    sound recording of, 1558
feminism and, 724, 1118, 1170, 2035,
    2043, 2809, 3012, 3714
    on feminist writing, 895
as fictional character, 2585
French-Canadian literature and, 469
influence
    on female Bildungsroman, 3700
    on George Woodcock, 2306
    on other writers, 865, 2311, 2366
influences on her, 2287, 3685; see titles of
    individual works
    Frye, Northrop, 2896
    Page, P. K., 3674
    Scott, F. R., 2811
later fiction, 551
as linguistic/literary example, 679, 2281,
    2305
on literature
    historical fiction, 2328
    science fiction, 3093, 3439
Margaret Atwood Society, 839, 1083,
    2631
meta-iconography of, 1692
news stories, 839
in other writers' work, 1679
as painter, 180, 301, 565, 1194-1195
photographs of, 2803, 2867
politics, 343, 927, 2035
    environmental, 3430
    nationalism, 2820
    of race, 728
    sexual, 1584
readership, 2301
    academic vs. mainstream, 2043
    universality, 3258
relations with media, 2794
relationship with; see also names of other
    writers
    Cohen, Matt, 2803
    Laurence, Margaret, 1641, 2543
    McClelland, Jack, 2393, 2587
    Munro, Alice, 3884
    Purdy, Al, 1167, 1171
as storyteller, 177, 329, 2563, 2628
techniques, 105
themes, 105, 466, 863, 1124, 1129, 1142,
    2555, 3045
Toronto and, 2569
on translation, 3219
on witches, 871

on writing, 290
Austen, Jane, 138
Auster, Paul, 2057, 3890
author, death of, 2054
authorial voice; *see* narrative voice
autobiography, 2804; *see also* life writing
    female, 1366
    in fiction
        Cat's Eye, 701, 873, 890, 1358, 1366,
            1623, 2827, 3872
        The Handmaid's Tale, 890, 1358
        Lady Oracle, 1358, 3705
        Murder in the Dark, 353
        Surfacing, 2355
    ironic, 174
    poststucturalist, 3718
Avison, Margaret, 3266

Baby M, and *The Handmaid's Tale*, 718
balance and parallelism, 2884
Baldwin, James, 2095
Bambara, Toni Cade, 3300
barbarism, 684
Barfoot, Joan, 2849
Barnes, Djuna, 1855
Barthes, Roland, 83, 482
Bashful Bob and Doleful Dorinda
    reviews of, 3723, 3895
Basho, 3686
Baxter, Charles, 1868
Beattie, Ann, 1162
Beauvoir, Simone de, 1872, 2334, 3868
Behn, Aphra, 152
Bellow, Saul, 1096
Best American Short Stories
    reviews of, 574
Bettelheim, Bruno, 131
"Betty"
    dramatic adaptation, 3202, 3420
Beynon, Frances, 1189
Bible, 497, 3693; *see also* religion
    Eve, 2367
    Jezebel, 545
    in novels
        Alias Grace, 3097
        The Handmaid's Tale, 545, 852, 1125,
            1614, 2309
        Surfacing, 167
    in "The Sin Eater"
        Gospel of Mark, 471, 486, 491, 535,
            537, 569
bibliographies, of Atwood; *see* Atwood,
    Margaret, bibliography
Bildungsroman
    Atwood's influence on, 3700

female, 363, 2347, 3700
    in novels
        Cat's Eye, 2347, 3092
        The Edible Woman, 2854
        Lady Oracle, 2854
        Surfacing, 363
    time in, 2347
biographies, of Atwood; *see* Atwood,
    Margaret, biography
biography, 839
    in *The Handmaid's Tale*, 335
    in *The Robber Bride*, 2079
Birdsell, Sandra, 909
birth; *see* reproduction
Bishop, Elizabeth, 3686
Blais, Marie-Claire, 469, 1865, 3520
Blind Assassin, The, 3090, 3247, 3471,
    3494-3495, 3535, 3704, 3867
    abjection, female, in, 3692
    approaches to
        Lacanian, 3704
        psychoanalytic, 3702
    as Canadian science fiction, 3690
    Cupid and Psyche in, 3702
    fallen women in, 3720
    food in, 3692
    as gothic, 3524, 3684
    imprisonment in, 3501
    interviews about, 2740, 2742-2743, 2746,
        2749, 2754, 2764, 2770, 2772, 2774-
        2775, 2779, 3018, 3020, 3024, 3033,
        3224-3225
    irony in, 3285
    language in, 3106
    male characters in, 3297
    as memoir, 3476
    narrative
        closure, 3499
        reader engagement, 3865
        specular, 3710
    as parody, 3705
    popular culture in, 3303
    realism in, 3702
    reviews of, 2905, 3115-3116, 3307, 3541
    reviews of audiobook, 2906-2907, 3117-
        3118, 3308, 3896
    self-destruction in, 3704
        drowning, 3049
    study guide, 3290
    translations of
        Bengali, 3561
        Catalan, 2956, 3370
        Chinese, 3158, 3381
        Czech, 2982
        Danish, 3132

Dutch, 2924
Estonian, 2973
Finnish, 2712, 2983
French, 2697, 2958, 3157
German, 2669
Greek, 2948
Italian, 2957, 3371
Japanese, 3369
Latvian, 2645
Lithuanian, 3317
Norwegian, 2926, 3339
Persian, 3316, 3553
Polish, 3186, 3411
Portuguese, 2967-2968
Russian, 3410, 3614, 3798
Serbian, 3409
Spanish, 2933, 3342
Swedish, 2667
Turkish, 2955
vision in, 3872
mirrors, 3704
as specular narrative, 3710
blindness; *see* sight
Bluebeard; *see* fairy tales
"Bluebeard's Egg," 540, 705, 1374
domesticity in, 3271
as fairy tale, 697, 1432, 1877
as romance, 2112
teaching, 1877
Bluebeard's Egg and Other Stories, 103,
149, 156, 897, 2876; *see also* titles of
individual stories
capitalism in, 1640
displacement in, 2385
as domestic fiction, 532
as fairy tale, 532, 1640
gender in, 1391
gothic in, 3527
language in, 1328, 2385
mythopoesis in, 532
as palimpsest, 317
realism in, 532
reviews of, 185
reviews of audiobook, 3119
study guide, 3290
subjectivity in, 1328
translations of
Czech, 3160
Finnish, 45
German, 1219
Italian, 2482
Japanese, 972
Spanish, 390
wilderness in, 1384
Bly, Robert, 2075

Bodily Harm, 88, 99, 155, 163, 311, 533,
1109, 1173, 1653, 1662, 2617
art and the artist in, 570, 2899
Atwood's art and, 565
the body in, 120, 2131
borders in, 479
cannibalism in, 350
Caribbean setting of, 472
censorship and, 2547, 3050
confinement in, 1629
creative process, 1142, 1175, 2387
critical reception of, 1142
death in, 2899
murder, 1336
feminism and, 348, 1397
gender in, 1870
and art, 570
and friendship, 1160
as gothic, 502, 719, 3082
as historiography, 526
irony in, 472
islands in, 3520
narrative structure, 691
natural consciousness in, 1895
pain in, 98
paranoia in, 358
and stalker novel, 1882
as parody, 526, 911
postmodern, 526
politics in, 2624
Canada vs. Quebec, 2602
postcolonialism and, 1596
power in
male, 567, 1882
state, 2800
public and private in, 2399
resistance in, 503, 1346, 2053
and language, 111
reviews of audiobook, 3542
as romance, 1121
subjectivity in, 1164
divided, 1650
translations of
Chinese, 240
Czech, 262
Dutch, 32
German, 442, 646, 1051, 2509
Polish, 2487
Serbian, 3190
travel in, 667, 2122, 2602
and self-knowledge, 1429
body, 864, 923, 1695, 2883, 3473
female, 120, 1449, 2124, 2131, 2356,
2806, 3095, 3108, 3237
appropriation of, 117, 1849, 2298

as Canada, 681, 695
  food and, 3270, 3275, 3286
  language and, 1642, 1837, 3275
  oppression and violence and, 496, 1823
  as performance, 2400
  subversion and, 1852, 3051
food and, 141, 671, 1593, 3270, 3275,
  3286
gendered, 2356, 3108, 3237
gothic and, 2616
language and, 1642, 1837, 2077, 2575,
  3079-3080, 3275
in novels, 3095
  Alias Grace, 2881
  Bodily Harm, 120, 2131
  Cat's Eye, 1642
  The Edible Woman, 141, 364, 671, 698,
    713, 1593, 1849, 2131, 3095, 3270,
    3275, 3856, 3862
  The Handmaid's Tale, 673, 698, 713,
    1091, 1449, 2044, 2298, 2400, 2890
  Lady Oracle, 117, 364, 2295, 2806,
    3108, 3237, 3270
  Surfacing, 698, 713
sexuality and, 1592
in short fiction
  "The Bog Man," 3287
  "Giving Birth," 1449, 2124
survival and, 2044
"The Bog Man," 3287
Boland, Eavan, 3104
Bones and Murder
  reviews of, 1699
book groups, 1370
  The Handmaid's Tale, 856, 1406
  how to read poetry, 2612
  The Robber Bride, 1090, 1406
book reviews; *see* titles of individual books
borders and boundaries, 483, 923, 2561
  in *Bodily Harm*, 479
  in *The Edible Woman*, 698
  in *The Handmaid's Tale*, 479, 698, 918,
    1651, 2273
  in *Surfacing*, 512, 698
Borman, Randy, 3057
Boullosa, Carmen, 2036
Bowering, George, 888, 908, 3502
Bradbury, Ray, 956, 1671, 2057, 3060
Braddon, Mary Elizabeth, 3063
bridges, 1411
Broner, E. M., 518
Brontë, Charlotte, 1825, 1835, 3280
Brooke, Frances, 1189, 2319
Brookner, Anita, 1900, 2101, 2874
Brooks, Gwendolyn, 3686

Brossard, Nicole, 1438, 2890
Brown, Rebecca, 1844
Buckler, Ernest, 528
bulemia, 930; *see also* body; food
Burdekin, Katharine, 2790, 3040
Burgess, Anthony, 1431, 3274
Butler, Octavia, 2790

Cadieux, Genevieve, 673
camp, 2834
Campbell, Joseph, 1881, 2353
Campion, Jane, 1589
Canada, representations of, 3517, 3688; *see*
  also identity, Canadian
Canadian West, 1337
"Canadian Coastlines"
  set to music, 653
Canadian identity; *see* identity, Canadian
Canadian literature, 739, 932, 1824, 2319
  Atwood in, 347, 467, 847, 859, 914, 1120,
    1631, 1840
  Atwood on, 894, 1421, 2581
  French, 1187
  ghosts in, 706
  history of, 347, 467, 1101
  identity and, 1903
  nationalism and, 1903
  naturalism and, 3081
  realism in, 1196, 2361
  reception of
    in Britain, 2630
    in Quebec, 3099
  Survival on, 894, 1421
  women's, 1853
Canadian Studies, 1880, 2087
Canlit Foodbook
  reviews of, 186
cannibalism, 350
  in *The Edible Woman*, 366, 564
  in *Wilderness Tips*, 2574, 3059
canon, 118
  Canadian, 1824
  revision of, 1686
capitalism, 1437, 1640, 3260
Captive
  interviews about, 2261
  reviews of, 2425
Caribbean
  in *Bodily Harm*, 472
Carmen, Bliss, 2099
carnival, 543, 1818
Carr, Emily, 1189
Carrier, Roch, 1865
Carroll, Lewis, 165, 319, 1609
Carson, Anne, 3873

Carter, Angela, 1138, 1176, 1365, 1657, 1866, 2092, 2103, 2128, 2335, 2550, 2883, 3084, 3280, 3301
  The Bloody Chamber, 1640, 1825, 3484, 3878
  Bluebeard in, 2123
  Heroes and Villains, 1647
  The Magic Toyshop, 1825
  The Passion of New Eve, 2806
Cartesian dualism, 1670
Castillo, Ana, 2600
Cather, Willa, 2600
Catholicism; *see* religion
Cat's Eye, 107, 475, 561, 745, 941, 1173, 1908, 2046, 2121, 2570, 2572, 2848, 3054, 3669
  adaptations of, musical, 2003
  aggression, women's, in, 3295
  aging in, 1582
  approaches to
    Canadian Studies, 1880
    feminist, 1880
    Foucault, Michel, 3719
    Kristeva, Julia, 1181
    object relations theory, 3043
    postcolonial, 1878
  art and the artist in, 531, 753, 874, 1880, 3698
    asocial, 3086
    female, 1180, 1583, 3891
    love and, 509
  autobiography in, 701, 873, 1358, 1366, 1623, 2827
    autobiographical subject, 3871
    vs. fiction, 890
  as Bildungsroman, 2347
  the body in, 1642
  bridges in, 1411
  children and childhood in, 720, 730, 1096, 1595
    adulthood and, 3296
    girls' relationships, 2276
  Christianity in, 507
  city in, 710, 3479
    Montreal, 2333
    Toronto, 514, 3479
  Clarendon lectures and, 3503
  colonialism in, 2111
  conflict, female, in, 921, 1595
  creative process, 2597
  creativity in, 1378
  desire in, 3292
  evil in, 2373
    female, 3038, 3683
  exile in, 3288

  as fantasy, 562, 672
  feminism in
    comedy and, 3523
    science and, 2047
  fetish objects in, 1666
  friendship in, 2271, 3659
    female, 1160, 1594, 2271, 2294
  gender in, 702, 2128
  as gothic, 1659, 2618, 3527
    the body in, 2616
  The Handmaid's Tale and, 1096
  as historiography, 3259
  identity in, 716, 1093, 2084, 3041, 3043, 3889
    self-discovery, 2127
  influences on
    Montgomery, L. M., 1323
    Shakespeare, 1149, 1400, 2039, 2621
  interviews about, 276, 278, 1082, 2268
  irony in, 562
  landscape in, 2371
  language in, 1688
  maps and mapping in, 3098
  masquerade and mimicry in, 700
  memory in, 716, 874, 1150, 1401
    identity and, 2071, 2838
    resistance and, 1891, 2386
  mirrors in, 2334
  models for characters, 3477
  mothers in, 300, 1659, 1684, 2283
  narrative structure, 691
    closure, 3504
  narrator in, 875
  nature vs. culture in, 1316
  politics in
    nationalist, 1117
    personal, 1394
  postmodernism in, 708
  power in, 478, 710, 3488
    gender and, 2088, 2128, 2271
  as quest, 1429, 3518
    spiritual, 507, 687
  resistance in, 1190, 2386
    to patriarchy, 1442
  revenge in, 748
  reviews of, 187, 575, 755, 958, 1459, 2137
  reviews of audiobook, 1700
  royal family in, 3241
  self-destruction in, 1595
  social control in, 1622
  space in, 1181, 2832
  study guide, 2814
  subjectivity in
    divided, 1650
    female, 1366, 1401

survival in, 1583
teaching, 1880
time in, 943, 1181, 1680, 2347
Toronto in, 3880
translations of
  Catalan, 440
  Chinese, 3159
  Danish, 232
  Dutch, 410
  Estonian, 1970
  Finnish, 235
  French, 37, 420, 626; reviewed, 582
  German, 411, 790, 1512, 2954
  Greek, 1755
  Hebrew, 1735
  Italian, 419, 3168
  Latvian, 3155
  Norwegian, 233
  Polish, 1513, 3368
  Portuguese, 39, 422
  Serbian, 3379
  Spanish, 421, 3170
  Swedish, 234
  Turkish, 791
trauma in, 3889
victimization in, 1419, 2088, 2294
vision in, 2617, 2827
  artistic, 753
visual imagery, 1198
voice in, 1410
  narrative, 742
women in
  marginalization, 1878
  odalisques, 1128
  Susie, 1114
  virgins, 672
  witches, 672
censorship, 3305
  Bodily Harm, 2547, 3050
  The Handmaid's Tale, 2051, 2547, 2802, 3050
characterization
  color and, 1868
  fragmentation and, 2898
characters, male; *see* men
Charna, Suzy McKee, 1852, 3877
Chaucer, Geoffrey, 1605
Cheever, John, 1634
children and childhood, 549, 2102
  in *Cat's Eye*, 720, 730, 1096
    girls' relationships, 2276
    search for adulthood, 3296
  in *The Handmaid's Tale*, 2897
  in *Lady Oracle*, 730
children's literature, 2836

Chodorow, Nancy, 928
Chopin, Kate, 1589, 2353
Christ, Carol, 2353
Christianity; *see* religion
"Circe"
  set to music, 2723
"Circe/Mud Poems," 1137, 1360, 2356, 3070
Circle Game, The, 100, 136, 166, 181, 884, 2100
  French translation of, 2481
  ghosts in, 2855
  as gothic, 134
  reviews of, 143
Cisneros, Sandra, 1855
city, 1349; *see also* Montreal; Toronto
  power and, 710, 2345
civilization, 684, 1340
Cixous, Hélène, 151, 728
Clark, Joan, 909
class, 125, 1686; *see also* servants
  in *Alias Grace*, 3522, 3708, 3857
  in *The Handmaid's Tale*, 3883
  in *Lady Oracle*, 1414
  in *Life Before Man*, 1415
Cleage, Pearl, 3300
Cliff, Michelle, 2624
clothing, 124, 898, 3870
  as performance, 3071
codes
  urban vs. rural, 1359
Cohen, Leonard, 559, 1196, 2299, 2327
Cohen, Matt, 2803
Colette, 3043
colonialism, 739, 2308
  the body and, 503, 1849
  identity and, 2111
color, 1643, 1868
comedy, 78, 298
  subversion and, 902
community, 1918, 3861
complicity, 1435
Conan, Laure, 1189
concealment, 3047
Conde, Maryse, 2819
confession, 1606, 3100, 3671
confinement, 1629
conflict, 921
Conn, Jan, 957
consciousness, 1895
  feminine, 678
conspiracy, 950
Cooke, Rose Terry, 2123
Cooley, Dennis, 2606
Cooper, James Fenimore, 1835

corruption, 2558
Coulter, Clare, 2826
Crate, Joan, 2287, 3718
Crawford, Isabella Valancy, 3245
creativity, 2053
criminality
  female, 2586, 3063, 3065, 3300
  murder, 1336, 2809, 3063, 3514
  punishment and, 3065
critical reception, 683, 1402, 1604
  by book reviewers, 1910
  feminist, 1376
  gender and, 1447
  lack of warmth, 135
  of novels, 179
    Bodily Harm, 1142
    The Edible Woman, 1604
    The Handmaid's Tale, 2375
    Lady Oracle, 1124
    Life Before Man, 1098
    Oryx and Crake, 3657
    The Robber Bride, 1604
    Surfacing, 568
  politics and, 343
  of short fiction, 1604
  of *Survival*, 1152
criticism, 891, 2375
  by Atwood, 705, 924, 2868; *see also*
    Second Words; *Survival*
  on Canadian poetry, 932
  feminist, 1131
  thematic, 3045
Crosbie, Lynn, 3662
Crozier, Lorna, 3266
Culleton, Beatrice, 1438
cult of true womanhood, 2879
culture, 513, 3701, 3889
  popular, 3303, 3486
    Atwood and, 1170
    gender and, 1870
    Lady Oracle, 947
  popular culture, 2105
Curious Pursuits
  reviews of, 3897
cyberpunk fiction, 954

Daly, Mary, 728, 2859
Dancing Girls and Other Stories, 86, 2876
  displacement in, 362
  as domestic fiction, 532
  as fairy tale, 532
  gender in, 1391
  mythopoesis in, 532
  realism in, 532, 1391
  as short fiction, 103

subjectivity in, and language, 1328
translations of
  German, 2995
  Italian, 602, 2682
  Japanese, 211, 2227
  Portuguese, 3336
  Russian, 3790
  Spanish, 2163
Dangarembga, Tsitsi, 1849, 2111
Danticat, Edwidge, 3109, 3238
Das, Kamala, 2835
daughters, 715, 1145, 1351; *see also*
  mothers
Davidson, Arnold E. [Ted], 2549, 2631
Davies, Robertson, 883
  on Atwood, 2554
De, Shobha, 3037, 3041
de Cespedes, Alba, 1872
death, 2626
  the artist and, 2899
  of the author, 2054
  murder, 1336, 2809, 3063, 3514
"Death by Landscape," 1901, 3489, 3666
  dramatic adaptation, 3202, 3420
"Death of a Young Son by Drowning," 3088
decolonization, 503; *see also* colonialism
defamiliarization, 1634, 3660
Defoe, Daniel, 3063
DeLillo, Don, 950, 1644, 1674
demography, 525
demonic, female, 1626
depression, 2874
Dernier homme, Le
  reviews of, 3900
Desai, Anita, 515, 1376, 1430, 2115, 3037
Descartes, René, 1670, 2106
Deshpande, Sashi, 1107
desire, 2363, 2551, 3252
  closeted, 3292
  female, 117, 1672, 2041, 2882
desolation; *see* hope and hopelessness
detective fiction
  in *Alias Grace*, 2304, 3510
Deux sollicitudes: entretiens
  reviews of, 2138, 2426, 3543
  reviews of English translation, 2431, 2643,
    2910, 3122
di Michele, Mary, 957
dialogic, 1405, 1613, 2565
dialog, 3488
diary, 550, 733, 1872
Dickens, Charles, 2077
Dickey, James, 168
Dickinson, Emily, 2376

Didion, Joan, 111, 566, 1674, 1835, 1855,
    1873
difference, 945, 3886
    cultural, 2625
discourse, 740, 1408, 3711
displacement, 1603
    carnival and, 1818
    in novels
        Bodily Harm, 2602
        Life Before Man, 2385
        Surfacing, 2385
    in short fiction, 928
        Bluebeard's Egg and Other Stories,
            2385
        Dancing Girls and Other Stories, 362
Doctorow, E. L., 950, 1958
documentary
    The Handmaid's Tale, 538, 3061
    The Journals of Susanna Moodie, 360,
        1151
dolls, 487
domesticity
    domestic abuse, 2874
    domestic fiction, 532
    domestic workers, 3291
    space of, 2357, 2791, 3861
    women's work, 1869
domination, 1352
Double Persephone, 94
Drabble, Margaret, 948, 1900, 2101, 2874
    A Natural Curiosity, 3287
    The Waterfall, 174, 1589, 1633
dreams, 1362
drowning, 3049
Du Maurier, Daphne, 3857
dualism, 732, 1377
    Cartesian, 1670
Duncan, Sara Jeannette, 934, 1189, 2064,
    2319
dystopias, 99, 855, 1876, 3040; *see also*
    utopias
    eugenics in, 3077
    feminist, 313, 1453, 2790
    gender and, 855, 1388, 1843
    The Handmaid's Tale, 99, 113, 176, 309,
        312, 335, 474, 498, 692, 900, 906, 1096,
        1146, 1843, 1876, 2323, 2343, 3060,
        3078, 3094, 3676-3677, 3696
        body in, 1453
        eugenics and, 3274
        female dystopia, 1646-1647, 2359, 2401
        feminism and, 1115, 1694, 1875, 2037,
            2344, 2594, 2790
        fundamentalist, 1665, 2072
        language in, 942, 1431, 2409, 2801

    leisure and, 3481
    love in, 2632
    mass culture and, 2105
    oppression in, 122, 1431
    postmodernist, 1326, 1339
    power in, 2409, 3052
    resistance in, 668, 1431
    salvation in, 1671
    science fiction, 2862
    as social commentary, 523
    space of, 2318
    storytelling in, 942
    time and, 2354, 2380
    utopian tradition and, 1115, 2056, 2553,
        3877
    women in, 668, 704
    imagination in, 1820
    memory in, 1820
    outsider, 3712
    transgressive, 3877

eating; *see* food
eating disorders; *see* food
ecofeminism, 527, 1850
ecology, 2824, 3255, 3668
    poetry and, 2822, 3265, 3680
Edible Woman, The, 144, 181, 320, 333,
    690, 1350, 1423, 2080, 2379, 2837, 2844,
    3669, 3868, 3881
    adaptations of
        dramatic, 3204; reviewed, 3314, 3733
        for radio; reviewed, 1928
    ambivalence and ambiguity in, 1608
    approaches to
        Lévi-Strauss, 131
        psychoanalytic, 131, 481
    as Bildungsroman, 2854
    the body in, 364, 698, 713, 3270, 3856,
        3862
        colonized, 1849
        eating disorders, 141, 671, 930, 1593
        female, 2131, 3270
    capitalism in, 1437, 3260
    city in, 710
    class in, 1415
    clothes in, 898
    compared to
        Fowles, John, 3687
        Surfacing, 2097
    creative process, 2387, 2873
        Jack McClelland and, 2393
    critical reception of, 1604
    as domestic fiction, 532
    as fairy tale, 131, 532, 564
    feminine consciousness in, 678, 1619

feminism and, 1397, 1413, 2617, 3856
  empowerment, 3036
  rejection of, 2798
fetish objects in, 1666
food in, 310, 364, 2882, 3663
  cannibalism, 564
  eating disorders, 141, 671, 930, 1593
  gender and, 3270, 3275
  vegetarianism, 292
gender in, 3270, 3275, 3862
  desire and, 2882
  masculinity, 3240
gothic in, 3527
influences on
  Lewis Carroll, 319, 1609
irony in, 327
language and, 884
maps and mapping in, 3098
mirror in, 85
models for characters, 3477
murder in, 1336
mythopoesis in, 532
nonsense in, 165
paranoia in, and stalker novel, 1882
power in, 710
realism in, 532
resistance in, 3270
reviews of, 576, 2139, 3309, 3898
schizophrenia in, 3260
sexuality in, 1119, 2882
space in, 1393
study guide, 1404, 2285
subjectivity in, 898, 1650
survival in, 1621
teaching, 1110, 1332
translations of
  Chinese, 2476
  Czech, 2241
  Danish, 2668, 2927
  French, 3767
  German, 593, 775, 2670
  Hebrew, 2185
  Italian, 3156
  Japanese, 1781
  Polish, 3588
  Portuguese, 3124
  Romanian, 247
  Russian, 1007
  Spanish, 3373, 3589
  Swedish, 773
victimization in, 147, 1355, 1419
vision in, 869
women in, 1633, 1834, 2108
  feminine sensibility, 1619
  Indonesian, 3036

ekphrasis, 3232
elegy, 1645, 3266
  Canadian, 3716, 3873
  Morning in the Burned House, 3066
Elgin, Suzette Haden, 1431, 1694, 1864,
  2801, 3877
Eliot, George, 741
Emecheta, Buchi, 1341
empowerment, 3036
Engel, Marian, 485, 1196, 2849, 3487, 3893
  Bear, 2332
  correspondence with Atwood, 3717
  Lunatic Villas, 1349
environmentalism, 1177, 3430
envy, 2415, 2421, 3722
Ephron, Nora, 174
epistolarity, 1597
  in *The Handmaid's Tale*, 331, 517, 904,
    3238
Erdrich, Louise, 923, 1888, 2090, 2294
eroticism, 3699
escape, 2849
Essai sur la littérature canadienne
  reviews of, 189
ethics, 365
ethnicity, 477, 1632, 1889
  feminism and, 2543
Etxebarría, Lucía, 3470
eugenics, 1598, 3077, 3274
evasion, 2312
Eve, 2367
evil, 1819, 2373
  female, 3038, 3084, 3683
exile, 955, 3288
experience, women's, 909

Fairbairn, Zoe, 1694
fairy tales, 1138, 1365, 2788, 3509, 3540
  adult, 131
  Bluebeard, 2123, 2322, 2789, 3279, 3525
    "Bluebeard's Egg," 3271
    Lady Oracle, 3855, 3878
    The Robber Bride, 3062
  Canadian, 920
  Cinderella, 3298
  Grimm brothers, 2792
  in novels
    The Edible Woman, 366, 532, 564
    The Handmaid's Tale, 1877, 3111, 3242
    Lady Oracle, 532, 2792
    Life Before Man, 532
    The Robber Bride, 2322, 3483
    Surfacing, 75, 505
  parody of, 74
  polymorphism of, 1640

Rapunzel, 2792
in short fiction
   Bluebeard's Egg and Other Stories, 532,
      1640; "Bluebeard's Egg," 1432, 1877,
      3271
   Dancing Girls and Other Stories, 532;
      "The Man from Mars," 74
   Wilderness Tips, 2579, 3490
Sleeping Beauty, 1432
faith vs. doubt, 1671
fantasy, 1897, 2588
   Alias Grace, 2787
   Cat's Eye, 562, 672
   The Handmaid's Tale, 562, 711, 1446,
      1856, 2396
   Lady Oracle, 153, 562, 3658
   The Robber Bride, 2787
   sexual, 2588
   Surfacing, 484, 562
Faulkner, William, 1159
"Female Body, The," 3051
female gothic; *see* gothic, female
female imaginary, 2627
femininity, 1099
   feminine sensibility, 1619
feminism, 170, 2038, 2384, 2885; *see also*
   anti-feminism; feminist theory; postfeminism
   aesthetics of, 351
   ambivalent, 3694
   Atwood's, 1118, 2035, 2809, 3714
      and non-feminist reader, 2043
   the body and, 117
   dystopia and, 176, 295, 309, 2037
   ethnicity and, 2543
   in fiction, 117, 1107, 1855
      Cat's Eye, 2047
      The Edible Woman, 1413, 2617, 2798
      The Handmaid's Tale, 154, 1118, 2054,
         2083, 2595, 3486, 3721; anti-feminism
         in, 1379, 3694; postmodernism in,
         1327, 2595; women's freedom and,
         1118
      Lady Oracle, 1436
      The Robber Bride, 2047
   hostility toward, 1379
   multiculturalism and, 1829
   nationalism and, 1192, 3110, 3487
   nature of, 1313
   poetics of, 95, 349, 351
   popular culture and, 3486
   postmodernism and, 536, 708, 1327, 2595,
      2617
   romance and, 321
   science and, 2047

utopia and, 295, 309, 313, 498, 520, 3885
feminist theory and criticism, 1131, 3714;
   see also gynocriticism
   diary and, 550
   in fiction
      Bodily Harm, 348
      The Edible Woman, 3856
      The Handmaid's Tale, 348, 521, 550
      Lady Oracle, 861
      Life Before Man, 518
   French feminism, 151, 518, 861
femme fatale, 3084
Ferguson, Trevor, 2852
Ferre, Rosario, 2819
fertility; *see* reproduction
fetish objects, 1666
fiction, 731, 2081, 3074; *see also* narrative
   form and structure; novels; short fiction;
   titles of individual books
   Atwood's
      development of, 927
      early work, 534, 2284
      later work, 551, 2619, 2637
   camp in, 2834
   Canadian, 739
   experimental, 2637
   female characters in, 2573
      heroes, 1176
   female subjectivity in, 731, 1099, 1392
   feminist, 117, 544, 1698, 3714
      diaries in, 1872
      escape narratives, 2849
      postmodernism and, 2617
   gothic, 1445
   historical, 2328
   Inter-American, 484, 2819
   Künstlerroman, 2544
   language in, 551, 739
   literature of science, 1674
   narrative, 919, 1392
      dual, 2102
   narrative voice in, 1179, 1888
   postmodernist, 1657, 2617, 2637
   post-realist, 1179
   quest novel, 1126
   speech acts, 725
   stalker novel, 1644
   survival in, 2573
   war novels, 1654
film, 944, 2083; *see also The Handmaid's*
   Tale [motion picture]
Findley, Timothy, 883, 919, 1446, 1836,
   2547
   on Atwood, 1345
fire, 3089

Flaubert, Gustave, 2831
folklore, 1194, 3536
food, 2883; *see also* cannibalism
  eating disorders, 3286
    anorexia, 141, 671, 930, 1593
    bulimia, 930
  female body and, 3270, 3275
  healing power of, 1898
  in novels, 292, 1658
    The Blind Assassin, 3692
    The Edible Woman, 292, 310, 364, 2882,
      3270, 3275, 3663
    Lady Oracle, 310, 364, 546, 3270
    Surfacing, 310
  politics of, 1892, 2870
  vegetarianism, 292
For the Birds
  reviews of, 577, 756, 959
Fossey, Dian, 3057
Foucault, Michel, 1599, 2106, 2604, 3719
Fowles, John, 3100, 3687
fragmentation, 2078, 2898, 3048
Frame, Janet, 1589
"Frankenstein Monster Song," 3623
Franklin, Sir John, 3507
Fraser, Sylvia, 2838
free trade, 2036
freedom, 1118, 3512
French, Marilyn, 913, 2083
  The Women's Room, 1599, 2083
French feminism, 151, 518, 861
Freud, Sigmund, 167, 352, 1446, 2787, 3251
friendship, female, 1160, 1594, 1885, 2271,
  2294, 3659
frontier, 2282
Frye, Northrop, 1320, 2073, 2282, 2622
  Canadian culture and, 1127, 2064, 2847,
    2896, 3268
  Cat's Eye and, 3523
  and *The Handmaid's Tale*, 1881
  The Handmaid's Tale and, 330
  Lady Oracle and, 323

Gale, Marilyn Kravitz, 2311
Gallant, Mavis, 514, 1179, 1187, 2132
games, 1094
Garcia, Cristina, 2600
gaze, 1681
  male, 1852
Gearhart, Sally Miller, 520, 527
gender, 294, 2878
  dystopia and; *see* dystopias
  elegy and, 1645
  genre and, 2125, 2790

insanity and, 2069
language and, 331, 2098
nation and, 2125, 2847
in novels, 125, 731, 1674, 1886, 2103
  Alias Grace, 3100, 3708
  Bodily Harm, 1870
  Cat's Eye, 702
  The Edible Woman, 3862
  feminist, 544
  The Handmaid's Tale, 520, 544, 702,
    1364, 1455, 1838, 1916, 2790
  The Robber Bride, 1585, 2617
  Surfacing, 1106, 1870, 2069
as performance, 2092, 2881, 3240
in poetry, 2098
  The Journals of Susanna Moodie, 1184
  You Are Happy, 1871
politics of, 2878
popular culture and, 1870
power and, 2128
regendering, 2571
science and, 1674
in short fiction, 345
  Bluebeard's Egg and Other Stories,
    1391
  Dancing Girls and Other Stories, 1391
  Good Bones, 2048
  Murder in the Dark, 2048
genetics, 3682; *see also* science
genre, 731, 2125; *see also* dystopias; fairy
  tales; fantasy; fiction; gothic; poetry;
  romance; short fiction
  revision of traditional forms, 1686, 2833
"Gertrude Talks Back," 1166, 1400
ghosts, 706, 1617, 2274, 2787, 2855
Gibbons, Stella, 3261
Gibson, William, 1388
Gilchrist, Ellen, 3075
Gilman, Charlotte Perkins
  Herland, 1341, 2879
  "The Yellow Wallpaper," 2829, 3878
"Giving Birth," 1186, 1449, 2124
  as female gothic, 1385
Glob, Peter Vilhelm, 3287
globalism, 2036
Glück, Louise, 3089
goddess, 2052, 2859, 2894, 3282
Godwin, Gail, 886
"Good Bones," 2826
Good Bones
  interview about, 842
  myth and folklore in, 3536
  review of stage adaptation, 1711
  reviews of, 960, 1199, 1465

translations of
   French, 1514, 1747, 2477; reviews of,
     1922
   German, 1502, 1963
   Swedish, 1002
Good Bones and Simple Murders
   reviews of, 1460, 3120, 3310-3311
Good Bones and Small Murders
   reviews of, 1701
Gordimer, Nadine, 668, 1147, 3894
Gordon, Mary, 923
gossip, 1859-1860
gothic, 134, 2093, 3244, 3262
   anxiety in, 2093
   in Atwood's criticism, 134, 3527
   Bluebeard in, 3878
   the body and, 2616
   concealment in, 3524
   female, 318, 1385, 1659, 2093
     Alias Grace, 3857
     The Blind Assassin, 3684
     Bodily Harm, 719
     Lady Oracle, 1403
   humor and, 3866
   intertextuality, 2618
   modern, 318, 1445
   mothers and, 1659
   northern, 2628
   in novels, 344, 2886
     Alias Grace, 3857
     The Blind Assassin, 3524, 3684
     Bodily Harm, 502, 719, 3082
     Cat's Eye, 2616, 2618, 3527
     The Edible Woman, 3527
     The Handmaid's Tale, 502, 3527, 3879
     Lady Oracle, 138, 153, 322, 344, 354,
       502, 690, 892, 1403, 2542, 3107,
       3527, 3866
     Life Before Man, 3527
     The Robber Bride, 2605, 3866
     Surfacing, 134, 318, 3527, 3866
   in poetry, 134, 3489, 3527
   postcolonial, 2605
   postmodern, 892
   psychological elements, 747
   revision of, 747
     alternative endings, 502
     parody, 3261
   in short fiction
     Bluebeard's Egg and Other Stories,
       3527
     "Death by Landscape," 1901, 3489
     Murder in the Dark, 3527
   sublime in, 892
   teaching, 3484

victimization and, 747
Gould, Lois, 711
government, 2360
Grant, George, 161
Grass, Günter, 525, 912
"Grave of the Famous Poet, The," 2363
Graves, Robert, 727
Grey Owl, 3057
"Grey Owl Syndrome, The," 2291
Griffin, Susan, 2311
Grimm brothers, 2792
Grosskurth, Phyllis, 2577
grotesque, 2270
Group of Seven, 2847
Gunnars, Kristjana, 1920
Gurney, Janice, 673
gynocriticism, 527, 1638; *see also* feminist
   theory and criticism

Haden, Suzette, 1694
"Hairball," 3863
Haldane, Charlotte Franken, 3274
"Half-Hanged Mary," 2866
The Handmaid's Tale, 118, 152, 163-164,
   179, 297, 308, 324, 328, 341, 476, 544,
   926, 1426, 1637, 1677, 2050, 2118, 2126,
   2278, 2288, 2302, 2342, 2350, 2368,
   2370, 2378, 2406, 2411, 2416, 2576,
   2629, 3293, 3482, 3528, 3533, 3669, 3713
   abortion in, 1879, 3678
   adaptations of
     film; *see Handmaid's Tale* [motion
       picture]; *Handmaid's Tale*, novel vs.
       film
     film script, 3497
     musical score, 1795, 2245
     opera, 2243, 2722, 3506; interviews
       about, 3637, 3643; reviewed, 3123,
       3552, 3734
     radio drama, 2720
     video release, 446, 3203; reviewed, 3315
   African Americans in, 2050
   Afterword, 1687, 2063, 2313, 2316, 3061,
     3672
     as narrative joke, 2330
   ambivalence and ambiguity in, 732, 2562,
     3694
   anti-Americanism in, 2308
   apocalypse in, 123, 2057
   approaches to, 1829
     Campbell, Joseph, 1881
     feminist, 1831
     Foucault, Michel, 2812
     Frye, Northrop, 330, 1881
     Mannheim, Karl, 1881

materialist, 883
postcolonial, 1832
psychoanalytic, 1446, 1831
Ricoeur, Paul, 1881
textual analysis by computer, 1148
Todorov, Tzvetan, 1446
archetypes in, 2413
artist in, 559
autobiography in, 890, 1358
Bible in, 1614, 2309
Gilead, 1125
handmaid, 852
Jezebel, 545
bibliography of criticism, 2309
the body in, 673, 698, 713, 1091, 2890
female, 1449, 2298, 2400
language and, 2575
as performance, 2400
survival and, 2044
book groups and, 856, 1406
borders and boundaries in, 479, 698, 918,
1651, 2273
Canadian canon and, 1331, 1824
capitalism in, 1437
carnival in, 543
Cat's Eye and, 1096
censorship and, 2051, 2547, 2802, 3050
children and childhood in, 2897
class in, 3883
colonialism in, 2308
complicity in, 1435
consciousness raising and, 470, 881
creative process, 1344
critical reception, 1089, 2375
by third world, 2331
cult of true womanhood, 2879
cyberpunk and, 954
demonic woman in, 1626
desire in, 2551, 3252
dialogics in, 1405
diary in, 550, 733
discourse in, 3711
as documentary, 538, 3061
domestic space in, 2337, 2357
domesticity in, 1869
dreams in, 1362
as dystopia, 99, 113, 122, 154, 176, 312,
334, 474, 668, 692, 900, 906, 942, 1096,
1146, 1453, 2323, 2343, 3078, 3094,
3677, 3696
anti-leisure, 3481
commentary on modern world, 523
dystopian tradition, 1876
eugenics and, 3274
female, 1646-1647, 2359, 2401

feminist, 498, 1694, 1875, 2037, 2344,
2594, 3676
feminist utopia and, 295, 309, 313, 1115,
2553, 3877
fundamentalist, 1665, 2072
gender in, 1843
individuality in, 2056
language in, 1431, 2409, 2801
love in, 2632
mass culture in, 2105
postmodernist, 1326
power in, 1339, 1431, 2409, 2807, 3052
salvation in, 1671
science fiction and, 2862
space of, 2318
time in, 2354, 2380
women in, 704
environmentalism in, 1177
envy in, 2415
epistolarity in, 331, 517, 904
eugenics in, 3274
evasion in, 2312
fairy tales and, 3111, 3242
teaching, 1877
faith vs. doubt in, 1671
as fantasy, 562, 711, 1856, 2396
unreal in, 1446
female quests in, 1126
feminism in, 2054, 3110, 3486, 3694,
3721
hostility to, 1379
postfeminism, 736
postmodernism and, 2595
women's freedom and, 1118
feminist theory and criticism, 348, 521
as fictional biography, 335
fragmentation in, 2078, 3048
freedom in, 3512
friendship in
female, 1160, 1594, 2271
games in
Scrabble, 1094
gaze in, 1161, 1681
gender in, 520, 544, 702, 1364, 1455,
1838, 1843, 1916
conflict, 1132
gender roles, 1694
genre and, 2790
narrative and, 1856
globalism and, 2036
goddess symbols, 2052
gossip in, 1859-1860
as gothic, 502, 3527, 3879
government in, 2360
heroes, female, in, 1342

as historiography, 97, 526, 542, 2036,
    2078, 2805
  irony and, 2317
  vs. private memory, 2329
  satire and, 314
  women's, 296, 2341
hope and hopelessness in, 1671
identity in, 1368, 1435
ideology in, 2280
illness and invalids in, 1182, 1325
  hysteria, 2846
  invalidation and, 1135
impurity in, 955
infertility in
  caused by pollution, 1177
influences on
  Chaucer, 1605
  Orwell's *1984*, 2582
  Plato's *Republic*, 2383
intertextuality in, 524, 1916
  "escaped nun" stories, 2351
  psychology, 335
interviews about, 2025, 3453, 3633
irony in, 493, 562, 2317, 2557, 3534
language in, 1431, 1665, 2409, 2801
  the body and, 2575
  consciousness raising and, 881
  oppression and, 1111, 2341
  subversion and, 1660, 2617
law in, 2607, 3243
literacy in, 521, 735, 1636
as literary history, 1101
love in, 2346
maps and mapping in, 1368
marginalization in, 2050
medicine in, 1607, 2607
memory in, 2329
  resistance and, 1362, 1891
as metafiction, 2343, 2420
mirrors in, 1161
misogyny in, 3044
mothers in, 300, 677, 860, 903, 1648,
    2065, 2635
  lost, 693
  surrogate, 718, 2853, 3277
myth in, 887, 1881, 2045
names and naming in, 357, 1191
narrative structure, 1450, 2300, 2349
  chronology, 2309
  closure, 3504
  plot, 560
narrative voice in, 887, 1664
narrators, 1141, 1339, 3675
  authority of, 3673

narratee and, 2296
  resistance of, 1676
nationalism in, 1192, 3110
Native Americans in, 2050
nature in, 696, 2583
  civilization and, 1340
  vs. nurture, 154
novel vs. film, 511, 1100, 1148, 1375,
    1607, 1691, 2590
Nunavut/Nunavit in, 542, 2063
olfactory imagery in, 933
oppression in, 1190, 1352, 2050
  fascism, 3067
  social control, 2307
  totalitarianism, 2076
orality and literacy in, 521, 1636
paranoia in, 358
as parody, 474, 526, 911, 2314, 2888,
    3102, 3711
patriarchy in, 303, 337, 1343, 1442
performance studies and, 946
politics in, 955, 2418, 2624
  fascism, 3067
  free trade, 2036
popular culture and, 3486
pornography in, 3678
postcolonialism and, 2420, 3091
postmodernism in, 104, 526, 536, 543,
    692, 708, 1884, 3667, 3885
  feminism and, 1327, 2595
  metafiction, 2343, 2420
power in, 478, 696, 1339, 1347, 1352,
    1599, 2558, 2807, 3037, 3052
  female, 2088
  female friendship and, 2271
  ideology and, 2280
  language and, 1431, 2409
  satire and, 1848
prisons in, 1866
protagonist, female, in, 1835, 2568
public vs. private in, 2399
race in, 2050
readers and, 2301, 3534
reading in, 296, 521, 1111
  and women's voices, 2067
realism in, 1673, 3055
regression in, 2548
religion in, 306, 337, 2635, 2859, 3242-
    3243
  Christianity, 1602
  government and, 2360
  Protestant fundamentalism, 955, 2608
  Puritans, 169, 303, 2560
  Roman Catholicism, 330, 853
  theocracy, 694

reproduction in, 3883
  birth, 1311
  eugenics, 1598, 3274
  pregnancy, 3235
  sterility and fertility, 2374
  technologies of, 669
resistance in, 1362, 1435, 1891, 2362,
  2397, 2558
  creativity and, 2053
  to patriarchy, 1442
  through narration, 1676, 3101
responsibility in, 953
reviews of, 191, 371, 578, 757, 1461, 2640
  French translation, 760
reviews of audiobook, 190, 961, 3899
revolution in, 668, 1389
rhetorical strategies in, 878
righteousness and fallibility in, 2392
risk in, 101
as romance, 721, 1338, 2861, 3085
sadomasochism in, 2117
satire in, 508, 1848, 1907, 2297
as science fiction, 746, 866, 1867, 3864
  feminist, 951, 1655, 1864
setting, 560, 746
sexuality in, 1600, 2346
  gender and, 3661
  slavery and, 2607
  surveillance of, 1607
shapeshifters in, 1905
silence in, 1580, 2382, 2397
society in, 523, 2307, 2799
  corruption, 2558
  decline of, 123
space in, 2318
  female, 1616
spectacle in, 2812, 3302
as speculative fiction, 860, 918, 1096
storytelling in, 887, 2313
  and Scheherazade, 306, 942
study guide, 1404, 1433, 1893, 2094,
  2269, 2303, 2324, 2422, 2567, 3072,
  3239, 3246, 3290, 3495
subjectivity in, 2890
  female, 2846
  split, 2359
subversion in, 1190, 1660, 2364, 2617,
  3243
  gossip, 1859
Sufism in, 367
surveillance in, 1161, 2310, 2812
survival in, 154, 1331, 1362, 1621, 2326
  the body and, 2044
  through witness, 2611
teaching, 556, 1139, 1824, 1826-1827,

  1845, 1917
  to boys, 1168
  in Germany, 3269
  politics, 299
  social roles, 545
  sociology, 504, 1851, 1867
  through film, 1863
  as utopia, 1909
  women's studies, 935
time in, 2321, 2354
translation and, 96
translations of
  Chinese, 2980, 3184
  Croatian, 46
  Danish, 54
  Finnish, 423, 2213
  French, 431; reviewed, 197, 374, 760
  German, 214, 774, 1730, 2173;
    reviewed, 188
  Greek, 226
  Italian, 24, 3584
  Japanese, 408, 2952
  Korean, 611, 3145
  Norwegian, 439
  Polish, 802, 2212
  Portuguese, 10
  Slovak, 2975
  Slovenian, 384
  Spanish, 2934, 3133; critical discussion
    of, 2058
  Turkish, 772
utopian tradition and, 521, 692, 1197,
  1881, 1909, 2601, 3306, 3885
  female, 1341
veil in, 3047
victimization in, 154, 499, 1343
  escaping, 1355, 1419
  through medicine, 862
  by women, 2088
violence in
  abduction, 2897
  murder, 1336
voice in, 1410
  narrative, 742, 887, 1664
witness in, 2369, 2610-2611
The Handmaid's Tale [motion picture], 446-
  447, 494, 2083, 2636, 3002
  feminism in, 2083, 2636
  film script, 3497
  film vs. novel, 511, 1100, 1148, 1375,
    1607, 1691, 2590
  interviews about, 455, 460-461, 464
  medicine in, 1607
  resistance in, 3478
  reviews of, 584, 762, 967, 1204, 1466

romance plot, 1122
    as science fiction film, 1143
    screenplay, computer analysis of, 1148
    sexuality in, 1607
    teaching, 1863
    uncanny in, 2290
    voyeurism in, 1607, 3670
hands, 356
"Happy Endings," 1136
harmony, creative, 1314
Harris, Bertha, 151
Harvor, Elizabeth, 909
Haushofer, Marlen, 2620
Hawthorne, Nathanial, 1862
Haycraft, Anna Margaret, 2883
Head, Bessie, 1341, 2901
healing, 1898, 1915
Hébert, Anne, 469, 1189, 2819, 3058, 3706
    Kamouraska, 2823, 3287, 3291
Heisenberg, Werner, 2376
"Helen of Troy Does Countertop Dancing"
    Hebrew translation of, 2190
Herbst, Josephine, 913
heritage; see culture
hero, female, 91, 1176, 1342
heroine, 729, 934, 1312, 3248; see also hero,
    female
heterosexuality; see sexuality
historiography, 2036
    irony and, 2317
    in The Journals of Susanna Moodie, 336,
        2864, 3706
    in "The Loneliness of the Military
        Historian," 2277
    in novels
        Alias Grace, 2819, 2823, 2864-2865,
            3083, 3109, 3513, 3706
        Bodily Harm, 526
        Cat's Eye, 3259
        The Handmaid's Tale, 97, 296, 526, 542,
            2036, 2078, 2317, 2329, 2341, 2805,
            3259
        Oryx and Crake, 3882
        The Robber Bride, 2272, 2864
    patchwork and, 3083
    women's history, 2341, 2819, 3706
Hoban, Russell, 1431
Hogen, Linda, 2398
Homans, Margaret, 728
Hood, Hugh, 1836
hope and hopelessness, 473, 1373, 1671,
    2363
Horwood, Harold
    on Atwood, 2830
Hulme, Keri, 3663

humanity, as homo faber, 3859
humour, 3076
    in Lady Oracle, 2295, 3108
    nationalism and, 2786
    in poetry, 1381
        Morning in the Burned House, 3053
    in representations of indigenous peoples,
        939
"Hurricane Hazel," 2104
Hurston, Zora Neale, 1868
Hutcheon, Linda, 2591, 2819
    critique of, 888
Huxley, Aldous, 1431, 1635, 3274, 3481
hysteria, 2846; see also insanity

"Icicle, The," 92
iconicity, 2845, 3073
identity, 731, 898, 917, 1095, 1172, 2817,
    3057, 3074
    Atwood on, 1649, 2622
    Canadian, 1649, 1829, 2073, 3268
        in Alias Grace, 3688
        innocence and, 548
        in The Journals of Susanna Moodie,
            1184
        in Lady Oracle, 3517
        in The Robber Bride, 3493
        in Survival, 1140, 1178, 1387
        victimization and, 1178
    cultural, 2272, 3057
    female, 1369, 3487, 3691
    in fiction, 731, 1163, 1174
        Alias Grace, 3688
        Bodily Harm, 1164
        Cat's Eye, 716, 1093, 2071, 2084, 3043,
            3889
        The Edible Woman, 898
        The Handmaid's Tale, 1368, 1435, 3235
        Lady Oracle, 916, 1185, 1613, 3517
        The Robber Bride, 2272, 2615, 3493
        short fiction, 1108
        Surfacing, 492, 898, 1368-1369, 1412
    intertextuality and, 2615
    in The Journals of Susanna Moodie, 1184
    marriage and, 1185
    memory and, 1913, 2071
    multiple, 1613
    national, 1184, 2055, 2104, 3112, 3263,
        3268
        gender and, 3487
    nationalism and, 1903
    place and, 1422, 2614
    pregnancy and, 3235
    wilderness and, 1858

ideology, 1330, 2280
  narrative and, 1392
illness and invalids
  in *The Handmaid's Tale*, 1135, 1182, 1325
imaginary, female, 2627
imagination, 1820
immigrants
  in fiction, 2619
    Alias Grace, 2887
    female coming-of-age, 2600
    The Robber Bride, 2619
    "Wilderness Tips," 1112-1113, 2116
  gendered, 1112, 2600
  Hungarian, 2116
  Irish, 2887
  in *The Journals of Susanna Moodie*, 488,
    1847
imprisonment, 1866, 3501
impurity, 955
"In Search of Rattlesnake Plantain," 3477
incest; *see* trauma
indigenous peoples, 939, 2050, 2332
individuality, 2056
infertility, 1177; *see also* reproduction
Ingalls, Rachel, 912
initiation, 3703
innocence, 500, 1386
  and Canadian character, 548
insanity
  gender and, 3516
  hysteria, 2846
  in novels, 359, 3529, 3715
    Alias Grace, 2604, 2843
    The Edible Woman, 3260
    The Handmaid's Tale, 2846
    Surfacing, 912, 2069, 3516
  schizophrenia, 912, 3260
Inter-American fiction, 484, 2819
Interlunar, 80, 519
  myth in, 2795
  poetics in, 3491
  postmodernism in, 708
  reviews of, 192, 372
intertextuality, 2900, 3283
  in *The Handmaid's Tale*, 335, 524, 1916,
    2351
  in *Lady Oracle*, 1825, 2113
  in *Life Before Man*, 858
  in *The Robber Bride*, 2615
intimacy, 2346
Ireland, 2856, 2887
Irigaray, Luce, 151, 322, 728, 867, 1161,
  2334
irony, 699, 899, 1196
  in *The Blind Assassin*, 3285

in *Bodily Harm*, 472
in *Cat's Eye*, 562
in *The Edible Woman*, 327
in *The Handmaid's Tale*, 174, 493, 562,
  2317, 2557, 3534
in *Lady Oracle*, 562
in *Life Before Man*, 2066
in *Surfacing*, 562
Irving, John, 902, 2083
Iser, Wolfgang, 78, 569
"Isis in Darkness," 3477
  dramatic adaptation, 3202, 3420
islands, 3520
Italy, 3517

Jackson, Shirley, 3251, 3280, 3857
James, Henry, 3521
James, Henry, Jr., 3528
Jameson, Anna Brownell, 1189
Jezebel; *see* Bible
Jia Pingwa, 2407, 2417
Johnston, George, 2797
Jones, D. G., 2064
Jones, Gayl, 3300
Jones, Gwyneth, 2396
Jong, Erica, 1910, 2849
Journals of Susanna Moodie, The, 148, 166,
  181, 901, 1097, 1322, 3299
  Afterword, 940
  as Canadian literature, 360
  compared to Moodie's poetry, 689
  as documentary, 360, 1151
  feminism and, 2384
  gender in, 1184
  ghosts in, 2855
  gothic in, 3489
  as historiography, 336, 2864, 3706
  immigrants in, 488, 1847
  as life writing, 1861
  as long poem, 703
  myth, 3104
  national identity in, 1184
  order in, 555
  reviews of, 159, 2140-2141, 2427, 3312
  setting
    Canadian, 722
    the North, 3489
    psychological, 722
    wilderness, 555, 722
  translations of
    Japanese, 816
    Spanish, 620
"Journey to the Interior," 1127
journeys; *see* travel
Jung, Carl, 1913, 2881

juvenilia, editing of, 2284

Keller, Nora Okja, 3109
Kelly, Mary, 1852
Kesey, Ken, 2812
Kierkegaard, Sören, 3521
King, Stephen, 2372
King, Thomas, 2626, 2786
Kingsolver, Barbara, 1915, 2372, 2600
Kingston, Maxine Hong, 182, 875
kitsch, *2834*
Kogawa, Joy, 2132, 3109
Kosinski, Jerzy, 3092
Kristeva, Julia, 83, 151, 518, 1181, 1900,
    2626
Kroetsch, Robert, 118, 876, 888, 1446,
    1858, 1920
Künstlerroman, 2544; *see also* art and the
    artist

labor
    homo faber, 3859
    women's, 1869
Labrador Fiasco
    reviews of, 2908
Lacan, Jacques, 487, 714, 2623
Lady Oracle, 1350, 1425, 2617, 3669
    anti-Americanism in, 685
    approaches to
        French feminism, 861
        Frye, Northrop, 323
        Irigaray, Luce, 322
    art and the artist in, 509, 750
    autobiography in, 857, 1358, 3705
    as Bildungsroman, 2854
    the body in, 117, 364, 2295
        anorexic, 930
        food and, 3270
        gendered, 2806, 3108, 3237, 3270
    Canada in, 2839
    capitalism in, 1414, 1437
    children and childhood in, 730
    comedy in, 298
    creative process, 1124
    creativity, feminine, in, 1378
    critical reception of, 1124
    depression in, 2874
    difference in, 182
        ethnicity, 182, 1889
        theories of Luce Irigaray, 322
    domestic abuse in, 2874
    as domestic fiction, 532
    drowning in, 3049
    evil, female, in, 3683
    as fairy tale, 532, 2792
        Bluebeard, 3855, 3878
        as fantasy, 153, 562, 3658
    female desire in, 117, 1319, 2041, 3048
    female friendship in, 1160
    feminism and, 1397, 1436
    food in, 310, 364, 546
        anorexia, 930
        female body and, 3270
    as gothic, 138, 1403, 3107, 3527, 3866,
        3878
        gender and, 153, 322, 354, 502, 690,
            2542
        parody of, 3261
        sublime in, 892
        teaching, 3484
    heroine in, 934
    humor in, 2295, 3108
    influences on
        Graves, Robert, 727
        Grimm brothers, 2792
        Montgomery, L. M., 885, 934, 1323
        Tennyson, Alfred, Lord, 2792
    intertextuality in, 1825, 2113
    irony in, 562
    as literary history, 1101
    male characters in, 2395
    maps and mapping in, 1418, 3098
    memory in, 1891
    metamorphosis in, 2546
    middle class in, 1414
    mirrors in, 85, 934, 2295
    models for characters, 3477
    mothers in, 714, 3107, 3505
        mother-daughter relationships, 298
    myth in, 532, 727
    narrated self in, 2552
    narrative, 3475
        structure, 691, 896
        voice, 670
    as parody, 1417, 3705
    popular culture and, 947
    quest; *see* travel
    resistance in, 916, 1393, 1417, 1834, 3270
        memory and, 1891
        to patriarchy, 857
    reviews of, 2642
    as romance, 323, 2831
    space in, 1393
    storytelling in, 298, 857
    subjectivity in
        community and, 1918
        confession and, 2552
        dialogic, 1613, 2565
        divided, 916, 1650
        marriage and, 1185

subversion in, 916, 1353, 1834
teaching, 3484
Toronto in, 1349, 2061, 3880
translations of
    Danish, 609, 2940
    Finnish, 1034
    French, 1973
    German, 793, 2480
    Latvian, 2662
    Polish, 249, 1987
    Portuguese, 1036, 3380
    Spanish, 1732, 2929
    Swedish, 627
    Turkish, 763
travel in, 88, 1443
    escape, 554
    picaresque, 3234
    quest, 506, 1825, 3234
vision in, 869
woman writer in, 688
"Landcrab"
    set to music, 1060
"The Landlady," 1381
landscape
    in *Cat's Eye*, 2371
    in "Circe/Mud Poems," 3070
    internal, 2391
    postmodern, 3070
    in *Surfacing*, 2391, 2398
language, 559, 744
    the body and, 1837, 2575, 3079-3080
    Canadian, 2305
    colonialism and, 739
    gender and, 331, 881, 1837, 2098, 2341
    in novels, 552, 739
        The Blind Assassin, 3106
        Bodily Harm, 111, 551
        Cat's Eye, 1660, 1688
        The Handmaid's Tale, 551, 559, 881,
            1665, 2341, 2409, 2617
        Life Before Man, 551, 2385
        Surfacing, 2348, 2385
    in poetry
        Two-Headed Poems, 510
    power and, 2409
    in short fiction, 1328
        Bluebeard's Egg and Other Stories, 551,
            2385
        "Loulou; or, The Domestic Life of
            Language," 551
    subjectivity and, 881, 1095, 1328
    subversion and, 2617
    tense and, 943
Latin America, 365
Laurence, Margaret, 82, 469, 485, 527, 541,
        555, 749, 893, 934, 1196, 1359, 1587,
        1603, 2066, 2106, 2547, 3487, 3520
    The Diviners, 506, 685, 861, 1151
    The Fire-Dwellers, 559
    relationship with Atwood, 1641, 2074,
        2543
    Stone Angel, 116
law, 1615, 2607, 3243, 3662
    panopticism and, 3695
Layton, Irving, 2797
Le Guin, Ursula K., 81, 520, 1852, 3868
Leacock, Stephen, 2786
Lecker, Robert, 2606
Lee, Harper, 1873
Lee, Sky, 1113
Lee, Vernon, 3084
leisure, repudiation of, 3481
Lessing, Doris, 81, 117, 150, 496, 550, 563,
        1161, 1385, 1659, 1872, 2565, 2624,
        2817, 2883, 3251, 3270
    Four-gated City, 704
    The Golden Notebook, 733, 896, 1180,
        3705
    *The Marriages Between Zones Three,
        Four, and Five*, 1914
    Memoirs of a Survivor, 2362
    "One off the Short List," 3039
LeSueur, Meridel, 913
Levertov, Denise, 1695
Levi, Primo, 3289
Lévi-Strauss, Claude, 131
Li Ang, 1330
liberation, women's, 1107
Life Before Man, 92, 145, 501, 532, 1098,
        1689, 2877
    approaches to
        French feminism, 518
    class in, 1415
    creative process, 1098
    critical reception, 1098
    displacement in, 2385
    as domestic fiction, 532
    ethnicity in, 477, 1632
    as fairy tale, 532
    female friendship in, 1160
    gothic in, 3527
    heterosexuality in, 1119
        marriage, 2617
    hope and hopelessness in, 1373
    intertextuality in, 858
    language in, 2385
    maps and mapping in, 3098
    men, sympathy for, in, 2065
    models for characters, 3477
    mythopoesis in, 532

reviews of audiobook, 3544
sexuality in, 2385
  heterosexuality, 1119
Shakespeare in, 1400
subjectivity in, 1650
teaching, 1827
time and, 110
Toronto in, 3880
translations of
  Czech, 3162
  Dutch, 1504
  German, 14, 388, 1487, 2451
  Russian, 3776
vision in, 869
life writing, 1861; *see also* autobiography;
  epistolarity
linearity vs. cyclicity, 1680
Lispector, Clarice, 2588
literacy, 735, 1636
  teaching, 2049
literature; *see also* Canadian literature
  Chinese, 2132
  feminist, 3887
  French-Canadian, 1187
  Indo-English, 140
  Indonesian, 3036
  Inter-American, 484, 2819
  settler women's, 2584
"Lives of the Poets," 925
Livesay, Dorothy, 158
"The Loneliness of the Military Historian,"
  2277
Lorde, Audre, 913
"Loulou; or, The Domestic Life of
  Language," 1383, 1837
love, 128, 509, 2632
Lowther, Pat, 3471
Lyotard, Jean-François, 867, 2591

MacDonald, Ann-Marie, 3720
MacEwan, Gwendolyn, 3471
"Machine. Gun. Nest," 1663
MacLennan, Hugh, 548, 778
MacPherson, Jay, 3873
madness; *see* insanity
Madonna, 1852
Magritte, René, 177
Malouf, David, 1158, 2407
"The Man from Mars," 74, 945, 2270
  dramatic adaptation, 3202, 3420
Mandel, Eli, 3502
Manguel, Alberto, 2626, 3697
Mannheim, Karl, 1881
Mantel, Hilary, 2085
maps and mapping, 325, 3112

in *Cat's Eye*, 3098
in *The Edible Woman*, 3098
in *The Handmaid's Tale*, 1368, 1853
in *Lady Oracle*, 1418, 3098
in *Life Before Man*, 3098
in *The Robber Bride*, 3098
in *Surfacing*, 326, 1368, 3893
Maraini, Dacia, 1872
Margaret Atwood: Conversations
  reviews of, 580
Margaret Atwood Society, 839, 1083
  founding member, 2631
marginalization, 1886
  of African Americans, 2050
  of indigenous peoples, 2050
  of women, 1878, 2050
Markandaya, Kamala, 2110
Marlatt, Daphne, 559, 1151, 2341, 3718
marriage, 359, 2040, 2617
masculinity, 1099, 3240; *see also* men
Maso, Carole, 3300
masquerade, 700
McCabe, Patrick, 3092
McClelland, Jack, 2393
  on Atwood, 2587
McCullers, Carson, 1873
McEwan, Ian, 2897, 3865
McFarland, Dennis, 2372
McGuane, Thomas, 1106
McQueen, Cilla, 3089
"Me, She, and It"
  translations of, Spanish, 2515, 2719
medicine, 862, 1607, 2607
melancholia, 1900, 2101, 2874
melancholy and mourning, 1668, 2813
Melville, Herman, 1862, 2376
memoir, feminist, 3476
memory, 489, 1820, 1913, 2071, 2578, 3500
  adult vs. child, 2102
  in *The Blind Assassin*, 3704
  in *Cat's Eye*, 716, 874, 1150, 1401
    identity and, 2071
    resistance and, 1891, 2386, 2838
  in *The Handmaid's Tale*, 2329
    resistance and, 1362, 1891
  in *Lady Oracle*, 1891
  recovered memory syndrome, 2372
  in *Surfacing*, 1150, 1438
men, representations of, 893, 929, 1099,
  3297
  elusive, 2070
  as immigrants, 1112
  reader sympathy and, 2066
Merkin, Daphne, 2818
mermaids; *see* sirens

metafiction, 1920, 2352
  The Handmaid's Tale, 2343, 2420
  Lady Oracle, 1443
metamorphosis; *see* transformation
Meurtre dans la nuit
  reviews of, 193
Michaels, Anne, 3718
midlife, 1582
Millay, Edna St. Vincent, 2123, 3280
Miller, Perry, 1344
Miller, Sue, 913
Millet, Kate, 913
mimicry, 700
mirrors, 85, 315, 1134
  in *The Blind Assassin*, 3704
  in *Cat's Eye*, 2334
  in *The Edible Woman*, 85
  in *The Handmaid's Tale*, 1161
  in *Lady Oracle*, 85, 316, 934, 2295
  in *The Robber Bride*, 1890
misogyny, 3044
modernism, 1452
Molloy, Sylvia, 3238
Montgomery, L. M., 1323, 2319, 3520
  Anne of Green Gables, 885, 934
Montreal, 2333
Moodie, Susanna, 82, 555, 2319, 2580,
  2638, 3471, 3490; *see also Alias Grace*;
  The Journals of Susanna Moodie
  Atwood reading Moodie, 539, 901
  poetry, 689
Moore, Lorrie, 2127
More, Thomas, 868
Morning in the Burned House, 1894, 2068,
  2325, 2795
  as elegy, 3066
  humor in, 3053, 3531
  interviews about, 1573, 1575
  mourning in, 2813
  reviews of, 1703, 1924, 2428
  translations of
    French, 3593
    German, 1734
    Swedish, 1757
Morrison, Toni, 150, 496, 1823, 1886, 1888,
  2090, 2787, 2860, 2901, 3294, 3300, 3705
  Beloved, 711, 922, 2089, 2818, 3238
  Jazz, 3097
  Sula, 3659
mother-daughter relationships; *see also*
  mothers
  in *Cat's Eye*, 2818
  in *The Handmaid's Tale*, 693
  in *Lady Oracle*, 298
  in *Surfacing*, 167

mothers, 867, 1351; *see also* mother-
  daughter relationships
  in novels, 344, 715, 1145, 1163, 2040,
    3251
    Cat's Eye, 300, 1684, 2283, 2818
    The Edible Woman, 723
    The Handmaid's Tale, 300, 677, 693,
      723, 860, 903, 1648, 1914, 2065,
      2635; surrogate, 718, 2853, 3277
    Lady Oracle, 298, 344, 714, 3107, 3505
    The Robber Bride, 1684
    Surfacing, 167, 184, 723
  oppressive, 1163
  in poetry, 2825
Mouré, Erin, 3873
mourning, 1668, 2813
Moving Targets: Writing with Intent
  interviews about, 3650, 3836
  reviews of, 3724, 3901
multiculturalism, Canadian, 1829
Munro, Alice, 478, 485, 544, 674, 680, 697,
  928, 934, 1179, 1187, 1189, 1587, 1836,
  2106, 2132, 2366, 2588, 3075, 3112
  Lives of Girls and Women, 1319, 2127,
    2542
  "Meneseteung," 2124
  Open Secrets, 2125
    "A Wilderness Station," 2361
  "Oranges and Apples," 1112-1113
  relationship with Atwood, 3884
murder, 1336, 2809, 3063, 3514
Murder in the Dark, 90, 103, 2850, 3515
  autobiography and, 353
  deconstruction in, 121
  gothic in, 3527
  interviews about, 2029
  postmodernism in, 361
  reviews of, 373, 581
  teaching, 1883
  translations of
    French; reviewed, 193
    German, 984, 2450, 2671
    Japanese, 3199
    Spanish, 2435
Murdoch, Iris, 2817, 3484
Murdock, Maureen, 2353
"Music in Circular Motions"
  set to music, 653
myth, 532, 887, 949, 1682, 1906, 2900,
  3521; *see also* goddess
  female, 2353
  feminist revisions of, 870, 2795
  in fiction, 3104
    Good Bones, 3536
    The Handmaid's Tale, 1881, 2045

Lady Oracle, 727
Surfacing, 2060, 2353
Greek
    Callisto, 175
    Circe, 368, 1137, 1360
    Cupid and Psyche, 3702
    Demeter, 108
    Eurydice, 468, 1354
    Kyklopes, 3068
    Orpheus, 1354
    Penelope, 1360
    Persephone, 1361
nationalism and, 949
in poetry
    Interlunar, 2795
    Morning in the Burned House, 2795
    You Are Happy, 1871
postmodernism and, 949
storytelling, 1137
survival and, 949
Wendigo, 2559
mythopoesis, 532, 887

Naipaul, V. S., 111, 3890
names and naming, 357, 1191, 1612
Namjoshi, Suniti, 2901, 3280
narrative
    authority, 2390, 3673
    gender and, 1392, 1856, 2878
    ideology and, 1392
    memory and, 2838, 3500
    politics of, 522, 2842, 2878
    resistance and, 1636, 3101
    sacred, 3860
    subjectivity and, 1392, 3475
narrative closure; *see* narrative form and
    structure
narrative discourse, 740, 1675
narrative form and structure, 1398, 2081,
    3236
    closure, 502, 3499, 3504
    dual narrative, 2102
    in novels, 1103, 2120, 2410
        Alias Grace, 3279, 3504
        The Blind Assassin, 3499
        Bodily Harm, 691
        Cat's Eye, 691, 3504
        The Handmaid's Tale, 560, 2349, 3504
        Lady Oracle, 691, 857
    perspective, 3675
    politics of, 522, 707
    religion and, 3279
    subversion of tradition, 2410
narrative voice, 1179, 1841, 1888, 2090
    in *Cat's Eye*, 742, 1410

in *The Handmaid's Tale*, 742, 887, 1410,
    1664
in *Lady Oracle*, 670
in poetry, 1333
in *Surfacing*, 342
narrators
    in *The Handmaid's Tale*, 1141, 1339,
        1676, 2296, 3675
    in *Lady Oracle*, 2552
    narratee and, 2296, 2552
    in poetry, 342
national identity; *see* identity, Canadian;
    identity, national
nationalism, 102, 1140, 1862, 2847, 3423
    Atwood's, 2820
    feminism and, 1192, 3110, 3487
    gender and, 2847
        in *Wilderness Tips*, 2125
    humor and, 2786
    identity and, 1184, 2055, 2104, 3112,
        3263, 3268, 3487
        in Canadian literature, 1903
    myth and, 949
    nature and, 2847
    race and, 2847
    sexuality and, 2381
natives; *see* indigenous peoples
naturalism, 3081
nature, 744, 2785; *see also*
    environmentalism
    culture and, 1316, 1340
    feminism and, 1313, 2785
    nation and, 2847
    in novels
        Cat's Eye, 1316
        The Handmaid's Tale, 154, 696, 1340,
            2583
        Surfacing, 109, 512, 558, 880, 1340,
            2785
    vs. nurture, 154
    in poetry, 3888
    in short fiction
        "Unearthing Suite," 744
    women and, 83, 880
Naylor, Gloria, 527, 1855, 2039
Negotiating with the Dead, 3867
    artistic value in, 3249
    creative process of, 3264
    interviews about, 3023
    models for characters, 3477
    reviews of, 3313, 3545-3546, 3725
    translations of
        Chinese, 3622
        Italian, 3165
        Swedish, 3324

Neruda, Pablo, 3686
New Oxford Book of Canadian Short Stories in English, The
    reviews of, 1704, 1925
New Oxford Book of Canadian Verse in English, The, 751
    reviews of, 194
newspapers, 2589
Nietzsche, Friedrich, 3483
"Night in the Royal Ontario Museum"
    set to music, 2517
Nin, Anaïs, 2335
nomadism; *see* travel
nonfiction, 1444; *see also* criticism; *Second Words*; *Survival*
    voice in, 1155
North, 938, 3253, 3489, 3503, 3893
"Notes Towards a Poem," 877, 1334-1335
Nourbese Philip, Marlene, 1438
novels, 164, 356, 726, 907, 948, 1380, 1408, 1628, 1693, 2062, 2115, 2869, 3046; *see also* domesticity; fiction; titles of individual books
    alienation in, 749, 1912
    art and the artist in, 3074
        photography, 482
    bodies in, 496, 1823
    borders and boundaries in, 479, 483, 512
    cannibalism in, 350
    character development in, 1193, 1356
    children and childhood in, 549, 715, 1145, 2600
    city in, 710
    color in, 1643
    coming-of-age, female, 2600
    creative harmony in, 1314
    critical approaches to
        phenomenology, 2365
        psychoanalysis, 2365
    drafts of; *see* Atwood, Margaret, creative process
    epistolarity in, 1597
    as fantasy, 562
    female characters in, 2573
        daughters, 715, 1145
        wives, 715
    female friendship in, 1160, 1594, 2294
    feminism in, 351, 1430, 1855
    first sentences in, 1635
    food in, 1658, 2870
    forms of address in, 2091
    gender and, 2103
    gender roles in, 496, 1163
    gothic in, 344, 2093
    immigration in, 2600

    innocence in, 500
    insanity in, 359, 3715
    irony in, 562
    language in, 551-552
    marriage in, 359, 2040
    masquerade and mimicry in, 700
    memory in, 1891
    mirrors in, 315-316
    mothers in, 344, 715, 1145, 1163, 2040
        Cat's Eye, 300
        The Edible Woman, 723
        The Handmaid's Tale, 300, 677, 693, 723
        Lady Oracle, 344, 714
        storytelling and, 867
        Surfacing, 184, 723
    names and naming in, 907
    narrative discourse in, 740, 1675
    narrative form and structure, 1103, 2120
    narrative voice in, 1841
    nature in, 710
        The Handmaid's Tale, 154
        Surfacing, 109, 512, 558
    postmodernism in, 950, 1855
        metafiction, 2352
    in postwar female tradition, 936
    power in, 551, 2423
    psychoanalysis and, 1887
    quests in, 340, 1873; *see also* individual titles
    short fiction and, 307
    stalker novel, 1882
    storytelling in, 867
    subjectivity in, 552, 3074
    survival in, 749, 1912, 2573
    traditional form
        breaking down, 1581
        transgression of, 2833
    transformation in, 2821
    Ukrainians in, 907
    victimization in, 304, 344, 1440, 2294
    violence in, 1440, 1823
Nunavut/Nunavit, 542, 2063
nuns, 2351

Oates, Joyce Carol, 680, 3280, 3294
occult, 3853
O'Connor, Flannery, 1385
odalisques, 1128
Oeil-de-chat
    reviews of, 582
O'Faolain, Nuala, 2856
Oliver, Mary, 1371
Ondaatje, Michael, 919, 957, 1836, 1858, 1862, 1920, 2407

oppression, 122, 496, 567, 1190, 1352, 2626
orality and literacy, 340, 521, 1636; *see also*
  literacy
Origin of Consciousness, The, 92
Orwell, George, 868, 900, 1141, 3040
    1984, 1431, 2056-2057, 2117, 2548,
      2582, 3481
    history vs. memory in, 2329
    Newspeak, 2330
Oryx and Crake, 3528, 3532, 3726-3727,
  3867
  as allegory, 3882
  critical reception, 3657
  exile and belonging in, 3861
  heritage in, 3701
  as historiography, 3882
  humanity in
    homo faber, 3859
    posthuman, 3665
  interviews about, 3434, 3436, 3438, 3445,
    3449, 3451-3452, 3454, 3456, 3462,
    3637, 3640, 3646, 3652, 3833, 3844,
    3849
  reviews of, 3547, 3902
  reviews of audiobook, 3548-3550, 3728-
    3729
  sacred narrative in, 3860
  science in, 3665, 3682
  survival in, 3689, 3701
  translations of
    Chinese, 3595
    Croatian, 3356
    Czech, 3791
    Danish, 3399
    Dutch, 3395
    Finnish, 3396
    French, 3768; reviewed, 3900
    German, 3400
    Italian, 3372
    Latvian, 3386
    Norwegian, 3398
    Polish, 3601
    Portuguese, 3608
    Spanish, 3609, 3783
    Swedish, 3397
Ostenso, Martha, 2600
Other, the, 322, 2626
Ovid, 175
"Owl Song"
  set to music, 2723
Oxford Book of Canadian Short Stories in
  English, The, 3245
  reviews of, 195, 1200

Pachter, Charles, 908
Paci, Frank, 3517
pacifism, 2841
Page, P. K., 3266, 3674, 3873
pain, 3699
palimpsest, 317
panopticon, 3695
paranoia, 358, 1644, 1882
parody
  of fairy tale, 74
  of gothic, 3261
  in novels
    The Blind Assassin, 3705
    Bodily Harm, 526, 911
    The Handmaid's Tale, 474, 526, 911,
      2314, 2888, 3102, 3711
    Lady Oracle, 3705
    Surfacing, 2810
past, Victorian, 1834, 3853
patriarchy, 303, 337, 857, 1099, 1343, 1442
Peck, M. Scott, 1819
The Penelopiad
  interviews about, 3832, 3834-3835, 3839,
    3842, 3845, 3848, 3850
  reviews of, 3903
  translations of
    French, 3765
    German, 3753
    Italian, 3763
    Korean, 3784
    Latvian, 3788
    Spanish, 3785
Perrault, Charles, 3280
Petry, Ann, 913
phallogocentrism, 2341
phenomenology, 1650, 1887, 2365
photography, 183, 482, 2857, 3894
physics, 943
picaresque, 3234
Picasso, Pablo, 355
Piercy, Marge, 527, 566, 912-913, 1156,
  1408, 1852, 3040
  Atwood on, 1428
    Braided Lives, 921
    He, She and It, 1655
    Woman on the Edge of Time, 1182,
      1341, 1864
Piñon, Nelida, 2819
Pinter, Harold, 3497
place, 2099, 3686
  identity and, 2614
"A Place: Fragments," 1154
"Plain Sense," 1363
Plath, Sylvia, 712, 864, 3868
Plato, 2383

Poems 1965-75
  reviews of, 758
Poems 1976-86
  reviews of, 963
"Poetic Significance," 1363
poetics
  feminist, 95, 349, 351
  of pain, 98
  Sanskrit, 2320
  technopoetics, 3491
poetry, 86, 94, 100, 164, 356, 519, 1407,
  1693, 2075, 2119, 2545, 2828, 3272,
  3283, 3511; *see also* individual poetry
  titles
  animals in, 173
  Atwood's development, 1333
  Canadian
    Atwood as critic, 932
    experimental, 3502
  comedy in, 78
  creative process, 1390, 2287
  documentary, 360
  ecology and, 2822, 3265, 3680
  experimental, 3502
  feminism and, 95, 349, 712, 738
  gender in, 87, 1871, 2835
    language, 2098
  how to read, 2612
  humor in, 1826
  identity in, 1172, 1857
  language in, 510, 2098
  later work, 1333, 1685
  metamorphosis in, 2340
  mothers in, 2825
    advice to daughters, 957
  myth in, 870, 3104
    Eurydice and Orpheus, 1354
    revisionist, 870
  narrative voice in, 342, 1333, 1826
  order in, 555
  place in, 3686
    Latin America, 365
    wilderness, 555
  poetic form
    elegy, 3716
    long poem, 703
  postcolonialism, 1395
  power in, 1871
  reality in, 1673
  set to music, 653, 3624; *see also*
    individual titles
  shamanism in, 171
  short fiction and, 307
  silence in, 2822
  teaching, to tenth grade, 1363

victimization in, 147
  by women, 870, 1092, 1137
The Poetry of Gwendolyn MacEwan
  reviews of, 1705, 2142
"Polarities," 144, 161, 1165, 1318, 3081
  dramatic adaptation, 3202, 3420
politics, 343, 927, 2418, 2624; *see also*
  nationalism
  body and language, 3080
  cultural nationalism, 102, 2847
  environmentalism, 3430
  of food, 2870
  gender, 85, 87, 2878
  gothic and, 2093
  identity, 2639
  leftist, 115
  narrative, 522, 707, 2842, 2878
  the personal and, 1394
  of risk, 101
  sexual, 180, 3093
  victimization in, 89
Politique de pouvoir
  reviews of, 1706
popular culture, 947, 3486
  Atwood and, 1170, 3303
  gender and, 1870
  popular fiction, 1170
pornography, 3678
postcolonialism, 1395, 1434
  Bodily Harm and, 1596
  The Handmaid's Tale and, 1832, 2420
  The Robber Bride and, 3886
  Surfacing and, 1321, 2566, 2584
postfeminism, 708, 736
posthuman, 3665
postmodernism, 183, 494, 1427, 1657
  Atwood's, 2035
  Canadian, 119, 183
    and carnival, 1818
  dystopia and, 1326, 3885
  female, 526
  feminist, 536, 708, 1327, 2595, 2617
  heroines in, 1312
  myth and, 949
  in novels, 950, 1855
    Bodily Harm, 526
    Cat's Eye, 708
    The Handmaid's Tale, 104, 526, 536,
      543, 692, 708, 1327, 1884, 2420,
      2595, 3667
  photography and, 183
  in poetry
    Interlunar, 708
  in short fiction
    "Loulou; or, The Domestic Life of

Language," 1383
Murder in the Dark, 361
Poulin, Jacques, 2602
Pound, Ezra, 158
power, 724, 1393, 1888
  Canadian, 3886
  the city and, 2345
  dialogue and, 3488
  female friendship and, 2271
  gender and, 1591, 2088, 2128, 2271, 3100,
    3516
  of narrator, 1339, 1888
  in novels, 710, 2423
    Alias Grace, 2271, 3100
    Bodily Harm, 551
    Cat's Eye, 478, 2271
    The Edible Woman, 1393
    The Handmaid's Tale, 478, 551, 696,
      1347, 1848, 2271, 2280, 2339, 2409,
      2558, 3037, 3052
    Lady Oracle, 1393
    Life Before Man, 551
    The Robber Bride, 1393, 1591, 2271,
      3886
    Surfacing, 513, 3516
  in poetry
    You Are Happy, 1871
  in short fiction
    "Loulou; or, The Domestic Life of
      Language," 551
  space and, 1393
  in *Survival*, 478
Power Politics, 84, 126, 144, 181, 490, 879,
  2835
  approaches to
    Rasa theory of emotion, 2320
  balance and parallelism in, 2884
  ghosts in, 2855
  as gothic, 134
  reviews of, 2143
  translations of
    French, 1532; reviews of, 1706
Pratt, Annis, 2353
pregnancy; *see* reproduction
Princess Prunella; *see Princess Prunella*
  and the Purple Peanut
Princess Prunella and the Purple Peanut
  interviews about, 1572, 1578, 1814
  reviews of, 1707, 1926, 2144
  translations of
    Danish, 2976
    French, 1770
    German, 2215
"Prisms"
  set to music, 653

private sphere, 2329, 2399, 2599, 3708
Procedures for Underground, 144, 162,
  1361
  reviews of, 159
professionalism, 1414-1415
"Progressive Insanities of a Pioneer," 2797
  musical adaptation, 2244
protagonist, female
  in *Alias Grace*, 2568, 2598
  in *The Handmaid's Tale*, 1835, 2568
Proulx, Annie, 3702
psychoanalysis; *see* therapy
psychoanalytic theory, 1650, 1821, 1887,
  2365, 3874
  object relations, 3043
psychology, 335
  gothic, 747
public vs. private, 2399, 3708
Puig, Manuel, 1600
Purdy, Alfred W.
  on Atwood, 1167, 1171, 3709
Pym, Barbara, 141, 902
Pynchon, Thomas, 950, 1408

Quebec, 2602
quests; *see also* travel
  female, 1126, 1821, 1873, 2294, 3518
  northern, 938
  in novels, 340, 1873, 2294
    Cat's Eye, 507, 687, 3518
    Lady Oracle, 506, 1825
    Surfacing, 75, 167-168, 506, 1821
Quiet Game and Other Early Works
  reviews of, 2429, 2909, 3121
quilts
  in *Alias Grace*, 2304, 2412, 2556, 3087
    as history, 2388, 3083
    as narrative art, 3537

race, 106, 728, 1113, 1686, 2050, 2584,
  2847
rape; *see* violence
"Rape Fantasies," 1857, 2902
  teaching, 2408, 3039
reader, implied, 3662
reading, 296
  as countertransference, 481
  dialogics and, 1405
  women's voices and, 2067
realism, 1196
  in *Alias Grace*, 2361
  in *The Blind Assassin*, 3702
  in *Bluebeard's Egg and Other Stories*, 532
  in *Dancing Girls and Other Stories*, 532
  in *The Edible Woman*, 532

in *The Handmaid's Tale*, 1673, 3055
in *Lady Oracle*, 532
in *Life Before Man*, 532
reality, 912, 1416, 1673
The Red Shoes, 2404
  audiobook, 2893
  excerpt from, 2403, 2405, 3105
  Swedish translation, 2892
regeneration, 139, 150, 175, 178, 669, 1311
regression, 2548
relationships, female, 2276; *see also* also
  friendship, female; mother-daughter
  relationships
religion, 2860, 3693; *see also* Bible;
  goddess; spirituality
  challenges to, 922
  Christianity, 306, 330, 337, 1602
    Catholicism, 507, 853
    Protestant fundamentalism, 2608
    Puritanism, 169, 303, 2560
  gnosticism, 2858, 3279
  mothers and, 2635
  in novels
    Alias Grace, 2858, 3279
    Cat's Eye, 507
    The Handmaid's Tale, 169, 303, 306,
      330, 337, 367, 853, 1602, 2360, 2560,
      2608, 2635, 3242-3243
    Surfacing, 563, 922, 937, 2089
  sacred narrative and, 3860
  shamanism, 171
  suffering and, 2858
  Sufi mysticism, 367
  voodoo, 3518
  women and, 694, 2635
Report der Magd, Der
  reviews of, 188
representation, 1330
  of Ukrainians, 907
reproduction
  birth, 139, 150, 669, 1311
  in *The Handmaid's Tale*, 3883
    birth and feminism, 669, 1311
    eugenics, 1598
    pregnancy, 77, 3235
    sterility and fertility, 1177, 2374
    technologies of, 77, 669
  in *Surfacing*
    sterility, 2060
Repše, Gundega, 3876
resistance, 2053
  in *Alias Grace*, 3526
  in *Cat's Eye*, 1442, 2386
  in *The Edible Woman*, 3270
  in *The Handmaid's Tale*, 1362, 1435,

1442, 2362
  narration and, 1676, 3101
  in *The Handmaid's Tale* [motion picture],
    3478
  in *Lady Oracle*, 3270
  memory and, 1891, 2386
  in *Surfacing*, 1661
responsibility, 953
revenge, 748
reviews; *see* titles of works
revision
  biblical, 3097
  feminist, of myth, 2795
  literary
    of canonical texts, 1686
    of picaresque, 3234
revolution
  in *Bodily Harm*, 503
  in *The Handmaid's Tale*, 668
  in *Surfacing*, 1661, 2617
  women and, 668
Reyes, Alina, 3084
rhetoric, 878, 888, 3278
Rhys, Jean, 2128, 2311, 3041, 3878
Ricci, Nino, 2095
Rich, Adrienne, 712, 1123, 1371, 2311
Richler, Mordecai, 876, 2852
Ricoeur, Paul, 547, 1881
Ritchie, Anne Thackeray, 3280
The Robber Bride, 1382, 1696, 2114, 2126
  approaches to
    Nietzsche, Friedrich, 3483
    postcolonialism, 3886
    postmodernist, 2591
  biography in, 2079
  Bluebeard in, 2322, 3062
  book groups and, 1090, 1406
  capitalism in, 1437
  clothes in, 3071, 3870
  creative process, 2597
  critical reception of, 1604
  cultural identity in, 2272
  dialogism in, 3483
  difference in, 3886
  envy in, 2421, 3722
  evil in, 1819, 2034
    female, 3038, 3096, 3256, 3530, 3683
    perception of, 2373
  exile in, 3288
  as fairy tale, 3483
  as fantasy, 2787
  feminism in, 2358
    science and, 2047
  foreignness in, 1620

friendship in, 1885
  female, 1594, 2271, 2294
gender in, 1585, 2617
as ghost story, 2274
as gothic, 2605, 3866
  postcolonial, 2605
as historiography, 2272, 2277, 2864, 3259
identity in, 3887
  Canadian, 3493
  intertextuality and, 2615
immigrants in, 2619
initiation in, 3703
interviews about, 1075, 1078, 1087, 1289, 1294
maps and mapping in, 1853, 3098
mirrors in, 1890
models for characters, 3477
mothers in, 1684
myth in
  goddess, 2052, 3282
  Wendigo, 2559
  White Goddess, 2381
names and naming in
  Zenia, 1612
nomadism in, 1885
picaresque in, 3234
postmodernism and, 3887
power in, 1393, 2540, 3488
  Canada and, 3886
  female, 1591, 2088, 2271
review of radio adaptation, 1712
reviews of, 1201, 1463, 1708, 2145
science and feminism in, 2047
space in, 1393
subversion in, 1834
survival in, 1590
teaching, 1090
translations of
  Croatian, 2485
  Czech, 1517
  Danish, 1266
  Dutch, 1217, 2664
  Estonian, 1990
  Finnish, 1268, 1991
  French, 1238, 1748; reviewed, 1702, 1923
  German, 1220, 1731
  Hebrew, 1964
  Italian, 2196
  Japanese, 2963
  Korean, 1994
  Latvian, 1753
  Norwegian, 1774
  Persian, 3182
  Polish, 1791

  Portuguese, 968, 1467
  Slovak, 2210
  Spanish, 1746
  Swedish, 1265
victimization in, 1419, 2294
  by women, 2088
villains in, 2872
  female, 3096, 3256, 3530
war in, 1885, 2277
Zenia, 1612, 2034, 2096, 2377
Roberts, Michele B., 2883
Robin, Régine, 1438, 2602
Robinson, Marilynne, 527, 875, 923, 2398, 2849, 3251
  Housekeeping, 687, 921, 1915
Rogers, Jane, 2635
romance, 675, 1116
  metaphysical, and J. R. R. Tolkein, 2596
  in novels
    Bodily Harm, 1121
    The Handmaid's Tale, 721, 1338, 2861, 3085
    Lady Oracle, 323, 2831
    Surfacing, 321
  in short fiction
    "Bluebeard's Egg," 2112
Rooke, Constance, 2606
Roy, Arundhati, 3289, 3663
Roy, Gabrielle, 1359, 3520
royalty, 3241
Rude Ramsay and the Roaring Radishes
  interviews about, 3431, 3433-3434, 3444, 3467, 3632
  reviews of, 3551, 3730
  translations of, German, 3795
Ruders, Poul, 3506
Russ, Joanna, 151, 1096, 1182, 1852, 3302

sacrifice, 2626
sadomasochism, 2117
Salinger, J. D., 2077, 2095
"The Salt Garden," 1451
Salzman, Mark, 3702
satire
  in *The Handmaid's Tale*, 508, 1848, 2297
  teaching, 1919
Scheherazade, 306, 942
schizophrenia, 912, 3260; *see also* insanity
science
  gender and, 1674, 2047, 2808
  genetics, 3665, 3682
  in novels
    Cat's Eye, 943, 2047
    Oryx and Crake, 3665, 3682
    The Robber Bride, 2047

physics, 943
postmodern, 2889
science fiction; *see also* speculative fiction
  Atwood on, 3093, 3439
  Canadian, 1388, 3690
  dystopias, 2862
  feminist, 77, 951, 1156, 1655, 1864
  The Handmaid's Tale [motion picture] as,
    1143
  in novels
    The Blind Assassin, 3690
    The Handmaid's Tale, 866, 951, 1655,
      1864, 2862, 3864
  reproductive technology in, 77
  teaching, 1867
  utopias, 480
Scott, F. R., 529, 2811
Second Words, 557, 1320, 1420, 1441
  Atwood as critic, 705
  gothic in, 3527
  victimization in, 157
Selected Poems: 1966-1984, 3527
  reviews of, 583, 759, 964
Selected Poems II, 3527
  reviews of, 196, 375
self; *see* identity; subjectivity
self-care, 1670
self-destruction, 1595, 3704
self-discovery, 140, 2127
self-mockery, 1818
semiotics, 146
sensory imagery
  olfactory, 933
  visual, 1198
serial killers, 2571
Servante écarlate, La
  reviews of, 197, 374, 760
servants, 3857
setting, 560
  Canadian, 722
    West, 1337
  Caribbean, 472
  domestic space, 2357, 2791, 3861
  in fiction
    Bodily Harm, 472
    Cat's Eye, 514
    The Handmaid's Tale, 560
    Lady Oracle, 1349
  future, 746
  kitchen, 2791
  Montreal, 2333
  in poetry
    The Journals of Susanna Moodie, 555,
      722
  Toronto, 514, 905, 1349, 2061, 3479, 3880

urban vs. rural, 1359
wilderness, 555, 722
Sexton, Anne, 712, 1138, 1365, 1592, 1640,
  2835, 3892
sexuality
  ambiguous, 2376
  the body and, 1592
  female, 117, 1189, 3048-3049
  heterosexuality, 1119
  intimacy and, 2346
  nationalism and, 2381
  in novels
    The Blind Assassin, 3049
    The Handmaid's Tale, 1607, 2346
    Lady Oracle, 117, 3048
    Life Before Man, 2385
    Surfacing, 2385
  in short fiction
    Bluebeard's Egg and Other Stories,
      2385
    "Walking on Water," 3049
    "The Whirlpool Rapids," 3049
  surveillance of, 1607
  water and, 3049
Shakespeare, William, 1400, 2039
  King Lear, 1149, 2084, 2621
  The Tempest, 506
shamanism, 171, 2895
shapeshifters, 1905
Shelley, Mary, 520, 1364, 2128
Sherman, Cindy, 1852
Shields, Carol, 909, 2319, 2580, 3471, 3490
  Small Ceremonies, 2839
  Swann, 2865
short fiction, 103, 356, 489, 1317, 1587,
  1628, 1693, 2634, 2891; *see also*
  domesticity
  Atwood on, 3093
  authority in, 2390
  Canadian literature and, 2876
  critical reception of, 1604
  cultural difference in, 2625
  defamiliarization in, 1634
  displacement in, 928
  gender in, 345, 1391, 2048, 2573
  genre, 307, 2048
  innocence in, 500
  language and power in, 551
  law in, 1615
  metalinguistic features of, 302
  place and time in, 2335
  reader's companion, 3103
  sexual fantasy in, 2588
  study guide, 3035

subjectivity in, 1108
  and language, 1328
survival in, 2573
woman as destroyer in, 882
women's experience in, 909
Sidwa, Bapsi, 3041
sight and blindness, 3872; *see also* vision
"Significant Moments in the Life of My
  Mother," 2104, 2639
silence, 1580, 2382, 2397, 2822
Silko, Leslie Marmon, 711, 2819
"The Sin Eater," 547
  Gospel of Mark and, 471, 486, 491, 535,
    537, 569
siren, 3301
  as storyteller, 1137
"Siren Song," 1137
  set to music, 2723
size, 3515
slavery, 2607
Sleeping Beauty; *see* fairy tales
Smart, Elizabeth, 1189
Smedley, Agnes, 913
Smiley, Jane, 2039, 2372
Smith, A. J. M., 529
Smith, Stevie, 2835
Smith, Zadie, 3869
"Snake Poems," 3079
social control, 1622, 2307
society, 2799
"Songs of the Transformed," 3267
space, 1422, 1625
  in "Circe/Mud Poems," 2356
  female, 1616, 2356
  female artist and, 559
  language and, 559
  in novels
    Cat's Eye, 2832
    The Edible Woman, 1393
    The Handmaid's Tale, 559
    Lady Oracle, 1393
    The Robber Bride, 1393
    Surfacing, 1625
  power and, 1393
  time and, 2832
Spark, Muriel, 902
spectacle, 2812, 3302
specular narrative, 3710
speculative fiction, 1431, 3302; *see also*
  science fiction
  Cat's Eye, 1096
  The Handmaid's Tale, 860, 918, 1096
speech
  speech act theory, 725, 1165
  women's, 340

"Speeches for Dr. Frankenstein"
  set to music, 653, 3205
"Spelling," 2623
Spence, Catherine Helen, 1146
spirituality, 482, 485; *see also* religion
  in *Cat's Eye*, 507, 687
  in *Morning in the Burned House*, 1894
Starhawk, 3712
state, 2360, 2800
"Statuary," 2336
stereotypes, cultural, 182
sterility; *see* reproduction
Stevenson, Lionel, 2786
storytelling, 177, 329, 489, 1104, 2563,
  2628, 3525
  clothes and, 3071
  comic, 298
  in novels, 867
    The Handmaid's Tale, 306, 887, 942,
    2313
    Lady Oracle, 298
  personal narration in, 1669
  women's, 867
*Strange Things: The Malevolent North in
  Canadian Literature*, 2606, 3253
  reviews of, 1710, 1927, 2146, 2430, 3731
strangers, 3474
study guide, 3480; *see* individual titles
  short fiction, 3035
subjectivity, 1187, 2565
  community and, 1918
  dialogic, 2565
  divided, 1650, 2359
  female, 731, 1366, 1392, 2391, 2846, 3887
  feminist, 738
  language and, 1328
  in novels
    Bodily Harm, 1650
    Cat's Eye, 1366
    The Handmaid's Tale, 1650, 2359, 2846,
    2890
    Lady Oracle, 1650, 1918, 2565
    Life Before Man, 1650
    The Robber Bride, 3887
    Surfacing, 2391
  in poetry, 738
  writing and, 1396
sublime, 892, 1454
subversion, 3058
  of female body, 3051
  language and, 1660
  of law and religion, 3243
  in novels
    Bodily Harm, 1346
    Cat's Eye, 1190, 1660

The Handmaid's Tale, 1190, 1835, 1859,
    2364, 3243
   Lady Oracle, 916, 1353
  of social order, 1346
  through gossip, 1859
  of traditional forms, 2410
Sufi mysticism; *see* religion
suicide, 2109
"The Sunrise"
  dramatic adaptation, 3202, 3420
Surfacing, 79, 86, 126-127, 142, 144, 166,
    181, 293, 338, 541, 686, 741, 859, 1109,
    1327, 1372, 2379, 2816, 2851, 3669
  abortion in, 566, 931
  adaptation in, 3057
  aging, and women, 1589
  Alberto Manguel on, 3697
  ambivalence and ambiguity in, 1822
  animals in, 3875
  approaches to
    Campbell, Joseph, 2353
    French feminist, 151
    Freud, Sigmund, 167, 352
    Kristeva, Julia, 83, 151
    postcolonial, 1321, 2566, 2584
    postmodernist, 1855
    psychoanalysis, 1821, 3874
    semiotic, 952
  art and the artist in, 682, 750, 944
  artificiality in, 2060
  autobiography in, 2355
  Biblical imagery in, 167
  the body in, 698, 713
  borders and boundaries in, 305, 512, 698
  Canada in, 548
    the U.S. and, 2419
  as Canadian literature, 1367, 1865
  civilization in
    barbarism and, 684
    nature and, 1340
  compared to
    Carrier, Roch, 1865
    The Edible Woman, 2097
  consciousness in, 1895
  creativity, feminine, in, 1378
  critical reception of, 568, 1376
  displacement in, 2385
  ecology in, 3255
    ecofeminism, 527, 1850
  as fairy tale, 505
  as fantasy, 484, 562
  as female Bildungsroman, 363
  female hero in, 91, 2353
  female imaginary in, 2627
  feminism in, 321, 1397, 1855, 2620, 3869

  gynocriticism, 527, 1638
  film in, 944
  food in, 310
  gender in, 1106, 2069, 3516
    popular culture and, 1870
  goddess in, 563, 2052, 2060
  as gothic, 134, 318, 3527, 3866
  healing in, 1915
  identity in, 492, 1368, 1412
    clothing and, 898
    female, 1369
  indigenous symbols in, 2332
  the individual in, 2299
  innocence in, 548, 1386
  insanity in, 2069, 3516
    schizophrenia, 912
  Inter-American fiction and, 484
  irony in, 562
  landscape in, 2398
    internal, 2391
  language in, 2348, 2385
  linearity in, 1680
  male oppression in, 567
  maps and mapping in, 326, 1368, 3893
  memory in, 1150, 1438
  mothers in, 175, 184
    mother-daughter relationships, 167
  murder in, 1336
  myth and, 168, 2060
    Callisto, 175
    Demeter, 108
    female monomyth, 2353
    Kyklopes, 3068
    matriarchal, 175
  narrative voice in, 342, 1828
  nature in, 109, 512, 558, 2785
    civilization and, 1340
    as feminist space, 2785
    women and, 880
  North in, 3253, 3893
  pacifism in, 2841
  as parody, 2810
  photography in, 3894
  power in, 146, 513, 3516
  race in, 106, 2584
  regeneration in, 175, 1132
  religion in, 116, 937, 2089
    challenges to, 922
  reproduction in
    sterility, 2060
  resistance in, 922, 1661
  reviews of, 1465
  revolt in, 2617
  as romance, 321
  sexuality in, 2385

space in
  and psychic growth, 1625
study guide, 2286
subjectivity in, 140, 1448
  female, 2391
  male, 2793
suicide in, 2109
teaching, 872
  in Canadian studies, 1844
  through film, 1863
transformation in, 2895
translations, analysis of, 346
translations of
  Chinese, 590
  Croatian, 616
  Czech, 2242
  Dutch, 2921
  Estonian, 2489
  French, 1221
  German, 386, 2172
  Greek, 377
  Hebrew, 2455
  Italian, 55, 2715
  Japanese, 1046
  Polish, 2240, 3621
  Portuguese, 248
  Slovak, 443
  Spanish, 218, 1262, 3611
  Swedish, 263
trauma in, 1618
travel in, 734, 1429, 2275
  quest, 75, 167-168, 506, 1821
the uncanny in, 352
United States in, 2130, 3069
victimization in, 89, 147, 1419, 1601
vision in, 869, 1416
water in, 512
wilderness in, 1384, 1627
as women's writing, 2539
surveillance, 2310, 2812, 3695
survival, 3699
  Atwood on, 2622, 3519
  the body and, 2044
  myth and, 949
  in novels, 749, 1912
    Bodily Harm, 3519
    Cat's Eye, 1583, 1590, 3519
    The Edible Woman, 1621
    The Handmaid's Tale, 154, 1331, 1362,
      1621, 2044, 2326, 2611, 3519
    Oryx and Crake, 3689, 3701
    Surfacing, 3519
  women and, 2573
Survival, 112, 166, 181, 557, 1348, 1409,
  3508

aging in, 2058
animals in, 1178, 3056
Canadian identity and, 695, 1140, 1387,
  3056
as Canadian literary criticism, 891, 894,
  1102, 1874, 2876, 3045
  literary history, 1101
Canadian literature and, 1367, 1421
Canadian Studies and, 2087
critical reception, 1152, 3045
  by public, 1152
  reviews of, 3732
epigraphs in, 161
female body in, 695
ghosts in, 706
gothic in, 134, 3527
influences on
  Frye, Northrop, 1320
  Scott, F. R., 2811
language and, 884
nation in, 3233
nature in, 3888
power in, 144, 478
Shakespearean revision in, 1400
sublime in, 1454
translations of
  Chinese, 634
  French; reviewed, 189
  Japanese, 1538
victimization in, 147, 157, 499, 1178
  creative nonvictims, 3474
Swan, Susan, 1151, 3234
Swift, Graham, 2897
Swift, Jonathan, 1907
Szymborska, Wislawa, 3511

Tamaro, Susanna, 1872
Tan, Amy, 2294, 2818
teaching, 2880, 3273
  Alias Grace
    in high school, 3254
    in International Baccalaureate program,
      3289
  Cat's Eye
    in Canadian Studies, 1880
  creative writing, 1911
  critical theory and praxis, 1904
  The Edible Woman, 1110, 1332
  The Handmaid's Tale, 299, 556, 1139,
    1845, 1917
    to boys, 1168
    as fairy tale, 1877
    in Germany, 3269
    social roles, 545
    sociology, 504, 1851

women's studies, 935
Lady Oracle
  as gothic, 3484
literacy and, 2049
Murder in the Dark, 1883
poetry, to tenth grade, 1363
"Rape Fantasies," 2408, 3039
The Robber Bride, 1090
satire, 1919
Surfacing, 872
Survival
  in Canadian Studies, 1844
Wilderness Tips, 1839
Tei, Karen, 3869
Tennyson, Alfred, Lord, 2792
Tepper, Sheri, 1694, 3302
territory, 2609
theory; *see* feminist theory and criticism;
  phenomenology; postcolonialism;
  postmodernism; psychoanalytic theory
therapy, Atwood's critique of, 1656
"They Eat Out"
  set to music, 2723
"This Is a Photograph of Me," 3232
Thomas, Audrey, 93, 541, 673, 697, 919,
  2390, 2638
Intertidal Life, 559
Songs My Mother Taught Me, 1319
Thomson, Tom, 3681
time
  in "Circe/Mud Poems," 2356
  dystopia and, 2354, 2380
  male, 2356
  in novels
    Cat's Eye, 943, 1181, 1680, 2347, 2832
    The Handmaid's Tale, 2321, 2354
    Life Before Man, 110
  in short fiction, 2335
  space and, 2832
Todorov, Tzvetan, 1446
Tolkein, J. R. R., 2596
tone, 3892
Toronto, 905, 3880
  Atwood's literary haunts, 2569
  in *Cat's Eye*, 514, 3479, 3880
  in *Lady Oracle*, 1349, 2061, 3880
  in *Life Before Man*, 3880
torture, 2626
Tostevin, Lola Lemire, 3873
totalitarianism, 2076
Traba, Marta, 1653
Tracy, Ann B., 3893
Traill, Catherine Parr, 82, 555
transformation, 876, 1640, 2095, 2340,
  2546, 2821, 2895, 3267

transgression, 571, 2558, 2833
translation, 96
  of Atwood, 346, 1697, 2852
    Soviet, 1588
  Atwood on, 3219
translations; *see* titles of works
translations, reviews of; *see* titles of works
Trapido, Barbara, 2039
trauma
  confession and, 3671
  historical, 3109
  incest, 1842
  in novels
    Alias Grace, 2829, 3109, 3671
    Cat's Eye, 3889
    Surfacing, 1618
  sexual, 2829
travel, 1371, 2602, 3234
  in the North, 938
  in novels, 340, 1873, 2294
    Bodily Harm, 667, 1429, 2122
    Cat's Eye, 507, 687, 1429, 2294, 3518
    Lady Oracle, 506, 1443, 1825, 3234
    The Robber Bride, 1885, 2294, 3234
    Surfacing, 75, 167-168, 506, 734, 1429,
      1821
  picaresque, 3234
  quests, 167-168, 507, 687, 938, 1825
    female, 75, 340, 506, 1126, 1821, 1873,
      2294, 3518
  for self-knowledge, 340, 1429, 1873
  spiritual, 507, 687, 734, 2294
"A Travel Piece," 3660
"Tricks with Mirrors"
  set to music, 2723
tricksters, 2628, 3531; *see also* folklore;
  myth
Triolet, Elsa, 3236
Troisième main, La
  reviews of, 1922
True Stories, 365, 1624
  adaptations of, musical, 2721
  reviews of, 133
  translations of, German, 2510
"True Trash," 1683
"The Trumpets of Summer"
  set to music, 3421
Turner Hospital, Janette, 909, 928
Tuttle, Lisa, 2801
Twain, Mark, 3068
Two Solicitudes: Conversations
  reviews of, 2431, 2643, 2910, 3122
"Two Stories about Emma," 674
Two-Headed Poems, 136, 510, 889, 1457
  reviews, 76

Tyler, Anne, 141, 2039, 2849

"Uglypuss," 1165
Ukrainians, 907
Unamuno, Miguel de, 3521
Uncanny, the, 352, 1446, 2290
"Uncles," 3477
"Under Glass," 473
underground, 1361
"Unearthing Suite," 744, 2104, 2402
uniform, 571
United States, 129, 1424, 2130, 2419, 3069;
    see also anti-Americanism
    relations with Canada, 136, 2419, 2593
universality, 2127
Up in the Tree
    translations of, German, 1234
Updike, John, 871, 2083
Urquhart, Jane, 1445, 2602
utopias, 176, 868, 2633; *see also* dystopias
    female, 81, 1341, 1388
    feminist, 295, 309, 313, 498, 520, 3885
    in *The Handmaid's Tale*, 176, 692, 1197,
        1341, 1881, 2601, 3091, 3306
        feminist, 295, 309, 3885
        literary tradition, 521
        postcolonial, 3091
        postmodern, 3885
    science fiction and, 480, 1388

vampire, 2872
van Gennep, Arnold, 1448
Van Herk, Aritha, 478, 1858, 2542, 3234
Varda, Agnès, 2122
"Variation on the Word *Sleep*," 1854
vegetarianism; *see* food
veil, 3047
victimization, 89, 2628
    animals, 1178
    Canadian identity and, 1178
    creative nonvictims, 3474
    in criticism
        Second Words, 157
        Survival, 147, 157, 499, 3474
    in fiction, 304, 1440
        Cat's Eye, 1419, 2088
        The Edible Woman, 147, 344, 1355,
            1419, 2088
        The Handmaid's Tale, 122, 154, 499,
            862, 1343, 1355, 1419, 2088
        The Robber Bride, 1419
        Surfacing, 89, 147, 1419, 1601
        Wilderness Tips, 3474
    friendship and, 2294
    gothic and, 747

medicine and, 862
myth and, 949
in poetry, 147
villains, female, 882, 3038, 3084, 3096,
    3256, 3530, 3683
Villanueva, Alma Luz, 734
violence, 1440
    murder, 1336, 2809, 3063, 3514
    rape fantasy, 1857
    women's, 3276, 3294
    in women's novels, 1823
virginity, 672
vision, in
    The Blind Assassin, 3710, 3872
    Cat's Eye, 2617, 2827
    artistic, 753
    The Edible Woman, 869
    Lady Oracle, 869
    Life Before Man, 869
    Surfacing, 869, 1416
voice, 742, 3892; *see also* narrative voice
    in *Alias Grace*
        middle voice, 3498
    post-realist, 1179
    in *Surfacing*, 1828, 2327
    women's, 867, 2327
Voleuse d'hommes, La
    reviews of, 1702, 1923
Vonarburg, Elisabeth, 1388
Vonnegut, Kurt, 912, 1671, 3060, 3481
voodoo; *see* religion
voyeurism, 3670; *see* surveillance
vulnerability, 2902

Waddington, Miriam, 928
Walker, Alice, 117, 527, 544, 550, 913,
    1161, 1913, 2901
    The Color Purple, 106, 182, 733, 896,
        921, 1341
"Walking on Water," 3049
war, 1885, 2277, 1654
Warner, Marina, 2039
water, 512, 923, 3049
Webster, Mary, 1344
"Weight," 1615
Weiler, Diana, 2055
Weitlzweig, Helen, 1349
Weldon, Fay, 174, 1823, 2613, 3235, 3261
Wells, H. G., 868, 3528
Welty, Eudora, 680, 1441, 2114
West, the, 1337
Wharton, Edith, 3857
    screen adaptations, 2636
"The Whirlpool Rapids," 3049
White, Patrick, 1611

Wideman, John Edgar, 1868
Wiebe, Rudy, 1196, 3662
wilderness, 1627, 1896, 2279
   attitudes towards, 1384
   in Canadian writing, 2389
      by women, 1896
   identity and, 1858
   language and, 884
   in poetry, 555, 722
"Wilderness Tips"
   immigrants in, 1112, 2116
   study guide, 1458
Wilderness Tips, 2876; *see also* individual
   story titles
   apocalypse in, 2574, 3059
   as Canadian literature, 1367
   cannibalism in, 2574, 3059
   fairy tales and, 2579, 3490
   gender in, 2125
   interviews about, 1297
   national identity in, 2125
   North in, 3253
   reviews of, 761, 966, 1203, 2147
   reviews of audiobook, 965, 2911
   strangers in, 3474
   subjectivity in, 1328
   teaching, 1839
   translations of
      Danish, 1044, 2232
      Dutch, 827
      French, 1760, 2207
      German, 640, 1276, 3414
      Italian, 1998, 2508
      Latvian, 3404
      Norwegian, 807
      Polish, 2674
      Swedish, 808
   wilderness in, 1627
Winterson, Jeanette, 1657, 1855, 2787, 2806
witches, 672, 2613
withdrawal, 515, 2275
witness, 2369, 2610-2611
Wittig, Monique, 117, 3043
wives, 715
Wolf, Christa, 1637, 2362, 2620
"Woman Skating," 1144
women, 553, 715; *see also* daughters;
   mothers; villains, female
   age and, 1589
   as author, 688
   as destroyer, 882
   fallen, 3720
   female demonic, 1626
   femme fatale, 3084
   marginalized, 1878

nature and, 83, 880
in novels
   Cat's Eye, 1878
   The Edible Woman, 1633, 1834
   The Handmaid's Tale, 668
   Lady Oracle, 688, 1834
   The Robber Bride, 1834
   Surfacing, 484, 880, 1589
position of, 1633
revolution and, 668
subversion and, 1834
survival and, 2573
war and, 2277
witches, 2613
women of color; *see* race
Woodcock, George, 2306
Woolf, Virginia, 741, 1380, 2128, 2376,
   2565
   artist, female, in, 1180
   To the Lighthouse, 570, 1436
   Three Guineas, 3067
work, women's, 1869
Wright, Judith, 2825
writers, 1823, 3471, 3890
   women, 688, 1452
   Canadian, 3471
writing; *see also* epistolarity
   and subjectivity, 1396
Writing with Intent
   reviews of, 3904

Xi Xi, 3270

Yeats, William Butler, 957
You Are Happy, 94, 100, 519, 1173, 1871
   as gothic, 134
   love in, 128
   myth in, 1871
"You Fit into Me," 863, 3858
   gendered interpretations of, 1183
"You Want to Go Back," 2099

Zamiatin, Yvgeny, 1664, 1671, 3661
Zhang Jie, 3270

About the Authors

Dr. **Shannon Hengen**, professor and chair of English at Laurentian University in Sudbury, Ontario, Canada, has published books, chapters in books, articles, and reviews of Margaret Atwood's work over approximately twenty years. In addition to seminars on Atwood, she teaches modern and contemporary writers in English, particularly those of North America, with a focus on female poets and dramatists, and in an interdisciplinary MA in Humanities.

Mr. **Ashley Thomson** is a librarian at Laurentian University and has coauthored or co-edited seven previous books: *The Directory of Canadian Private Residential Schools* (Toronto: Methuen, 1986); *The Bibliography of Ontario History, 1976-1986* (Toronto: Dundurn, 1989); *Temagami: A Debate on Wilderness* (Toronto: Dundurn, 1990); *At the End of the Shift: Mines and Single-Industry Towns in Northern Ontario* (Toronto: Dundurn, 1992); *Sudbury: Rail Town to Regional Capital* (Toronto: Dundurn, 1993); *The Bibliography of Northern Ontario, 1966-1991* (Toronto: Dundurn, 1994); *The Handbook of Canadian Boarding Schools* (Toronto: Dundurn, 1999).